MOTORIST'S BRITAIN

C000003854

Contents

Map pages	inside front cover
Route planner	II–VII
Motorways	VIII–XIV
Restricted junctions	VIII–XI
M25 London Orbital motorway	XII
M6 Toll motorway	XIII
Smart motorways	XIV
Road map symbols	1
Road maps	2–115
Britain 1:250,000 scale Some islands are shown at slightly smaller scales	2–111
Ireland 1:1,000,000 scale	112–115
District maps	116–127
Birmingham	116–117
Glasgow	118–119
London	120–123
Manchester	124–125
Tyne & Wear	126–127
Street map symbols	128
Town plans	129–141
Central London	142–157
Central London street map	142–151
Central London index	152–157
Index to place names	158–194
County, administrative area map	158

41st edition June 2018

© AA Media Limited 2018

Revised version of the atlas formerly known as *Complete Atlas of Britain*. Original edition printed 1979.

Cartography: All cartography in this atlas edited, designed and produced by the Mapping Services Department of AA Publishing (A05624).

This atlas contains Ordnance Survey data © Crown copyright and database right 2018 and Royal Mail data © Royal Mail copyright and database right 2018.

Contains public sector information licensed under the Open Government Licence v3.0

Ireland mapping contains data from openstreetmap.org © OpenStreetMap contributors

Publisher's Notes: Published by AA Publishing (a trading name of AA Media Limited, whose registered office is Fanum House, Basing View, Basingstoke, Hampshire RG21 4EA, UK. Registered number 06112600).

ISBN: 978 0 7495 7956 2

A CIP catalogue record for this book is available from The British Library.

Disclaimer: The contents of this atlas are believed to be correct at the time of the latest revision, it will not contain any subsequent amended, new or temporary information including diversions and traffic control or enforcement systems. The publishers cannot be held responsible or liable for any loss or damage occasioned to any person acting or refraining from action as a result of any use or reliance on material in this atlas, nor for any errors, omissions or changes in such material. This does not affect your statutory rights.

The publishers would welcome information to correct any errors or omissions and to keep this atlas up to date. Please write to the Atlas Editor, AA Publishing, The Automobile Association, Fanum House, Basing View, Basingstoke, Hampshire RG21 4EA, UK. E-mail: *roadatlasfeedback@theaa.com*

Acknowledgements: AA Publishing would like to thank the following for information used in the creation of this atlas: Cadw, English Heritage, Forestry Commission, Historic Scotland, National Trust and National Trust for Scotland, RSPB, The Wildlife Trust, Scottish Natural Heritage, Natural England, The Countryside Council for Wales. Award winning beaches from 'Blue Flag' and 'Keep Scotland Beautiful' (summer 2017 data): for latest information visit *www.blueflag.org* and *www.keepscotlandbeautiful.org*. Transport for London (Central London Map), Nexus (Newcastle district map).

Ireland mapping: Republic of Ireland census 2011 © Central Statistics Office and Northern Ireland census 2011 © NISRA (population data); Irish Public Sector Data (CC BY 4.0) (Gaeltacht); Logainm.ie (placenames); Roads Service and Transport Infrastructure Ireland

Printer: Wyndeham Peterborough Ltd, UK

Scale 1:250,000
or 3.95 miles to 1 inch

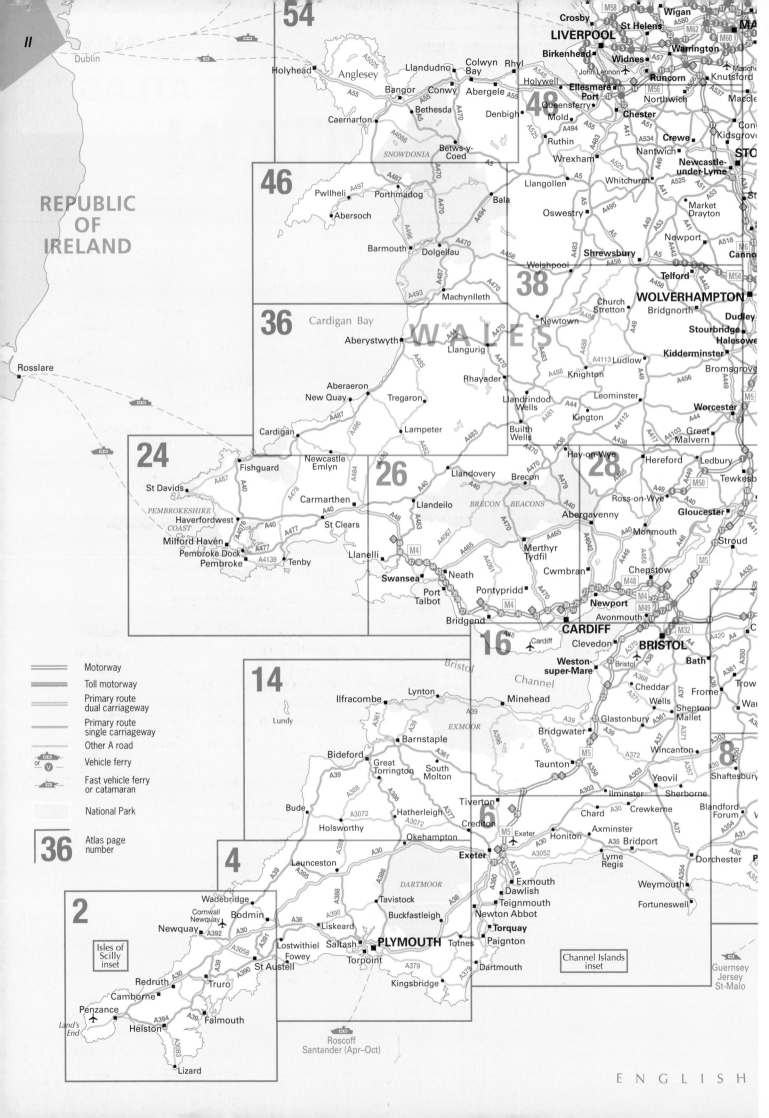

ENGLAND

Rotterdam (Europoort) Zeebrugge

Cleethorpes · Brigg · Market Rasen · Louth · Mablethorpe
Doncaster · Doncaster Sheffield Bawtry · Gainsborough · Retford · Worksop
Rotherham · SHEFFIELD · Chesterfield · Mansfield · Newark-on-Trent · Sleaford · Horncastle · Skegness
Glossop · Stockport · Buxton · Bakewell · Matlock · Alfreton · Lincoln
PEAK DISTRICT · Leek · Ashbourne · Ilkeston · DERBY · NOTTINGHAM · Grantham · Boston · The Wash

Sheringham · Cromer · North Walsham
Hunstanton · Aylsham · Fakenham · Caister-on-Sea
Dereham · Norwich · THE BROADS · Great Yarmouth
Swaffham · Lowestoft
King's Lynn · Downham Market · Attleborough · Bungay · Beccles
Spalding · Bourne · Wisbech · March · Chatteris · Diss · Southwold

STOKE-ON-TRENT · Stafford · Burton upon Trent · Loughborough · Melton Mowbray · Oakham · Stamford · Peterborough
Rugeley · Lichfield · Tamworth · LEICESTER · Wigston · Market Harborough · Corby · Ely · Thetford
Walsall · Nuneaton · Hinckley · Kettering · Huntingdon · Newmarket · Bury St Edmunds · Stowmarket · Aldeburgh
BIRMINGHAM · COVENTRY · Rugby · Northampton · St Neots · Cambridge · Sudbury · Woodbridge · Ipswich
Warwick · Royal Leamington Spa · Daventry · Bedford · Royston · Haverhill · Halstead · Felixstowe · Harwich
Redditch · Stratford-upon-Avon · Evesham · Banbury · Towcester · Brackley · Milton Keynes · Baldock · Stevenage · Stansted · Braintree · Colchester · Hook of Holland
Cheltenham · Stow-on-the-Wold · Chipping Norton · Bicester · Leighton Buzzard · Dunstable · Luton · Bishop's Stortford · Witham · Maldon · Clacton-on-Sea

Cirencester · Burford · Witney · Oxford · Thame · Aylesbury · Hertford · Harlow · Chelmsford · Burnham-on-Crouch
Swindon · Faringdon · Wantage · Abingdon-on-Thames · High Wycombe · Watford · St Albans · Hatfield · Brentwood · Southend-on-Sea
Chippenham · Marlborough · Newbury · Maidenhead · Beaconsfield · Slough · LONDON · Basildon · Canvey Island · Margate
Devizes · Reading · Windsor · Bracknell · Heathrow · Richmond · Dartford · Tilbury · Sheerness · Ramsgate
Staines-upon-Thames · Woking · Leatherhead · Croydon · Swanley · Rochester · Chatham · Gravesend · Canterbury · Sandwich · Deal
Basingstoke · Guildford · Dorking · Reigate · Redhill · Sevenoaks · Maidstone · Deal
Andover · Farnham · Alton · East Grinstead · Tonbridge · Royal Tunbridge Wells · Ashford · Channel Tunnel Terminal · Dover
Amesbury · Winchester · Petersfield · Billingshurst · Horsham · Crawley · Gatwick · Crowborough · Tenterden · Hythe · Folkestone · Dunkirk
Wilton · Salisbury · Romsey · Eastleigh · Midhurst · SOUTH DOWNS · Heathfield · New Romney · Calais
SOUTHAMPTON · Chichester · Arundel · Shoreham-by-Sea · Lewes · Rye · Calais / Coquelles Terminal
Bournemouth · Ringwood · Lymington · Gosport · Portsmouth · Bognor Regis · Worthing · Brighton · Newhaven · Hastings · Bexhill
Swanage · Isle of Wight · Sandown · Shanklin · Eastbourne

Cherbourg (May–Aug)
Guernsey · Jersey · St-Malo · Caen (Ouistreham) · le Havre (Jan–Oct) · Bilbao (Jan–Oct) · Santander (Jan–Oct)
Cherbourg

FRANCE
CHANNEL
Dieppe

0 10 20 30 miles
0 10 20 30 40 kilometres

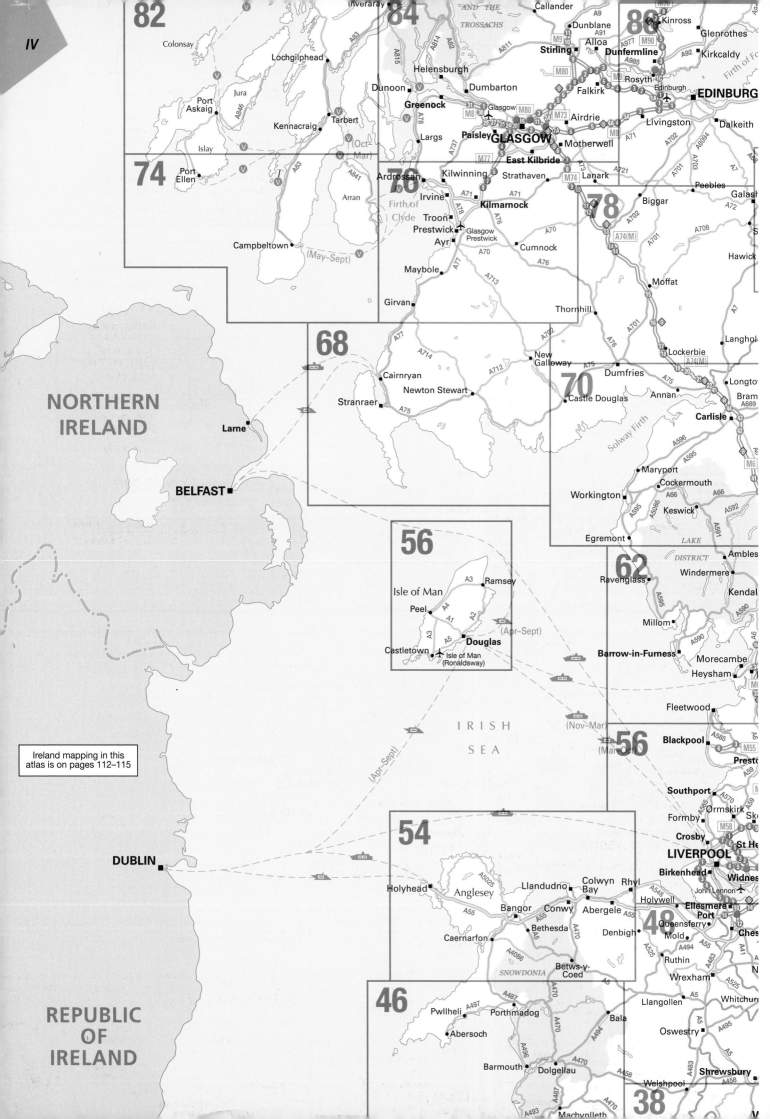

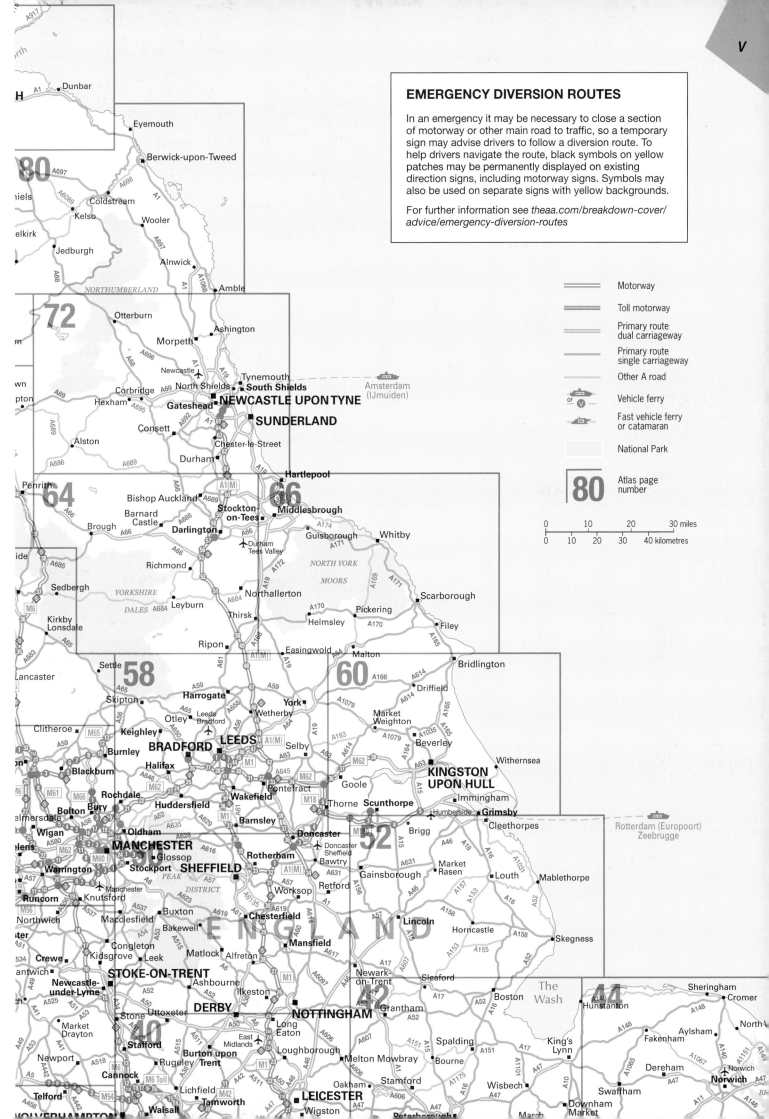

EMERGENCY DIVERSION ROUTES

In an emergency it may be necessary to close a section of motorway or other main road to traffic, so a temporary sign may advise drivers to follow a diversion route. To help drivers navigate the route, black symbols on yellow patches may be permanently displayed on existing direction signs, including motorway signs. Symbols may also be used on separate signs with yellow backgrounds.

For further information see *theaa.com/breakdown-cover/ advice/emergency-diversion-routes*

════════	Motorway
════════	Toll motorway
════════	Primary route dual carriageway
────────	Primary route single carriageway
────────	Other A road
🚢 or V	Vehicle ferry
🚢	Fast vehicle ferry or catamaran
☐	National Park
80	Atlas page number

0   10   20   30 miles
0   10   20   30   40 kilometres

80

Dunbar
A1
Eyemouth
A697
A6089
Coldstream
Kelso
Berwick-upon-Tweed
A698
A1
Wooler
Jedburgh
A68
A697
A68
Alnwick
72
NORTHUMBERLAND
A1068
Amble
A68
Otterburn
A696
Ashington
Morpeth
A1
A69
Newcastle
A68
A696
North Shields
South Shields
Tynemouth
Amsterdam (IJmuiden)
Corbridge
A69
A69
Gateshead
NEWCASTLE UPON TYNE
Hexham
A695
A692
SUNDERLAND
A689
Consett
A693
Chester-le-Street
Alston
A686
Durham
A19
A689
Hartlepool
Penrith
A68
A1(M)
64
Bishop Auckland
A689
Stockton-on-Tees
66
A66
Barnard Castle
A688
Middlesbrough
Brough
A66
A174
Darlington
A66
Guisborough
A171
Whitby
A685
Durham Tees Valley
Richmond
A66
NORTH YORK MOORS
A169
A171
ide
A66
A1
YORKSHIRE DALES
A684
Northallerton
A19
A172
Scarborough
Sedbergh
A683
Leyburn
A684
Thirsk
A170
Pickering
A170
Filey
M6
Kirkby Lonsdale
Ripon
A165
A61
A19
A1(M)
Easingwold
A64
Malton
Bridlington
A65
Settle
A1(M)
A166
A614
Lancaster
58
A59
A59
60
Driffield
Skipton
A59
York
A1079
A614
A614
Harrogate
A65
Wetherby
A64
Market Weighton
A165
Clitheroe
A656
Otley
Leeds Bradford
A58
A19
A1035
Beverley
M65
Keighley
A650
A658
A1079
A164
Burnley
BRADFORD
LEEDS
A1(M)
Selby
A163
M62
Halifax
A63
A63
Withernsea
M61
M66
Rochdale
A646
M62
Wakefield
Pontefract
A645
Goole
KINGSTON UPON HULL
Bolton
Bury
Huddersfield
A629
M18
Thorne
Scunthorpe
A15
Immingham
Wigan
Oldham
A62
M1
Barnsley
A635
Doncaster
M180
Grimsby
A580
M60
A628
A616
Rotherham
Doncaster Sheffield
52
Brigg
Cleethorpes
Rotterdam (Europoort) Zeebrugge
Warrington
M62
MANCHESTER
Stockport
Glossop
SHEFFIELD
Bawtry
A1(M)
A631
A46
A18
M56
Runcorn
Knutsford
PEAK DISTRICT
A57
Worksop
A631
Gainsborough
Market Rasen
A16
Louth
Mablethorpe
Northwich
A537
Macclesfield
Buxton
A619
A57
A1
A46
A157
A52
Crewe
Congleton
Bakewell
Chesterfield
A614
Retford
A156
A158
Lincoln
Skegness
Kidsgrove
Leek
A515
Matlock
Alfreton
Mansfield
A617
Horncastle
A158
A155
STOKE-ON-TRENT
Ashbourne
Ilkeston
A6097
Newark-on-Trent
A17
Sleaford
Boston
The Wash
44
Sheringham
Cromer
Newcastle-under-Lyme
A50
DERBY
NOTTINGHAM
42
Grantham
A52
Hunstanton
A148
Stone
Uttoxeter
A50
A511
Long Eaton
A606
A607
A52
A17
King's Lynn
A148
Aylsham
Stafford
A515
East Midlands
Loughborough
A46
Melton Mowbray
Spalding
A151
A17
A10
Fakenham
A1067
Dereham
A47
Norwich
Cannock
Burton upon Trent
M1
Bourne
Stamford
Wisbech
Swaffham
A11
Telford
Lichfield
M42
LEICESTER
A47
A47
Downham Market
Newport
Rugeley
Tamworth
WOLVERHAMPTON
Walsall
Wigston

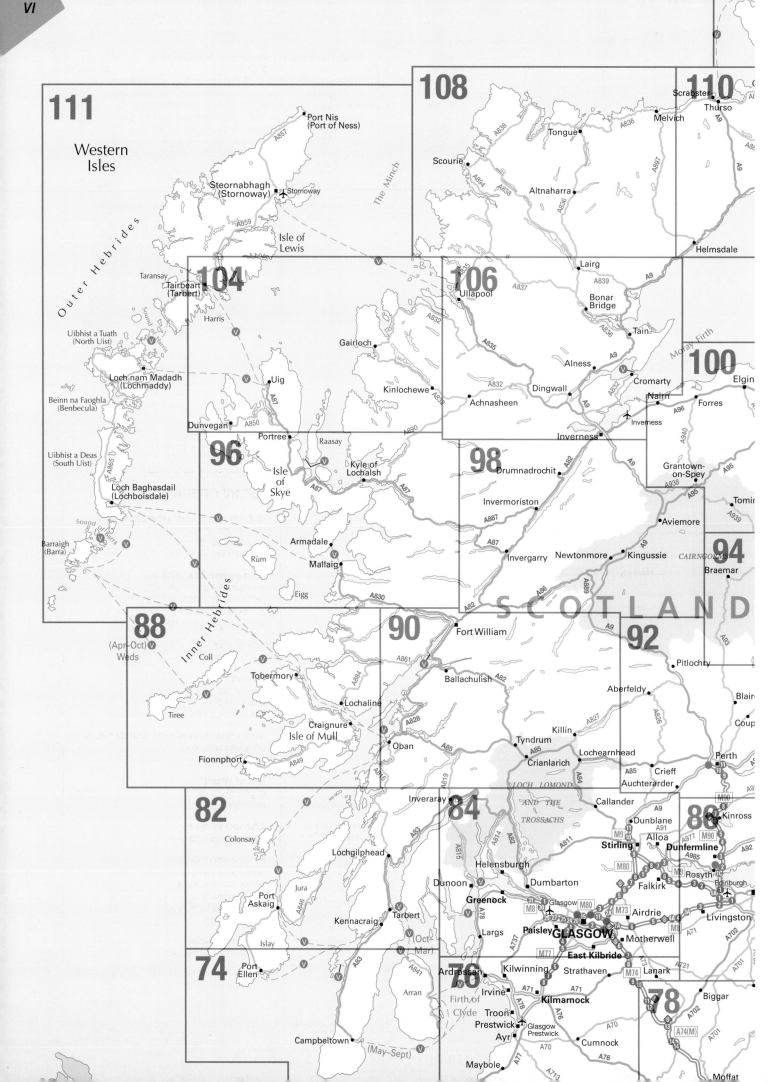

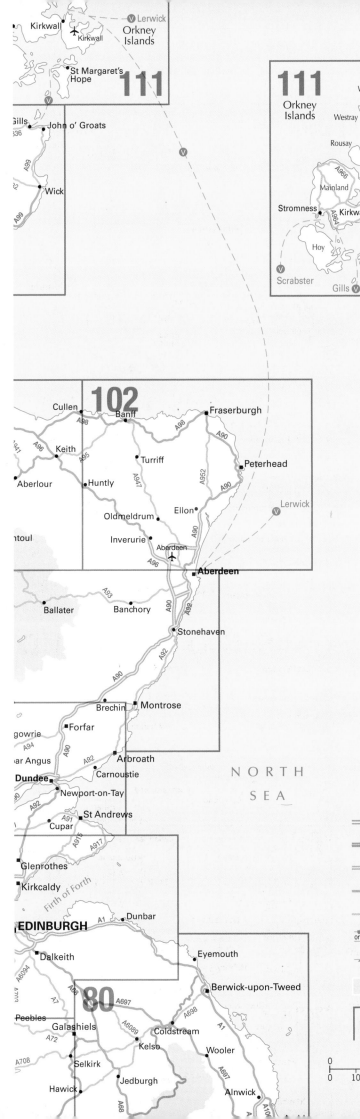

111 Orkney Islands

Papa Westray
North Ronaldsay
Westray
Rousay
Eday
Sanday
Mainland
Stronsay
A966
Shapinsay
Lerwick
Stromness
A964
Kirkwall
Kirkwall
A960
Aberdeen
Hoy
St Margaret's Hope
Scrabster
A961
South Ronaldsay
Gills

111 Shetland Islands

Unst
A968
Yell
Fetlar
A968
Out Skerries
Scatsta
A970
Vidlin
Whalsay
Papa Stour
A971
Mainland
Scalloway
Lerwick
Foula
A970
Bressay
Sumburgh
Kirkwall Aberdeen
Fair Isle

Kirkwall
Orkney Islands
Lerwick
111
St Margaret's Hope
Gills
John o' Groats
Wick

102
Cullen
Banff
Fraserburgh
A98
A90
Keith
Turriff
Peterhead
A941
A96
A95
A947
A952
A90
Aberlour
Huntly
Oldmeldrum
Ellon
A90
Inverurie
Aberdeen
A96
Aberdeen
Lerwick

A93
Ballater
Banchory
A90
A92
Stonehaven
A92
Brechin
Montrose
Forfar
A94
A90
A92
Arbroath
Dundee
Carnoustie
Newport-on-Tay
A92
A91
St Andrews
A915
Cupar
A917
Glenrothes
Firth of Forth
Kirkcaldy
EDINBURGH
A1
Dunbar
Dalkeith
Eyemouth
80
A697
Berwick-upon-Tweed
A1
Peebles
A72
A698
A6091
Coldstream
A708
Galashiels
Kelso
Wooler
Selkirk
A697
Jedburgh
Hawick
A68
Alnwick

NORTH SEA

FERRY OPERATORS

Hebrides and west coast Scotland
calmac.co.uk
skyeferry.co.uk
western-ferries.co.uk

Orkney and Shetland
northlinkferries.co.uk
pentlandferries.co.uk
orkneyferries.co.uk
shetland.gov.uk/ferries

Isle of Man
steam-packet.com

Ireland
irishferries.com
poferries.com
stenaline.co.uk

North Sea (Scandinavia and Benelux)
dfdsseaways.co.uk
poferries.com

Isle of Wight
wightlink.co.uk
redfunnel.co.uk

Channel Islands
condorferries.co.uk

France and Belgium
brittany-ferries.co.uk
condorferries.co.uk
eurotunnel.com
dfdsseaways.co.uk
poferries.com

Northern Spain
brittany-ferries.co.uk

Motorway
Toll motorway
Primary route dual carriageway
Primary route single carriageway
Other A road
or   Vehicle ferry
Fast vehicle ferry or catamaran
National Park
92 Atlas page number

0   10   20   30 miles
0   10   20   30   40 kilometres

Restricted junctions

Motorway and primary route junctions which have access or exit restrictions are shown on the map pages thus:

M1 London - Leeds

Northbound
Access only from A1 (northbound)

Southbound
Exit only to A1 (southbound)

Northbound
Access only from A41 (northbound)

Southbound
Exit only to A41 (southbound)

Northbound
Access only from M25 (no link from A405)

Southbound
Exit only to M25 (no link from A405)

Northbound
Access only from A414

Southbound
Exit only to A414

Northbound
Exit only to M45

Southbound
Access only from M45

Northbound
Exit only to M6 (northbound)

Southbound
Exit only to A14 (southbound)

Northbound
Exit only, no access

Southbound
Access only, no exit

Northbound
Access only from A42

Southbound
No restriction

Northbound
No exit, access only

Southbound
Exit only, no access

Northbound
Exit only, no access

Southbound
Access only, no exit

Northbound
Exit only to M621

Southbound
Access only from M621

Northbound
Exit only to A1(M) (northbound)

Southbound
Access only from A1(M) (southbound)

M2 Rochester - Faversham

Westbound
No exit to A2 (eastbound)

Eastbound
No access from A2 (westbound)

M3 Sunbury - Southampton

Northeastbound
Access only from A303, no exit

Southwestbound
Exit only to A303, no access

Northbound
Exit only, no access

Southbound
Access only, no exit

Northeastbound
Access from M27 only, no exit

Southwestbound
No access to M27 (westbound)

M4 London - South Wales

For junctions 1 & 2 see London district map on pages 120–123

Westbound
Exit only to M48

Eastbound
Access only from M48

Westbound
Access only from M48

Eastbound
Exit only to M48

Westbound
Exit only, no access

Eastbound
Access only, no exit

Westbound
Exit only, no access

Eastbound
Access only, no exit

Westbound
Exit only to A48(M)

Eastbound
Access only from A48(M)

Westbound
Exit only, no access

Eastbound
No restriction

Westbound
Access only, no exit

Eastbound
No access or exit

M5 Birmingham - Exeter

Northeastbound
Access only, no exit

Southwestbound
Exit only, no access

Northeastbound
Access only from A417 (westbound)

Southwestbound
Exit only to A417 (eastbound)

Northeastbound
Exit only to M49

Southwestbound
Access only from M49

Northeastbound
No access, exit only

Southwestbound
No exit, access only

M6 Toll Motorway

See M6 Toll motorway map on page XIII

M6 Rugby - Carlisle

Northbound
Exit only to M6 Toll

Southbound
Access only from M6 Toll

Northbound
Exit only to M42 (southbound) and A446

Southbound
Exit only to A446

Northbound
Access only from M42 (southbound)

Southbound
Exit only to M42

Northbound
Exit only, no access

Southbound
Access only, no exit

Northbound
Exit only to M54

Southbound
Access only from M54

Northbound
Access only from M6 Toll

Southbound
Exit only to M6 Toll

Westbound
Exit only to A483

Eastbound
Access only from A483

Northbound
No restriction

Southbound
Access only from M56 (eastbound)

Northbound
Exit only to M56 (westbound)

Southbound
Access only from M56 (eastbound)

Northbound
Access only, no exit

Southbound
Exit only, no access

Northbound
Exit only, no access

Southbound
Access only, no exit

Northbound
Access only from M61

Southbound
Exit only to M61

Northbound
Exit only, no access

Southbound
Access only, no exit

Northbound
Exit only, no access

Southbound
Access only, no exit

M8 Edinburgh - Bishopton

For junctions 7A to 28A see Glasgow district map on pages 118–119

Westbound
Exit only, no access

Eastbound
Access only, no exit

Westbound
Access only, no exit

Eastbound
Exit only, no access

Westbound
Access only, no exit

Eastbound
Exit only, no access

M9 Edinburgh - Dunblane

Northwestbound
Access only, no exit

Southeastbound
Exit only, no access

Northwestbound
Exit only, no access

Southeastbound
Access only, no exit

Northwestbound
Access only, no exit

Southeastbound
Exit only to A905

Northwestbound
Exit only to M876
(southwestbound)

Southeastbound
Access only from M876
(northeastbound)

M11 London - Cambridge

Northbound
Access only from A406
(eastbound)

Southbound
Exit only to A406

Northbound
Exit only, no access

Southbound
Access only, no exit

Northbound
Exit only, no access

Southbound
No direct access,
use jct 8

Northbound
Exit only to A11

Southbound
Access only from A11

Northbound
Exit only, no access

Southbound
Access only, no exit

Northbound
Exit only, no access

Southbound
Access only, no exit

M20 Swanley - Folkestone

Northwestbound
Staggered junction; follow
signs - access only

Southeastbound
Staggered junction; follow
signs - exit only

Northwestbound
Exit only to M26
(westbound)

Southeastbound
Access only from M26
(eastbound)

Northwestbound
Access only from A20

Southeastbound
For access follow signs -
exit only to A20

Northwestbound
No restriction

Southeastbound
For exit follow signs

Northwestbound
Access only, no exit

Southeastbound
Exit only, no access

M23 Hooley - Crawley

Northbound
Exit only to A23
(northbound)

Southbound
Access only from A23
(southbound)

Northbound
Access only, no exit

Southbound
Exit only, no access

M25 London Orbital Motorway

See M25 London Orbital motorway map on
page *XII*

M26 Sevenoaks - Wrotham

Westbound
Exit only to clockwise
M25 (westbound)

Eastbound
Access only from
anticlockwise M25
(eastbound)

Westbound
Access only from M20
(northwestbound)

Eastbound
Exit only to M20
(southeastbound)

M27 Cadnam - Portsmouth

Westbound
Staggered junction; follow
signs - access only from
M3 (southbound). Exit
only to M3 (northbound)

Eastbound
Staggered junction; follow
signs - access only from
M3 (southbound). Exit
only to M3 (northbound)

Westbound
Exit only, no access

Eastbound
Access only, no exit

Westbound
Staggered junction; follow
signs - exit only to M275
(southbound)

Eastbound
Staggered junction; follow
signs - access only from
M275 (northbound)

M40 London - Birmingham

Northwestbound
Exit only, no access

Southeastbound
Access only, no exit

Northwestbound
Exit only, no access

Southeastbound
Access only, no exit

Northwestbound
Exit only to M40/A40

Southeastbound
Access only from
M40/A40

Northwestbound
Exit only, no access

Southeastbound
Access only, no exit

Northwestbound
Access only, no exit

Southeastbound
Exit only, no access

Northwestbound
Access only, no exit

Southeastbound
Exit only, no access

M42 Bromsgrove - Measham

See Birmingham district map on pages
116–117

M45 Coventry - M1

Westbound
Access only from A45
(northbound)

Eastbound
Exit only, no access

Westbound
Access only from M1
(northbound)

Eastbound
Exit only to M1
(southbound)

M48 Chepstow

Westbound
Access only from M4
(westbound)

Eastbound
Exit only to M4
(eastbound)

Westbound
No exit to M4 (eastbound)

Eastbound
No access from M4
(westbound)

M53 Mersey Tunnel - Chester

Northbound
Access only from M56
(westbound). Exit only to
M56 (eastbound)

Southbound
Access only from M56
(westbound). Exit only to
M56 (eastbound)

M54 Telford - Birmingham

Westbound
Access only from M6
(northbound)

Eastbound
Exit only to M6
(southbound)

M56 Chester - Manchester

For junctions 1,2,3,4 & 7 see Manchester
district map on pages 124–125

Westbound
Access only, no exit

Eastbound
No access or exit

Westbound
No exit to M6
(southbound)

Eastbound
No access from M6
(northbound)

Westbound
Exit only to M53

Eastbound
Access only from M53

Westbound
No access or exit

Eastbound
No restriction

M57 Liverpool Outer Ring Road

Northwestbound
Access only, no exit

Southeastbound
Exit only, no access

Northwestbound
Access only from A580
(westbound)

Southeastbound
Exit only, no access

M58 Liverpool - Wigan

Westbound
Exit only, no access

Eastbound
Access only, no exit

M60 Manchester Orbital

See Manchester district map on pages
124–125

M61 Manchester - Preston

Northwestbound
No access or exit

Southeastbound
Exit only, no access

Northwestbound
Exit only to M6
(northbound)

Southeastbound
Access only from M6
(southbound)

M62 Liverpool - Kingston upon Hull

Westbound
Access only, no exit

Eastbound
Exit only, no access

Westbound
No access to A1(M) (southbound)

Eastbound
No restriction

M65 Preston - Colne

Northeastbound
Exit only, no access

Southwestbound
Access only, no exit

Northeastbound
Access only, no exit

Southwestbound
Exit only, no access

M66 Bury

Northbound
Exit only to A56 (northbound)

Southbound
Access only from A56 (southbound)

Northbound
Exit only, no access

Southbound
Access only, no exit

M67 Hyde Bypass

Westbound
Access only, no exit

Eastbound
Exit only, no access

Westbound
Exit only, no access

Eastbound
Access only, no exit

Westbound
Exit only, no access

Eastbound
No restriction

M69 Coventry - Leicester

Northbound
Access only, no exit

Southbound
Exit only, no access

M73 East of Glasgow

Northbound
No exit to A74 and A721

Southbound
No exit to A74 and A721

Northbound
No access from or exit to A89. No access from M8 (eastbound)

Southbound
No access from or exit to A89. No exit to M8 (westbound)

M74 and A74(M) Glasgow - Gretna

Northbound
Exit only, no access

Southbound
Access only, no exit

Northbound
Access only, no exit

Southbound
Exit only, no access

Northbound
No access from A74 and A721

Southbound
Access only, no exit to A74 and A721

Northbound
Access only, no exit

Southbound
Exit only, no access

Northbound
No access or exit

Southbound
Exit only, no access

Northbound
No restriction

Southbound
Access only, no exit

Northbound
Access only, no exit

Southbound
Exit only, no access

Northbound
Exit only, no access

Southbound
Exit only, no access

Northbound
Exit only, no access

Southbound
Access only, no exit

Northbound
Exit only, no access

Southbound
Access only, no exit

M77 Glasgow - Kilmarnock

Northbound
No exit to M8 (westbound)

Southbound
No access from M8 (eastbound)

Northbound
Access only, no exit

Southbound
Exit only, no access

Northbound
Access only, no exit

Southbound
Exit only, no access

Northbound
Access only, no exit

Southbound
No restriction

Northbound
Exit only, no access

Southbound
Exit only, no access

M80 Glasgow - Stirling

For junctions 1 & 4 see Glasgow district map on pages 118–119

Northbound
Exit only, no access

Southbound
Access only, no exit

Northbound
Access only, no exit

Southbound
Exit only, no access

Northbound
Exit only to M876 (northeastbound)

Southbound
Access only from M876 (southwestbound)

M90 Edinburgh - Perth

Northbound
No exit, access only

Southbound
Exit only to A90 (eastbound)

Northbound
Exit only to A92 (eastbound)

Southbound
Access only from A92 (westbound)

Northbound
Access only, no exit

Southbound
Exit only, no access

Northbound
No access from A912
No exit to A912 (southbound)

Southbound
No access from A912 (northbound).
No exit to A912

M180 Doncaster - Grimsby

Westbound
Access only, no exit

Eastbound
Exit only, no access

M606 Bradford Spur

Northbound
Exit only, no access

Southbound
No restriction

M621 Leeds - M1

Clockwise
Access only, no exit

Anticlockwise
Exit only, no access

Clockwise
No exit or access

Anticlockwise
No restriction

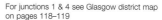

Clockwise
Access only, no exit

Anticlockwise
Exit only, no access

Clockwise
Exit only, no access

Anticlockwise
Access only, no exit

Clockwise
Exit only to M1 (southbound)

Anticlockwise
Access only from M1 (northbound)

M876 Bonnybridge - Kincardine Bridge

Northeastbound
Access only from M80 (northbound)

Southwestbound
Exit only to M80 (southbound)

Northeastbound
Exit only to M9 (eastbound)

Southwestbound
Access only from M9 (westbound)

A1(M) South Mimms - Baldock

Northbound
Exit only, no access

Southbound
Access only, no exit

Northbound
No restriction

Southbound
Exit only, no access

Northbound
Access only, no exit

Southbound
No access or exit

A1(M) Pontefract - Bedale

Northbound
No access to M62 (eastbound)

Southbound
No restriction

Northbound
Access only from M1 (northbound)

Southbound
Exit only to M1 (southbound)

A1(M) Scotch Corner - Newcastle upon Tyne

Northbound
Exit only to A66(M) (eastbound)

Southbound
Access only from A66(M) (westbound)

Northbound
No access. Exit only to A194(M) & A1 (northbound)

Southbound
No exit. Access only from A194(M) & A1 (southbound)

A3(M) Horndean - Havant

Northbound
Access only from A3

Southbound
Exit only to A3

Northbound
Exit only, no access

Southbound
Access only, no exit

A38(M) Birmingham Victoria Road (Park Circus)

Northbound
No exit

Southbound
No access

A48(M) Cardiff Spur

Westbound
Access only from M4 (westbound)

Eastbound
Exit only to M4 (eastbound)

Westbound
Exit only to A48 (westbound)

Eastbound
Access only from A48 (eastbound)

A57(M) Manchester Brook Street (A34)

Westbound
No exit

Eastbound
No access

A58(M) Leeds Park Lane and Westgate

Northbound
No restriction

Southbound
No access

A64(M) Leeds Clay Pit Lane (A58)

Westbound
No exit (to Clay Pit Lane)

Eastbound
No access (from Clay Pit Lane)

A66(M) Darlington Spur

Westbound
Exit only to A1(M) (southbound)

Eastbound
Access only from A1(M) (northbound)

A74(M) Gretna - Abington

Northbound
Exit only, no access

Southbound
No exit

A194(M) Newcastle upon Tyne

Northbound
Access only from A1(M) (northbound)

Southbound
Exit only to A1(M) (southbound)

A12 M25 - Ipswich

Northeastbound
Access only, no exit

Southwestbound
No restriction

Northeastbound
Exit only, no access

Southwestbound
Access only, no exit

Northeastbound
Exit only, no access

Southwestbound
Access only, no exit

Northeastbound
Access only, no exit

Southwestbound
Exit only, no access

Northeastbound
No restriction

Southwestbound
Access only, no exit

Northeastbound
Exit only, no access

Southwestbound
Access only, no exit

Northeastbound
Access only, no exit

Southwestbound
Exit only, no access

Northeastbound
Exit only, no access

Southwestbound
Access only, no exit

Northeastbound
Exit only (for Stratford St Mary and Dedham)

Southwestbound
Access only

A14 M1 - Felixstowe

Westbound
Exit only to M6 & M1 (northbound)

Eastbound
Access only from M6 & M1 (southbound)

Westbound
Exit only, no access

Eastbound
Access only, no exit

Westbound
Exit only to M11 (for London)

Eastbound
Access only, no exit

Westbound
Exit only to A14 (northbound)

Eastbound
Access only, no exit

Northeastbound
Access only, no exit

Southwestbound
No restriction

Northeastbound
Exit only, no access

Southwestbound
Access only, no exit

Northeastbound
Exit only, no access

Southwestbound
Access only, no exit

Westbound
Access only, no exit

Eastbound
Exit only, no access

Westbound
Exit only to A11 Access only from A1303

Eastbound
Access only from A11

Westbound
Access only from A11

Eastbound
Exit only to A11

Westbound
Exit only, no access

Eastbound
Access only, no exit

Westbound
Access only, no exit

Eastbound
Exit only, no access

A55 Holyhead - Chester

Westbound
Exit only, no access

Eastbound
Access only, no exit

Westbound
Access only, no exit

Eastbound
Exit only, no access

Westbound
Exit only, no access

Eastbound
No access or exit.

Westbound
No restriction

Eastbound
No access or exit

Westbound
Exit only, no access

Eastbound
No access or exit

Westbound
Exit only, no access

Eastbound
Access only, no exit

Westbound
Exit only to A5104

Eastbound
Access only from A5104

Refer also to atlas pages 20–21

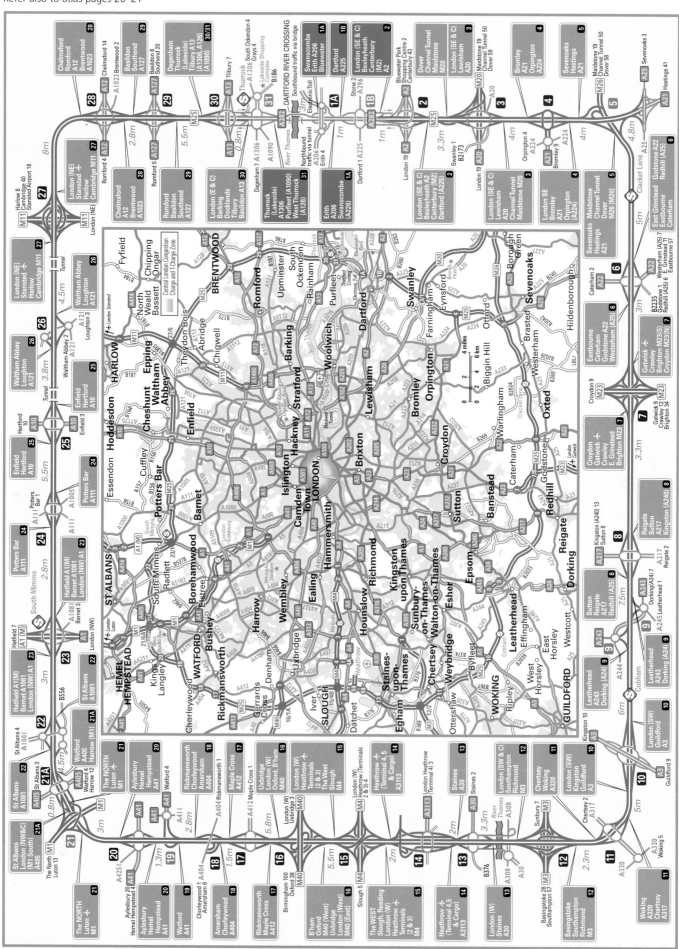

Refer also to atlas page 40

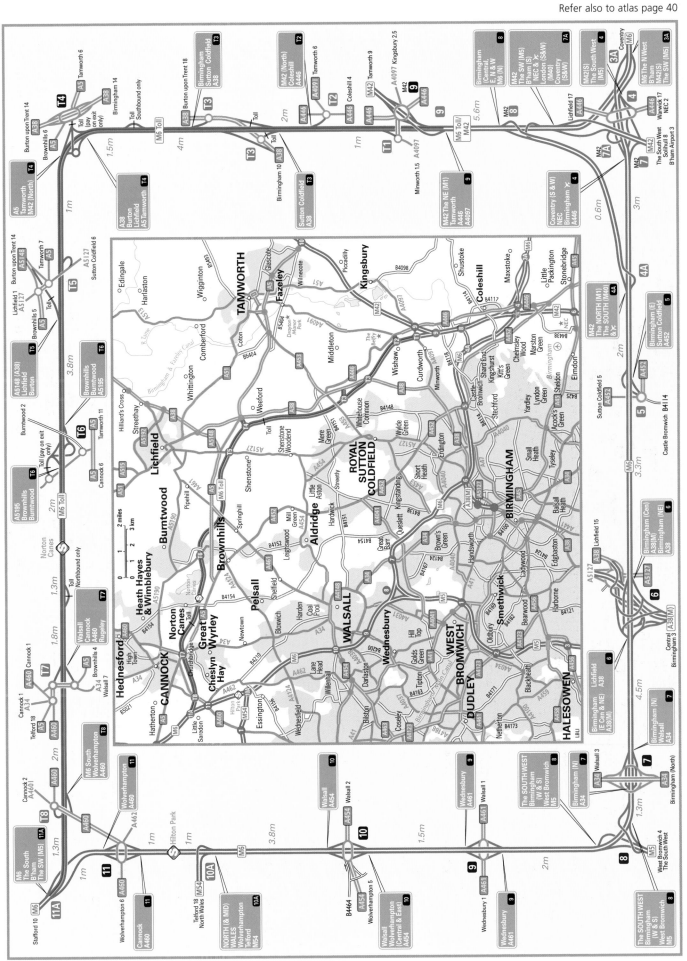

Smart motorways

Since Britain's first motorway (the Preston Bypass) opened in 1958, motorways have changed significantly. A vast increase in car journeys over the last 60 years has meant that motorways quickly filled to capacity. To combat this, the recent development of **smart motorways** uses technology to monitor and actively manage traffic flow and congestion.

How they work

Smart motorways utilise various active traffic management methods, monitored through a regional traffic control centre:

- Traffic flow is monitored using CCTV
- Speed limits are changed to smooth traffic flow and reduce stop-start driving
- Capacity of the motorway can be increased by either temporarily or permanently opening the hard shoulder to traffic
- Warning signs and messages alert drivers to hazards and traffic jams ahead
- Lanes can be closed in the case of an accident or emergency by displaying a red X sign

- Emergency refuge areas are located regularly along the motorway where there is no hard shoulder available

The map shows the main motorway network with the three different types of smart motorway in operation or planned to open over the next five years:

Controlled motorway
Variable speed limits without hard shoulder (the hard shoulder is used in emergencies only)

Hard shoulder running
Variable speed limits with part-time hard shoulder (the hard shoulder is open to traffic at busy times when signs permit)

All lane running
Variable speed limits with hard shoulder as permanent running lane (there is no hard shoulder); this is standard for all new smart motorway schemes since 2013

Standard motorway

Quick tips

- Never drive in a lane closed by a red X

- Keep to the speed limit shown on the gantries
- A solid white line indicates the hard shoulder – do not drive in it unless directed or in the case of an emergency
- A broken white line indicates a normal running lane
- Exit the smart motorway where possible if your vehicle is in difficulty. In an emergency, move onto the hard shoulder where there is one, or the nearest emergency refuge area
- Put on your hazard lights if you break down

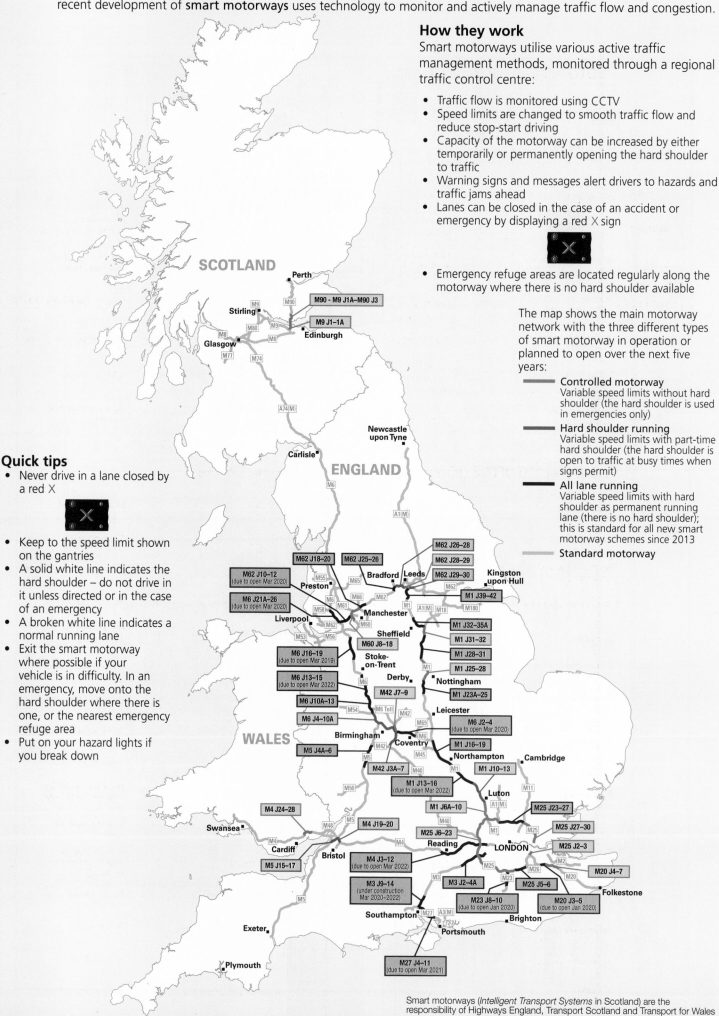

Smart motorways (*Intelligent Transport Systems* in Scotland) are the responsibility of Highways England, Transport Scotland and Transport for Wales

Motoring information

M4	Motorway with number	Primary route service area	Road tunnel	International freight terminal

Toll T4 Toll	Toll motorway with toll station	BATH Primary route destination	Road toll, steep gradient (arrows point downhill)	24-hour Accident & Emergency hospital
6	Motorway junction with and without number	A1123 Other A road single/dual carriageway	Distance in miles between symbols	Crematorium
5	Restricted motorway junctions	B2070 B road single/dual carriageway	Vehicle ferry	Park and Ride (at least 6 days per week)
Fleet	Motorway service area, rest area	Minor road more than 4 metres wide, less than 4 metres wide	Fast vehicle ferry or catamaran	City, town, village or other built-up area
	Motorway and junction under construction	Roundabout	Railway line, in tunnel	Height in metres, mountain pass
A3	Primary route single/dual carriageway	Interchange/junction	Railway/tram station, level crossing	Snow gates (on main routes)
	Primary route junction with and without number	Narrow primary/other A/B road with passing places (Scotland)	Tourist railway	National boundary
	Restricted primary route junctions	Road under construction	Airport (major/minor), heliport	County, administrative boundary

Touring information To avoid disappointment, check opening times before visiting

Scenic route	Garden	Waterfall	Motor-racing circuit
Tourist Information Centre	Arboretum	Hill-fort	Air show venue
Tourist Information Centre (seasonal)	Country park	Roman antiquity	Ski slope (natural, artificial)
Visitor or heritage centre	Agricultural showground	Prehistoric monument	National Trust site
Picnic site	Theme park	Battle site with year	National Trust for Scotland site
Caravan site (AA inspected)	Farm or animal centre	Steam railway centre	English Heritage site
Camping site (AA inspected)	Zoological or wildlife collection	Cave or cavern	Historic Scotland site
Caravan & camping site (AA inspected)	Bird collection	Windmill, monument	Cadw (Welsh heritage) site
Abbey, cathedral or priory	Aquarium	Beach (award winning)	Other place of interest
Ruined abbey, cathedral or priory	RSPB site	Lighthouse	Boxed symbols indicate attractions within urban areas
Castle	National Nature Reserve (England, Scotland, Wales)	Golf course (AA listed)	World Heritage Site (UNESCO)
Historic house or building	Local nature reserve	Football stadium	National Park and National Scenic Area (Scotland)
Museum or art gallery	Wildlife Trust reserve	County cricket ground	Forest Park
Industrial interest	Forest drive	Rugby Union national stadium	Sandy beach
Aqueduct or viaduct	National trail	International athletics stadium	Heritage coast
Vineyard, brewery or distillery	Viewpoint	Horse racing, show jumping	Major shopping centre

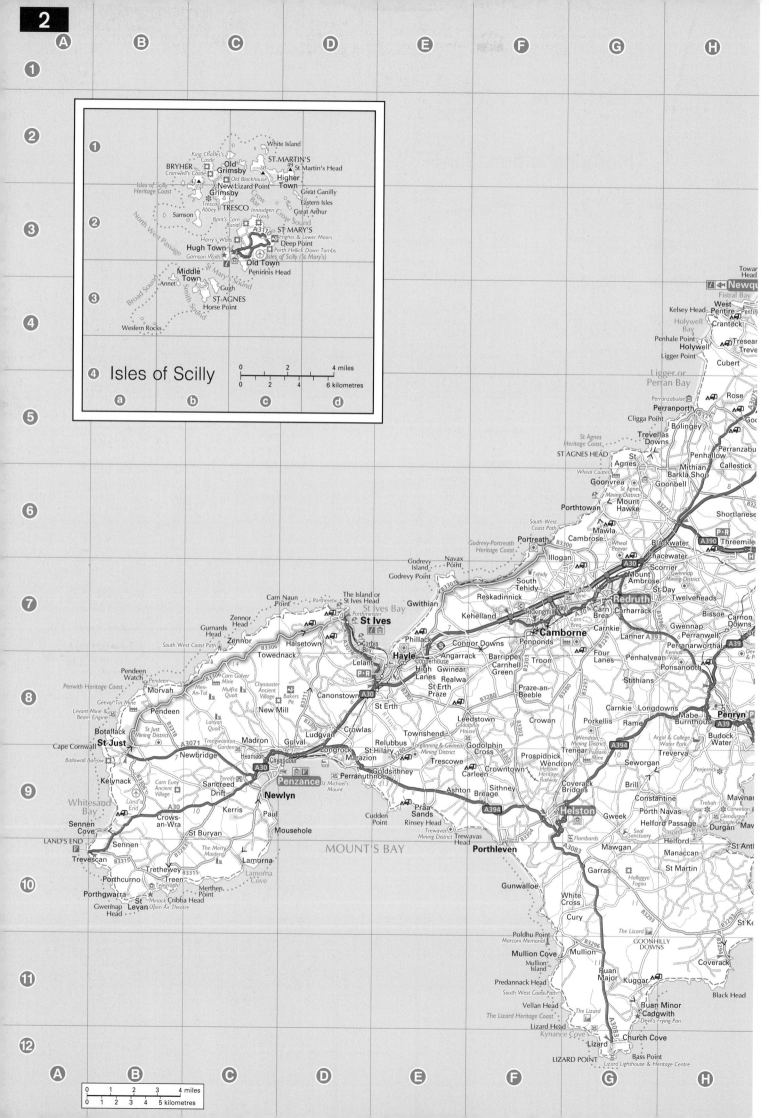

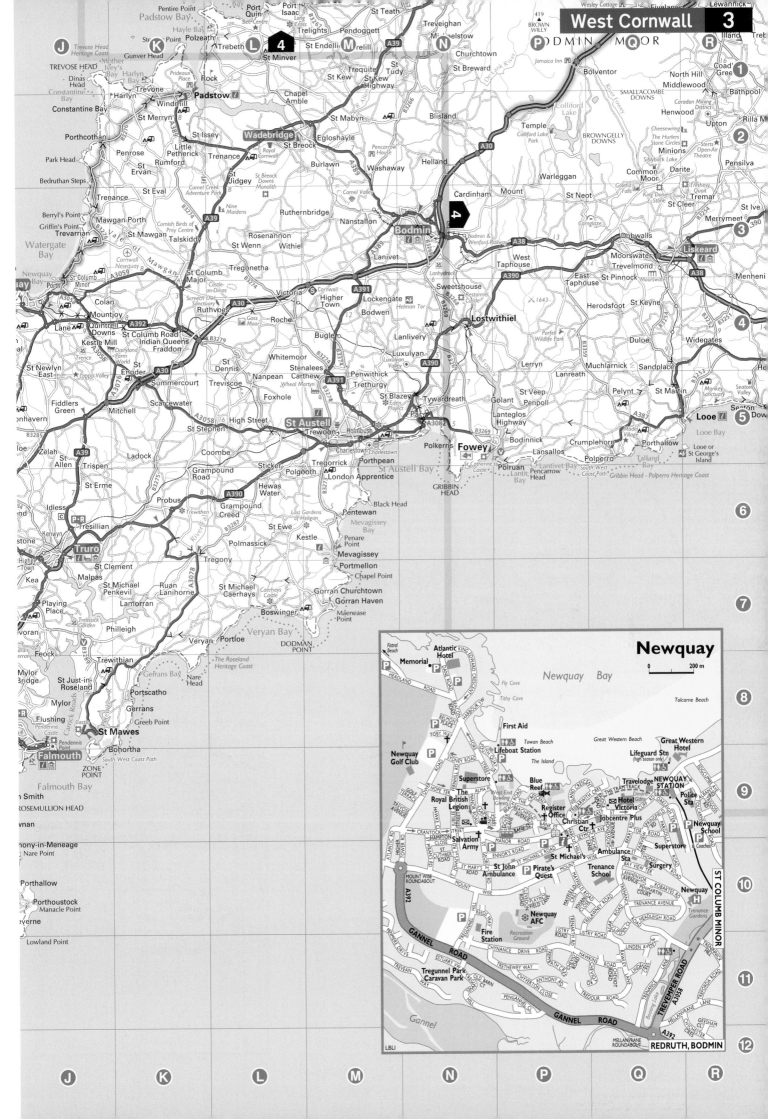

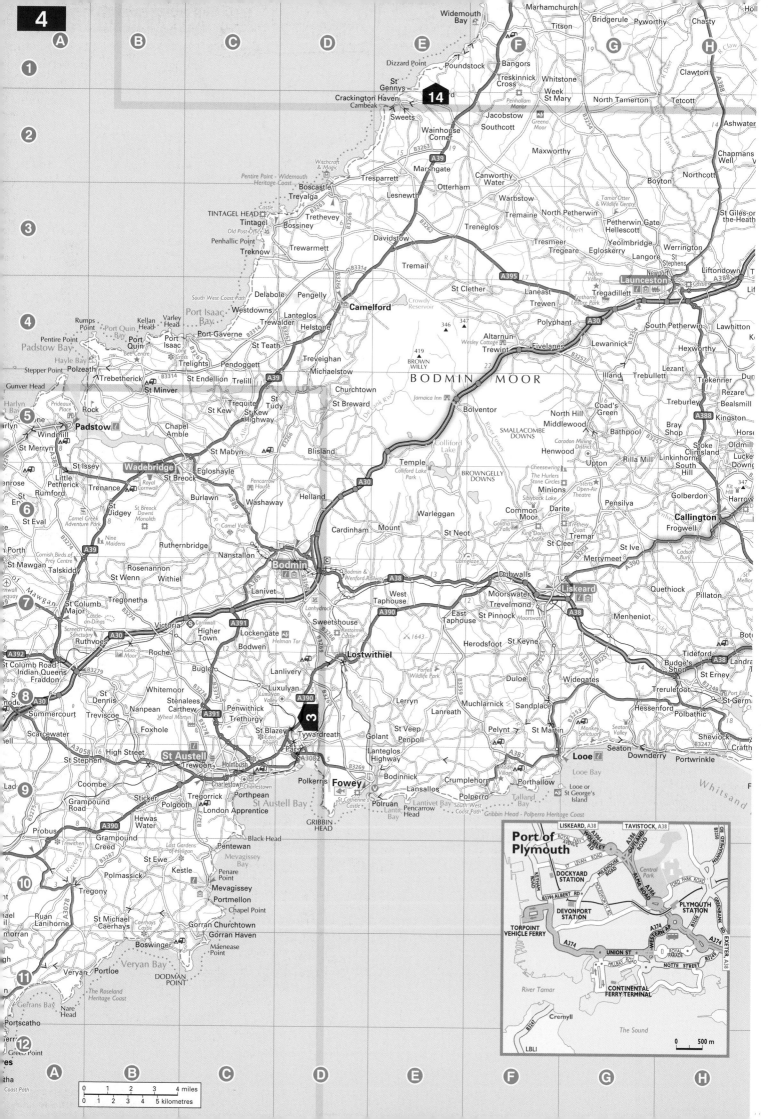

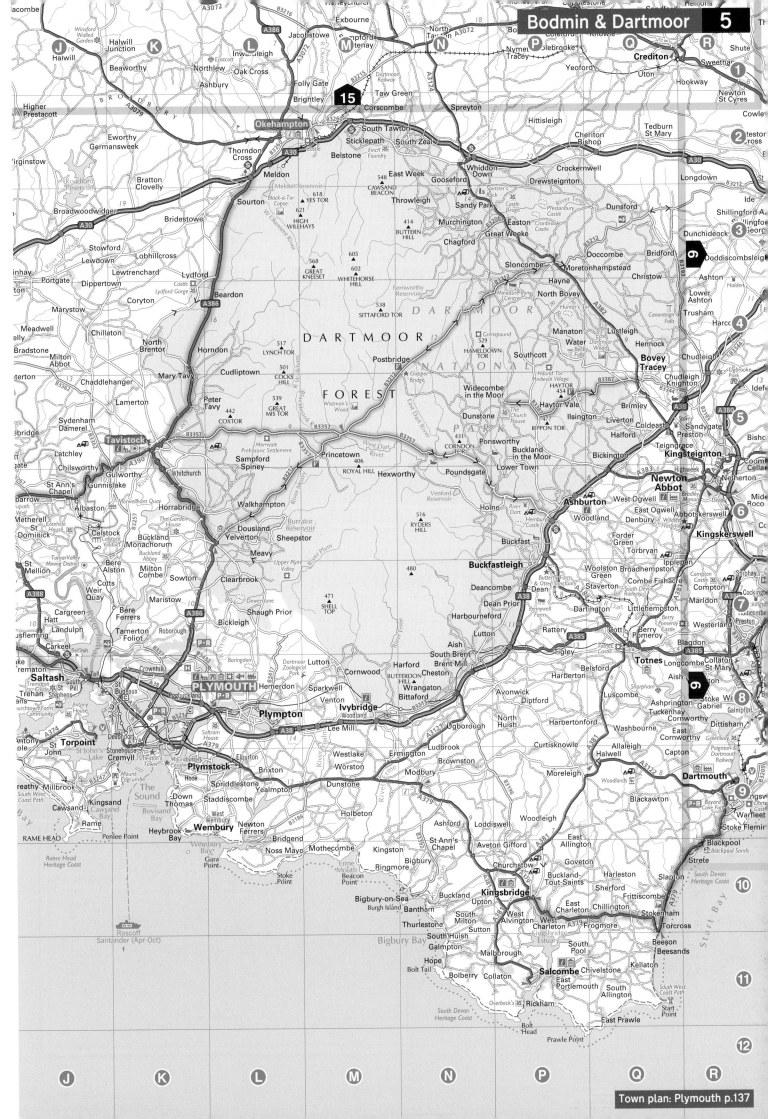

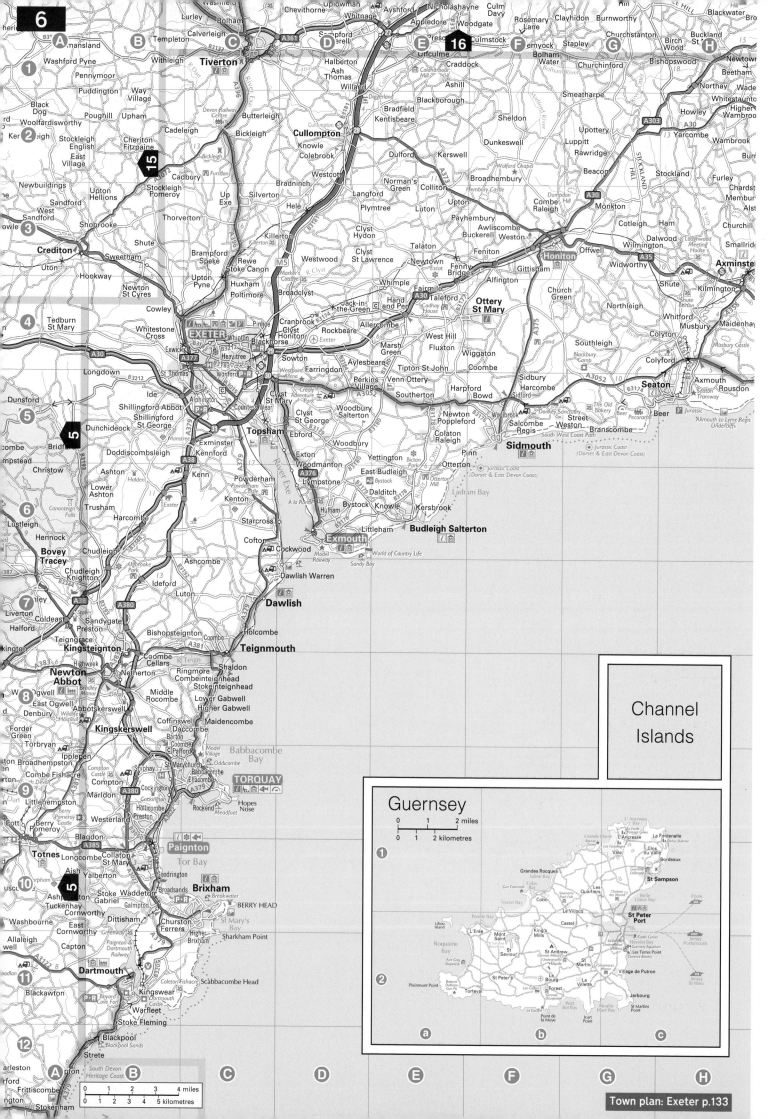

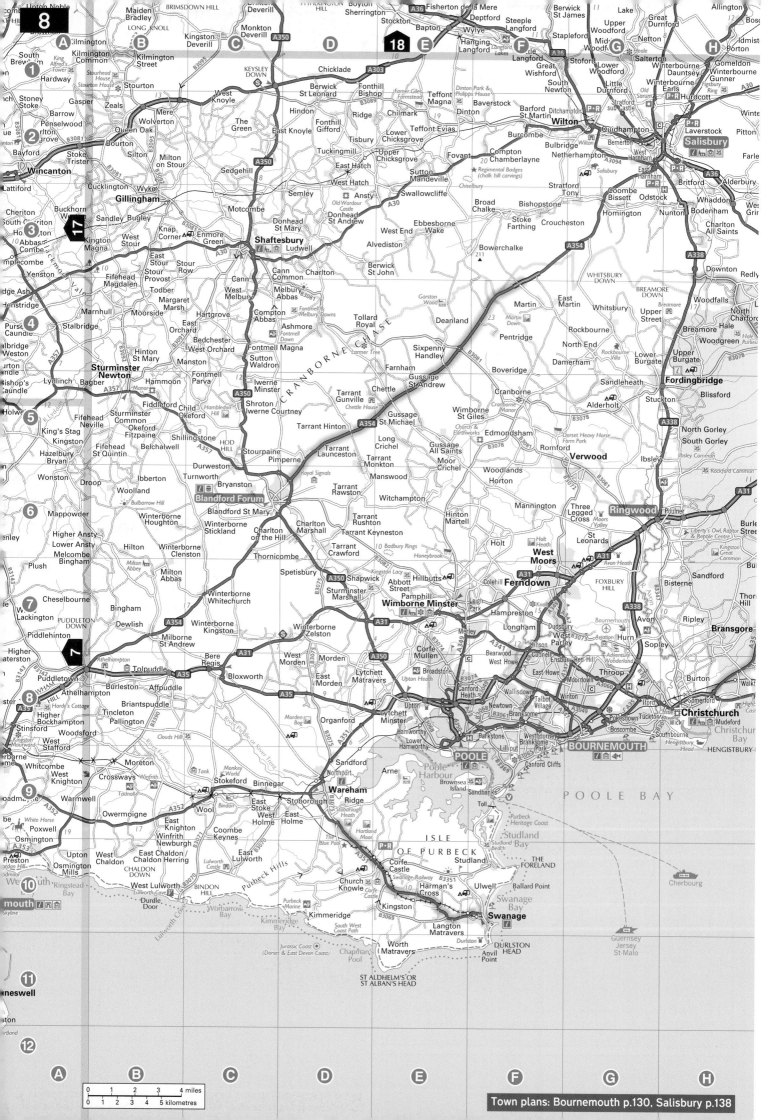

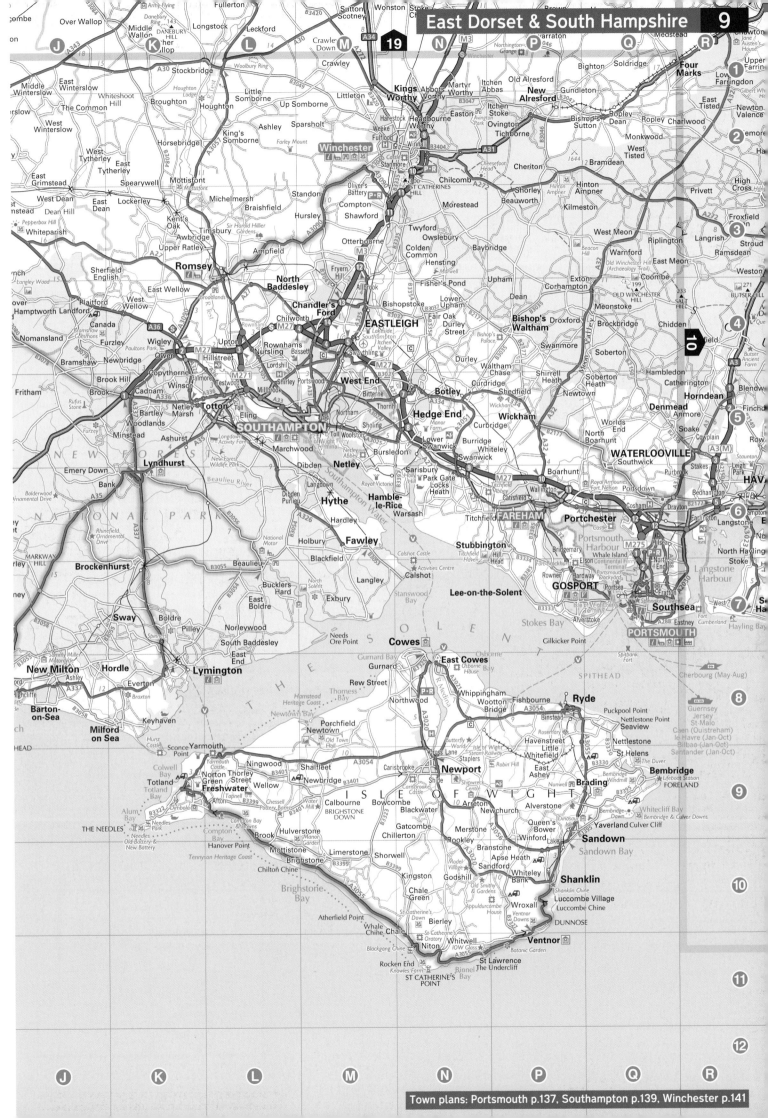

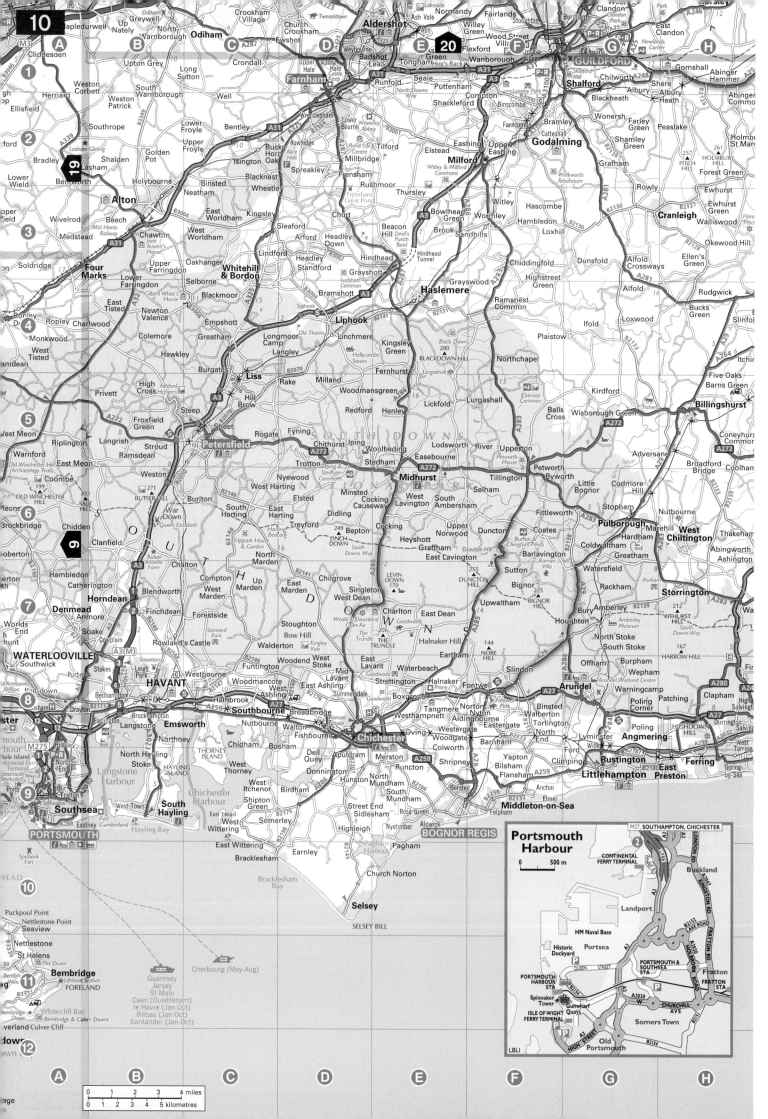

Town plan: Brighton p.131

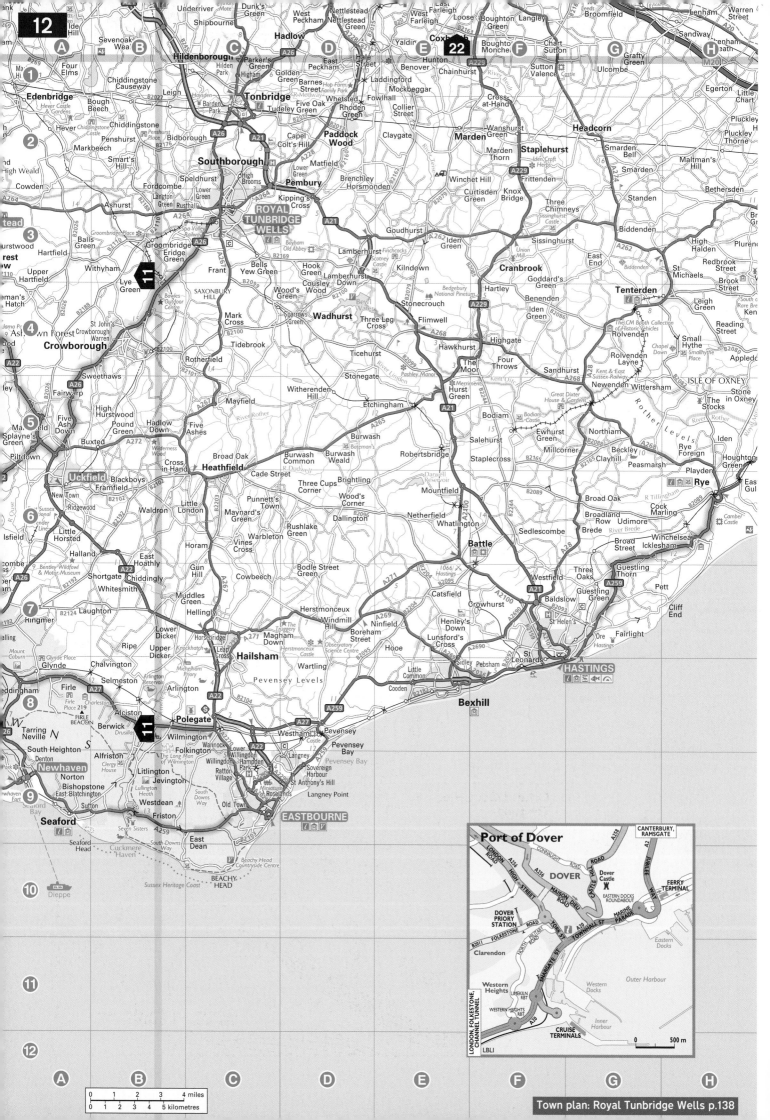

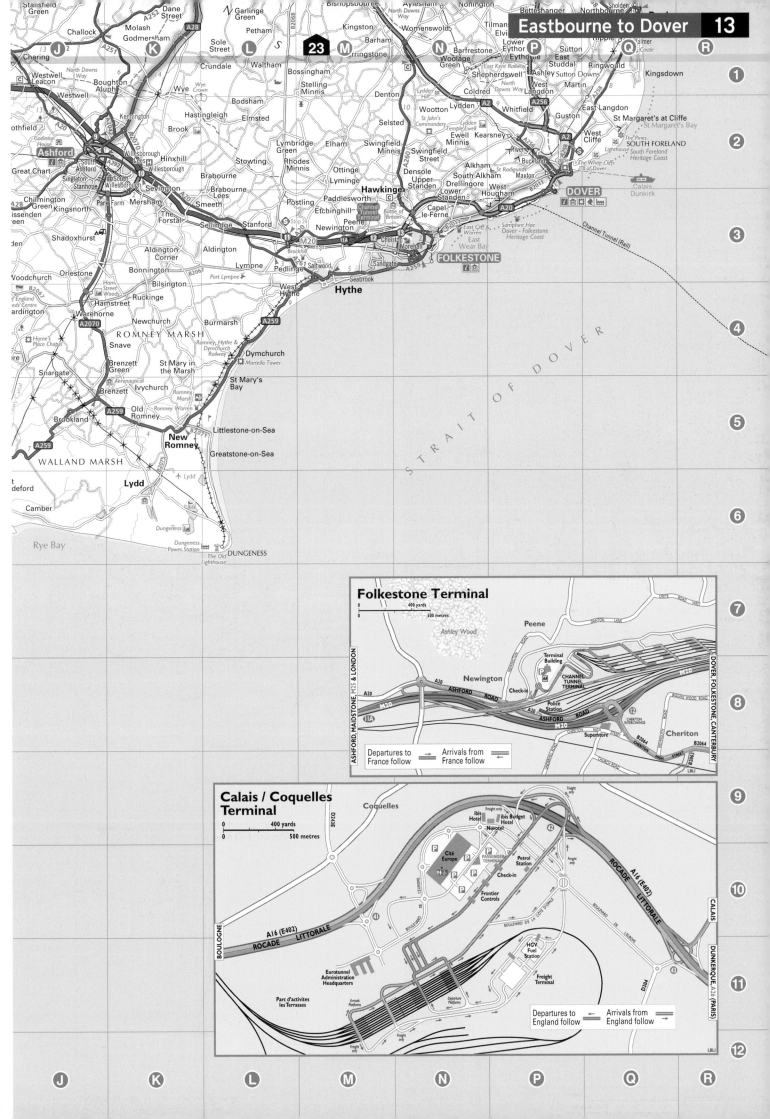

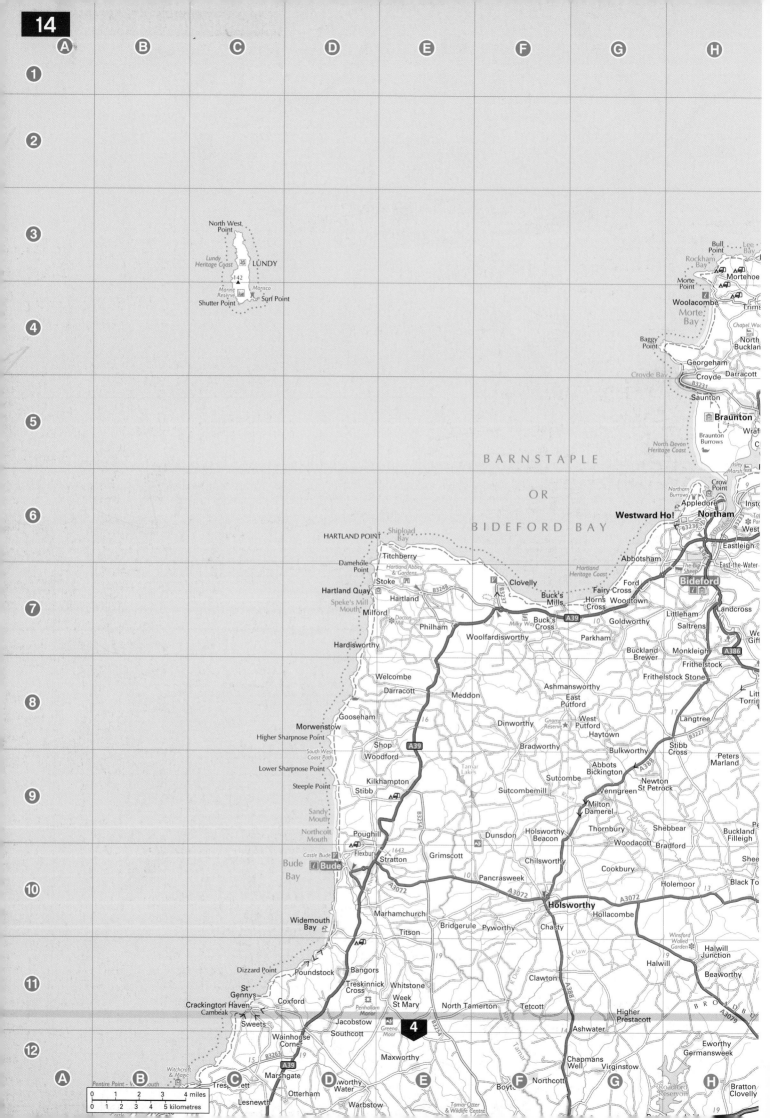

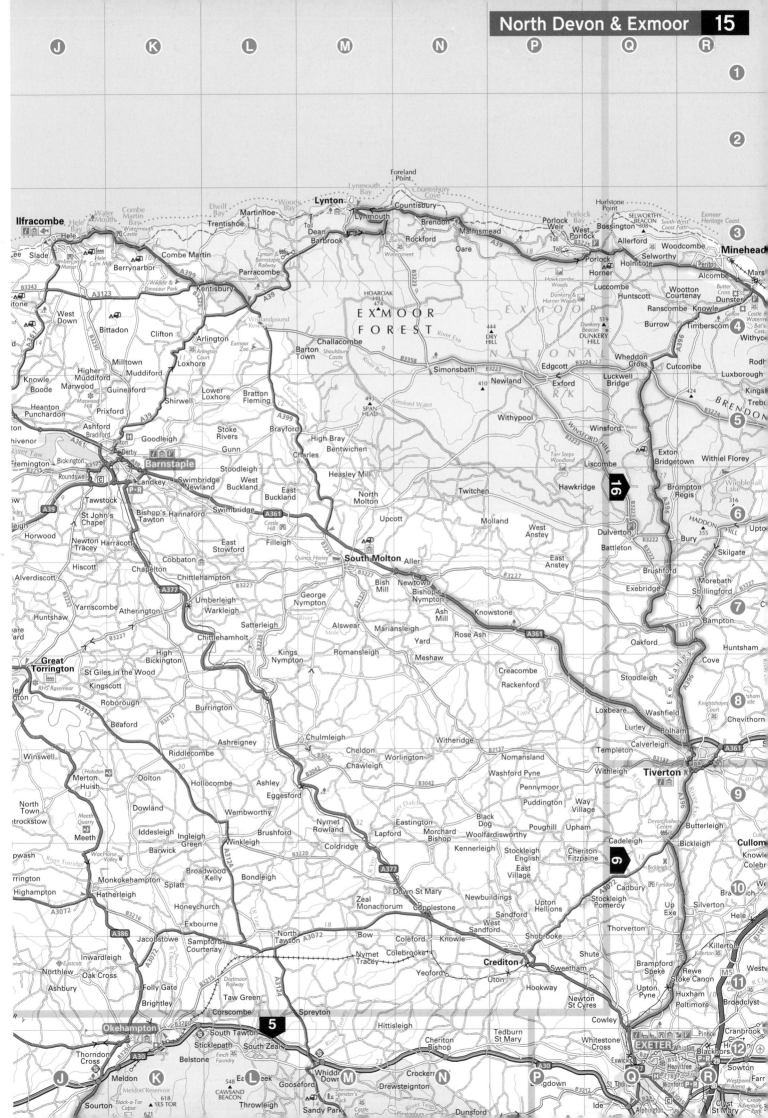

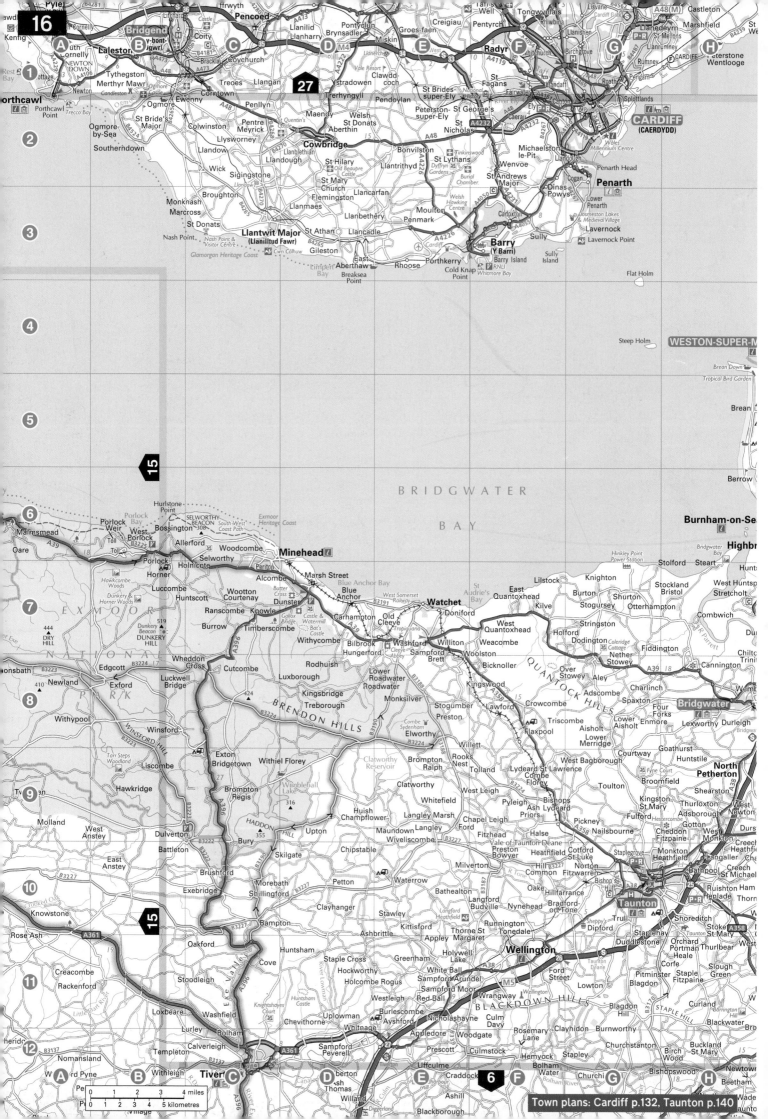

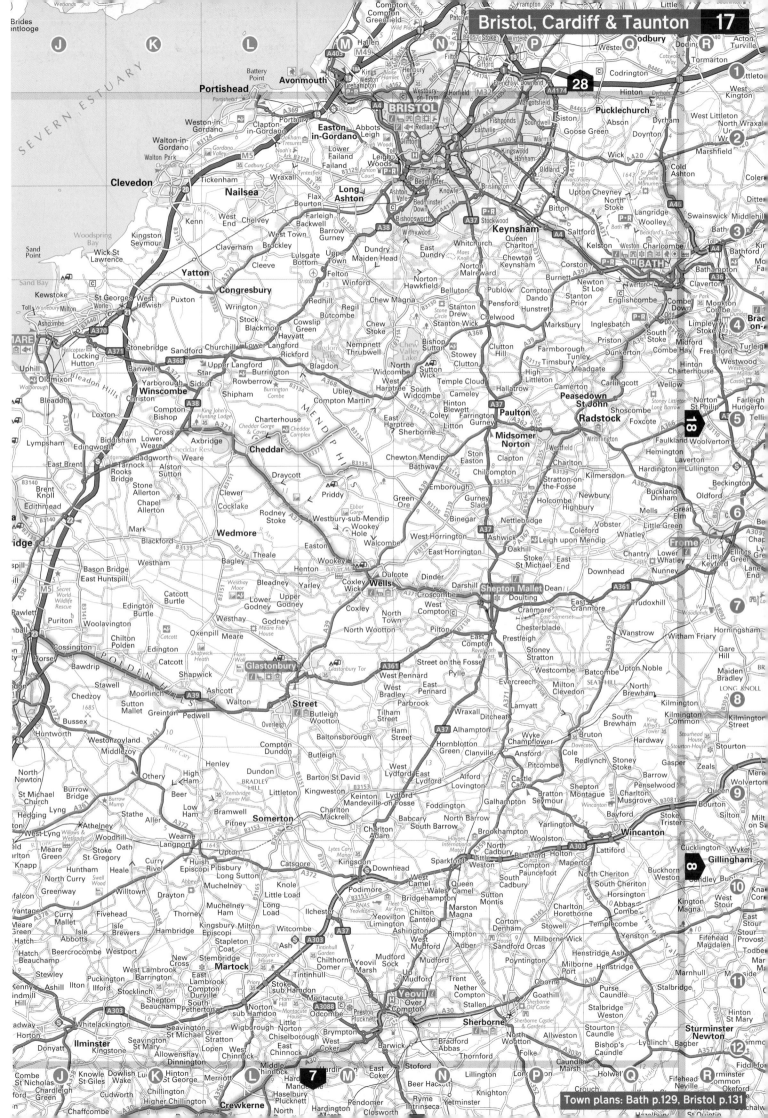

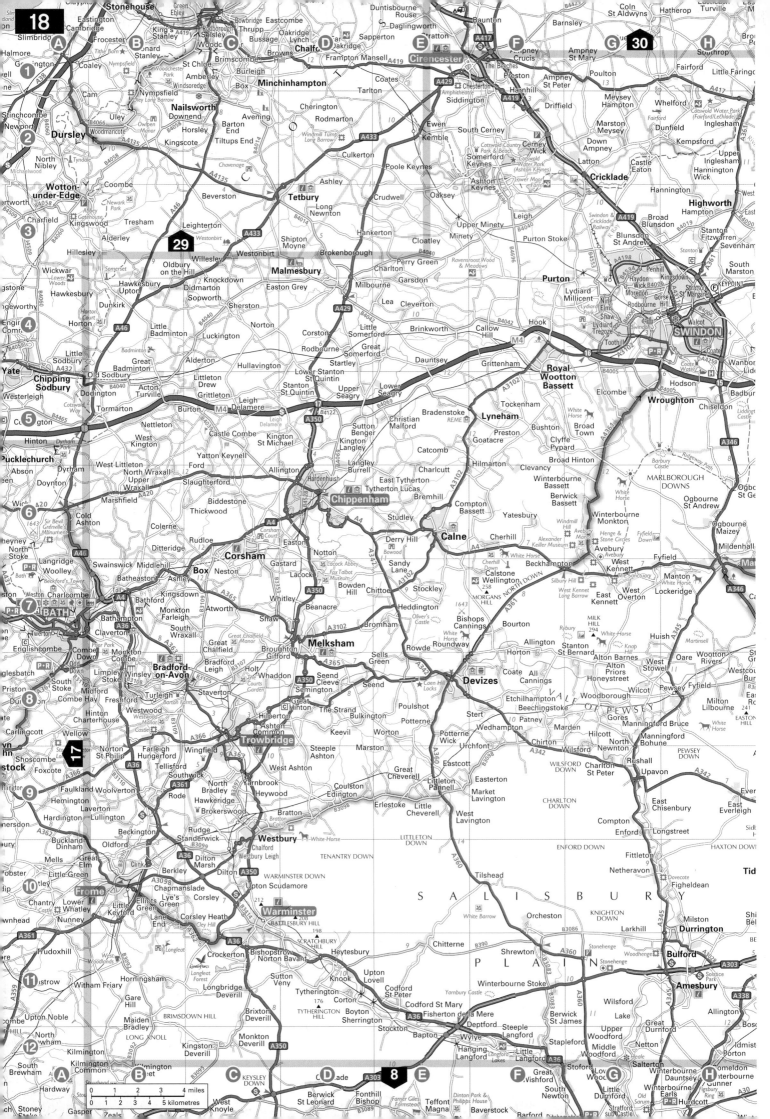

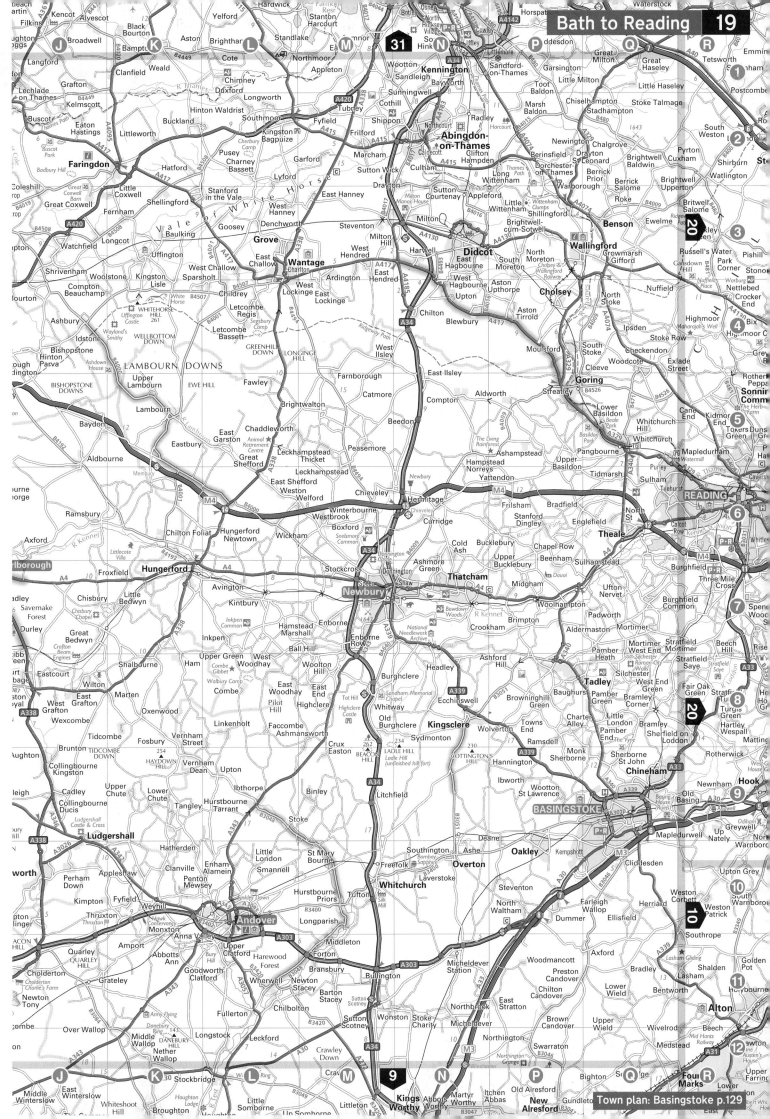

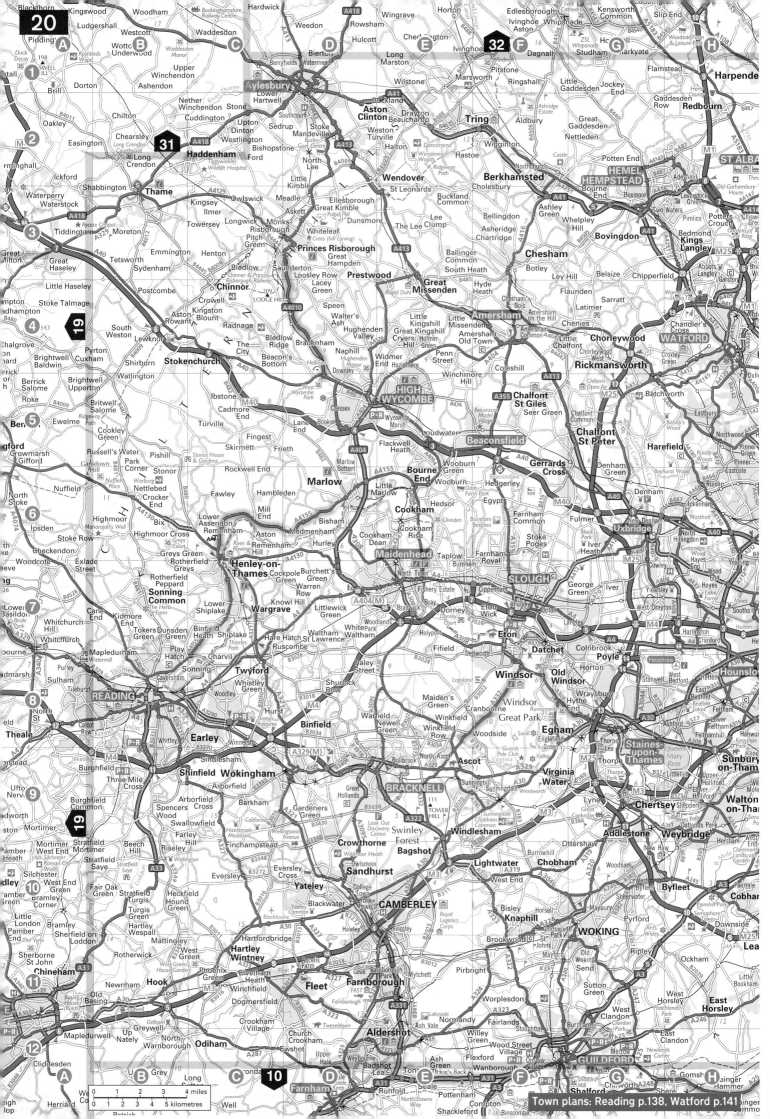

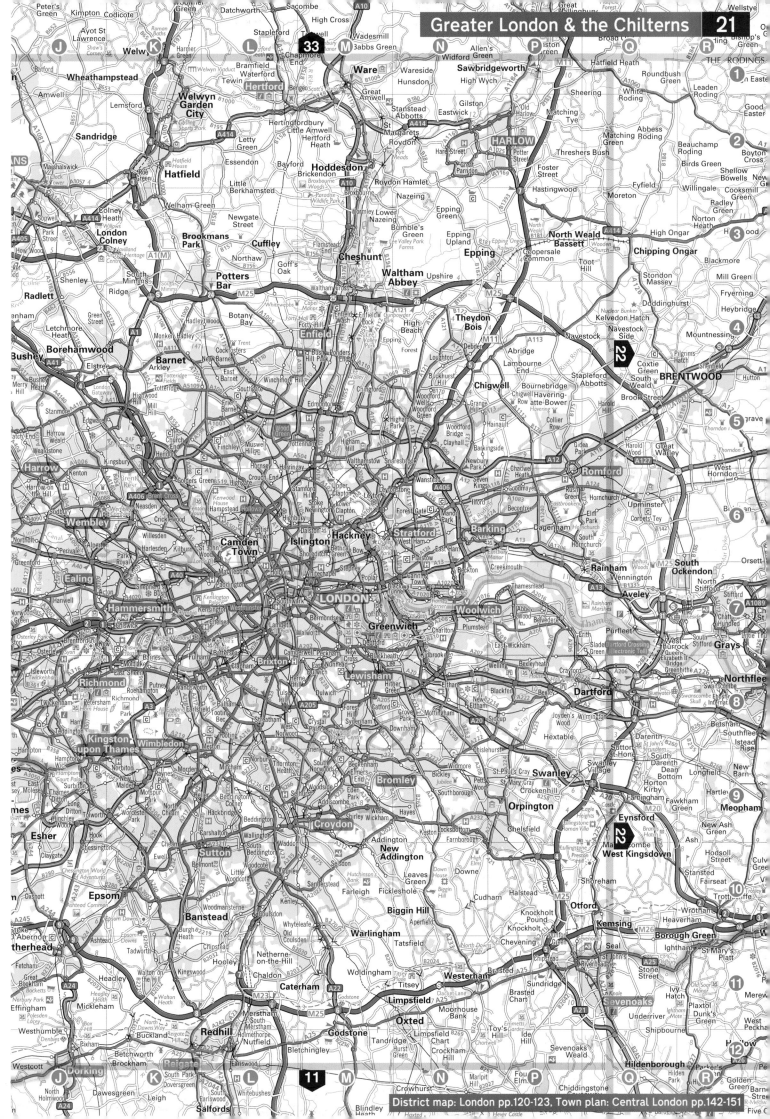

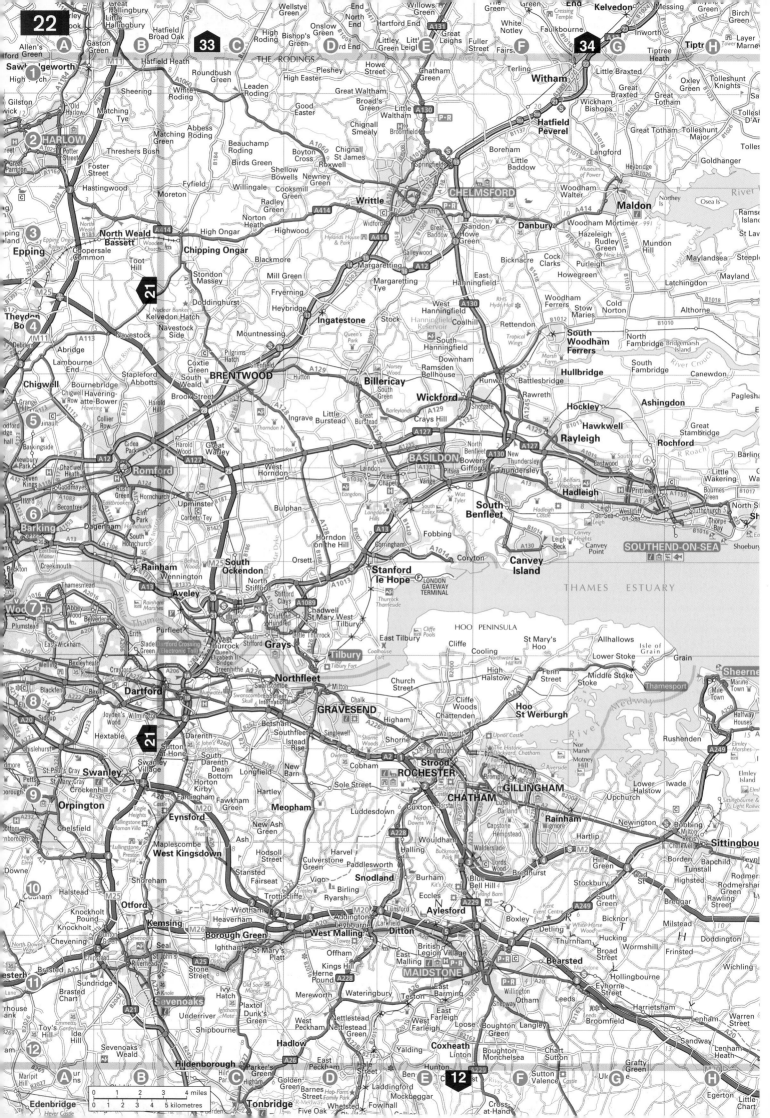

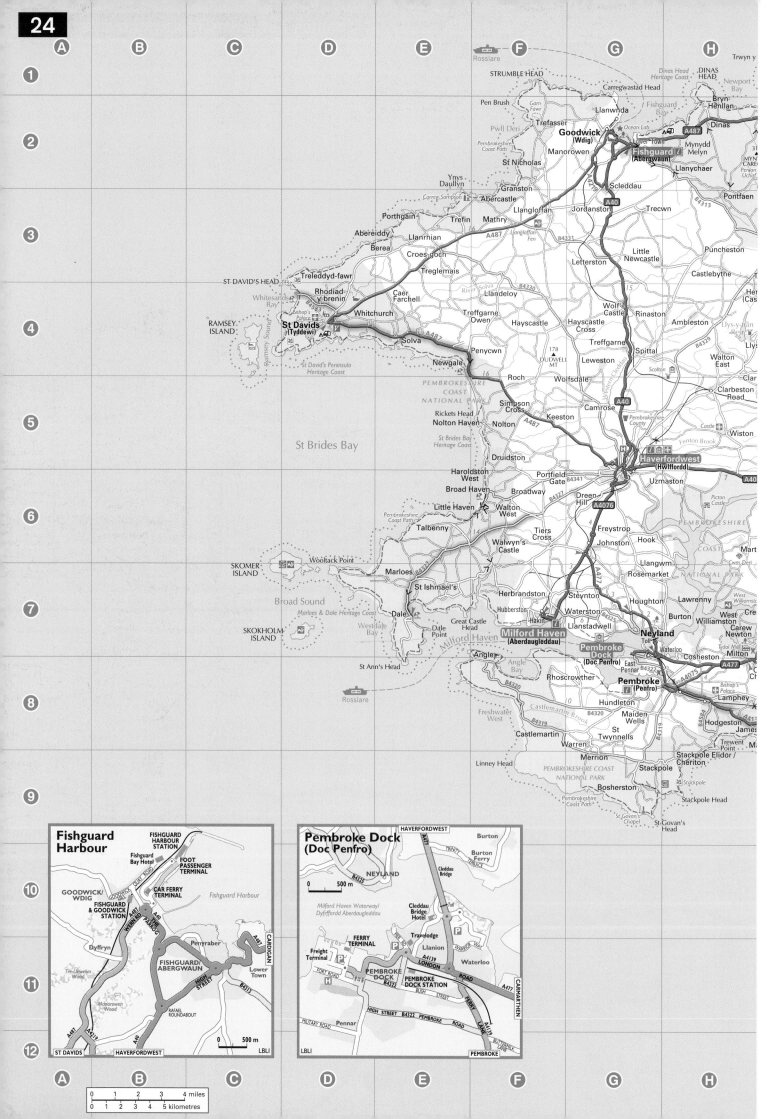

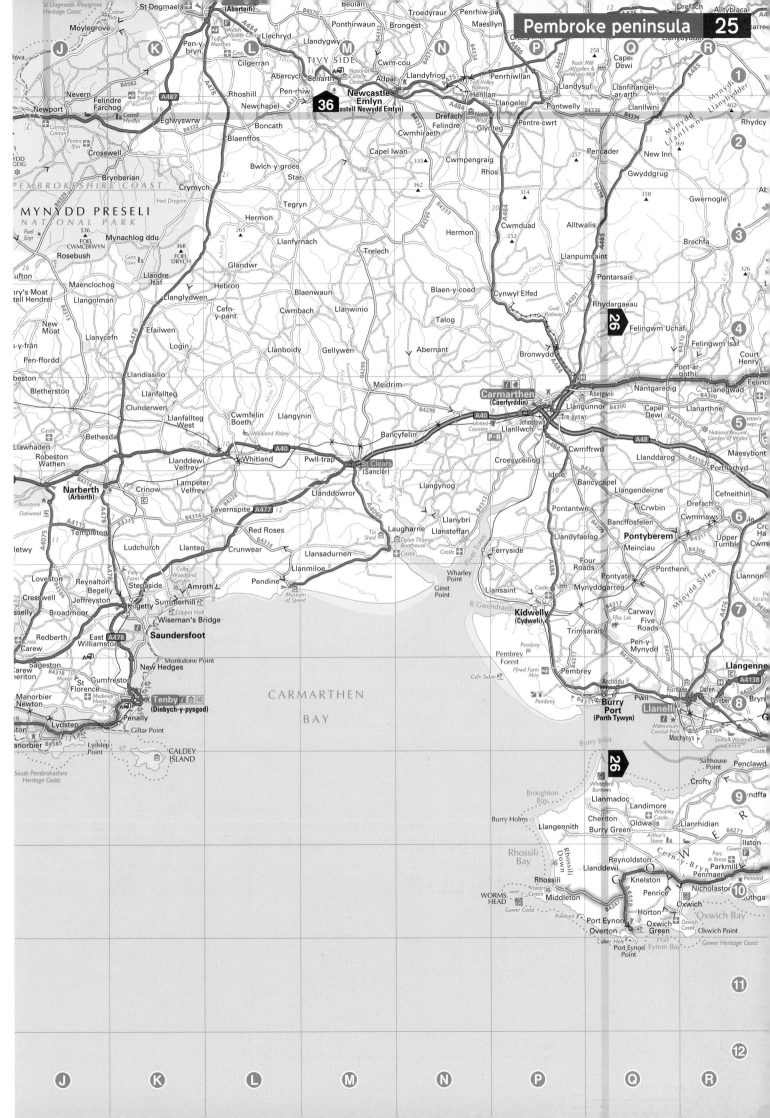

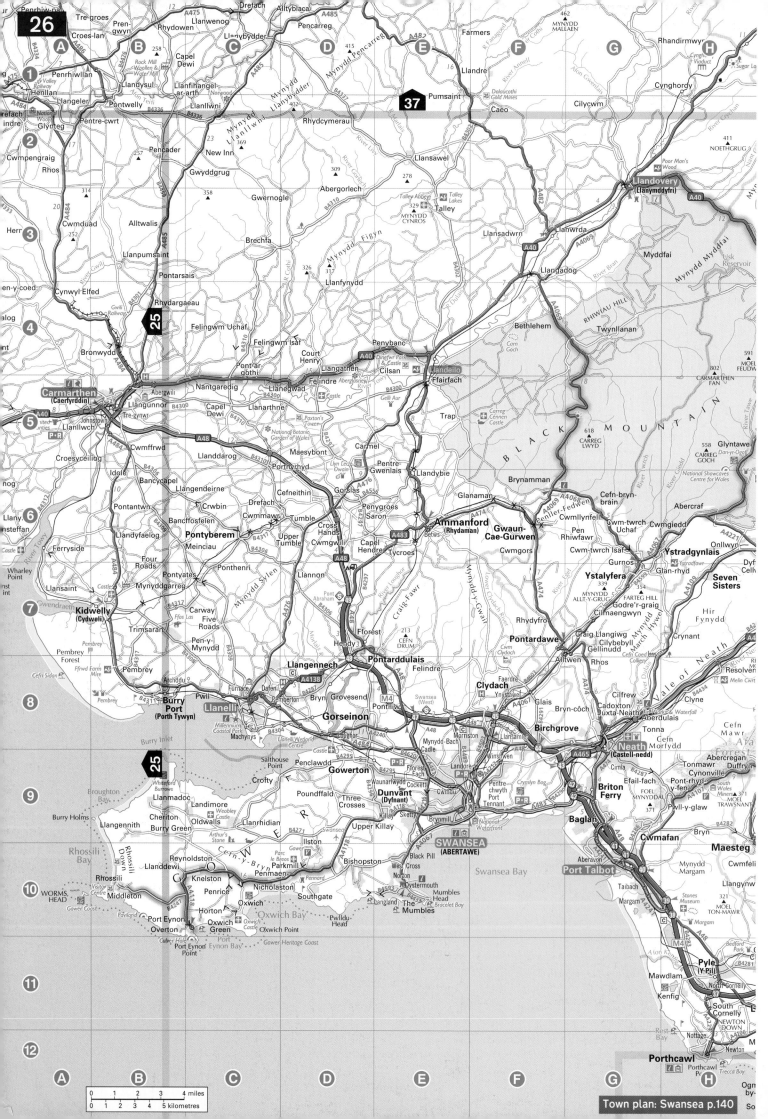

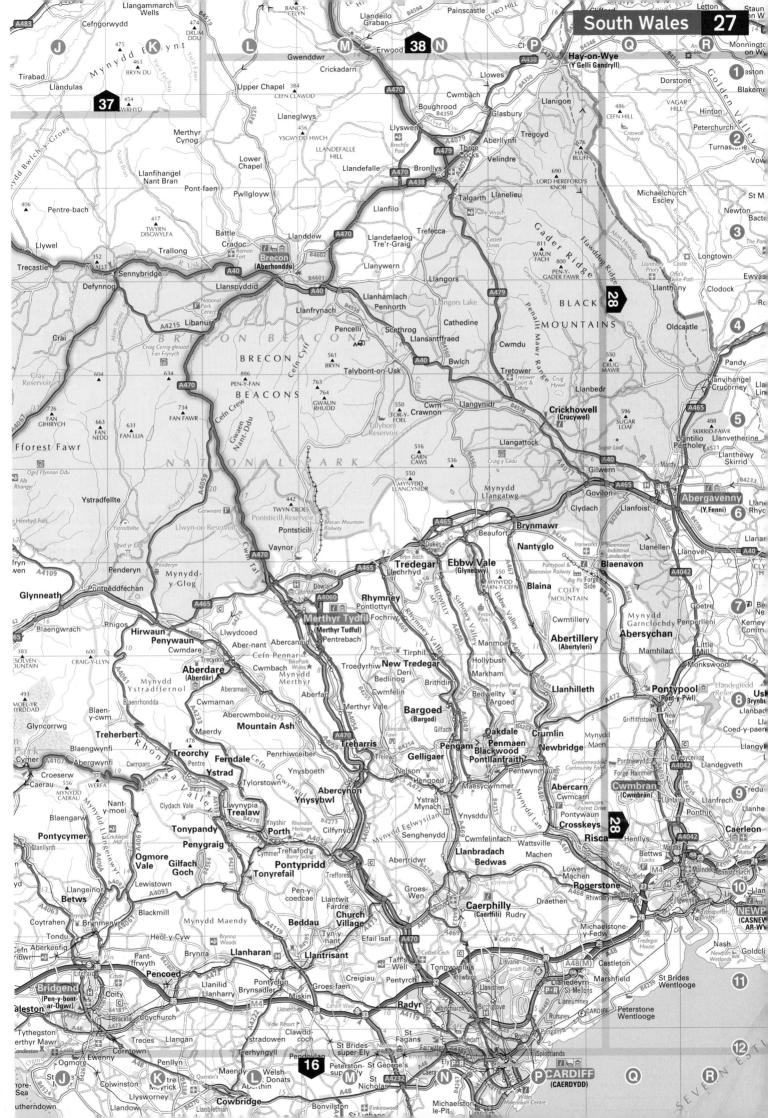

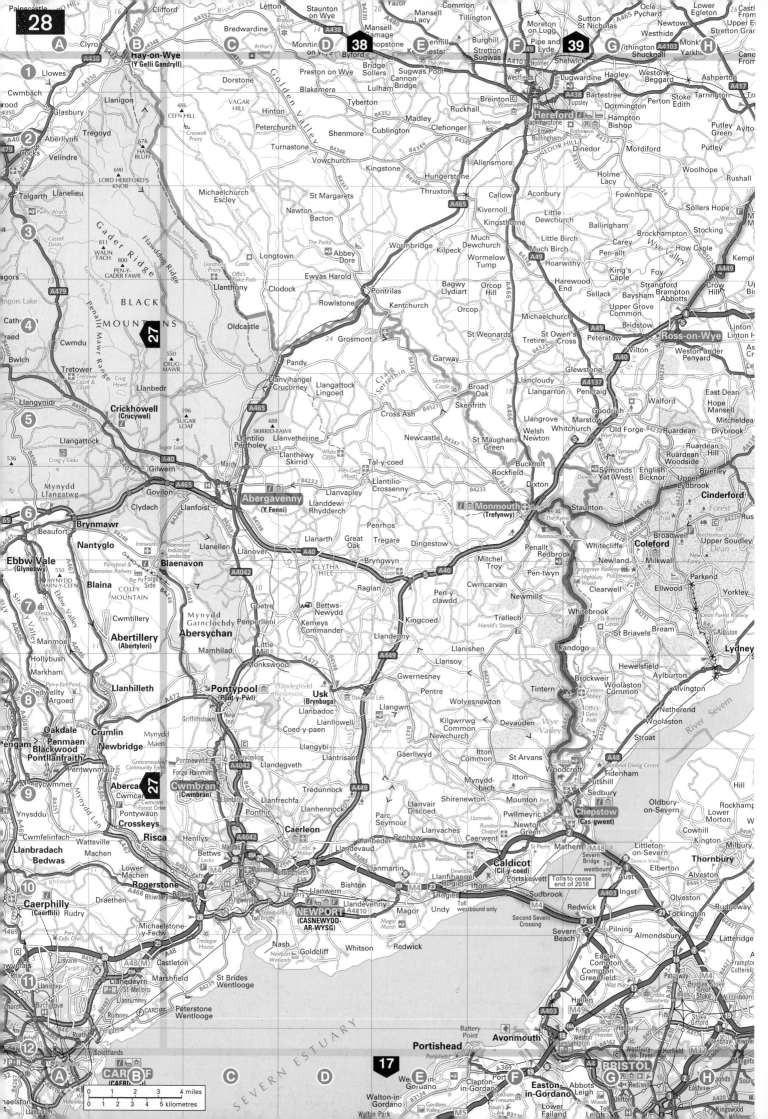

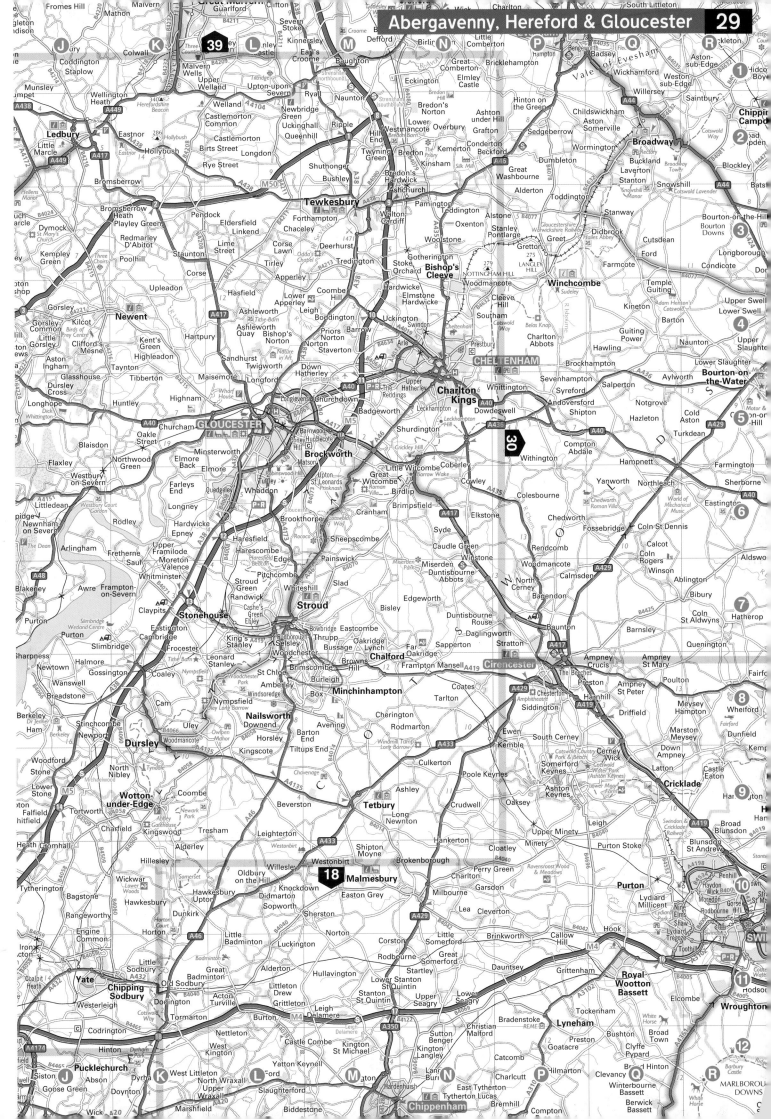

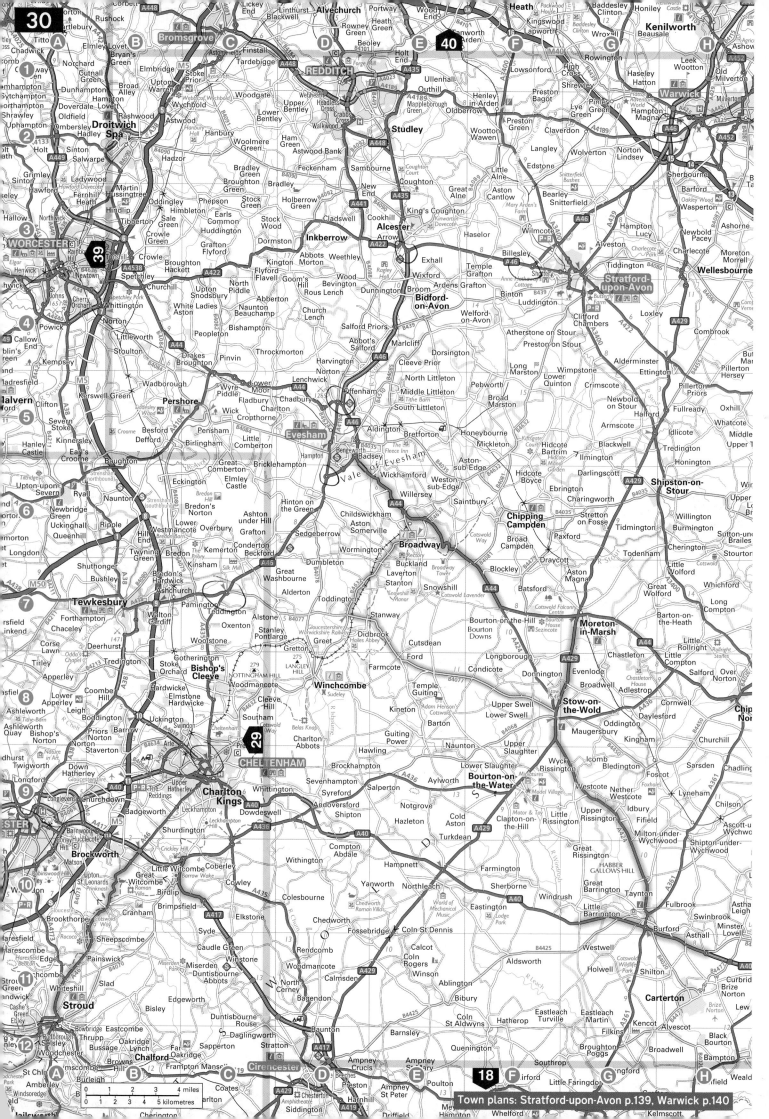

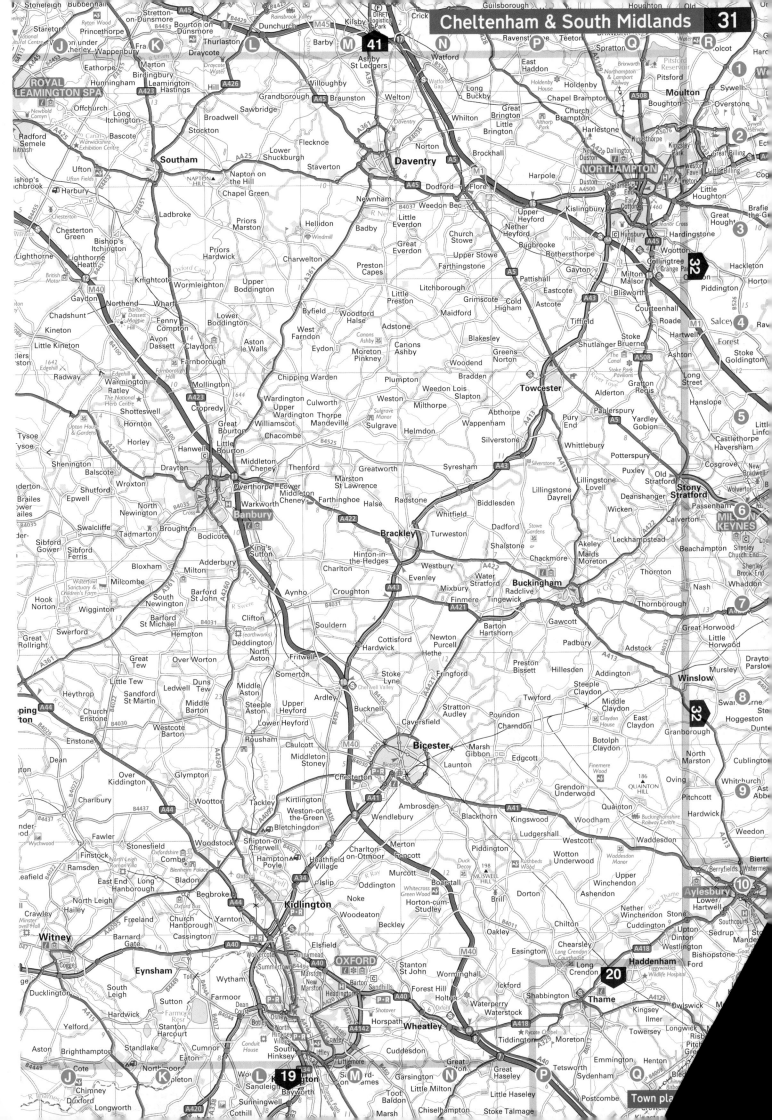

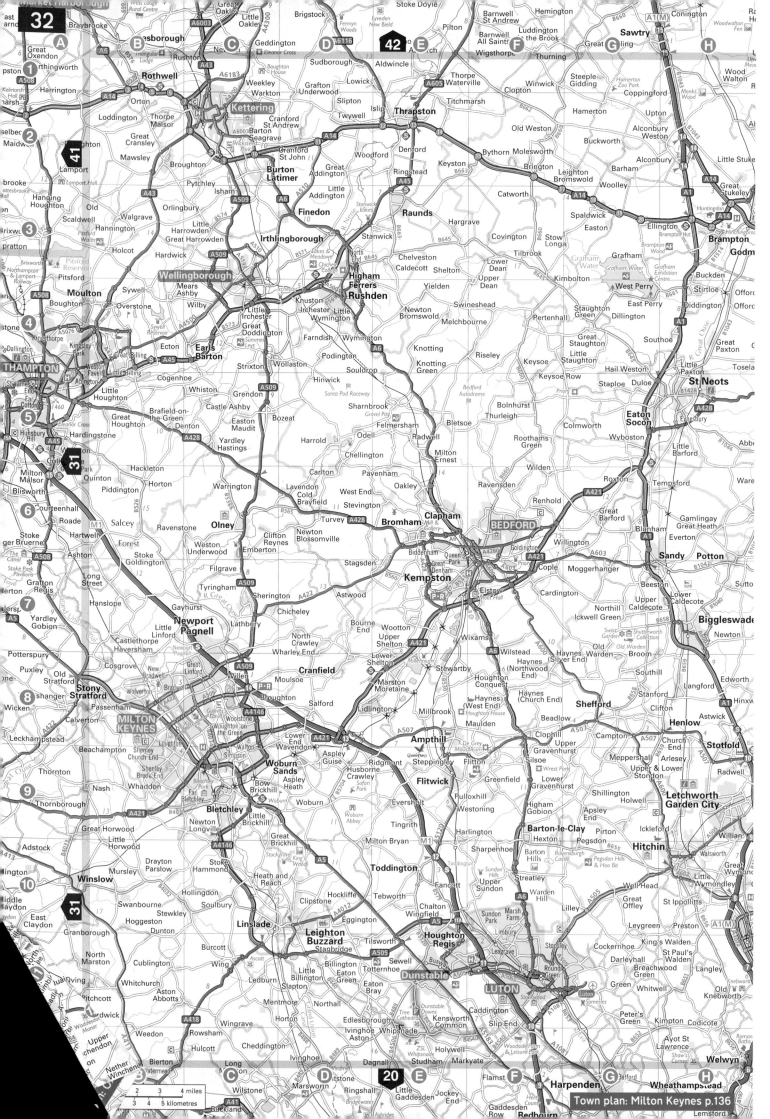

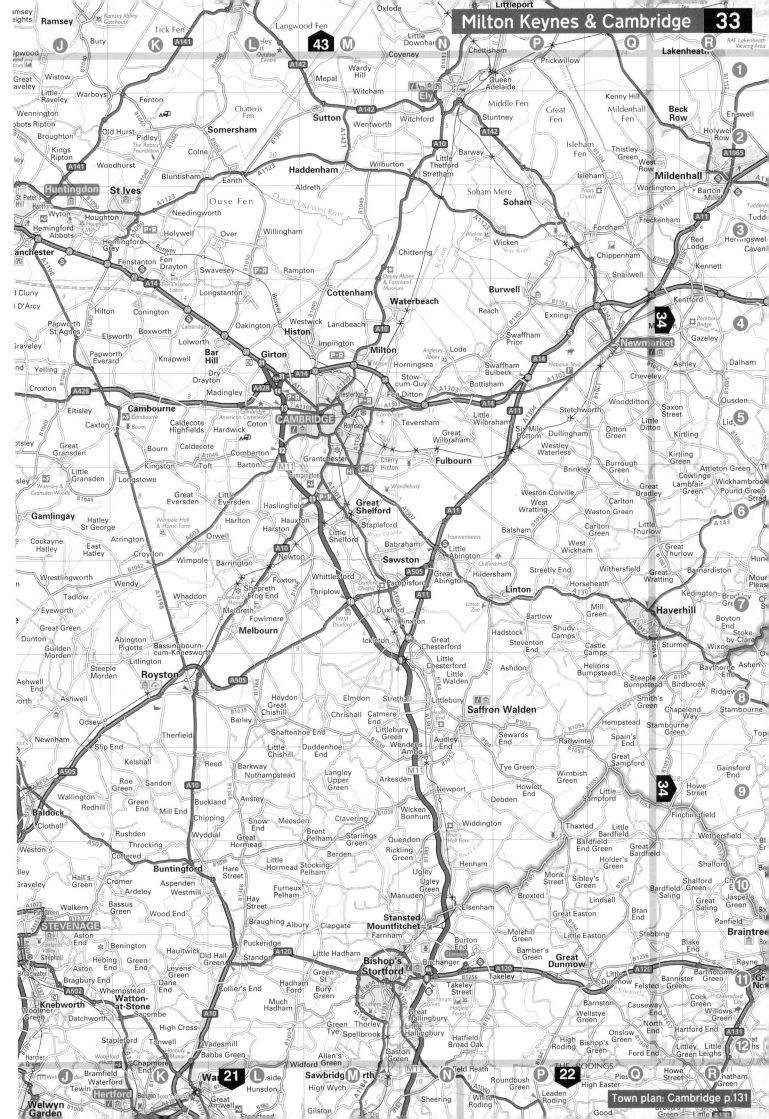

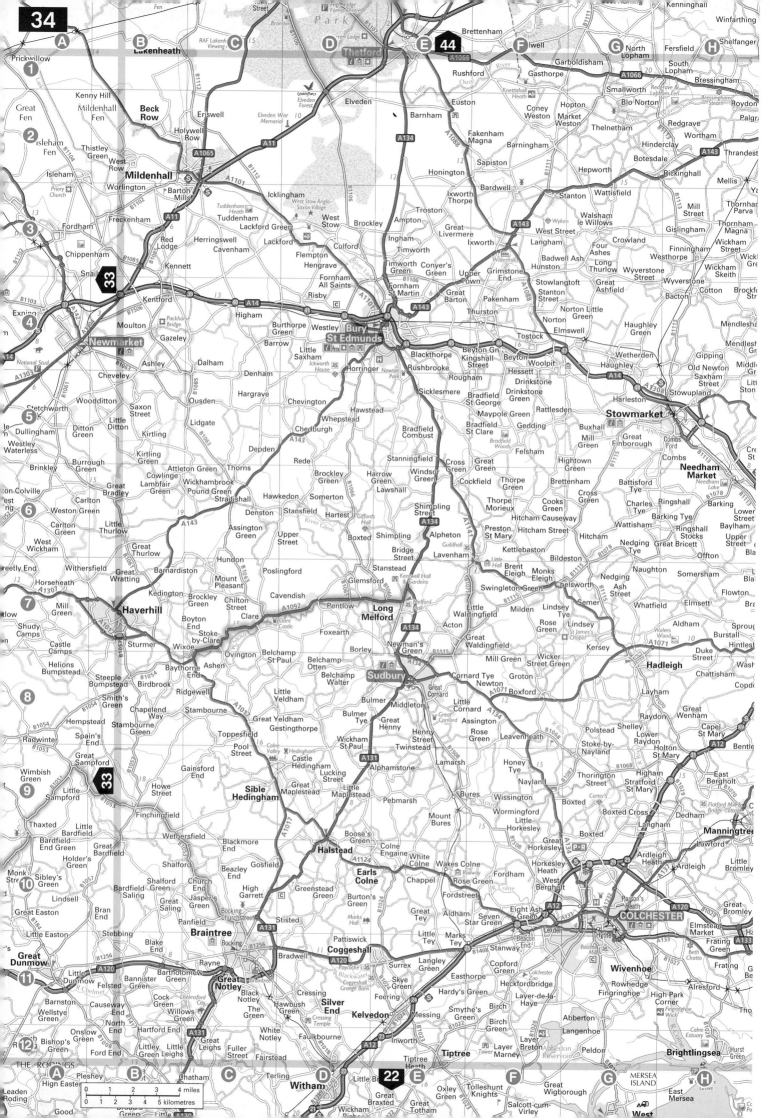

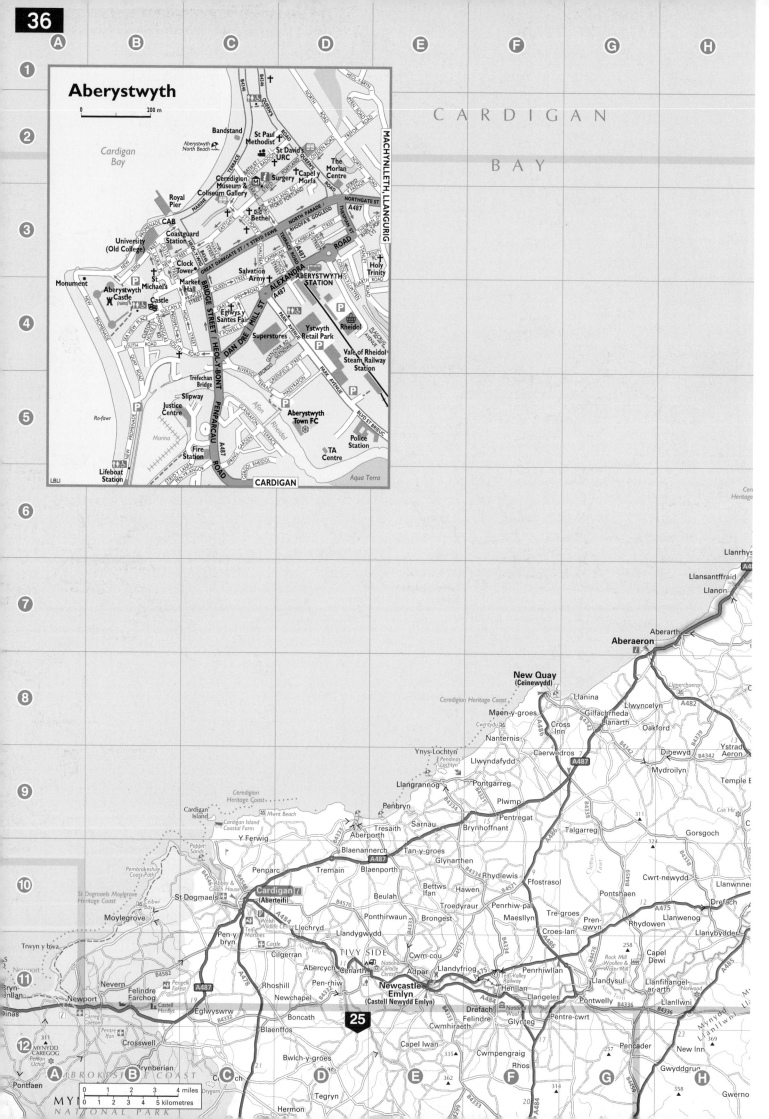

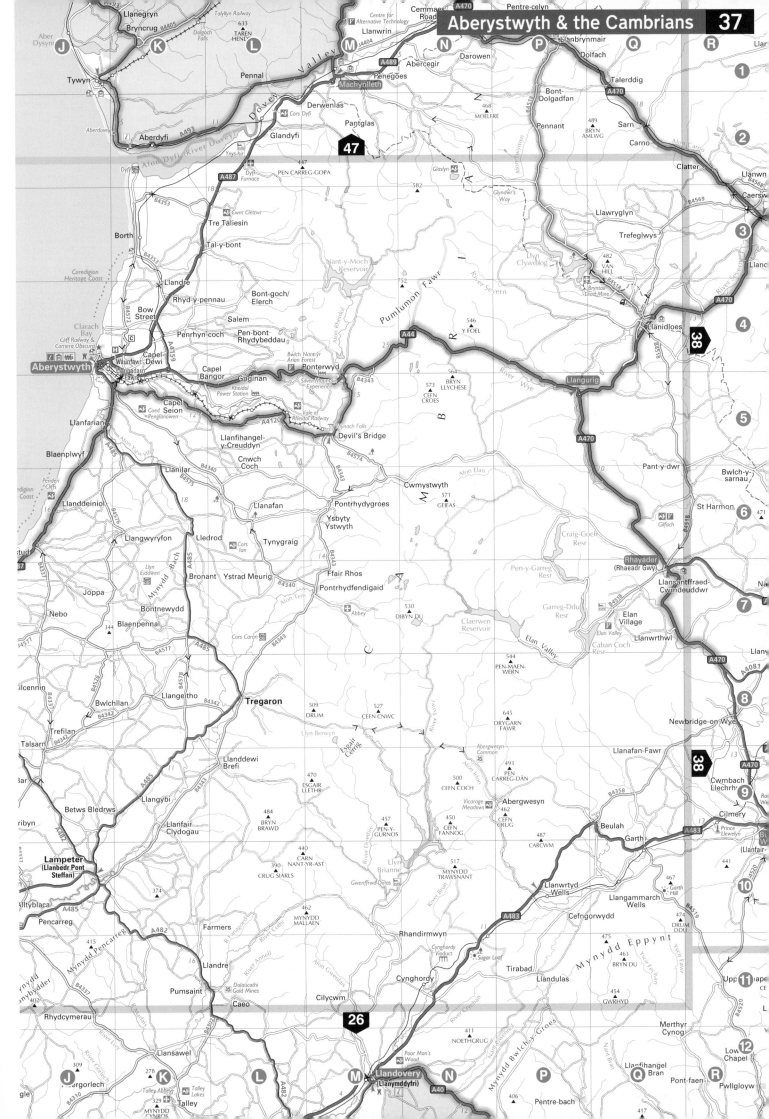

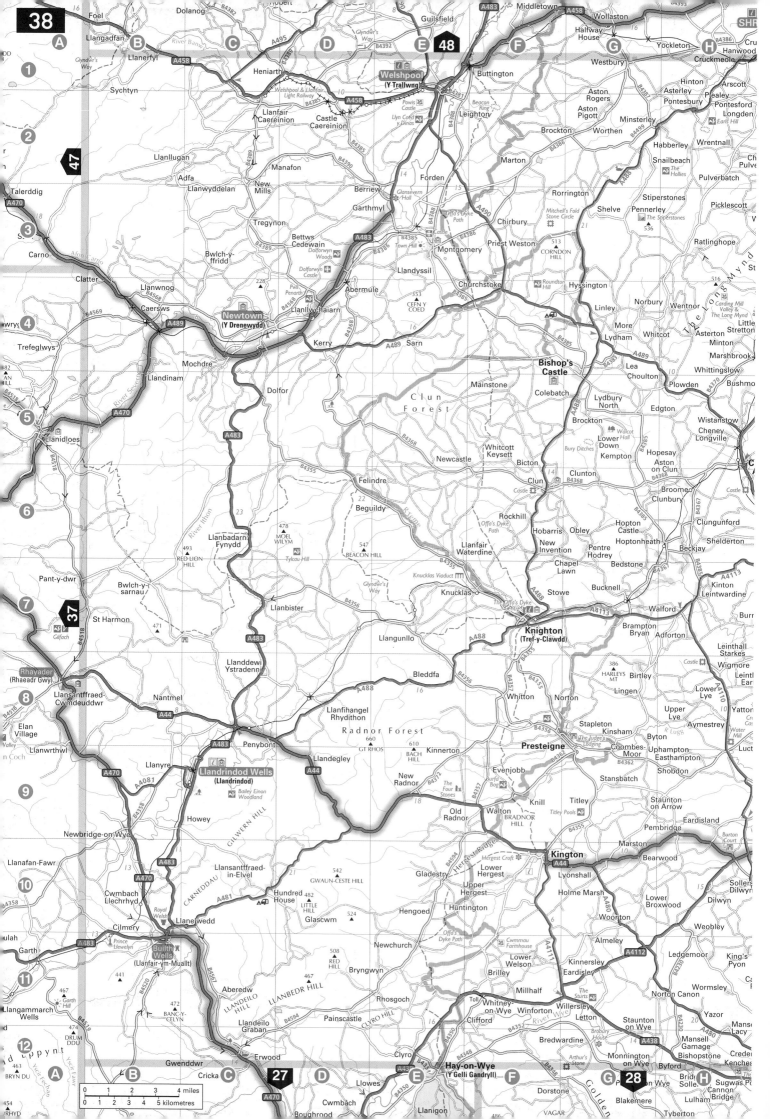

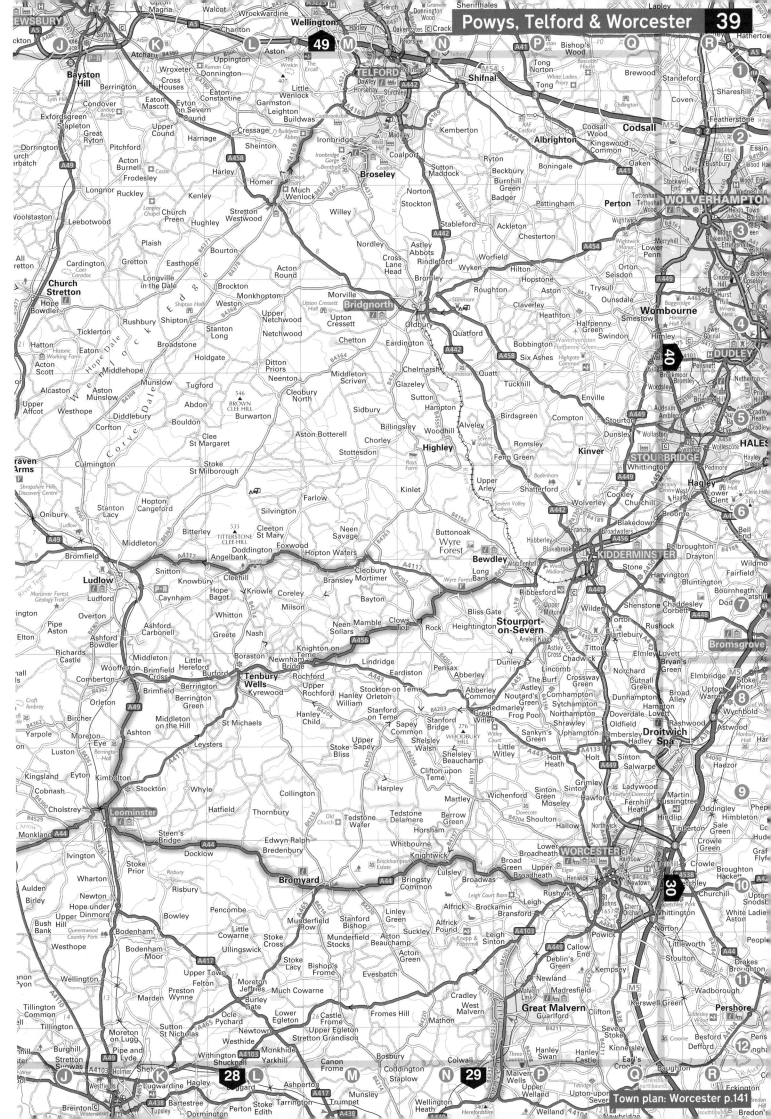

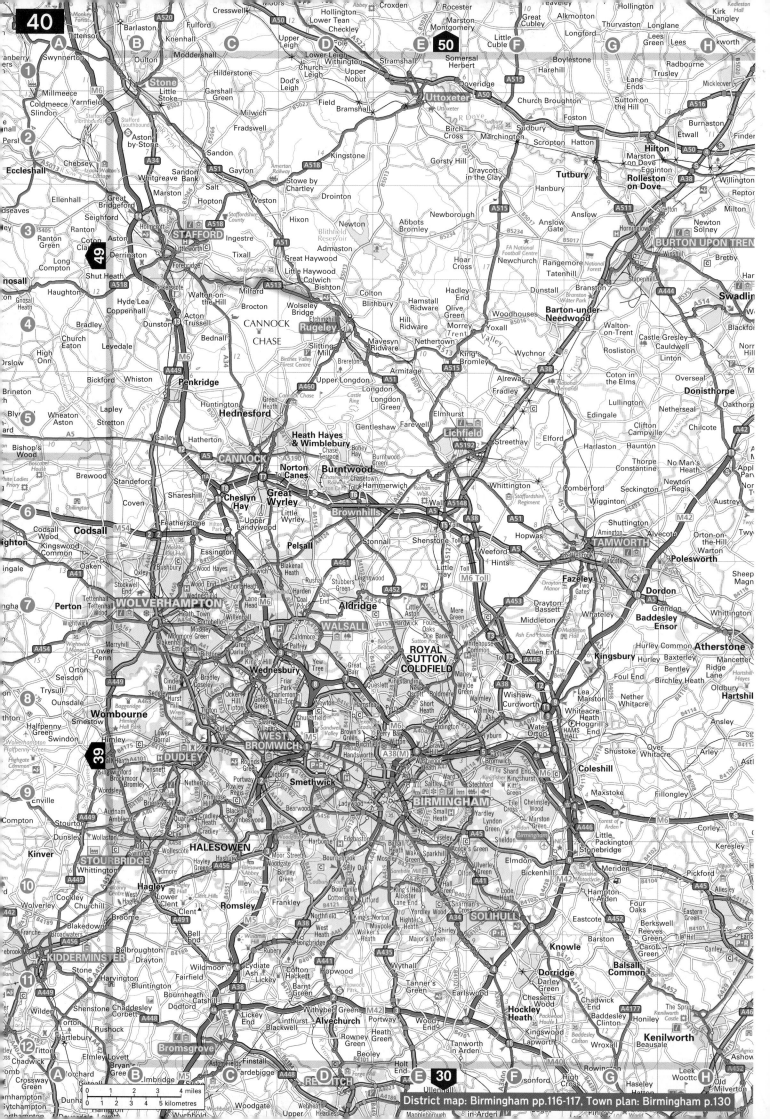

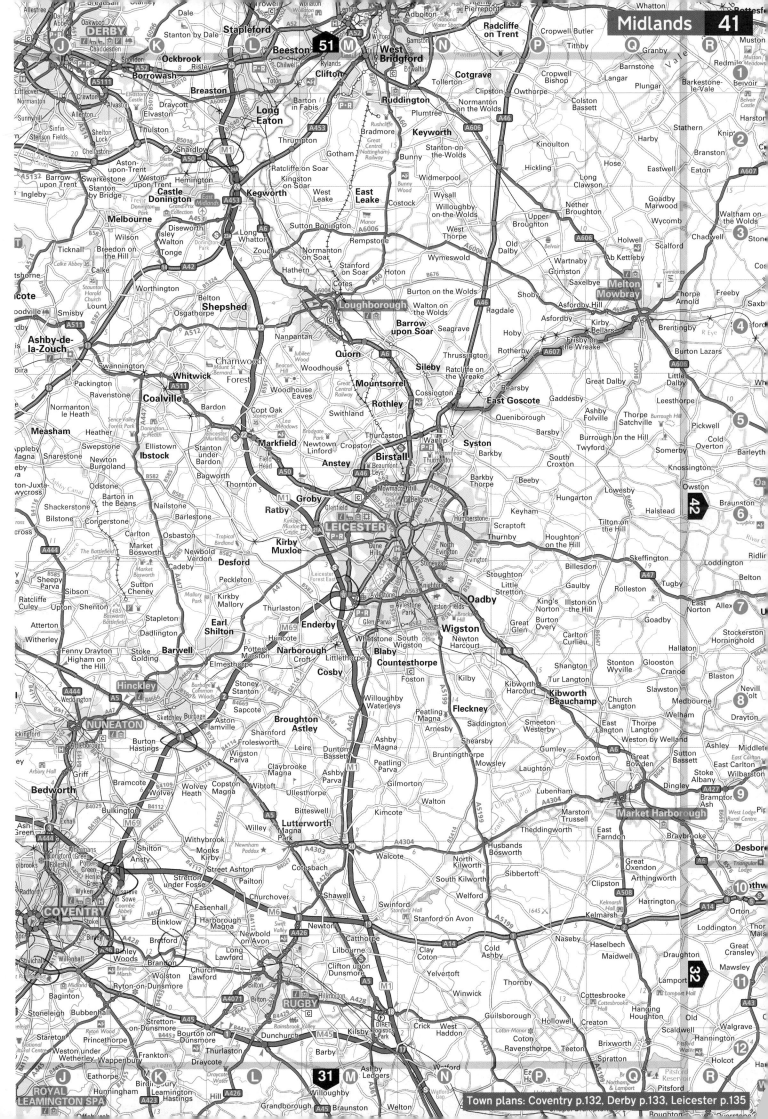

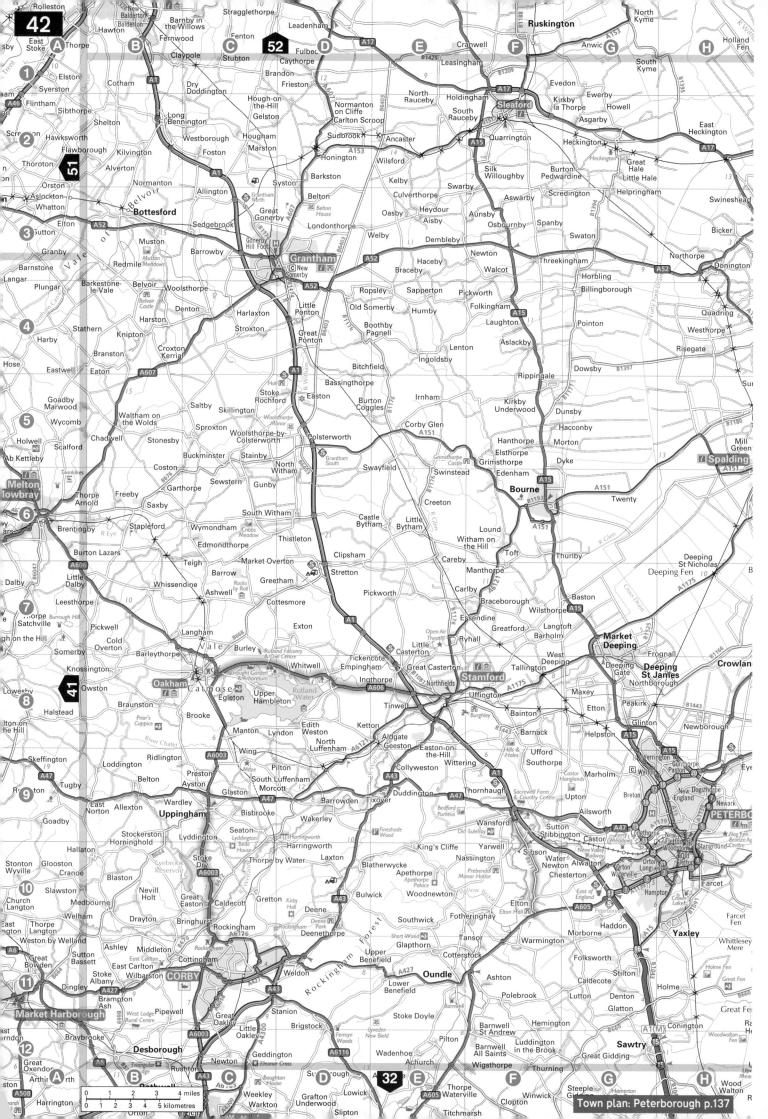

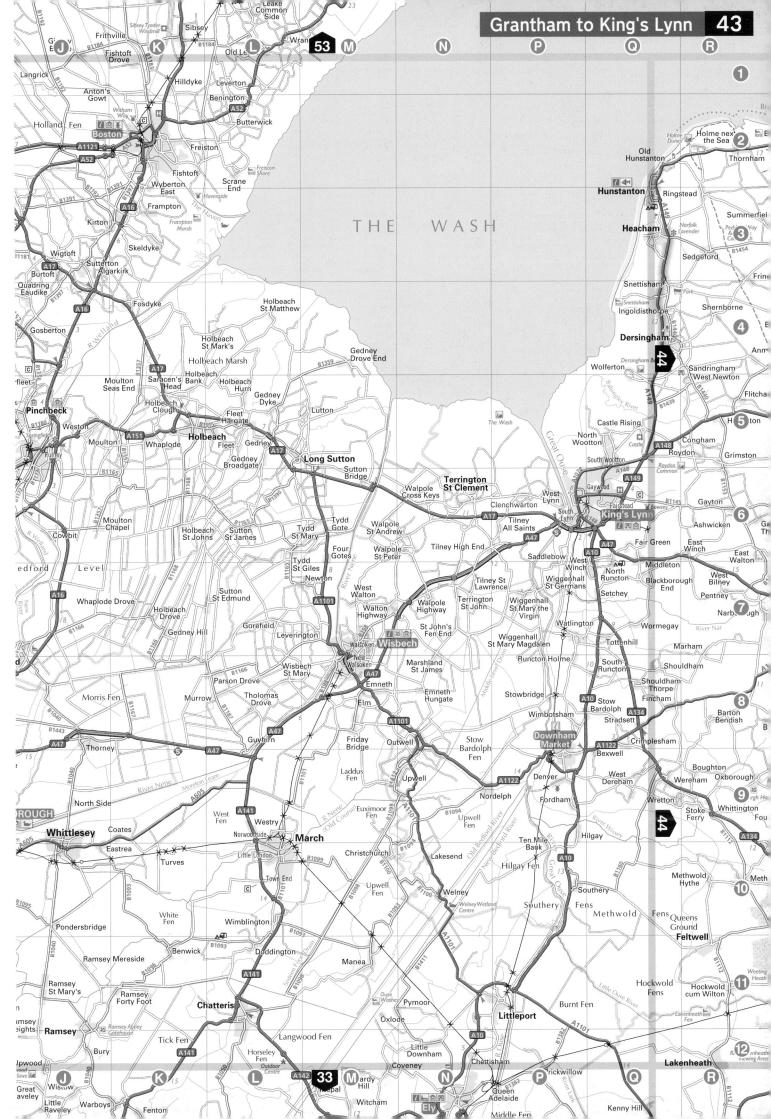

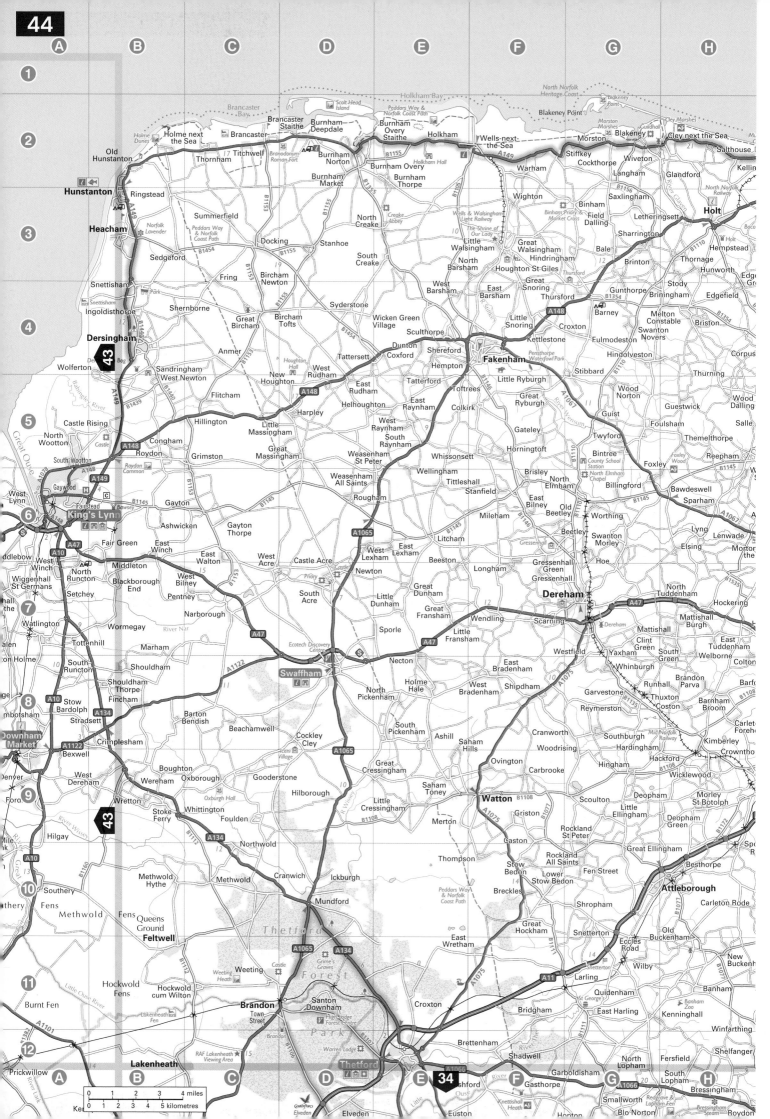

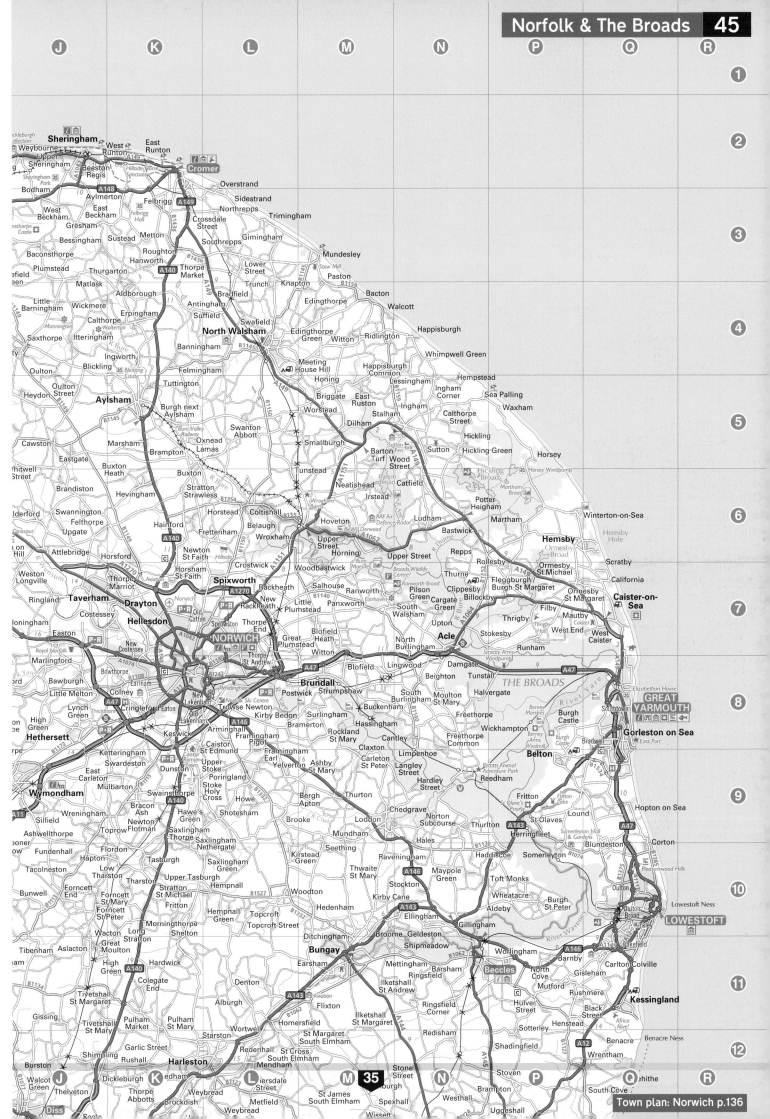

CAERNARFON BAY

54

LLEYN PENINSULA

Llanwnda
Rhostryfan
Llandwrog
Groeslon
Carmel
Penygroes
Talysarn
Pontllyfni
Llanllyfni
Nebo
Clynnog-fawr
Nasareth
Pant Glas
Coeau Tan y Bwlch
522
Y GYRN-DDU
Trefor
Llanaelhaearn
Bryncir
Garn-Dolbenmaen
Dolbenn
Trwyn y Grolech
Porth Nefyn
564
YR EIFL
Tre'r Ceiri
Llithfaen
Pistyll
St Cybi's Well
Llangybi
Carreg Ddu
Morfa Nefyn
Nefyn
Y Ffôr
Llanystumdwy
Chwilog
Pentrefelin
Edern
Bodfuan
B4354
Criccieth
Porth Ysgaden
Tudweiliog
Llannor
Abererch
Penarth Fawr Medieval House
Pen-ychain
LLEYN
Efailnewydd
Tremadog Bay
Porth Colman
Dinas
371 Garn Fadrun
Llaniestyn
Rhyd-y-clafdy
Pwllheli
Pen-y-graig
Sarn Meyllteyrn
Bryn-mawr
Penrhos
Llangwnnadl
Botwnnog
Llanbedrog
Bryncroes
Rhoshirwaun
Llangian
Trwyn Llanbedrog
St Tudwal's Road
Porthoer
Plas yn Rhiw
Y Rhiw
Llanengan
Abersoch
Aberdaron
Llanfaelrhys
Porth Neigwl or Hell's Mouth
Bwlchtocyn
Marchros
St Tudwal's Island East
Aberdaron Bay
Porth Ysgo
St Tudwal's Island West
Porth Geiriad
Bardsey Sound
Lleyn Heritage Coast
St Mary's
Ynys Enlli
BARDSEY ISLAND

CARDIGAN

BAY

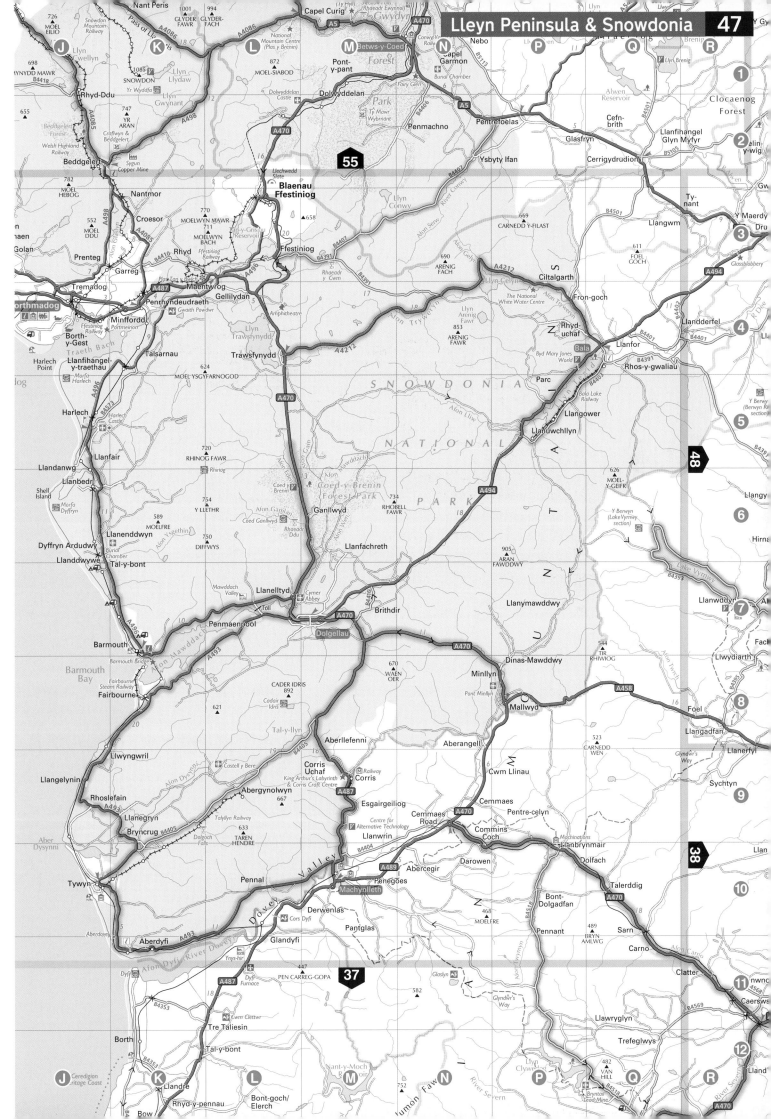

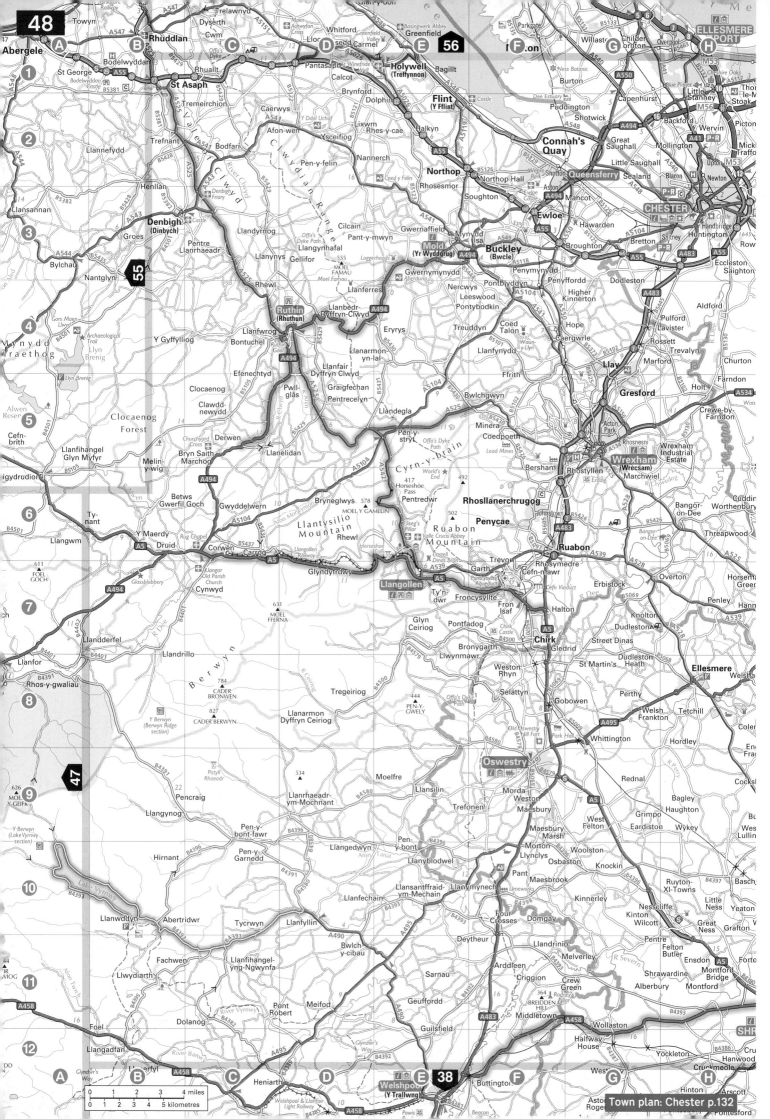

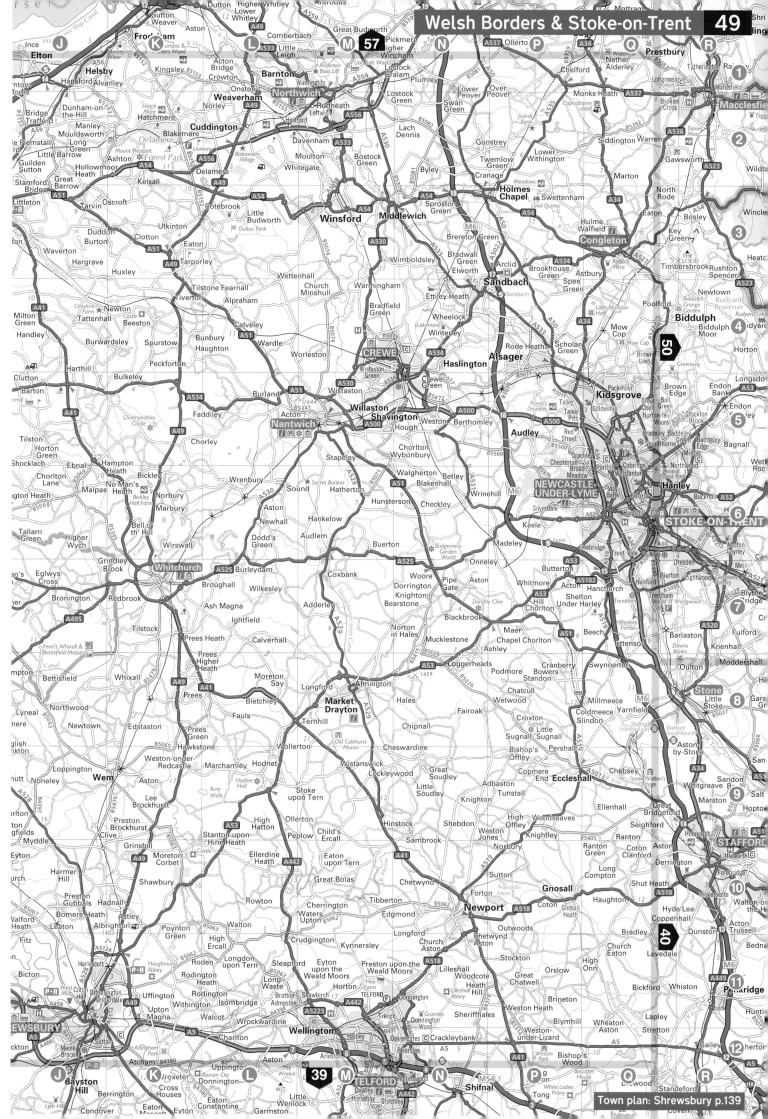

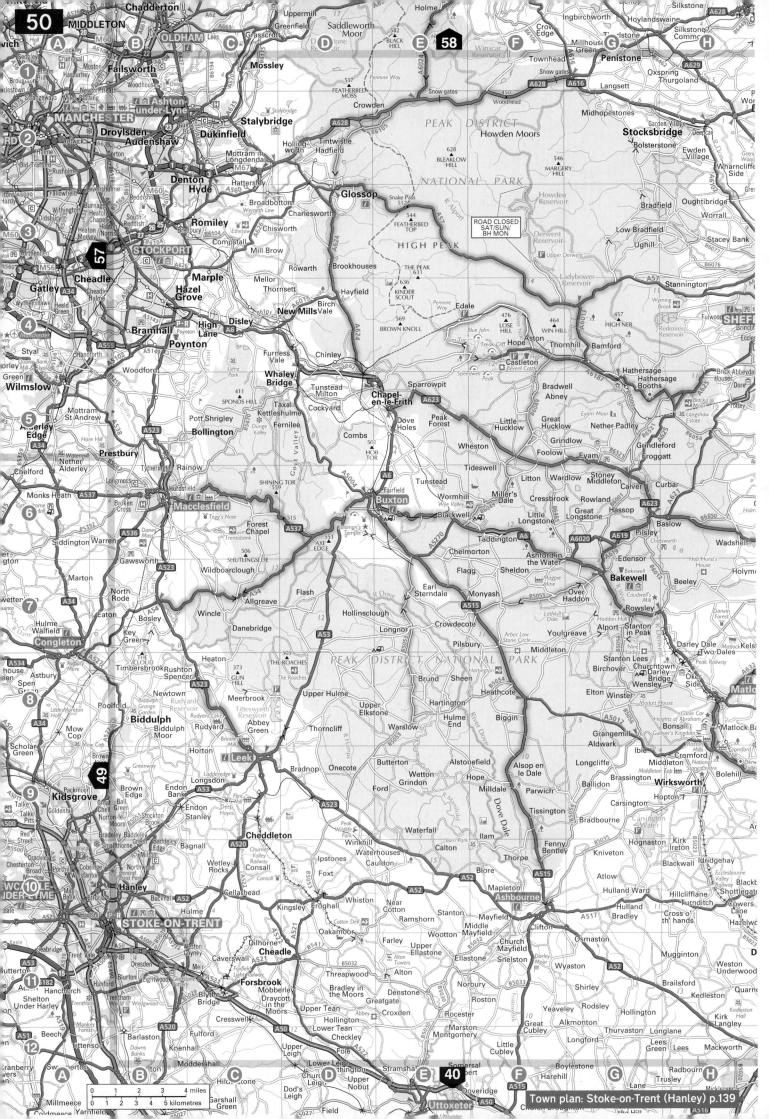

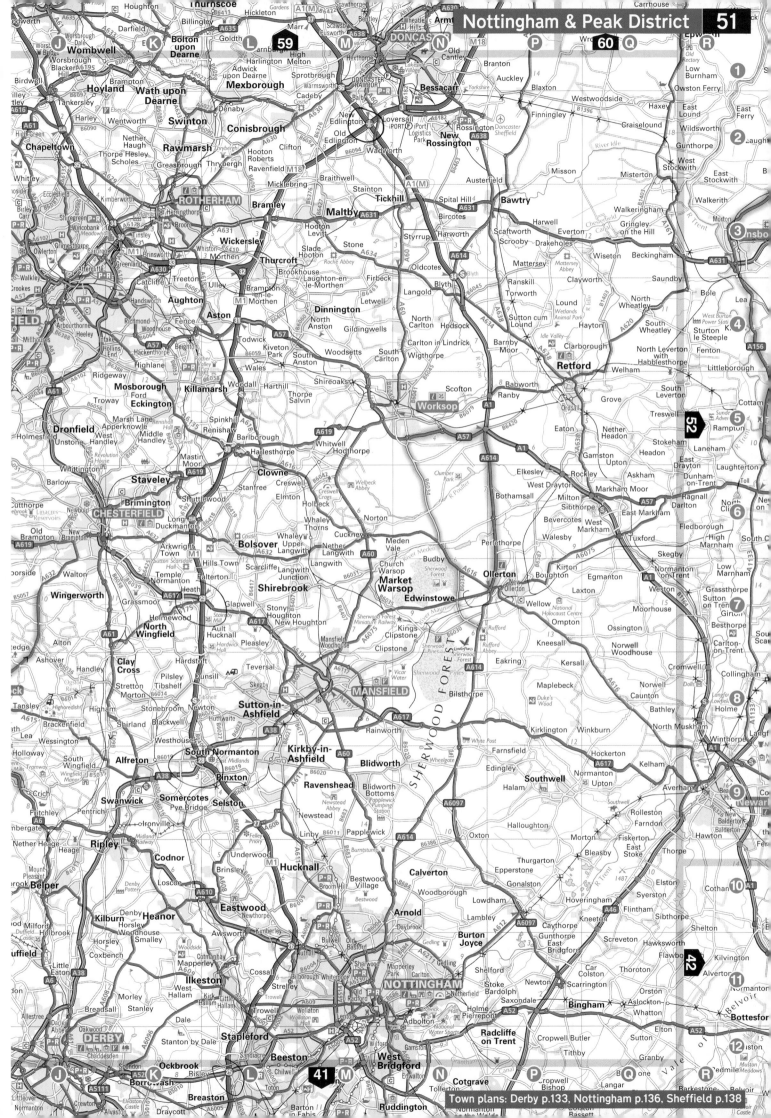

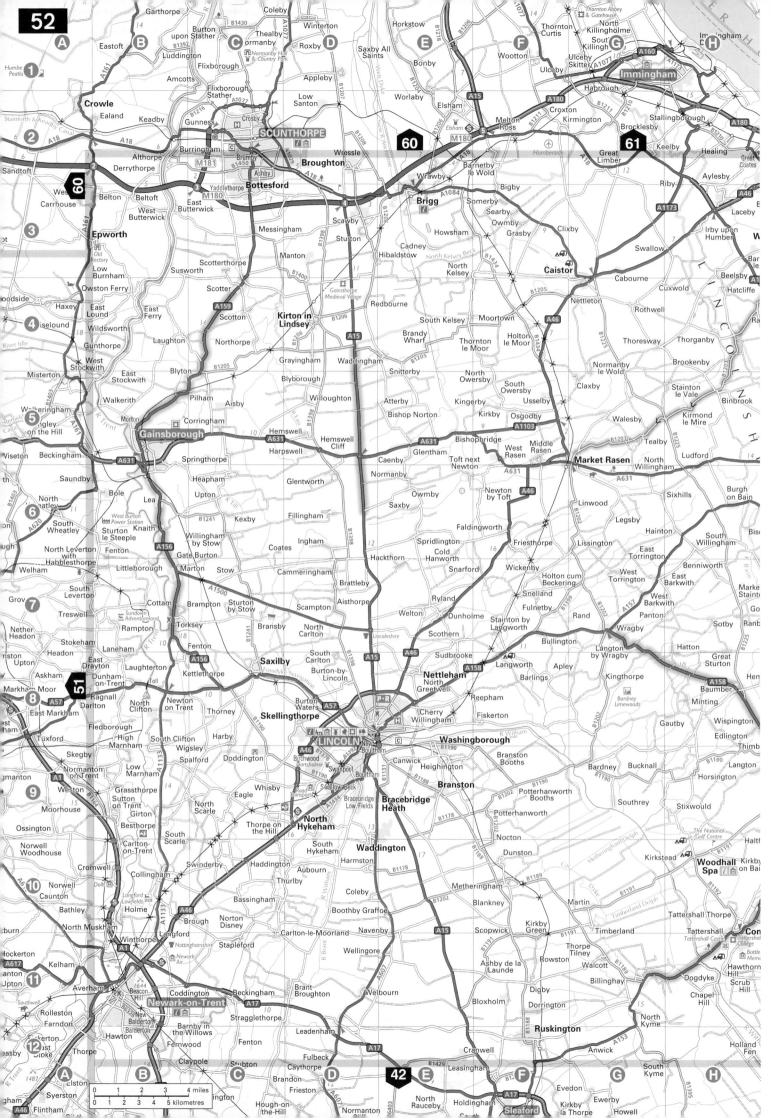

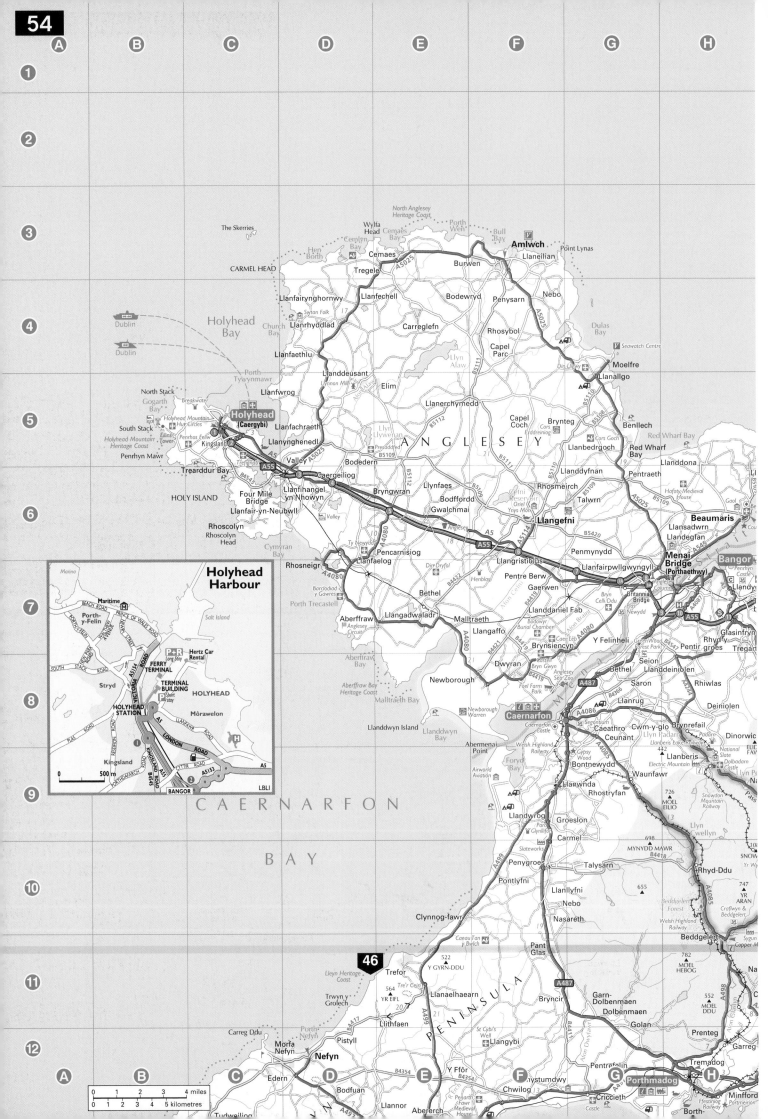

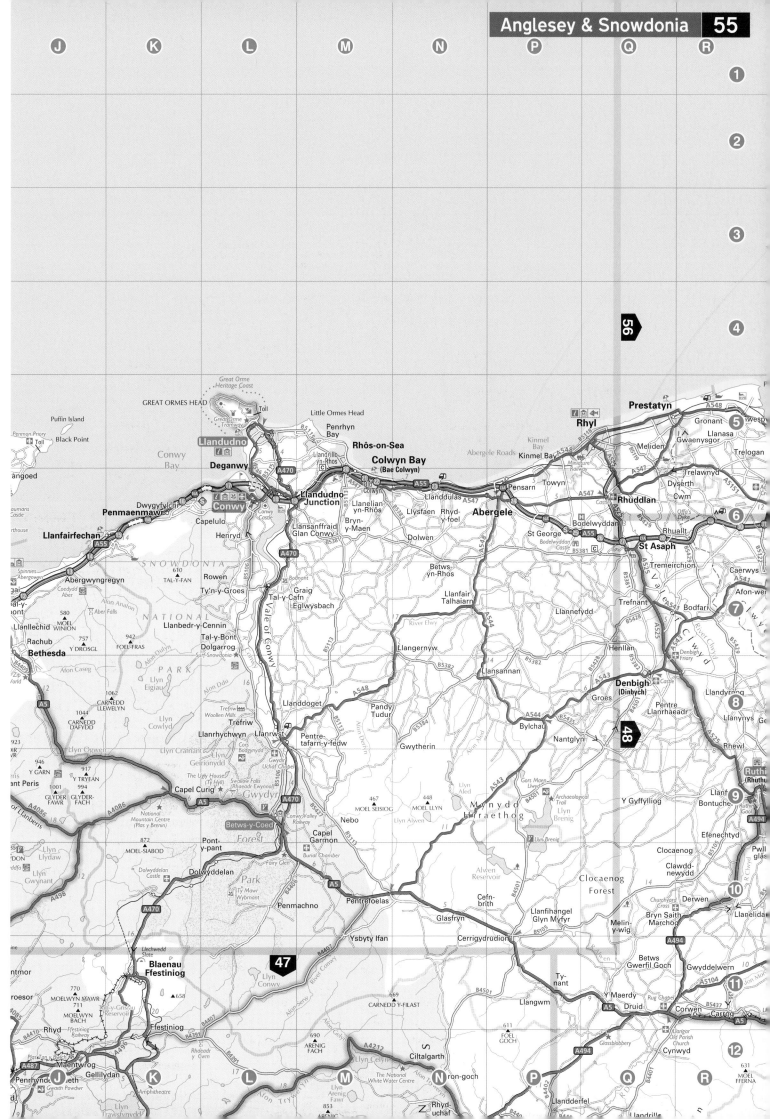

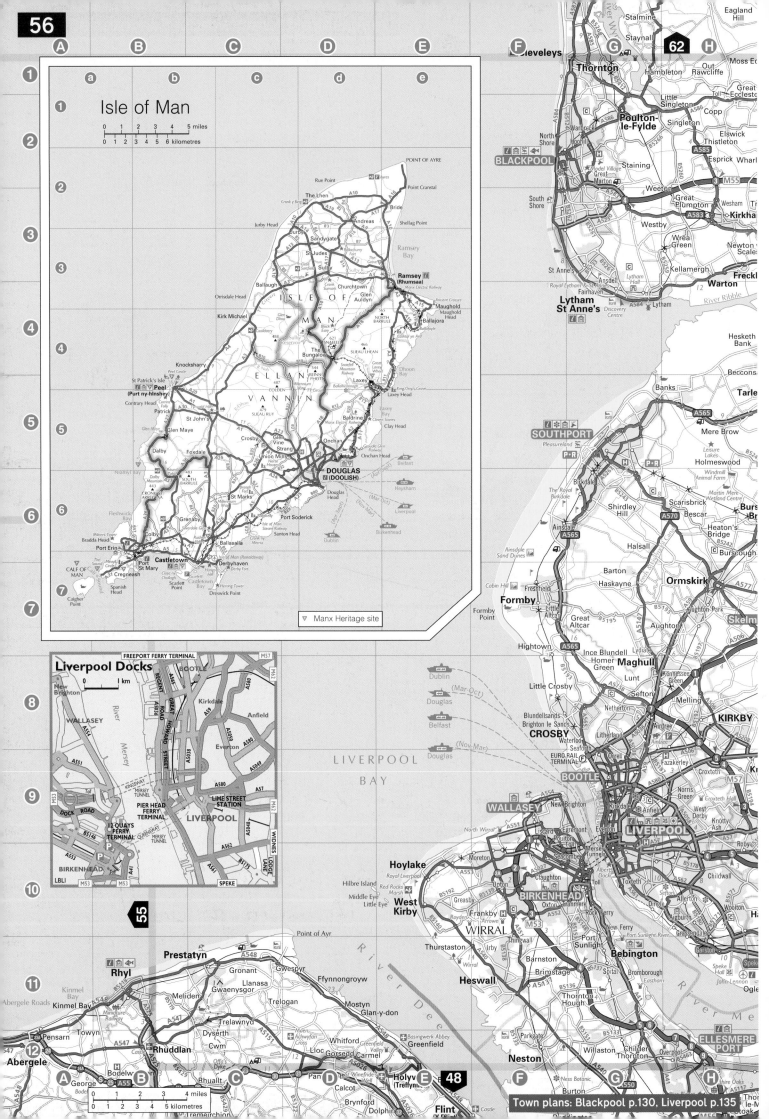

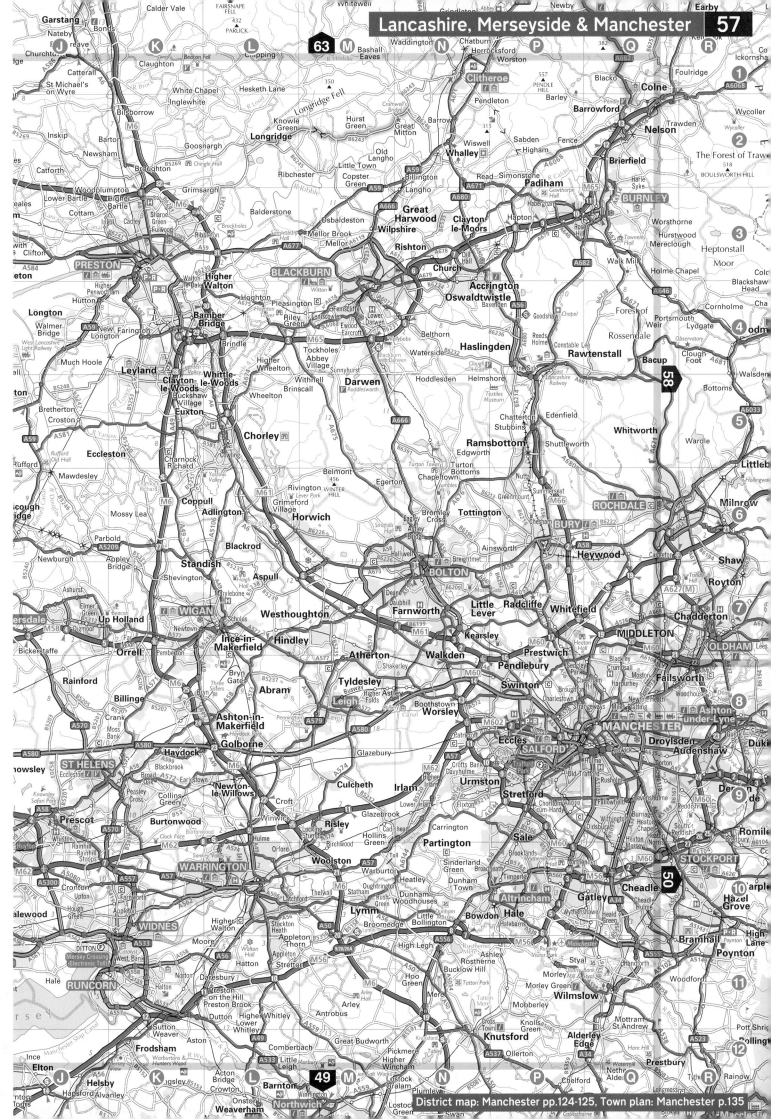

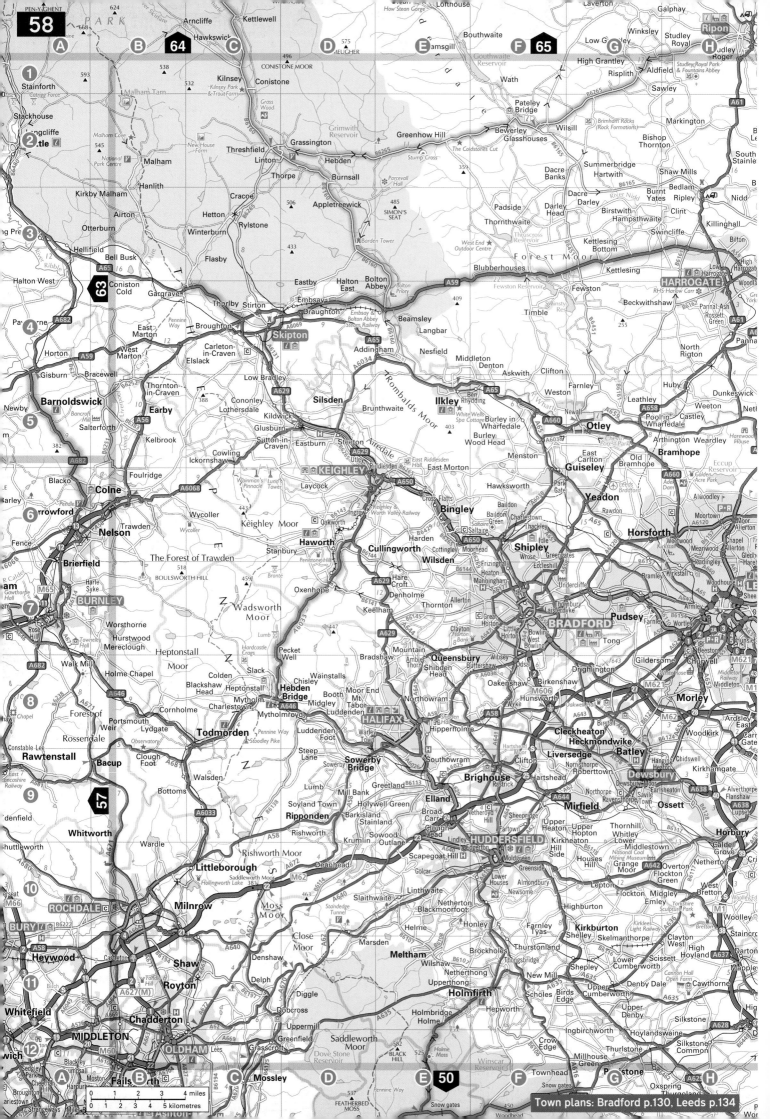

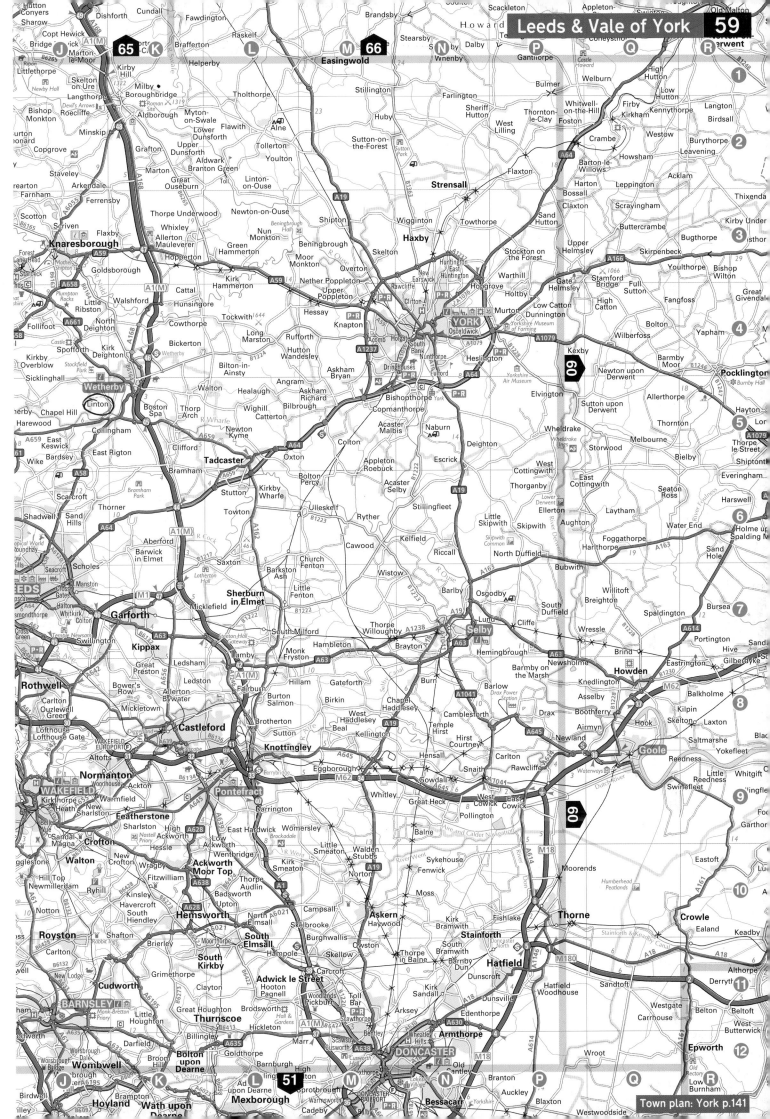

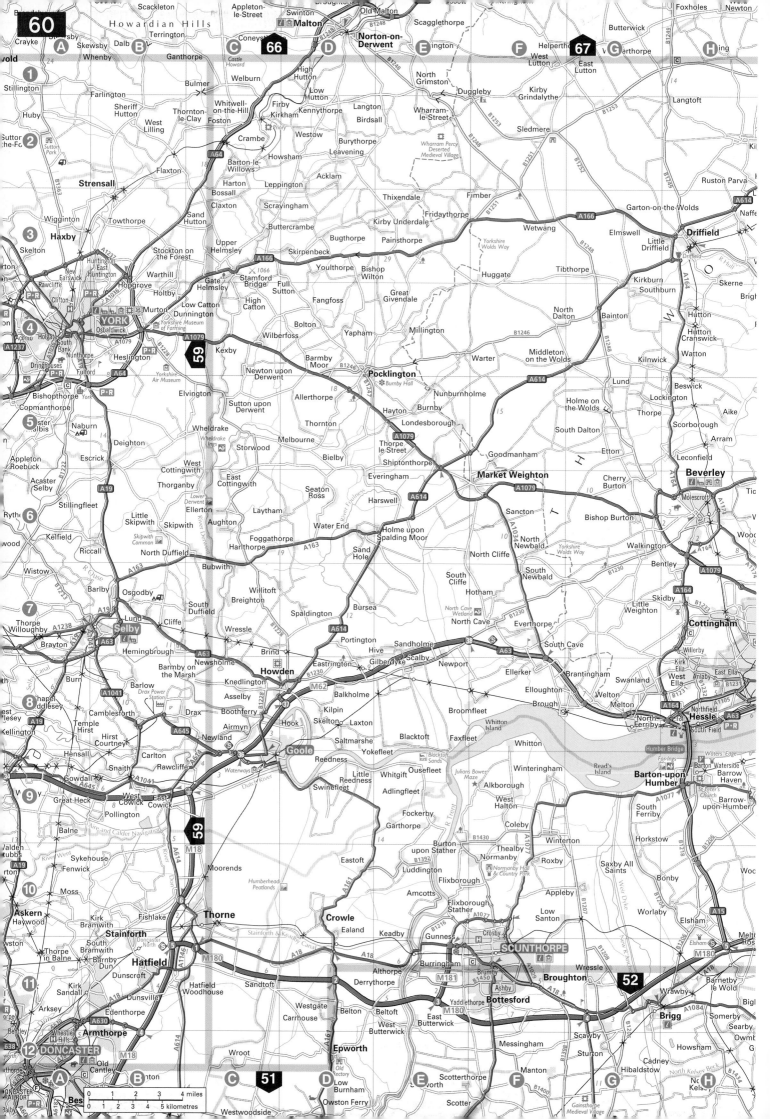

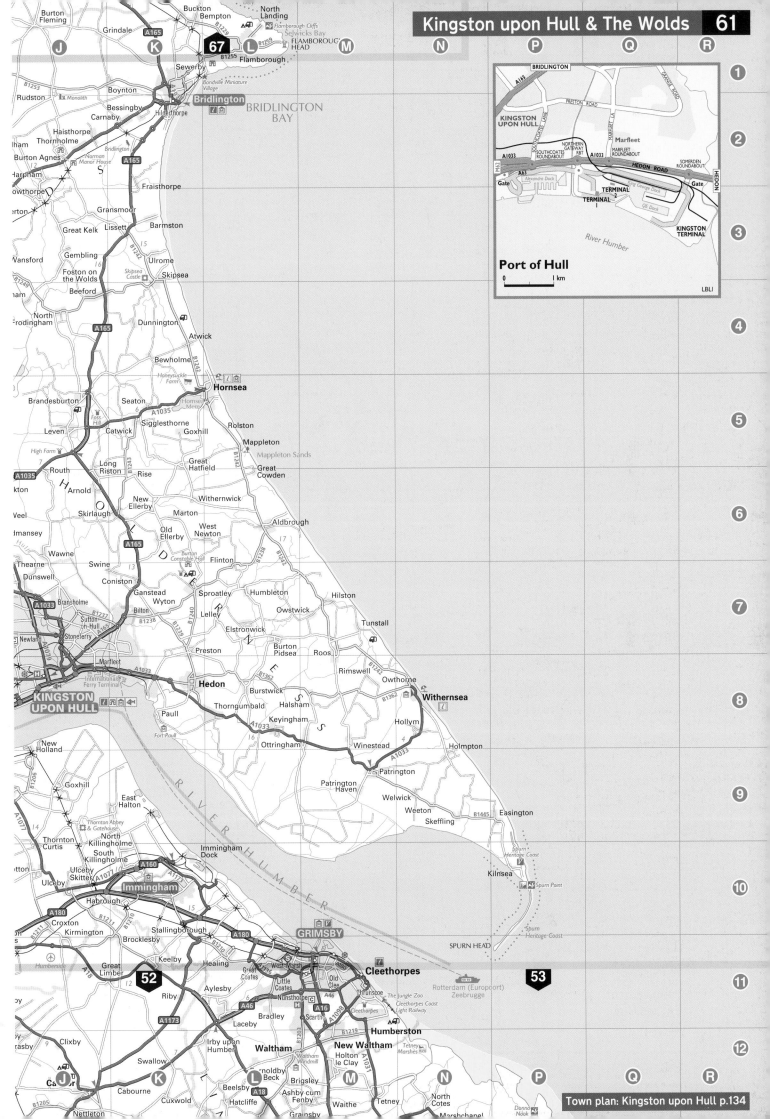

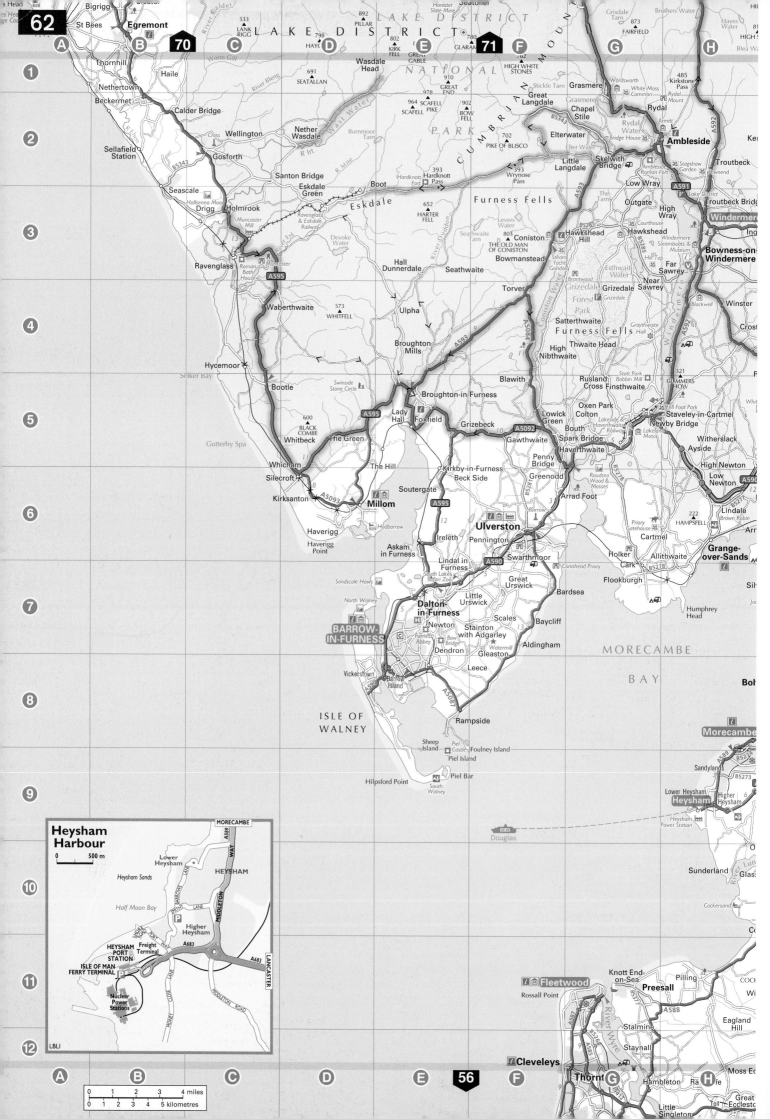

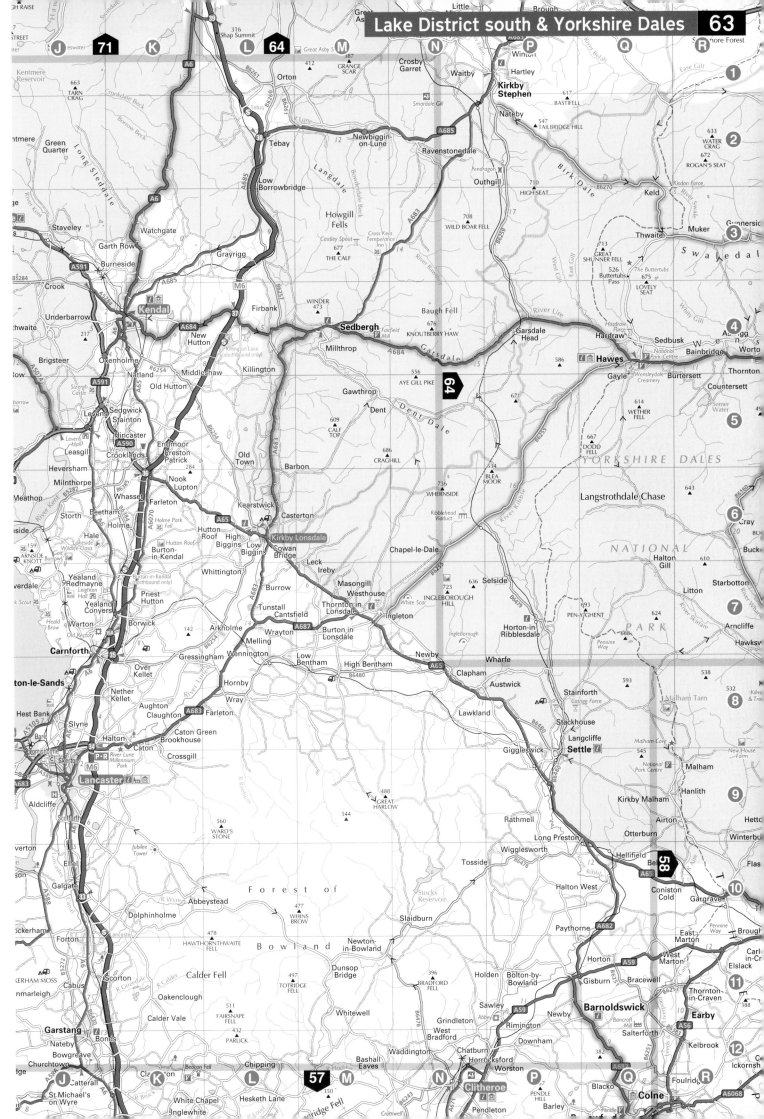

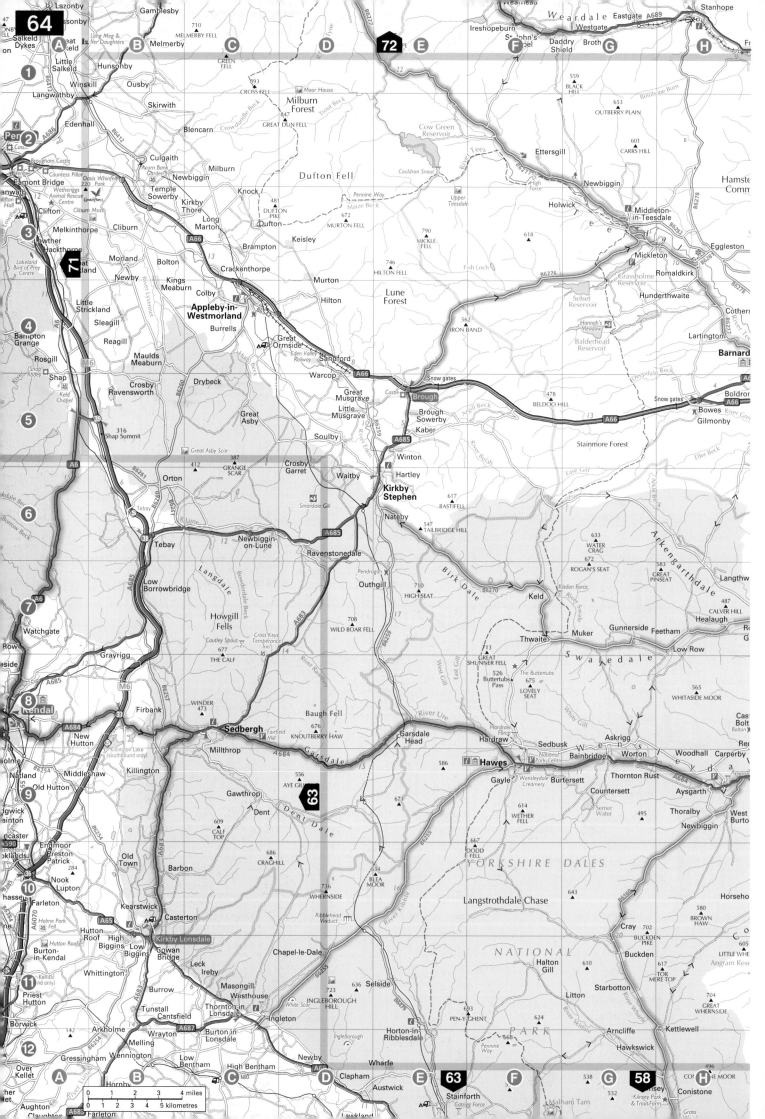

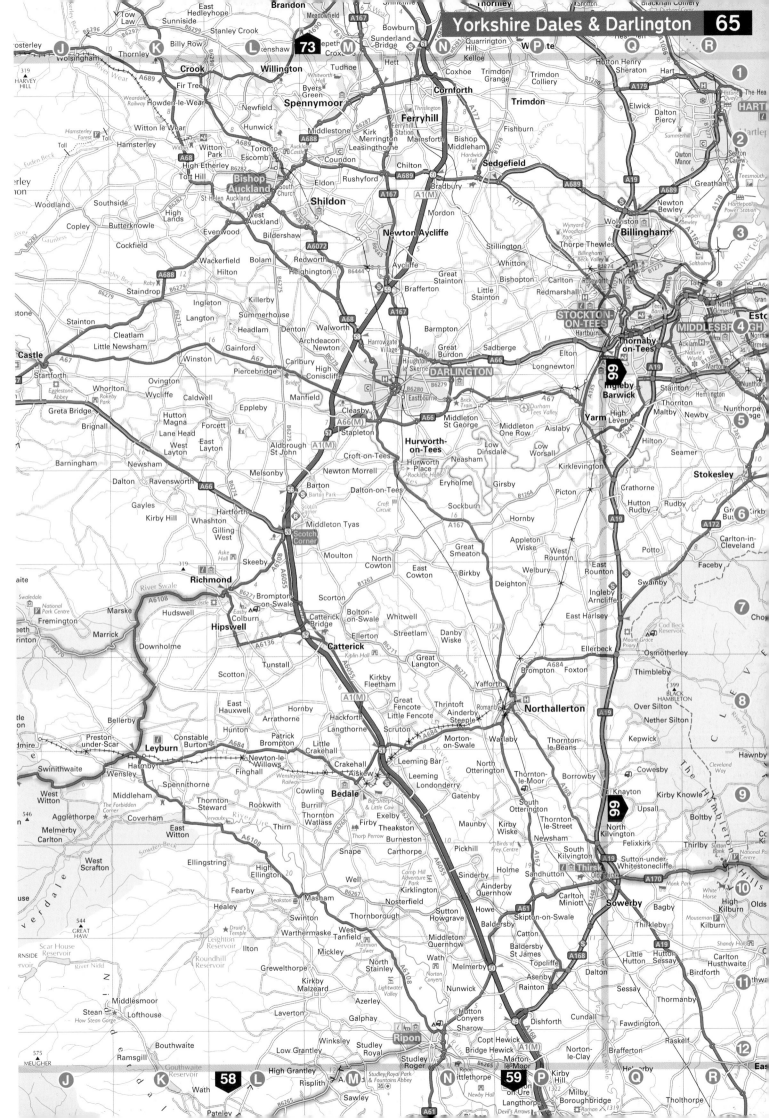

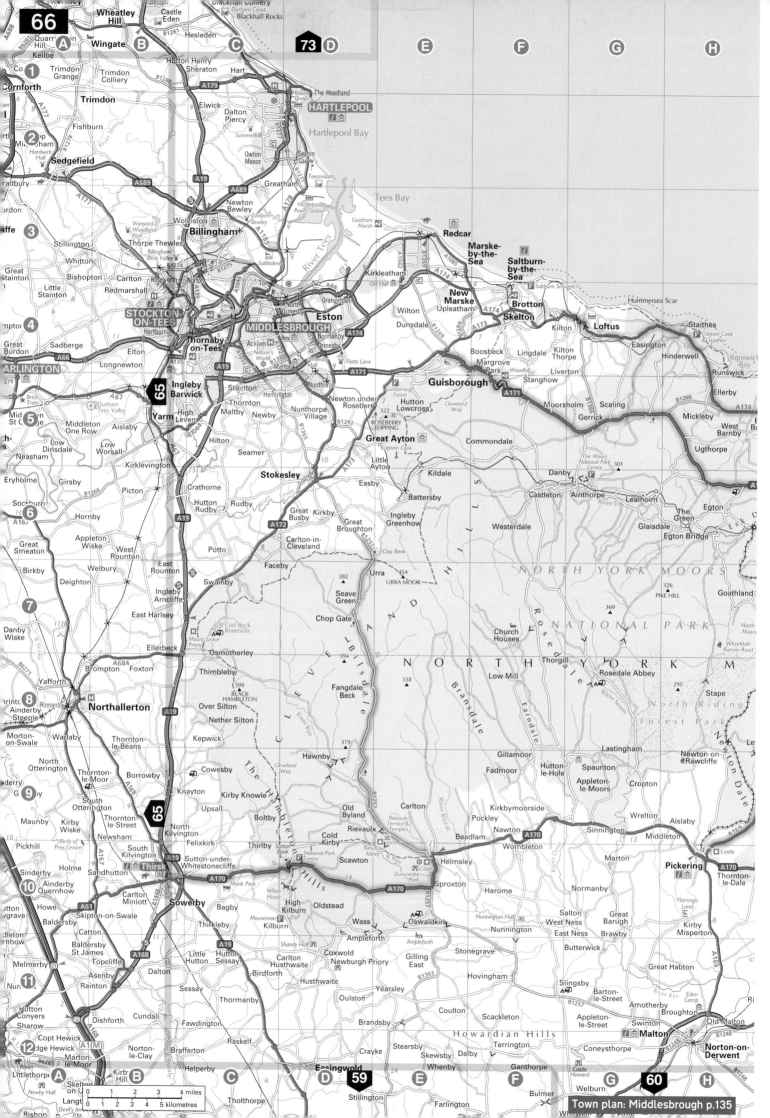

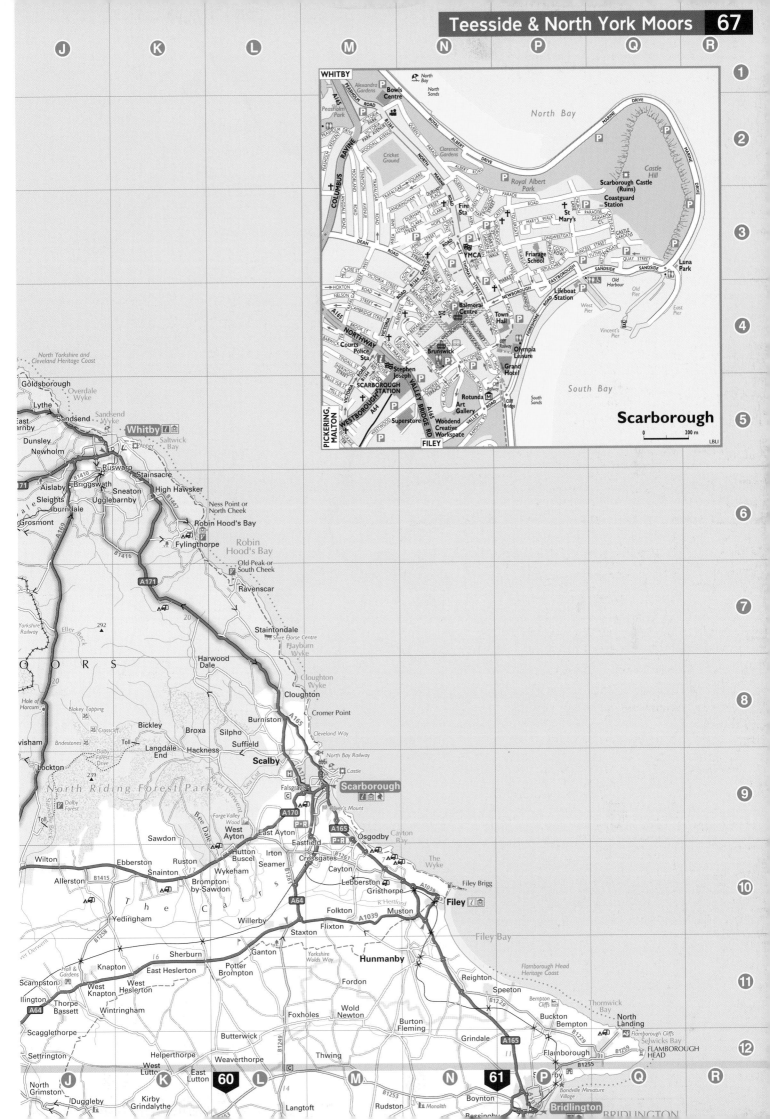

Scarborough

WHITBY

North Bay

South Bay

0   200 m

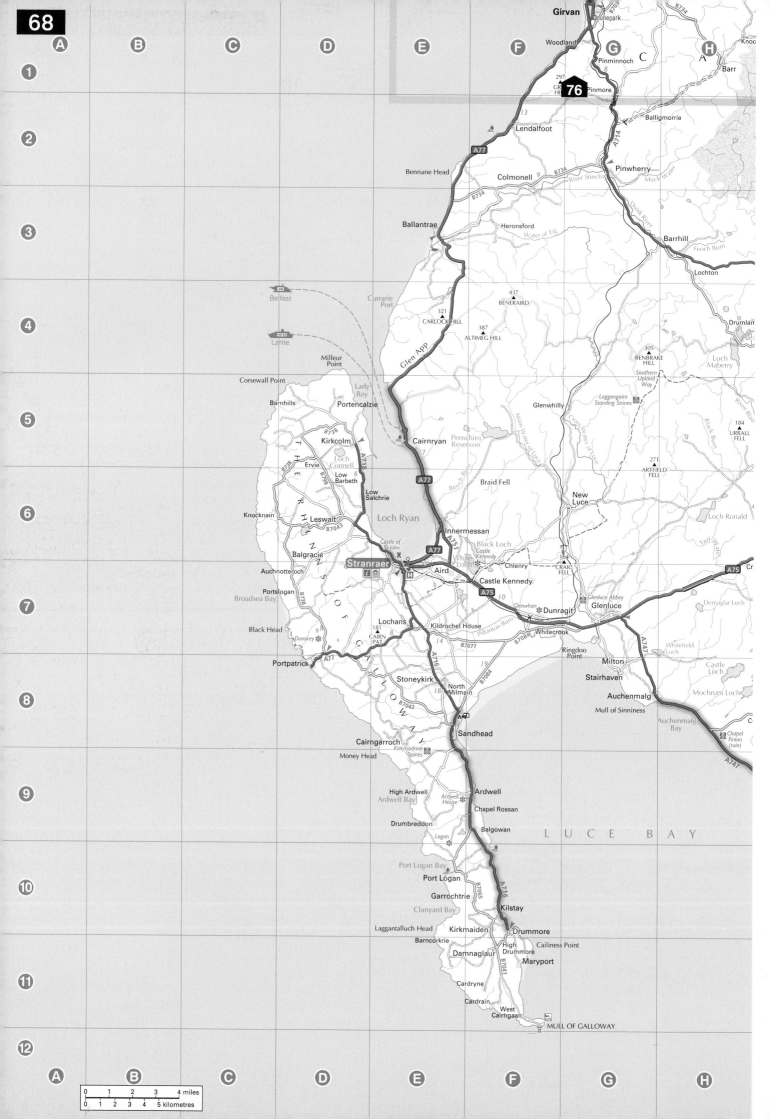

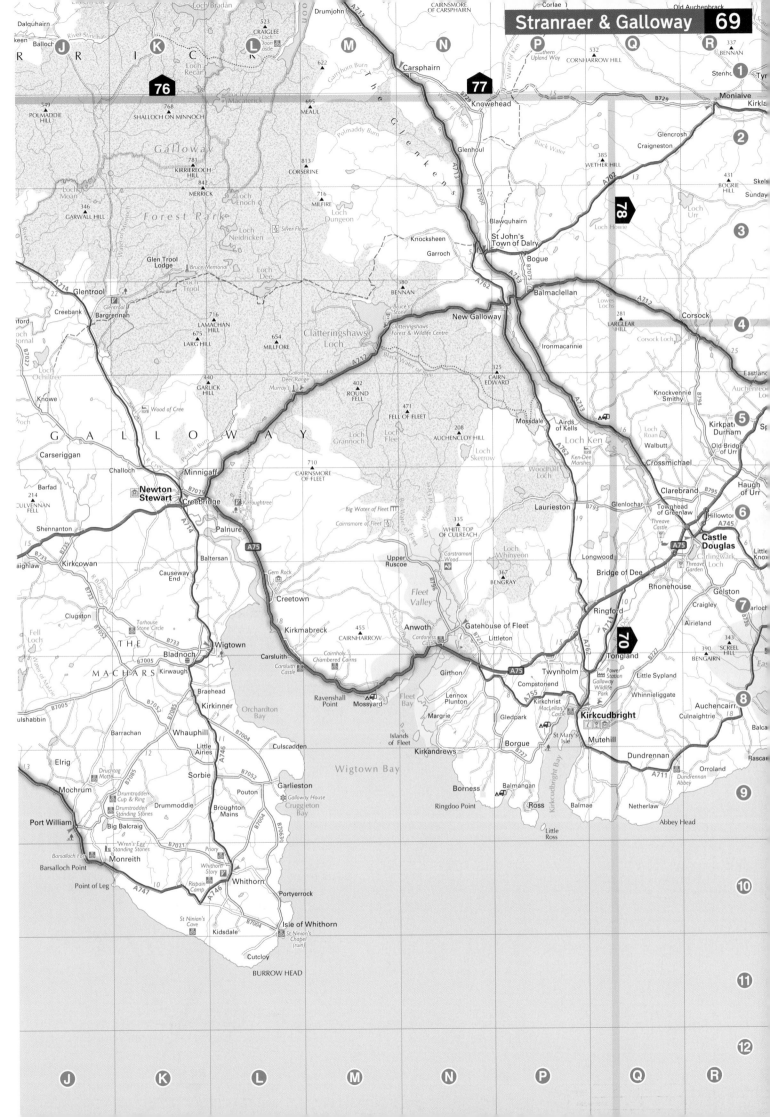

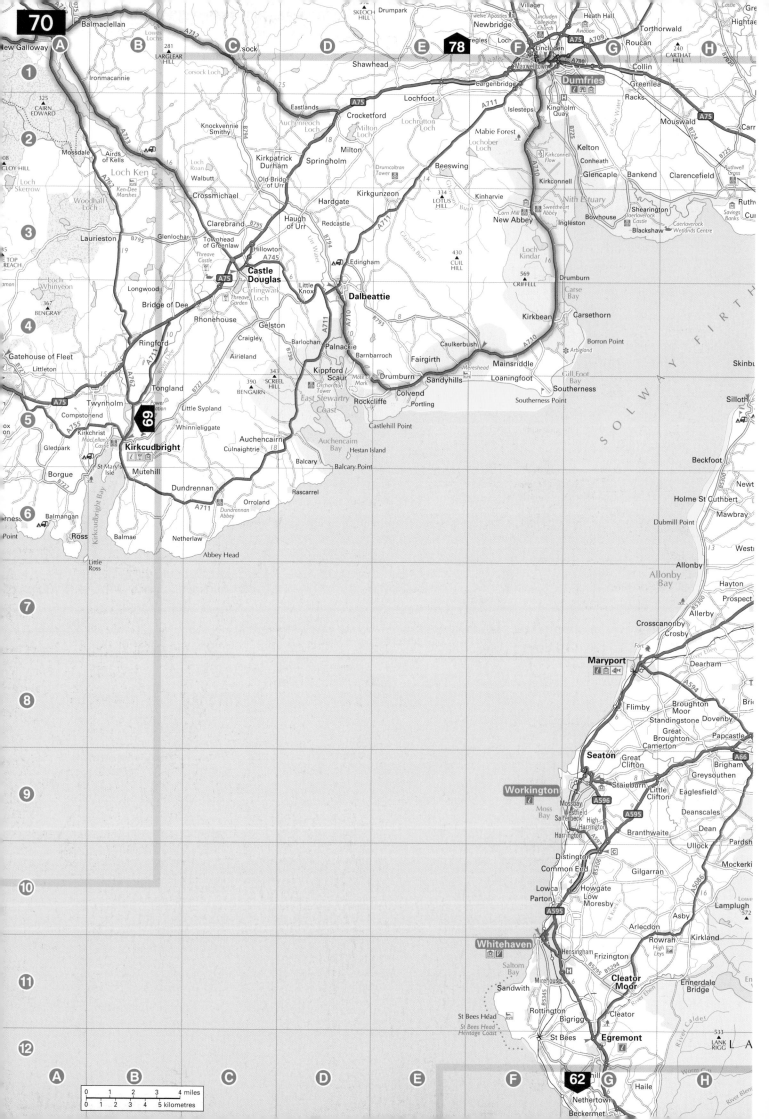

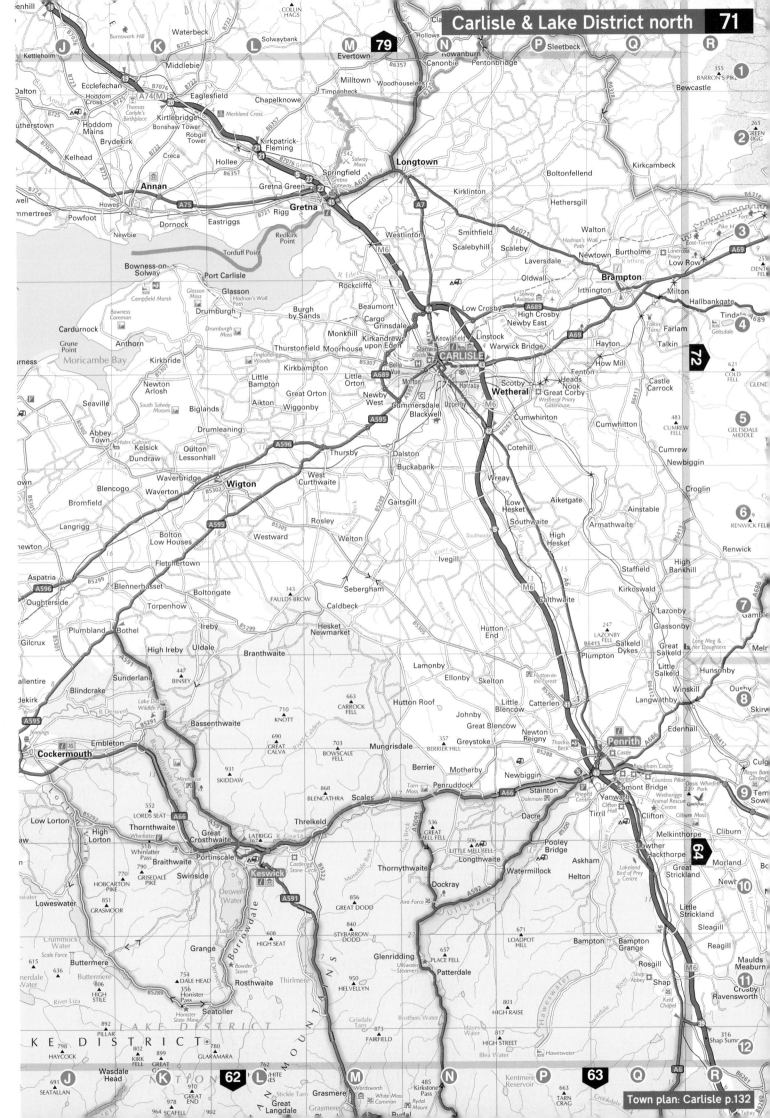

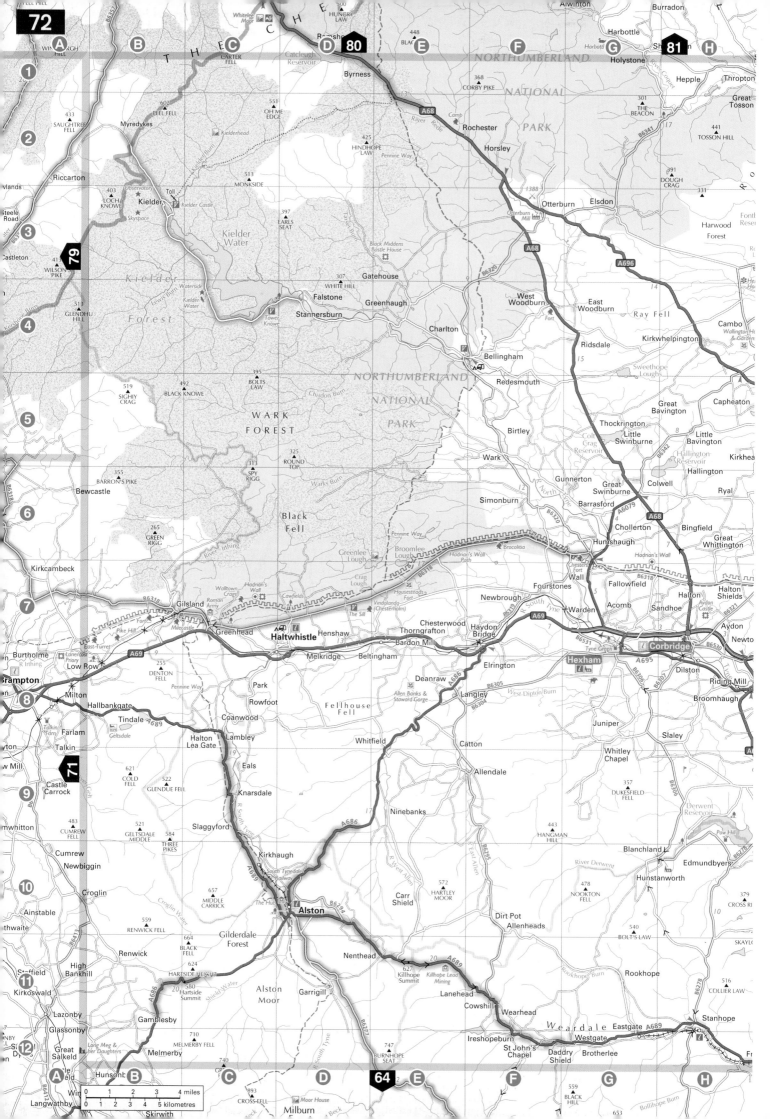

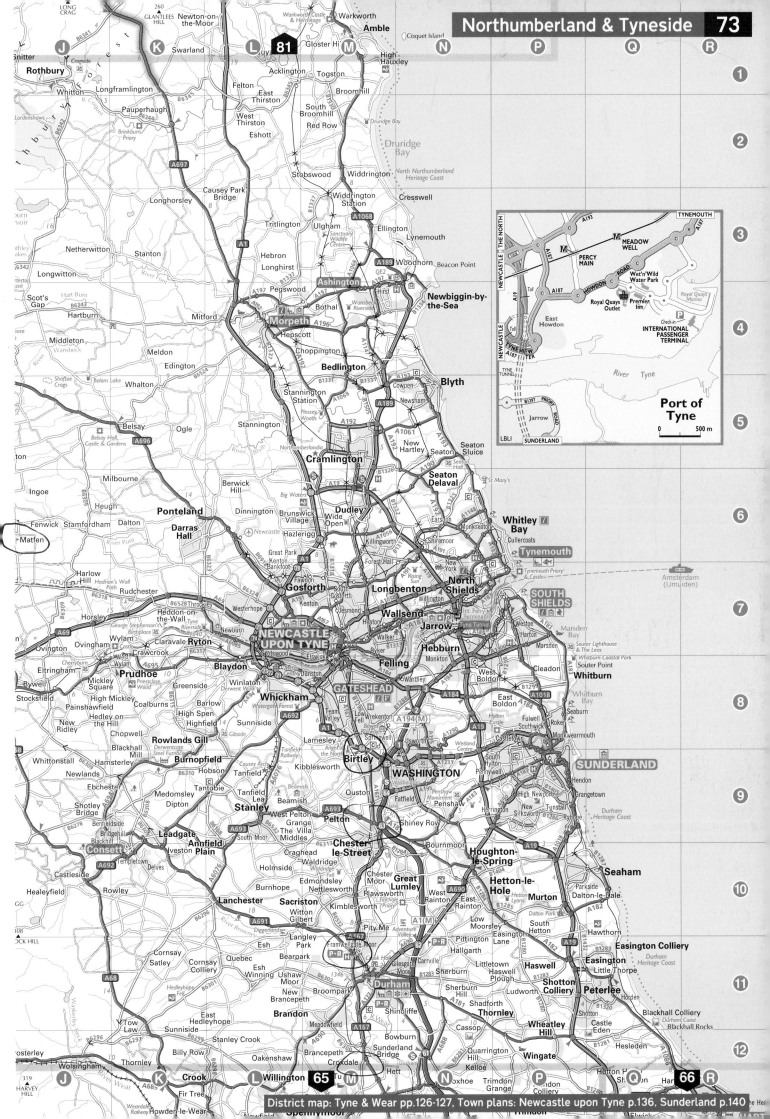

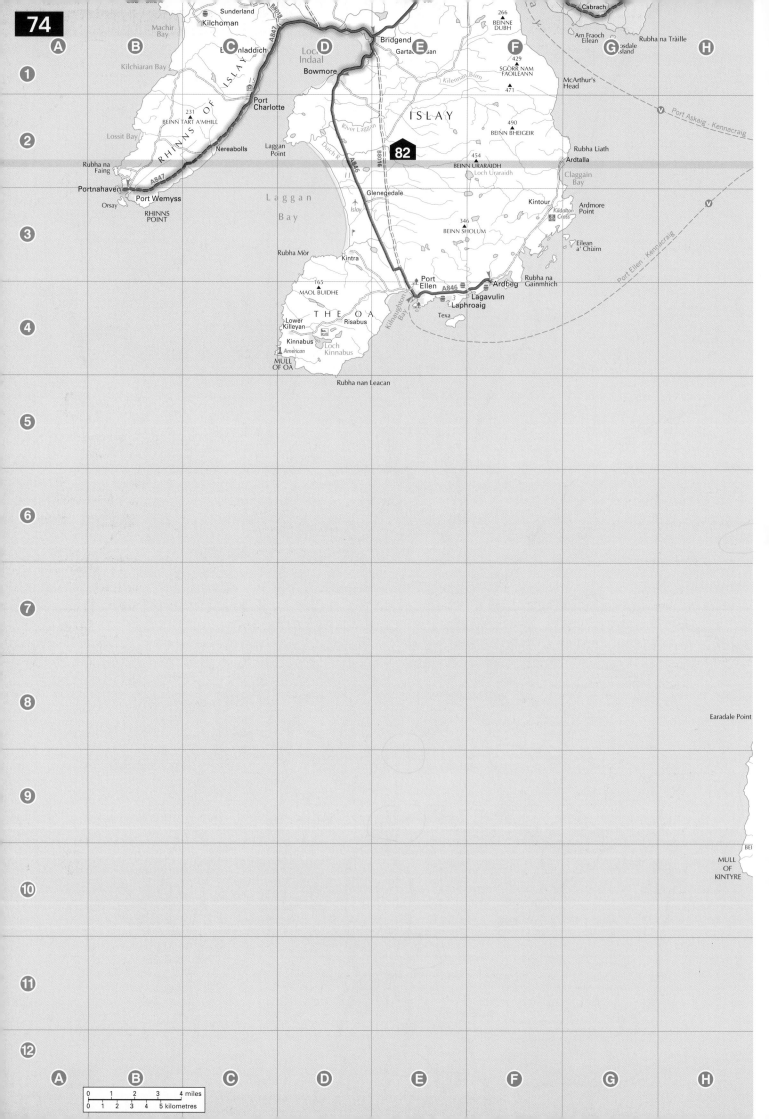

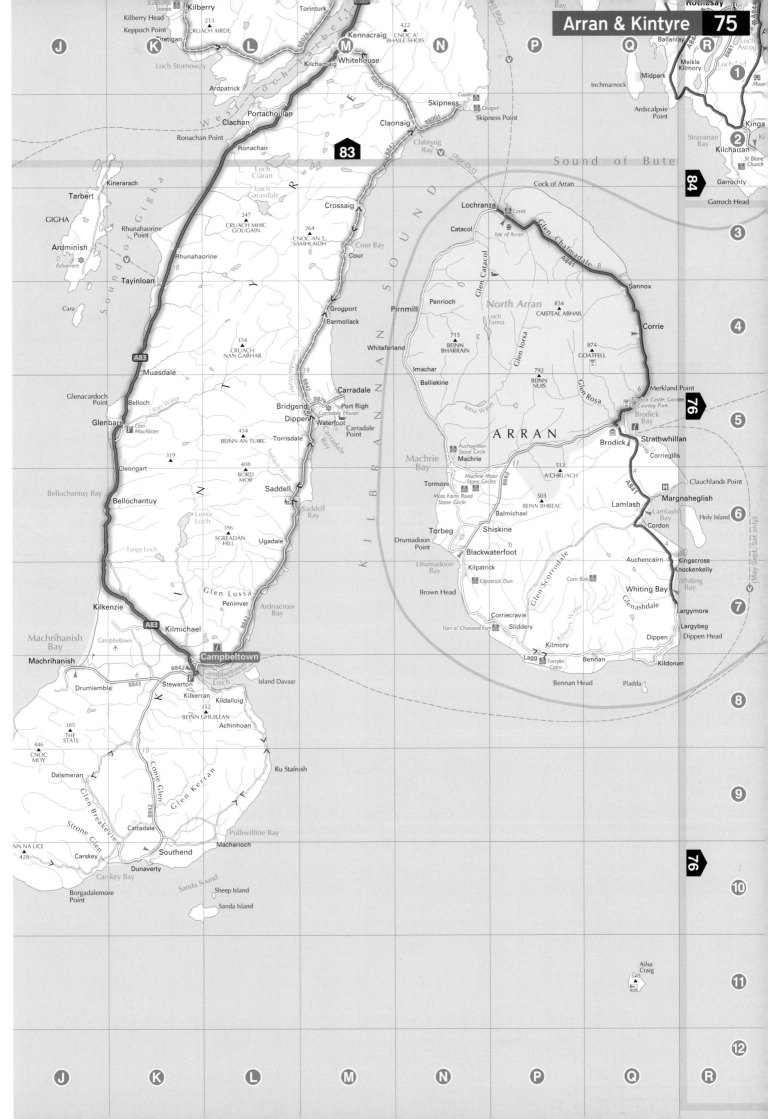

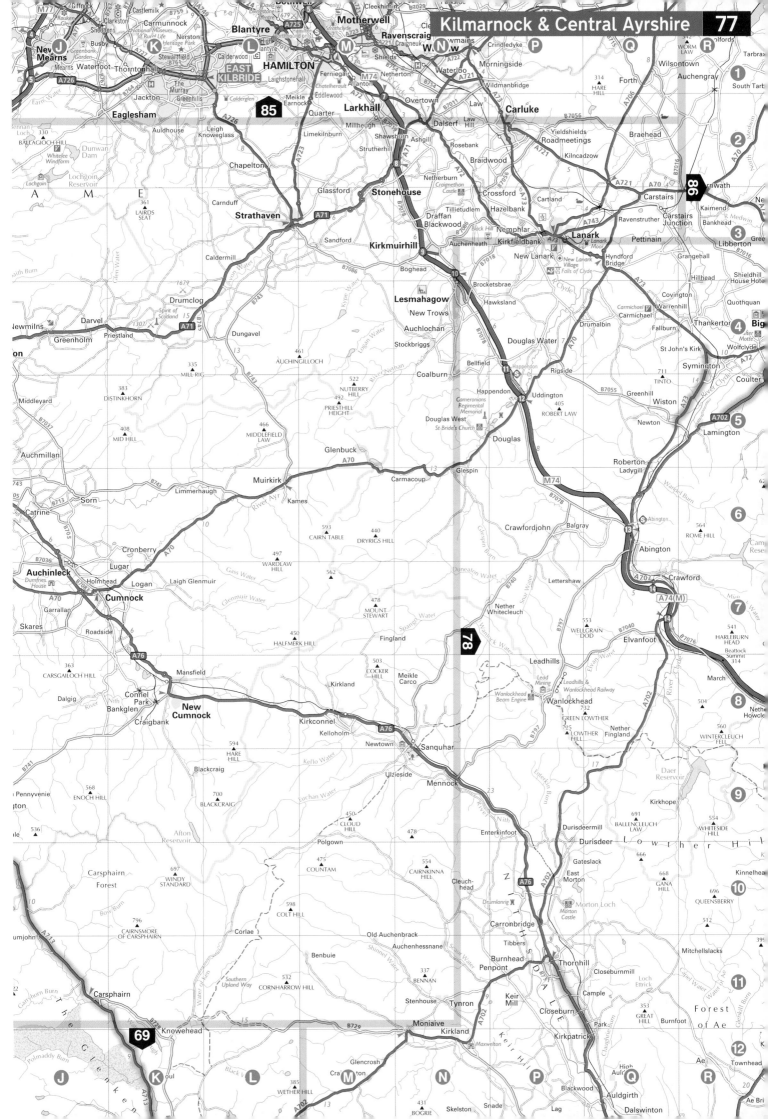

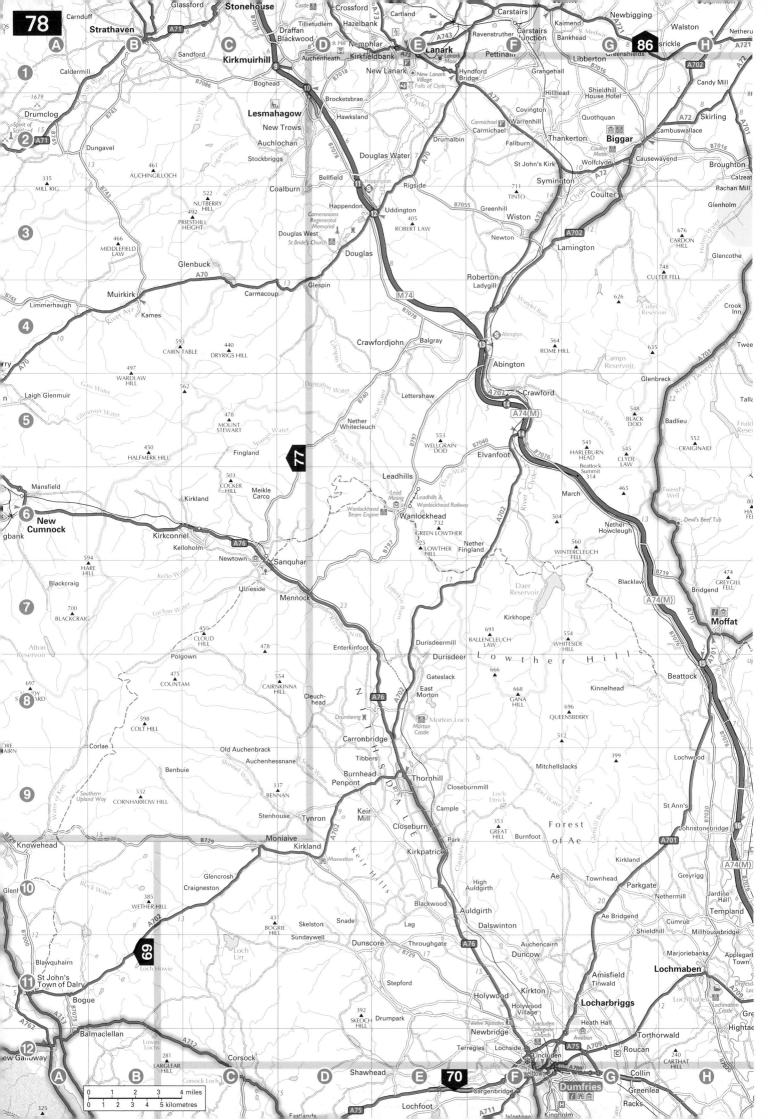

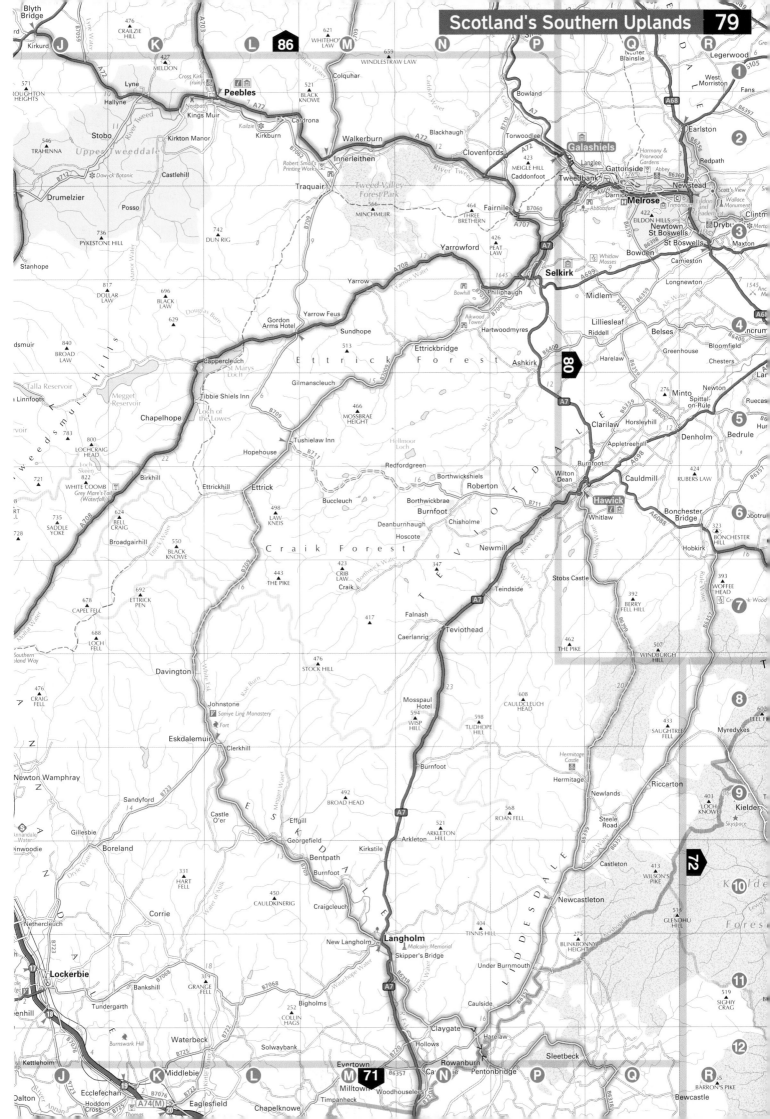

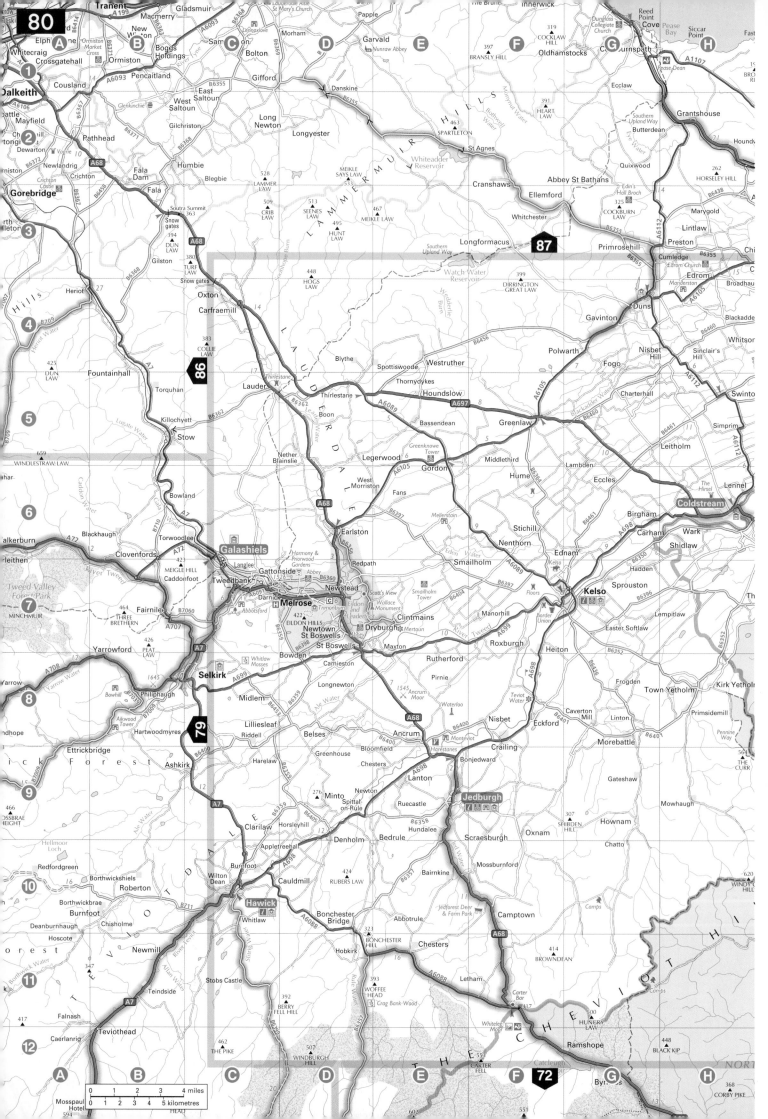

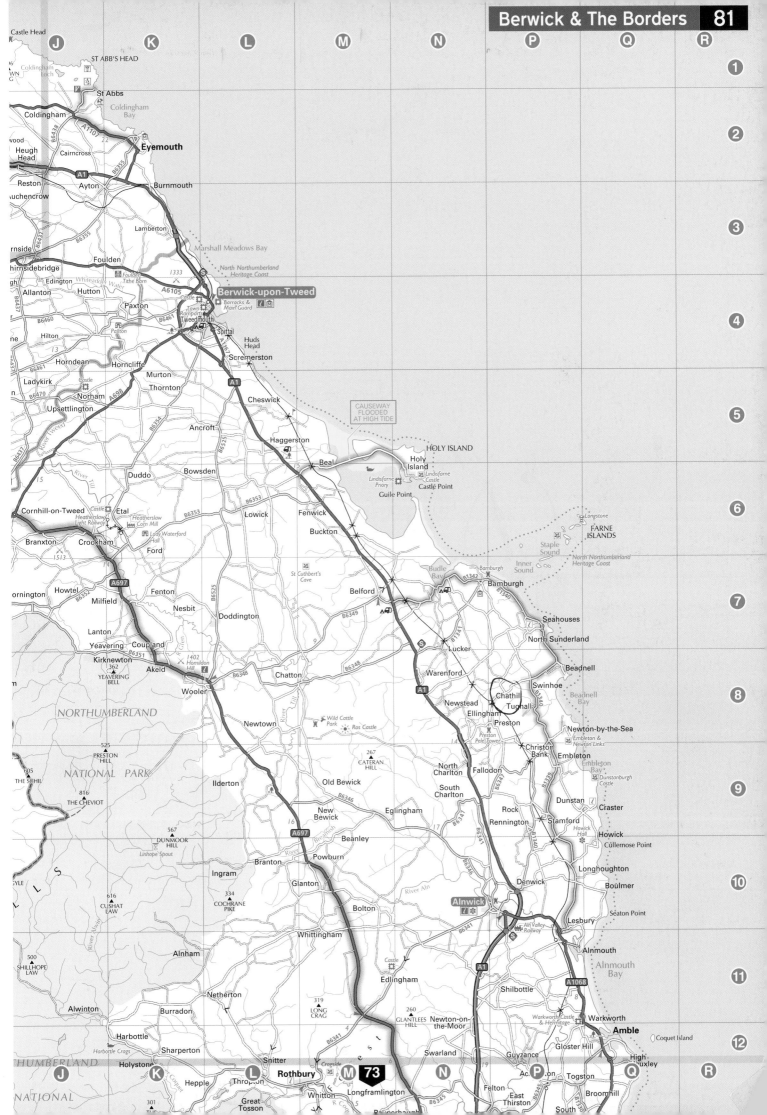

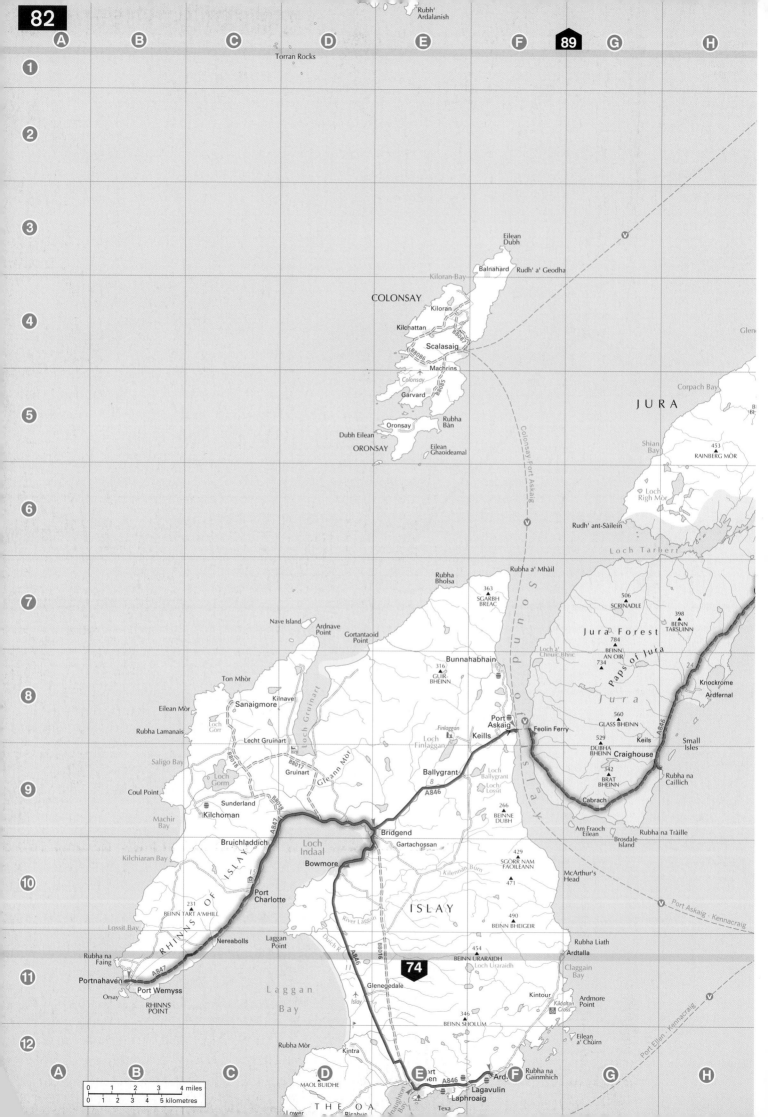

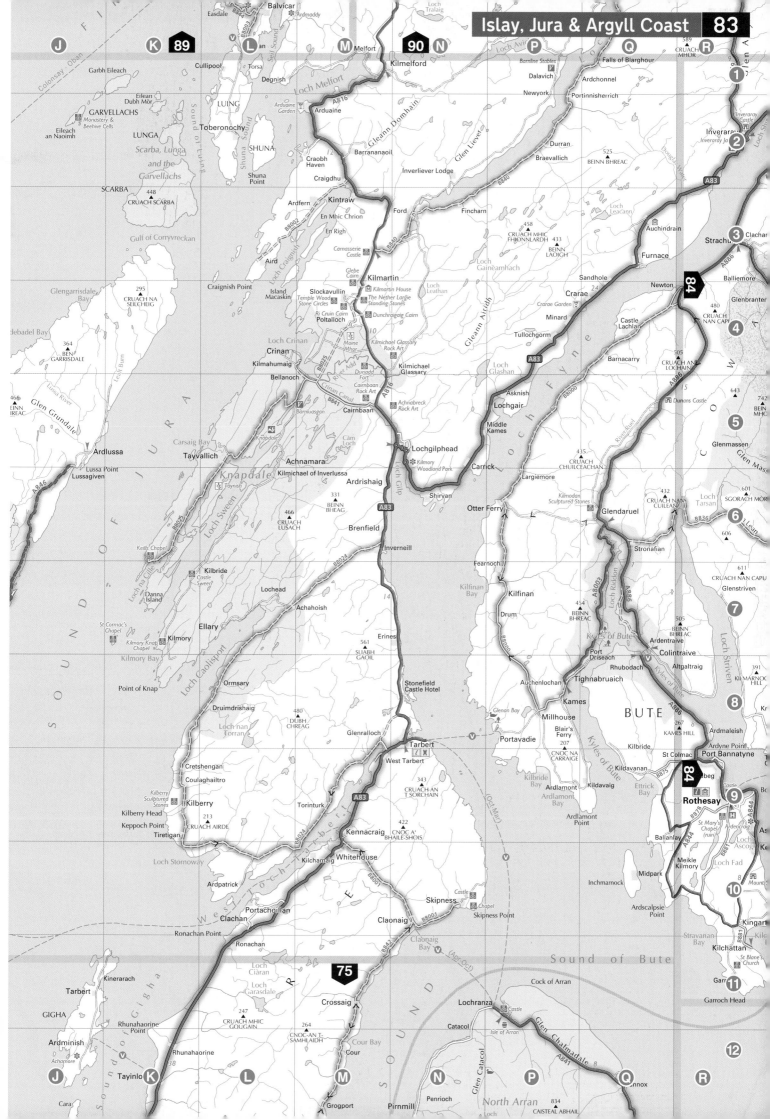

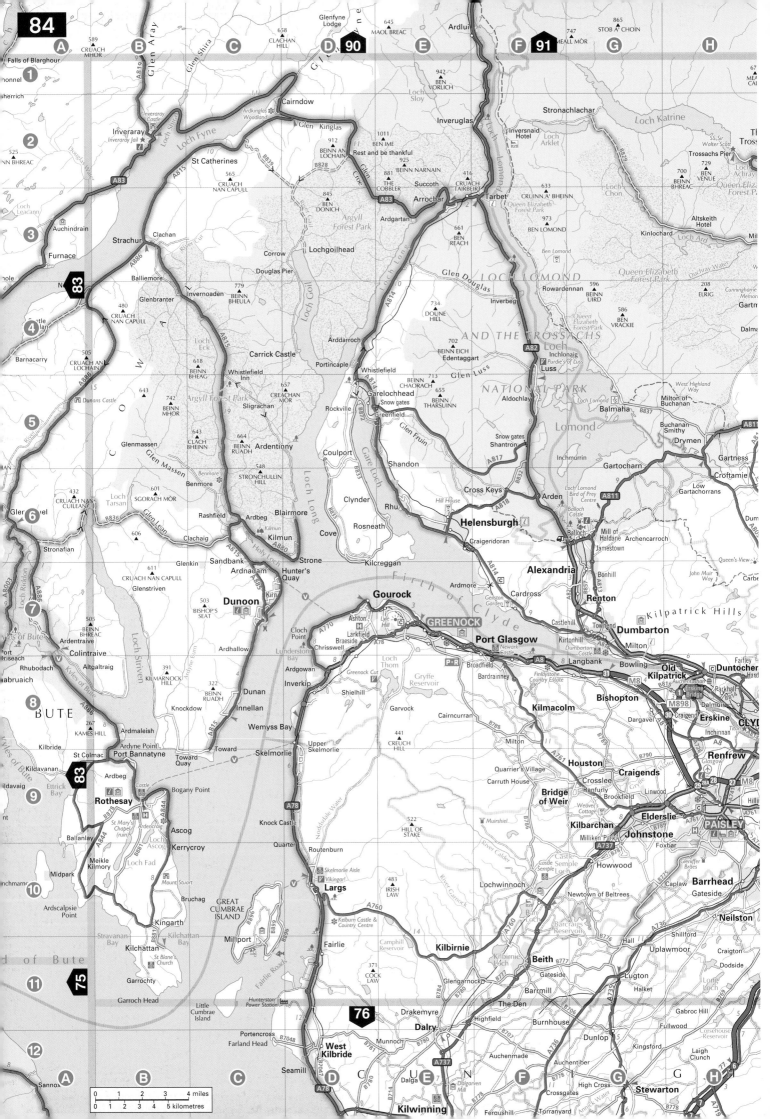

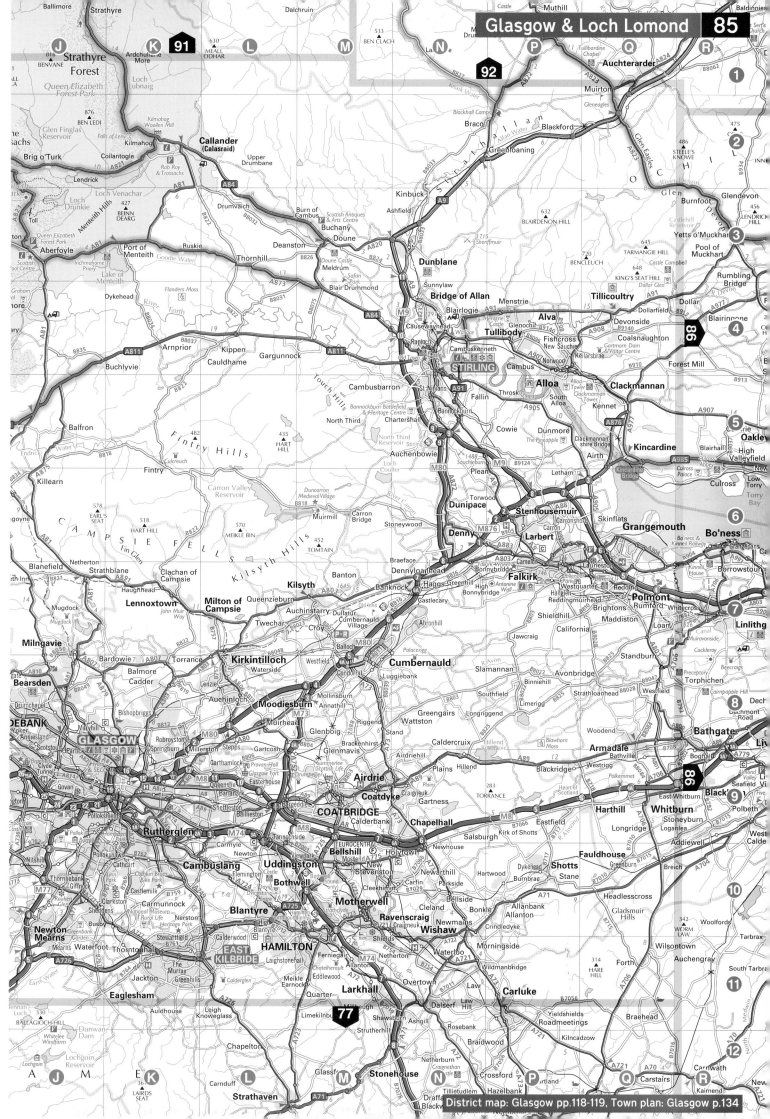

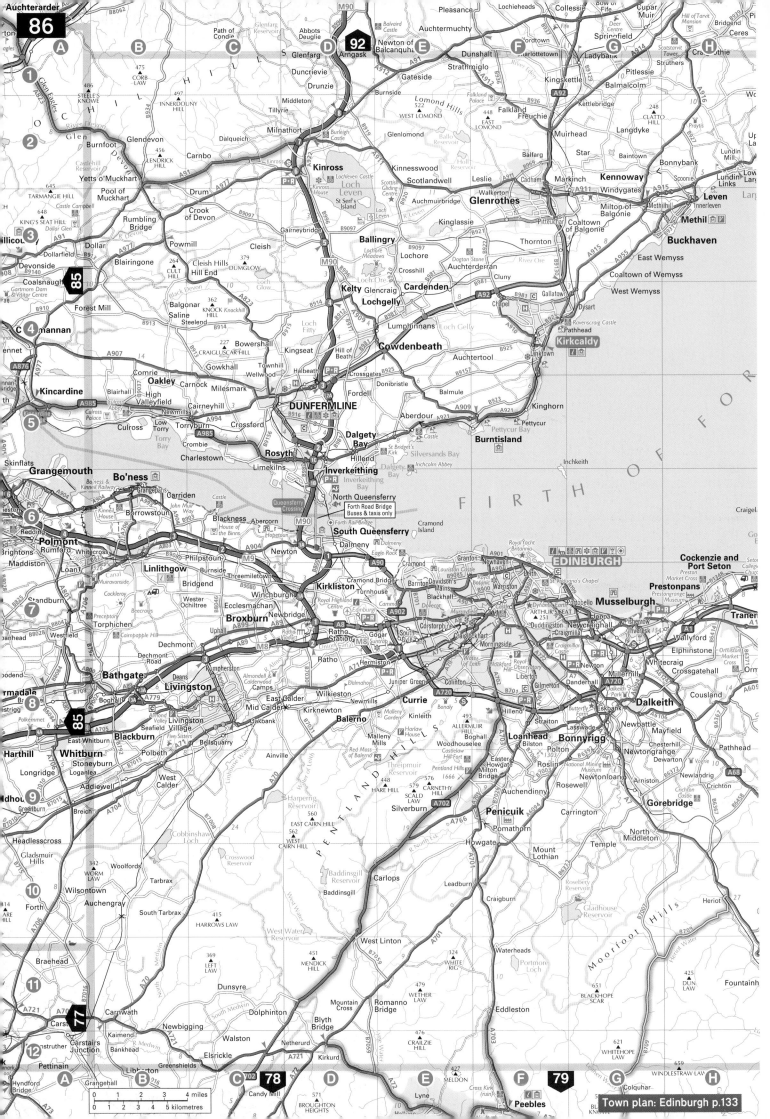

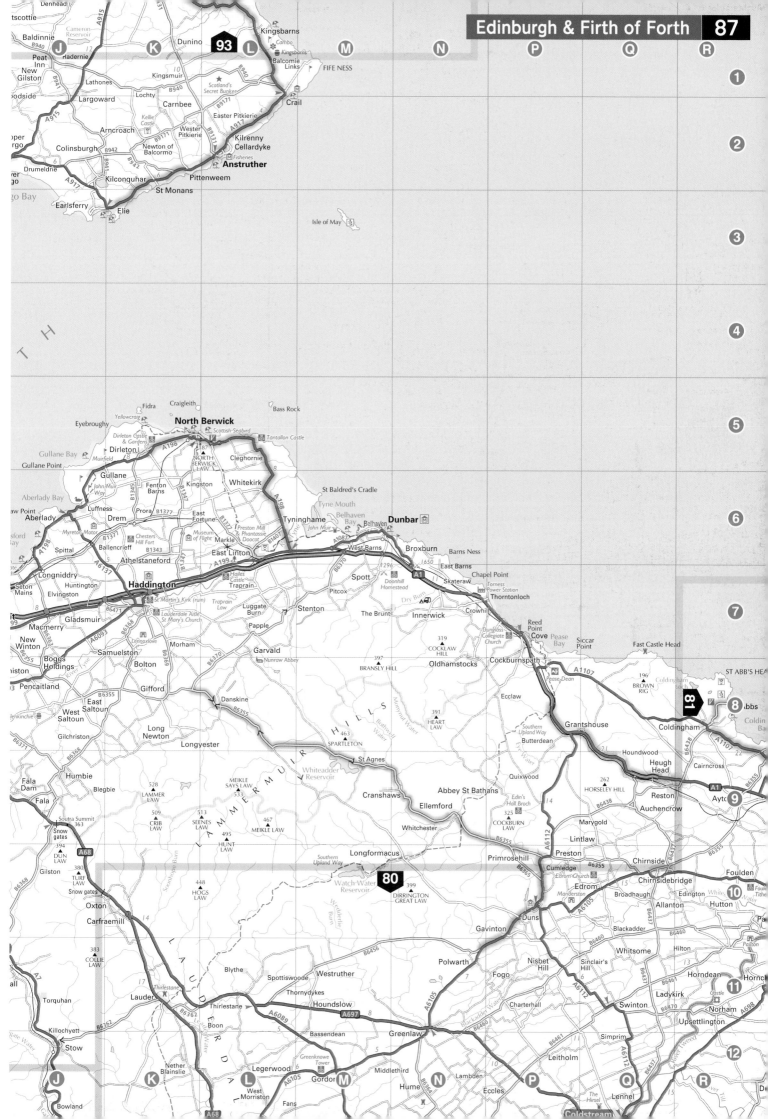

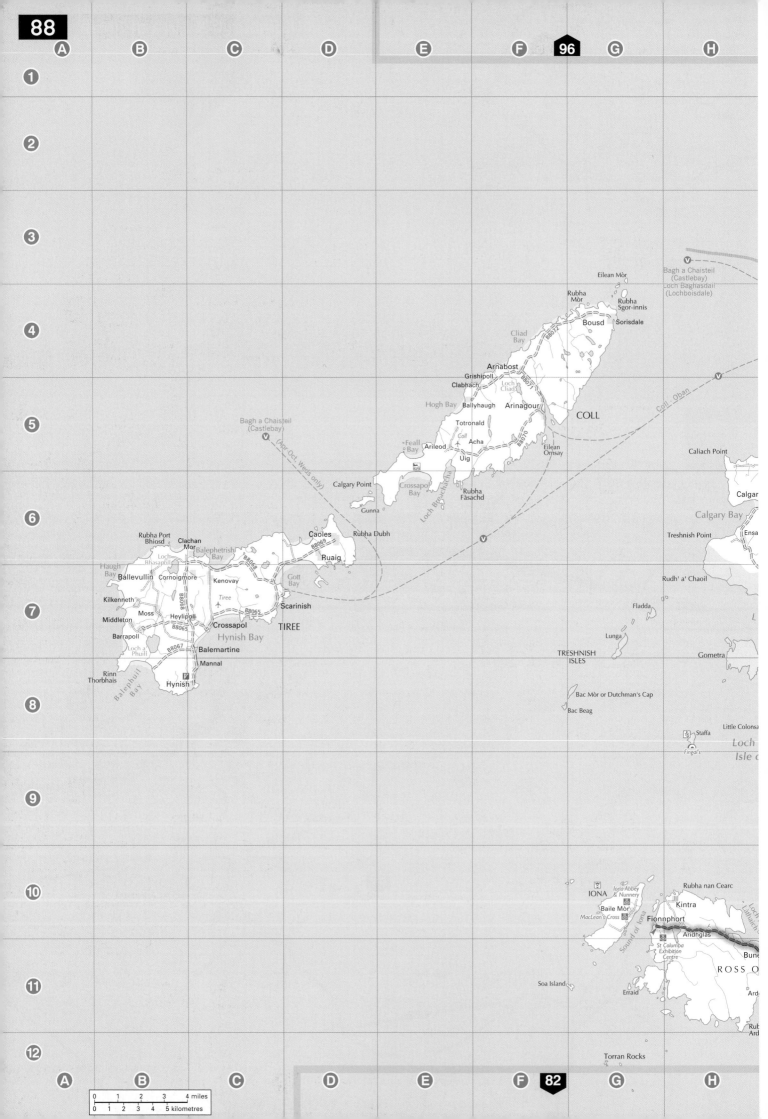

A   B   C   D   E   F   **96**   G   H

1
2
3
4
5
6
7
8
9
10
11
12

A   B   C   D   E   F   **82**   G   H

Eilean Mòr
Bagh a Chaisteil (Castlebay)
Loch Baghasdail (Lochboisdale)
Rubha Mòr
Rubha Sgor-innis
Bousd
Sorisdale
Cliad Bay
Arnabost
Grishipoll
Clabhach
Loch Cliad
Hogh Bay   Ballyhaugh   Arinagour
COLL
Coll - Oban
Bagh a Chaisteil (Castlebay)
Totronald
Feall Bay
Arileod   Coll   Acha
Uig
Caliach Point
Eilean Ornsay
Calgary Point
Crossapol Bay
Rubha Fàsachd
Loch Breachacha
Calgar
Gunna
Calgary Bay
Rubha Port Bhiosd
Clachan Mòr
Caoles
Rùbha Dubh
Treshnish Point
Ensa
Balephetrish Bay
B8069
Ruaig
Haugh Bay
Loch Bhasapoll
B8068
Rudh' a' Chaoil
Ballevullin   Cornoigmore
Kenovay
Gott Bay
Fladda
Kilkenneth
Tiree
B8068
Scarinish
Lunga
Moss   Heylipoll
B8065
TRESHNISH ISLES
Gometra
Middleton
TIREE
Crossapol
Hynish Bay
Barrapoll
Loch a' Phuill
B8067
Balemartine
Bac Mòr or Dutchman's Cap
Mannal
Bac Beag
Rinn Thorbhais
Balephuill Bay
Hynish
Little Colonsa
Staffa
Loch
Isle o
Fingal's

Rubha nan Cearc
Iona Abbey & Nunnery
IONA
Kintra
Baile Mòr
MacLean's Cross
Fionnphort
Aridhglas
Sound of Iona
St Columba Exhibition Centre
Bune
ROSS O
Soa Island
Ardi
Erraid
Rub
Ard
Torran Rocks

0   1   2   3   4 miles
0   1   2   3   4   5 kilometres

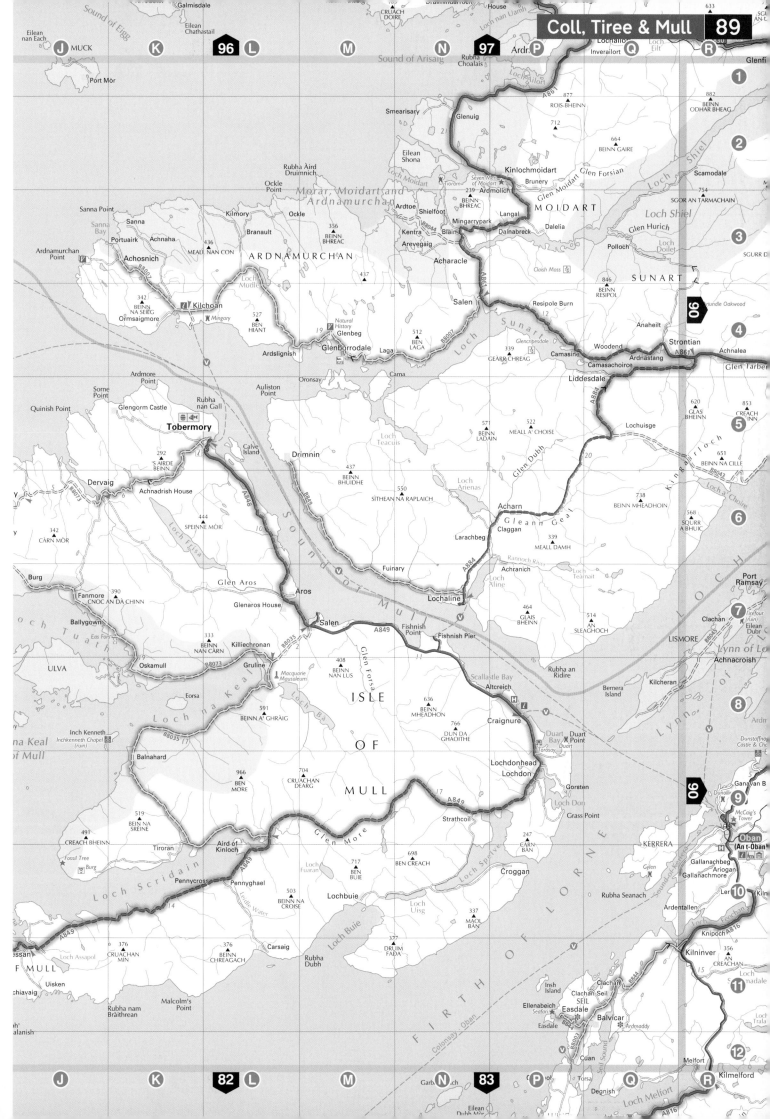

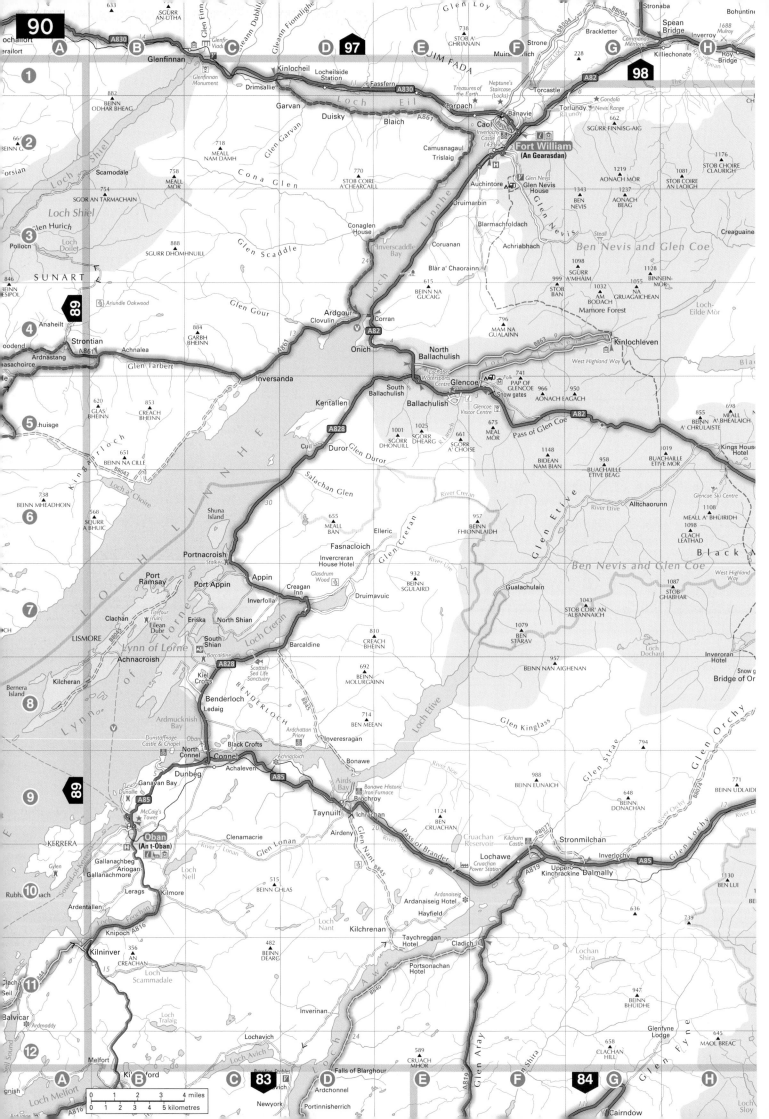

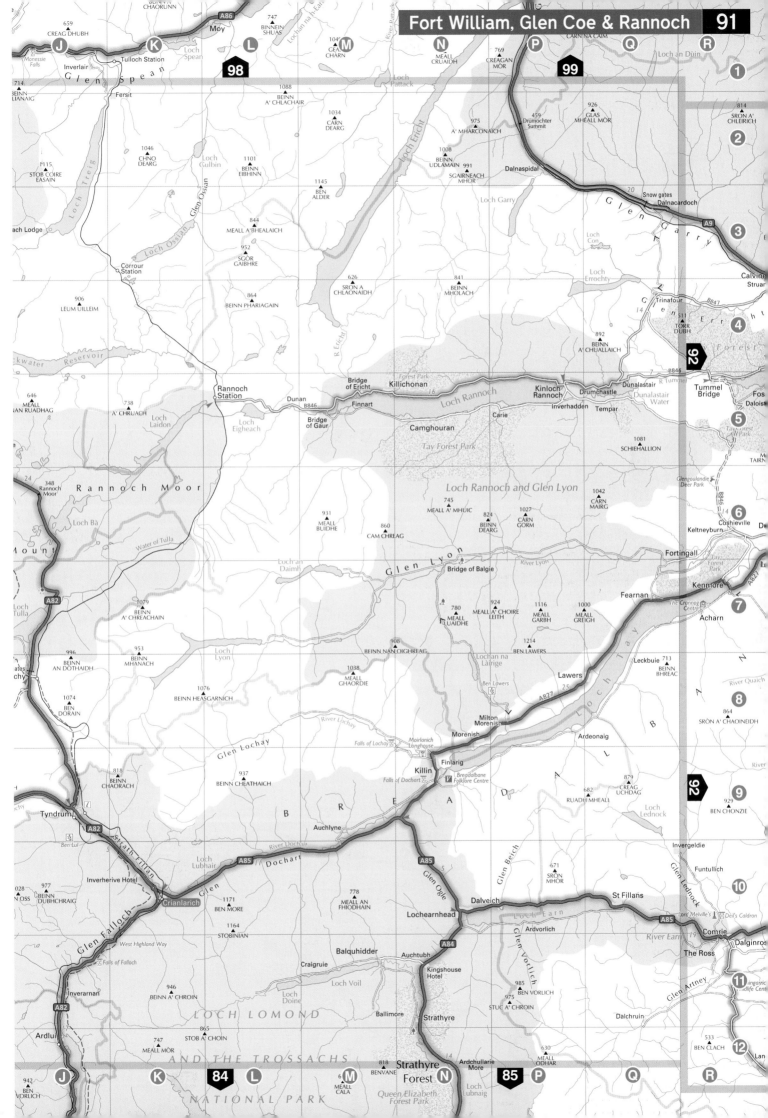

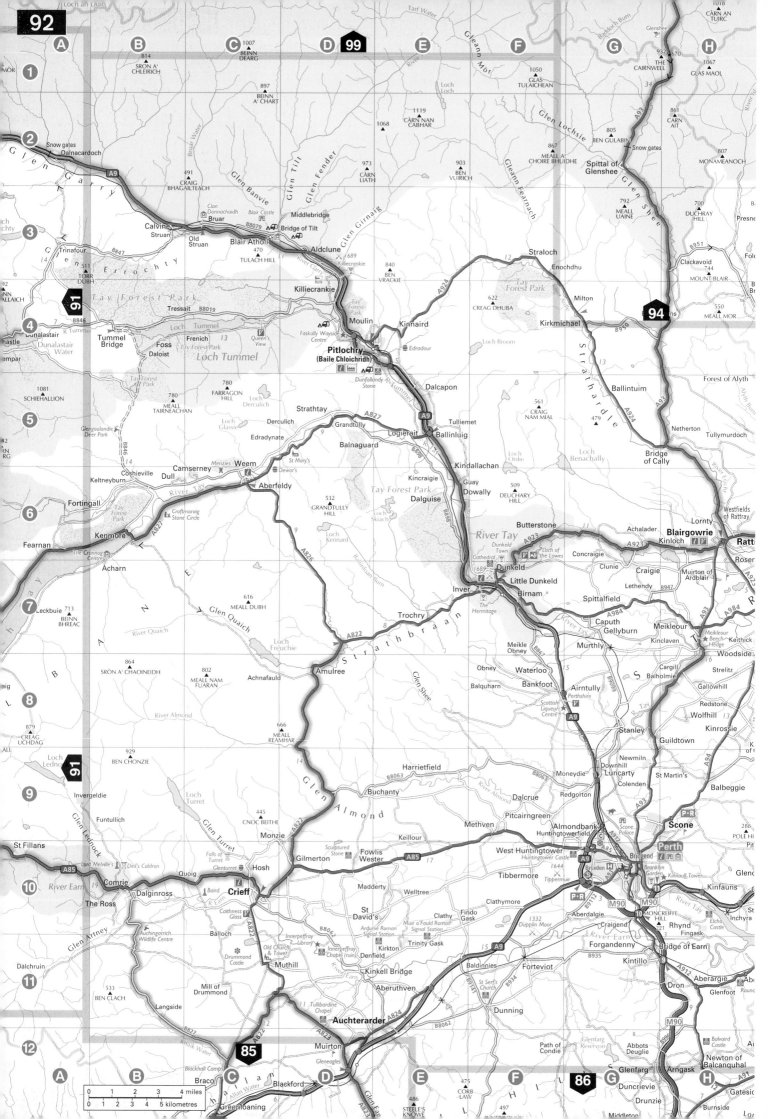

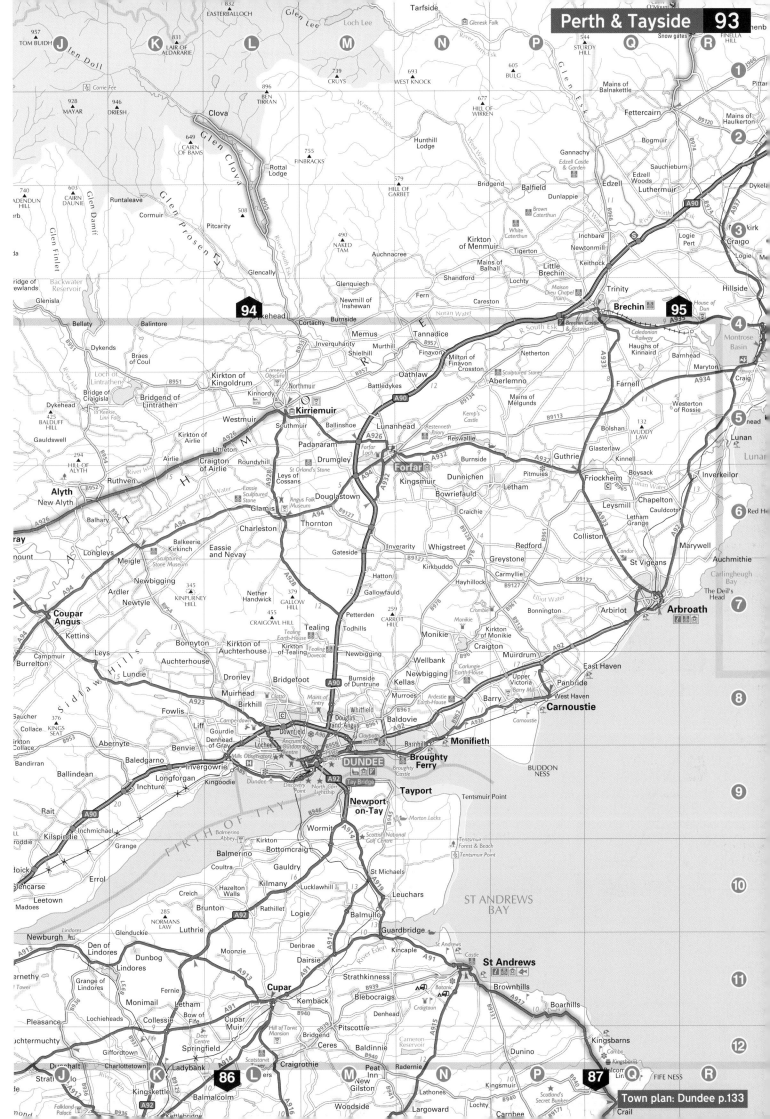

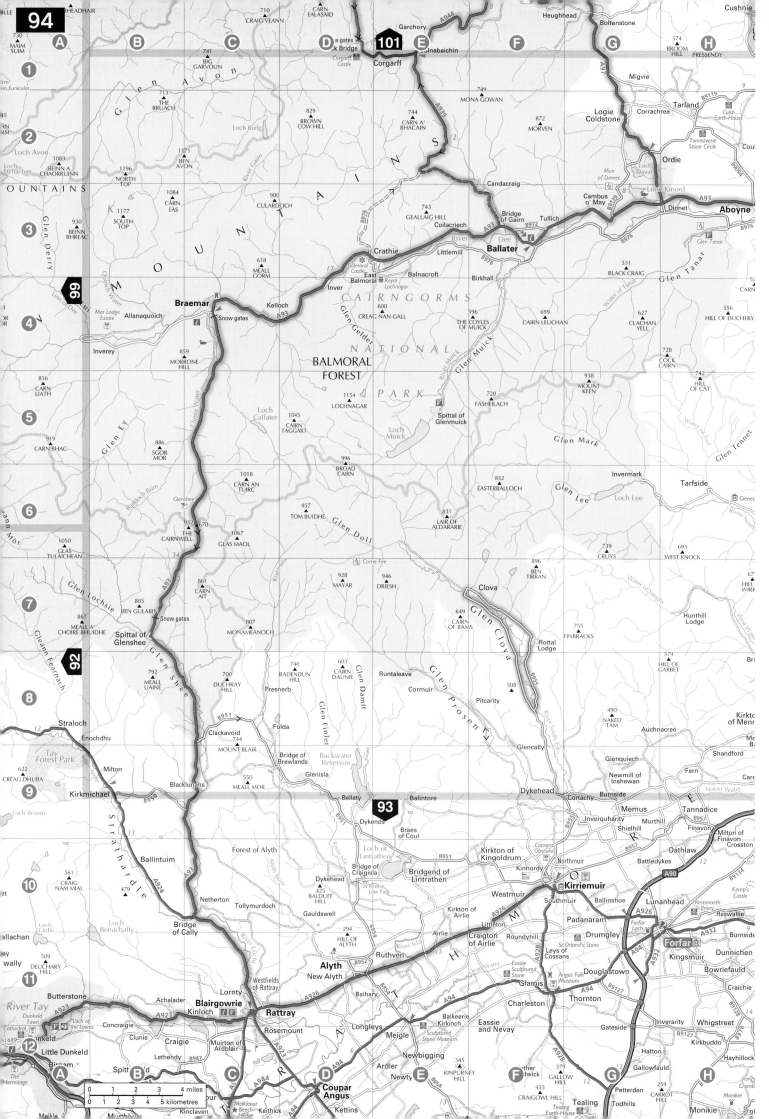

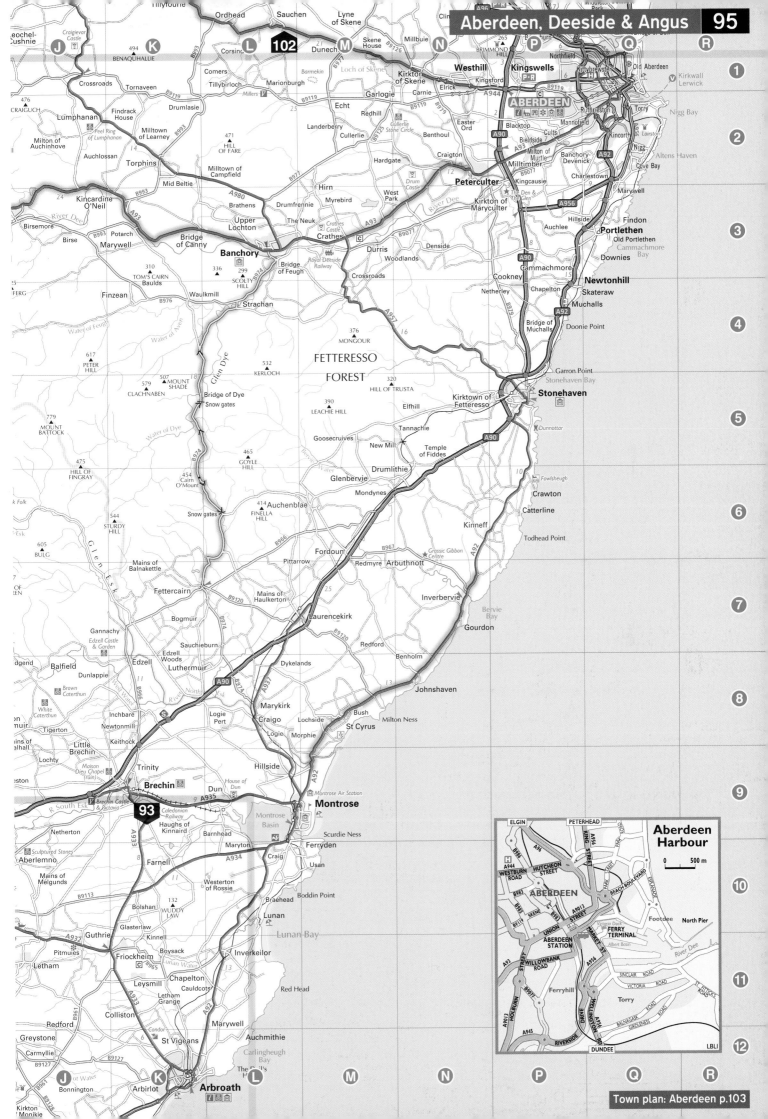

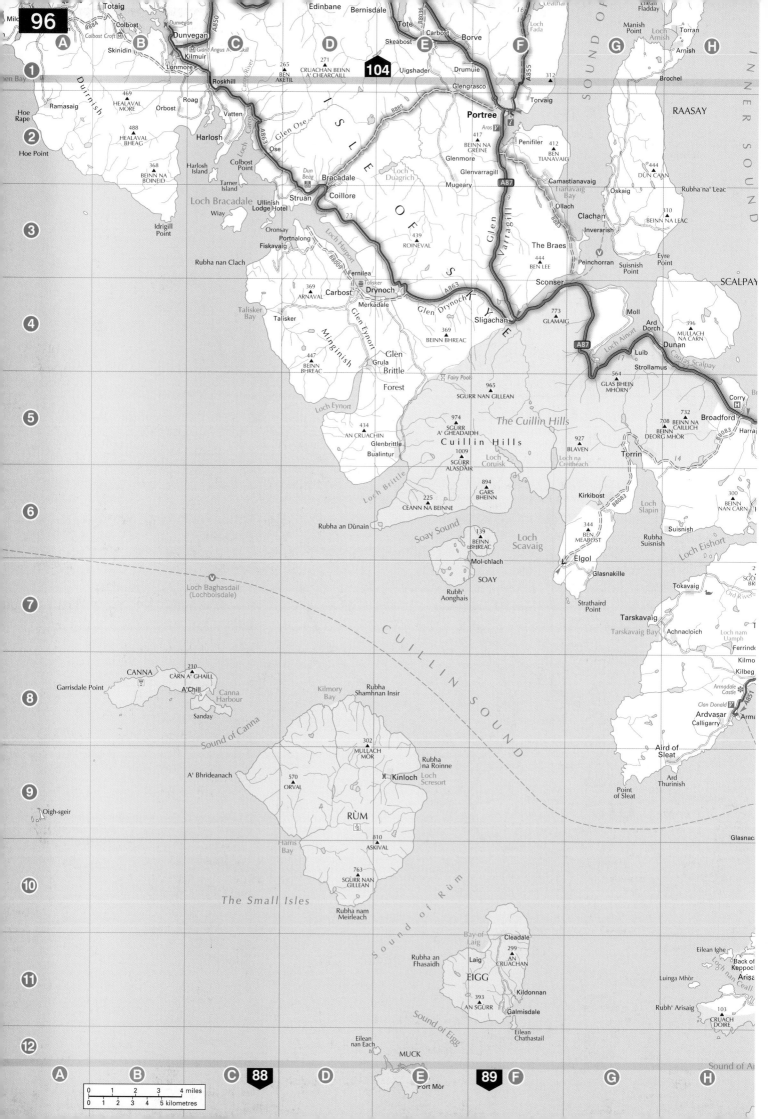

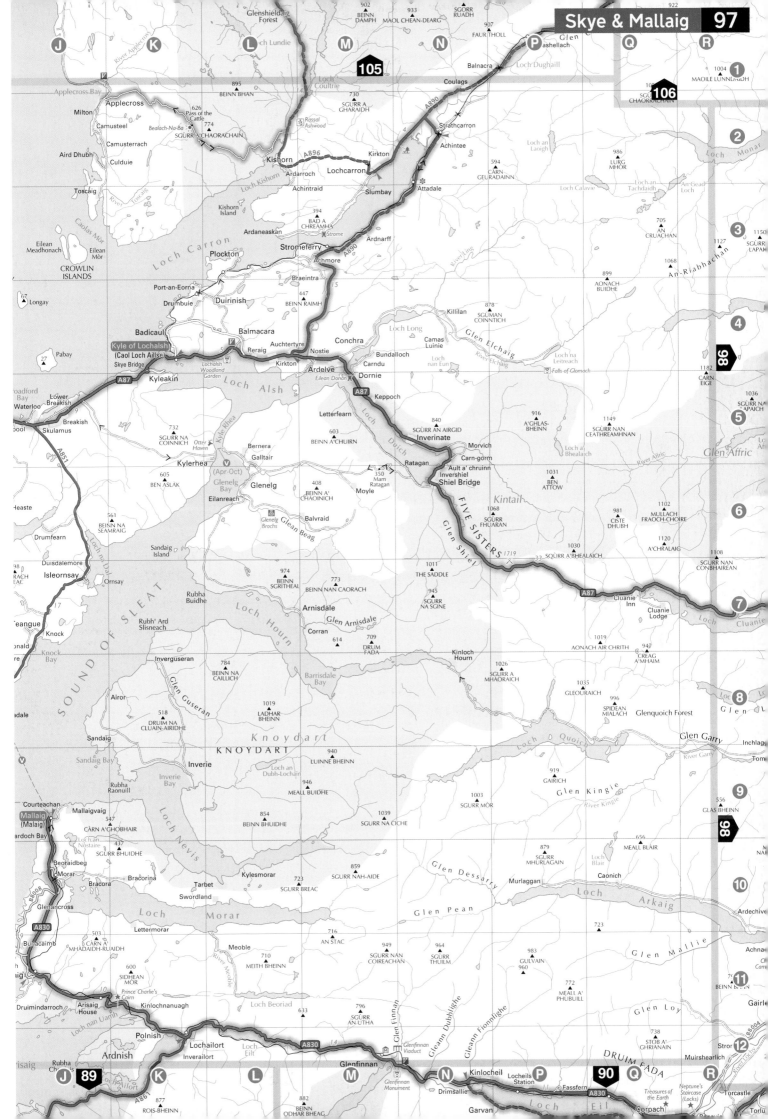

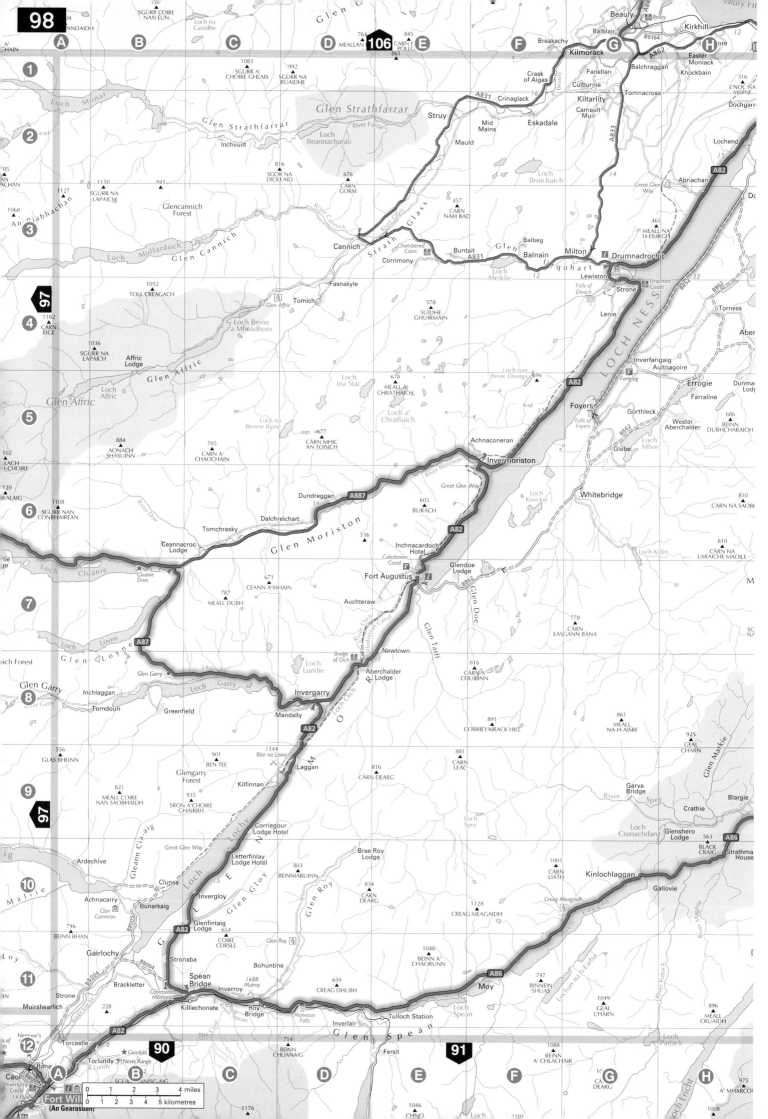

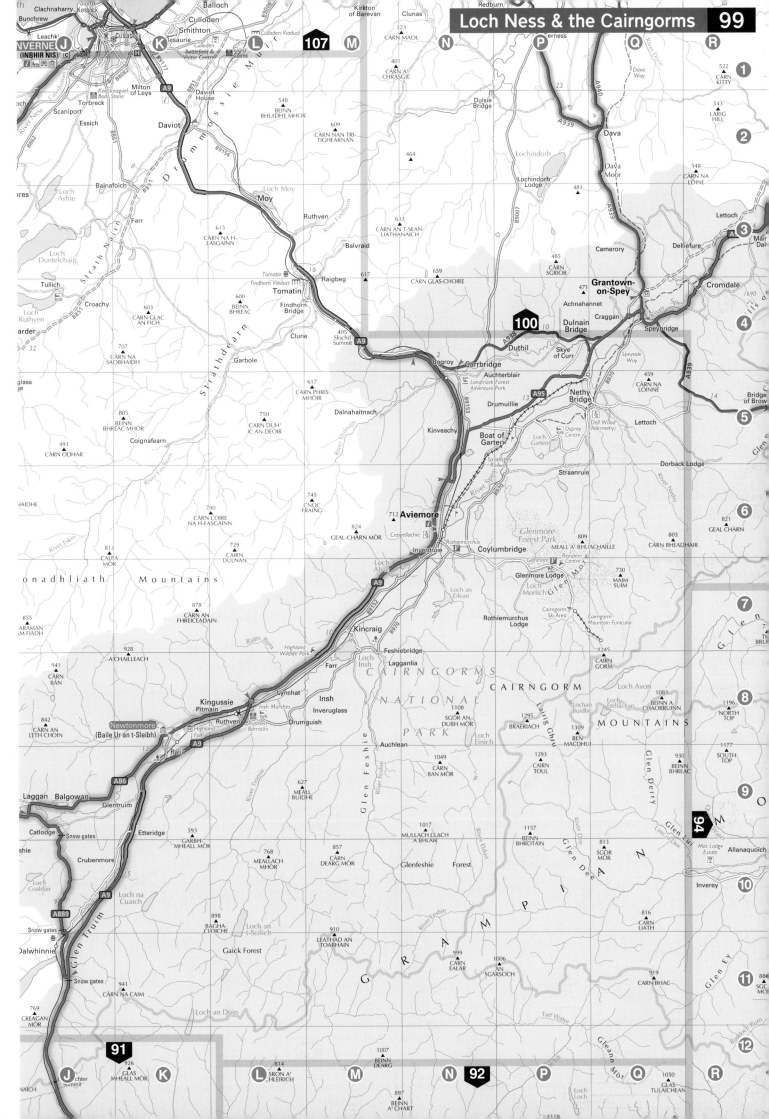

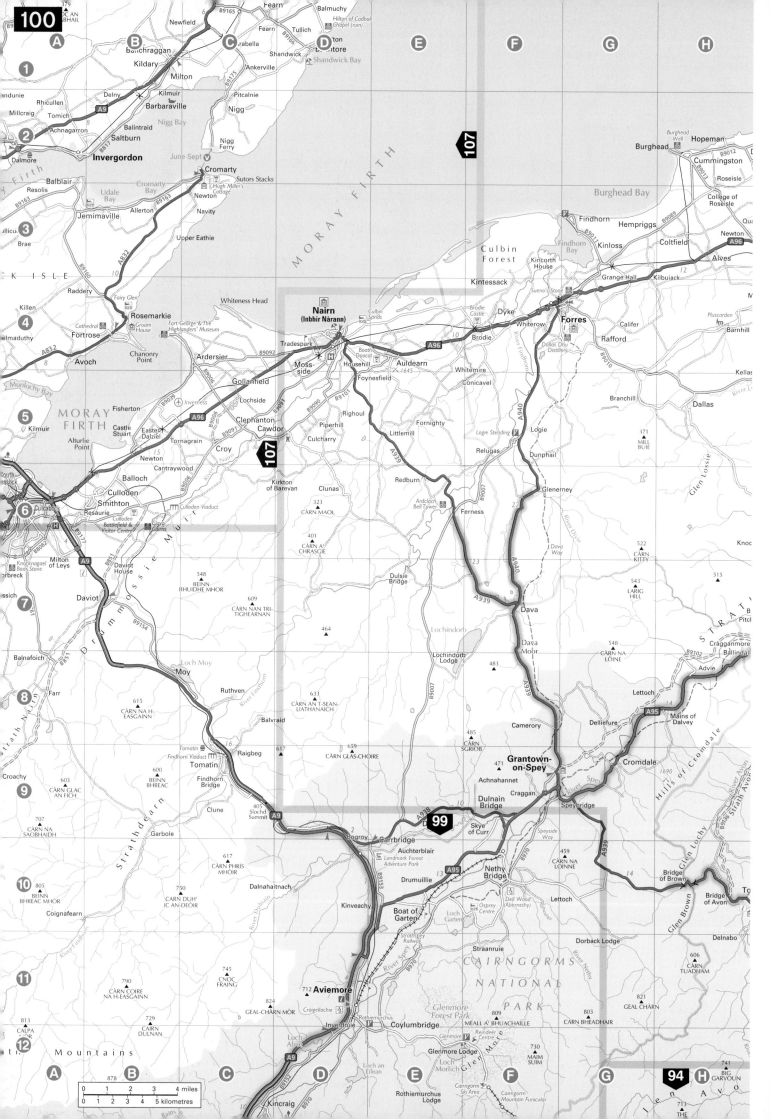

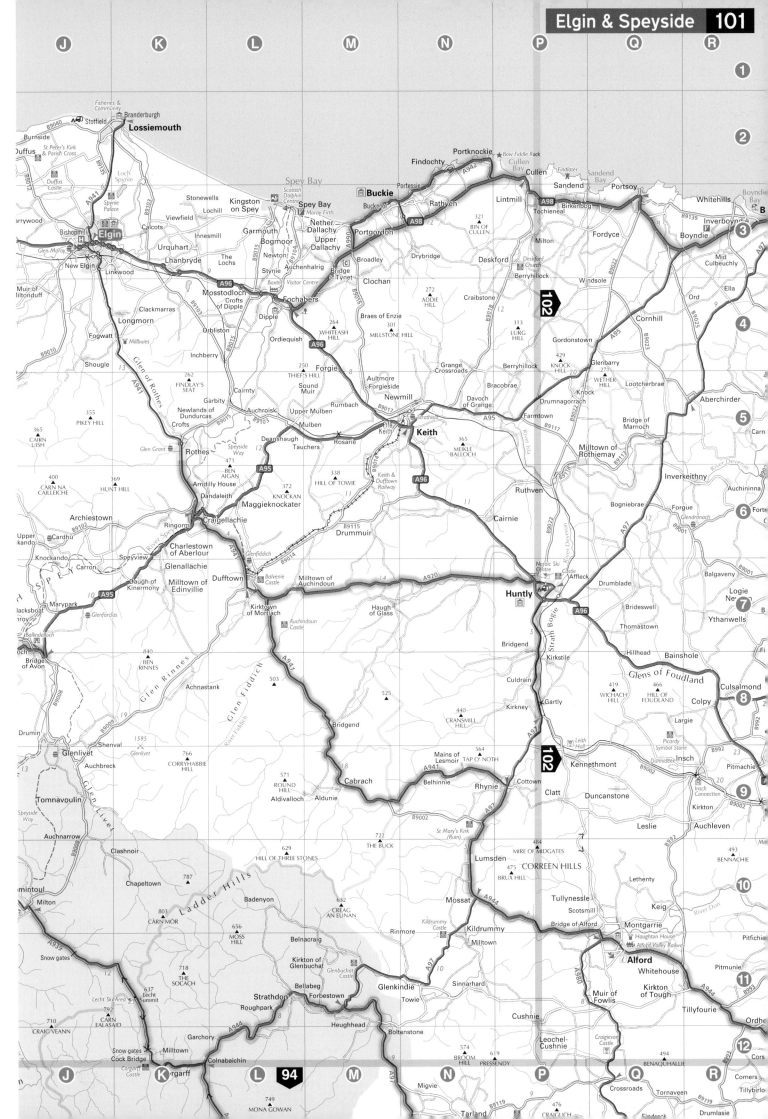

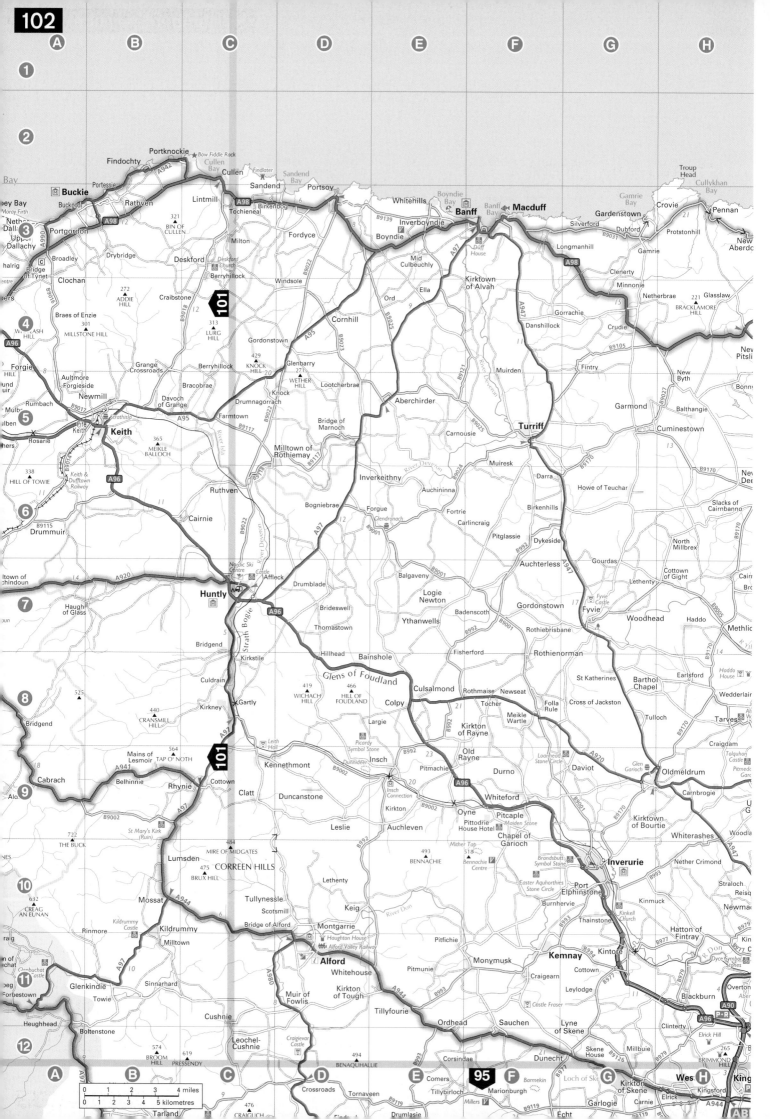

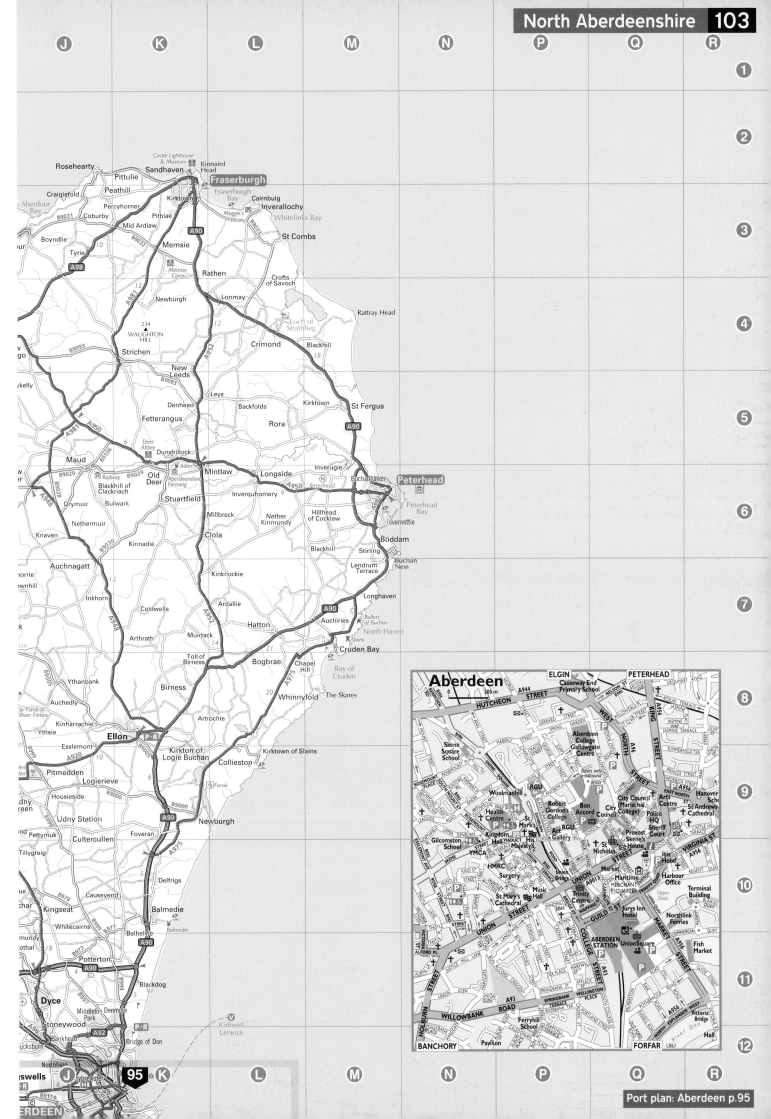

J K L M N P Q R

Rosehearty
Pittulie
Sandhaven
Castle Lighthouse
& Museum
Kinnaird Head
Kirktown
Fraserburgh
Craigiefold
Peathill
Fraserburgh Bay
Cairnbulg
Inverallochy
Aberdour Bay
Percyhorner
Coburty
Pitblae
Maggie's Floosie
Whitelinks Bay
Boyndlie
Mid Ardlaw
Memsie
St Combs
Tyrie
B9032
A90
Memsie Cairn
Rathen
Crofts of Savoch
Newburgh
Lonmay
234 WAUGHTON HILL
Rattray Head
Strichen
Crimond
Blackhill
Loch of Strathbeg
New Leeds
B9093
Leys
Backfolds
Kirktown
St Fergus
Denhead
Rora
A90
Fetterangus
Deer Abbey
Dunshillock
Inverugie
River Ugie
Buchanhaven
Peterhead
Maud
Railway
Old Deer
Mintlaw
Aberdeenshire Farming
Longside
Peterhead
Blackhill of Clackriach
Bulwark
Stuartfield
Inverquhomery
Peterhead Bay
Drymuir
Invernettie
Nethermuir
Millbreck
Nether Kinmundy
Hillhead of Cocklaw
Boddam
Knaven
Clola
Blackhill
Stirling
Kinnadie
Kinknockie
Lendrum Terrace
Buchan Ness
Auchnagatt
Coldwells
Ardallie
Longhaven
Inkhorn
A952
Hatton
A90
Auchiries
Bullers of Buchan
North Haven
Arthrath
Muirtack
Slains
Toll of Birness
Bogbrae
Cruden Bay
Birness
Chapel Hill
Bay of Cruden
Ythanbank
A975
Whinnyfold
The Skares
Auchedly
Artrochie
Kinharrachie
Car Tomb of William Forbes
Ythsie
Ellon
Kirktown of Slains
Esslemont
A920
Kirkton of Logie Buchan
Collieston
Pitmedden
Forvie
Logierieve
Housieside
B9000
Udny Station
B9000
Newburgh
Pettymuk
Foveran
Cultercullen
A975
Tillygreig
Delfrigs
Kingseat
Causeyend
Balmedie
Whitecairns
Belhelvie
Balmedie
A90
Potterton
Dyce
Blackdog
Stoneywood
Middleton Denmore Park
A92
Kirkwall Lerwick
Bankhead
Bridge of Don

Aberdeen

ELGIN
PETERHEAD
Causeway End Primary School
HUTCHEON STREET
A944
NELSON ST
URQUHART ROAD
WEST
NORTH
KING
Jasmine Terrace
Skene Square School
Aberdeen College Gallowgate Centre
Summerfield Ter
RGU
Robert Gordon's College
Woolmanhill
Bon Accord
City Council (Marischal College)
Arts Centre
St Andrews Cathedral
Hanover School
Health Centre
St Mark's
City Council
Police HQ
Castle Hill
Gilcomston School
Art Gallery
RGU
Provost Skene's House
St Nicholas
Virginia St
YMCA
His Majesty's
Kingdom Hall
VIADUCT
Market
Ibis Hotel
HMRC
Union Bridge
Maritime
Harbour Office
Surgery
MERCHANT QUARTER
St Mary's Cathedral
Music Hall
Trinity Centre
Upper Dock
Terminal Building
Jurys Inn Hotel
GUILD ST
Northlink Ferries
UNION STREET
ABERDEEN STATION
UnionSquare
Fish Market
ALFORD PL
COLLEGE STREET
MARKET STREET
Victoria Bridge
WILLOWBANK ROAD
Ferryhill School
NORTH ESPLANADE WEST
Hall
BANCHORY
Pavilion
FORFAR
River Dee

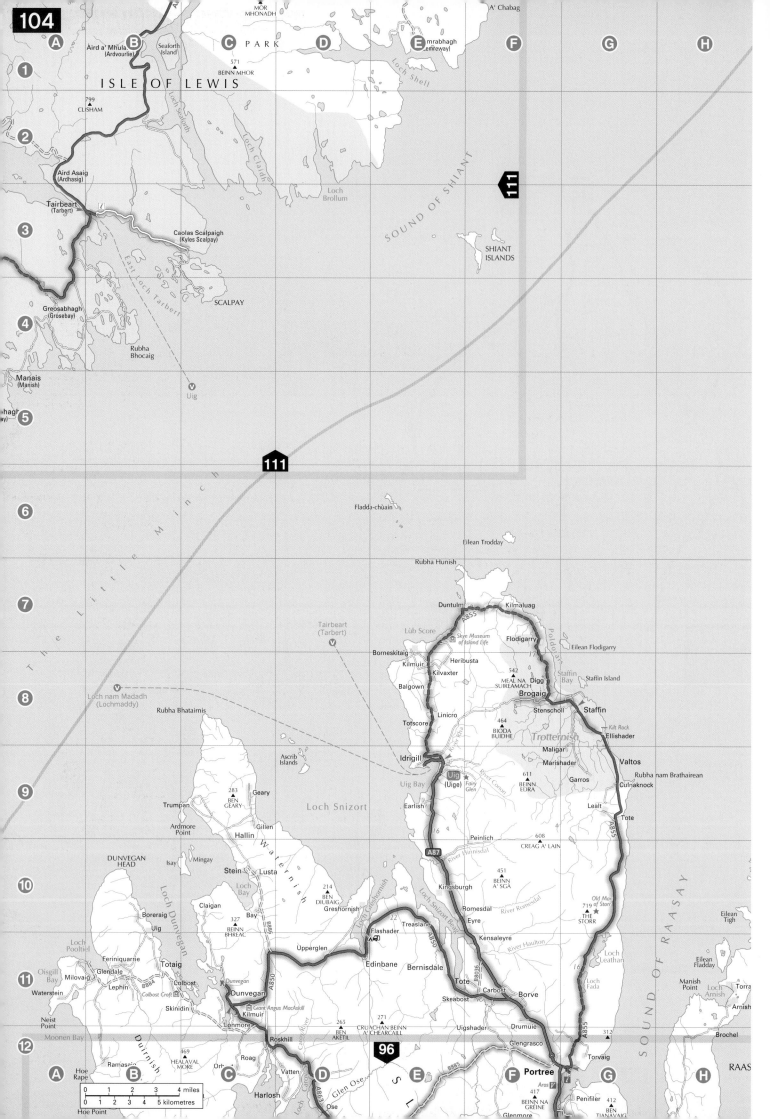

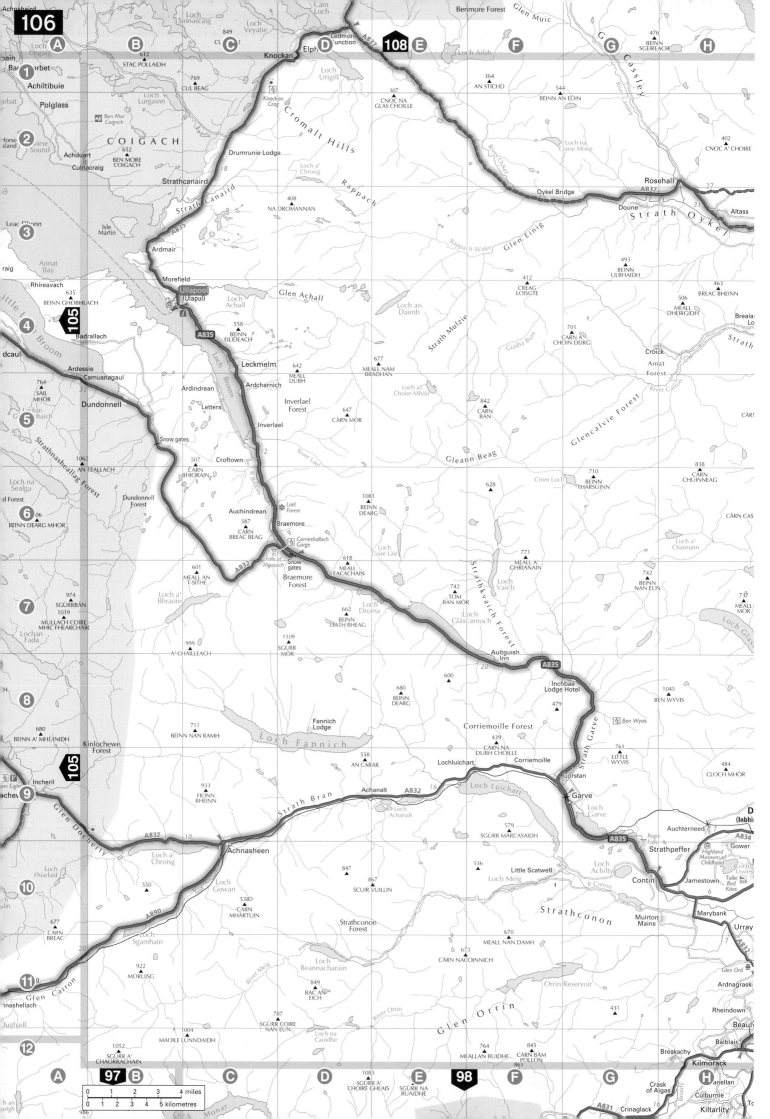

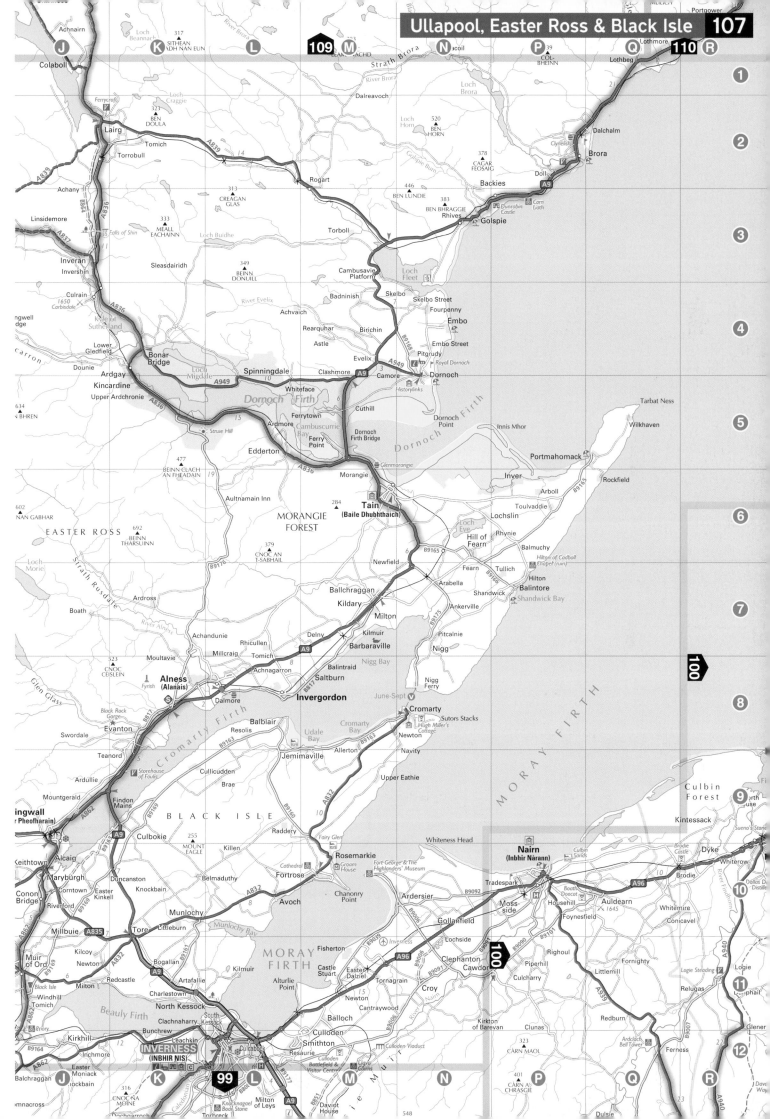

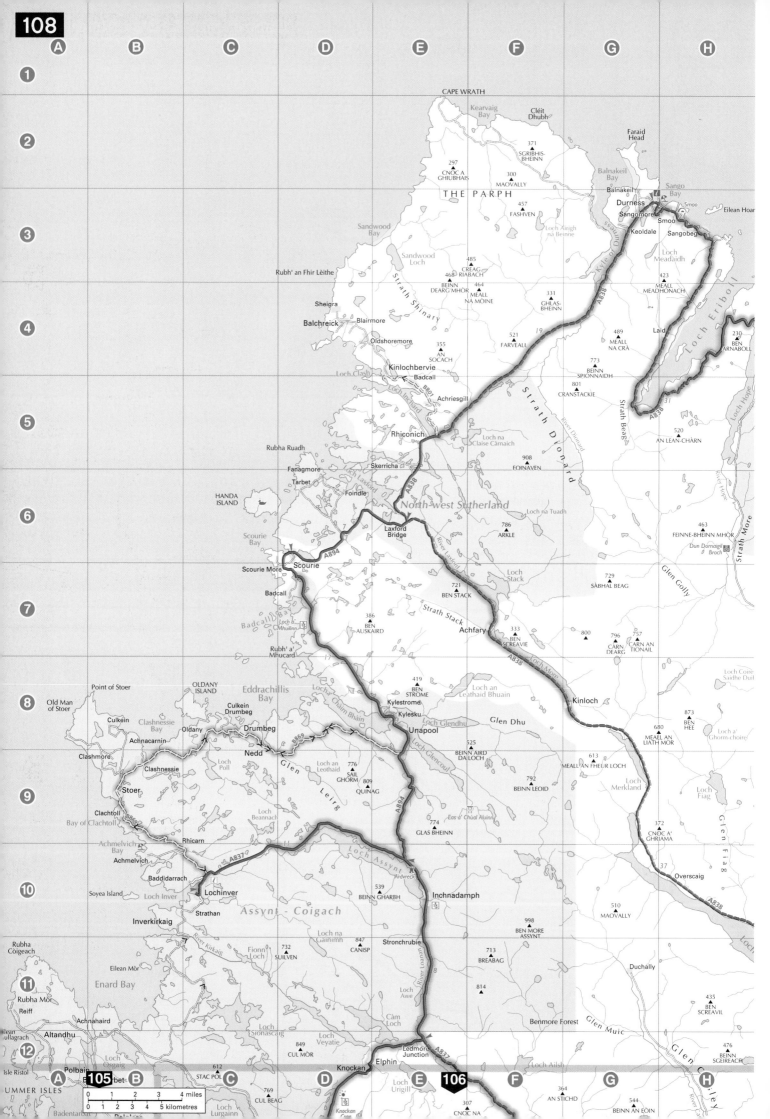

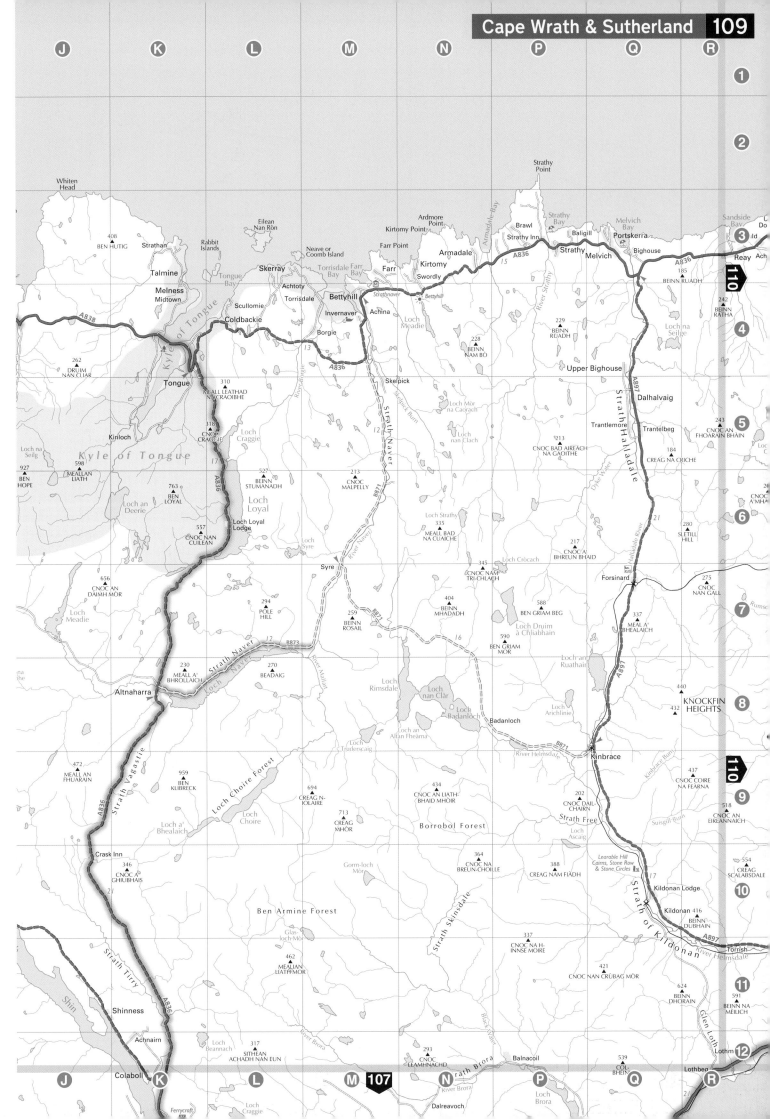

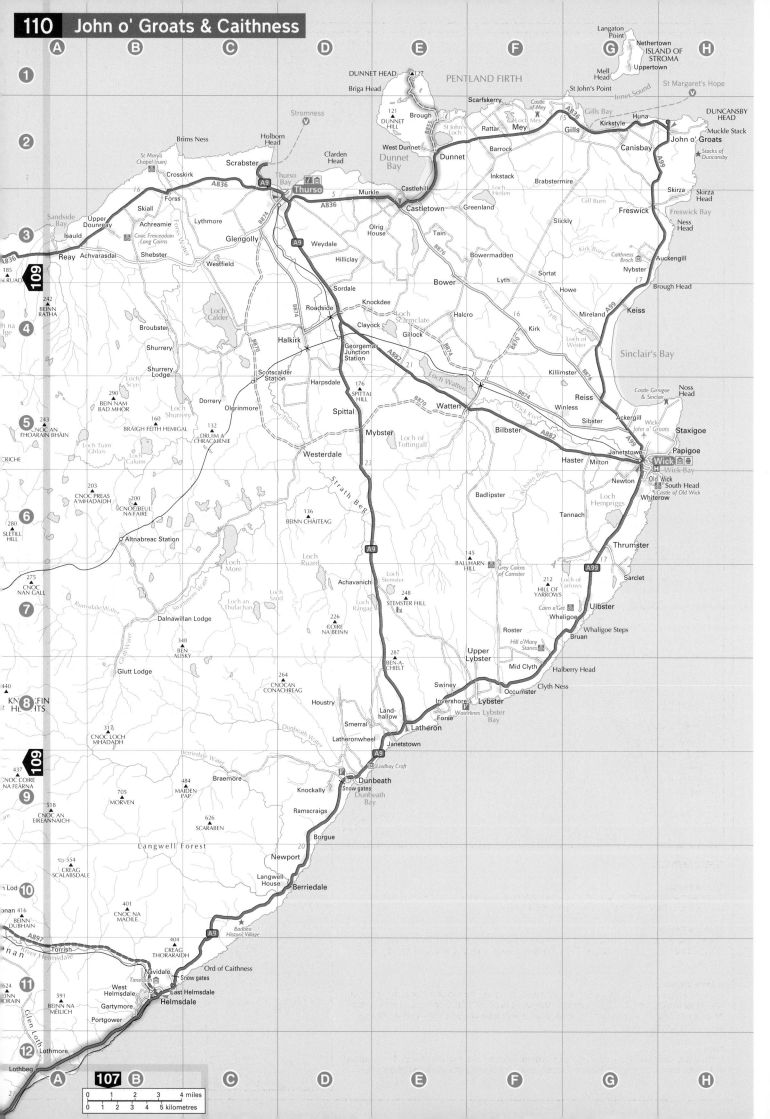

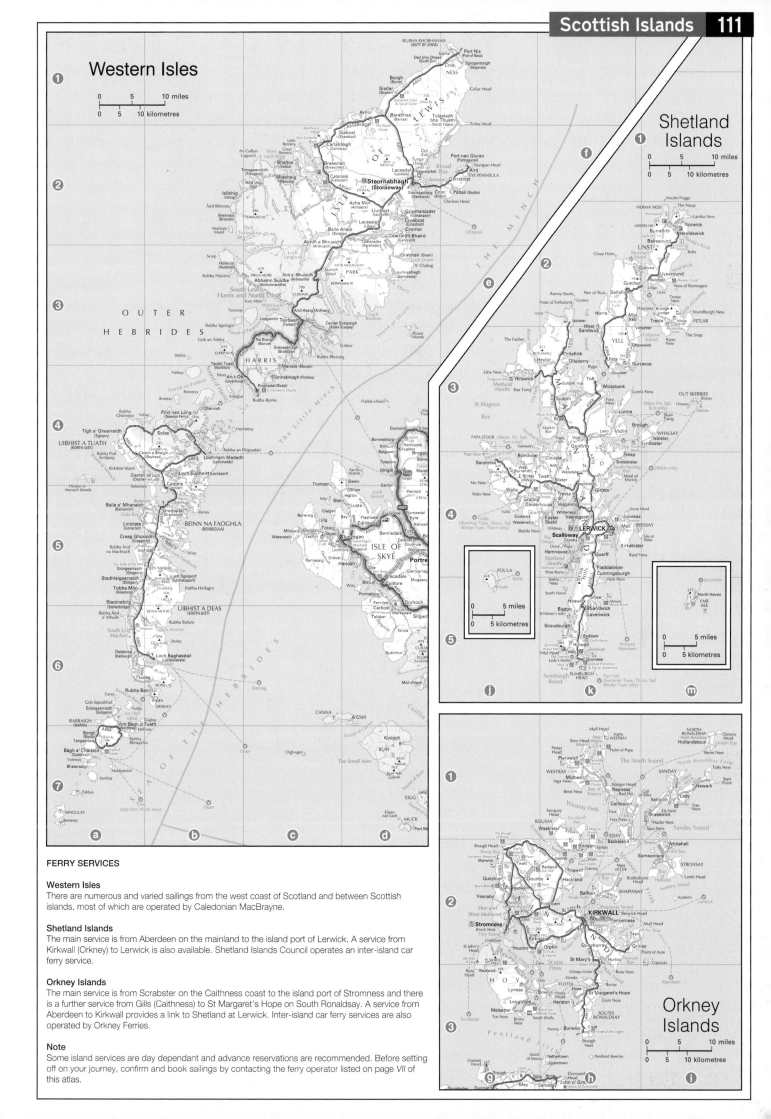

Western Isles

Shetland Islands

Orkney Islands

FERRY SERVICES

Western Isles

There are numerous and varied sailings from the west coast of Scotland and between Scottish islands, most of which are operated by Caledonian MacBrayne.

Shetland Islands

The main service is from Aberdeen on the mainland to the island port of Lerwick. A service from Kirkwall (Orkney) to Lerwick is also available. Shetland Islands Council operates an inter-island car ferry service.

Orkney Islands

The main service is from Scrabster on the Caithness coast to the island port of Stromness and there is a further service from Gills (Caithness) to St Margaret's Hope on South Ronaldsay. A service from Aberdeen to Kirkwall provides a link to Shetland at Lerwick. Inter-island car ferry services are also operated by Orkney Ferries.

Note

Some island services are day dependant and advance reservations are recommended. Before setting off on your journey, confirm and book sailings by contacting the ferry operator listed on page *VII* of this atlas.

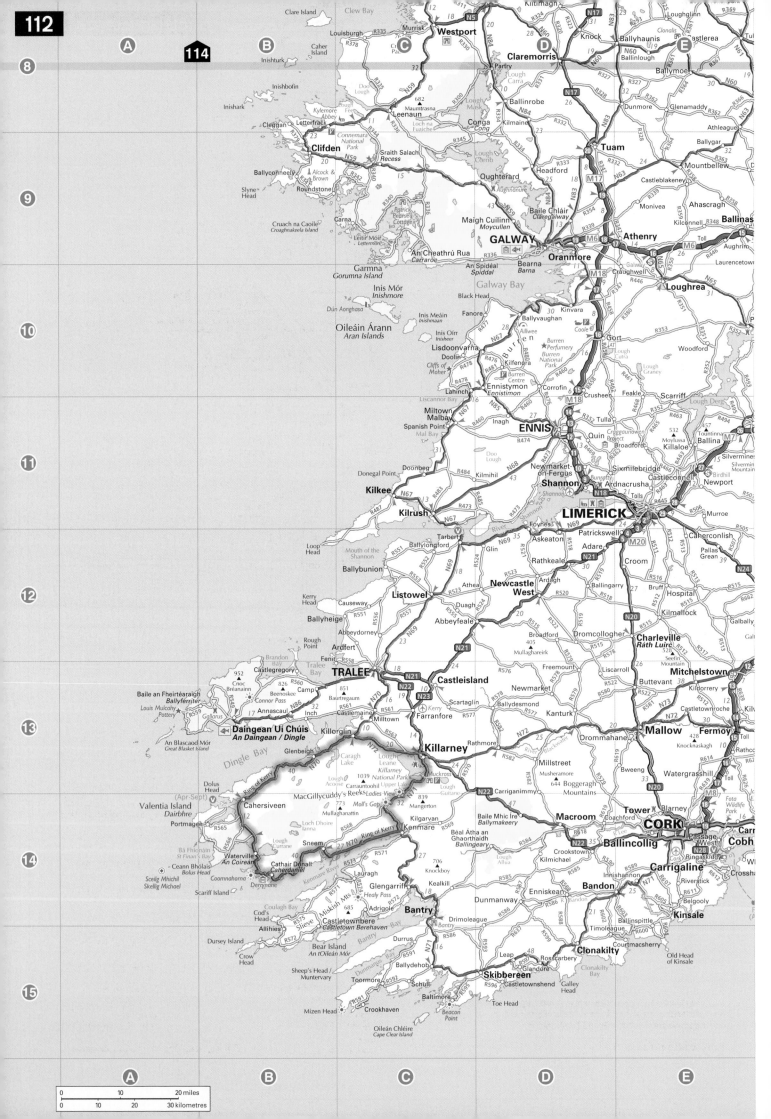

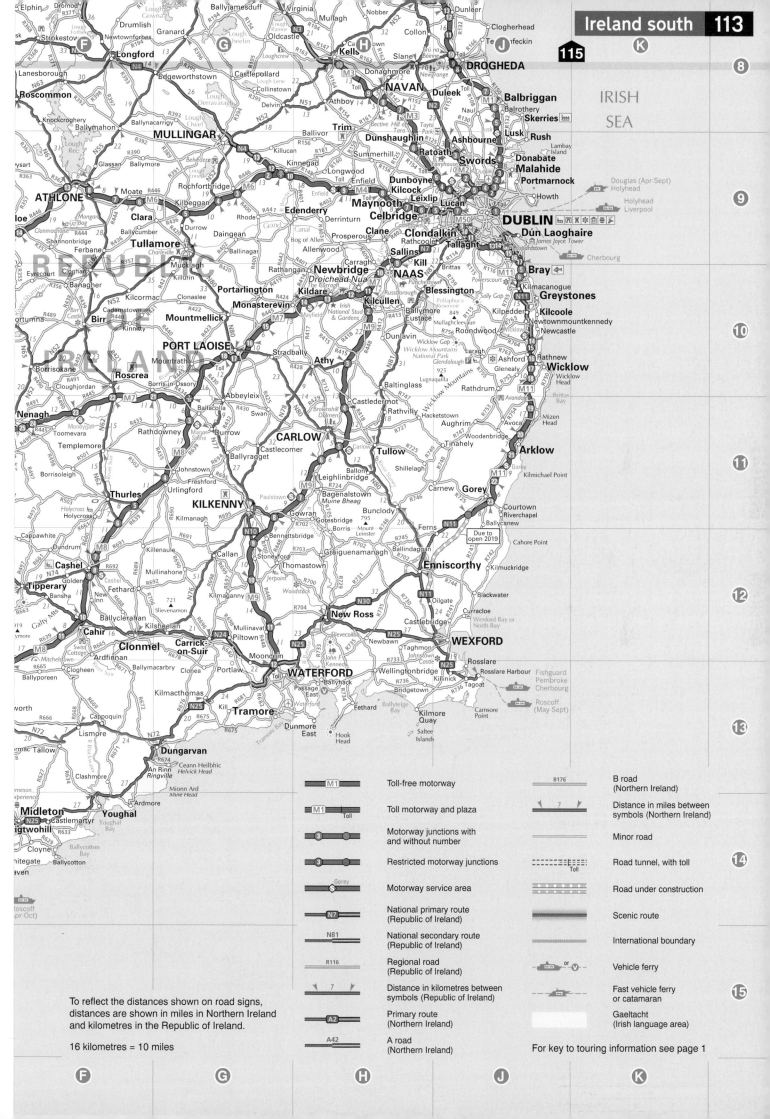

Ireland index

Abbeydorney....C12
Abbeyfeale....D12
Abbeyleix....G11
Adare....D12
Adrigole....C14
Aghalee....J5
Ahascragh....E9
Ahoghill....J4
Allenwood....H9
Allihies....B15
An Bun Beag....E4
An Charraig....E5
An Cheathrú Rua....C9
An Clochán Liath....E4
An Coireán....B14
An Daingean....B13
An Fál Carrach....F3
Annahilt....J6
Annalong....J7
Annascaul....B13
An Rinn....G13
An Spidéal....D9
Antrim....J5
Ardagh....D12
Ardara....E5
Ardee....H8
Ardfert....C12
Ardfinnan....F12
Ardglass....K6
Ardmore....F14
Ardnacrusha....E11
Arklow....J11
Armagh....H6
Armoy....J3
Arvagh....G7
Ashbourne....J9
Ashford....J10
Askeaton....D12
Athboy....H8
Athea....D12
Athenry....E9
Athleague....E8
Athlone....F9
Athy....H10
Augher....G6
Aughnacloy....H6
Aughrim....E9
Aughrim....J11
Avoca....J11

Bagenalstown....H11
Baile an Fheirtéaraigh....B13
Baile Chláir....D9
Baile Mhic Íre....D14
Bailieborough....H7
Balbriggan....J8
Ballacolla....G11
Ballina....D7
Ballina....E11
Ballinafad....E7
Ballinagar....G9
Ballinamallard....G6
Ballinamore....F7
Ballinasloe....E9
Ballincollig....E14
Ballindaggan....H12
Ballingarry....D12
Ballingeary....D14
Ballinlough....E8
Ballinrobe....D8
Ballinspittle....E15
Ballintra....F5
Ballivor....H9
Ballon....H11
Ballybay....H7
Ballybofey....F5
Ballybunion....C12
Ballycanew....J11
Ballycarry....K5
Ballycastle....J3

Ballycastle....C6
Ballyclare....J5
Ballyclerahan....F12
Ballyconneely....B9
Ballyconnell....G7
Ballycotton....F14
Ballycumber....F9
Ballydehob....C15
Ballydesmond....D13
Ballyfarnan....E7
Ballyferriter....B13
Ballygally....J4
Ballygar....E9
Ballygawley....H6
Ballygawley....E6
Ballygowan....K5
Ballyhack....H13
Ballyhaise....G7
Ballyhalbert....K5
Ballyhaunis....E8
Ballyheige....C12
Ballyjamesduff....G8
Ballyliffin....G3
Ballylongford....C12
Ballymacarbry....F13
Ballymahon....F8
Ballymakeery....D14
Ballymena....J4
Ballymoe....E8
Ballymoney....H4
Ballymore....F9
Ballymore Eustace....H10
Ballymote....E7
Ballynacarrigy....G8
Ballynahinch....J6
Ballynure....J5
Ballyporeen....F13
Ballyragget....G11
Ballyshannon....F5
Ballyvaughan....D10
Ballywalter....K5
Balrothery....J8
Baltinglass....H10
Baltimore....C15
Banagher....F10
Banbridge....J6
Bandon....E14
Bangor....K5
Bangor Erris....C7
Bansha....F12
Bantry....C14
Barna....D9
Béal an Mhuirthead....B6
Béal Átha an Ghaorthaidh....D14
Bearna....D9
Belcoo....F6
Belfast....J5
Belgooly....E14
Bellaghy....H4
Belleek....F6
Belmullet....B6
Belturbet....G7
Benburb....H6
Bennettsbridge....G12
Beragh....G5
Bessbrook....J6
Birr....F10
Blacklion....F6
Blackwater....J12
Blarney....E14
Blessington....H10
Borris....H11
Borris-in-Ossory....F10
Borrisokane....F11
Borrisoleigh....F11
Boyle....E7
Bray....J10
Bridgetown....H13
Brittas....J9
Broadford....E11

Broadford....D12
Broughshane....J4
Bruff....E12
Bunbeg....E4
Bunclody....H11
Buncrana....G3
Bundoran....E6
Bunnyconnellan....D7
Bushmills....H3
Buttevant....E13
Bweeng....E13

Cadamstown....F10
Caherconlish....E12
Caherdaniel....B14
Cahersiveen....B14
Cahir....F12
Caledon....H6
Callan....G12
Camp....B13
Carndonagh....G3
Cappawhite....F12
Cappoquin....F13
Carlanstown....H8
Carlingford....J7
Carlow....H11
Carna....C9
Carnew....J11
Carnlough....J4
Carragh....H9
Carraig Airt....F3
Carraroe....C9
Carrick....E5
Carrickart....F3
Carrickfergus....K5
Carrickmacross....H7
Carrickmore....G5
Carrick-on-Shannon....F7
Carrick-on-Suir....G12
Carrigaline....E14
Carrigallen....F7
Carriganimmy....D13
Carrigtwohill....E14
Carryduff....J5
Cashel....F12
Castlebar....D8
Castlebellingham....J7
Castleblakeney....E9
Castleblayney....H7
Castlebridge....J12
Castlecomer....G11
Castleconnell....E11
Castlederg....G5
Castledermot....H11
Castlegregory....B13
Castleisland....C13
Castlemaine....C13
Castlemartyr....F14
Castlepollard....G8
Castlerea....E8
Castlerock....H3
Castletownbere....B15
Castletownroche....E13
Castletownshend....D15
Castlewellan....J6
Cathair Dónall....B14
Causeway....C12
Cavan....G7
Celbridge....H9
Charlestown....D7
Charleville....E12
Cill Charthaigh....E5
Clady....G4
Clane....H9
Clara....G9
Claregalway....D9
Claremorris....D8
Clashmore....F13
Claudy....G4
Cleggan....B8
Clifden....B9

Cliffoney....E6
Cloghan....F10
Clogheen....F13
Clogher....G6
Clogherhead....J8
Clogh Mills....J4
Clonakilty....D15
Clonaslee....G10
Clondalkin....J9
Clonea....G13
Clones....G7
Clonmany....G3
Clonmel....F12
Clough....K6
Cloughjordan....F10
Cloyne....F14
Coachford....D14
Coagh....H5
Coalisland....H5
Cobh....E14
Coleraine....H3
Collinstown....G8
Collon....H8
Collooney....E7
Comber....K5
Cong....D9
Conna....E13
Convoy....F4
Cookstown....H5
Cootehill....G7
Cork....E14
Corrofin....D10
Courtmacsherry....E15
Courtown....J11
Craigavon....J6
Craughwell....E10
Creeslough....F4
Croithlí....E4
Crolly....E4
Crookhaven....C15
Crookstown....D14
Croom....E12
Crosshaven....E14
Crossmaglen....H7
Crossmolina....D7
Crumlin....J5
Crusheen....D10
Culdaff....G3
Cullybackey....J4
Culmore....G4
Curracloe....J12
Curry....E7
Cushendall....J3
Cushendun....J3

Daingean....G9
Daingean Uí Chúis....B13
Delvin....G8
Derrinturn....H9
Derry....G4
Derrygonnelly....F6
Derrylin....G6
Dervock....H3
Dingle....B13
Doagh....J5
Donabate....J9
Donaghadee....K5
Donaghmore....H5
Donaghmore....H8
Donegal....F5
Donemana....G4
Doolin....C10
Doonbeg....C11
Downings....F3
Downpatrick....K6
Dowra....F6
Draperstown....H5
Drimoleague....D14
Drogheda....J8
Droichead Nua....H10
Dromahair....E6
Dromara....J6

Dromcollogher....D12
Dromiskin....J7
Drommahane....E13
Dromod....F8
Dromore....J6
Dromore....G5
Dromore West....D6
Drumaness....K6
Drumfries....G3
Drumkeeran....F7
Drumlish....F8
Drumquin....G5
Drumshanbo....F7
Duagh....C12
Dublin....J9
Duleek....J8
Dunboyne....J9
Dundalk....J7
Dundonald....K5
Dundrum....F12
Dunfanaghy....F3
Dungannon....H5
Dungarvan....G13
Dungiven....H4
Dunglow....E4
Dún Laoghaire....J9
Dunlavin....H10
Dunleer....J8
Dunloy....J4
Dunmanway....D14
Dunmore....E8
Dunmore East....H13
Dunshaughlin....H9
Durrow....G11
Durrow....G9
Durrus....C15
Dysart....E9

Easky....D6
Edenderry....H9
Edgeworthstown....G8
Eglinton....G4
Elphin....F8
Enfield....H9
Ennis....D11
Enniscorthy....H12
Enniscrone....D6
Enniskean....D14
Enniskillen....F6
Ennistymon....D10
Eyrecourt....F10

Fahan....G3
Falcarragh....F3
Fanore....D10
Farranfore....C13
Feakle....E11
Fenagh....F7
Fenit....B13
Ferbane....F9
Fermoy....E13
Ferns....J12
Fethard....F12
Fethard....H13
Fintona....G6
Fivemiletown....G6
Foxford....D7
Foynes....D12
Freemount....D13
Frenchpark....E8
Freshford....G11

Galbally....E12
Galway....D9
Garrison....F6
Garvagh....H4
Gilford....J6
Glandore....D15
Glaslough....H6
Glassan....F9
Gleann Cholm Cille....E5
Glenamaddy....E8

Glenarm....J4
Glenavy....J5
Glenbeigh....B13
Glencolumbkille....E5
Glenealy....J10
Glengarriff....C14
Glenties....E5
Glin....D12
Golden....F12
Goresbridge....H11
Gorey....J11
Gort....D10
Gortin....G5
Gowran....H11
Graiguenamanagh....H12
Granard....G8
Grange....E6
Greencastle....H3
Greencastle....G5
Greenore....J7
Greyabbey....K5
Greystones....J10
Gulladuff....H4

Hacketstown....H11
Headford....D9
Hillsborough....J6
Hilltown....J6
Holycross....F11
Holywood....K5
Hospital....E12
Howth....J9

Inagh....D11
Inch....B13
Inishcrone....D6
Innishannon....E14
Irvinestown....F6

Johnstown....G11

Kanturk....D13
Keadue....F7
Keady....H6
Kealkill....C14
Keel....B7
Kells....H8
Kenmare....C14
Kesh....F5
Kilbeggan....G9
Kilcar....E5
Kilcock....H9
Kilconnell....E9
Kilcoole....J10
Kilcormac....F10
Kilcullen....H10
Kildare....H10
Kildorrery....E13
Kilfenora....D10
Kilgarvan....C14
Kilkee....C11
Kilkeel....J7
Kilkenny....G11
Kill....H9
Kill....G13
Killala....D6
Killaloe....E11
Killarney....C13
Killashandra....G7
Killenaule....F12
Killinick....J13
Killorglin....C13
Killough....K6
Killucan....G9
Killurin....G10
Killybegs....E5
Killyleagh....K6
Kilmacanogue....J10
Kilmacrenan....F4
Kilmacthomas....G13
Kilmaganny....G12
Kilmaine....D8

Kilmallock....E12
Kilmanagh....G11
Kilmichael....D14
Kilmihil....C11
Kilmore Quay....H13
Kilmuckridge....J12
Kilpedder....J10
Kilrea....H4
Kilrush....C11
Kilsheelan....G12
Kiltimagh....D8
Kilworth....E13
Kingscourt....H7
Kinlough....E6
Kinnegad....G9
Kinnitty....F10
Kinsale....E14
Kinvara....D10
Kircubbin....K5
Knock....D8
Knockcroghery....F8

Lahinch....C10
Lanesborough....F8
Laragh....J10
Larne....K4
Lauragh....C14
Laurencetown....F10
Leap....D15

Leenaun....C8
Leighlinbridge....H11
Leixlip....H9
Letterfrack....B8
Letterkenny....F4
Lifford....G4
Limavady....H4
Limerick....E11
Lisbellaw....G6
Lisburn....J5
Liscarroll....D13
Lisdoonvarna....D10
Lismore....F13
Lisnaskea....G6
Listowel....C12
Londonderry....G4
Longford....F8
Longwood....H9
Loughbrickland....J6
Loughgilin....E8
Loughrea....E10
Louisburgh....C8
Lucan....J9
Lurgan....J6
Lusk....J9

Macroom....D14
Maghera....H4
Magherafelt....H5

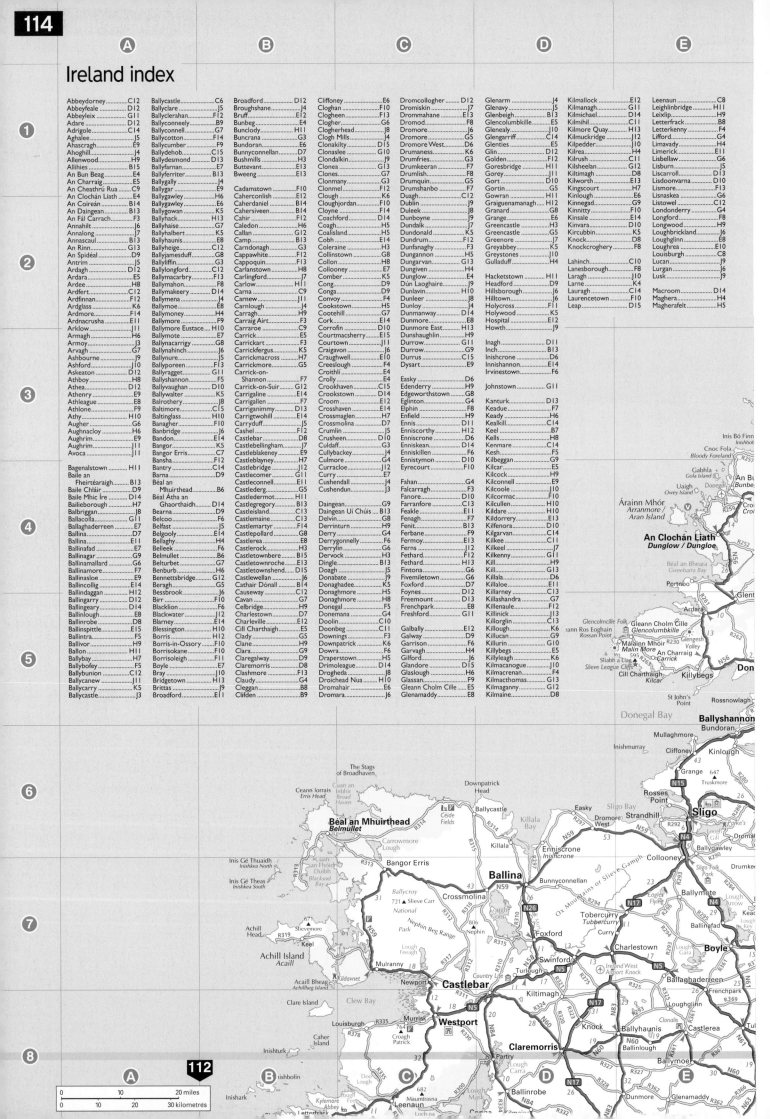

112

| 0 | 10 | 20 miles |
| 0 | 10 | 20 | 30 kilometres |

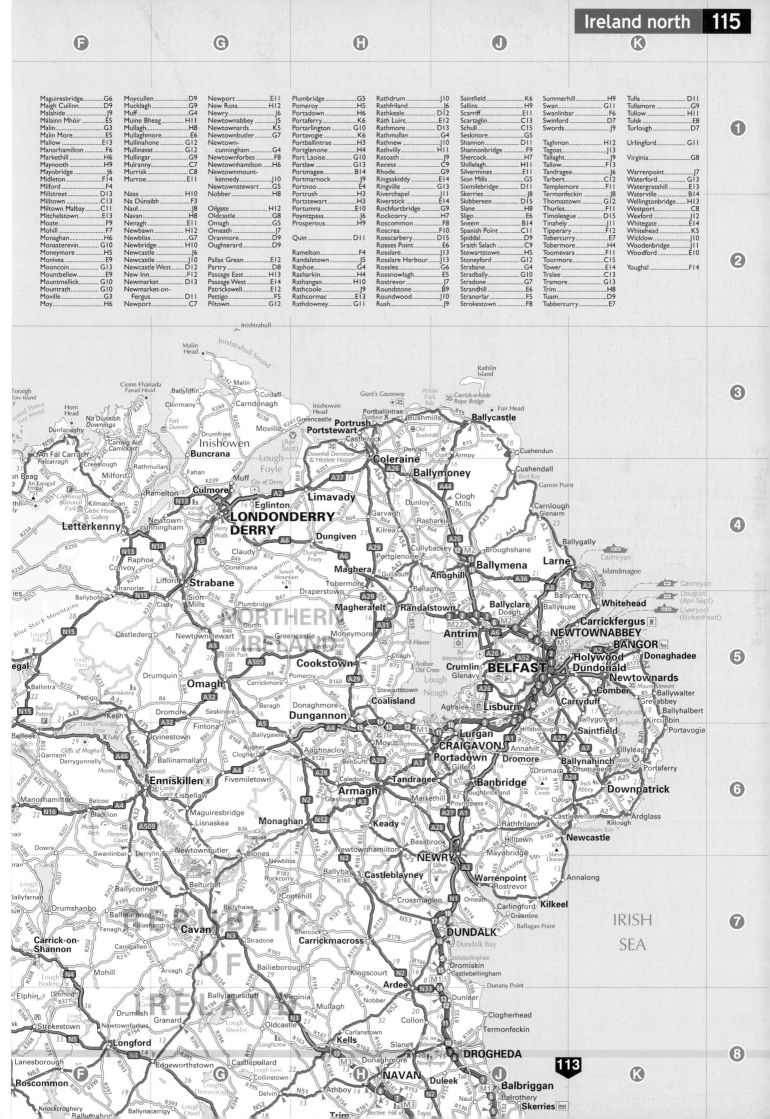

Maguiresbridge......G6
Maigh Cuilinn......D9
Malahide......J9
Málainn Mhóir......E5
Malin......G3
Malin More......E5
Mallow......E13
Manorhamilton......F6
Markethill......H6
Maynooth......H9
Mayobridge......J6
Midleton......F14
Milford......F4
Millstreet......D13
Milltown......C13
Miltown Malbay......C11
Mitchelstown......E13
Moate......F9
Mohill......F7
Monaghan......H6
Monasterevin......G10
Moneymore......H5
Monivea......E9
Mooncoin......G13
Mountbellew......E9
Mountmellick......G10
Mountrath......G10
Moville......G3
Moy......H6

Moycullen......D9
Mucklagh......G9
Muff......G4
Muine Bheag......H11
Mullagh......H8
Mullaghmore......E6
Mullinahone......G12
Mullinavat......G12
Mullingar......G9
Mulranny......C7
Murrisk......C8
Murroe......E11
Naas......H10
Na Dúnaibh......F3
Naul......J8
Navan......H8
Nenagh......E11
Newbawn......H12
Newbliss......G7
Newbridge......H10
Newcastle......J6

Newport......E11
New Ross......H12
Newry......J6
Newtownabbey......J5
Newtownards......K5
Newtownbutler......G7
Newtown-cunningham......G4
Newtownforbes......F8
Newtownhamilton......H6
Newtownmount-kennedy......J10
Newtownstewart......H5
Nobber......H8

Oilgate......H12
Oldcastle......G8
Omagh......G5
Omeath......J7
Oranmore......D9
Oughterard......D9

Pallas Green......E12
Partry......D8
Passage East......H13
Passage West......E14
Patrickswell......E12
Pettigo......F5
Piltown......G13

Plumbridge......G5
Pomeroy......H5
Portadown......H6
Portaferry......K6
Portarlington......G10
Portavogie......K6
Portballintrae......H3
Portglenone......H4
Port Laoise......G10
Portlaw......G13
Portmagee......B14
Portmarnock......J9
Portnoo......E4
Portrush......H3
Portstewart......H3
Portumna......E10
Poyntzpass......J6
Prosperous......H9

Quin......D11

Ramelton......F4
Randalstown......J5
Raphoe......G4
Rasharkin......H4
Rathangan......H10
Rathcoole......J9
Rathcormac......E13
Rathdowney......G11

Rathdrum......J10
Rathfriland......J6
Rathkeale......D12
Ráth Luirc......E12
Rathmore......D13
Rathmullan......G4
Rathnew......J10
Rathvilly......H11
Ratoath......J9
Recess......C9
Ringaskiddy......E14
Ringville......D13
Riverchapel......J11
Riverstick......E14
Rochfortbridge......G9
Rockcorry......H7
Roscommon......F8
Roscrea......F10
Rosscarbery......D15
Rosses Point......E6
Rosslare......G6
Rosslare Harbour......J13
Rosslea......G6
Rossnowlagh......E5
Rostrevor......J7
Roundstone......B9
Roundwood......J10
Rush......J9

Saintfield......K6
Sallins......H9
Scarriff......E11
Scartaglin......C13
Schull......C15
Seskinore......G5
Shannon......D11
Shannonbridge......F9
Shercock......H7
Shillelagh......H11
Silvermines......E11
Sion Mills......G5
Sixmilebridge......D11
Skerries......J8
Skibbereen......D15
Slane......H8
Sligo......E6
Sneem......B14
Spanish Point......C11
Spiddal......C9
Sraith Salach......C9
Stewartstown......H5
Stoneyford......G12
Strabane......G4
Stradbally......G10
Stradone......G7
Stranorlar......F8
Strokestown......F8

Summerhill......H9
Swan......G11
Swanlinbar......F6
Swinford......D7
Swords......J9

Taghmon......H12
Tagoat......J13
Tallaght......J9
Tallow......F13
Tandragee......J6
Tarbert......C12
Templemore......F11
Termonfeckin......J7
Thomastown......G12
Thurles......F11
Timoleague......D15
Tinahely......J11
Tipperary......F12
Tobercurry......E7
Tobermore......H4
Toomevara......F11
Toormore......C15
Tower......E14
Tralee......C13
Tramore......G13
Trim......H8
Tuam......D9
Tubbercurry......E7

Tulla......D11
Tullamore......G9
Tullow......H11
Tulsk......E8
Turlough......D7

Urlingford......G11

Virginia......G8

Warrenpoint......J7
Waterford......G13
Watergrasshill......E13
Waterville......B14
Wellingtonbridge......H13
Westport......C8
Wexford......J12
Whitegate......E14
Whitehead......K5
Wicklow......J10
Woodenbridge......J11
Woodford......E10

Youghal......F14

Town plan : Central London p.142–151

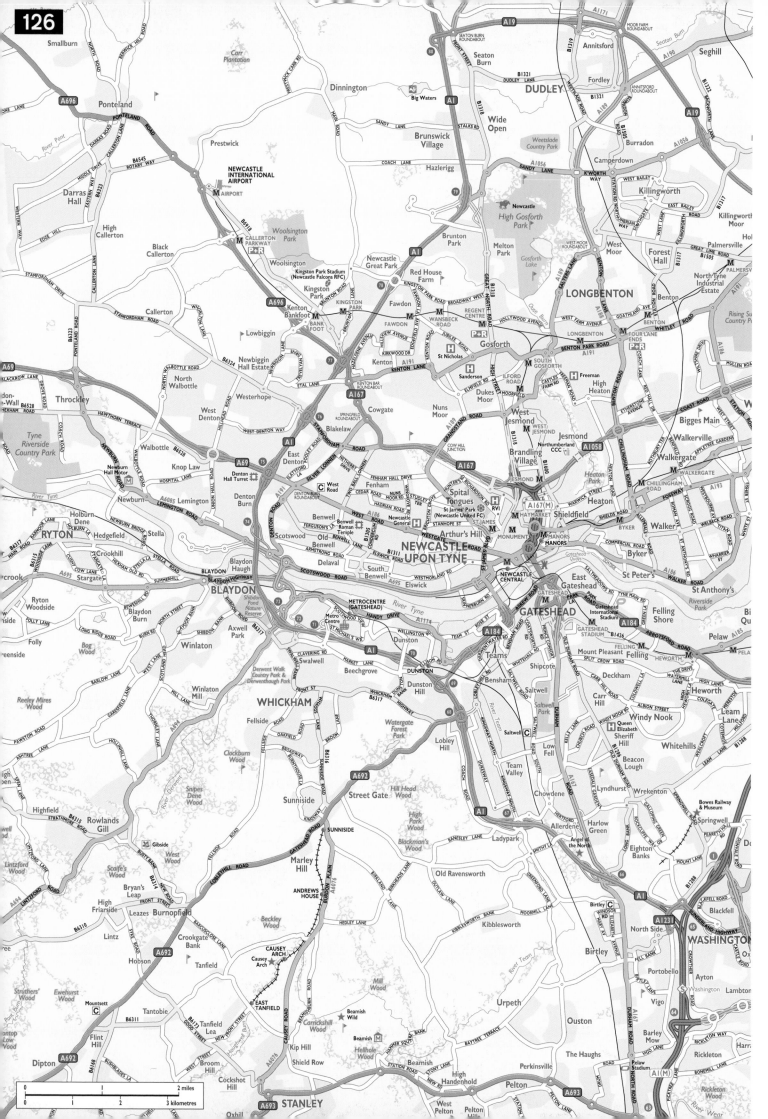

St Mary's Island
St Mary's

Seaton Delaval
Bates Cottages
Holywell
East Holywell
Earsdon
Backworth
Shiremoor
Murton
Monkseaton
Whitley Bay
WHITLEY BAY
Links Art Gallery
Whitley Bay
Promenade
West Monkseaton
West Monkseaton
MONKSEATON
West Allotment
New York
North Tyneside General
Marden Park Nature Reserve
Marden
CULLERCOATS
Cullercoats
Blue Reef
Longsands South
Northumberland Park
West Allotment
North Shields
Billy Mill
Preston
TYNEMOUTH
King Edwards Bay
Tynemouth Priory & Castle
TYNEMOUTH
Stephenson Railway
West Chirton
NORTH SHIELDS
NORTH SHIELDS
Amsterdam (IJmuiden)
Willington Square
Silverlink Roundabout
North Tyneside Steam Railway
Howdon Interchange
Waterville Road
Meadow Well
Arbeia Roman Fort & Museum
The Lawe
Sandhaven
SOUTH SHIELDS
SOUTH SHIELDS
Holy Cross
Willington
Howdon
Percy Main
WALLSEND
Point Pleasant
Segedunum Roman Fort & Baths
East Howdon
Willington Quay
Tyne Tunnel
River Tyne
Westoe
Harton
Cauldwell
Marsden Rock
JARROW
Jarrow Hall
St Paul's Monastery
East Jarrow
Tyne Dock
Temple Town
CHICHESTER
Marsden
Marsden Bay
Hebburn Colliery
Simonside
South Shields General
Harton Nook
Cleadon Park
Souter Lighthouse & The Leas
HEBBURN
Hebburn New Town
Riverside Park
Monkton
Primrose
West Harton
Whiteleas
Nevinson Avenue
Whitburn Coastal Park
Brockley Whins
South Shields
BROCKLEY WHINS
Biddick Hall
Hedworth
FELLGATE
Fellgate
Boldon Colliery
Cleadon
Whitburn
Wardley
West Boldon
East Boldon
EAST BOLDON
South Bents
Folingsby
Testos Roundabout
Greyhound Stadium
Seaburn
Whitburn Bay
Downhill
Witherwack
Carley Hill
Marley Pots
High Southwick
Roker
Roker
Hylton Castle
Castletown
Southwick
Monkwearmouth
STADIUM OF LIGHT
Sunderland Harbour
Usworth
Low Southwick
Queen Alexandra Bridge
Deptford
Stadium of Light (Sunderland AFC)
National Glass Centre
Concord
Sulgrave
Hylton Plantation
PALLION
Ayre's Quay
St Peter's
Bishopwearmouth
SUNDERLAND
Albany
Hertburn
South Hylton
SOUTH HYLTON
Pallion
Millfield
MILLFIELD
UNIVERSITY
PARK LANE
Washington Old Hall
Washington Village
Barmston
Teal Farm
Washington Wetland Centre
Pennywell
Ford
Sunderland Royal
Sunderland
SUNDERLAND
Hendon
The Princess Anne Park
Biddick
Columbia
High Barnes
Barnes Park
Ashbrooke
Sunderland Eye Infirmary
Hillview
Grangetown
Fatfield
Mount Pleasant
Penshaw
Penshaw Monument
Herrington Country Park
Hastings Hill
Grindon
Thorney Close
Plains Farm
Humbledon
Springwell
Silksworth Sports Complex & Ski Centre
Middle Herrington
East Herrington
New Silksworth
Tunstall
Farrington
Biddick Gill Wood
Shiney Row
New Herrington
Silksworth
Ryhope

NORTH SEA

Street map symbols

Town, port and airport plans

② Motorway and junction	→ One-way, gated/ closed road	● Railway station	**P** Car park
④ Primary road single/ dual carriageway and numbered junction	Restricted access road	○ Light rapid transit system station	**P+R** Park and Ride (at least 6 days per week)
37 A road single/ dual carriageway and numbered junction	Pedestrian area	✕ Level crossing	Bus/coach station
B road single/ dual carriageway	Footpath	Tramway	**H** Hospital
Local road single/ dual carriageway	Road under construction	Airport, heliport	**H** 24-hour Accident & Emergency hospital
Other road single/ dual carriageway, minor road	Road tunnel	® Railair terminal	Beach (award winning)
Building of interest	Lighthouse	Theatre or performing arts centre	City wall
Ruined building	Castle	Cinema	Escarpment
i Tourist Information Centre	Castle mound	† Abbey, chapel, church	Cliff lift
V Visitor or heritage centre	• Monument, statue	✡ Synagogue	River/canal, lake
◉ World Heritage Site (UNESCO)	✉ Post Office	☾ Mosque	Lock, weir
M Museum	Public library	⚑ Golf course	☀ **Viewpoint**
English Heritage site	Shopping centre	Racecourse	Park/sports ground
Historic Scotland site	Shopmobility	Nature reserve	Cemetery
Cadw (Welsh heritage) site	Football stadium	Aquarium	Woodland
National Trust site	Rugby stadium	Agricultural showground	Built-up area
National Trust Scotland site	County cricket ground	Toilet, with facilities for the less able	Beach

Central London street map (see pages 142–151)

⊖ London Underground station	⊖ London Overground station
⊖ Docklands Light Railway (DLR) station	Central London Congestion Charge and T-Charge Zone boundary

Royal Parks

Green Park	Park open 5am–midnight. Constitution Hill and The Mall closed to traffic Sundays and public holidays 8am–dusk.
Grosvenor Square Garden	Park open 7:30am–dusk.
Hyde Park	Park open 5am–midnight. Park roads closed to traffic midnight–5am.
Kensington Gardens	Park open 6am–dusk.
Regent's Park	Park open 5am–dusk. Park roads closed to traffic midnight–7am, except for residents.
St James's Park	Park open 5am–midnight. The Mall closed to traffic Sundays and public holidays 8am–dusk.
Victoria Tower Gardens	Park open dawn–dusk.

Traffic regulations in the City of London include security checkpoints and restrict the number of entry and exit points.

Note: Oxford Street is closed to through-traffic (except buses & taxis) 7am–7pm Monday–Saturday.

Central London Congestion Charge Zone (CCZ)

The charge for driving or parking a vehicle on public roads in this Central London area, during operating hours, is £11.50 per vehicle per day in advance or on the day of travel. Alternatively you can pay £10.50 by registering with CC Auto Pay, an automated payment system. Drivers can also pay the next charging day after travelling in the zone but this will cost £14. Payment permits entry, travel within and exit from the CCZ by the vehicle as often as required on that day.

The CCZ operates between 7am and 6pm, Mon–Fri only. There is no charge at weekends, on public holidays or between 25th Dec and 1st Jan inclusive.

For up to date information on the CCZ, exemptions, discounts or ways to pay, visit *www.tfl.gov.uk/modes/driving/congestion-charge*

T-Charge (Toxicity Charge)

All vehicles in Central London need to meet minimum exhaust emission standards or pay a £10 daily Emission Surcharge. It applies to the same area covered by the Congestion Charge and operates during the same hours (between 7am and 6pm Monday to Friday). The surcharge is in addition to the Congestion Charge.

The minimum emmission standards are Euro 4/IV for both petrol and diesel vehicles (different standards may apply to certain specialist vehicle types). The surcharge will largely apply to pre-2006 vehicles.

For further information visit *www.tfl.gov.uk/t-charge*

The Ultra Low Emission Zone (ULEZ) is planned to replace the T-Charge in April 2019 with even stricter standards. For details visit *www.tfl.gov.uk/ultra-low-emission-zone*

Town plans

Aberdeen 103
Aberystwyth 36
Basingstoke 129
Bath 129
Birmingham 130
Blackpool 130
Bournemouth 130
Bradford 130
Brighton 131
Bristol 131
Cambridge 131
Canterbury 131
Cardiff 132
Carlisle 132
Chester 132
Coventry 132
Derby 133
Dundee 133
Edinburgh 133
Exeter 133
Glasgow 134
Ipswich 134
Kingston upon Hull 134
Leeds 134
Leicester 135
Liverpool 135
LONDON 142–151
Manchester 135

Middlesbrough 135
Milton Keynes 136
Newcastle upon Tyne 136
Newquay 3
Norwich 136
Nottingham 136
Oxford 137
Peterborough 137
Plymouth 137
Portsmouth 137
Ramsgate 23
Reading 138
Royal Tunbridge Wells 138
Salisbury 138
Scarborough 67
Sheffield 138
Shrewsbury 139
Southampton 139
Stoke-on-Trent (Hanley) 139
Stratford-upon-Avon 139
Sunderland 140
Swansea 140
Taunton 140
Warwick 140
Watford 141
Winchester 141
Worcester 141
York 141

Ferry Ports

Aberdeen Harbour 95
Dover, Port of 12
Fishguard Harbour 24
Harwich International Port 35
Heysham Harbour 62
Holyhead Harbour 54
Hull, Port of 61
Liverpool Docks 56
Newhaven Harbour 11
Pembroke Dock 24
Plymouth, Port of 4
Port of Tyne 73
Portsmouth Harbour 10

Channel Tunnel

Folkestone Terminal 13
Calais / Coquelles Terminal 13

Central London

Basingstoke | Bath

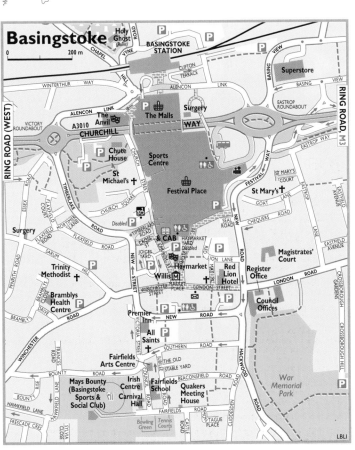

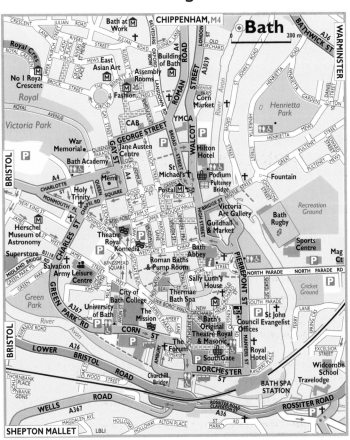

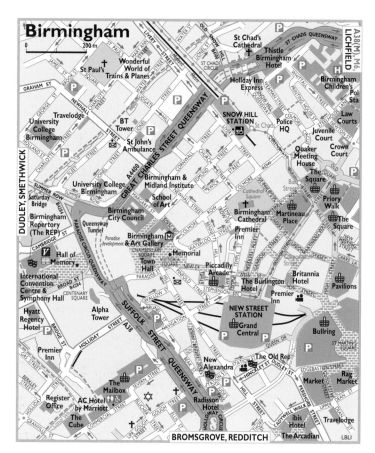

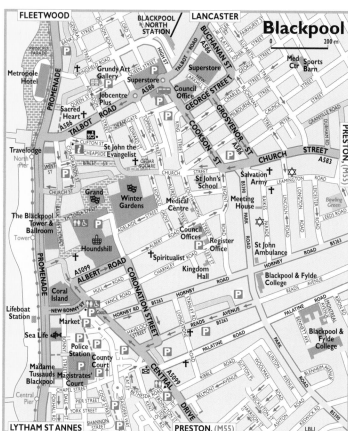

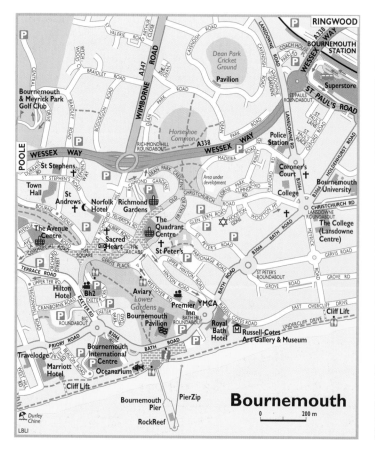

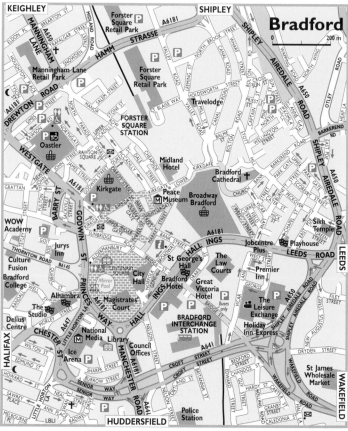

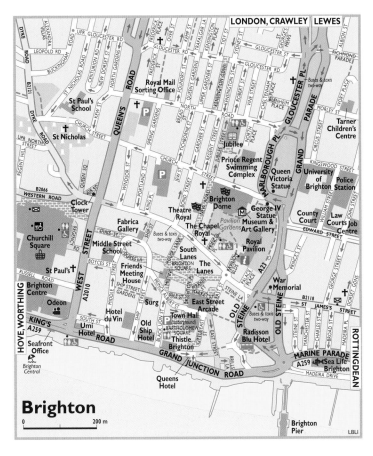

Brighton

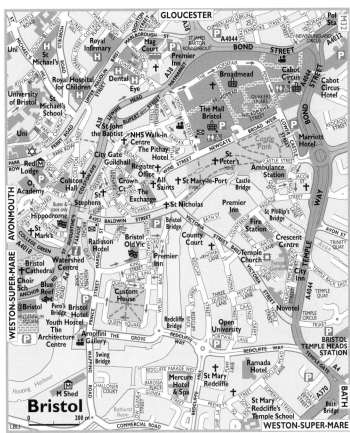

Bristol

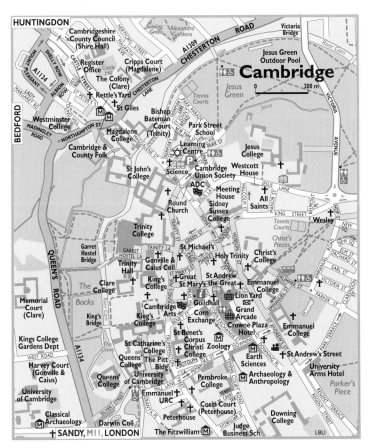

Cambridge

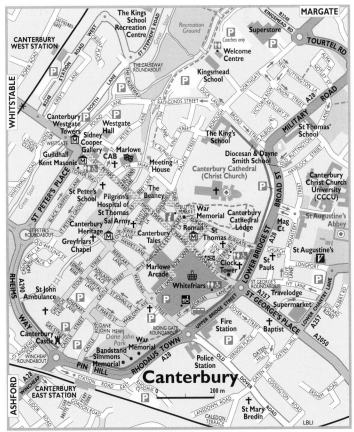

Canterbury

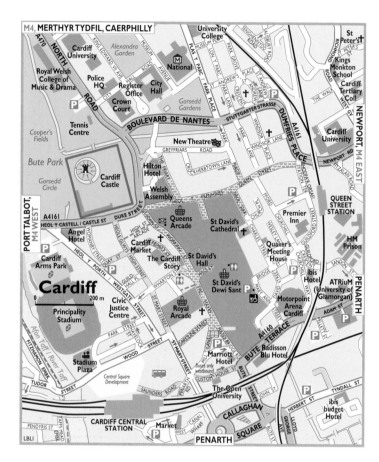

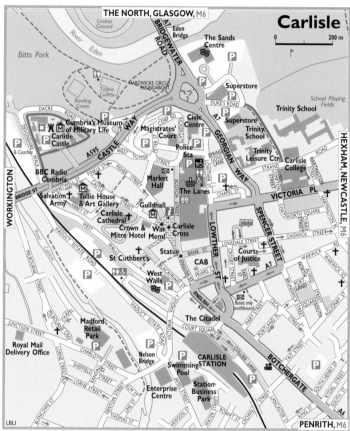

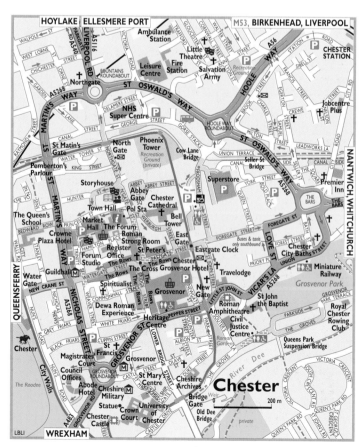

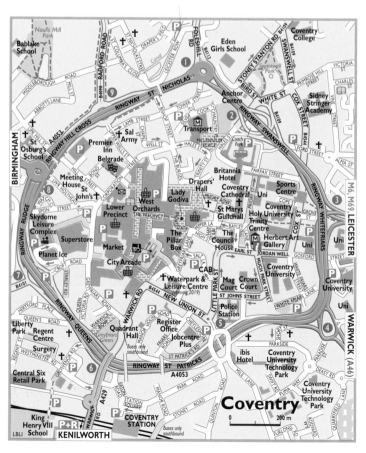

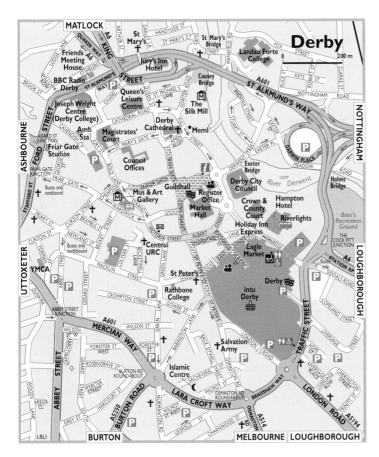

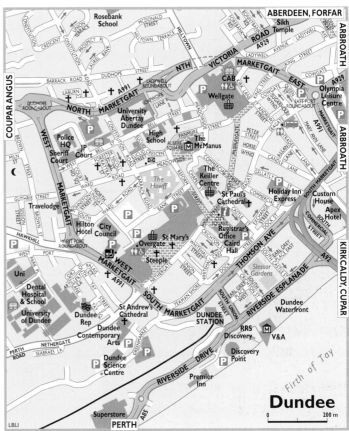

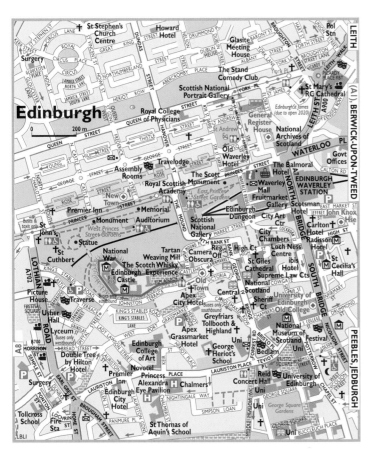

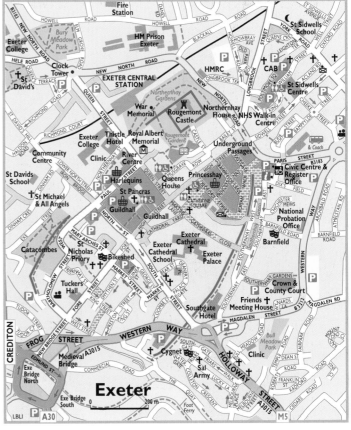

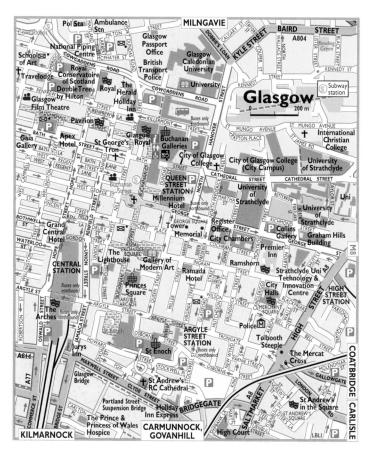

Glasgow

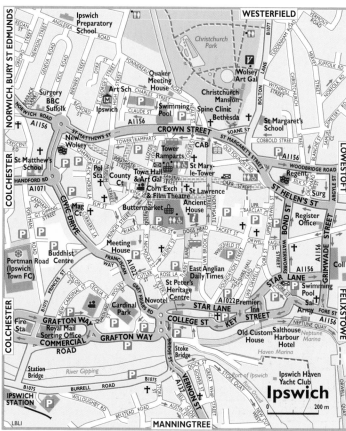

Ipswich

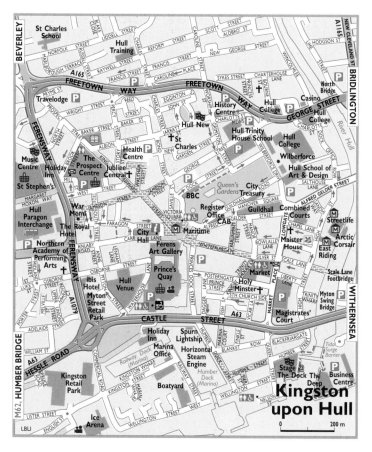

Kingston upon Hull

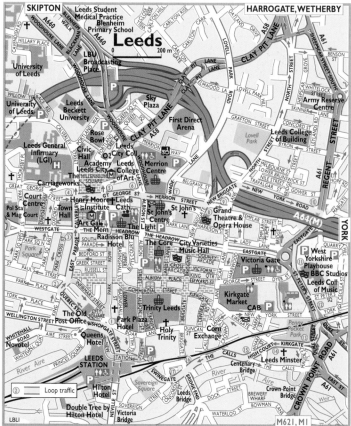

Leeds

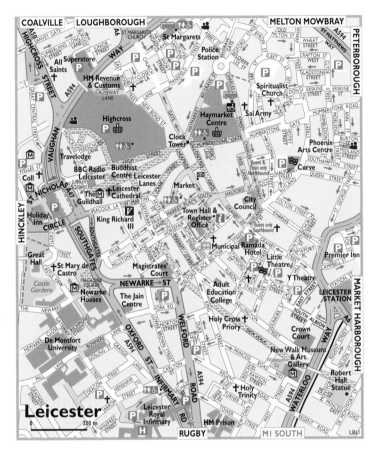

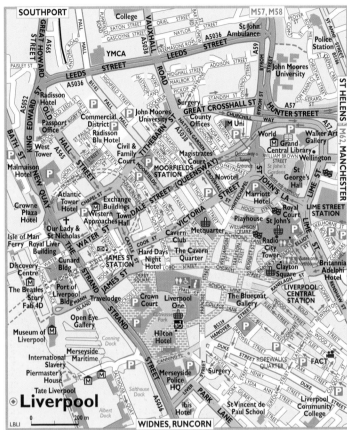

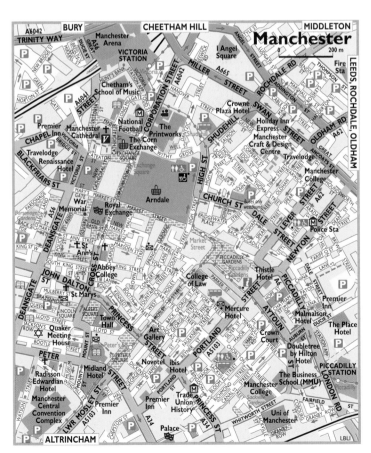

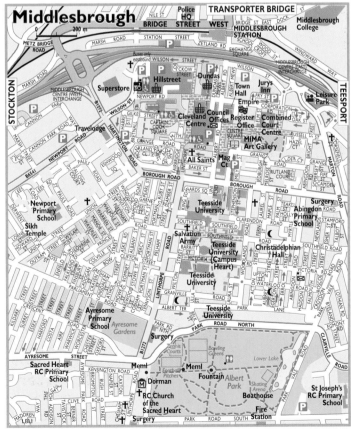

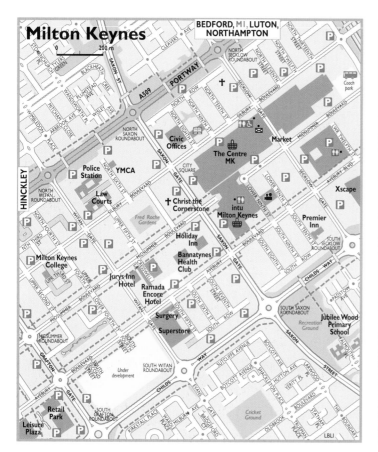

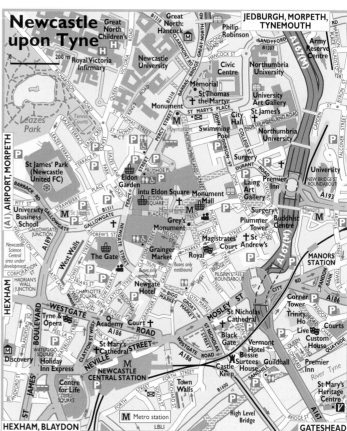

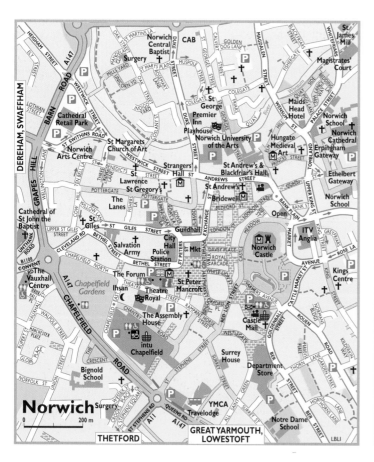

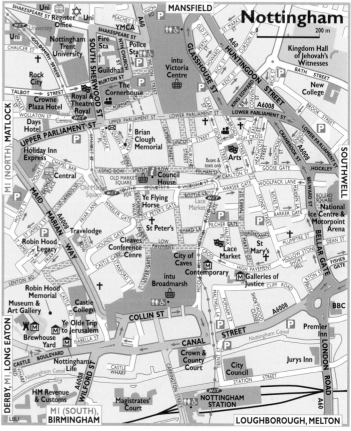

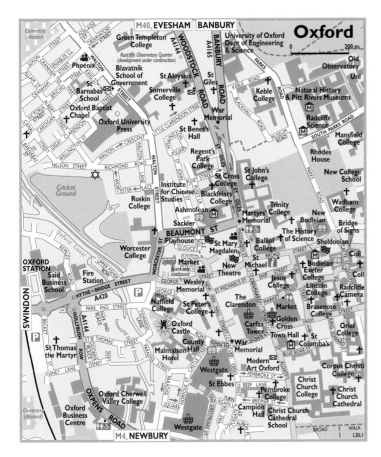

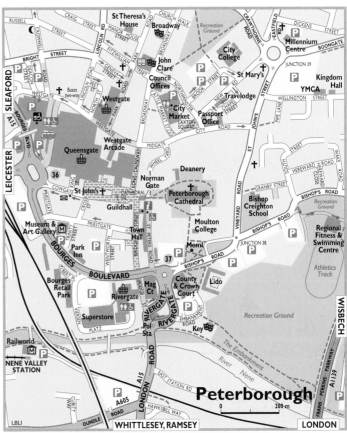

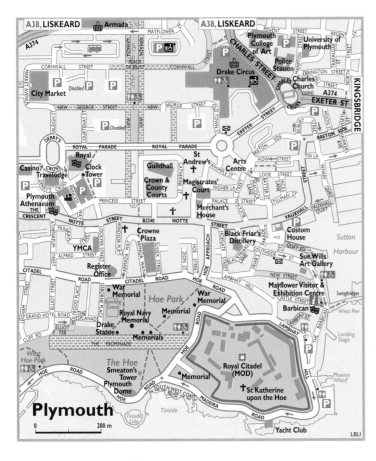

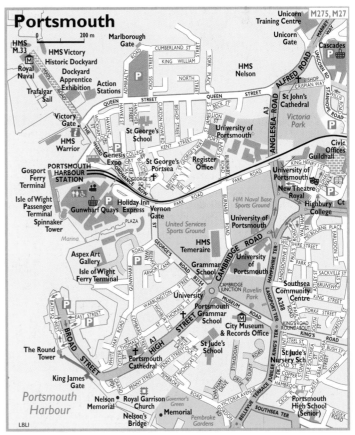

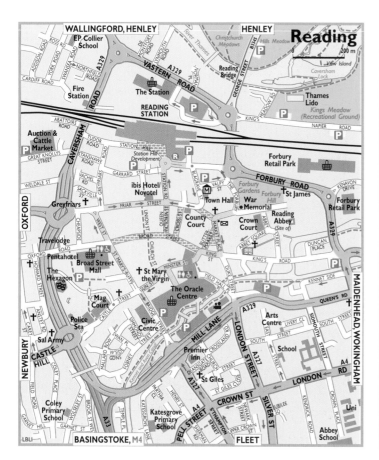

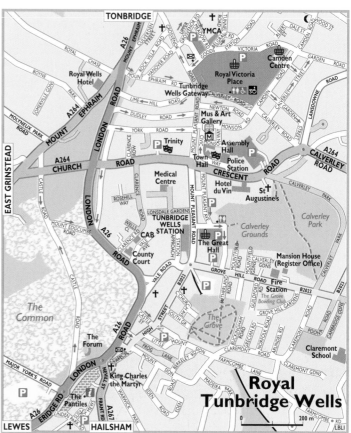

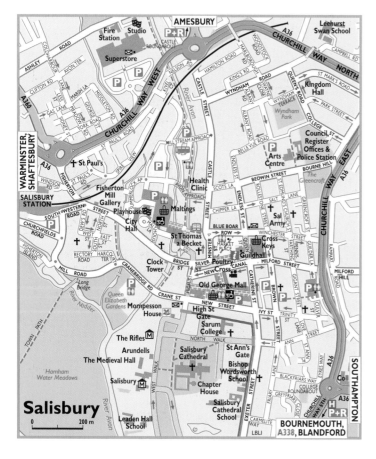

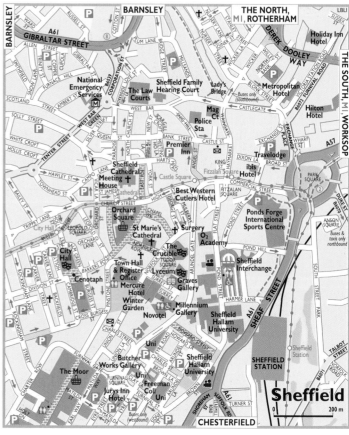

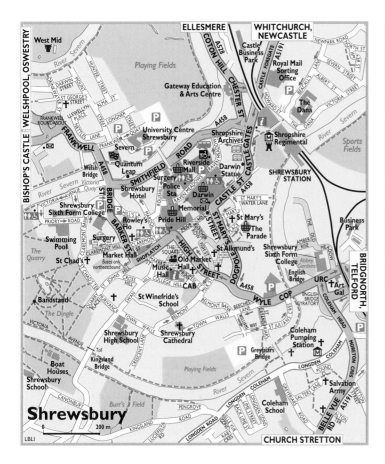

Shrewsbury

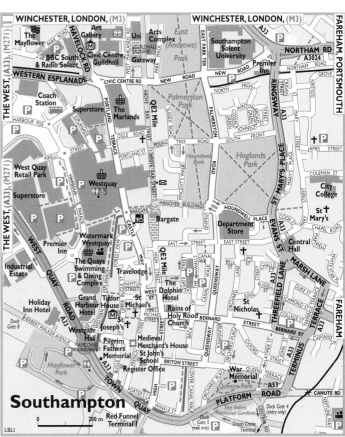

Southampton

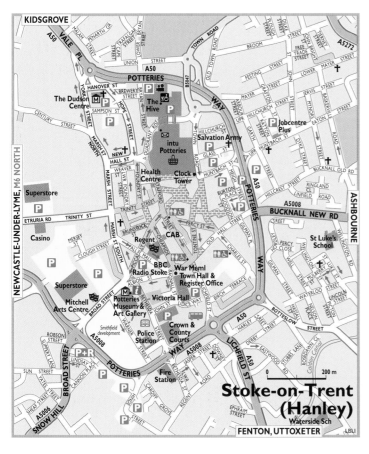

Stoke-on-Trent (Hanley)

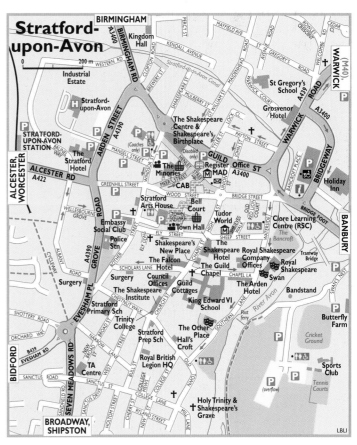

Stratford-upon-Avon

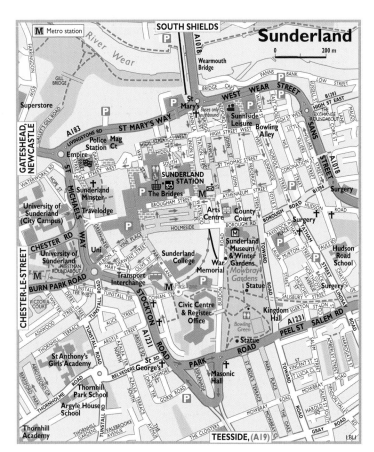

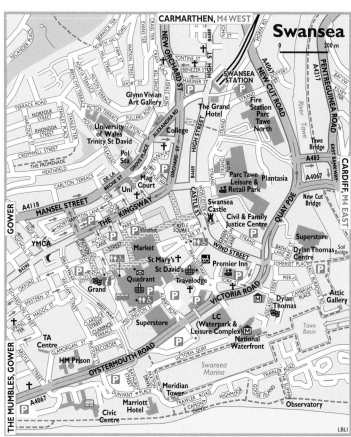

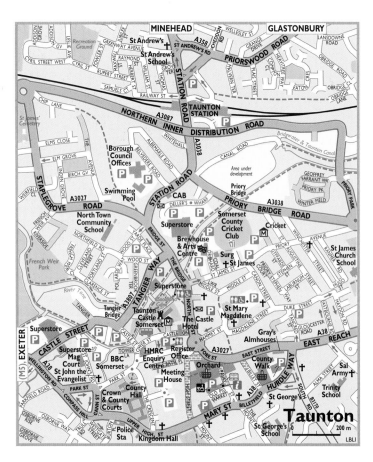

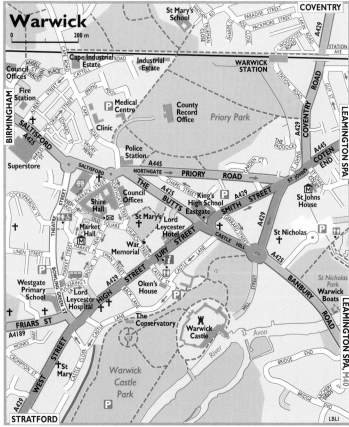

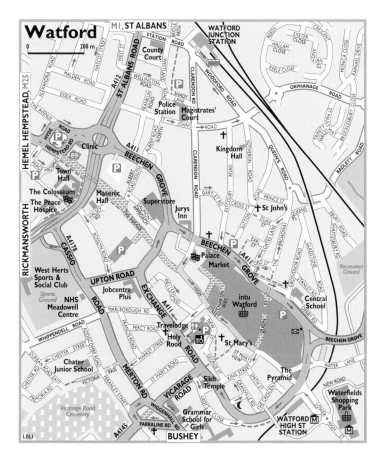

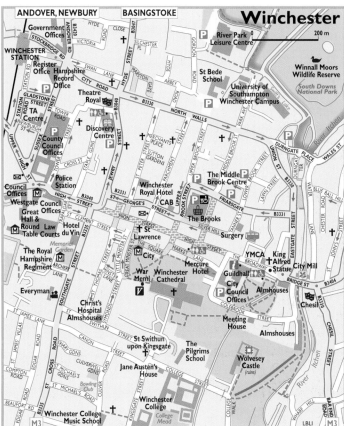

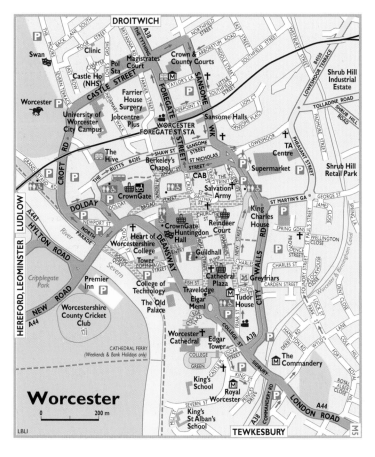

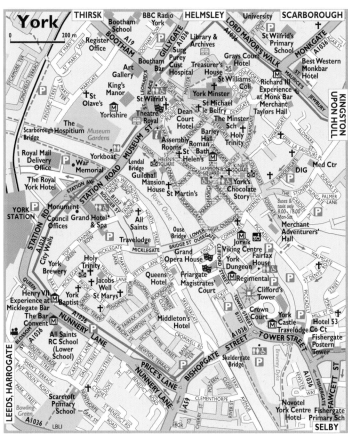

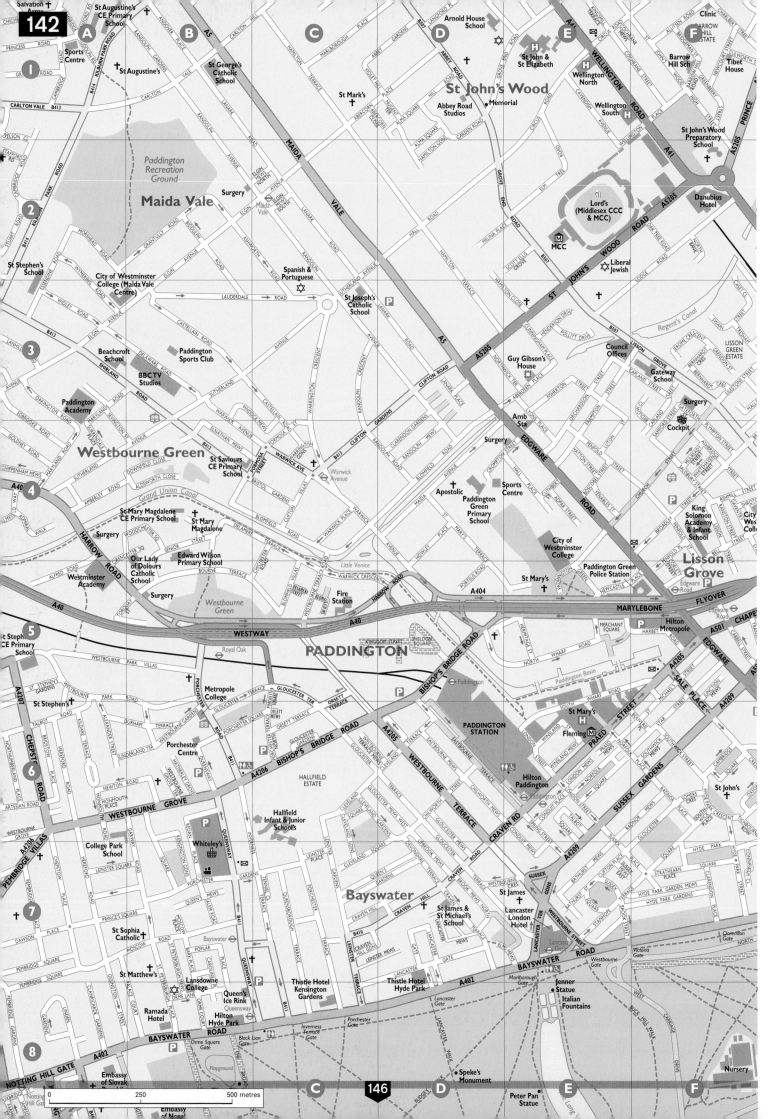

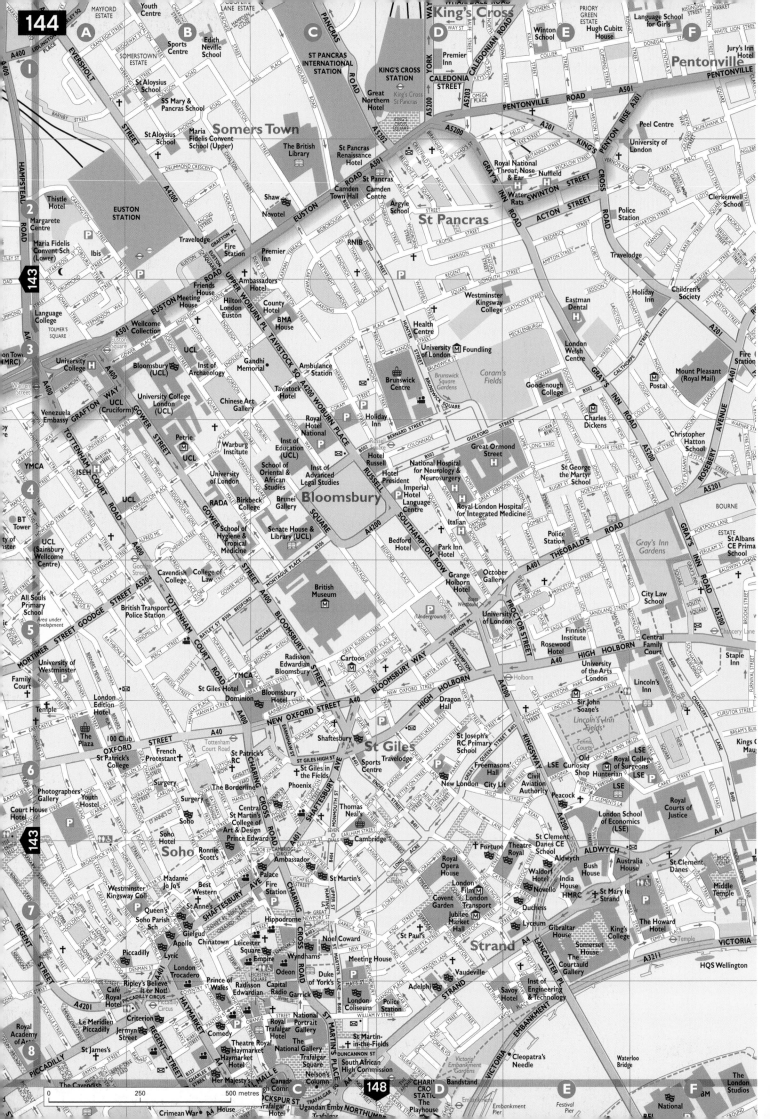

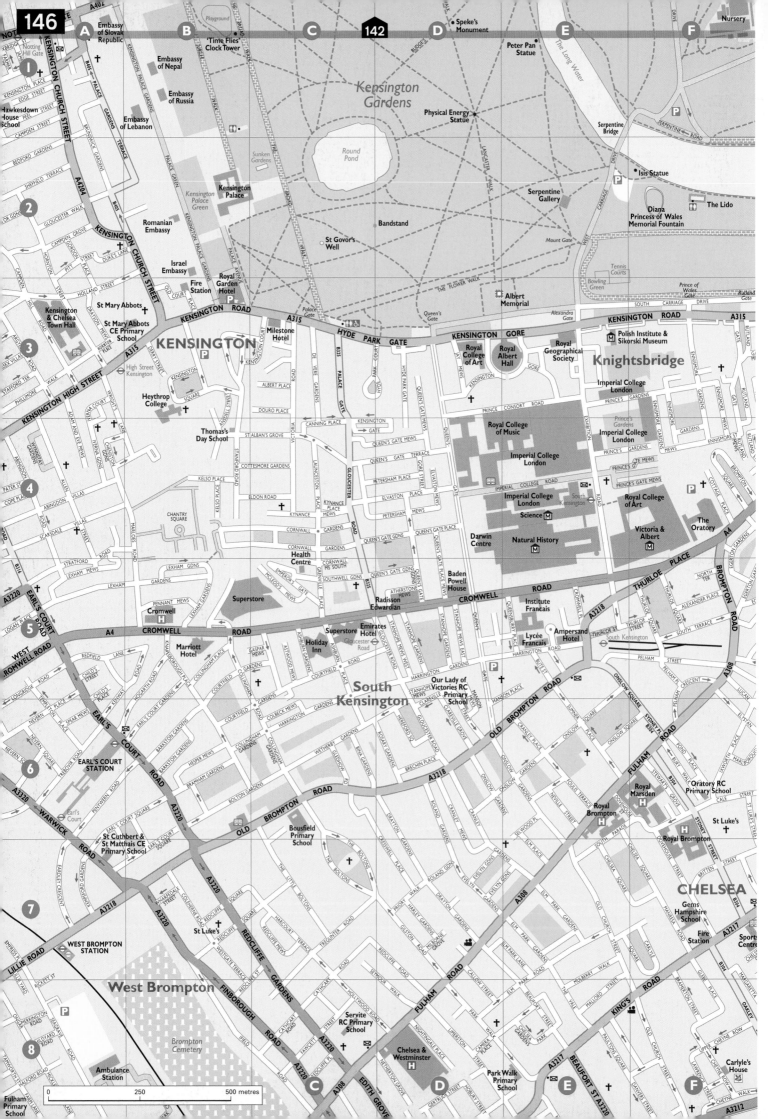

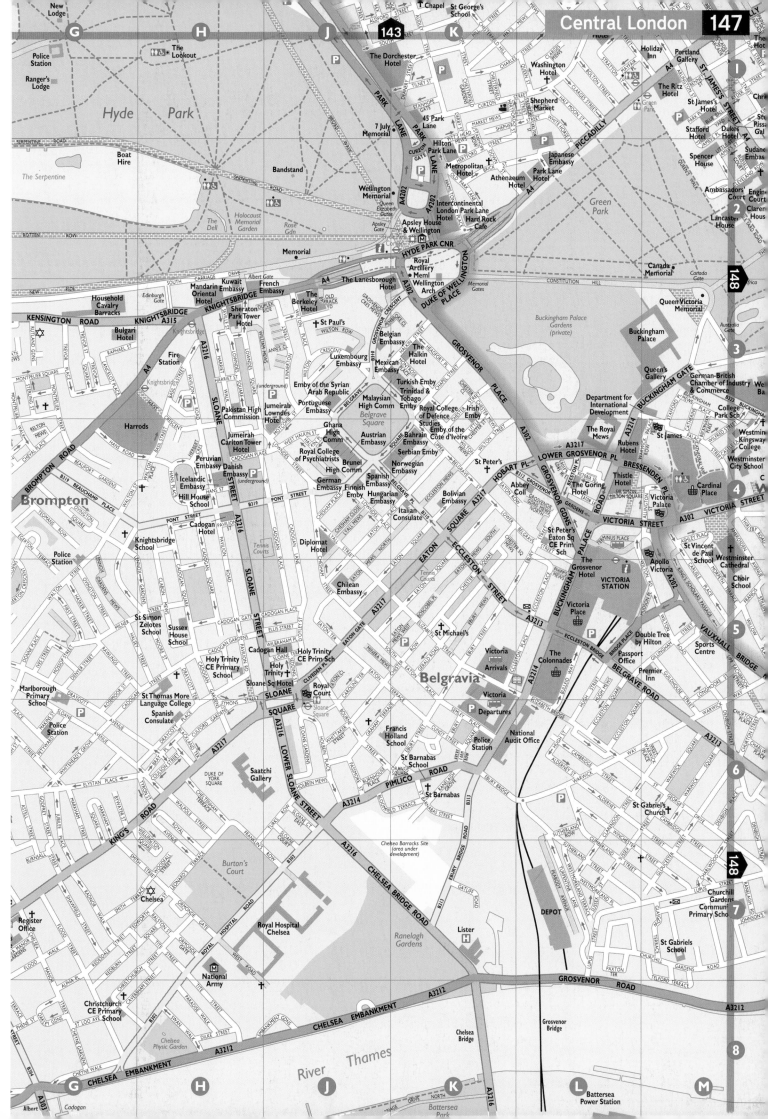

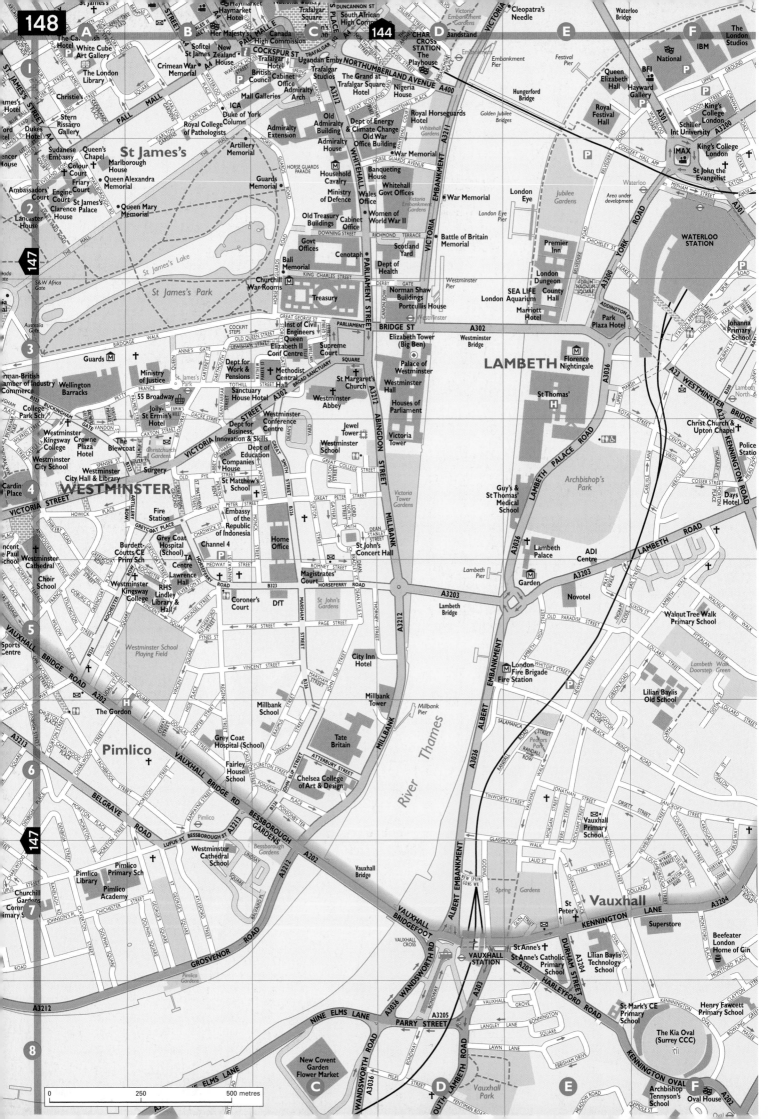

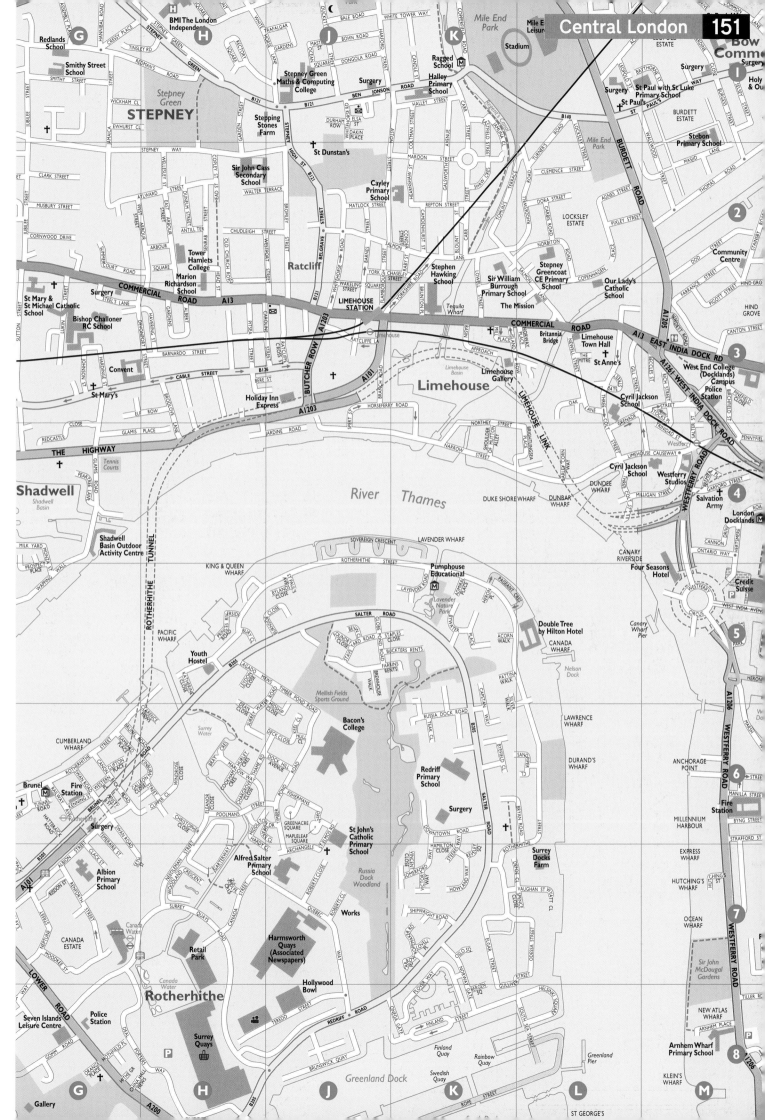

Central London index

This index lists street and station names, and top places of tourist interest shown in red. Names are listed in alphabetical order and written in full, but may be abbreviated on the map. Each entry is followed by its Postcode District and then the page number and grid reference to the square in which the name is found. Names are asterisked (*) in the index where there is insufficient space to show them on the map.

A

Abbey Gardens NW8 ... 142 C1
Abbey Orchard Street SW1P ... 148 B4
Abbey Road NW8 ... 142 D1
Abbey Street SE1 ... 150 B7
Abchurch Lane EC4N ... 145 L7
Abercorn Close NW8 ... 142 C1
Abercorn Place NW8 ... 142 C1
Aberdeen Place NW8 ... 142 E3
Aberdour Street SE1 ... 149 M5
Abingdon Road W8 ... 146 A4
Abingdon Street SW1P ... 148 C3
Abingdon Villas W8 ... 146 A4
Ackroyd Drive E3 ... 151 L1
Acorn Walk SE16 ... 151 K5
Acton Street WC1X ... 144 E2
Adam and Eve Mews W8 ... 146 A3
Adam's Row W1K ... 143 K8
Adam Street WC2N ... 144 D8
Addington Street SE1 ... 148 E3
Addle Hill EC4V ... 145 H7
Adelina Grove E1 ... 150 F1
Adeline Place WC1B ... 144 B5
Adler Street E1 ... 150 D2
Admiral Place SE16 ... 151 K5
Admiral Walk W9 ... 142 A4
Adpar Street W2 ... 142 E4
Agar Street WC2N ... 144 D8
Agdon Street EC1V ... 145 H3
Agnes Street E14 ... 151 L2
Ainsty Street SE16 ... 151 G6
Air Street W1B ... 144 A8
Alaska Street SE1 ... 148 F2
Albany Road SE5 ... 149 L8
Albany Street NW1 ... 143 L1
Albemarle Street W1S ... 143 L8
Albemarle Way EC1V ... 145 H4
Alberta Street SE17 ... 149 H6
Albert Bridge SW3 ... 147 G8
Albert Embankment SE1 ... 148 D7
Albert Gardens E1 ... 151 H3
Albert Gate SW1X ... 147 H2
Albert Place W8 ... 146 C3
Albion Gate W2 ... 143 G7
Albion Place EC1M ... 145 H4
Albion Street SE16 ... 151 G7
Albion Street W2 ... 143 G7
Aldenham Street NW1 ... 144 A1
Aldermanbury EC2V ... 145 K6
Alderney Mews SE1 ... 149 K4
Alderney Street SW1V ... 147 L6
Aldersgate Street EC1A ... 145 J4
Aldford Street W1K ... 143 J8
Aldgate EC3M ... 150 B3
Aldgate ⊖ EC3N ... 150 B3
Aldgate East ⊖ E1 ... 150 C2
Aldgate High Street EC3N ... 150 B3
Aldgate Square EC3N ... 150 B3
Aldsworth Close W9 ... 142 B4
Aldwych WC2E ... 144 E7
Alexander Place SW7 ... 146 F5
Alexander Street W2 ... 142 A6
Alexandra Gate SW7 ... 146 E3
Alfred Mews WC1E ... 144 B4
Alfred Place WC1E ... 144 B4
Alfred Road W2 ... 142 A5
Alice Street SE1 ... 149 M4
Alie Street E1 ... 150 C3
Allen Street W8 ... 146 A4
Allhallows Lane EC4R ... 145 L8
Allington Street SW1E ... 147 M4
Allitsen Road NW8 ... 142 F1
Allsop Place NW1 ... 143 H4
Alma Square NW8 ... 142 D1
Alpha Place SW3 ... 147 G8
Alsace Road SE17 ... 149 M7
Alscot Road SE1 ... 150 C8
Alvey Street SE17 ... 149 M6
Ambergate Street SE17 ... 149 H7
Amberley Road W9 ... 142 A4
Ambrosden Avenue SW1P ... 148 A4
Amelia Street SE17 ... 149 J6
America Square EC3N ... 150 B3
America Street SE1 ... 149 J2
Ampton Street WC1X ... 144 E2
Amwell Street EC1R ... 144 F2
Anchorage Point E14 ... 151 M6
Andover Place NW6 ... 142 B1
Angel ⊖ N1 ... 145 G1
Angela Hooper Place * SW1E ... 148 A4
Angel Junction N1 ... 145 G1
Angel Lane EC4R ... 145 L8
Angel Street EC1A ... 145 J6
Ann Moss Way SE16 ... 150 F8
Ann's Close SW1X ... 147 J3
Ansdell Street W8 ... 146 B4
Antill Terrace E1 ... 151 H2
Antizan Street E1 ... 150 B2
Apple Tree Yard SW1Y ... 144 A8
Appold Street EC2A ... 145 M4
Apsley Gate W1J ... 147 J2
Apsley House & Wellington
  Museum W1J ... 147 K2
Aquinas Street SE1 ... 149 G1
Arbour Square E1 ... 151 H2
Archangels SE16 ... 151 J7
Archer Street W1B ... 144 B7
Arch Street SE1 ... 149 J4
Arden Estate N1 ... 145 M1
Argyle Square WC1H ... 144 D2
Argyle Street WC1H ... 144 D2
Argyll Road W8 ... 146 A3
Argyll Street W1F ... 143 M6
Arlington Street SW1A ... 147 M1
Arlington Way EC1R ... 145 G2
Arne Street WC2H ... 144 D6
Arneway Street SW1P ... 148 B5
Arnhem Place E14 ... 151 M8
Arnold Estate SE1 ... 150 C7
Arnside Street SE17 ... 149 K8
Artesian Road W11 ... 142 A6
Arthur Street EC4V ... 145 L7
Artichoke Hill E1W ... 150 E4
Artillery Lane E1 ... 150 A1
Artillery Row SW1P ... 148 B4
Arundel Street WC2R ... 144 F7

Ashbridge Street NW8 ... 142 F4
Ashburn Gardens SW7 ... 146 C5
Ashburn Place SW7 ... 146 C5
Ashby Street EC1V ... 145 H2
Ashfield Street E1 ... 150 E2
Ashford Street N1 ... 145 M2
Ashley Place SW1P ... 147 M4
Ashmill Street NW1 ... 142 F4
Ashmole Street SW8 ... 148 F8
Ashworth Road W9 ... 142 B2
Assam Street E1 ... 150 C2
Assembly Place E1 ... 151 G1
Astell Street SW3 ... 147 G6
Aston Street E14 ... 151 K1
Astwood Mews SW7 ... 146 C5
Atherstone Mews SW7 ... 146 D5
Atterbury Street SW1P ... 148 C6
Attneave Street WC1X ... 144 F3
Augustus Street NW1 ... 143 L1
Aulton Place SE11 ... 149 G7
Austin Friars EC2N ... 145 L6
Australia Gate SW1A ... 147 M3
Austral Street SE11 ... 149 H5
Aveline Street SE11 ... 148 F7
Ave Maria Lane EC1A ... 145 H6
Avery Farm Row SW1W ... 147 K6
Avery Row W1K ... 143 L7
Aybrook Street W1U ... 143 J5
Aylesbury Road SE17 ... 149 L7
Aylesbury Street EC1R ... 145 H4
Aylesford Street SW1V ... 148 B7
Aylward Street E1 ... 151 G2
Ayres Street SE1 ... 149 K2

B

Babmaes Street SW1Y ... 144 B8
Bache's Street N1 ... 145 L2
Back Church Lane E1 ... 150 D3
Back Hill EC1R ... 145 G4
Bacon Grove SE1 ... 150 B8
Bainbridge Street WC1A ... 144 C6
Bakers Mews W1U ... 143 J6
Baker's Row EC1R ... 145 G4
Baker Street NW1 ... 143 H4
Baker Street W1U ... 143 J5
Baker Street ⊖ NW1 ... 143 H4
Balcombe Street NW1 ... 143 G3
Balderton Street W1K ... 143 J7
Baldwin's Gardens EC1N ... 144 F5
Baldwin Street EC1V ... 145 L2
Bale Road E1 ... 151 J1
Balfe Street N1 ... 144 D1
Balfour Mews W1K ... 143 K8
Balfour Place W1K ... 143 J8
Balfour Street SE17 ... 149 K5
Balvaird Place SW1V ... 148 C7
Baltic Street East EC1Y ... 145 J3
Baltic Street West EC1Y ... 145 J4
Balvaird Place SW1V ... 148 C7
Bank ⊖ EC2R ... 145 L6
Bank End SE1 ... 149 K1
Bankside SE1 ... 145 J8
Banner Street EC1Y ... 145 K3
Banyard Road SE16 ... 150 E8
Barbican ⊖ EC1A ... 145 J4
Barbican Estate EC2Y ... 145 J5
Barge House Street SE1 ... 149 G1
Bark Place W2 ... 142 B7
Barkston Gardens SW5 ... 146 B6
Barley Corn Way E14 ... 151 L4
Barlow/Congreve
  Estate SE17 ... 149 M5
Barlow Place W1J ... 143 L7
Barlow Street SE17 ... 149 L5
Barnardo Street E1 ... 151 H3
Barnby Street NW1 ... 144 A1
Barnes Street E14 ... 151 J2
Barnham Street SE1 ... 150 A6
Baron's Place SE1 ... 149 G3
Baron Street N1 ... 145 G1
Barrett Street W1U ... 143 K6
Barrow Hill Estate NW8 ... 142 F1
Barrow Hill Road NW8 ... 142 F1
Barter Street WC1A ... 144 D5
Bartholomew Close EC1A ... 145 J5
Bartholomew Lane EC2R ... 145 L6
Bartholomew Street SE1 ... 149 L5
Bartlett Court EC4A ... 145 G6
Barton Street SW1P ... 148 C4
Basil Street SW3 ... 147 H4
Basin Approach E14 ... 151 K3
Basinghall Lane EC2V ... 145 K5
Basinghall Street EC2V ... 145 K5
Bastwick Street EC1V ... 145 J3
Bateman's Buildings W1D ... 144 B6
Bateman Street W1D ... 144 B6
Bath Street EC1V ... 145 K2
Bath Terrace SE1 ... 149 J4
Bathurst Mews W2 ... 142 E7
Bathurst Street W2 ... 142 E7
Battle Bridge Lane SE1 ... 149 M1
Batty Street E1 ... 150 D2
Bayley Street WC1B ... 144 B5
Baylis Road SE1 ... 148 F3
Bayswater W2 ... 142 B7
Bayswater Road W2 ... 142 B7
Baythorne Street E3 ... 151 L1
Beaconsfield Road SE17 ... 149 M7
Beak Street W1F ... 144 A7
Bear Gardens SE1 ... 145 J8
Bear Grove SE1 ... 149 H1
Bear Lane SE1 ... 149 H1
Beauchamp Place SW3 ... 147 G4
Beaufort Gardens SW3 ... 147 G4
Beaufort Street SW3 ... 146 E8
Beaumont Place W1T ... 144 A4
Beaumont Street W1G ... 143 K4
Beccles Street E14 ... 151 M3
Beckett Street SE1 ... 149 L3
Beckway Street SE17 ... 149 M6
Bedale Street SE1 ... 149 L1
Bedford Avenue WC1B ... 144 C5
Bedfordbury WC2N ... 144 C7
Bedford Gardens W8 ... 146 A2

Bedford Place WC1N ... 144 D4
Bedford Row WC1R ... 144 E4
Bedford Square WC1B ... 144 B5
Bedford Street WC2E ... 144 D7
Bedford Way WC1H ... 144 C3
Bedlow Close NW8 ... 142 F3
Beech Street EC2Y ... 145 J4
Beeston Place SW1W ... 147 L4
Belgrave Mews North * SW1X ... 147 J3
Belgrave Mews South * SW1X ... 147 K4
Belgrave Place SW1X ... 147 J4
Belgrave Road SW1V ... 147 L5
Belgrave Road SW1V ... 148 A6
Belgrave Square SW1X ... 147 J3
Belgrave Street E1 ... 151 J2
Belgrove Street WC1H ... 144 D2
Bell Lane E1 ... 150 B1
Bell Street NW1 ... 142 F4
Bell Yard WC2A ... 144 F6
Belvedere Road SE1 ... 148 E2
Benjamin Street EC1M ... 145 H4
Ben Jonson Road E1 ... 151 J1
Bennett Street SW1A ... 147 M1
Ben Smith Way SE16 ... 150 D7
Benson Quay E1W ... 150 F4
Bentinck Mews W1U ... 143 K6
Bentinck Street W1U ... 143 K6
Bere Street E1W ... 151 H3
Bergen Square SE16 ... 151 K8
Berkeley Mews W1H ... 143 H6
Berkeley Square W1J ... 143 L8
Berkeley Street W1J ... 143 L8
Bermondsey ⊖ ⊖ SE16 ... 150 E7
Bermondsey Spa SE16 ... 150 C8
Bermondsey Square SE1 ... 150 A8
Bermondsey Street SE1 ... 150 A6
Bermondsey Wall East SE16 ... 150 E7
Bermondsey Wall
  Estate SE16 ... 150 C1
Bermondsey Wall West SE16 ... 150 C6
Bernard Street WC1N ... 144 D4
Berners Mews W1T ... 144 A5
Berners Place W1F ... 144 A6
Berners Street W1T ... 144 A5
Bernhardt Crescent NW8 ... 142 F3
Berryfield Road SE17 ... 149 J6
Berry Street EC1V ... 145 H3
Berwick Street W1F ... 144 A6
Bessborough Gardens SW1V ... 148 C6
Bessborough Street SW1V ... 148 B6
Betterton Street WC2H ... 144 D6
Bevenden Street N1 ... 145 L2
Bevin Close SE16 ... 151 J5
Bevington Street SE16 ... 150 D7
Bevin Way WC1X ... 144 F1
Bevis Marks EC3A ... 150 A2
Bewley Street E1 ... 150 F3
Bickenhall Street W1U ... 143 H4
Bidborough Street WC1H ... 144 C2
Biddulph Road W9 ... 142 B2
Big Ben (Elizabeth
  Tower) SW1A ... 148 D3
Bigland Street E1 ... 150 E3
Billiter Square EC3M ... 150 A3
Billiter Street EC3M ... 150 A3
Bina Gardens SW5 ... 146 C6
Bingham Place W1U ... 143 J4
Binney Street W1K ... 143 K7
Birchfield Street E14 ... 151 M3
Birchin Lane EC3V ... 145 L7
Birdcage Walk SW1H ... 148 A3
Birde Lane EC4Y ... 145 H6
Bird Street W1C ... 143 K6
Birkenhead Street N1 ... 144 D1
Bishop's Bridge Road W2 ... 142 C6
Bishopsgate EC2M ... 150 A2
Bishops Square E1 ... 150 B1
Bishop's Terrace SE11 ... 149 G5
Bittern Street SE1 ... 149 J3
Blackall Street EC2A ... 145 M3
Blackburne's Mews W1K ... 143 J7
Blackfriars ⊖ EC4V ... 145 H7
Blackfriars Bridge SE1 ... 145 H8
Black Friars Lane EC4V ... 145 H7
Blackfriars Road SE1 ... 149 H3
Blackhorse Court SE1 ... 149 L4
Black Lion Gate W2 ... 142 B8
Black Prince Road SE11 ... 148 E6
Blackwood Street SE17 ... 149 K6
Blandford Street W1U ... 143 H5
Blenheim Street W1S ... 143 L7
Bletchley Street N1 ... 145 K1
Blomfield Mews W2 ... 142 C5
Blomfield Road W9 ... 142 C4
Blomfield Street EC2M ... 145 M5
Blomfield Villas W2 ... 142 C5
Bloomfield Terrace SW1W ... 147 J6
Bloomsbury Square WC1A ... 144 D5
Bloomsbury Street WC1B ... 144 C5
Bloomsbury Way WC1A ... 144 C5
Blount Street E14 ... 151 K2
Blue Ball Yard SW1A ... 147 M1
Bohn Road E1 ... 151 J1
Bolsover Street W1W ... 143 L4
Bolton Gardens SW5 ... 146 B6
Bolton Street W1J ... 147 L1
Bond Street ⊖ W1C ... 143 K6
Bondway SW8 ... 148 D8
Bonhill Street EC2A ... 145 L4
Bonnington Square SW8 ... 148 E8
Boot Street N1 ... 145 M2
Borough ⊖ SE1 ... 149 K3
Borough High Street SE1 ... 149 K3
Borough Road SE1 ... 149 H3
Boscobel Place SW1W ... 147 K5
Boscobel Street NW8 ... 142 E4
Boss Street SE1 ... 150 B6
Boston Place NW1 ... 143 G4
Botolph Lane EC3R ... 145 M7
Boundary Lane SE17 ... 149 K8
Boundary Row SE1 ... 149 G2
Bourdon Street W1K ... 143 L7
Bourlet Close W1W ... 143 M5
Bourne Estate EC1N ... 144 F4
Bourne Street SW1W ... 147 J6
Bourne Terrace W2 ... 142 B5
Bouverie Place W2 ... 142 F6
Bouverie Street EC4Y ... 145 G6

Bowland Yard * SW1X ... 147 J3
Bow Lane EC4M ... 145 K6
Bowling Green Lane EC1R ... 145 G3
Bowling Green Place SE1 ... 149 L2
Bowling Green Street SE11 ... 148 F8
Bowling Green Walk N1 ... 145 M2
Bowsell Street WC1N ... 144 D4
Bow Street WC2E ... 144 D7
Boyd Street E1 ... 150 D3
Boyfield Street SE1 ... 149 H3
Boyle Street W1S ... 143 M7
Boyson Road SE17 ... 149 K8
Brackland Terrace SW3 ... 147 H6
Brackley Street EC1Y ... 145 J4
Bradenham Close SE17 ... 149 K8
Brad Street SE1 ... 149 G2
Braganza Street SE17 ... 149 H7
Braham Street E1 ... 150 C3
Bramerton Street SW3 ... 146 F7
Bramham Gardens SW5 ... 146 B6
Branch Road E14 ... 151 J3
Brandon Estate SE17 ... 149 H8
Brandon Street SE17 ... 149 K6
Brangton Road SE11 ... 148 F7
Bray Crescent SE16 ... 151 H6
Bray Place SW3 ... 147 H6
Bread Street EC4M ... 145 K7
Bream's Buildings EC4A ... 144 F6
Brechin Place SW7 ... 146 D6
Breezer's Hill E1W ... 150 D4
Brendon Street W1H ... 143 G5
Bressenden Place SW1W ... 147 L4
Brettell Street SE17 ... 149 L7
Brewers Green SW1H ... 148 A3
Brewer Street W1F ... 144 A7
Brewhouse Lane E1W ... 150 F6
Brewhouse Walk SE16 ... 151 J5
Brick Court WC2R ... 144 F7
Brick Lane E1 ... 150 C1
Brick Street W1J ... 147 K2
Bridewell Place EC4V ... 145 H7
Bridgeman Street NW8 ... 142 F1
Bridge Place SW1V ... 147 L5
Bridgeport Place E1W ... 150 D4
Bridge Street EC4V ... 145 J7
Bridge Street SW1A ... 148 D3
Bridgewater Street EC2Y ... 145 J4
Bridgeway Street NW1 ... 144 A1
Bridle Lane W1F ... 144 A7
Bridstow Place W2 ... 142 A6
Brightlingsea Place E14 ... 151 L4
Brill Place NW1 ... 144 C1
Briset Street EC1M ... 145 H4
Bristol Gardens W9 ... 142 B4
Britannia Street WC1X ... 144 E2
Britannia Walk N1 ... 145 L2
Britannia Way N1 ... 145 K1
Britten Street SW3 ... 146 F7
Britton Street EC1M ... 145 H4
Broadbent Street W1K ... 143 L7
Broadgate Circle EC2M ... 145 M5
Broadley Street NW8 ... 142 F4
Broadley Terrace NW1 ... 142 F4
Broadstone Place W1U ... 143 J5
Broad Walk NW1 ... 143 K1
Broad Walk W2 ... 143 H7
Broadwall SE1 ... 149 G1
Broadway SW1H ... 148 B4
Broadwick Street W1F ... 144 A7
Brockham Street SE1 ... 149 K4
Brodlove Lane E1W ... 151 H3
Bromley Street E1 ... 151 J2
Brompton Road SW3 ... 147 G4
Brompton Road SW3 ... 146 F5
Brompton Square SW3 ... 146 F4
Bronti Close SE17 ... 149 K7
Brook Drive SE11 ... 149 G5
Brooke Street EC1N ... 144 F5
Brook Gate W2 ... 143 H8
Brook Mews North W2 ... 142 D7
Brook's Mews W1K ... 143 K7
Brook Street W1K ... 143 K7
Brook Street W2 ... 142 F7
Brown Heart Gardens W1K ... 143 K7
Browning Mews W1G ... 143 K5
Browning Street SE17 ... 149 K6
Brownlow Mews WC1N ... 144 E3
Brownlow Street WC1V ... 144 E5
Brown Street W1H ... 143 G6
Brunel Road SE16 ... 151 G6
Brune Street E1 ... 150 B1
Brunswick Close SE1 ... 150 A6
Brunswick Gardens W8 ... 146 A1
Brunswick Place N1 ... 145 L2
Brunswick Quay SE16 ... 151 J8
Brunswick Square WC1N ... 144 D3
Brunton Place E14 ... 151 K3
Brushfield Street E1 ... 150 B1
Bruton Lane W1J ... 143 L8
Bruton Place W1J ... 143 L7
Bruton Street W1J ... 143 L8
Bryan Road SE16 ... 151 K6
Bryanstone Mews West W1H ... 143 G5
Bryanston Mews East W1H ... 143 G5
Bryanston Place W1H ... 143 G5
Bryanston Square W1H ... 143 H5
Bryanston Street W1C ... 143 H7
Buck Hill Walk W2 ... 142 E8
Buckingham Gate SW1E ... 147 L3
Buckingham Mews SW1E ... 147 M3
Buckingham Palace SW1A ... 147 L3
Buckingham Palace
  Road SW1W ... 147 L5
Buckingham Palace
  Road SW1W ... 147 M4
Buckland Street N1 ... 145 L1
Buckle Street E1 ... 150 C2
Bucknall Street WC2H ... 144 C6
Buckters Rents SE16 ... 151 J5
Budge's Walk W2 ... 146 D2
Bulleid Way SW1V ... 147 L5
Bulstrode Street W1U ... 143 K5
Bunhill Row EC1Y ... 145 L3
Burdett Estate E14 ... 151 M1
Burdett Road E14 ... 151 L2
Burdett Street SE1 ... 148 F3
Burgess Street E14 ... 151 M1
Burge Street SE1 ... 149 L4

Burlington Arcade W1J ... 143 M8
Burlington Gardens W1S ... 143 M8
Burnhouse Place SW1W ... 147 J6
Burnsall Street SW3 ... 147 G7
Burnside Close SE16 ... 151 J5
Burrell Street SE1 ... 149 H1
Burslem Street E1 ... 150 D3
Burton Grove SE17 ... 149 L7
Burton Street WC1H ... 144 C3
Burwood Place W2 ... 143 G6
Bury Close SE16 ... 151 H5
Bury Court EC3A ... 150 A2
Bury Place WC1A ... 144 D5
Bury Street EC3A ... 150 A2
Bury Street SW1Y ... 148 A1
Bury Walk SW3 ... 146 F6
Bushell Street E1W ... 150 D5
Bush Lane EC4V ... 145 L7
Butcher Row E14 ... 151 J3
Bute Street SW7 ... 146 E5
Butler Place SW1H ... 148 B4
Butler's Wharf SE1 ... 150 C6
Buttesland Street N1 ... 145 L2
Byefield Close SE16 ... 151 K6
Bylands Close SE16 ... 151 J5
Byng Place WC1E ... 144 B4
Byng Street E14 ... 151 M6
Byward Street EC3R ... 150 A4
Byng Street E14 ... 151 K5
Bywater Street SW3 ... 147 G6

C

Cabbell Street NW1 ... 142 F5
Cable Street E1 ... 150 F3
Cadiz Street SE17 ... 149 K7
Cadogan Gardens SW3 ... 147 H5
Cadogan Gate SW1X ... 147 H5
Cadogan Lane SW1X ... 147 J4
Cadogan Place SW1X ... 147 J4
Cadogan Square SW1X ... 147 H5
Cadogan Street SW3 ... 147 G6
Caledonian Road N1 ... 144 D1
Caledonia Street N1 ... 144 D1
Cale Street SW3 ... 146 F6
Callow Street SW3 ... 146 D7
Calshot Street N1 ... 144 E1
Calthorpe Street WC1X ... 144 E3
Cambridge Circus WC2H ... 144 C7
Cambridge Gardens NW6 ... 142 A1
Cambridge Gate NW1 ... 143 L3
Cambridge Road NW6 ... 142 A1
Cambridge Road NW6 ... 142 A2
Cambridge Square W2 ... 142 F6
Cambridge Street SW1V ... 147 L6
Cambridge Terrace NW1 ... 143 L3
Cambridge Terrace
  Mews NW1 ... 143 L3
Camdenhurst Street E14 ... 151 K2
Camera Place SW10 ... 146 D8
Camomile Street EC3A ... 150 A2
Campden Grove W8 ... 146 A2
Campden Hill Road W8 ... 146 A2
Campden Street W8 ... 146 A1
Camperdown Street E1 ... 150 C3
Canada Estate SE16 ... 151 G7
Canada Gate SW1A ... 147 M3
Canada Street SE16 ... 151 H7
Canada Water ⊖ ⊖ SE16 ... 151 G7
Canada Wharf SE16 ... 151 L5
Canal Street SE5 ... 149 L8
Canary Riverside E14 ... 151 L4
Candle Street E1 ... 151 K1
Canning Place W8 ... 146 C4
Cannon Drive E14 ... 151 M4
Cannon Street EC4N ... 145 K7
Cannon Street ⊖ EC4R ... 145 K7
Cannon Street Road E1 ... 150 E3
Canon Beck Road SE16 ... 151 G6
Canon Row SW1A ... 148 D3
Canton Street E14 ... 151 M3
Capeners Close * SW1X ... 147 J3
Capland Street NW8 ... 142 E3
Capper Street WC1E ... 144 A4
Capstan Way SE16 ... 151 K5
Carbis Road E14 ... 151 L2
Carburton Street W1W ... 143 L4
Cardigan Street SE11 ... 148 F6
Cardington Street NW1 ... 144 A2
Carey Street WC2A ... 144 F6
Carlisle Avenue EC3N ... 150 B3
Carlisle Lane SE1 ... 148 E4
Carlisle Place SW1P ... 147 M5
Carlisle Street W1D ... 144 B6
Carlos Place W1K ... 143 K7
Carlton Gardens SW1Y ... 148 B2
Carlton Hill NW6 ... 142 B1
Carlton House Terrace SW1Y ... 148 B1
Carlton Street SW1Y ... 148 L1
Carlton Vale NW6 ... 142 A1
Carlton Vale NW6 ... 142 B1
Carlyle Square SW3 ... 146 F7
Carmelite Street EC4Y ... 145 G7
Carnaby Street W1F ... 143 M7
Caroline Place W2 ... 142 B7
Caroline Street E1 ... 151 H3
Caroline Terrace SW1W ... 147 J5
Carpenter Street W1K ... 143 K7
Carrington Street W1J ... 147 K1
Carr Street E14 ... 151 K1
Carteret Street SW1H ... 148 B3
Carter Lane EC4V ... 145 H7
Carter Place SE17 ... 149 K7
Carter Street SE17 ... 149 J7
Carthusian Street EC1M ... 145 J4
Carting Lane WC2E ... 144 D8
Cartwright Gardens WC1H ... 144 C2
Cartwright Street E1 ... 150 C4
Casey Close NW8 ... 142 F3
Casson Street E1 ... 150 C1
Castellain Road W9 ... 142 B3
Castlebrook Close SE11 ... 149 G5
Castle Lane SW1E ... 147 M4
Catesby Street SE17 ... 149 L6
Cathay Street SE16 ... 150 F7
Cathcart Road SW10 ... 146 C8

Cathedral Walk SW1E 147 M4
Catherine Place SW1E 147 M4
Catherine Street WC2E 144 D7
Cato Street W1H 143 G5
Causton Street SW1P 148 B6
Cavell Street E1 ..... 150 F1
Cavendish Avenue NW8 ..... 142 E1
Cavendish Place W1G 143 L6
Cavendish Square W1G 143 L6
Cavendish Street N1 ..... 145 L1
Caversham Street SW3 ..... 147 G8
Caxton Street SW1H 148 B4
Cayton Street EC1V 145 K2
Centaur Street SE1 ..... 148 F4
Central Street EC1V 145 J2
Chadwell Street EC1R 145 G1
Chadwick Street SW1P 148 B4
Chagford Street NW1 ..... 143 H4
Chalton Street NW1 ..... 144 B1
Chambers Street SE16 ..... 150 D7
Chamber Street E1 ..... 150 C3
Chambers Wharf SE16 ..... 150 D6
Chancel Street SE1 ..... 149 H1
Chancery Lane WC2A 144 F5
Chancery Lane ⊖ WC1V 144 F5
Chandos Place WC2N 144 C8
Chandos Street W1G 143 L6
Chantry Square W8 ..... 146 B4
Chapel Market N1 ..... 144 F1
Chapel Street NW1 ..... 142 F5
Chapel Street SW1X 147 K3
Chaplin Close SE1 ..... 149 G3
Chapman Street E1 ..... 150 E3
Chapter Road SE17 ..... 149 H7
Chapter Street SW1P 148 B6
Chargrove Close SE16 ..... 151 H6
Charing Cross ≥⊖ WC2N 148 D1
Charing Cross Road WC2H 144 B6
Charing Cross Road WC2N 144 C7
Charlbert Street NW8 ..... 142 F1
Charles II Street SW1Y 144 B8
Charles Square N1 ..... 145 M2
Charles Street W1J 147 K1
Charleston Street SE17 ..... 149 K6
Charlotte Road EC2A 145 M3
Charlotte Street W1T 144 A4
Charlwood Place SW1V 148 A6
Charlwood Street SW1V 147 M7
Charlwood Street SW1V 148 A6
Charrington Street NW1 ..... 144 B1
Charterhouse Square EC1M 145 H4
Charterhouse Street EC1M 145 G5
Chart Street N1 ..... 145 L2
Chaseley Street E14 ..... 151 J2
Chatham Street SE17 ..... 149 L5
Cheapside EC2V 145 K6
Chelsea Bridge SW1W 147 K8
Chelsea Bridge Road SW1W 147 J7
Chelsea Embankment SW3 ..... 147 G8
Chelsea Manor Gardens SW3 ..... 146 F7
Chelsea Manor Street SW3 ..... 147 G7
Chelsea Park Gardens SW3 ..... 146 E8
Chelsea Physic Garden SW3 ..... 147 H8
Chelsea Square SW3 ..... 146 E7
Cheltenham Terrace SW3 ..... 147 H6
Chenies Mews WC1E 144 B4
Chenies Street WC1E 144 B4
Cheniston Gardens W8 ..... 146 A4
Chepstow Place W2 ..... 142 A7
Chepstow Road W2 ..... 142 A6
Chequer Street EC1Y 145 K3
Cherbury Street N1 ..... 145 L1
Cherry Garden Street SE16 ..... 150 E7
Chesham Close SW1X 147 J4
Chesham Place SW1X 147 J4
Chesham Street SW1X 147 J4
Chester Close SW1X 147 K3
Chester Close North NW1 ..... 143 L2
Chester Close South NW1 ..... 143 L2
Chesterfield Gardens W1J 147 K1
Chesterfield Hill W1J 143 K8
Chesterfield Street W1J 147 K1
Chester Gate NW1 ..... 143 L2
Chester Mews SW1X 147 K3
Chester Place NW1 ..... 143 L1
Chester Road NW1 ..... 143 K2
Chester Row SW1W 147 K5
Chester Square SW1W 147 K5
Chester Square Mews SW1W 147 K4
Chester Street SW1X 147 K4
Chester Terrace NW1 ..... 143 L2
Chester Way SE11 ..... 149 G6
Cheval Place SW7 ..... 147 G4
Cheval Street E14 ..... 151 M7
Cheyne Gardens SW3 ..... 147 G8
Cheyne Row SW3 ..... 146 F8
Cheyne Walk SW3 ..... 146 F8
Chicheley Street SE1 ..... 148 E2
Chichester Road NW6 ..... 142 A1
Chichester Road W2 ..... 142 C5
Chichester Street SW1V 148 A7
Chicksand Street E1 ..... 150 C1
Chigwell Hill E1W 150 E4
Child's Place SW5 ..... 146 A5
Child's Street SW5 ..... 146 A5
Chiltern Street W1U 143 J4
Chilworth Mews W2 ..... 142 D6
Chilworth Street W2 ..... 142 D6
China Hall Mews SE16 ..... 151 G8
Chippenham Mews W9 ..... 142 A4
Chiswell Street EC1Y 145 K4
Chitty Street W1T 144 A4
Christchurch Street SW3 ..... 147 G8
Christian Street E1 ..... 150 D3
Christina Street EC2A 145 M3
Christopher Close SE16 ..... 151 H6
Christopher Street EC2A 145 L4
Chudleigh Street E1 ..... 151 H2
Chumleigh Street SE5 ..... 149 M8
Churchill Gardens Road SW1V 147 L7
Churchill War Rooms SW1A 148 C3
Church Street NW8 ..... 142 E4
Church Way NW1 ..... 144 B2
Churchyard Row SE1 ..... 149 H5
Churton Place SW1V 148 A6
Churton Street SW1V 148 A6
Circus Road NW8 ..... 142 E1
Cirencester Square W2 ..... 142 A5
City Garden Row N1 ..... 145 J1
City Road EC1V 145 J1
City Road EC1V 145 L3
City Thameslink ≥ EC4M 145 H6
Clabon Mews SW1X 147 H5
Clack Street SE16 ..... 151 G7
Clanricarde Gardens W2 ..... 142 A8

Claremont Square N1 ..... 144 F1
Clarence Gardens NW1 ..... 143 L2
Clarence Mews SE16 ..... 151 G6
Clarendon Gardens W9 ..... 142 D4
Clarendon Gate W2 ..... 142 F7
Clarendon Place W2 ..... 142 F7
Clarendon Street SW1V 147 L6
Clareville Grove SW7 ..... 146 D6
Clareville Street SW7 ..... 146 D6
Clarges Mews W1J 147 L1
Clarges Street W1J 147 L1
Clark Street E1 ..... 150 F2
Claverton Street SW1V 148 A7
Clave Street E1W 150 F5
Clay Street W1U 143 H5
Clayton Street SE11 ..... 148 F8
Cleaver Square SE11 ..... 149 G7
Cleaver Street SE11 ..... 149 G7
Clegg Street E1W 150 F5
Clemence Street E14 ..... 151 L2
Clements Lane EC4N 145 L7
Clement's Road SE16 ..... 150 E8
Clenston Mews W1H 143 H6
Clere Street EC2A 145 L3
Clerkenwell Close EC1R 145 G3
Clerkenwell Green EC1R 145 G4
Clerkenwell Road EC1M 145 G4
Cleveland Gardens W2 ..... 142 C6
Cleveland Mews W1T 143 M4
Cleveland Place SW1Y 148 A1
Cleveland Row SW1A 148 A2
Cleveland Square W2 ..... 142 C6
Cleveland Street W1T 143 M4
Cleveland Terrace W2 ..... 142 D6
Clifford Street W1S 143 M7
Clifton Gardens W9 ..... 142 C4
Clifton Place SE16 ..... 151 G6
Clifton Place W2 ..... 142 E7
Clifton Road W9 ..... 142 D3
Clifton Street EC2A 145 M3
Clifton Villas W9 ..... 142 C4
Clink Street SE1 ..... 149 K1
Clipper Close SE16 ..... 151 H6
Clipstone Mews W1W 143 M4
Clipstone Street W1W 143 L4
Cliveden Place SW1W 147 J5
Cloak Lane EC4R 145 K7
Cloth Fair EC1A 145 J5
Cloth Street EC1A 145 J5
Cluny Place SE1 ..... 150 A8
Cobb Street E1 ..... 150 B2
Cobourg Street NW1 ..... 144 A2
Coburg Close SW1P 148 A5
Cochrane Mews NW8 ..... 142 E1
Cochrane Street NW8 ..... 142 E1
Cock Lane EC1A 145 H5
Cockspur Street SW1Y 148 C1
Codling Close * E1W 150 D5
Coin Street SE1 ..... 149 G1
Coke Street E1 ..... 150 D2
Colbeck Mews SW7 ..... 146 C6
Colebrook Row N1 ..... 145 H1
Coleherne Road SW10 ..... 146 B7
Coleman Street EC2R 145 L6
Cole Street SE1 ..... 149 K3
Coley Street WC1X 144 F3
College Hill EC4R 145 K7
College Street EC4R 145 K7
Collett Road SE16 ..... 150 D8
Collier Street N1 ..... 144 E1
Collingham Gardens SW5 ..... 146 B6
Collingham Place SW5 ..... 146 B5
Collingham Road SW5 ..... 146 B5
Colnbrook Street SE1 ..... 149 H4
Colombo Street SE1 ..... 149 H1
Colonnade WC1N 144 D4
Coltman Street E14 ..... 151 L2
Commercial Road E1 ..... 150 D2
Commercial Road E14 ..... 151 K3
Commercial Street E1 ..... 150 B1
Compton Street EC1V 145 H3
Concert Hall Approach SE1 ..... 148 E2
Conder Street E14 ..... 151 K2
Conduit Mews W2 ..... 142 E6
Conduit Place W2 ..... 142 E6
Conduit Street W1S 143 L7
Congreve Street SE17 ..... 149 M5
Connaught Close W2 ..... 142 F7
Connaught Place W2 ..... 143 G7
Connaught Square W2 ..... 143 G6
Connaught Street W2 ..... 143 G6
Cons Street SE1 ..... 149 G2
Constitution Hill SW1A 147 L3
Content Street SE17 ..... 149 K5
Conway Street W1T 143 M4
Cookham Crescent SE16 ..... 151 H6
Cook's Road SE17 ..... 149 H8
Coombs Street N1 ..... 145 J1
Cooper's Lane Estate NW1 ..... 144 B1
Cooper's Road EC3N 150 B3
Copenhagen Place E14 ..... 151 L2
Cope Place W8 ..... 146 A4
Copley Court SE17 ..... 149 J8
Copley Street E1 ..... 151 H2
Copperfield Road E3 ..... 151 K1
Copperfield Street SE1 ..... 149 J2
Copthall Avenue EC2R 145 L6
Coptic Street WC1A 144 C5
Coral Street SE1 ..... 149 G3
Coram Street WC1H 144 C3
Cork Square E1W 150 E5
Cork Street W1S 143 M8
Corlett Street NW1 ..... 142 F5
Cornhill EC3V 145 L6
Cornwall Gardens SW7 ..... 146 C4
Cornwall Mews South SW7 ..... 146 C5
Cornwall Road SE1 ..... 148 F1
Cornwall Road SE1 ..... 149 G2
Cornwall Road SE1 ..... 150 E3
Cornwall Terrace Mews NW1 ..... 143 H4
Cornwood Drive E1 ..... 151 G2
Coronet Street N1 ..... 145 M2
Corporation Row EC1R 145 G3
Corsham Street N1 ..... 145 L2
Cosser Street SE1 ..... 148 F4
Cosway Street NW1 ..... 143 G4
Cottage Place SW3 ..... 146 F4
Cottesmore Gardens W8 ..... 146 B4
Cottons Lane SE1 ..... 149 M1
Coulson Street SW3 ..... 147 H6
Counter Street SE1 ..... 149 M1
County Street SE1 ..... 149 K5
Courtenay Square SE11 ..... 148 F7
Courtenay Street SE11 ..... 148 F6
Courtfield Gardens SW5 ..... 146 B5
Courtfield Mews * SW5 ..... 146 C5
Courtfield Road SW7 ..... 146 C5

Court Street E1 ..... 150 E1
Cousin Lane SE1 ..... 145 K8
Covent Garden ⊖ WC2E 144 D7
Covent Garden WC2E 144 D7
Coventry Street W1D 144 B8
Cowcross Street EC1M 145 H4
Cowper Street EC2A 145 L3
Crail Row SE17 ..... 149 L5
Cramer Street W1U 143 J5
Crampton Street SE17 ..... 149 J6
Cranbourn Street WC2H 144 C7
Cranleigh Street NW1 ..... 144 A1
Cranley Gardens SW7 ..... 146 D6
Cranley Mews SW7 ..... 146 D6
Cranley Place SW7 ..... 146 E6
Cranston Estate N1 ..... 145 L1
Cranwood Street EC1V 145 L2
Craven Hill W2 ..... 142 C7
Craven Hill Gardens W2 ..... 142 C7
Craven Hill Gardens W2 ..... 142 C7
Craven Road W2 ..... 142 D7
Craven Street WC2N 148 D1
Craven Terrace W2 ..... 142 D7
Crawford Passage EC1R 145 G3
Crawford Place W1H 143 G5
Crawford Street W1H 143 H5
Creechurch Lane EC3A 150 A3
Creed Lane EC4V 145 H7
Cresswell Place SW10 ..... 146 D6
Cressy Place E1 ..... 151 G1
Crestfield Street WC1H 144 D2
Crimscott Street SE1 ..... 150 A8
Crispin Street E1 ..... 150 B1
Cromer Street WC1H 144 D2
Crompton Street W2 ..... 142 D4
Cromwell Mews * SW7 ..... 146 E5
Cromwell Place SW7 ..... 146 E5
Cromwell Road SW5 ..... 146 B5
Cromwell Road SW7 ..... 146 E5
Crondall Court N1 ..... 145 M1
Crondall Street N1 ..... 145 L1
Cropley Street N1 ..... 145 K1
Crosby Row SE1 ..... 149 L3
Cross Lane EC3R 150 A4
Crosswall EC3N 150 B3
Crowder Street E1 ..... 150 E3
Crucifix Lane SE1 ..... 150 A6
Cruikshank Street WC1X 144 F1
Crutched Friars EC3N 150 A3
Cuba Street E14 ..... 151 M6
Cubitt Street WC1X 144 E2
Culford Gardens SW3 ..... 147 H6
Culling Road SE16 ..... 150 F7
Cullum Street EC3M 145 M7
Culross Street W1K 143 J8
Culworth Street NW8 ..... 142 F1
Cumberland Gardens WC1X 144 F2
Cumberland Gate W2 ..... 143 H7
Cumberland Market NW1 ..... 143 L2
Cumberland Street SW1V 147 L6
Cumberland Terrace NW1 ..... 143 K1
Cumberland Terrace Mews NW1 ..... 143 L1
Cumberland Wharf SE16 ..... 151 G6
Cumming Street N1 ..... 144 E1
Cundy Street SW1W 147 K6
Cunningham Place NW8 ..... 142 E3
Cureton Street SW1P 148 C6
Curlew Street SE1 ..... 150 B6
Cursitor Street EC4A 144 F6
Curtain Road EC2A 145 M3
Curtain Road EC2A 145 M4
Curzon Gate W2 ..... 147 K2
Curzon Street W1J 147 K1
Cuthbert Street W2 ..... 142 E4
Cutler Street EC3A 150 A2
Cynthia Street N1 ..... 144 F1
Cypress Place W1T 144 A4
Cyrus Street EC1V 145 H3

D

Dacre Street SW1H 148 B3
Dakin Place E1 ..... 151 J1
Dallington Street EC1V 145 H3
Damien Street E1 ..... 150 F2
Dane Street WC1R 144 E5
Dansey Place W1D 144 B7
Dante Road SE11 ..... 149 H5
Danvers Street SW3 ..... 146 F8
D'Arblay Street W1F 144 A6
Dartford Street SE17 ..... 149 K8
Dartmouth Street SW1H 148 B3
Darwin Street SE17 ..... 149 L5
Date Street SE17 ..... 149 K7
Davenant Street E1 ..... 150 D1
Daventry Street NW1 ..... 142 F4
Davidge Street SE1 ..... 149 H3
Davies Mews W1K 143 K7
Davies Street W1K 143 K7
Dawes Street SE17 ..... 149 L6
Dawson Place W2 ..... 142 A7
Deal Porters Way SE16 ..... 151 G8
Deal Street E1 ..... 150 D1
Dean Bradley Street SW1P 148 C5
Dean Close SE16 ..... 151 H6
Deancross Street E1 ..... 150 F3
Deanery Street W1K 147 K1
Dean Farrar Street SW1H 148 B3
Dean Ryle Street SW1P 148 C5
Dean's Buildings SE17 ..... 149 L6
Dean Stanley Street SW1P 148 C4
Dean Street W1D 144 B6
Dean's Yard SW1P 148 C4
Decima Street SE1 ..... 149 M4
Deck Close SE16 ..... 151 J6
Defoe Close SE16 ..... 151 K7
Delamere Street W2 ..... 142 C5
Delamere Terrace W2 ..... 142 B4
De Laune Street SE17 ..... 149 H7
Delaware Road W9 ..... 142 B3
Dellow Street E1 ..... 150 F3
Delverton Road SE17 ..... 149 H7
Denbigh Place SW1V 147 M6
Denbigh Mews SW1V 147 M6
Denbigh Street SW1V 148 A6
Denman Street W1D 144 B7
Denmark Street WC2H 144 C6
Denny Close SE11 ..... 149 G6
Denny Street SE11 ..... 149 G6
Denyer Street SW3 ..... 147 G5
Derby Gate SW1A 148 D3
Derby Street W1J 147 K1
Dering Street W1S 143 L6
Derry Street W8 ..... 146 B3

De Vere Gardens W8 ..... 146 C3
Deverell Street SE1 ..... 149 L4
Devonport Street E1 ..... 151 G3
Devonshire Close W1G 143 K4
Devonshire Mews South W1G 143 K4
Devonshire Mews West W1G 143 K4
Devonshire Place W1G 143 K4
Devonshire Place Mews W1G 143 K4
Devonshire Row EC2M 150 A2
Devonshire Square EC2M 150 A2
Devonshire Street W1G 143 K4
Devonshire Terrace W2 ..... 142 D7
De Walden Street W1G 143 K5
Dickens Estate SE16 ..... 150 D7
Dickens Square SE1 ..... 149 K4
Dilke Street SW3 ..... 147 H8
Dingley Place EC1V 145 K2
Dingley Road EC1V 145 J2
Discovery Walk E1W 150 E5
Disney Place SE1 ..... 149 K2
Distaff Lane EC4V 145 J7
Distin Street SE11 ..... 148 F6
Dockhead SE1 ..... 150 C7
Dockley Road SE16 ..... 150 D8
Dock Street E1 ..... 150 D4
Doddington Grove SE17 ..... 149 H7
Doddington Place SE17 ..... 149 H8
Dodson Street SE1 ..... 149 G3
Dod Street E14 ..... 151 M2
Dolben Street SE1 ..... 149 H2
Dolland Street SE11 ..... 148 E7
Dolphin Square SW1V 148 A7
Dolphin Square SW1V 148 B7
Dombey Street WC1N 144 E4
Dominion Street EC2A 145 L5
Donegal Street N1 ..... 144 F1
Dongola Road E1 ..... 151 J1
Donne Place SW3 ..... 147 G5
Doon Street SE1 ..... 148 F1
Doric Way NW1 ..... 144 B2
Dorset Rise EC4Y 145 G7
Dorset Square NW1 ..... 143 H4
Dorset Street W1U 143 H5
Doughty Mews WC1N 144 E3
Doughty Street WC1N 144 E3
Douglas Street SW1P 148 B6
Douro Place W8 ..... 146 C3
Douthwaite Square * E1W 150 D5
Dovehouse Street SW3 ..... 146 F6
Dover Street W1J 147 L1
Dover Street W1S 143 L8
Dowgate Hill EC4R 145 K7
Downfield Close W9 ..... 142 B4
Downing Street SW1A 148 C2
Down Street W1J 147 K2
Downtown Road SE16 ..... 151 K6
D'Oyley Street SW1X 147 J5
Draco Street SE17 ..... 149 J8
Drake Close SE16 ..... 151 H6
Draycott Avenue SW3 ..... 147 G5
Draycott Place SW3 ..... 147 H6
Draycott Terrace SW3 ..... 147 H5
Drayson Mews W8 ..... 146 A3
Drayton Gardens SW10 ..... 146 D6
Druid Street SE1 ..... 150 A6
Druid Street SE1 ..... 150 B6
Drummond Crescent NW1 ..... 144 B2
Drummond Gate * SW1V 148 B6
Drummond Road SE16 ..... 150 E8
Drummond Street NW1 ..... 144 A3
Drury Lane WC2B 144 D6
Dryden Court SE11 ..... 149 G5
Dryden Street WC2B 144 D6
Duchess Mews W1G 143 L5
Duchess Street W1B 143 L5
Duchy Street SE1 ..... 149 G1
Duckett Street E1 ..... 151 J1
Duck Lane W1F 144 B6
Dufferin Street EC1Y 145 K4
Duke of Wellington Place SW1W 147 K3
Duke of York Square SW3 ..... 147 H6
Duke of York Street SW1Y 148 A1
Duke Shore Wharf E14 ..... 151 K4
Duke's Lane W8 ..... 146 A2
Duke's Place EC3A 150 B2
Duke's Road WC1H 144 C2
Duke Street W1K 143 K7
Duke Street W1U 143 J6
Duke Street Hill SE1 ..... 149 M1
Duke Street St James's SW1Y 148 A1
Dunbar Wharf E14 ..... 151 L4
Duncannon Street WC2N 144 C8
Duncan Terrace N1 ..... 145 H1
Dundee Street E1W 150 E5
Dundee Wharf E14 ..... 151 L4
Dunelm Street E1 ..... 151 H2
Dunlop Place SE16 ..... 150 C8
Dunraven Street W1K 143 H7
Dunster Court EC3R 150 A3
Duplex Ride SW1X 147 H3
Durand's Wharf SE16 ..... 151 L6
Durham Row E1 ..... 151 J1
Durham Street SE11 ..... 148 E7
Durham Terrace W2 ..... 142 A6
Dyott Street WC1A 144 C6
Dysart Street EC2A 145 M4

E

Eagle Close EC1M 145 H4
Eagle Street WC1R 144 E5
Eardley Crescent SW5 ..... 146 A7
Earlham Street WC2H 144 C6
Earl's Court ≥⊖ SW5 ..... 146 A6
Earl's Court Gardens SW5 ..... 146 A6
Earl's Court Road SW5 ..... 146 A6
Earl's Court Square SW5 ..... 146 A6
Earlstoke Street EC1V 145 H2
Earl Street EC2A 145 M4
Earnshaw Street WC2H 144 C6
East Arbour Street E1 ..... 151 H2
Eastbourne Mews W2 ..... 142 D6
Eastbourne Terrace W2 ..... 142 D6
Eastcastle Street W1W 144 A6
Eastcheap EC3M 145 M7
Eastfield Street E14 ..... 151 L1
East India Dock Road E14 ..... 151 M3
East Lane SE16 ..... 150 D7
Easton Street WC1X 144 F3
East Poultry Avenue EC1A 145 H5
East Road N1 ..... 145 L2
East Smithfield E1W 150 C4

East Street SE17 ..... 149 L6
Eaton Close SW1W 147 J5
Eaton Gate SW1W 147 J5
Eaton Lane SW1W 147 L4
Eaton Mews North SW1W 147 J5
Eaton Mews South SW1W 147 K5
Eaton Mews West SW1W 147 J4
Eaton Row SW1W 147 K4
Eaton Square SW1W 147 K5
Eaton Terrace SW1W 147 J5
Ebbisham Drive SW8 ..... 148 E8
Ebury Bridge SW1W 147 K6
Ebury Bridge Road SW1W 147 K7
Ebury Mews SW1W 147 K5
Ebury Square SW1W 147 K6
Ebury Street SW1W 147 K5
Eccleston Bridge SW1W 147 L5
Eccleston Mews SW1X 147 K4
Eccleston Place SW1W 147 L5
Eccleston Square SW1V 147 L6
Eccleston Street SW1X 147 K4
Edbrooke Road W9 ..... 142 A3
Edge Street W8 ..... 146 A1
Edgware Road W2 ..... 142 F5
Edgware Road ⊖ NW1 ..... 142 F5
Edinburgh Gate SW1X 147 H3
Edith Grove SW10 ..... 146 C8
Edwards Mews W1H 143 J6
Egerton Crescent SW3 ..... 146 F5
Egerton Gardens SW3 ..... 146 F5
Egerton Terrace SW3 ..... 147 G4
Eglington Court SE17 ..... 149 J8
Elba Place SE17 ..... 149 K5
Eldon Place EC2M 145 L5
Eldon Road W8 ..... 146 B4
Eleanor Close SE16 ..... 151 H6
Elephant & Castle SE1 ..... 149 J4
Elephant & Castle ≥⊖ SE1 ..... 149 J5
Elephant Lane SE16 ..... 150 F6
Elephant Road SE17 ..... 149 J5
Elf Row E1W 151 G3
Elgar Street SE16 ..... 151 K7
Elgin Avenue W9 ..... 142 B2
Elgin Mews North W9 ..... 142 C2
Elgin Mews South W9 ..... 142 C2
Elia Mews N1 ..... 145 H1
Elia Street N1 ..... 145 H1
Elim Estate SE1 ..... 149 M3
Elim Street SE1 ..... 149 M3
Elizabeth Bridge SW1V 147 L6
Elizabeth Street SW1W 147 K5
Ellen Street E1 ..... 150 D3
Elliott's Row SE11 ..... 149 H5
Ellis Street SW1X 147 J5
Elmfield Way W9 ..... 142 A4
Elm Park Gardens SW10 ..... 146 E7
Elm Park Lane SW3 ..... 146 E7
Elm Park Road SW3 ..... 146 E8
Elm Place SW7 ..... 146 E7
Elms Mews W2 ..... 142 D7
Elm Street WC1X 144 F4
Elm Tree Road NW8 ..... 142 E2
Elnathan Mews W9 ..... 142 B4
Elsa Street E1 ..... 151 J1
Elsted Street SE17 ..... 149 L6
Elvaston Mews SW7 ..... 146 D4
Elvaston Place SW7 ..... 146 D4
Elverton Street SW1P 148 B5
Ely Place EC1N 145 G5
Elystan Place SW3 ..... 147 G6
Elystan Street SW3 ..... 146 F6
Embankment ⊖ WC2N 148 D1
Embankment Gardens SW3 ..... 147 H8
Embankment Place WC2N 148 D1
Emba Street SE16 ..... 150 D7
Emerald Street WC1N 144 E4
Emerson Street SE1 ..... 149 J1
Emery Hill Street SW1P 148 A5
Emery Street SE1 ..... 149 G3
Emperor's Gate SW7 ..... 146 C5
Empire Square SE1 ..... 149 L3
Empress Place SW6 ..... 146 A7
Endell Street WC2H 144 C6
Endsleigh Gardens WC1H 144 B3
Endsleigh Place WC1H 144 B3
Endsleigh Street WC1H 144 B3
Enford Street W1H 143 G5
English Grounds SE1 ..... 149 M1
Enid Street SE16 ..... 150 C8
Ennismore Gardens SW7 ..... 146 F3
Ennismore Gardens Mews SW7 ..... 146 F3
Ennismore Mews SW7 ..... 146 F3
Ennismore Street SW7 ..... 146 F4
Ensign Street E1 ..... 150 D4
Epworth Street EC2A 145 L3
Erasmus Street SW1P 148 C6
Errol Street EC1Y 145 K4
Essendine Road W9 ..... 142 A3
Essex Street WC2R 144 F7
Essex Villas W8 ..... 146 A3
Europa Place EC1V 145 J2
Euston ≥⊖ NW1 ..... 144 B2
Euston Road NW1 ..... 144 B3
Euston Square NW1 ..... 144 A3
Euston Square ⊖ NW1 ..... 144 A3
Euston Street NW1 ..... 144 A3
Evelyn Gardens SW7 ..... 146 D7
Evelyn Walk N1 ..... 145 L1
Eversholt Street NW1 ..... 144 A1
Everton Buildings NW1 ..... 143 M2
Ewer Street SE1 ..... 149 J2
Ewhurst Close E1 ..... 151 G1
Exchange Square EC2A 145 M4
Exeter Street WC2E 144 D7
Exhibition Road SW7 ..... 146 E3
Exmouth Market EC1R 145 G3
Exon Street SE17 ..... 149 M6
Exton Street SE1 ..... 148 F2
Eyre Street Hill EC1R 144 F4

F

Fairclough Street E1 ..... 150 D3
Fair Street SE1 ..... 150 B6
Falmouth Road SE1 ..... 149 K4
Fann Street EC1M 145 J4
Fanshaw Street N1 ..... 145 M1
Fareham Street W1D 144 B6
Farmer Street W8 ..... 146 A1
Farm Lane SW6 ..... 146 A8
Farm Street W1K 143 K8
Farnham Place SE1 ..... 149 J1

Farrance Street E14 .... 151 M3
Farringdon ⇌ EC1M 145 G4
Farringdon Lane EC1R 145 G4
Farringdon Road EC1R 144 F3
Farringdon Street EC1M 145 H5
Farrins Rents SE16 .... 151 K7
Farrow Place SE16 .... 151 K7
Farthing Fields * E1W 150 E5
Fashion Street E1 .... 150 B1
Faunce Street SE17 .... 149 H7
Fawcett Street SW10 .... 146 C8
Featherstone Street EC1Y 145 L3
Fenchurch Avenue EC3M 150 A3
Fenchurch Buildings EC3M 150 A3
Fenchurch Place EC3M 150 A3
Fenchurch Street EC3M 150 A3
Fenchurch Street ⇌ EC3M 150 A3
Fendall Street SE1 .... 150 B8
Fenning Street SE1 .... 149 M2
Fentiman Road SW8 .... 148 D8
Fernsbury Street WC1X 144 F3
Fetter Lane EC4A 145 G6
Fieldgate Street E1 .... 150 D2
Fielding Street SE17 .... 149 J7
Field Street WC1X 144 E1
Finborough Road SW10 .... 146 B8
Finch Lane EC3V 145 L6
Finland Street SE16 .... 151 K8
Finsbury Circus EC2M 145 L5
Finsbury Estate EC1R 145 G3
Finsbury Market EC2A 145 M4
Finsbury Square EC2A 145 L4
Finsbury Street EC2Y 145 L4
First Street SW3 .... 147 G5
Fishermans Drive SE16 .... 151 J6
Fisher Street WC1R 144 D5
Fisherton Street NW8 .... 142 E3
Fish Street Hill EC3R 145 L7
Fitzalan Street SE11 .... 148 F5
Fitzhardinge Street W1H 143 J6
Fitzroy Square W1T 143 M4
Fitzroy Street W1T 143 M4
Flamborough Street E14 .... 151 J3
Flank Street E1 .... 150 C4
Flaxman Terrace WC1H 144 C2
Fleet Street EC4A 145 G6
Fleming Road SE17 .... 149 H8
Fletcher Street E1 .... 150 D3
Flint Street SE17 .... 149 L6
Flitcroft Street WC2H 144 C6
Flockton Street SE16 .... 150 D7
Flood Street SW3 .... 147 G7
Flood Walk SW3 .... 147 G7
Floral Street WC2E 144 C7
Foley Street W1W 143 M5
Forbes Street E1 .... 150 D3
Fordham Street E1 .... 150 D2
Ford Square E1 .... 150 F2
Fore Street EC2Y 145 K5
Formosa Street W9 .... 142 C4
Forset Street W1H 143 G6
Forsyth Gardens SE17 .... 149 H8
Fort Street E1 .... 150 B1
Fortune Street EC1Y 145 K4
Forum Magnum Square SE1 .... 148 E3
Foster Lane EC2V 145 J6
Foulis Terrace SW7 .... 146 E6
Foundry Close SE16 .... 151 J5
Fournier Street E1 .... 150 B1
Fowey Close E1W 150 E5
Frampton Street NW8 .... 142 E4
Francis Street SW1P 148 A5
Frankland Close SE16 .... 150 F8
Franklin's Row SW3 .... 147 H6
Frazier Street SE1 .... 149 G3
Frean Street SE16 .... 150 C4
Frederick Close W2 .... 143 G7
Frederick Street WC1X 144 E2
Frederic Mews * SW1X 147 J3
Freemantle Street SE17 .... 149 M6
Friend Street EC1V 145 H2
Frith Street W1D 144 B6
Fulbourne Street E1 .... 150 E1
Fulford Street SE16 .... 150 F7
Fulham Road SW10 .... 146 D8
Fulham Road SW3 .... 146 F6
Furnival Street EC4A 144 F5
Fynes Street SW1P 148 B5

G

Gabriel's Wharf SE1 .... 149 G1
Gainsford Street SE1 .... 150 B6
Galleon Close SE16 .... 151 G6
Galsworthy Avenue E14 .... 151 K2
Galway Street EC1V 145 K2
Gambia Street SE1 .... 149 H2
Garden Road NW8 .... 142 D1
Garden Row SE1 .... 149 H4
Garden Street E1 .... 151 H1
Garden Terrace * SW1V 148 B6
Garden Walk EC2A 145 M3
Gard Street EC1V 145 J2
Garford Street E14 .... 151 M4
Garnault Place EC1R 145 G3
Garnet Street E1W 150 F4
Garrett Street EC1Y 145 K3
Garrick Street WC2E 144 C7
Garterway SE16 .... 151 H7
Garway Road W2 .... 142 B6
Gaspar Mews SW7 .... 146 C5
Gataker Street * SE16 .... 150 E8
Gate Mews SW7 .... 146 F3
Gateforth Street NW8 .... 142 F3
Gate Mews NW1 .... 143 L3
Gatesborough Street * EC2A 145 M3
Gate Street WC2A 144 E5
Gatliff Road SW1W 147 K7
Gaunt Street SE1 .... 149 J4
Gayfere Street SW1P 148 C4
Gaywood Street SE1 .... 149 H4
Gaza Street SE17 .... 149 H7
Gedling Place SE1 .... 150 C7
Gee Street EC1V 145 J3
George Mathers Road SE11 .... 149 H5
George Row SE16 .... 150 C7
George Street W1H 143 H6
George Yard W1K 143 K7
Geraldine Street SE1 .... 149 H4
Gerald Road SW1W 147 K5
Gerrard Street W1D 144 B7
Gerridge Street SE1 .... 149 G3
Gertrude Street SW10 .... 146 D8
Gibson Road SE11 .... 148 E5
Gilbert Place WC1A 144 C5

Gilbert Road SE11 .... 149 G5
Gilbert Street W1K 143 K7
Gildea Street W1W 143 L5
Gillingham Street SW1V 147 M5
Gill Street E14 .... 151 L3
Gilston Road SW10 .... 146 D7
Giltspur Street EC1A 145 H5
Gladstone Street SE1 .... 149 H4
Glamis Place E1W 151 G4
Glamis Road E1W 151 G4
Glasgow Terrace SW1V 147 M7
Glasshill Street SE1 .... 149 J3
Glasshouse Street W1B 144 A8
Glasshouse Walk SE11 .... 148 D7
Glasshouse Yard EC1 .... 145 J4
Glebe Place SW3 .... 146 F7
Gledhow Road SW5 .... 146 C6
Glentworth Street NW1 .... 143 H4
Globe Pond Road SE16 .... 151 J5
Globe Street SE1 .... 149 K3
Gloucester Court * EC3R 150 A4
Gloucester Gardens W2 .... 142 C6
Gloucester Mews W2 .... 142 D6
Gloucester Mews West W2 .... 142 C6
Gloucester Place W1H 143 H3
Gloucester Place W1U 143 H5
Gloucester Place Mews W1U 143 H5
Gloucester Road SW7 .... 146 C4
Gloucester Road SW6 .... 146 D6
Gloucester Road ⇌ SW7 .... 146 C5
Gloucester Square W2 .... 142 F6
Gloucester Street SW1V 147 M7
Gloucester Terrace W2 .... 142 B5
Gloucester Terrace W2 .... 142 D6
Gloucester Walk W8 .... 146 A2
Gloucester Way EC1R 145 G2
Glyn Street SE11 .... 148 E7
Godfrey Street SW3 .... 147 G6
Goding Street SE11 .... 148 D7
Godliman Street EC4V 145 J7
Godwin Close N1 .... 145 K1
Golden Hinde II SE1 .... 149 L1
Golden Jubilee Bridge WC2N 148 D1
Golden Lane EC1Y 145 J4
Golden Square W1F 144 A7
Golding Street E1 .... 150 E3
Goldney Road W9 .... 142 A4
Goldsmith Street EC2V 145 K6
Gomm Road SE16 .... 151 G8
Goodge Place W1T 144 A5
Goodge Street W1T 144 A5
Goodge Street ⇌ W1T 144 B5
Goodwin Close SE16 .... 150 C8
Gordon Place W8 .... 146 A2
Gordon Square WC1H 144 B3
Gordon Street WC1H 144 B3
Gore Street SW7 .... 146 D4
Goring Street * EC3A 150 A2
Gosfield Street W1W 143 L5
Goslett Yard WC2H 144 B6
Goswell Road EC1V 145 H1
Gough Street WC1X 144 F3
Goulston Street E1 .... 150 B2
Gower Mews WC1E 144 B5
Gower Place NW1 .... 144 A3
Gower Street WC1E 144 B3
Gower's Walk E1 .... 150 D2
Gracechurch Street EC3V 145 M7
Grafton Place NW1 .... 144 B2
Grafton Street W1S 143 L8
Grafton Way W1T 144 A4
Graham Street N1 .... 145 J1
Graham Terrace SW1W 147 J6
Granby Terrace NW1 .... 143 M1
Grand Avenue EC1A 145 H5
Grange Road SE1 .... 150 B8
Grange Walk SE1 .... 150 A8
Grange Yard SE1 .... 150 B8
Grantully Road W9 .... 142 B2
Granville Place W1H 143 J6
Granville Road NW6 .... 142 A1
Granville Square WC1X 144 F2
Grape Street WC2H 144 C6
Gravel Lane E1 .... 150 B2
Gray's Inn Road WC1X 144 D2
Gray's Inn Square WC1R 144 F5
Gray Street SE1 .... 149 G3
Great Castle Street W1G 143 L6
Great Central Street NW1 .... 143 G4
Great Chapel Street W1D 144 B6
Great College Street SW1P 148 C4
Great Cumberland
   Place W1H 143 H6
Great Dover Street SE1 .... 149 K3
Great Eastern Street EC2A 145 M3
Great George Street SW1P 148 C3
Great Guildford Street SE1 .... 149 J1
Great James Street WC1N 144 E4
Great Marlborough
   Street W1F 143 M7
Great Maze Pond SE1 .... 149 L2
Great New Portland
   Street * W1W 144 C7
Greatorex Street E1 .... 150 D1
Great Ormond Street WC1N 144 D4
Great Percy Street WC1X 144 F2
Great Peter Street SW1P 148 B4
Great Portland Street W1W 143 L4
Great Portland
   Street ⇌ W1W 143 L4
Great Pulteney Street W1F 144 A7
Great Queen Street WC2B 144 D6
Great Russell Street WC1B 144 C5
Great Scotland Yard SW1A 148 C1
Great Smith Street SW1P 148 C4
Great Suffolk Street SE1 .... 149 H2
Great Sutton Street EC1V 145 H4
Great Titchfield Street W1W 143 M4
Great Tower Street EC3M 145 M7
Great Tower Street EC3R 150 A4
Great Winchester
   Street EC2N 145 L6
Great Windmill Street W1D 144 B7
Greek Street W1D 144 B6
Greenacre Square SE16 .... 151 J6
Green Bank E1W 150 E5
Greenberry Street NW8 .... 142 F1
Greencoat Place SW1P 148 A5
Green Coat Row SW1P 148 A4
Greenfield Road E1 .... 150 D2
Greenham Close SE1 .... 148 F3
Green Park ⇌ W1J 147 M1
Green Street W1K 143 J7
Greenwell Street W1W 143 L4
Green Street E1 .... 151 K2
Grenade Street E14 .... 151 L4

Grendon Street NW8 .... 142 F3
Grenville Place SW7 .... 146 C5
Gresham Street EC2V 145 J6
Gresse Street W1T 144 B5
Greville Street EC1N 145 G5
Greycoat Place SW1P 148 B4
Greycoat Street SW1P 148 B4
Grigg's Place SE1 .... 150 A8
Grosvenor Bridge SW8 .... 147 L8
Grosvenor Crescent SW1X 147 J3
Grosvenor Crescent
   Mews SW1X 147 J3
Grosvenor Gardens SW1W 147 L4
Grosvenor Gardens Mews
   East SW1W 147 L4
Grosvenor Gardens Mews
   North SW1W 147 L4
Grosvenor Gardens Mews
   South * SW1W 147 L4
Grosvenor Gate W2 .... 143 H8
Grosvenor Hill W1K 143 L7
Grosvenor Place SW1X 147 K3
Grosvenor Road SW1V 147 L8
Grosvenor Square W1K 143 J7
Grosvenor Street W1K 143 K7
Grosvenor Terrace SE5 .... 149 J8
Grove End Road NW8 .... 142 D2
Guildhouse Street SW1V 147 M5
Guilford Street WC1N 144 D4
Guinness Square SE1 .... 149 M5
Gulliver Street SE16 .... 151 K8
Gunpowder Square EC4A 145 G6
Gun Street E1 .... 150 B1
Gunthorpe Street E1 .... 150 C2
Gutter Lane EC2V 145 J6
Guy Street SE1 .... 149 L3

H

Haberdasher Street N1 .... 145 L2
Haddonhall Estate SE1 .... 149 M4
Hainton Close E1 .... 150 F3
Halcrow Street * E1 .... 150 F2
Half Moon Street W1J 147 L1
Halford Road SW6 .... 146 A8
Halifield Estate W2 .... 142 C6
Hall Place W2 .... 142 E4
Hall Road NW8 .... 142 D2
Hall Street EC1V 145 H2
Halpin Place SE17 .... 149 M6
Halsey Street SW3 .... 147 G5
Hamilton Close NW8 .... 142 D2
Hamilton Close SE16 .... 151 K7
Hamilton Gardens NW8 .... 142 D2
Hamilton Place W1J 147 K2
Hamilton Terrace NW8 .... 142 C1
Hamlet Way SE1 .... 149 L3
Hammett Street EC3N 150 B4
Hampden Close NW1 .... 144 B1
Hampden Gurney Street W2 .... 143 H6
Hampstead Road NW1 .... 143 M2
Hampton Street SE17 .... 149 J6
Hanbury Street E1 .... 150 C1
Hand Court WC1V 144 E5
Handel Street WC1N 144 D3
Hankey Place SE1 .... 149 L3
Hannibal Road E1 .... 151 G1
Hanover Square W1S 143 L6
Hanover Street W1S 143 L7
Hans Crescent SW3 .... 147 H3
Hanson Street W1W 143 M4
Hans Place SW1X 147 H4
Hans Road SW3 .... 147 G4
Hans Street SW1X 147 H4
Hanway Place W1T 144 B6
Hanway Street W1T 144 B6
Harbet Road W2 .... 142 F5
Harbour Street WC1N 144 E4
Harcourt Street W1H 143 G5
Harcourt Terrace SW10 .... 146 C7
Hardinge Street E1W 151 G3
Hardwick Street EC1R 145 G2
Hardwidge Street SE1 .... 149 M2
Hardy Close SE16 .... 151 H6
Harewood Place W1G 143 L6
Harewood Row NW1 .... 143 G4
Harewoood Avenue NW1 .... 143 G4
Harford Street E1 .... 151 J1
Harleyford Road SE11 .... 148 E8
Harley Gardens SW10 .... 146 D7
Harley Place W1G 143 K5
Harley Street W1G 143 K4
Harmsworth Street SE17 .... 149 G7
Harold Estate SE1 .... 150 A8
Harper Road SE1 .... 149 K4
Harriet Street SW1X 147 H3
Harriet Walk SW1X 147 H3
Harrington Gardens SW7 .... 146 C6
Harrington Road SW7 .... 146 E5
Harrington Square NW1 .... 143 M1
Harrington Street NW1 .... 143 M2
Harrison Street WC1H 144 D2
Harrods SW1X 147 G3
Harrowby Street W1H 143 G6
Harrow Place E1 .... 150 B2
Harrow Road W2 .... 142 A4
Hart Street EC3R 150 A3
Hasker Street SW3 .... 147 G5
Hastings Street WC1H 144 C2
Hatfields SE1 .... 149 G1
Hatherley Grove W2 .... 142 B6
Hatteraick Road SE16 .... 151 G6
Hatton Garden EC1N 145 G4
Hatton Street W2 .... 142 F3
Hatton Wall EC1N 145 G4
Havering Street E1 .... 151 H3
Haverstock Street N1 .... 145 J1
Hawke Place * SE16 .... 151 H6
Haydon Street EC3N 150 B3
Hayes Place NW1 .... 143 G4
Hay Hill W1J 143 L8
Hayles Street SE11 .... 149 H5
Haymarket SW1Y 144 B8
Hayne Street EC1A 145 J4
Hay's Lane SE1 .... 149 M1
Hay's Mews W1J 143 L8
Haywood Place EC1R 145 K3
Headfort Place SW1X 147 K3
Head Street E1 .... 151 H2
Hearnshaw Street E14 .... 151 K2
Hearn Street EC2A 145 M4

Heathcote Street WC1N 144 E3
Heddon Street W1B 143 M7
Heddon Street W1S 144 A7
Hedger Street SE11 .... 149 H5
Heiron Street SE17 .... 149 J8
Hellings Street E1W 150 D5
Helmet Row EC1V 145 K3
Helsinki Square SE16 .... 151 L8
Henderson Drive NW8 .... 142 E3
Heneage Lane EC3A 150 A3
Heneage Street E1 .... 150 C1
Henrietta Place W1G 143 L6
Henrietta Street WC2E 144 D7
Henriques Street E1 .... 150 D2
Henshaw Street SE17 .... 149 L5
Herbal Hill EC1R 145 G4
Herbert Crescent SW1X 147 H4
Herbrand Street WC1H 144 C3
Hercules Road SE1 .... 148 F4
Hereford Road W2 .... 142 A6
Hereford Square SW7 .... 146 D6
Hermitage Street W2 .... 142 E5
Hermitage Wall E1W 150 D5
Hermit Street EC1V 145 H2
Heron Place SE16 .... 151 K5
Heron Quay E14 .... 151 M5
Herrick Street SW1P 148 C6
Hertford Street W1J 147 K2
Hertsmere Road E14 .... 151 M4
Hesper Mews SW5 .... 146 B6
Hessel Street E1 .... 150 E3
Hewett Street EC2A 145 M3
Heygate Street SE17 .... 149 J5
Hide Place SW1P 148 B6
High Holborn WC1V 144 E5
High Street
   Kensington ⇌ W8 .... 146 A3
Hildyard Road SW6 .... 146 A8
Hilliards Court E1W 150 F5
Hillingdon Street SE17 .... 149 J8
Hill Road NW8 .... 142 D1
Hills Place W1F 143 M6
Hill Street W1J 143 K8
Hinde Street W1U 143 K6
Hind Grove E14 .... 151 M3
Hindgrove Area E14 .... 151 M3
Hithe Grove SE16 .... 151 G8
HMS Belfast SE1 .... 150 A5
Hobart Place SW1W 147 K4
Hobury Street SW10 .... 146 D8
Hogarth Road SW5 .... 146 B6
Holbein Mews SW1W 147 J6
Holbein Place SW1W 147 J6
Holborn EC1N 145 G5
Holborn ⇌ WC2B 144 E5
Holborn Circus EC1N 145 G5
Holborn Viaduct EC1A 145 G5
Holford Street WC1X 144 F2
Holland Street SE1 .... 149 H1
Holland Street W8 .... 146 A3
Hollen Street W1F 144 A6
Holles Street W1C 143 L6
Hollywood Road SW10 .... 146 C8
Holyoak Road SE11 .... 149 H5
Holyrood Street SE1 .... 149 M2
Holyrood Street SE1 .... 150 A6
Holywell Row EC2A 145 M4
Homefield Street * N1 .... 145 M1
Homer Row W1H 143 G5
Homer Street W1H 143 G5
Hooper Street E1 .... 150 D3
Hopetown Street E1 .... 150 C1
Hopkins Street W1F 144 A7
Hopton Street SE1 .... 149 H1
Hopwood Road SE17 .... 149 L8
Hornton Place W8 .... 146 A3
Hornton Street W8 .... 146 A2
Horse & Dolphin Yard W1D 144 B7
Horseferry Road E14 .... 151 J3
Horseferry Road SW1P 148 B4
Horse Guards Avenue SW1A 148 C2
Horse Guards Parade SW1A 148 C2
Horse Guards Road SW1A 148 C2
Horselydown Lane SE1 .... 150 B6
Horsley Street SE17 .... 149 K8
Hosier Lane EC1A 145 H5
Hothfield Place SE16 .... 151 G8
Hotspur Street SE11 .... 148 F6
Houghton Street WC2A 144 E6
Houndsditch EC3A 150 A2
Houses of Parliament SW1A 148 D3
Howick Place SW1E 148 A4
Howland Street W1T 144 A4
Howland Way SE16 .... 151 K7
Howley Place W2 .... 142 D4
Hoxton Square N1 .... 145 M2
Hoxton Street N1 .... 145 M1
Hudson Place SW1V 147 M5
Hugh Mews SW1V 147 L6
Hugh Street SW1V 147 L5
Hugh Street SW1V 147 L6
Hull Close SE16 .... 151 J6
Hull Street EC1V 145 J2
Hungerford Bridge SE1 .... 148 E1
Hunter Close SE1 .... 149 M4
Hunter Street WC1N 144 D3
Huntley Street WC1E 144 A4
Huntsman Street SE17 .... 149 M6
Huntsworth Mews NW1 .... 143 H3
Hurley Crescent SE16 .... 151 H6
Hutching's Street E14 .... 151 M7
Hutton Street EC4Y 145 G7
Hyde Park W2 .... 147 G1
Hyde Park Corner W1J 147 K2
Hyde Park Corner ⇌ W1J 147 K2
Hyde Park Court SW7 .... 146 D3
Hyde Park Crescent W2 .... 142 F6
Hyde Park Garden Mews W2 .... 142 F7
Hyde Park Gardens W2 .... 142 F7
Hyde Park Gate SW7 .... 146 C3
Hyde Park Gate SW7 .... 146 D3
Hyde Park Square W2 .... 142 F7
Hyde Park Street W2 .... 142 F7

I

Idol Lane EC3R 145 M7
Ifield Road SW10 .... 146 B8
Iliffe Street SE17 .... 149 J6
Iliffe Yard SE17 .... 149 J6
Imperial College Road SW7 .... 146 D4
Imperial War Museum SE1 .... 149 G4
India Street EC3N 150 B3
Ingestre Place W1F 144 A7
Ingleton Street EC1R 144 F1

Ingram Close SE11 .... 148 E5
Inner Circle NW1 .... 143 J2
Inverness Terrace W2 .... 142 B6
Inverness Terrace Gate W2 .... 142 C8
Invicta Plaza SE1 .... 149 H1
Inville Road SE17 .... 151 L7
Ironmonger Lane EC2V 145 K6
Ironmonger Row EC1V 145 K2
Irving Street WC2N 144 C8
Isambard Place SE16 .... 151 G6
Island Row E14 .... 151 K3
Iverna Court W8 .... 146 A4
Iverna Gardens W8 .... 146 A4
Ives Street SW3 .... 147 G5
Ivor Place NW1 .... 143 G4
Ixworth Place SW3 .... 146 F6

J

Jacob Street SE1 .... 150 C6
Jamaica Gate SE16 .... 151 G8
Jamaica Road SE1 .... 150 C7
Jamaica Road SE16 .... 150 E7
Jamaica Street E1 .... 151 G2
Jamaica Wharf SE1 .... 150 C6
James Street W1U 143 K6
James Street WC2E 144 D7
Jameson Street W8 .... 142 A1
Jamuna Close E14 .... 151 K1
Janeway Street SE16 .... 150 D7
Jardine Road E1W 151 J4
Java Wharf SE1 .... 150 C6
Jay Mews SW7 .... 146 D3
Jermyn Street SW1Y 144 A8
Jerome Crescent NW8 .... 142 F3
Jewery Street EC3N 150 B3
Joan Street SE1 .... 149 G2
Jockey's Fields WC1R 144 E4
Johanna Street SE1 .... 148 F3
John Adam Street WC2N 144 D8
John Carpenter Street EC4Y 145 G7
John Felton Road SE16 .... 150 D7
John Fisher Street E1 .... 150 C4
John Islip Street SW1P 148 C5
John Prince's Street W1G 143 L6
John Roll Way SE16 .... 150 D7
John Ruskin Street SE5 .... 149 J8
John Slip Street SW1P 148 C6
John's Mews WC1N 144 E4
Johnson's Place SW1V 148 A7
Johnson Street E1 .... 151 G3
John Street WC1N 144 E4
Joiner Street SE1 .... 149 L1
Jonathan Street SE11 .... 148 E6
Jubilee Place SW3 .... 147 G6
Jubilee Street E1 .... 151 G2
Jubilee Walk W8 .... 146 B1
Judd Street WC1H 144 C2
Junction Mews W2 .... 142 F5
Juxon Street SE11 .... 148 E5

K

Katherine Close SE16 .... 151 H5
Kean Street WC2B 144 E6
Keel Close SE16 .... 151 J6
Keeley Street WC2B 144 E6
Keeton's Road SE16 .... 150 E7
Kell Street SE1 .... 149 H3
Kelso Place W8 .... 146 B4
Kemble Street WC2B 144 E6
Kempsford Gardens SW5 .... 146 A7
Kempsford Road SE11 .... 149 G6
Kendall Place W1U 143 J5
Kendal Street W2 .... 143 G6
Kennet Street E1W 150 D5
Kenning Street SE16 .... 151 G6
Kennings Way SE11 .... 149 G7
Kennington ⇌ SE11 .... 149 H7
Kennington Lane SE11 .... 148 E7
Kennington Oval SE11 .... 148 E8
Kennington Park
   Gardens SE11 .... 149 G8
Kennington Park Place SE11 .... 149 G7
Kennington Park Road SE11 .... 149 G7
Kennington Road SE1 .... 148 F4
Kennington Road SE11 .... 149 G5
Kennnington Oval SE11 .... 148 F8
Kenrick Place W1U 143 J5
Kensington Church Street W8 .... 146 A1
Kensington Court W8 .... 146 B3
Kensington Gardens W2 .... 146 C1
Kensington Gardens
   Square W2 .... 142 B6
Kensington Gate W8 .... 146 C4
Kensington Gore SW7 .... 146 D3
Kensington High Street W8 .... 146 A4
Kensington Palace
   Gardens W8 .... 146 B1
Kensington Palace
   Gardens W8 .... 146 B2
Kensington Place W8 .... 146 A1
Kensington Road SW7 .... 147 G3
Kensington Road W8 .... 146 B3
Kensington Square W8 .... 146 B3
Kenton Street WC1H 144 C3
Kenway Road SW5 .... 146 A6
Keystone Close N1 .... 144 D1
Keyworth Street SE1 .... 149 H4
Kia Oval (Surrey County
   Cricket Ground) SE11 .... 148 F8
Kilburn Park Road NW6 .... 142 A2
Kildare Terrace W2 .... 142 A6
Killick Street N1 .... 144 E1
Kinburn Street SE16 .... 151 H6
Kinder Street E1 .... 150 E2
King & Queen Wharf SE16 .... 151 H5
King and Queen Street SE17 .... 149 K6
King Charles Street SW1A 148 C3
Kingdom Street W2 .... 142 C5
King Edward Street EC1A 145 J6
King Edward Walk SE1 .... 149 G4
King James Street SE1 .... 149 H3
Kingly Street W1F 143 M7
King's Arms Yard EC2R 145 L6
King's Bench Street SE1 .... 149 H2
Kingscote Street EC4V 145 H7
King's Cross ⇌ N1C 144 D1
King's Cross Road WC1X 144 E2
King's Cross Square N1C 144 D1
King's Cross St
   Pancras ⊖ N1C 144 D1

Kingsgate Walk * SW1E 148 A4
King's Head Yard SE1 ...... 149 L1
King's Mews WC1N 144 F4
Kingsmill Terrace NW8 ..... 142 E1
King Square EC1V 145 J2
King's Road SW3 .... 146 E8
King's Scholars
  Passage SW1P 147 M5
King's Stairs Close SE16 .... 150 F6
King Street WC2E 144 D7
King Street SW1Y 148 A1
King Street EC2V 145 K6
Kingsway WC2B 144 E6
King William Street EC4N ... 145 L7
Kinnerton Place
  North * SW1X 147 J3
Kinnerton Place
  South * SW1X 147 J3
Kinnerton Street SW1X 147 J3
Kinnerton Yard * SW1X 147 J3
Kipling Estate SE1 .... 149 L3
Kipling Street SE1 .... 149 L3
Kirby Estate SE16 .... 150 D7
Kirby Grove SE1 .... 149 M3
Kirby Street EC1N 145 G4
Knaresborough Place SW5 ... 146 B5
Knightrider Street EC4V 145 H7
Knightsbridge SW1X 147 H3
Knightsbridge ⊖ SW3 ...... 147 H3
Knox Street W1H 143 H4
Kynance Mews SW7 .... 146 C4
Kynance Place SW7 .... 146 C4

L

Lackington Street EC2A 145 L4
Lafone Street SE1 .... 150 B6
Lagado Mews SE16 .... 151 H5
Lambeth Bridge SW1P 148 D5
Lambeth High Street SE1 .... 148 E5
Lambeth Hill EC4V 145 J7
Lambeth North ⊖ SE1 ...... 148 F3
Lambeth Palace Road SE1 ... 148 E4
Lambeth Road SE1 .... 148 F4
Lambeth Walk SE11 .... 148 F5
Lamb's Conduit Street WC1N . 144 E4
Lamb's Passage EC1Y 145 K4
Lamb Street E1 .... 150 B1
Lamb Way SE1 .... 150 A7
Lamlash Street SE11 .... 149 H5
Lanark Place W9 .... 142 D3
Lanark Road W9 .... 142 B1
Lancaster Gate W2 .... 142 D7
Lancaster Gate W2 .... 142 D8
Lancaster Gate ⊖ W2 ...... 142 E7
Lancaster Mews W2 .... 142 D7
Lancaster Place WC2E 144 E7
Lancaster Street SE1 .... 149 H3
Lancaster Terrace W2 ...... 142 E7
Lancaster Walk W2 .... 142 D8
Lancelot Place SW7 .... 147 G3
Lancing Street NW1 .... 144 B2
Lanesborough Place * SW1X . 147 J3
Langdale Street E1 .... 150 E3
Langford Place NW8 .... 142 D1
Langham Place W1B 143 L5
Langham Street W1W 143 L5
Langham Street W1W 143 M5
Langley Lane SW8 .... 148 D8
Langley Street WC2H 144 C7
Langton Close WC1X 144 E3
Lanhill Road W9 .... 142 A1
Lansdowne Place SE1 ...... 149 L4
Lant Street SE1 .... 149 J3
Larcom Street SE17 .... 149 K6
Lauderdale Road W9 .... 142 B3
Laud Street SE11 .... 148 E7
Launcelot Street SE1 .... 148 F3
Launceston Place W8 .... 146 C4
Laurence Pountney
  Lane EC4V 145 L7
Lavender Road SE16 .... 151 K5
Lavender Wharf SE16 ...... 151 K4
Lavington Street SE1 .... 149 J1
Lawn Lane SW8 .... 148 D8
Lawrence Street SW3 .... 146 F8
Lawrence Wharf SE16 ...... 151 L6
Law Street SE1 .... 149 L4
Laxton Place NW1 .... 143 L3
Laystall Street EC1R 144 F4
Leadenhall Street EC3A 150 A3
Leadenhall Street EC3V 145 M6
Leake Street SE1 .... 148 E2
Leather Lane EC1N 145 G4
Leathermarket Street SE1 ... 149 M3
Leeke Street WC1X 144 E2
Lees Place W1K 143 J7
Leicester Square ⊖ WC2H .. 144 C7
Leicester Square WC2H 144 C7
Leicester Street WC2H 144 B7
Leigh Street WC1H 144 C3
Leinster Gardens W2 .... 142 C6
Leinster Mews W2 .... 142 C7
Leinster Place W2 .... 142 C7
Leinster Square W2 .... 142 A7
Leinster Terrace W2 .... 142 C7
Leman Street E1 .... 150 C3
Lennox Gardens SW1X 147 G4
Lennox Gardens Mews SW1X . 147 G5
Leonard Street EC2A 145 L3
Leopold Estate E3 .... 151 M1
Leopold Street E3 .... 151 L1
Leroy Street SE1 .... 149 M5
Lever Street EC1V 145 J2
Lewisham Street SW1H 148 B3
Lexham Gardens W8 .... 146 A5
Lexham Mews W8 .... 146 A5
Lexington Street W1F 144 A7
Leyden Street E1 .... 150 B2
Leydon Close SE16 .... 151 H5
Library Street SE1 .... 149 H3
Lidlington Place NW1 ...... 144 A1
Lilestone Street NW8 ...... 142 F3
Lilley Close E1W 150 D5
Lillie Road SW6 .... 146 A7
Lillie Yard SW6 .... 146 A7
Lime Close E1W 150 D5
Limeburner Lane EC4M 145 H6
Lime Street EC3M 145 M6
Limehouse Causeway E14 ... 151 L4
Limehouse Link E14 .... 151 L3
Limehouse ⊖ E14 .... 151 J3
Limerston Street SW10 ..... 146 D8
Lime Street EC3M 145 M6
Lincoln's Inn Fields WC2A ... 144 E6
Linden Gardens W2 .... 142 A8

Lindley Street E1 .... 150 F1
Lindsay Square SW1V 148 B7
Lindsey Street EC1A 145 H4
Linhope Street NW1 .... 143 G3
Linsey Street SE16 .... 150 D8
Lisle Street WC2H 144 B7
Lisson Green Estate NW8 ... 142 F3
Lisson Grove NW1 .... 143 G4
Lisson Grove NW8 .... 142 F3
Lisson Street NW1 .... 142 F4
Litchfield Street WC2H 144 C7
Little Argyll Street W1F 143 M6
Little Britain EC1A 145 J5
Little Chester Street SW1X .. 147 K4
Little George Street SW1P ... 148 C3
Little Marlborough
  Street W1F 144 A7
Little New Street EC4A 145 G6
Little Portland Street W1G ... 143 L6
Little Russell Street WC1A ... 144 C5
Little St James's Street SW1A . 147 M2
Little Sanctuary SW1A 148 C3
Little Somerset Street E1 ... 150 B3
Little Titchfield Street W1W . 143 M5
Liverpool Grove SE17 ...... 149 K7
Liverpool Street EC2M 145 M5
Liverpool Street ⊖ EC2M ... 145 M5
Lizard Street EC1V 145 K3
Llewellyn Street SE16 ...... 150 D7
Lloyd Baker Street WC1X ... 144 F2
Lloyd's Avenue EC3N 150 B3
Lloyd Square WC1X 144 F2
Lloyds Row EC1R 145 G2
Lloyd's Street WC1X 144 F2
Locksley Estate E14 .... 151 L2
Locksley Street E14 .... 151 L1
Lockyer Street SE1 .... 149 L3
Lodge Road NW8 .... 142 F3
Loftie Street SE16 .... 150 D7
Logan Place W8 .... 146 A5
Lolesworth Close E1 .... 150 B1
Lollard Street SE11 .... 148 F5
Lollard Street SE11 .... 148 F6
Loman Street SE1 .... 149 J2
Lomas Street E1 .... 150 D1
Lombard Lane EC4Y 145 G6
Lombard Street EC3V 145 L7
London Bridge EC4R 145 L8
London Bridge ⊖≥ SE1 .... 149 L1
London Bridge Street SE1 ... 149 L1
London Dungeon SE1 ...... 148 E2
London Eye SE1 .... 148 E2
London Mews W2 .... 142 E6
London Road SE1 .... 149 H4
London Street EC3R 150 A3
London Street W2 .... 142 E6
London Transport
  Museum WC2E 144 D7
London Wall EC2M 145 K5
London Zoo ZSL NW1 ...... 143 J1
Long Acre WC2E 144 D7
Longford Street NW1 ...... 143 L3
Long Lane EC1A 145 J5
Long Lane SE1 .... 149 L3
Longmoore Street SW1V ... 147 M5
Longridge Road SW5 ...... 146 A5
Longville Road SE11 .... 149 H5
Long Walk SE1 .... 150 A8
Long Yard WC1N 144 E4
Lord North Street SW1P 148 C4
Lord's Cricket Ground NW8 . 142 E2
Lorenzo Street WC1X 144 E1
Lorrimore Road SE17 ...... 149 J8
Lorrimore Square SE17 ..... 149 H8
Lothbury EC2R 145 L6
Loughborough Street SE11 . 148 F7
Lovat Lane EC3R 145 M7
Love Lane EC2V 145 K6
Lovell Place SE16 .... 151 K7
Lowell Street E14 .... 151 K2
Lower Belgrave Street SW1W . 147 K4
Lower Grosvenor Place SW1W . 147 L4
Lower James Street W1F 144 A7
Lower John Street W1F 144 A7
Lower Marsh SE1 .... 148 F3
Lower Road SE16 .... 151 G7
Lower Sloane Street SW1W . 147 J6
Lower Thames Street EC3R .. 150 A4
Lower Thames Street EC3R .. 145 M8
Lowndes Close * SW1X 147 J4
Lowndes Place SW1X 147 J4
Lowndes Square SW1X 147 H3
Lowndes Street SW1X 147 J4
Lucan Place SW3 .... 146 F5
Lucey Road SE16 .... 150 C8
Ludgate Circus EC4M 145 H6
Ludgate Hill EC4M 145 H6
Luke Street EC2A 145 M3
Lukin Street E1 .... 151 G3
Lumley Street W1K 143 K7
Lupus Street SW1V 147 L7
Lupus Street SW1V 148 B7
Luton Street NW8 .... 142 E4
Luxborough Street W1U 143 J4
Lyall Mews SW1X 147 J4
Lyall Street SW1X 147 J4
Lyons Place NW8 .... 142 E3
Lytham Street SE17 .... 149 K7

M

Macclesfield Road EC1V 145 J2
Macclesfield Street * W1D .. 144 B7
Mace Close E1W 150 E5
Macklin Street WC2B 144 D6
Mackworth Street NW1 .... 143 M2
Macleod Street SE17 ...... 149 K7
Madame Tussauds NW1 .... 143 J4
Maddox Street W1S 143 M7
Magdalen Street SE1 ...... 149 M2
Magee Street SE11 .... 148 F8
Maguire Street SE1 .... 150 C6
Maida Avenue W9 .... 142 D4
Maida Vale W9 .... 142 C2
Maida Vale ⊖ W9 .... 142 C2
Maiden Lane SE1 .... 149 K1
Maiden Lane WC2E 144 D7
Major Road SE16 .... 150 D7
Makins Street SW3 .... 147 G6
Malet Street WC1E 144 B4
Mallord Street SW3 .... 146 E8
Mallory Street NW8 ...... 142 F3
Mallow Street EC1Y 145 L3
Malta Street EC1V 145 H3
Maltby Street SE1 .... 150 B7

Manchester Square W1U ... 143 J6
Manchester Street W1U 143 J5
Manciple Street SE1 ...... 149 L3
Mandeville Place W1U 143 K6
Manette Street W1D 144 B6
Manilla Street E14 .... 151 M6
Manningford Close EC1V ... 145 H2
Manor Place SE17 .... 149 J7
Manresa Road SW3 .... 146 F7
Mansell Street E1 .... 150 C3
Mansfield Mews W1G 143 L5
Mansfield Street W1G 143 L5
Mansion House ⊖ EC4V ... 145 K7
Manson Mews SW7 .... 146 D5
Manson Place SW7 .... 146 D6
Mapleleaf Square SE16 .... 151 J6
Maples Place E1 .... 150 F1
Maple Street W1T 143 M4
Marble Arch ⊖ W1C 143 H7
Marchmont Street WC1H ... 144 C3
Margaret Street W1W 143 L6
Margaretta Terrace SW3 ... 146 F7
Margery Street WC1X 144 F3
Marigold Street SE16 ..... 150 E7
Marine Street SE16 .... 150 C7
Market Mews W1J 147 K1
Market Place W1W 143 M6
Markham Square SW3 ..... 147 G6
Markham Street SW3 ..... 147 G6
Mark Lane EC3R 150 A4
Marlborough Gate W2 ..... 142 E7
Marlborough Place NW8 ... 142 C1
Marlborough Road SW1A .. 148 A2
Marlborough Street SW3 ... 146 F6
Marloes Road W8 .... 146 B4
Marlow Way SE16 .... 151 H6
Maroon Street E14 .... 151 K2
Marshall Street W1F 144 A7
Marshalsea Road SE1 ..... 149 K2
Marsham Street SW1P 148 C5
Marsh Wall E14 .... 151 M5
Martha's Buildings EC1V ... 145 K3
Martha Street E1 .... 150 F3
Martin Lane EC4V 145 L7
Maryland Road W9 .... 142 A4
Marylands Road W9 ...... 142 A4
Marylebone ⊖≥ NW1 ..... 143 G4
Marylebone Flyover W2 ... 142 E5
Marylebone High Street W1U . 143 K5
Marylebone Lane W1U 143 K6
Marylebone Lane W1U 143 K6
Marylebone Road NW1 .... 143 G4
Marylebone Street W1G ... 143 K5
Marylee Way SE11 .... 148 F6
Masjid Lane E14 .... 151 K2
Mason Street SE17 .... 149 M5
Massinger Street SE17 .... 149 M6
Masters Street E1 .... 151 J1
Matlock Street E14 .... 151 J2
Matthew Parker Street SW1H . 148 C3
Maunsel Street SW1P 148 B5
Mayfair Place W1J 147 L1
Mayflower Street SE16 .... 150 F7
Mayford Estate NW1 ...... 144 A1
Maynards Quay E1W 150 F4
May's Street WC2N 144 C8
McAuley Close SE1 .... 148 F4
McLeod's Mews SW7 ..... 146 C5
Meadcroft Road SE11 ..... 149 G8
Meadcroft Road SE11 ..... 149 H8
Meadow Road SW8 ...... 148 E8
Meadow Row SE1 .... 149 J5
Mead Row SE1 .... 148 F4
Meakin Estate SE1 .... 149 M4
Mecklenburgh Square WC1N . 144 E3
Medway Street SW1P 148 B5
Meeting House Alley E1W .. 150 E5
Melbourne Street WC1H ... 144 H4
Melcombe Place NW1 ..... 143 G4
Melcombe Street NW1 .... 143 H4
Melina Place NW8 .... 142 D2
Melior Street SE1 .... 149 M2
Melton Street NW1 .... 144 A2
Memorial Gates SW1W 147 K3
Mepham Street SE1 ...... 148 F2
Mercer Street WC2H 144 C7
Merchant Square W2 ..... 142 E5
Merlin Street EC1R 144 F2
Mermaid Court SE1 ...... 149 K2
Merrick Square SE1 ...... 149 K4
Merrington Road SW6 .... 146 A8
Merrow Street SE17 ...... 149 L7
Methley Street SE11 ...... 148 F6
Meymott Street SE1 ...... 149 G2
Micawber Street N1 ...... 145 K1
Micklethwaite Lane SW6 .. 146 A8
Middlesex Street E1 ...... 150 A1
Middlesex Street E1 ...... 150 B2
Middle Street EC1A 145 J5
Middle Temple WC2R 144 F7
Middle Temple Lane EC4Y .. 144 F7
Middleton Drive SE16 ..... 151 H6
Midland Road NW1 .... 144 C1
Midship Close SE16 ...... 151 H6
Milborne Grove SW10 .... 146 D7
Milcote Street SE1 .... 149 H3
Miles Street SW8 .... 148 D8
Milford Lane WC2R 144 F7
Milk Street EC2V 145 K6
Milk Yard E1W 151 G4
Millbank SW1P 148 D4
Millennium Bridge SE1 .... 145 J8
Millennium Harbour E14 ... 151 M6
Milligan Street E14 ...... 151 L4
Millman Mews WC1N 144 E4
Millman Street WC1N 144 E4
Mill Place E14 .... 151 K3
Millstream Road SE1 ..... 150 B7
Mill Street SE1 .... 150 C7
Mill Street W1S 143 L7
Milner Street SW3 .... 147 G5
Milton Street EC2Y 145 K4
Milverton Street SE11 .... 149 G7
Minera Mews SW1W 147 J5
Minories EC3N 150 B3
Mitchell Street EC1V 145 J3
Mitre Road SE1 .... 149 G3
Mitre Street EC3A 150 A3
Molyneux Street W1H 143 G5
Monck Street SW1P 148 C4
Monkton Street SE11 ..... 148 F5
Monkwell Square EC2Y ... 145 K5
Monmouth Place W2 ..... 142 A6
Monmouth Road W2 ..... 142 A6
Monmouth Street WC2H ... 144 C6
Montague Close SE1 ...... 149 L1
Montague Place EC3R 150 A3
Montague Place WC1B 144 C5
Montague Street SE1 ..... 149 K2
Montague Street WC1B ... 144 C5

Montagu Mansions W1U ... 143 H5
Montagu Mews North W1H . 143 H5
Montagu Mews West W1H . 143 H6
Montagu Place W1H 143 H5
Montagu Row W1U 143 H5
Montagu Square W1H 143 H5
Montagu Street W1H 143 H6
Montford Place SE11 ..... 148 F7
Monthorpe Road E1 ...... 150 C1
Montpelier Square SW7 ... 147 G3
Montpelier Street SW7 .... 147 G3
Montpelier Walk SW7 ..... 146 G3
Montrose Place SW1X 147 K3
Monument ⊖ EC4R 145 L7
Monument Street EC3R ... 145 L7
Monument Street EC3R ... 145 M7
Monza Street E1W 151 G4
Moodkee Street SE16 ..... 151 G7
Moore Street SW3 .... 147 H5
Moorfields EC2Y 145 L5
Moorgate EC2R 145 L6
Moorgate ⊖≥ EC2Y 145 L5
Moor Lane EC2Y 145 K5
Moor Street W1D 144 C7
Mora Street EC1V 145 K2
Morecambe Street SE17 ... 149 K6
Moreland Street EC1V 145 H2
More London SE1 .... 150 A5
Moreton Place SW1V 148 A6
Moreton Street SW1V 148 B6
Moreton Terrace SW1V ... 148 A6
Morgan's Lane SE1 .... 149 M2
Morgan's Lane SE1 .... 150 A5
Morley Street SE1 .... 149 G3
Mornington Crescent NW1 . 143 M1
Mornington Place NW1 ... 143 L1
Mornington Terrace NW1 .. 143 L1
Morocco Street SE1 ...... 150 A7
Morpeth Terrace SW1P 147 M5
Morris Street E1 .... 150 F3
Morshead Road W9 ...... 142 A2
Mortimer Market WC1E ... 144 A4
Mortimer Street W1T 144 A5
Mortimer Street W1W 143 M5
Morton Place SE1 .... 148 F4
Morwell Street WC1B 144 B5
Moscow Place W2 .... 142 B7
Moscow Road W2 .... 142 B7
Mossop Street SW3 ...... 147 G5
Motcomb Street SW1X 147 J4
Mount Gate W2 .... 146 E2
Mount Mills EC1V 145 J3
Mount Pleasant WC1X 144 F4
Mount Row W1K 143 K8
Mount Street W1K 143 K8
Mount Street Mews W1K .. 143 K8
Mount Terrace E1 .... 150 E1
Moxon Street W1U 143 J5
Mulberry Street E1 ...... 150 D2
Mulberry Walk SW3 ..... 146 E8
Mulready Street NW8 .... 142 F4
Mundy Street N1 .... 145 M2
Munster Square W1 ...... 143 L3
Munton Road SE17 ...... 149 K5
Murphy Street SE1 ...... 148 F3
Murray Grove N1 .... 145 K1
Musbury Street E1 ...... 151 G2
Muscovy Street EC3N 150 A4
Museum of London EC2Y .. 145 J5
Museum Street WC1A 144 C5
Myddelton Passage EC1R .. 145 G2
Myddelton Square EC1R ... 145 G1
Myddelton Street EC1R ... 145 G3
Myrdle Street E1 .... 150 D2

N

Naoroji Street WC1X 144 F2
Napier Grove N1 .... 145 K1
Narrow Street E14 .... 151 K4
Nash Street NW1 .... 143 L2
Nassau Street W1W 143 M5
Nathaniel Close * E1 ..... 150 C2
National Portrait
  Gallery WC2H 144 C8
Natural History Museum SW7 . 146 E4
Neal Street WC2H 144 C6
Neathouse Place * SW1V .. 147 M5
Neckinger SE1 .... 150 C8
Needleman Street SE16 ... 151 H7
Nelson Close NW6 .... 142 A1
Nelson Place N1 .... 145 H1
Nelson's Column WC2N ... 144 C8
Nelson Square SE1 ...... 149 H2
Nelson Street E1 .... 150 E2
Nelson Terrace N1 ...... 145 H1
Neptune Street SE16 ..... 151 G7
Nesham Street E1W 150 D4
Netherton Grove SW10 ... 146 D8
Netley Street NW1 ...... 143 M2
Nevern Place SW5 ...... 146 A6
Nevern Square SW5 ..... 146 A6
Neville Street SW7 ...... 146 E6
Newark Street E1 .... 150 E2
New Atlas Wharf E14 .... 151 M8
New Bond Street W1S ... 143 L7
New Bond Street W1S ... 143 M7
New Bridge Street EC4V .. 145 H6
New Broad Street EC2M .. 145 M5
New Burlington Street W1S . 143 M7
Newburn Street SE11 .... 148 F7
Newbury Street EC1A 145 J5
Newcastle Place W2 ..... 142 E5
New Cavendish Street W1G . 143 L5
New Change EC4M 145 J6
New Church Road SE5 .... 149 L8
Newcomen Street SE1 ... 149 L2
New Compton Street WC2H . 144 C6
Newcourt Street NW8 .... 142 F1
Newell Street E14 .... 151 L3
New Fetter Lane EC4A ... 145 G6
Newgate Street WC1A ... 145 H6
New Goulston Street E1 .. 150 B2
Newham's Row SE1 ..... 150 A7
Newington Butts SE11 ... 149 H5
Newington Causeway SE1 . 149 J4
New Kent Road SE1 ..... 149 K5
Newlands Quay E1W 150 F4
Newman Street W1T 144 A5
New North Place EC2A ... 145 M3
New North Road N1 ..... 145 L1
New North Street WC1N .. 144 D4
New Oxford Street WC1A . 144 C6
Newport Street SE11 .... 148 E5
New Quebec Street W1H .. 143 H6

New Ride SW7 .... 146 E3
New Road E1 .... 150 E2
New Row WC2N 144 C7
New Spring Gardens Walk SE1 . 148 D7
New Square WC2A 144 F6
New Street EC2M 150 A2
New Street Square EC4A .. 145 G6
Newton Road W2 ...... 142 A6
Newton Street WC2B ... 144 D5
New Union Street EC2Y .. 145 K5
Nicholas Lane EC3V 145 L7
Nicholson Street SE1 ... 149 H1
Nightingale Place SW10 . 146 D8
Nile Street N1 .... 145 K2
Nine Elms Lane SW8 ... 148 C8
Noble Street EC2V 145 J6
Noel Road N1 .... 145 H1
Noel Street W1F 144 A6
Norbiton Road E14 .... 151 L2
Norfolk Crescent W2 ... 143 G6
Norfolk Place W2 ..... 142 E6
Norfolk Square W2 .... 142 E6
Norman Street EC1V ... 145 J3
Norris Street SW1Y 144 B8
Northampton Road EC1R . 145 G3
Northampton Square EC1V . 145 H2
North Audley Street W1K . 143 J7
North Bank NW8 ...... 142 F2
Northburgh Street EC1V . 145 H3
North Carriage Drive W2 . 142 F7
Northdown Street N1 ... 144 D1
Northey Street E14 .... 151 K4
North Gower Street NW1 . 144 A2
Northington Street WC1N . 144 E4
North Mews WC1N 144 E4
North Ride W2 .... 143 G7
North Row W1K 143 J7
North Tenter Street E1 .. 150 C3
North Terrace SW3 .... 146 F5
Northumberland Alley EC3N . 150 B3
Northumberland
  Avenue WC2N 148 C1
Northumberland Place W2 . 142 A6
Northumberland
  Street WC2N 148 C1
North Wharf Road W2 .. 142 E5
Northwick Terrace NW8 . 142 D3
Norway Gate SE16 .... 151 K7
Norway Place E14 ..... 151 L3
Norwich Street EC4A ... 144 F5
Nottingham Place W1U .. 143 J4
Nottingham Street W1U . 143 J4
Notting Hill Gate W11 .. 142 A8
Notting Hill Gate ⊖ W11 . 146 A1
Nugent Terrace NW8 ... 142 D1
Nutford Place W1H 143 G6

O

Oakden Street SE11 .... 149 G5
Oakington Road W9 .... 142 A3
Oak Lane E14 .... 151 L3
Oakley Close EC1V 145 H1
Oakley Gardens SW3 ... 147 G8
Oakley Square NW1 ... 144 A1
Oakley Street SW3 .... 146 F8
Oak Tree Road NW8 ... 142 F2
Oat Lane EC2V 145 J5
Occupation Road SE17 .. 149 J6
Ocean Square E1 ..... 151 J1
Odessa Street SE16 ... 151 L7
Ogle Street W1W 143 M5
Old Bailey EC4M 145 H6
Old Barrack Yard SW1X . 147 J3
Old Bond Street W1S .. 143 M8
Old Broad Street EC2N . 145 M6
Old Brompton Road SW5 . 146 B6
Old Brompton Road SW7 . 146 D6
Old Burlington Street W1S . 143 M7
Oldbury Place W1U 143 J4
Old Castle Street E1 ... 150 B2
Old Cavendish Street W1G . 143 L6
Old Church Road E1 ... 151 H2
Old Church Street SW3 . 146 E7
Old Compton Street W1D . 144 B7
Old Court Place W8 ... 146 B3
Old Gloucester Street WC1N . 144 D4
Old Jamaica Road SE16 . 150 C7
Old Jewry EC2R 145 K6
Old Kent Road SE1 .... 149 M5
Old Marylebone Road NW1 . 143 G5
Old Montague Street E1 . 150 C1
Old North Street WC1X . 144 E5
Old Paradise Street SE11 . 148 E5
Old Park Lane W1J 147 K2
Old Pye Street SW1P ... 148 B4
Old Queen Street SW1H . 148 B3
Old Square WC2A 144 F6
Old Street EC1V 145 J3
Old Street ⊖≥ EC1Y ... 145 L3
Old Street Junction EC1Y . 145 L3
Oliver's Yard EC1Y 145 L3
Olney Road SE17 ..... 149 J8
O'Meara Street SE1 ... 149 K2
Omega Place N1 ...... 144 D1
Onega Gate SE16 ..... 151 K8
Ongar Road SW6 ..... 146 A8
Onslow Gardens SW7 .. 146 D6
Onslow Square SW7 .. 146 E6
Onslow Square SW7 .. 146 E6
Ontario Street SE1 .... 149 J4
Ontario Way E14 ..... 151 M4
Opal Street SE1 ...... 149 H6
Orange Place SE16 ... 151 G8
Orange Square SW1W . 147 K6
Orange Street WC2H .. 144 B8
Orb Street SE17 ..... 149 L6
Orchardson Street NW8 . 142 E4
Orchard Street W1H .. 143 J6
Ordehall Street WC1N .. 144 E4
Orient Street SE11 ... 149 H5
Orme Court W2 ...... 142 B8
Orme Lane W2 ...... 142 B8
Orme Square Gate W2 . 142 B8
Ormond Close WC1N .. 144 D4
Ormonde Gate SW3 .. 147 H7
Ormond Yard SW1Y .. 144 A8
Orsett Mews W2 ..... 142 C6
Orsett Street SE11 ... 148 E6
Orsett Terrace W2 ... 142 C5
Orton Street E1W 150 D5
Osbert Street SW1V .. 148 B6
Osborn Street E1 .... 150 C2
Oslo Square SE16 .... 151 K7

Osnaburgh Street NW1 .... 143 L3
Osnaburgh Terrace NW1 .... 143 L3
Ossington Buildings W1U 143 J5
Ossington Street W2 .... 142 A7
Ossulston Street NW1 .... 144 B1
Oswin Street SE11 .... 149 H5
Othello Close SE1 .... 149 H6
Otto Street SE17 .... 149 H8
Outer Circle NW1 .... 143 H3
Outer Circle NW1 .... 143 K1
Oval ⊖ SE11 .... 148 F8
Oval Way SE11 .... 148 E7
Ovington Square SW3 .... 147 G4
Ovington Street SW3 .... 147 G5
Owen Street EC1V 145 G1
Oxendon Street SW1Y 144 B8
Oxford Circus ⊖ W1B 143 M6
Oxford Road NW6 .... 142 A1
Oxford Square W2 .... 142 F6
Oxford Street W1C 143 L6
Oxford Street W1A 144 A6

P

Pace Place E1 .... 150 E3
Pacific Wharf SE16 .... 151 H5
Paddington ⊖≉ W2 .... 142 D6
Paddington Green W2 .... 142 E5
Paddington Street W1U 143 J5
Pageant Crescent SE16 .... 151 K5
Page Street SW1P 148 B5
Paget Street EC1V 145 H2
Pakenham Street WC1X 144 E2
Palace Avenue W8 .... 146 B2
Palace Court W2 .... 142 A7
Palace Gardens Terrace W8 ..... 146 A1
Palace Gate W8 .... 146 C3
Palace Green W8 .... 146 B2
Palace Place SW1E 147 M4
Palace Street SW1E 147 M4
Pall Mall SW1Y 148 A1
Pall Mall East SW1Y 148 B1
Palmer Street SW1H 148 B3
Pancras Lane EC4N 145 K6
Pancras Road N1C 144 C1
Panton Street SW1Y 144 B8
Paradise Street SE16 .... 150 E7
Paradise Walk SW3 .... 147 H8
Pardoner Street SE1 .... 149 L4
Pardon Street EC1V 145 H3
Parfett Street E1 .... 150 D2
Paris Garden SE1 .... 149 G1
Park Crescent W1B 143 K4
Park Crescent
    Mews West W1G 143 K4
Parker's Row SE1 .... 150 C7
Parker Street WC2B 144 D6
Park Lane W1K 143 H7
Park Lane W1 .... 147 J1
Park Place SW1A 147 M1
Park Road NW1 .... 143 H3
Park Square East NW1 .... 143 L3
Park Square Mews NW1 .... 143 K3
Park Square West NW1 .... 143 K3
Park Street SE1 .... 149 K1
Park Street W1K 143 J7
Park Village East NW1 .... 143 L1
Park Walk SW10 .... 146 D8
Park West Place W2 .... 143 G6
Parliament Street SW1A 148 C2
Parry Street SW8 .... 148 D8
Passmore Street SW1W 147 J6
Paternoster Square EC4M 145 J6
Pater Street W8 .... 146 A4
Pattina Walk SE16 .... 151 K5
Paul Street EC2A 145 M3
Paultons Square SW3 .... 146 E8
Paveley Street NW1 .... 143 G3
Pavilion Road SW1X 147 H3
Pavilion Street SW1X 147 H4
Paxton Terrace SW1V 147 L7
Peabody Avenue SW1V 147 L7
Peabody Estate SE1 .... 149 J1
Peacock Street SE17 .... 149 J6
Pearl Street E1W 150 F5
Pearman Street SE1 .... 149 G3
Pear Tree Court EC1R 145 G4
Peartree Lane E1W 151 G4
Pear Tree Street EC1V 145 J3
Peel Street W8 .... 146 A1
Peerless Street EC1V 145 K2
Pelham Crescent SW7 .... 146 F5
Pelham Place SW7 .... 146 F5
Pelham Street SW7 .... 146 F5
Pelier Street SE17 .... 149 K8
Pemberton Row EC4A 145 G6
Pembridge Gardens W2 .... 142 A8
Pembridge Place W2 .... 142 A7
Pembridge Square W2 .... 142 A7
Pembridge Villas W11 .... 142 A7
Pembroke Close SW1X 147 J3
Penang Street E1W 150 F5
Penfold Place NW8 .... 142 F5
Penfold Street NW8 .... 142 E4
Pennant Mews W8 .... 146 B5
Pennington Street E1W 150 D4
Pennyfields E14 .... 151 M4
Penrose Grove SE17 .... 149 J7
Penrose Street SE17 .... 149 J7
Penryn Road SE16 .... 150 E7
Penton Place SE17 .... 149 H6
Penton Rise WC1X 144 E2
Penton Street N1 .... 144 F1
Pentonville Road N1 .... 144 E1
Penywern Road SW5 .... 146 A6
Pepper Street SE1 .... 149 J2
Pepys Street EC3N 150 A4
Percival Street EC1V 145 H3
Percy Circus WC1X 144 F2
Percy Street W1T 144 B5
Perkin's Rent SW1P 148 B4
Petersham Mews SW7 .... 146 C4
Petersham Place SW7 .... 146 C4
Peter Street W1F 144 B7
Peto Place NW1 .... 143 L3
Petticoat Lane E1 .... 150 B2
Petty France SW1H 148 A3
Petty Wales EC3R 150 A4
Petyward SW3 .... 147 G6
Phelp Street SE17 .... 149 L7
Phene Street SW3 .... 147 G8
Phillimore Walk W8 .... 146 A3
Philpot Lane EC3M 145 M7
Philpot Street E1 .... 150 E2
Phipp's Mews SW1W 147 L5

Phipp Street EC2A 145 M3
Phoenix Place WC1X 144 F3
Phoenix Road NW1 .... 144 B1
Phoenix Street WC2H 144 C6
Piccadilly W1J 147 L2
Piccadilly Arcade SW1Y 147 M1
Piccadilly Circus W1B 144 A8
Piccadilly Circus W1J 144 B8
Pickard Street EC1V 145 J2
Picton Place W1U 143 K6
Pier Head E1W 150 E6
Pigott Street E14 .... 151 M3
Pilgrimage Street SE1 .... 149 L3
Pimlico ⊖ SW1V 148 B6
Pimlico Road SW1W 147 J6
Pinchin Street E1 .... 150 D3
Pindar Street EC2A 145 M4
Pindock Mews W9 .... 142 B3
Pine Street EC1R 144 F3
Pitfield Street N1 .... 145 M1
Pitsea Street E1 .... 151 H3
Pitt's Head Mews W1J 147 K2
Pitt Street W8 .... 146 A2
Pixley Street E14 .... 151 L2
Platina Street * EC2A 145 L3
Plover Way SE16 .... 151 K8
Plumbers Row E1 .... 150 D2
Plumtree Court EC4A 145 G5
Plympton Street NW8 .... 142 F4
Pocock Street SE1 .... 149 H2
Poland Street W1F 144 A6
Pollen Street W1S 143 L7
Pollitt Drive NW8 .... 142 E3
Polperrom SE11 .... 149 G5
Polygon Road NW1 .... 144 B1
Pond Place SW3 .... 146 F6
Ponler Street E1 .... 150 E3
Ponsonby Place SW1P 148 C6
Ponsonby Terrace SW1P 148 C6
Ponton Road SW1V 148 B8
Pont Street SW1X 147 H4
Poolmans Street SE16 .... 151 H6
Pope Street SE1 .... 150 B7
Poplar Place W2 .... 142 B7
Poppin's Court EC4A 145 H6
Porchester Gardens W2 .... 142 B7
Porchester Gate W2 .... 142 C8
Porchester Place W2 .... 143 G6
Porchester Road W2 .... 142 B5
Porchester Square W2 .... 142 B6
Porchester Terrace W2 .... 142 C7
Porchester Terrace
    North W2 .... 142 C6
Porlock Street SE1 .... 149 L3
Porter Street NW1 .... 143 H4
Porteus Road W2 .... 142 D5
Portia Place W1B 143 L4
Portland Place W1B 143 L5
Portland Square E1W 150 E5
Portland Street SE17 .... 149 L7
Portman Close W1H 143 J6
Portman Mews South W1H 143 J6
Portman Square W1H 143 J6
Portman Street W1H 143 J6
Portpool Lane EC1N 144 F4
Portsea Place W2 .... 143 G6
Portsmouth Street WC2A 144 E6
Portsoken Street E1 .... 150 B3
Portugal Street WC2A 144 E6
Potier Street SE1 .... 149 L4
Potters Fields SE1 .... 150 B6
Pottery Street SE16 .... 150 E7
Poultry EC2V 145 K6
Powis Place WC1N 144 D4
Praed Mews W2 .... 142 E6
Praed Street W2 .... 142 E6
Pratt Walk SE1 .... 148 E5
Premier Place E14 .... 151 M4
Prescot Street E1 .... 150 C3
Preston Close SE1 .... 149 M5
Price's Street SE1 .... 149 H1
Prideaux Place WC1X 144 F2
Primrose Street EC2A 150 A1
Prince Albert Road NW8 .... 142 F1
Prince Consort Road SW7 ...... 146 D3
Princelet Street E1 .... 150 C1
Prince of Wales Gate SW7 ..... 146 F3
Princes Arcade SW1Y 144 A8
Prince's Gardens SW7 .... 146 E3
Prince's Gate Mews SW7 .... 146 E4
Princes Riverside Road SE16 .. 151 H5
Prince's Square W2 .... 142 A7
Princess Road NW6 .... 142 A1
Princess Street SE1 .... 149 H4
Princes Street W1B 143 L6
Prince's Street EC2R 145 L6
Princeton Street WC1R 144 E5
Prioress Street SE1 .... 149 L4
Priory Green Estate N1 .... 144 E1
Priory Walk SW10 .... 146 D7
Proctor Street WC1V 144 E5
Prospect Place E1W 151 G5
Prospect Street SE16 .... 150 E7
Provident Court W1K 143 J7
Provost Street N1 .... 145 L1
Prusom Street E1W 150 F5
Pudding Lane EC3R 145 M7
Pumphouse Mews E1 .... 150 D3
Purbrook Street SE1 .... 150 A7
Purcell Street N1 .... 145 M1
Purchese Street NW1 .... 144 B1

Q

Quebec Way SE16 .... 151 J7
Queen Anne's Gate SW1H 148 B3
Queen Anne Street W1G 143 K5
Queen Elizabeth Street SE1 ... 150 B6
Queen Mother Gate W2 .... 147 J2
Queensborough Terrace W2 ..... 142 B8
Queensberry Place SW7 .... 146 E5
Queen's Gardens SW7 .... 142 C7
Queen's Gate SW7 .... 146 D3
Queen's Gate W7 .... 146 D4
Queen's Gate Gardens SW7 ..... 146 D5
Queen's Gate Mews SW7 .... 146 D4
Queen's Gate Place SW7 .... 146 D4
Queen's Gate Place
    Mews SW7 .... 146 D4
Queen's Gate Terrace SW7 ..... 146 C4
Queen's Mews W2 .... 142 B7
Queen Square WC1N 144 D4
Queen's Row SE17 .... 149 K7
Queen Street EC4N 145 K7
Queen Street W1J 147 L1

Queen Street Place EC4R 145 K7
Queen's Walk SE1 .... 150 A5
Queen's Walk SW1A 147 M2
Queensway W2 .... 142 B8
Queensway ⊖ W2 .... 142 B8
Queen Victoria Street EC4V ... 145 J7
Quick Street N1 .... 145 H1

R

Raby Street E14 .... 151 K2
Radcliffe Road SE1 .... 150 B8
Radcot Street SE11 .... 149 G7
Radnor Mews W2 .... 142 E6
Radnor Place W2 .... 142 F6
Radnor Street EC1V 145 K3
Radnor Walk SW3 .... 147 G7
Railway Approach SE1 .... 149 L1
Railway Avenue SE16 .... 151 G6
Railway Street N1 .... 144 D1
Raine Street E1W 150 F5
Ralston Street SW3 .... 147 H7
Ramillies Place W1F 143 M6
Ramillies Street W1F 143 M6
Rampart Street E1 .... 150 E2
Rampayne Street SW1V 148 B6
Randall Road SE11 .... 148 D6
Randall Row SE11 .... 148 D6
Randolph Avenue W9 .... 142 B1
Randolph Crescent W9 .... 142 C3
Randolph Gardens NW6 .... 142 B1
Randolph Mews W9 .... 142 D4
Randolph Road W9 .... 142 C4
Ranelagh Grove SW1W 147 K6
Ranelagh Road SW1V 148 A7
Rangoon Street * EC3N 150 B3
Ranston Street NW8 .... 142 F4
Raphael Street SW7 .... 147 G3
Ratcliffe Cross Street E1W ... 151 J3
Ratcliffe Lane E14 .... 151 J3
Raven Row E1 .... 150 F1
Ravensdon Street SE11 .... 149 G7
Ravey Street EC2A 145 M3
Rawlings Street SW3 .... 147 G5
Rawstone Street EC1V 145 H2
Ray Street EC1R 145 G4
Reardon Place E1W 150 E5
Reardon Street E1W 150 E5
Rectory Square E1 .... 151 H1
Redan Place W2 .... 142 B6
Redburn Street SW3 .... 147 G7
Redcastle Close E1W 151 G4
Redcliffe Gardens SW10 .... 146 B7
Redcliffe Mews SW10 .... 146 C7
Redcliffe Place SW10 .... 146 C8
Redcliffe Road SW10 .... 146 C7
Redcliffe Square SW10 .... 146 B7
Redcliffe Street SW10 .... 146 B8
Redcross Way SE1 .... 149 K2
Redesdale Street SW3 .... 147 G7
Redfield Lane SW5 .... 146 A5
Redhill Street NW1 .... 143 L1
Red Lion Row SE5 .... 149 K8
Red Lion Square WC1R 144 E5
Red Lion Street WC2B 144 E5
Redman's Road E1 .... 151 G1
Red Place W1K 143 J7
Redriff Road SE16 .... 151 J8
Reedworth Street SE11 .... 149 G6
Reeves Mews W1K 143 J8
Regal Close E1 .... 150 D1
Regan Way N1 .... 145 M1
Regency Street SW1P 148 B5
Regent Place W1B 144 A7
Regent's Park ⊖ W1B 143 L4
Regent's Park NW1 .... 143 J1
Regent's Park Estate NW1 ..... 143 L2
Regent Square WC1H 144 D2
Regent Street SW1Y 144 B8
Regent Street W1S 143 M7
Relton Mews SW7 .... 147 G4
Remington Street N1 .... 145 H1
Remnant Street WC2A 144 E6
Renforth Street SE16 .... 151 G7
Renfrew Road SE11 .... 149 H5
Rennie Street SE1 .... 149 H1
Rephidim Street SE1 .... 149 M4
Repton Street E14 .... 151 K2
Reveley Square SE16 .... 151 K7
Rex Place W1K 143 J8
Rhodeswell Road E14 .... 151 L2
Rich Street E14 .... 151 M3
Rickett Street SW6 .... 146 A8
Ridgmount Street WC1E 144 B4
Ridgmount Gardens WC1E 144 B4
Riding House Street W1W 143 M5
Riley Road SE1 .... 150 B7
Ripley's Believe It or Not! W1J 144 B8
Risborough Street SE1 .... 149 J2
Risdon Street SE16 .... 151 G7
Rissinghill Street N1 .... 144 F1
River Street EC1R 144 F2
Rivington Street EC2A 145 M3
Robert Adam Street W1U 143 J6
Roberts Close SE16 .... 151 J7
Robert Street NW1 .... 143 L2
Rochester Row SW1P 148 A5
Rochester Street SW1P 148 B5
Rockingham Street SE1 .... 149 J4
Rocliffe Street N1 .... 145 H1
Roding Mews E1W 150 D5
Rodmarton Street W1U 143 H5
Rodney Place SE17 .... 149 K5
Rodney Road SE17 .... 149 K5
Rodney Street N1 .... 144 E1
Roger Street WC1N 144 E4
Roland Gardens SW7 .... 146 D6
Roland Way SE17 .... 149 L7
Romford Street E1 .... 150 E2
Romilly Street W1D 144 B7
Romney Street SW1P 148 C5
Rood Lane EC3M 145 M7
Ropemaker Road SE16 .... 151 K7
Ropemaker Street EC2Y 145 L4
Roper Lane SE1 .... 150 B7
Rope Street SE16 .... 151 K8
Rope Walk Gardens SE1 .... 150 E2
Rosary Gardens SW7 .... 146 D6
Roscoe Street EC1Y 145 K3
Rose Alley SE1 .... 145 K8
Rosebery Avenue EC1R 144 F3
Rosemoor Street SW3 .... 147 G6
Rose Street WC2E 144 C7

Rossmore Road NW1 .... 143 G3
Rotary Street SE1 .... 149 H3
Rotherhithe ⊖ SE16 .... 151 G6
Rotherhithe Street SE16 ...... 151 G6
Rotherhithe Street SE16 ...... 151 J4
Rotherhithe Tunnel SE16 ...... 151 H5
Rothsay Street SE1 .... 149 M4
Rotten Row W2 .... 146 F2
Rouel Road SE16 .... 150 C8
Roupell Street SE1 .... 149 G2
Royal Albert Hall SW7 .... 146 E3
Royal Avenue SW3 .... 147 H6
Royal Hospital Road SW3 ...... 147 H7
Royal Mint Street E1 .... 150 C4
Royal Oak ⊖ W2 .... 142 B5
Royal Oak Yard SE1 .... 150 A7
Royal Opera House WC2E 144 D7
Royal Road SE17 .... 149 H8
Royal Street SE1 .... 148 E3
Rudolph Road NW6 .... 142 A1
Rugby Street WC1N 144 E4
Rum Close E1W 150 F4
Rupack Street SE16 .... 150 F7
Rupert Street W1D 144 B7
Rushworth Street SE1 .... 149 H2
Russell Court SW1 .... 148 A2
Russell Square WC1B 144 C4
Russell Square ⊖ WC1B 144 D4
Russell Street WC2B 144 D7
Russia Dock Road SE16 .... 151 K6
Rutherford Street SW1P 148 B5
Rutland Gardens SW7 .... 147 G3
Rutland Gate SW7 .... 146 F3
Rutland Mews SW7 .... 146 F4
Rutland Street SW7 .... 146 F4
Ryder Street SW1Y 148 A1

S

Sackville Street W1S 144 A8
Saffron Hill EC1N 145 G4
Saffron Street EC1N 145 G4
Sail Street SE11 .... 148 F5
St Agnes Place SE11 .... 149 G8
St Alban's Grove W8 .... 146 B4
St Alban's Street SW1Y 144 B8
St Alphage Garden EC2Y 145 K5
St Andrews Hill EC4V 145 H7
St Andrew's Place NW1 .... 143 L3
St Andrew Street EC4A 145 G5
St Anne's Court W1F 144 B6
St Ann's Street SW1P 148 C4
St Anselm's Place W1K 143 K7
St Barnabas Street SW1W 147 K6
St Botolph Street EC3N 150 B2
St Bride Street EC4A 145 G6
St Chad's Street WC1H 144 D2
St Clare Street EC3N 150 B3
St Clements Lane WC2A 144 E6
St Cross Street EC1N 145 G4
St Dunstan's Hill EC3R 145 M8
St Dunstan's Lane EC3R 145 M7
St Elmos Road SE16 .... 151 J7
St Ermin's Hill SW1H 148 B3
St George's Circus SE1 .... 149 H3
St George's Drive SW1V 147 M6
St George's Estate E1 .... 150 D3
St George's Lane * EC3R 145 M7
St George's Road SE1 .... 149 G4
St George's Square SW1V 148 B7
St George Street W1S 143 L7
St Giles High Street WC2H 144 C6
St Helen's Place EC3A 145 M6
St James Market * SW1Y 144 B8
St James's Park ⊖ SW1H 148 B3
St James's Park SW1A 148 B3
St James's Place SW1A 147 M2
St James's Road SE16 .... 150 D8
St James's Square SW1Y 148 A1
St James's Street SW1A 147 M1
St John's Lane EC1M 145 H4
St John's Place EC1M 145 H4
St John's Square EC1V 145 H4
St John Street EC1V 145 H2
St John's Wood High
    Street NW8 .... 142 F1
St John's Wood Road NW8 ...... 142 E3
St Katharine's Way E1W 150 C5
St Leonard's Terrace SW3 ..... 147 H7
St Loo Avenue SW3 .... 147 G8
St Luke's Close EC1V 145 K3
St Luke's Street SW3 .... 146 F6
St Manningtree E1 .... 150 C2
St Mark Street E1 .... 150 C3
St Martin's Lane WC2 .... 144 C7
St Martin's le Grand EC1A 145 J6
St Martin's Place WC2N 144 C8
St Mary at Hill EC3R 145 M8
St Mary Axe EC3A 150 A3
St Mary Church Street SE16 ... 150 F7
St Mary's Gardens SE11 .... 149 G5
St Mary's Terrace W2 .... 142 D4
St Mary's Walk SE11 .... 149 G5
St Matthew Street SW1P 148 B4
St Michael's Street W2 .... 142 F6
St Olav's Square SE16 .... 150 F7
St Oswald's Place SE11 .... 148 E7
St Oswulf Street * SW1P 148 C6
St Pancras
    International ≉ N1C 144 C1
St Paul's ⊖ EC1A 145 J6
St Paul's Avenue SE16 .... 151 J5
St Paul's Cathedral EC4M 145 J6
St Paul's Churchyard EC4M 145 J6
St Paul's Way E1 .... 151 H1
St Petersburgh Mews W2 .... 142 B7
St Petersburgh Place W2 ...... 142 B7
St Saviours Wharf SE1 .... 150 C6
St Stephen's Gardens W2 ...... 142 A5
St Swithin's Lane EC4N 145 L7
St Thomas Street SE1 .... 149 L2
St Vincent Street W1U 143 J5
Salamanca Street SE11 .... 148 D6
Salem Road W2 .... 142 B7
Sale Place W2 .... 142 F5
Salisbury Court EC4Y 145 G6
Salisbury Place W1H 143 H4
Salisbury Street NW8 .... 142 F4
Salmon Lane E14 .... 151 L2
Salter Road SE16 .... 151 H6
Salter Street E14 .... 151 M4
Samford Street NW8 .... 142 F4
Sampson Street E1W 150 D5
Sancroft Street SE11 .... 148 F6

Sandford Row SE17 .... 149 L6
Sandland Street WC1R 144 E5
Sandpiper Close SE16 .... 151 L6
Sandwich Street WC1H 144 C2
Sandy's Row E1 .... 150 B1
Sans Walk EC1R 145 G3
Sardinia Street WC2A 144 E6
Savage Gardens EC3N 150 B3
Savile Row W1S 143 M7
Savoy Hill WC2R 144 E8
Savoy Place WC2R 144 D8
Savoy Street WC2E 144 E7
Sawyer Street SE1 .... 149 J2
Scala Street W1T 144 A5
Scandrett Street E1W 150 E5
Scarborough Street E1 .... 150 C3
Scarsdale Villas W8 .... 146 A4
Schooner Close * SE16 .... 151 H6
Science Museum SW7 .... 146 E4
Scoresby Street SE1 .... 149 H2
Scotch House Junction SW1X ... 147 H3
Scotland Place SW1A 148 C1
Scott Ellis Grove NW8 .... 142 E2
Scott Lidgett Crescent SE16 .. 150 D7
Scrutton Street EC2A 145 M3
Seaford Street WC1H 144 D2
Seagrave Road SW6 .... 146 A8
Sea Life London
    Aquarium 148 E3
Searles Road SE1 .... 149 L5
Sebastian Street EC1V 145 H2
Secker Street SE1 .... 148 F2
Sedan Way SE17 .... 149 M6
Sedding Street SW1X 147 J5
Seddon Street WC1X 144 E3
Seething Lane EC3N 150 A4
Sekforde Street EC1R 145 H3
Selfridges W1A 143 J6
Selsey Street E14 .... 151 M1
Selwood Place SW7 .... 146 E6
Semley Place SW1W 147 K6
Senior Street W2 .... 142 B4
Senrab Street E1 .... 151 H2
Serle Street WC2A 144 F6
Serpentine Bridge W2 .... 146 F2
Serpentine Road W2 .... 146 F2
Seth Street SE16 .... 151 G7
Settles Street E1 .... 150 D2
Seven Dials WC2H 144 C6
Seville Street SW1X 147 H3
Sevington Street W9 .... 142 A3
Seward Street EC1V 145 J3
Seymour Mews W1H 143 J6
Seymour Place W1H 143 G5
Seymour Street W1H 143 H6
Seymour Street W2 .... 143 G7
Seymour Walk SW10 .... 146 C7
Shad Thames SE1 .... 150 B6
Shad Thames SE1 .... 150 C6
Shadwell ⊖≉ E1 .... 150 F3
Shadwell Gardens E1 .... 150 F3
Shaftesbury Avenue W1D 144 B7
Shaftesbury Avenue WC2H 144 C6
Shaftesbury Street N1 .... 145 K1
Shakespeare's Globe SE1 ...... 149 J8
Shand Street SE1 .... 150 A6
Sharsted Street SE17 .... 149 H7
Shaw Crescent E14 .... 151 K2
Shawfield Street SW3 .... 147 G7
Sheffield Terrace W8 .... 146 A2
Sheldon Square W2 .... 142 D5
Shelmerdine Close E3 .... 151 M1
Shelton Street WC2H 144 D6
Shepherdess Walk N1 .... 145 K1
Shepherd Street W1J 147 K1
Sheraton Street W1F 144 B6
Sherborne Lane EC4N 145 L7
Sherwood Street W1D 144 A7
Ship and Mermaid Row SE1 ..... 149 M2
Shipwright Road SE16 .... 151 K7
Shirland Road W9 .... 142 A3
Shoe Lane EC4A 145 G5
Shorter Street EC3N 150 B4
Shorts Gardens WC2H 144 C6
Short Street SE1 .... 149 G2
Shoulder of Mutton Alley E14 . 151 K4
Shouldham Street W1H 143 G5
Shroton Street NW1 .... 142 F4
Siddons Lane W1H 143 H4
Sidmouth Street WC1N 144 D3
Sidney Square E1 .... 150 F2
Sidney Street E1 .... 150 F1
Silex Street SE1 .... 149 H3
Silk Street EC2Y 145 K4
Silver Walk SE16 .... 151 K5
Silvester Street SE1 .... 149 K3
Singer Street EC2A 145 L3
Sir John Soane's
    Museum WC2A 144 E5
Sir Simon Milton Square SW1V . 147 L4
Skinner Place * SW1W 147 J6
Skinners Lane EC4V 145 K7
Skinner Street EC1R 145 G3
Slippers Place SE16 .... 150 F8
Sloane Avenue SW3 .... 147 G6
Sloane Court SW3 .... 147 J6
Sloane Court East SW3 .... 147 J6
Sloane Gardens SW1W 147 J6
Sloane Square SW1W 147 J6
Sloane Square ⊖ SW1W 147 J6
Sloane Street SW1X 147 J3
Sloane Terrace SW1X 147 J5
Smeaton Street E1W 150 E5
Smithfield Street EC1A 145 H5
Smith Square SW1P 148 C4
Smith Street SW3 .... 147 G7
Smith Terrace SW3 .... 147 G7
Smithy Street E1 .... 151 H1
Snowden Street EC2A 145 M4
Snow Hill EC1A 145 H5
Snowsfields SE1 .... 149 L2
Soho Square W1D 144 B6
Soho Street W1D 144 B6
Somerford Way SE16 .... 151 K7
Somers Crescent W2 .... 142 F6
Somerset House WC2R 144 E7
Somerstown Estate NW1 .... 144 A1
Sondes Street SE17 .... 149 L7
South & West Africa Gate SW1A 148 A3
Southall Place SE1 .... 149 L3
Southampton Buildings WC2A ... 144 F5
Southampton Place WC1A 144 D5
Southampton Row WC1B 144 D4
Southampton Street WC2E 144 D7
South Audley Street W1K 143 K8
South Carriage Drive SW1X 147 H3
South Carriage Drive SW7 ..... 146 F3

South Eaton Place SW1W 147 J5
Southern Street N1 ...... 144 E1
South Kensington ⊖ SW7 ...... 146 E4
South Kensington ⊖ SW7 ...... 146 E5
South Lambeth Road SW8 ...... 148 D8
South Molton Lane W1K 143 K7
South Molton Street W1K 143 K7
South Parade SW3 ...... 146 E7
South Place EC2M 145 L5
South Sea Street SE16 ...... 151 L8
South Square WC1R 144 F5
South Street W1K 147 J1
South Tenter Street E1 ...... 150 C3
South Terrace SW7 ...... 146 F5
Southwark ⊖ SE1 ...... 149 H2
Southwark Bridge SE1 ...... 145 K8
Southwark Bridge Road SE1 ...... 149 J3
Southwark Park Road SE16 ...... 150 E8
Southwark Street SE1 ...... 149 H1
Southwell Gardens SW7 ...... 146 C5
South Wharf Road W2 ...... 142 E6
Southwick Mews W2 ...... 142 F6
Southwick Place W2 ...... 142 F6
Southwick Street W2 ...... 142 F6
Sovereign Close E1W 150 F4
Sovereign Crescent SE16 ...... 151 J4
Spanish Place W1U 143 J5
Spa Road SE16 ...... 150 C8
Spear Mews SW5 ...... 146 A6
Spelman Street E1 ...... 150 C1
Spence Close SE16 ...... 151 K7
Spencer Street EC1V 145 H2
Spenser Street SW1E 148 A4
Spert Street E14 ...... 151 J4
Spital Square E1 ...... 150 A1
Spring Gardens SW1A 148 C1
Spring Street W2 ...... 142 E6
Spurgeon Street SE1 ...... 149 L4
Spur Road SE1 ...... 148 F3
Stables Way SE11 ...... 148 F7
Stable Yard Road SW1A 148 A2
Stacey Street WC2H 144 C6
Stafford Place SW1E 147 M3
Stafford Road NW6 ...... 142 A2
Stafford Street W1S 143 M8
Stafford Terrace W8 ...... 146 A3
Stainer Street SE1 ...... 149 L2
Stainsby Road E14 ...... 151 M4
Stalham Street SE16 ...... 150 F8
Stamford Street SE1 ...... 149 G1
Stanford Place SE1 ...... 149 M6
Stanford Road W8 ...... 146 B4
Stanford Street * SW1V 148 B6
Stanhope Close * SE1 ...... 151 H6
Stanhope Gardens SW7 ...... 146 D5
Stanhope Gate W1K 147 K1
Stanhope Mews SW7 ...... 146 D5
Stanhope Mews East SW7 ...... 146 D5
Stanhope Mews West SW7 ...... 146 D5
Stanhope Place W2 ...... 143 G7
Stanhope Place Gate W2 ...... 143 G7
Stanhope Row W1J 147 K1
Stanhope Street NW1 ...... 143 M1
Stanhope Terrace W2 ...... 142 E7
Stannary Street SE11 ...... 149 G7
Staples Close SE16 ...... 151 J5
Staple Street SE1 ...... 149 L3
Starcross Street NW1 ...... 144 A2
Star Street W2 ...... 142 F6
Station Approach SE1 ...... 148 F3
Stave Yard Road SE16 ...... 151 J5
Stead Street SE17 ...... 149 K6
Steedman Street SE17 ...... 149 J5
Steel's Lane E1 ...... 151 G3
Steeres Way SE16 ...... 151 K7
Stephenson Way NW1 ...... 144 A3
Stephen Street W1T 144 B5
Stepney Green E1 ...... 151 H1
Stepney High Street E1 ...... 151 J1
Stepney Way E1 ...... 150 E1
Sterling Street SW7 ...... 147 G3
Stevedore Street E1W 150 E5
Stevens Street SE1 ...... 150 A7
Steward Street * E1 ...... 150 B1
Stewart's Grove SW3 ...... 146 F6
Stew Lane EC4V 145 J7
Stillington Street SW1P 148 A5
Stockholm Way E1W 150 D5
Stocks Place E14 ...... 151 M3
Stone Buildings WC2A 144 F5
Stonecutter Street EC4A 145 G6
Stoney Lane E1 ...... 150 B2
Stoney Street SE1 ...... 149 K1
Stopford Road SE17 ...... 149 J7
Store Street WC1E 144 B5
Storey's Gate SW1H 148 C3
Storks Road SE16 ...... 150 D8
Stoughton Close SE11 ...... 148 E6
Stourcliffe Street W1H 143 G6
Strafford Street E14 ...... 151 M6
Strand WC2R 144 D8
Stratford Place W1C 143 K6
Stratford Road W8 ...... 146 A5
Strathearn Place W2 ...... 142 F7
Stratton Street W1J 147 L1
Strutton Ground SW1P 148 B4
Strype Street E1 ...... 150 B2
Stuart Road NW6 ...... 142 A2
Stukeley Street WC2B 144 D6
Sturgeon Road SE17 ...... 149 J7
Sturge Street SE1 ...... 149 J3
Sturt Street N1 ...... 145 K1
Stutfield Street E1 ...... 150 D3
Sudley Street N1 ...... 145 H1
Sudrey Street SE1 ...... 149 J3
Suffolk Lane EC4V 145 L7
Suffolk Street SW1Y 144 B8
Sugar Quay Walk EC3R 150 A4
Sullivan Road SE11 ...... 149 G5
Summercourt Road E1 ...... 151 G2
Summers Street EC1R 144 F4
Sumner Place SW7 ...... 146 E6
Sumner Street SE1 ...... 149 J1
Sunderland Terrace W2 ...... 142 A6
Sun Passage SE16 ...... 150 D8
Sun Street EC2M 145 M4
Surrendale Place W9 ...... 142 A4
Surrey Quays Road SE16 ...... 151 H7
Surrey Row SE1 ...... 149 H2
Surrey Square SE17 ...... 149 M6
Surrey Street WC2E 144 E7
Surrey Water Road SE16 ...... 151 H6
Sussex Gardens W2 ...... 142 E6
Sussex Mews East W2 ...... 142 E7
Sussex Place NW1 ...... 143 H3
Sussex Place W2 ...... 142 E6
Sussex Square W2 ...... 142 E7

Sussex Street SW1V 147 L7
Sutherland Avenue W9 ...... 142 A4
Sutherland Row SW1V 147 L6
Sutherland Square SE17 ...... 149 J7
Sutherland Street SW1V 147 L7
Sutton Row W1D 144 B6
Sutton Street E1 ...... 151 G3
Suttons Way EC1Y 145 K4
Swain Street NW8 ...... 142 F3
Swallow Place W1B 143 L6
Swallow Street W1B 144 A8
Swan Lane EC4R 145 L8
Swan Mead SE1 ...... 149 M4
Swan Road SE16 ...... 151 G6
Swan Street SE1 ...... 149 K3
Swan Walk SW3 ...... 147 H8
Swedenborg Gardens E1 ...... 150 E4
Sweeney Crescent SE1 ...... 150 C7
Swinton Street WC1X 144 E2
Sydney Place SW7 ...... 146 F6
Sydney Street SW3 ...... 146 F6
Symons Street SW3 ...... 147 H6

T

Tabard Gardens Estate SE1 ...... 149 L3
Tabard Street SE1 ...... 149 L3
Tabernacle Street EC2A 145 L3
Tachbrook Street SW1V 148 A6
Talbot Road W2 ...... 142 A6
Talbot Square W2 ...... 142 E6
Talbot Yard SE1 ...... 149 L2
Tallis Street EC4Y 145 G7
Tamworth Street SW6 ...... 146 A8
Tanner Street SE1 ...... 150 A7
Taplow Street N1 ...... 145 K1
Tarling Street E1 ...... 150 F3
Tarver Road SE17 ...... 149 H7
Tate Britain SW1P 148 C6
Tate Modern SE1 ...... 145 J8
Tatum Street SE17 ...... 149 M6
Taunton Place NW1 ...... 143 G3
Tavistock Place WC1H 144 C3
Tavistock Square WC1H 144 C3
Tavistock Street WC2E 144 D7
Taviton Street WC1H 144 B3
Teak Close SE16 ...... 151 K6
Tedworth Square SW3 ...... 147 G7
Telford Terrace SW1V 147 M7
Temeraire Street SE16 ...... 151 G6
Temple ⊖ WC2R 144 F7
Temple Avenue EC4Y 145 G7
Temple Lane EC4Y 145 G7
Temple Place WC2R 144 F7
Templeton Place SW5 ...... 146 A5
Tench Street E1W 150 E5
Tenniel Close W2 ...... 142 C7
Tennis Street SE1 ...... 149 L2
Tenterden Street W1S 143 L6
Tenterground E1 ...... 150 B1
Teredo Street SE16 ...... 151 J8
Terminus Place SW1V 147 L4
Thame Road SE16 ...... 151 H6
Thanet Street WC1H 144 C2
Thavies Inn EC4A 145 G6
Thayer Street W1U 143 K5
The Arches WC2N 144 D8
The Boltons SW10 ...... 146 C7
The British Library NW1 ...... 144 C2
The British Museum WC1B 144 C5
The Broad Walk W2 ...... 142 B8
The Broad Walk W8 ...... 146 C2
The Cut SE1 ...... 149 G2
Theed Street SE1 ...... 149 G2
The Flower Walk W2 ...... 146 D3
The Grange SE1 ...... 150 B8
The Highway E1W 150 E4
The Little Boltons SW10 ...... 146 C7
The Mall SW1A 148 B2
The Mitre E14 ...... 151 L3
The Monument EC3R 145 L7
The National Gallery WC2N 144 C8
Theobald's Road WC1X 144 E4
Theobald Street SE1 ...... 149 L5
The Oval (Surrey County Cricket Ground) SE11 ...... 148 F8
The Shard SE1 ...... 149 L2
The Vale SW3 ...... 146 E8
Thirleby Road SW1P 148 A4
Thomas More Street E1W 150 D4
Thomas Road E14 ...... 151 M2
Thoresby Street N1 ...... 145 K1
Thorney Street SW1P 148 C5
Thornton Place W1H 143 H4
Thrale Street SE1 ...... 149 K1
Thrawl Street E1 ...... 150 C1
Threadneedle Street EC2R 145 L6
Three Colt Street E14 ...... 151 L3
Three Oak Lane SE1 ...... 150 B6
Throgmorton Avenue EC2N 145 L6
Throgmorton Street EC2N 145 L6
Thurland Road SE16 ...... 150 D8
Thurloe Place SW7 ...... 146 F5
Thurloe Square SW7 ...... 146 F5
Thurloe Street SW7 ...... 146 E5
Thurlow Street SE17 ...... 149 M7
Tichbourne Row W2 ...... 142 F6
Tiller Road E14 ...... 151 M8
Tillman Street E1 ...... 150 E3
Tilney Street W1J 147 K1
Timber Pond Road SE16 ...... 151 J6
Tinsley Street E1 ...... 151 G1
Tinworth Street SE11 ...... 148 D6
Tisdall Place SE17 ...... 149 L6
Tite Street SW3 ...... 147 H8
Tiverton Street SE1 ...... 149 J4
Token House Yard EC2R 145 L6
Tolmer's Square NW1 ...... 144 A3
Tomlin's Terrace E14 ...... 151 K2
Tonbridge Street WC1H 144 D2
Tooley Street SE1 ...... 149 L1
Tooley Street SE1 ...... 150 A6
Tor Gardens W8 ...... 146 A2
Torquay Street W2 ...... 142 A5
Torrens Street EC1V 145 G1
Torrington Place SE1 ...... 150 D5
Torrington Place WC1E 144 B4
Torrington Square WC1E 144 B4
Tothill Street SW1H 148 B3
Tottenham Court Road ⊖ W1T 144 A4
Tottenham Court Road W1D 144 A5
Tottenham Street W1T 144 A5
Toulmin Street SE1 ...... 149 J3
Tower Bridge EC3N 150 B5
Tower Bridge Approach EC3N 150 B5

Tower Bridge Road SE1 ...... 150 A7
Tower Bridge Wharf E1W 150 C5
Tower Gateway ⊖ EC3N 150 B4
Tower Hill EC3N 150 B4
Tower Hill ⊖ EC3N 150 B4
Tower of London EC3N 150 B4
Tower Place EC3R 150 A4
Tower Street WC2H 144 C7
Townsend Street SE17 ...... 149 M5
Toynbee Street E1 ...... 150 B1
Trafalgar Gardens E1 ...... 151 H1
Trafalgar Square WC2N 144 C8
Trafalgar Street SE17 ...... 149 L7
Transept Street NW1 ...... 142 F5
Trebeck Street W1J 147 L1
Trebovir Road SW5 ...... 146 A6
Tregunter Road SW10 ...... 146 C7
Trenton Road SE16 ...... 150 E8
Tresham Crescent NW8 ...... 142 F3
Trevor Place SW7 ...... 147 G3
Trevor Square SW7 ...... 147 G3
Trevor Street SW7 ...... 147 G3
Trinidad Street E14 ...... 151 M4
Trinity Church Square SE1 ...... 149 K3
Trinity Square EC3N 150 B4
Trinity Street SE1 ...... 149 K3
Trump Street EC2V 145 K6
Tudor Street EC4Y 145 G7
Tufton Street SW1P 148 C4
Tunnel Road SE16 ...... 151 G6
Turks Row SW3 ...... 147 J6
Turner's Road E3 ...... 151 L2
Turner Street E1 ...... 150 E2
Turnmill Street EC1N 145 G4
Turpentine Lane SW1V 147 L7
Turquand Street SE17 ...... 149 K6
Tyers Gate SE1 ...... 149 M3
Tyers Street SE11 ...... 148 E7
Tyers Terrace SE11 ...... 148 E7
Tyron Street SW3 ...... 147 H6
Tysoe Street EC1R 145 G3

U

Udall Street SW1P 148 A5
Ufford Street SE1 ...... 149 G3
Ulster Place NW1 ...... 143 K4
Umberston Street E1 ...... 150 E2
Undershaft EC3A 150 A2
Underwood Road E1 ...... 150 D1
Underwood Street N1 ...... 145 K1
Union Street SE1 ...... 149 H2
University Street WC1E 144 A4
Upbrook Mews W2 ...... 142 D6
Upper Belgrave Street SW1X 147 K4
Upper Berkeley Street W1H 143 H6
Upper Brook Street W1K 143 J7
Upper Cheyne Row SW3 ...... 146 F8
Upper Grosvenor Street W1K 143 J8
Upper Ground SE1 ...... 148 F1
Upper Harley Street NW1 ...... 143 K3
Upper James Street W1F 144 A7
Upper John Street W1F 144 A7
Upper Marsh SE1 ...... 148 E3
Upper Montagu Street W1H 143 H5
Upper St Martin's WC2H 144 C7
Upper Tachbrook Street SW1V 148 A5
Upper Thames Street EC4V 145 J7
Upper Wimpole Street W1G 143 K4
Upper Woburn Place WC1H 144 B2
Urlwin Street SE5 ...... 149 J8
Uxbridge Street W8 ...... 146 A1

V

Valentine Place SE1 ...... 149 G3
Vandon Passage SW1H 148 A3
Vandon Street SW1H 148 A4
Vandy Street EC2A 145 M4
Varden Street E1 ...... 150 E2
Varndell Street NW1 ...... 143 M2
Vauban Street SE16 ...... 150 C8
Vaughan Street SE16 ...... 151 L7
Vaughan Way E1W 150 D5
Vauxhall ⇄ ⊖ SW8 ...... 148 D7
Vauxhall Bridge SW1V 148 C7
Vauxhall Bridgefoot SE1 ...... 148 D7
Vauxhall Bridge Road SW1V 147 M5
Vauxhall Cross SE1 ...... 148 D7
Vauxhall Grove SW8 ...... 148 D8
Vauxhall Street SE11 ...... 148 E6
Vauxhall Walk SE11 ...... 148 E6
Venables Street W2 ...... 142 E4
Vere Street W1G 143 K6
Vernon Place WC1A 144 D5
Vernon Rise WC1X 144 E2
Verulam Street WC1X 144 F4
Vestry Street N1 ...... 145 L2
Victoria ⇄ ⊖ SW1V 147 L5
Victoria & Albert Museum SW7 ...... 146 F4
Victoria Embankment SW1A 148 D2
Victoria Embankment WC2R 144 F7
Victoria Gate W2 ...... 142 F7
Victoria Road W8 ...... 146 C4
Victoria Square SW1W 147 L4
Victoria Street SW1E 147 L4
Victory Place SE17 ...... 149 K5
Victory Way SE16 ...... 151 K7
Vigo Street W1S 143 M8
Villa Street SE17 ...... 149 L7
Villiers Street WC2N 144 D8
Vincent Close SE16 ...... 151 K7
Vincent Square SW1P 148 B5
Vincent Street SW1P 148 B5
Vincent Terrace N1 ...... 145 H1
Vince Street EC1V 145 L2
Vine Court E1 ...... 150 D1
Vinegar Street E1W 150 E5
Vine Hill EC1R 144 F4
Vine Lane SE1 ...... 150 A6
Vine Street EC3N 150 B3
Violet Hill NW8 ...... 142 C1
Virgil Street SE1 ...... 148 F4
Virginia Street E1W 150 D4
Viscount Street EC2Y 145 J4

W

Wadding Street SE17 ...... 149 K6
Wakefield Street WC1H 144 D3
Wakeling Street E14 ...... 151 J3

Wakley Street EC1V 145 H2
Walbrook EC4N 145 L7
Walcorde Avenue SE17 ...... 149 K6
Walcot Square SE11 ...... 149 G5
Walden Street E1 ...... 150 E2
Wallwood Street E14 ...... 151 M1
Walnut Tree Walk SE11 ...... 148 F5
Walpole Street SW3 ...... 147 H6
Walter Terrace E1 ...... 151 H2
Walton Place SW3 ...... 147 H4
Walton Street SW3 ...... 147 G4
Walworth Place SE17 ...... 149 K7
Walworth Road SE17 ...... 149 J5
Wandsworth Road SW8 ...... 148 C8
Wansey Street SE17 ...... 149 K6
Wapping ⊖ E1W 150 F5
Wapping High Street E1W 150 F4
Wapping Lane E1W 150 F4
Wapping Wall E1W 151 G5
Warden's Grove SE1 ...... 149 J2
Wardour Street W1F 144 B6
Warner Street EC1R 144 F4
Warren Street W1T 143 M4
Warren Street ⊖ NW1 ...... 143 M3
Warrington Crescent W9 ...... 142 C3
Warrington Gardens W9 ...... 142 C4
Warwick Avenue W9 ...... 142 B3
Warwick Avenue ⊖ W9 ...... 142 C4
Warwick Crescent W2 ...... 142 C5
Warwick House Street SW1Y 148 B1
Warwick Lane EC4M 145 H6
Warwick Place W9 ...... 142 C4
Warwick Road SW5 ...... 146 A6
Warwick Row SW1E 147 L4
Warwick Square SW1V 147 M6
Warwick Street W1B 144 A7
Warwick Way SW1V 147 L6
Waterhouse Square EC1N 145 G5
Waterloo ⇄ ⊖ SE1 ...... 148 F2
Waterloo Bridge SE1 ...... 148 E1
Waterloo Bridge WC2R 144 E8
Waterloo East ⇄ SE1 ...... 149 G2
Waterloo Place SW1Y 148 B1
Waterloo Road SE1 ...... 148 F1
Waterloo Road SE1 ...... 149 G2
Waterman Way E1W 150 E5
Waterside Close SE16 ...... 150 D7
Watling Street EC4N 145 K7
Watney Street E1 ...... 150 F3
Watts Street E1W 150 E5
Waveney Close E1W 150 D5
Waverton Street W1J 147 K1
Weavers Lane SE1 ...... 150 A6
Webber Row SE1 ...... 149 G3
Webber Street SE1 ...... 149 H3
Webb Street SE1 ...... 150 A8
Webster Road SE16 ...... 150 D8
Weigh House Street W1K 143 K7
Welbeck Street W1G 143 K5
Welbeck Way W1G 143 K6
Welland Mews E1W 150 E5
Wellclose Square E1 ...... 150 D4
Wellesley Street E1 ...... 151 H2
Wellesley Terrace N1 ...... 145 K2
Wellington Arch W1J 147 K2
Wellington Square SW3 ...... 147 H6
Wellington Place NW8 ...... 142 E2
Wellington Road NW8 ...... 142 E1
Wellington Street WC2E 144 D7
Wells Mews W1T 144 A5
Wells Street W1T 144 A5
Wells Way SE5 ...... 149 M8
Wenlock Road N1 ...... 145 K1
Wenlock Street N1 ...... 145 K1
Wentworth Street E1 ...... 150 B2
Werrington Street NW1 ...... 144 A1
Wesley Street W1G 143 K5
West Arbour Street E1 ...... 151 G2
Westbourne Crescent W2 ...... 142 D7
Westbourne Gardens W2 ...... 142 B6
Westbourne Gate W2 ...... 142 D6
Westbourne Grove W2 ...... 142 A6
Westbourne Grove Terrace W2 ...... 142 B6
Westbourne Park Road W2 ...... 142 A5
Westbourne Park Villas W2 ...... 142 A5
Westbourne Street W2 ...... 142 D6
Westbourne Terrace W2 ...... 142 D6
Westbourne Terrace Mews W2 ...... 142 C6
Westbourne Terrace Road W2 ...... 142 C5
West Brompton ⇄ ⊖ SW5 ...... 146 A7
West Carriage Drive W2 ...... 146 E2
Westcott Road SE17 ...... 149 H8
West Cromwell Road SW5 ...... 146 A5
Western Place SE16 ...... 151 G6
Westferry ⊖ E14 ...... 151 M4
Westferry Circus E14 ...... 151 M5
Westferry Road E14 ...... 151 M5
West Gardens E1W 150 F4
Westgate Terrace SW10 ...... 146 B7
West Halkin Street SW1X 147 J4
West Harding Street EC4A 145 G6
West India Avenue E14 ...... 151 M5
West India Dock Road E14 ...... 151 M3
Westland Place N1 ...... 145 K2
West Lane SE16 ...... 150 E7
Westminster ⊖ SW1A 148 D3
Westminster Abbey SW1P 148 C3
Westminster Bridge SE1 ...... 148 D3
Westminster Bridge Road SE1 ...... 148 F3
Westmoreland Place SW1V 147 L7
Westmoreland Road SE17 ...... 149 K8
Westmoreland Street W1G 143 K5
Westmoreland Terrace SW1V 147 L7
Weston Rise WC1X 144 E1
Weston Street SE1 ...... 149 M2
Weston Street SE1 ...... 149 M3
Westport Street E1 ...... 151 H2
West Poultry Avenue EC1A 145 H5
West Road SW3 ...... 147 H7
West Smithfield EC1A 145 H5
West Square SE11 ...... 149 H4
West Street WC2H 144 C6
West Tenter Street E1 ...... 150 C3
West Warwick Place SW1V 147 M6
Westway W2 ...... 142 B5
Wetherby Gardens SW5 ...... 146 C6
Weyhill Road E1 ...... 150 D2
Weymouth Mews W1G 143 L5
Weymouth Street W1G 143 K5
Wharfdale Road N1 ...... 144 D1
Wharfedale Street SW10 ...... 146 B7
Wharf Road N1 ...... 145 J1
Wharton Street WC1X 144 F2
Wheatley Street W1G 143 K5
Whetstone Park WC2A 144 E5
Whidborne Street WC1H 144 D2
Whiskin Street EC1R 145 G2

Whitcomb Street WC2H 144 B8
Whitechapel ⇄ ⊖ E1 ...... 150 E1
Whitechapel Estate E1 ...... 150 C4
Whitechapel High Street E1 ...... 150 C2
Whitechapel Road E1 ...... 150 D1
Whitecross Street EC1Y 145 K3
Whitefriars Street EC4Y 145 G6
Whitehall SW1A 148 C2
Whitehall Court SW1A 148 D2
Whitehall Place SW1A 148 D1
White Hart Street SE11 ...... 149 G6
White Hart Yard SE1 ...... 149 L2
Whitehaven Street NW8 ...... 142 F4
Whitehead's Grove SW3 ...... 147 G6
White Horse Lane E1 ...... 151 H1
Whitehorse Road E1 ...... 151 J1
White Horse Street W1J 147 L1
White Kennett Street E1 ...... 150 B2
White Lion Hill EC4V 145 H7
White Lion Street N1 ...... 144 F1
White's Grounds SE1 ...... 150 A7
White's Row E1 ...... 150 B1
White Tower Way E1 ...... 151 J1
Whitfield Place W1T 144 A4
Whitfield Street W1T 144 A4
Whitgift Street SE11 ...... 148 E5
Whittaker Street SW1W 147 J6
Whittlesey Street SE1 ...... 149 G2
Wicker Street E1 ...... 150 E3
Wickham Close E1 ...... 151 G1
Wickham Street SE11 ...... 148 E7
Wicklow Street WC1X 144 E2
Widegate Street E1 ...... 150 A1
Widley Road W9 ...... 142 A3
Wigmore Place W1G 143 K5
Wigmore Street W1U 143 K6
Wigton Place SE11 ...... 149 G7
Wilbraham Place SW1X 147 J5
Wilcox Place * SW1E 148 A4
Wild Court WC2B 144 E6
Wild's Rents SE1 ...... 149 M4
Wild Street WC2B 144 D6
Wilfred Street SW1E 147 M4
Wilkes Street E1 ...... 150 B1
William IV Street WC2N 144 C8
William Mews SW1X 147 H3
William Road NW1 ...... 143 M3
Willow Place SW1P 148 A5
Willow Street EC2A 145 M3
Wilmington Square WC1X 144 F3
Wilmington Street WC1X 144 F2
Wilson Grove SE16 ...... 150 E7
Wilson Street EC2A 145 L4
Wilton Crescent SW1X 147 J3
Wilton Mews SW1X 147 K4
Wilton Place SW1X 147 J3
Wilton Road SW1V 147 M5
Wilton Row SW1X 147 J3
Wilton Street SW1X 147 K4
Wimpole Mews W1G 143 K5
Wimpole Street W1G 143 K5
Winchester Street SW1V 147 L6
Winchester Walk SE1 ...... 149 K1
Wincott Street SE11 ...... 149 G5
Windmill Road SE11 ...... 148 F7
Windmill Street W1T 144 B5
Windrose Close SE16 ...... 151 H6
Windsor Terrace N1 ...... 145 K1
Wine Close E1W 150 F5
Winnett Street W1D 144 B7
Winsland Mews W2 ...... 142 E6
Winsland Street W2 ...... 142 E6
Winsley Street W1W 144 A6
Winthrop Street E1 ...... 150 E1
Woburn Place WC1H 144 C3
Woburn Square WC1H 144 C4
Wodeham Gardens E1 ...... 150 E1
Wolfe Crescent SE16 ...... 151 H7
Wolseley Street SE1 ...... 150 C7
Woodbridge Street EC1R 145 G3
Woodchester Square W9 ...... 142 B4
Woodfall Street SW3 ...... 147 H7
Woodland Crescent SE16 ...... 151 H7
Woodseer Street E1 ...... 150 C1
Woods Mews W1K 143 J7
Woods Place SE1 ...... 150 A8
Woodstock Street W1C 143 K6
Wood Street EC2V 145 K6
Woolaston Close SE1 ...... 149 J5
Wooler Street SE17 ...... 149 L7
Wootton Street SE1 ...... 149 G2
Worgan Street SE11 ...... 148 E6
Worgan Street SE16 ...... 151 H8
Wormwood Street EC2M 145 M5
Worship Street EC2A 145 M4
Wren Street WC1X 144 E3
Wright's Lane W8 ...... 146 A3
Wyatt Close SE16 ...... 151 L7
Wyclif Street EC1V 145 H2
Wymering Road W9 ...... 142 A2
Wynard Terrace SE11 ...... 148 F7
Wyndham Place W1H 143 H5
Wyndham Street W1H 143 G4
Wynnstay Gardens W8 ...... 146 A4
Wynyat Street EC1V 145 H2
Wythburn Place W1H 143 H6

Y

Yalding Road SE16 ...... 150 C8
Yardley Street WC1X 144 F2
Yeomans Row SW3 ...... 147 G4
York Boulevard WC2N 144 D8
York Bridge NW1 ...... 143 J3
York Gate NW1 ...... 143 J4
York Road SE1 ...... 148 E2
Yorkshire Road E14 ...... 151 K3
York Square E14 ...... 151 J2
York Street W1H 143 G5
York Street W1U 143 H5
York Terrace East NW1 ...... 143 J4
York Terrace West NW1 ...... 143 J4
York Way N1 ...... 144 D1

Z

Zoar Street SE1 ...... 149 J1
ZSL London Zoo NW1 ...... 143 J1

This index lists places appearing in the main map section of the atlas in alphabetical order. The reference following each name gives the atlas page number and grid reference of the square in which the place appears. The map shows counties, unitary authorities and administrative areas, together with a list of the abbreviated name forms used in the index. The top 100 places of tourist interest are indexed in red, World Heritage sites in green, motorway service areas in blue, airports in blue *italic* and National Parks in green *italic*.

Scotland

Abers	**Aberdeenshire**
Ag & B	**Argyll and Bute**
Angus	**Angus**
Border	**Scottish Borders**
C Aber	**City of Aberdeen**
C Dund	**City of Dundee**
C Edin	**City of Edinburgh**
C Glas	**City of Glasgow**
Clacks	**Clackmannanshire (1)**
D & G	**Dumfries & Galloway**
E Ayrs	**East Ayrshire**
E Duns	**East Dunbartonshire (2)**
E Loth	**East Lothian**
E Rens	**East Renfrewshire (3)**
Falk	**Falkirk**
Fife	**Fife**
Highld	**Highland**
Inver	**Inverclyde (4)**
Mdloth	**Midlothian (5)**
Moray	**Moray**
N Ayrs	**North Ayrshire**
N Lans	**North Lanarkshire (6)**
Ork	**Orkney Islands**
P & K	**Perth & Kinross**
Rens	**Renfrewshire (7)**
S Ayrs	**South Ayrshire**
S Lans	**South Lanarkshire**
Shet	**Shetland Islands**
Stirlg	**Stirling**
W Duns	**West Dunbartonshire (8)**
W Isls	**Western Isles (Na h-Eileanan an Iar)**
W Loth	**West Lothian**

Wales

Blae G	**Blaenau Gwent (9)**
Brdgnd	**Bridgend (10)**
Caerph	**Caerphilly (11)**
Cardif	**Cardiff**
Carmth	**Carmarthenshire**
Cerdgn	**Ceredigion**
Conwy	**Conwy**
Denbgs	**Denbighshire**
Flints	**Flintshire**
Gwynd	**Gwynedd**
IoA	**Isle of Anglesey**
Mons	**Monmouthshire**
Myr Td	**Merthyr Tydfil (12)**
Neath	**Neath Port Talbot (13)**
Newpt	**Newport (14)**
Pembks	**Pembrokeshire**
Powys	**Powys**
Rhondd	**Rhondda Cynon Taff (15)**
Swans	**Swansea**
Torfn	**Torfaen (16)**
V Glam	**Vale of Glamorgan (17)**
Wrexhm	**Wrexham**

Channel Islands & Isle of Man

Guern	**Guernsey**
Jersey	**Jersey**
IoM	**Isle of Man**

England

BaNES	**Bath & N E Somerset (18)**
Barns	**Barnsley (19)**
Bed	**Bedford**
Birm	**Birmingham**
Bl w D	**Blackburn with Darwen (20)**
Bmouth	**Bournemouth**
Bolton	**Bolton (21)**
Bpool	**Blackpool**
Br & H	**Brighton & Hove (22)**
Br For	**Bracknell Forest (23)**
Bristl	**City of Bristol**
Bucks	**Buckinghamshire**
Bury	**Bury (24)**
C Beds	**Central Bedfordshire**
C Brad	**City of Bradford**
C Derb	**City of Derby**
C KuH	**City of Kingston upon Hull**
C Leic	**City of Leicester**
C Nott	**City of Nottingham**

C Pete	**City of Peterborough**
C Plym	**City of Plymouth**
C Port	**City of Portsmouth**
C Sotn	**City of Southampton**
C Stke	**City of Stoke-on-Trent**
C York	**City of York**
Calder	**Calderdale (25)**
Cambs	**Cambridgeshire**
Ches E	**Cheshire East**
Ches W	**Cheshire West and Chester**
Cnwll	**Cornwall**
Covtry	**Coventry**
Cumb	**Cumbria**
Darltn	**Darlington (26)**
Derbys	**Derbyshire**
Devon	**Devon**
Donc	**Doncaster (27)**
Dorset	**Dorset**
Dudley	**Dudley (28)**
Dur	**Durham**
E R Yk	**East Riding of Yorkshire**
E Susx	**East Sussex**
Essex	**Essex**
Gatesd	**Gateshead (29)**
Gloucs	**Gloucestershire**
Gt Lon	**Greater London**
Halton	**Halton (30)**
Hants	**Hampshire**
Hartpl	**Hartlepool (31)**
Herefs	**Herefordshire**
Herts	**Hertfordshire**
IoS	**Isles of Scilly**
IoW	**Isle of Wight**
Kent	**Kent**
Kirk	**Kirklees (32)**
Knows	**Knowsley (33)**
Lancs	**Lancashire**
Leeds	**Leeds**
Leics	**Leicestershire**
Lincs	**Lincolnshire**
Lpool	**Liverpool**
Luton	**Luton**

M Keyn	**Milton Keynes**
Manch	**Manchester**
Medway	**Medway**
Middsb	**Middlesbrough**
N Linc	**North Lincolnshire**
N Som	**North Somerset (34)**
N Tyne	**North Tyneside (35)**
N u Ty	**Newcastle upon Tyne**
N York	**North Yorkshire**
NE Lin	**North East Lincolnshire**
Nhants	**Northamptonshire**
Norfk	**Norfolk**
Notts	**Nottinghamshire**
Nthumb	**Northumberland**
Oldham	**Oldham (36)**
Oxon	**Oxfordshire**
Poole	**Poole**
R & Cl	**Redcar & Cleveland**
Readg	**Reading**
Rochdl	**Rochdale (37)**
Rothm	**Rotherham (38)**
Rutlnd	**Rutland**
S Glos	**South Gloucestershire (39)**
S on T	**Stockton-on-Tees (40)**
S Tyne	**South Tyneside (41)**
Salfd	**Salford (42)**
Sandw	**Sandwell (43)**
Sefton	**Sefton (44)**
Sheff	**Sheffield**
Shrops	**Shropshire**
Slough	**Slough (45)**
Solhll	**Solihull (46)**
Somset	**Somerset**
St Hel	**St Helens (47)**
Staffs	**Staffordshire**
Sthend	**Southend-on-Sea**
Stockp	**Stockport (48)**
Suffk	**Suffolk**
Sundld	**Sunderland**
Surrey	**Surrey**
Swindn	**Swindon**
Tamesd	**Tameside (49)**
Thurr	**Thurrock (50)**
Torbay	**Torbay**
Traffd	**Trafford (51)**
W & M	**Windsor & Maidenhead (52)**
W Berk	**West Berkshire**
W Susx	**West Sussex**
Wakefd	**Wakefield (53)**
Warrtn	**Warrington (54)**
Warwks	**Warwickshire**
Wigan	**Wigan (55)**
Wilts	**Wiltshire**
Wirral	**Wirral (56)**
Wokham	**Wokingham (57)**
Wolves	**Wolverhampton (58)**
Worcs	**Worcestershire**
Wrekin	**Telford & Wrekin (59)**
Wsall	**Walsall (60)**

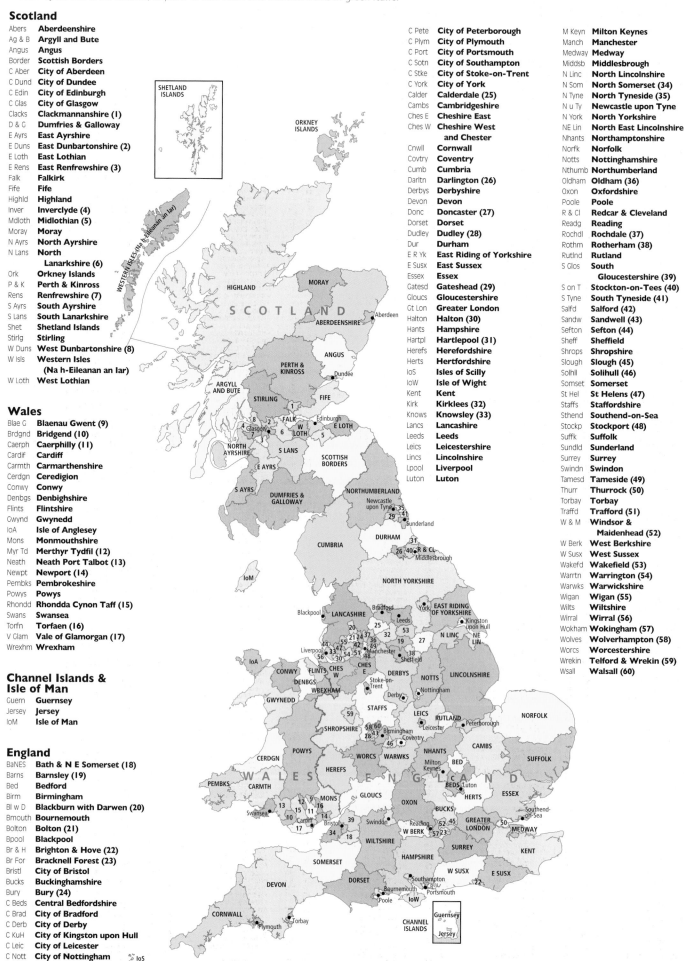

A

Abbas Combe Somset 17 Q10
Abberley Worcs 39 N8
Abberley Common Worcs 39 N8
Abberton Essex 34 G11
Abberton Worcs 30 C4
Abbess Roding Essex 22 C2
Abbeydale Sheff 50 H4
Abbey Dore Herefs 28 D3
Abbey Green Staffs 50 C8
Abbey St Bathans Border 87 P9
Abbeystead Lancs 63 K10
Abbey Town Cumb 71 J5
Abbey Valley Crematorium Derbys 51 K9
Abbey Village Lancs 57 M4
Abbey Wood Gt Lon 21 P7
Abbotrule Border 80 E10
Abbots Bickington Devon 14 G9
Abbots Bromley Staffs 40 E3
Abbotsbury Dorset 7 N6
Abbots Deuglie P & K 92 G12
Abbotsham Devon 14 H6
Abbotskerswell Devon 6 B8
Abbots Langley Herts 20 H3
Abbots Leigh N Som 17 M2
Abbotsley Cambs 32 H5
Abbots Morton Worcs 30 D3
Abbots Ripton Cambs 32 H2
Abbot's Salford Warwks 30 E4
Abbots Worthy Hants 9 N2
Abbotts Ann Hants 19 K11
Abbott Street Dorset 8 E7
Abdon Shrops 39 L5
Aberaeron Cerdgn 36 G7
Aberaman Rhondd 27 L8
Aberangell Gwynd 47 N8
Aberarder Highld 99 J4
Aberargie P & K 92 H11
Aberarth Cerdgn 36 H7
Aberavon Neath 26 G10
Abercanaid Myr Td 27 M7
Abercarn Caerph 27 P9
Abercastle Pembks 24 F3
Abercegir Powys 47 N10
Aberchalder Lodge Highld 98 D8
Aberchirder Abers 102 E5
Abercorn W Loth 86 C6
Abercraf Powys 26 H6
Abercregan Neath 26 H9
Abercwmboi Rhondd 27 L8
Abercych Pembks 36 D11
Abercynon Rhondd 27 M9
Aberdalgie P & K 92 G10
Aberdaron Gwynd 46 C6
Aberdeen C Aber 95 Q1
Aberdeen Airport C Aber 103 J11
Aberdeen Crematorium C Aber 95 P2
Aberdour Fife 86 E5
Aberdulais Neath 26 G8
Aberdyfi Gwynd 47 K11
Abereiddy Pembks 24 E3
Abererch Gwynd 46 G4
Aberfan Myr Td 27 M8
Aberfeldy P & K 92 C6
Aberffraw IoA 54 E7
Aberford Leeds 59 K6
Aberfoyle Stirlg 85 J3
Abergavenny Mons 28 C6
Abergele Conwy 55 P6
Abergorlech Carmth 26 D3
Abergwesyn Powys 37 P9
Abergwili Carmth 25 Q5
Abergwynfi Neath 27 J9
Abergwyngregyn Gwynd 55 J7
Abergynolwyn Gwynd 47 L9
Aberkenfig Brdgnd 27 J11
Aberlady E Loth 87 J6
Aberlemno Angus 93 N5
Aberllefenni Gwynd 47 M8
Aberllynfi Powys 27 N2
Aberlour, Charlestown of Moray 101 K6
Abermule Powys 38 D4
Abernant Carmth 25 N4
Abernethy P & K 92 H11
Abernyte P & K 93 J8
Aberporth Cerdgn 36 D9
Abersoch Gwynd 46 E6
Abersychan Torfn 28 B7
Aberthin V Glam 16 D2
Abertillery Blae G 27 P7
Abertridwr Caerph 27 N10
Abertridwr Powys 48 B10
Aberuthven P & K 92 E11
Aberystwyth Cerdgn 37 J4
Aberystwyth Crematorium Cerdgn 37 K4
Abingdon-on-Thames Oxon 19 N2
Abinger Common Surrey 10 H2
Abinger Hammer Surrey 10 H1
Abington Nhants 32 A5
Abington S Lans 78 F4
Abington Pigotts Cambs 33 K7
Abington Services S Lans 78 F4
Abingworth W Susx 10 H6
Ab Kettleby Leics 41 Q3
Ablington Gloucs 30 E11
Abney Derbys 50 G5
Aboyne Abers 95 J3
Abhainn Suidhe W Isls 111 C3
Abram Wigan 57 L8
Abriachan Highld 98 H2
Abridge Essex 21 P4
Abronhill N Lans 85 N7
Abson S Glos 17 Q2
Abthorpe Nhants 31 N5
Aby Lincs 53 L7
Acaster Malbis C York 59 N5
Acaster Selby N York 59 M6
Accrington Lancs 57 N3
Accrington Crematorium Lancs 57 N3
Acha Ag & B 88 F5
Achahoish Ag & B 83 L7
Achalader P & K 92 G6
Achaleven Ag & B 90 C9
Acha Mor W Isls 111 d2
Achanalt Highld 106 D9

Achandunie Highld 107 K7
Achany Highld 107 J3
Acharacle Highld 89 N3
Acharn Highld 89 P6
Acharn P & K 92 B6
Achavanich Highld 110 E7
Achduart Highld 105 Q2
Achfary Highld 108 F7
A'Chill Highld 96 C8
Achiltibuie Highld 105 Q1
Achina Highld 109 M4
Achinhoan Ag & B 75 L8
Achintee Highld 97 N2
Achintraid Highld 97 L2
Achmelvich Highld 108 B10
Achmore Highld 97 M3
Achmore W Isls 111 d2
Achnacarnin Highld 108 B8
Achnacarry Highld 98 B10
Achnacloich Ag & B 90 C7
Achnaconeran Highld 98 F5
Achnacroish Ag & B 90 B7
Achnadrish House Ag & B 89 K6
Achnafauld P & K 92 D8
Achnagarron Highld 107 L8
Achnaha Highld 89 K3
Achnahaird Highld 108 A11
Achnahannet Highld 107 F9
Achnairn Highld 109 K12
Achnalea Highld 90 B4
Achnamara Ag & B 83 L5
Achnasheen Highld 106 C10
Achnashellach Highld 105 Q11
Achnastank Moray 101 K8
Achosnich Highld 89 K3
Achranich Highld 89 P6
Achreamie Highld 110 B3
Achriabhach Highld 90 F3
Achriesgill Highld 108 E5
Achtoty Highld 109 M3
Achurch Nhants 42 E12
Achvaich Highld 107 L4
Achvarasdal Highld 110 B3
Ackergill Highld 110 G5
Acklam Middsb 66 C4
Acklam N York 60 D2
Ackleton Shrops 39 P3
Acklington Nthumb 73 M1
Ackton Wakefd 59 K9
Ackworth Moor Top Wakefd 59 K10
Acle Norfk 45 N7
Acock's Green Birm 40 E10
Acol Kent 23 P9
Acomb C York 59 M4
Acomb Nthumb 72 G7
Aconbury Herefs 28 F3
Acton Ches E 49 L5
Acton Gt Lon 21 K7
Acton Staffs 49 P7
Acton Suffk 34 E7
Acton Beauchamp Herefs 39 M11
Acton Bridge Ches W 49 L1
Acton Burnell Shrops 39 K2
Acton Green Herefs 39 M11
Acton Park Wrexhm 48 G5
Acton Round Shrops 39 L3
Acton Scott Shrops 39 J4
Acton Trussell Staffs 40 C4
Acton Turville S Glos 18 B5
Adbaston Staffs 49 N9
Adber Dorset 17 N11
Adbolton Notts 51 N12
Adderbury Oxon 31 L7
Adderley Shrops 49 M7
Addiewell W Loth 86 B9
Addingham C Brad 58 E4
Addington Bucks 31 Q8
Addington Gt Lon 21 M9
Addington Kent 22 D10
Addiscombe Gt Lon 21 M9
Addlestone Surrey 20 G9
Addlethorpe Lincs 53 N9
Adeyfield Herts 20 H2
Adfa Powys 38 C2
Adforton Herefs 38 H7
Adisham Kent 23 N11
Adlestrop Gloucs 30 G8
Adlingfleet E R Yk 60 E9
Adlington Lancs 57 L6
Admaston Staffs 40 D3
Admaston Wrekin 49 L11
Adpar Cerdgn 36 E11
Adsborough Somset 16 H9
Adscombe Somset 16 G8
Adstock Bucks 31 Q7
Adstone Nhants 31 N4
Adversane W Susx 10 H5
Advie Highld 100 H8
Adwick le Street Donc 59 M11
Adwick upon Dearne Donc 51 L1
Ae D & G 78 G10
Ae Bridgend D & G 78 G10
Afan Forest Park Neath 26 H8
Affleck Abers 102 H7
Affpuddle Dorset 8 B8
Affric Lodge Highld 98 B3
Afon-wen Flints 48 D2
Afton IoW 9 L9
Agecroft Crematorium Salfd 57 P8
Agglethorpe N York 65 J9
Aigburth Lpool 56 H10
Aike E R Yk 60 H5
Aiketgate Cumb 71 P6
Aikton Cumb 71 L5
Ailsworth C Pete 42 G9
Ainderby Quernhow N York 65 N10
Ainderby Steeple N York 65 N8
Aingers Green Essex 35 J11
Ainsdale Sefton 56 F6
Ainstable Cumb 71 Q6
Ainsworth Bury 57 N6
Ainthorpe N York 66 G6
Aintree Sefton 56 H8
Ainville W Loth 86 D9
Aird Ag & B 83 L3
Aird D & G 68 E7
Aird W Isls 111 e2
Aird a' Mhulaidh W Isls 111 c3
Aird Asaig W Isls 111 c3
Aird Dhubh Highld 97 J2
Airdeny Ag & B 90 D9
Aird of Kinloch Ag & B 89 L9
Aird of Sleat Highld 96 H9
Airdrie N Lans 85 M9

Airdriehill N Lans 85 N9
Airds of Kells D & G 69 P5
Aird Uig W Isls 111 c2
Airidh a bhruaich W Isls 111 c3
Airieland D & G 70 C4
Airlie Angus 93 K5
Airmyn E R Yk 60 C8
Airntully P & K 92 G8
Airor Highld 97 J8
Airth Falk 85 Q5
Aisby Lincs 42 E3
Aisby Lincs 52 C5
Aish Devon 5 N7
Aish Devon 6 A10
Aisholt Somset 16 G8
Aiskew N York 65 M9
Aislaby N York 66 H9
Aislaby N York 67 J6
Aislaby S on T 65 P5
Aisthorpe Lincs 52 D7
Aith Shet 111 k4
Akeld Nthumb 81 K8
Akeley Bucks 31 P6
Akenham Suffk 35 K6
Albaston Cnwll 5 J6
Alberbury Shrops 48 G11
Albourne W Susx 11 K6
Albrighton Shrops 39 P2
Albrighton Shrops 49 J10
Alburgh Norfk 45 L11
Albury Herts 33 M10
Albury Surrey 10 G1
Albury Heath Surrey 10 G2
Alcaig Highld 107 J10
Alcaston Shrops 39 J5
Alcester Warwks 30 E3
Alcester Lane End Birm 40 E10
Alciston E Susx 11 P8
Alcombe Somset 16 C7
Alconbury Cambs 32 H2
Alconbury Weston Cambs 32 H2
Aldborough N York 59 K2
Aldborough Norfk 45 K4
Aldbourne Wilts 19 J5
Aldbrough E R Yk 61 L6
Aldbrough St John N York 65 L5
Aldbury Herts 20 F2
Aldcliffe Lancs 63 J9
Aldclune P & K 92 D3
Aldeburgh Suffk 35 P5
Aldeby Norfk 45 P10
Aldenham Herts 21 J4
Alderbury Wilts 8 H2
Alderford Norfk 45 J6
Alderholt Dorset 8 G5
Alderley Gloucs 29 K10
Alderley Edge Ches E 57 Q12
Aldermans Green Covtry 41 J10
Aldermaston W Berk 19 P7
Alderminster Warwks 30 G4
Aldershot Hants 20 D12
Alderton Gloucs 30 D7
Alderton Nhants 31 Q5
Alderton Suffk 35 M8
Alderton Wilts 18 C4
Aldfield N York 58 H1
Aldford Ches W 48 H4
Aldgate Rutlnd 42 E8
Aldham Essex 34 F10
Aldham Suffk 34 H7
Aldingbourne W Susx 10 E8
Aldingham Cumb 62 F7
Aldington Kent 13 K3
Aldington Worcs 30 E5
Aldington Corner Kent 13 K3
Aldivalloch Moray 101 M9
Aldochlay Ag & B 84 F5
Aldreth Cambs 33 M3
Aldridge Wsall 40 D7
Aldringham Suffk 35 P5
Aldsworth Gloucs 30 F11
Aldunie Moray 101 M9
Aldwark Derbys 50 G8
Aldwark N York 59 L2
Aldwick W Susx 10 E9
Aldwincle Nhants 32 E1
Aldworth W Berk 19 P5
Alexandria W Duns 84 G7
Aley Somset 16 G8
Alfington Devon 6 F4
Alfold Surrey 10 G3
Alfold Crossways Surrey 10 G3
Alford Abers 102 D11
Alford Lincs 53 M8
Alford Somset 17 N9
Alford Crematorium Lincs 53 M8
Alfreton Derbys 51 K9
Alfrick Worcs 39 N10
Alfrick Pound Worcs 39 N10
Alfriston E Susx 11 P9
Algarkirk Lincs 43 J3
Alhampton Somset 17 P8
Alkborough N Linc 60 F9
Alkham Kent 13 N2
Alkmonton Derbys 50 F12
Allaleigh Devon 5 Q9
Allanaquoich Abers 94 B4
Allanbank N Lans 85 P10
Allanton Border 81 J4
Allanton N Lans 85 P10
Allanton S Lans 85 M11
Allaston Gloucs 28 H7
Allbrook Hants 9 M4
All Cannings Wilts 18 G8
Allendale Nthumb 72 F9
Allen End Warwks 40 F7
Allenheads Nthumb 72 F10
Allen's Green Herts 33 M12
Allensmore Herefs 28 F2
Allenton C Derb 41 J2
Aller Devon 15 N7
Aller Somset 17 K9
Allerby Cumb 70 H7
Allercombe Devon 6 D4
Allerford Somset 16 B6
Allerston N York 67 J10
Allerthorpe E R Yk 60 D5
Allerton C Brad 58 E7
Allerton Highld 107 M8
Allerton Lpool 56 H10
Allerton Bywater Leeds 59 K8
Allerton Mauleverer N York 59 K3
Allesley Covtry 40 H10
Allestree C Derb 51 J11
Allexton Leics 42 B9
Allgreave Ches E 50 C7

Allhallows Medway 22 G7
Alligin Shuas Highld 105 M10
Allington Dorset 7 L4
Allington Lincs 42 C3
Allington Wilts 18 D5
Allington Wilts 18 F8
Allington Wilts 18 H11
Allithwaite Cumb 62 H6
Alloa Clacks 85 P4
Allonby Cumb 70 H7
Alloway S Ayrs 76 F7
Allowenshay Somset 17 K12
All Stretton Shrops 39 J3
Alltchaorunn Highld 90 G6
Alltwalis Carmth 25 Q3
Alltwen Neath 26 G7
Alltyblaca Cerdgn 36 H10
Allweston Dorset 17 P12
Almeley Herefs 38 G11
Almington Staffs 49 N8
Almodington W Susx 10 D9
Almondbank P & K 92 F9
Almondbury Kirk 58 F10
Almondsbury S Glos 28 H11
Alne N York 59 L2
Alness Highld 107 L8
Alnham Nthumb 81 L11
Alnmouth Nthumb 81 P11
Alnwick Nthumb 81 P10
Alperton Gt Lon 21 J6
Alphamstone Essex 34 E9
Alpheton Suffk 34 E6
Alphington Devon 6 C5
Alport Derbys 50 G7
Alpraham Ches E 49 L4
Alresford Essex 34 H11
Alrewas Staffs 40 F5
Alsager Ches E 49 P4
Alsop en le Dale Derbys 50 F9
Alston Cumb 72 D10
Alston Devon 7 J3
Alstone Gloucs 29 N3
Alstonefield Staffs 50 F9
Alston Sutton Somset 17 K6
Alswear Devon 15 M7
Altandhu Highld 108 A12
Altarnun Cnwll 4 H4
Altass Highld 106 H3
Altcreich Ag & B 89 N8
Altgaltraig Ag & B 83 Q8
Althorne Essex 22 H4
Althorpe N Linc 60 E11
Altnabreac Station Highld 110 B6
Altnaharra Highld 109 K8
Altofts Wakefd 59 J9
Alton Derbys 51 J7
Alton Hants 10 B3
Alton Staffs 50 E11
Alton Barnes Wilts 18 G8
Alton Pancras Dorset 7 Q3
Alton Priors Wilts 18 G8
Alton Towers Staffs 50 E11
Altrincham Traffd 57 P10
Altrincham Crematorium Traffd 57 N10
Altskeith Hotel Stirlg 84 H3
Alva Clacks 85 P4
Alvanley Ches W 49 J1
Alvaston C Derb 41 K2
Alvechurch Worcs 40 D11
Alvecote Warwks 40 G6
Alvediston Wilts 8 E3
Alveley Shrops 39 N5
Alverdiscott Devon 15 J7
Alverstoke Hants 9 P7
Alverstone IoW 9 P9
Alverthorpe Wakefd 58 H9
Alverton Notts 42 B2
Alves Moray 100 H3
Alvescot Oxon 30 H12
Alveston S Glos 28 H10
Alveston Warwks 30 G3
Alvingham Lincs 53 K5
Alvington Gloucs 28 H8
Alwalton C Pete 42 G10
Alwinton Nthumb 81 J11
Alwoodley Leeds 58 H6
Alyth P & K 93 J6
Am Bàgh a Tuath W Isls 111 a7
Ambergate Derbys 51 J9
Amberley Gloucs 29 L8
Amberley W Susx 10 G7
Amble Nthumb 81 Q12
Amblecote Dudley 40 B9
Ambler Thorn C Brad 58 E8
Ambleside Cumb 62 G2
Ambleston Pembks 24 H4
Ambrosden Oxon 31 N9
Amcotts N Linc 60 E10
Amersham Bucks 20 F4
Amersham Common Bucks 20 F4
Amersham Old Town Bucks 20 F4
Amersham on the Hill Bucks 20 F4
Amesbury Wilts 18 H11
Amhuinnsuidhe W Isls 111 c3
Amington Staffs 40 G6
Amisfield D & G 78 G11
Amlwch IoA 54 F3
Ammanford Carmth 26 E6
Amotherby N York 66 G11
Ampfield Hants 9 L3
Ampleforth N York 66 E10
Ampney Crucis Gloucs 30 E12
Ampney St Mary Gloucs 18 G1
Ampney St Peter Gloucs 18 G1
Amport Hants 19 K11
Ampthill C Beds 32 E8
Ampton Suffk 34 E3
Amroth Pembks 25 K7
Amulree P & K 92 D8
Amwell Herts 21 J2
Anaheilt Highld 89 Q4
Ancaster Lincs 42 E2
Ancells Farm Hants 20 D11
Ancroft Nthumb 81 L5
Ancrum Border 80 E8
Ancton W Susx 10 F9
Anderby Lincs 53 N8
Andover Hants 19 L10
Andoversford Gloucs 30 D9
Andreas IoM 56 d2
Anerley Gt Lon 21 M9
Anfield Lpool 56 G9
Anfield Crematorium Lpool 56 G9
Angarrack Cnwll 2 E7
Angelbank Shrops 39 L7

Angle Pembks 24 F8
Anglesey IoA 54 F5
Anglesey Abbey Cambs 33 N4
Angmering W Susx 10 H8
Angram N York 59 M5
Ankerville Highld 107 N7
Anlaby E R Yk 60 H8
Anmer Norfk 44 C4
Anmore Hants 9 Q5
Annan D & G 71 K3
Annandale Water Services D & G 78 H9
Annat Highld 105 N10
Annathill N Lans 85 M8
Anna Valley Hants 19 L11
Annbank S Ayrs 76 G6
Anne Hathaway's Cottage Warwks 30 F3
Annfield Plain Dur 73 L9
Anniesland C Glas 85 J8
Ansdell Lancs 56 G3
Ansford Somset 17 P9
Ansley Warwks 40 H8
Anslow Staffs 40 G3
Anslow Gate Staffs 40 G3
Anstey Herts 33 L9
Anstey Leics 41 M6
Anstruther Fife 87 L2
Ansty W Susx 11 L5
Ansty Warwks 41 J9
Ansty Wilts 8 E3
Anthorn Cumb 71 K4
Antingham Norfk 45 L4
An t-Ob W Isls 111 c4
Antonine Wall 85 P7
Anton's Gowt Lincs 43 J1
Antony Cnwll 5 J8
Antrobus Ches W 57 M11
Anwick Lincs 52 G12
Anwoth D & G 69 N7
Aperfield Gt Lon 21 N10
Apethorpe Nhants 42 E10
Apley Lincs 52 G8
Apperknowle Derbys 51 J5
Apperley Gloucs 29 M3
Appin Ag & B 90 C7
Appleby N Linc 60 G10
Appleby-in-Westmorland Cumb 64 C4
Appleby Magna Leics 40 H5
Appleby Parva Leics 40 H6
Applecross Highld 97 J2
Appledore Devon 14 H6
Appledore Devon 16 E12
Appledore Kent 13 J4
Appleford Oxon 19 N3
Applegarth Town D & G 78 H11
Appleshaw Hants 19 K10
Appleton Halton 57 K10
Appleton Oxon 19 M1
Appleton Warrtn 57 L11
Appleton-le-Moors N York 66 G9
Appleton-le-Street N York 66 G11
Appleton Roebuck N York 59 M6
Appleton Thorn Warrtn 57 M11
Appleton Wiske N York 65 P6
Appletreehall Border 80 C10
Appletreewick N York 58 D3
Appley Somset 16 E10
Appley Bridge Lancs 57 K7
Apse Heath IoW 9 P10
Apsley End C Beds 32 G9
Apuldram W Susx 10 D9
Arabella Highld 107 N7
Arbirlot Angus 93 Q7
Arboll Highld 107 P6
Arborfield Wokham 20 C9
Arborfield Cross Wokham 20 C9
Arbourthorne Sheff 51 J4
Arbroath Angus 93 Q7
Arbuthnott Abers 95 N6
Archddu Carmth 25 Q8
Archdeacon Newton Darltn 65 M4
Archencarroch W Duns 84 G6
Archiestown Moray 101 J6
Arclid Ches E 49 P3
Ardallie Abers 103 L7
Ardanaiseig Hotel Ag & B 90 E10
Ardaneaskan Highld 97 L3
Ardarroch Highld 97 L2
Ardbeg Ag & B 74 F4
Ardbeg Ag & B 84 B9
Ardbeg Ag & B 84 C6
Ardcharnich Highld 106 C5
Ardchiavaig Ag & B 89 J11
Ardchonnel Ag & B 83 P1
Ardchullarie More Stirlg 91 N12
Arddarroch Ag & B 84 D4
Arddleen Powys 48 F11
Ard Dorch Highld 96 G4
Ardechive Highld 98 A10
Ardeer N Ayrs 76 E4
Ardeley Herts 33 K9
Ardelve Highld 97 M4
Arden Ag & B 84 F6
Ardens Grafton Warwks 30 E4
Ardentallen Ag & B 90 B10
Ardentinny Ag & B 84 D5
Ardentraive Ag & B 83 Q7
Ardeonaig Stirlg 91 P8
Ardersier Highld 107 N10
Ardessie Highld 105 Q5
Ardfern Ag & B 83 M3
Ardfernal Ag & B 82 H3
Ardgartan Ag & B 84 E3
Ardgay Highld 107 K4
Ardgour Highld 90 D4
Ardgowan Inver 84 D8
Ardhallow Ag & B 84 C7
Ardhasig Highld 111 c3
Ardheslaig Highld 105 L10
Ardindrean Highld 106 C5
Ardingly W Susx 11 M4
Ardington Oxon 19 M3
Ardlamont Ag & B 83 P9
Ardleigh Essex 34 H10
Ardleigh Heath Essex 34 H10
Ardler P & K 93 J7
Ardley Oxon 31 M8
Ardlui Ag & B 91 J12
Ardlussa Ag & B 82 J5
Ardmair Highld 106 B3
Ardmaleish Ag & B 84 B8
Ardminish Ag & B 75 J3
Ardmolich Highld 89 P2

160 Ardmore – Barabhas

Ardmore Ag & B 84 F7
Ardmore Highld 107 L5
Ardnadam Ag & B 84 C7
Ardnagrask Highld 106 H11
Ardnamurchan Highld 89 L3
Ardnarff Highld 97 M3
Ardnastang Highld 89 Q4
Ardpatrick Ag & B 83 L10
Ardrishaig Ag & B 83 M6
Ardross Highld 107 K7
Ardrossan N Ayrs 76 D3
Ardsley East Leeds 58 H8
Ardslignish Highld 89 L4
Ardtalla Ag & B 82 G11
Ardtoe Highld 89 M3
Arduaine Ag & B 83 M2
Ardullie Highld 107 J9
Ardvasar Highld 96 H8
Ardvorlich P & K 91 P10
Ardvourlie W Isls 111 c3
Ardwell D & G 68 F9
Ardwick Manch 57 Q9
Areley Kings Worcs 39 P7
Arevegaig Highld 89 N3
Arford Hants 10 D3
Argoed Caerph 27 N8
Argyll Forest Park Ag & B 84 D3
Aribruach W Isls 111 c3
Aridhglas Ag & B 88 H10
Arileod Ag & B 88 E5
Arinagour Ag & B 88 F5
Ariogan Ag & B 90 B10
Arisaig Highld 97 J11
Arisaig House Highld 97 J11
Arkendale N York 59 K2
Arkesden Essex 33 M9
Arkholme Lancs 63 L7
Arkleton D & G 79 N10
Arkley Gt Lon 21 K4
Arksey Donc 59 M11
Arkwright Town Derbys 51 K6
Arle Gloucs 29 N4
Arlecdon Cumb 70 G10
Arlesey C Beds 32 H9
Arleston Wrekin 49 M12
Arley Ches E 57 M11
Arley Warwks 40 H8
Arlingham Gloucs 29 J6
Arlington Devon 15 K4
Arlington E Susx 12 B8
Armadale Highld 96 H8
Armadale Highld 109 N3
Armadale W Loth 85 Q8
Armathwaite Cumb 71 Q6
Arminghall Norfk 45 L8
Armitage Staffs 40 E4
Armley Leeds 58 H7
Armscote Warwks 30 G5
Armthorpe Donc 59 N12
Arnabost Ag & B 88 F4
Arncliffe N York 64 G12
Arncroach Fife 87 K2
Arndilly House Moray 101 K6
Arne Dorset 8 E9
Arnesby Leics 41 N8
Arngask P & K 92 H12
Arnisdale Highld 97 L7
Arnish Highld 104 H11
Arniston Mdloth 86 G9
Arnol W Isls 111 d1
Arnold E R Yk 61 J6
Arnold Notts 51 N10
Arnprior Stirlg 85 K4
Arnside Cumb 63 J6
Aros Ag & B 89 L7
Arrad Foot Cumb 62 F6
Arram E R Yk 60 H5
Arran N Ayrs 75 P5
Arrathorne N York 65 L8
Arreton IoW 9 N9
Arrina Highld 105 L10
Arrington Cambs 33 K6
Arrochar Ag & B 84 E3
Arrow Warwks 30 E3
Arscott Shrops 38 H1
Artafallie Highld 107 K11
Arthington Leeds 58 H5
Arthingworth Nhants 41 Q10
Arthrath Abers 103 K7
Artrochie Abers 103 L8
Arundel W Susx 10 G8
Asby Cumb 70 H10
Ascog Ag & B 84 B9
Ascot W & M 20 E9
Ascott-under-Wychwood Oxon 30 H9
Asenby N York 65 P11
Asfordby Leics 41 P4
Asfordby Hill Leics 41 Q4
Asgarby Lincs 42 G2
Ash Kent 22 C9
Ash Kent 23 P10
Ash Somset 17 L11
Ash Surrey 20 E12
Ashampstead W Berk 19 P5
Ashbocking Suffk 35 K6
Ashbourne Derbys 50 F10
Ashbrittle Somset 16 E11
Ashburton Devon 5 P6
Ashbury Devon 15 J11
Ashbury Oxon 19 J4
Ashby N Linc 52 C2
Ashby by Partney Lincs 53 L9
Ashby cum Fenby NE Lin 53 J4
Ashby de la Launde Lincs 52 F11
Ashby-de-la-Zouch Leics 41 J4
Ashby Folville Leics 41 P5
Ashby Magna Leics 41 M9
Ashby Parva Leics 41 M9
Ashby Puerorum Lincs 53 K8
Ashby St Ledgers Nhants 31 M1
Ashby St Mary Norfk 45 M9
Ashchurch Gloucs 29 N3
Ashcombe Devon 6 C6
Ashcombe N Som 17 J4
Ashcott Somset 17 L8
Ashdon Essex 33 P8
Ashdown Forest E Susx 11 P4
Ashe Hants 19 N10
Asheldham Essex 23 J3
Ashen Essex 34 C8
Ashendon Bucks 31 P10
Asheridge Bucks 20 F3
Ashfield Stirlg 85 N3
Ashfield cum Thorpe Suffk 35 K4
Ashfield Green Suffk 35 L3
Ashford Devon 5 N9
Ashford Devon 15 J5
Ashford Kent 13 J2
Ashford Surrey 20 H8
Ashford Bowdler Shrops 39 K7
Ashford Carbonell Shrops 39 K7
Ashford Hill Hants 19 P8
Ashford in the Water Derbys 50 G6
Ashgill S Lans 77 N2
Ash Green Surrey 20 E12
Ash Green Warwks 41 J9
Ashill Devon 6 E1
Ashill Norfk 44 E8
Ashill Somset 17 J11
Ashingdon Essex 22 G5
Ashington Nthumb 73 M4
Ashington Somset 17 N11
Ashington W Susx 11 J7
Ashkirk Border 79 P4
Ashleworth Gloucs 29 L4
Ashleworth Quay Gloucs 29 L4
Ashley Cambs 34 B5
Ashley Ches E 57 P11
Ashley Devon 15 L9
Ashley Gloucs 29 N9
Ashley Hants 9 J8
Ashley Hants 9 L2
Ashley Kent 13 P1
Ashley Nhants 42 B11
Ashley Staffs 49 N7
Ashley Wilts 18 B7
Ashley Green Bucks 20 F3
Ash Magna Shrops 49 K7
Ashmansworth Hants 19 M8
Ashmansworthy Devon 14 F8
Ash Mill Devon 15 N7
Ashmore Dorset 8 D4
Ashmore Green W Berk 19 N6
Ashorne Warwks 30 H3
Ashover Derbys 51 J8
Ashow Warwks 40 H12
Ashperton Herefs 28 H1
Ashprington Devon 5 Q8
Ash Priors Somset 16 F9
Ashreigney Devon 15 L9
Ash Street Suffk 34 G7
Ashtead Surrey 21 J10
Ash Thomas Devon 6 D1
Ashton Ches W 49 J2
Ashton Cnwll 2 F9
Ashton Devon 6 B6
Ashton Herefs 39 K8
Ashton Inver 84 D7
Ashton Nhants 31 Q4
Ashton Nhants 42 F11
Ashton Common Wilts 18 D8
Ashton-in-Makerfield Wigan 57 L8
Ashton Keynes Wilts 18 F2
Ashton under Hill Worcs 30 C6
Ashton-under-Lyne Tamesd 50 C2
Ashton Vale Bristl 17 N3
Ashurst Hants 9 K5
Ashurst Kent 11 P3
Ashurst Lancs 57 J7
Ashurst W Susx 11 J6
Ashurstwood W Susx 11 N3
Ash Vale Surrey 20 E11
Ashwater Devon 5 J2
Ashwell Herts 33 J8
Ashwell Rutlnd 42 C7
Ashwell End Herts 33 J8
Ashwellthorpe Norfk 45 J9
Ashwick Somset 17 P6
Ashwicken Norfk 44 B6
Askam in Furness Cumb 62 E6
Askern Donc 59 M10
Askerswell Dorset 7 M4
Askett Bucks 20 D3
Askham Cumb 71 Q10
Askham Notts 51 Q6
Askham Bryan C York 59 M5
Askham Richard C York 59 M5
Asknish Ag & B 83 P5
Askrigg N York 64 G8
Askwith N York 58 F5
Aslackby Lincs 42 F4
Aslacton Norfk 45 J11
Aslockton Notts 51 Q11
Aspatria Cumb 71 J7
Aspenden Herts 33 K10
Aspley Guise C Beds 32 D9
Aspley Heath C Beds 32 D9
Aspull Wigan 57 L7
Asselby E R Yk 60 C8
Assington Suffk 34 F8
Assington Green Suffk 34 C6
Astbury Ches E 49 Q3
Astcote Nhants 31 P4
Asterby Lincs 53 J7
Asterley Shrops 38 G1
Asterton Shrops 38 H4
Asthall Oxon 30 H10
Asthall Leigh Oxon 30 H10
Astle Highld 107 M4
Astley Shrops 49 K10
Astley Warwks 40 H9
Astley Wigan 57 M8
Astley Worcs 39 P8
Astley Abbots Shrops 39 N3
Astley Bridge Bolton 57 N6
Astley Cross Worcs 39 P8
Aston Birm 40 E9
Aston Ches E 49 L6
Aston Ches W 57 K12
Aston Derbys 50 F4
Aston Flints 48 F3
Aston Herts 33 J11
Aston Oxon 31 J12
Aston Rothm 51 L4
Aston Shrops 39 P4
Aston Shrops 49 K9
Aston Staffs 40 B3
Aston Staffs 49 N7
Aston Wokham 20 C6
Aston Wrekin 49 L12
Aston Abbotts Bucks 32 C11
Aston Botterell Shrops 39 L5
Aston-by-Stone Staffs 40 B2
Aston Cantlow Warwks 30 F3
Aston Clinton Bucks 20 E2
Aston Crews Herefs 29 J4
Aston End Herts 33 J11
Aston Fields Worcs 40 C12
Aston Flamville Leics 41 L8
Aston Ingham Herefs 29 J4
Aston le Walls Nhants 31 L4
Aston Magna Gloucs 30 G7
Aston Munslow Shrops 39 K5
Aston on Clun Shrops 38 H6
Aston Pigott Shrops 38 G2
Aston Rogers Shrops 38 G2
Aston Rowant Oxon 20 B4
Aston Somerville Worcs 30 D6
Aston-sub-Edge Gloucs 30 F6
Aston Tirrold Oxon 19 P4
Aston-upon-Trent Derbys 41 K2
Aston Upthorpe Oxon 19 P4
Astwick C Beds 32 H8
Astwood M Keyn 32 D7
Astwood Worcs 30 C2
Astwood Bank Worcs 30 D2
Aswarby Lincs 42 F3
Aswardby Lincs 53 L9
Atcham Shrops 39 K1
Athelhampton Dorset 8 B8
Athelington Suffk 35 K3
Athelney Somset 17 J9
Athelstaneford E Loth 87 K6
Atherington Devon 15 K7
Atherstone Warwks 40 H7
Atherstone on Stour Warwks 30 G4
Atherton Wigan 57 M8
Atlow Derbys 50 G10
Attadale Highld 97 N3
Atterby Lincs 52 E5
Attercliffe Sheff 51 J3
Atterton Leics 41 J7
Attingham Park Shrops 49 K12
Attleborough Norfk 44 H10
Attleborough Warwks 41 J8
Attlebridge Norfk 45 J6
Attleton Green Suffk 34 C6
Atwick E R Yk 61 K4
Atworth Wilts 18 C7
Aubourn Lincs 52 D10
Auchbreck Moray 101 J9
Auchedly Abers 103 J8
Auchenblae Abers 95 M6
Auchenbowie Stirlg 85 N5
Auchencairn D & G 70 D5
Auchencairn D & G 78 F11
Auchencairn N Ayrs 75 Q6
Auchencrow Border 87 Q9
Auchendinny Mdloth 86 F9
Auchengray S Lans 86 B10
Auchenhalrig Moray 101 M3
Auchenheath S Lans 77 N3
Auchenhessnane D & G 77 N11
Auchenlochan Ag & B 83 P8
Auchenmade N Ayrs 76 F2
Auchenmalg D & G 68 G8
Auchentiber N Ayrs 76 F2
Auchindrain Ag & B 83 Q3
Auchindrean Highld 106 C6
Auchininna Abers 102 E6
Auchinleck E Ayrs 77 J7
Auchinloch N Lans 85 L8
Auchinstarry N Lans 85 M7
Auchintore Highld 90 F2
Auchiries Abers 103 M7
Auchlean Highld 99 M9
Auchlee Abers 95 P3
Auchleven Abers 102 E9
Auchlochan S Lans 77 N4
Auchlossan Abers 95 J2
Auchlyne Stirlg 91 M9
Auchmillan E Ayrs 77 J5
Auchmithie Angus 93 R6
Auchmuirbridge Fife 86 E3
Auchnacree Angus 94 H8
Auchnagatt Abers 103 J7
Auchnarrow Moray 101 J9
Auchnotteroch D & G 68 D7
Auchroisk Moray 101 L5
Auchterarder P & K 92 E12
Auchteraw Highld 98 E7
Auchterblair Highld 99 N5
Auchtercairn Highld 105 M7
Auchterderran Fife 86 E3
Auchterhouse Angus 93 L8
Auchterless Abers 102 F7
Auchtermuchty Fife 93 J12
Auchterneed Highld 106 H9
Auchtertool Fife 86 E4
Auchtertyre Highld 97 L4
Auchtubh Stirlg 91 N11
Auckengill Highld 110 G3
Auckley Donc 51 P1
Audenshaw Tamesd 50 B2
Audlem Ches E 49 M6
Audley Staffs 49 P5
Audley End Essex 33 N8
Audley End House & Gardens Essex 33 N8
Audnam Dudley 40 B9
Aughton E R Yk 60 C6
Aughton Lancs 56 H7
Aughton Lancs 63 K8
Aughton Rothm 51 L4
Aughton Wilts 19 J9
Aughton Park Lancs 56 H7
Auldearn Highld 100 E4
Aulden Herefs 39 J10
Auldgirth D & G 78 E10
Auldhouse S Lans 77 K2
Ault a' chruinn Highld 97 N5
Aultbea Highld 105 N5
Aultgrishin Highld 105 L5
Aultguish Inn Highld 106 F8
Ault Hucknall Derbys 51 L7
Aultmore Moray 101 M5
Aultnagoire Highld 98 H4
Aultnamain Inn Highld 107 L6
Aunsby Lincs 42 F3
Aust S Glos 28 G10
Austerfield Donc 51 P2
Austrey Warwks 40 H6
Austwick N York 63 N8
Authorpe Lincs 53 L7
Avebury Wilts 18 G6
Avebury Wilts 18 G6
Aveley Thurr 22 C7
Avening Gloucs 29 M8
Averham Notts 51 Q9
Aveton Gifford Devon 5 N10
Aviemore Highld 99 N6
Avington W Berk 19 L7
Avoch Highld 107 L10
Avon Hants 8 G7
Avonbridge Falk 85 Q8
Avon Dassett Warwks 31 K4
Avonmouth Bristl 28 F12
Avonwick Devon 5 P8
Awbridge Hants 9 K3
Awliscombe Devon 6 F3
Awre Gloucs 29 J7
Awsworth Notts 51 L11
Axbridge Somset 17 L5
Axford Hants 19 Q11
Axford Wilts 19 J6
Axminster Devon 6 H3
Axmouth Devon 6 H5
Aycliffe Dur 65 M3
Aydon Nthumb 72 H7
Aylburton Gloucs 28 H8
Aylesbeare Devon 6 D4
Aylesbury Bucks 20 D1
Aylesbury Crematorium Bucks 32 B12
Aylesby NE Lin 52 H3
Aylesford Kent 22 E10
Aylesham Kent 23 N11
Aylestone C Leic 41 M7
Aylestone Park C Leic 41 N7
Aylmerton Norfk 45 K3
Aylsham Norfk 45 K5
Aylton Herefs 28 H2
Aylworth Gloucs 30 E9
Aymestrey Herefs 38 H8
Aynho Nhants 31 L7
Ayot St Lawrence Herts 32 H12
Ayr S Ayrs 76 F7
Aysgarth N York 64 H9
Ayshford Devon 16 E11
Ayside Cumb 62 H5
Ayston Rutlnd 42 C9
Ayton Border 81 J3
Azerley N York 65 M11

B

Babbacombe Torbay 6 C9
Babbs Green Herts 33 L12
Babcary Somset 17 N9
Babraham Cambs 33 N6
Babworth Notts 51 P5
Backaland Ork 111 h1
Backfolds Abers 103 L5
Backford Ches W 48 H2
Backies Highld 107 N3
Back of Keppoch Highld 97 J11
Backwell N Som 17 L3
Baconsthorpe Norfk 45 J3
Bacton Herefs 28 D3
Bacton Norfk 45 M4
Bacton Suffk 34 H4
Bacup Lancs 57 Q4
Badachro Highld 105 L7
Badanloch Highld 109 N8
Badbury Swindn 18 H5
Badby Nhants 31 M3
Badcall Highld 108 D7
Badcall Highld 108 E5
Badcaul Highld 105 Q4
Baddeley Edge C Stke 50 B9
Baddeley Green C Stke 50 B9
Baddesley Clinton Warwks 40 G11
Baddesley Ensor Warwks 40 H7
Baddidarrach Highld 108 C10
Baddinsgill Border 86 D10
Badenscoth Abers 102 F7
Badentarbet Highld 105 Q1
Badenyon Abers 101 L10
Badger Shrops 39 N3
Badgeworth Gloucs 29 M5
Badgworth Somset 17 K5
Badicaul Highld 97 K4
Badingham Suffk 35 M3
Badlesmere Kent 23 J11
Badlieu Border 78 H5
Badlipster Highld 110 F6
Badluarach Highld 105 P4
Badninish Highld 107 M4
Badrallach Highld 105 Q4
Badsey Worcs 30 E5
Badshot Lea Surrey 10 D1
Badsworth Wakefd 59 L10
Badwell Ash Suffk 34 G3
Bagber Dorset 17 Q12
Bagby N York 66 C10
Bag Enderby Lincs 53 K8
Bagendon Gloucs 30 D11
Bàgh a' Chaisteil W Isls 111 a7
Bagillt Flints 48 E1
Baginton Warwks 41 J11
Baglan Neath 26 G9
Bagley Shrops 48 H9
Bagley Somset 17 L7
Bagnall Staffs 50 B10
Bagshot Surrey 20 E10
Bagstone S Glos 29 J10
Bagworth Leics 41 K6
Bagwy Llydiart Herefs 28 E4
Baildon C Brad 58 F6
Baildon Green C Brad 58 F6
Baile Ailein W Isls 111 d2
Baile a' Mhanaich W Isls 111 b5
Baile Mòr Ag & B 88 G10
Baillieston C Glas 85 L9
Bainbridge N York 64 G9
Bainshole Abers 102 D8
Bainton C Pete 42 F8
Bainton E R Yk 60 G4
Baintown Fife 86 G2
Bairnkine Border 80 E10
Bakewell Derbys 50 G7
Bala Gwynd 47 Q4
Balallan W Isls 111 d2
Balbeg Highld 98 F3
Balbeggie P & K 92 H9
Balblair Highld 106 H12
Balblair Highld 107 L8
Balby Donc 51 M1
Balcary D & G 70 D5
Balchraggan Highld 98 G1
Balchreick Highld 108 D4
Balcombe W Susx 11 L4
Balcomie Links Fife 87 M1
Baldersby N York 65 N10
Baldersby St James N York 65 P11
Balderstone Lancs 57 L3
Balderton Notts 52 B12
Baldinnie Fife 93 M12
Baldinnies P & K 92 F11
Baldock Herts 33 J9
Baldock Services Herts 32 H9
Baldovie C Dund 93 M8
Baldrine IoM 56 d5
Baldslow E Susx 12 F7
Bale Norfk 44 G3
Baledgarno P & K 93 K9
Balemartine Ag & B 88 C7
Balerno C Edin 86 D8
Balfarg Fife 86 F2
Balfield Angus 95 J8
Balfour Ork 111 h2
Balfron Stirlg 85 J5
Balgaveny Abers 102 E7
Balgonar Fife 86 B4
Balgowan D & G 68 F9
Balgowan Highld 99 J9
Balgown Highld 104 E8
Balgracie D & G 68 D7
Balgray S Lans 78 E4
Balham Gt Lon 21 L8
Balhary P & K 93 J6
Balholmie P & K 92 H8
Baligill Highld 109 P3
Balintore Angus 93 K4
Balintore Highld 107 P7
Balintraid Highld 107 M8
Balivanich W Isls 111 b5
Balkeerie Angus 93 K6
Balkholme E R Yk 60 D8
Ballachulish Highld 90 E5
Ballajora IoM 56 e4
Ballanlay Ag & B 83 Q9
Ballantrae S Ayrs 68 E3
Ballasalla IoM 56 b6
Ballater Abers 94 F3
Ballaugh IoM 56 c3
Ballchraggan Highld 107 M7
Ballencrieff E Loth 87 J6
Ballevullin Ag & B 88 B7
Ball Green C Stke 50 B9
Ball Hill Hants 19 M8
Ballidon Derbys 50 G9
Balliekine N Ayrs 75 N5
Balliemore Ag & B 84 B3
Balligmorrie S Ayrs 68 G2
Ballimore Stirlg 91 M11
Ballindalloch Moray 101 J7
Ballindean P & K 93 J9
Ballinger Common Bucks 20 E3
Ballingham Herefs 28 G3
Ballingry Fife 86 E3
Ballinluig P & K 92 E5
Ballinshoe Angus 93 M5
Ballintuim P & K 92 G5
Balloch Highld 107 M11
Balloch N Lans 85 M7
Balloch P & K 92 C10
Balloch S Ayrs 76 F11
Balloch W Duns 84 G6
Balls Cross W Susx 10 F5
Balls Green E Susx 11 P3
Ballygown Ag & B 89 J7
Ballygrant Ag & B 82 E9
Ballyhaugh Ag & B 88 E5
Balmacara Highld 97 L4
Balmaclellan D & G 69 P4
Balmae D & G 69 P9
Balmaha Stirlg 84 G5
Balmalcolm Fife 86 G1
Balmangan D & G 69 P9
Balmedie Abers 103 K10
Balmerino Fife 93 L10
Balmichael N Ayrs 75 P6
Balmore E Duns 85 K8
Balmuchy Highld 107 P6
Balmule Fife 86 E5
Balmullo Fife 93 M10
Balnacoil Highld 109 P12
Balnacra Highld 105 P12
Balnacroft Abers 94 E3
Balnafoich Highld 99 K2
Balnaguard P & K 92 E5
Balnahard Ag & B 82 F3
Balnahard Ag & B 89 K9
Balnain Highld 98 F3
Balnakeil Highld 108 G3
Balne N York 59 N9
Balquharn P & K 92 F8
Balquhidder Stirlg 91 M11
Balsall Common Solhll 40 G11
Balsall Heath Birm 40 E9
Balscote Oxon 31 K6
Balsham Cambs 33 P6
Baltasound Shet 111 m2
Baltersan D & G 69 K6
Balthangie Abers 102 H5
Baltonsborough Somset 17 M8
Balvicar Ag & B 89 Q11
Balvraid Highld 97 M6
Balvraid Highld 99 M3
Bamber Bridge Lancs 57 K4
Bamber's Green Essex 33 P11
Bamburgh Nthumb 81 N7
Bamburgh Castle Nthumb 81 N7
Bamford Derbys 50 G4
Bampton Cumb 71 Q11
Bampton Devon 16 C10
Bampton Oxon 30 H12
Bampton Grange Cumb 71 Q11
Banavie Highld 90 F2
Banbury Oxon 31 L6
Banbury Crematorium Oxon 31 L5
Bancffosfelen Carmth 25 C6
Banchory Abers 95 L3
Banchory-Devenick Abers 95 P2
Bancycapel Carmth 25 P6
Bancyfelin Carmth 25 N5
Bandirran P & K 93 J9
Banff Abers 102 F3
Bangor Gwynd 54 H7
Bangor Crematorium Gwynd 54 H7
Bangor-on-Dee Wrexhm 48 H6
Bangors Cnwll 14 D11
Banham Norfk 44 H11
Bank Hants 9 K6
Bankend D & G 70 G2
Bankfoot P & K 92 F8
Bankglen E Ayrs 77 K8
Bankhead C Aber 103 J12
Bankhead S Lans 86 B12
Banknock Falk 85 N7
Banks Lancs 56 H5
Bankshill D & G 79 K11
Banningham Norfk 45 K4
Bannister Green Essex 34 B11
Bannockburn Stirlg 85 N5
Banstead Surrey 21 K10
Bantham Devon 5 N10
Banton N Lans 85 M7
Banwell N Som 17 K4
Bapchild Kent 22 H10
Bapton Wilts 18 E12
Barabhas W Isls 111 d1

Barassie S Ayrs	76	F5
Barbaraville Highld	107	M7
Barbieston S Ayrs	76	G7
Barbon Cumb	63	L6
Barbrook Devon	15	M3
Barby Nhants	41	M12
Barcaldine Ag & B	90	D7
Barcombe E Susx	11	N7
Barcombe Cross E Susx	11	N6
Barden Park Kent	12	C2
Bardfield End Green Essex	33	Q9
Bardfield Saling Essex	34	B10
Bardney Lincs	52	G9
Bardon Leics	41	K5
Bardon Mill Nthumb	72	E7
Bardowie E Duns	85	K8
Bardrainney Inver	84	F8
Bardsea Cumb	62	F7
Bardsey Leeds	59	J5
Bardsey Island Gwynd	46	B7
Bardwell Suffk	34	F3
Bare Lancs	63	J8
Barfad D & G	69	L6
Barford Norfk	45	J8
Barford Warwks	30	H2
Barford St John Oxon	31	K7
Barford St Martin Wilts	8	F2
Barford St Michael Oxon	31	K7
Barfrestone Kent	23	N12
Bargeddie N Lans	85	L9
Bargoed Caerph	27	N8
Bargrennan D & G	69	J4
Barham Cambs	32	G2
Barham Kent	23	N12
Barham Suffk	35	J6
Barham Crematorium Kent	13	N1
Bar Hill Cambs	33	L4
Barholm Lincs	42	F7
Barkby Leics	41	N5
Barkby Thorpe Leics	41	N5
Barkestone-le-Vale Leics	41	R1
Barkham Wokham	20	C9
Barking Gt Lon	21	N6
Barking Suffk	34	H6
Barkingside Gt Lon	21	N5
Barking Tye Suffk	34	H6
Barkisland Calder	58	D9
Barkla Shop Cnwll	2	H5
Barkston Lincs	42	D2
Barkston Ash N York	59	L7
Barkway Herts	33	L9
Barlanark C Glas	85	L9
Barlaston Staffs	50	B11
Barlavington W Susx	10	F6
Barlborough Derbys	51	L5
Barlby N York	59	N7
Barlestone Leics	41	K6
Barley Herts	33	L8
Barley Lancs	57	P1
Barleythorpe Rutlnd	42	C8
Barling Essex	22	H5
Barlings Lincs	52	F8
Barlochan D & G	70	D4
Barlow Derbys	51	J6
Barlow Gatesd	73	K8
Barlow N York	59	N8
Barmby Moor E R Yk	60	D4
Barmby on the Marsh E R Yk	59	P8
Barmollack Ag & B	75	M4
Barmouth Gwynd	47	K7
Barmpton Darltn	65	N4
Barmston E R Yk	61	K3
Barnacarry Ag & B	83	Q4
Barnack C Pete	42	F8
Barnard Castle Dur	65	J4
Barnard Gate Oxon	31	K11
Barnardiston Suffk	34	B7
Barnbarroch D & G	70	D4
Barnburgh Donc	59	L12
Barnby Suffk	45	P11
Barnby Dun Donc	59	N11
Barnby in the Willows Notts	52	C11
Barnby Moor Notts	51	P4
Barncorkrie D & G	68	E11
Barnes Gt Lon	21	K7
Barnes Street Kent	12	D1
Barnet Gt Lon	21	K4
Barnetby le Wold N Linc	52	F2
Barney Norfk	44	G4
Barnham Suffk	34	E2
Barnham W Susx	10	F8
Barnham Broom Norfk	44	H8
Barnhead Angus	93	R4
Barnhill C Dund	93	N8
Barnhill Moray	100	H4
Barnhills D & G	68	D5
Barningham Dur	65	J5
Barningham Suffk	34	F2
Barnoldby le Beck NE Lin	52	H3
Barnoldswick Lancs	63	Q11
Barns Green W Susx	10	H5
Barnsley Barns	59	J11
Barnsley Gloucs	30	E12
Barnsley Crematorium Barns	59	J12
Barnstaple Devon	15	K5
Barnston Essex	33	Q11
Barnston Wirral	56	F11
Barnstone Notts	41	Q3
Barnt Green Worcs	40	D11
Barnton C Edin	86	E7
Barnton Ches W	49	L1
Barnwell All Saints Nhants	42	F12
Barnwell St Andrew Nhants	42	F12
Barnwood Gloucs	29	M5
Barr S Ayrs	76	E11
Barra W Isls	111	a7
Barra Airport W Isls	111	a6
Barrachan D & G	69	J8
Barraigh W Isls	111	a7
Barrananaoil Ag & B	83	M2
Barrapoll Ag & B	88	B7
Barrasford Nthumb	72	G6
Barrhead E Rens	84	H10
Barrhill S Ayrs	68	H3
Barrington Cambs	33	L6
Barrington Somset	17	K11
Barripper Cnwll	2	H6
Barrock Highld	110	F2
Barrow Gloucs	29	M4
Barrow Lancs	57	N2
Barrow Rutlnd	42	C7
Barrow Somset	17	Q9
Barrow Suffk	34	C4
Barrowby Lincs	42	C3
Barrowden Rutlnd	42	D9
Barrowford Lancs	57	Q2
Barrow Gurney N Som	17	M3
Barrow Haven N Linc	60	H9
Barrow-in-Furness Cumb	62	E8
Barrow Island Cumb	62	E8
Barrow-upon-Humber N Linc	60	H9
Barrow upon Soar Leics	41	M4
Barrow upon Trent Derbys	41	J2
Barry Angus	93	P8
Barry V Glam	16	F3
Barry Island V Glam	16	F3
Barsby Leics	41	P5
Barsham Suffk	45	N11
Barston Solhll	40	G10
Bartestree Herefs	28	G1
Barthol Chapel Abers	102	H8
Bartholomew Green Essex	34	C11
Barthomley Ches E	49	N5
Bartley Hants	9	K5
Bartley Green Birm	40	D10
Bartlow Cambs	33	P7
Barton Cambs	33	L5
Barton Ches W	49	J5
Barton Gloucs	30	E8
Barton Lancs	56	G7
Barton Lancs	57	K2
Barton N York	65	M6
Barton Oxon	31	M11
Barton Torbay	6	C8
Barton Bendish Norfk	44	B8
Barton End Gloucs	29	L8
Barton Hartshorn Bucks	31	N7
Barton in Fabis Notts	41	M2
Barton in the Beans Leics	41	K6
Barton-le-Clay C Beds	32	F9
Barton-le-Street N York	66	G11
Barton-le-Willows N York	60	C2
Barton Mills Suffk	34	C3
Barton-on-Sea Hants	9	J8
Barton-on-the-Heath Warwks	30	G7
Barton Park Services N York	65	L6
Barton St David Somset	17	M9
Barton Seagrave Nhants	32	C2
Barton Stacey Hants	19	M11
Barton Town Devon	15	L4
Barton Turf Norfk	45	M5
Barton-under-Needwood Staffs	40	F4
Barton-upon-Humber N Linc	60	H9
Barton Waterside N Linc	60	H9
Barvas W Isls	111	d1
Barway Cambs	33	N2
Barwell Leics	41	K8
Barwick Devon	15	K10
Barwick Somset	17	M12
Barwick in Elmet Leeds	59	K6
Baschurch Shrops	48	H10
Bascote Warwks	31	K2
Bashall Eaves Lancs	63	M12
Basildon Essex	22	E5
Basildon & District Crematorium Essex	22	E6
Basingstoke Hants	19	Q9
Basingstoke Crematorium Hants	19	P10
Baslow Derbys	50	G6
Bason Bridge Somset	17	J7
Bassaleg Newpt	28	C10
Bassendean Border	80	E5
Bassenthwaite Cumb	71	K8
Bassett C Sotn	9	M4
Bassingbourn-cum-Kneesworth Cambs	33	K7
Bassingham Lincs	52	C10
Bassingthorpe Lincs	42	D5
Bassus Green Herts	33	K10
Baston Lincs	42	G7
Bastwick Norfk	45	N6
Batchworth Herts	20	G5
Batcombe Dorset	7	N3
Batcombe Somset	17	Q8
Batford Herts	21	J1
Bath BaNES	17	Q4
Bath, City of BaNES	17	Q3
Bathealton Somset	16	E10
Batheaston BaNES	18	B7
Bathford BaNES	18	B7
Bathgate W Loth	86	B8
Bathley Notts	51	Q8
Bathpool Cnwll	4	G5
Bathpool Somset	16	H10
Bath Side Essex	35	L9
Bathville W Loth	85	Q9
Bathway Somset	17	N6
Batley Kirk	58	G9
Batsford Gloucs	30	F7
Battersby N York	66	E6
Battersea Gt Lon	21	L7
Battisford Tye Suffk	34	G6
Battle E Susx	12	E7
Battle Powys	27	L3
Battledykes Angus	93	M5
Battlesbridge Essex	22	F5
Battleton Somset	16	C10
Baughton Worcs	29	M1
Baughurst Hants	19	P8
Baulds Abers	95	K4
Baulking Oxon	19	K3
Baumber Lincs	52	H8
Baunton Gloucs	30	D12
Baverstock Wilts	8	F2
Bawburgh Norfk	45	J8
Bawdeswell Norfk	44	H6
Bawdrip Somset	17	J8
Bawdsey Suffk	35	M8
Bawtry Donc	51	P3
Baxenden Lancs	57	P4
Baxterley Warwks	40	H7
Bay Highld	104	C10
Bayble W Isls	111	e2
Baybridge Hants	9	N3
Baycliff Cumb	62	F7
Baydon Wilts	19	K5
Bayford Herts	21	L2
Bayford Somset	17	Q9
Bayhead W Isls	111	a4
Baylham Suffk	34	H6
Baysham Herefs	28	G4
Bayston Hill Shrops	39	J1
Baythorne End Essex	34	C8
Bayton Worcs	39	M7
Bayworth Oxon	19	N1
Beachampton Bucks	31	Q6
Beachamwell Norfk	44	C8
Beachy Head E Susx	12	C10
Beacon Devon	6	G2
Beacon End Essex	34	F10
Beacon Hill Notts	52	B11
Beacon Hill Surrey	10	E3
Beacon's Bottom Bucks	20	C4
Beaconsfield Bucks	20	F5
Beaconsfield Services Bucks	20	F5
Beadlam N York	66	F9
Beadlow C Beds	32	F8
Beadnell Nthumb	81	P8
Beaford Devon	15	K8
Beal N York	59	M8
Beal Nthumb	81	M6
Bealsmill Cnwll	4	H5
Beaminster Dorset	7	L3
Beamish Dur	73	L9
Beamish Museum Dur	73	L9
Beamsley N York	58	E4
Beanacre Wilts	18	D7
Beanley Nthumb	81	M9
Beardon Devon	5	L4
Beare Green Surrey	11	J2
Bearley Warwks	30	F3
Bearpark Dur	73	M11
Bearsden E Duns	85	J8
Bearsted Kent	22	F11
Bearstone Shrops	49	N7
Bearwood Birm	40	D9
Bearwood Herefs	38	H10
Bearwood Poole	8	F7
Beattock D & G	78	H8
Beauchamp Roding Essex	22	C2
Beauchief Sheff	51	J4
Beaufort Blae G	27	N6
Beaulieu Hants	9	L7
Beauly Highld	107	J11
Beaumaris IoA	54	H6
Beaumaris Castle IoA	54	H6
Beaumont Cumb	71	M4
Beaumont Essex	35	J10
Beaumont Jersey	7	b2
Beaumont Leys C Leic	41	M6
Beausale Warwks	40	G12
Beauworth Hants	9	P3
Beaworthy Devon	14	H11
Beazley End Essex	34	C10
Bebington Wirral	56	G11
Bebside Nthumb	73	M4
Beccles Suffk	45	N11
Becconsall Lancs	57	J4
Beckbury Shrops	39	N2
Beckenham Gt Lon	21	M9
Beckenham Crematorium Gt Lon	21	M9
Beckermet Cumb	62	B2
Beckfoot Cumb	70	H5
Beckford Worcs	29	N2
Beckhampton Wilts	18	G7
Beckingham Lincs	52	C11
Beckingham Notts	51	R3
Beckington Somset	18	B9
Beckjay Shrops	38	H6
Beckley E Susx	12	G5
Beckley Oxon	31	M10
Beck Row Suffk	34	B2
Beck Side Cumb	62	E6
Beckton Gt Lon	21	N7
Beckwithshaw N York	58	H4
Becontree Gt Lon	21	P6
Bedale N York	65	M9
Bedchester Dorset	8	C4
Beddau Rhondd	27	M10
Beddgelert Gwynd	54	H11
Beddingham E Susx	11	N8
Beddington Gt Lon	21	L9
Beddington Corner Gt Lon	21	L9
Bedfield Suffk	35	K4
Bedford Bed	32	F6
Bedford Crematorium Bed	32	F6
Bedhampton Hants	10	B8
Bedingfield Suffk	35	K3
Bedlam N York	58	H2
Bedlington Nthumb	73	M5
Bedlinog Myr Td	27	M8
Bedminster Bristl	17	N2
Bedminster Down Bristl	17	N3
Bedmond Herts	20	H3
Bednall Staffs	40	C4
Bedrule Border	80	E10
Bedstone Shrops	38	G7
Bedwas Caerph	27	N10
Bedwellty Caerph	27	N8
Bedworth Warwks	41	J9
Beeby Leics	41	P6
Beech Hants	10	B3
Beech Staffs	49	Q7
Beech Hill W Berk	20	B9
Beechingstoke Wilts	18	G8
Beedon W Berk	19	N5
Beeford E R Yk	61	J4
Beeley Derbys	50	H7
Beelsby NE Lin	52	H3
Beenham W Berk	19	P7
Beer Devon	6	G5
Beer Somset	17	M9
Beercrocombe Somset	17	J11
Beer Hackett Dorset	7	N2
Beesands Devon	5	Q11
Beesby Lincs	53	M7
Beeson Devon	5	Q11
Beeston C Beds	32	G7
Beeston Ches W	49	K4
Beeston Leeds	58	H7
Beeston Norfk	44	E7
Beeston Notts	51	M12
Beeston Regis Norfk	45	J2
Beeswing D & G	70	E2
Beetham Cumb	63	J6
Beetham Somset	6	H1
Beetley Norfk	44	F6
Begbroke Oxon	31	L10
Begelly Pembks	25	K7
Beguildy Powys	38	E6
Beighton Norfk	45	N8
Beighton Sheff	51	K4
Beinn Na Faoghla W Isls	111	b5
Beith N Ayrs	84	F11
Bekesbourne Kent	23	M11
Belaugh Norfk	45	L6
Belbroughton Worcs	40	B11
Belchalwell Dorset	8	B5
Belchamp Otten Essex	34	D8
Belchamp St Paul Essex	34	D8
Belchamp Walter Essex	34	D8
Belchford Lincs	53	J8
Belford Nthumb	81	M7
Belgrave C Leic	41	N6
Belhaven E Loth	87	M6
Belhelvie Abers	103	K10
Belhinnie Abers	101	N9
Bellabeg Abers	101	L11
Bellanoch Ag & B	83	M5
Bellaty Angus	93	J4
Bell Busk N York	58	B3
Belleau Lincs	53	L7
Bell End Worcs	40	C11
Bellerby N York	65	K8
Belle Vue Cumb	71	M4
Belle Vue Wakefd	59	J9
Bellfield S Lans	78	D2
Bellingdon Bucks	20	F3
Bellingham Nthumb	72	F4
Belloch Ag & B	75	K5
Bellochantuy Ag & B	75	K6
Bell o' th' Hill Ches W	49	K6
Bellshill N Lans	85	M10
Bellshill Nthumb	81	M7
Bellside N Lans	85	N10
Bellsquarry W Loth	86	C8
Bells Yew Green E Susx	12	C3
Belluton BaNES	17	N4
Belmaduthy Highld	107	K10
Belmont Bl w D	57	M6
Belmont Gt Lon	21	K10
Belmont S Ayrs	76	F7
Belmont Shet	111	m2
Belnacraig Abers	101	M11
Belper Derbys	51	J10
Belsay Nthumb	73	K5
Belses Border	80	D8
Belsford Devon	5	P8
Belsize Herts	20	G4
Belstead Suffk	35	J8
Belstone Devon	5	M2
Belthorn Lancs	57	N4
Beltinge Kent	23	M9
Beltingham Nthumb	72	E7
Beltoft N Linc	52	B3
Belton Leics	41	K4
Belton Lincs	42	D3
Belton Lincs	52	B3
Belton Norfk	45	P9
Belton Rutlnd	42	B9
Belton House Lincs	42	D3
Beltring Kent	12	E2
Belvedere Gt Lon	21	P7
Belvoir Leics	42	B4
Bembridge IoW	9	Q9
Bemerton Wilts	8	G2
Bempton E R Yk	67	P12
Benacre Suffk	45	Q12
Benbecula W Isls	111	b5
Benbecula Airport W Isls	111	b5
Benbuie D & G	77	M11
Benderloch Ag & B	90	C8
Benenden Kent	12	F4
Benfieldside Dur	73	J9
Bengeo Herts	21	L1
Bengeworth Worcs	30	D5
Benhall Green Suffk	35	N5
Benhall Street Suffk	35	M5
Benholm Abers	95	N7
Beningbrough N York	59	M3
Benington Herts	33	J11
Benington Lincs	43	L2
Benllech IoA	54	G5
Benmore Ag & B	84	C6
Bennan N Ayrs	75	Q8
Ben Nevis Highld	90	G3
Benniworth Lincs	52	H7
Benover Kent	12	E1
Ben Rhydding C Brad	58	F5
Benslie N Ayrs	76	F3
Benson Oxon	19	Q3
Benthoul C Aber	95	N2
Bentley Donc	59	M11
Bentley E R Yk	60	H7
Bentley Hants	10	C2
Bentley Suffk	35	J8
Bentley Warwks	40	H8
Bentley Crematorium Essex	22	C4
Bentpath D & G	79	M10
Bentwichen Devon	15	M5
Bentworth Hants	19	Q11
Benvie Angus	93	K8
Benville Dorset	7	M3
Benwick Cambs	43	K11
Beoley Worcs	40	E12
Beoraidbeg Highld	97	J10
Bepton W Susx	10	D6
Berden Essex	33	M10
Bere Alston Devon	5	J6
Bere Ferrers Devon	5	K7
Bere Regis Dorset	8	C8
Bergh Apton Norfk	45	M9
Berinsfield Oxon	19	P2
Berkeley Gloucs	29	J8
Berkhamsted Herts	20	F3
Berkley Somset	18	B10
Berkswell Solhll	40	G10
Bermondsey Gt Lon	21	M7
Bernera Highld	97	L5
Bernisdale Highld	104	E11
Berrick Prior Oxon	19	Q2
Berrick Salome Oxon	19	Q3
Berriedale Highld	110	D10
Berrier Cumb	71	N9
Berriew Powys	38	E2
Berrington Shrops	39	K2
Berrington Worcs	39	L10
Berrington Green Worcs	39	L10
Berrow Somset	16	H6
Berrow Worcs	39	N9
Berrow Green Worcs	39	N9
Berryfields Bucks	20	C1
Berryhillock Moray	101	P3
Berryhillock Moray	101	P5
Berrynarbor Devon	15	K3
Berry Pomeroy Devon	5	Q7
Bersham Wrexhm	48	F6
Berwick E Susx	11	P8
Berwick Bassett Wilts	18	G6
Berwick Hill Nthumb	73	L6
Berwick St James Wilts	18	F11
Berwick St John Wilts	8	D3
Berwick St Leonard Wilts	8	D2
Berwick-upon-Tweed Nthumb	81	L4
Bescar Lancs	56	H5
Besford Worcs	30	B5
Bessacarr Donc	51	N1
Bessingby E R Yk	61	K2
Bessingham Norfk	45	J3
Besthorpe Norfk	44	H10
Besthorpe Notts	52	B9
Bestwood Village Notts	51	M10
Beswick E R Yk	60	H5
Betchworth Surrey	21	K12
Bethel Gwynd	54	G8
Bethel IoA	54	E7
Bethersden Kent	12	H3
Bethesda Gwynd	55	J8
Bethesda Pembks	25	J5
Bethlehem Carmth	26	F4
Bethnal Green Gt Lon	21	M6
Betley Staffs	49	N6
Betsham Kent	22	D8
Betteshanger Kent	23	P11
Bettiscombe Dorset	7	K3
Bettisfield Wrexhm	49	J8
Bettws Newpt	28	C10
Bettws Cedewain Powys	38	D3
Bettws Ifan Cerdgn	36	E10
Bettws-Newydd Mons	28	D7
Bettyhill Highld	109	M4
Betws Brdgnd	27	J10
Betws Carmth	26	E6
Betws Bledrws Cerdgn	37	K9
Betws Gwerfil Goch Denbgs	48	B6
Betws-y-Coed Conwy	55	L9
Betws-yn-Rhos Conwy	55	N6
Beulah Cerdgn	36	E10
Beulah Powys	37	Q9
Bevercotes Notts	51	P6
Beverley E R Yk	60	H6
Beverston Gloucs	29	M9
Bewcastle Cumb	71	Q1
Bewdley Worcs	39	P7
Bewerley N York	58	F2
Bewholme E R Yk	61	K4
Bexhill E Susx	12	E8
Bexley Gt Lon	21	P8
Bexleyheath Gt Lon	21	P8
Bexwell Norfk	43	Q9
Beyton Suffk	34	F4
Beyton Green Suffk	34	F4
Bhaltos W Isls	111	c2
Bhatarsaigh W Isls	111	a7
Bibury Gloucs	30	E11
Bicester Oxon	31	N9
Bickenhill Solhll	40	F10
Bicker Lincs	42	H3
Bickerstaffe Lancs	57	J7
Bickerton N York	59	K4
Bickford Staffs	40	B5
Bickington Devon	5	Q6
Bickington Devon	15	J6
Bickleigh Devon	5	L7
Bickleigh Devon	6	C2
Bickley Ches W	49	K6
Bickley Gt Lon	21	N9
Bickley N York	67	K8
Bicknacre Essex	22	F3
Bicknoller Somset	16	F8
Bicknor Kent	22	G10
Bicton Shrops	38	F5
Bicton Shrops	49	J11
Bidborough Kent	12	C2
Biddenden Kent	12	G3
Biddenham Bed	32	E6
Biddestone Wilts	18	C6
Biddisham Somset	17	K5
Biddlesden Bucks	31	N6
Biddulph Staffs	50	B8
Biddulph Moor Staffs	50	B8
Bideford Devon	14	H6
Bidford-on-Avon Warwks	30	E4
Bielby E R Yk	60	D5
Bieldside C Aber	95	P2
Bierley IoW	9	N10
Bierton Bucks	32	B12
Big Balcraig D & G	69	K8
Bigbury Devon	5	N10
Bigbury-on-Sea Devon	5	N10
Bigby Lincs	52	F3
Biggar S Lans	78	G2
Biggin Derbys	50	F8
Biggin Hill Gt Lon	21	N10
Biggleswade C Beds	32	H7
Bigholms D & G	79	M10
Bighouse Highld	109	Q3
Bighton Hants	9	Q1
Biglands Cumb	71	L5
Bignor W Susx	10	F7
Bigrigg Cumb	70	G11
Big Sand Highld	105	L6
Bigton Shet	111	k5
Bilborough C Nott	51	M11
Bilbrook Somset	16	D7
Bilbrough N York	59	M5
Bilbster Highld	110	F5
Bildershaw Dur	65	L3
Bildeston Suffk	34	G6
Billericay Essex	22	D5
Billesdon Leics	41	Q7
Billesley Warwks	30	F3
Billingborough Lincs	42	G4
Billinge St Hel	57	K8
Billingford Norfk	35	J2
Billingford Norfk	44	G6
Billingham S on T	66	C3
Billinghay Lincs	52	G11
Billingley Barns	59	K12
Billingshurst W Susx	10	H5
Billingsley Shrops	39	N5
Billington C Beds	32	D11
Billington Lancs	57	N2
Billockby Norfk	45	N7
Billy Row Dur	73	L12
Bilsborrow Lancs	57	K2
Bilsby Lincs	53	M8
Bilsham W Susx	10	F9
Bilsington Kent	13	K3
Bilson Green Gloucs	29	J6
Bilsthorpe Notts	51	N8
Bilston Mdloth	86	F8
Bilston Wolves	40	C8
Bilstone Leics	41	J6
Bilton E R Yk	61	K7
Bilton N York	58	H3
Bilton Warwks	41	L11
Bilton-in-Ainsty N York	59	L4
Binbrook Lincs	52	H5
Bincombe Dorset	7	P6
Binegar Somset	17	N6
Binfield Br For	20	D8
Binfield Heath Oxon	20	C7
Bingfield Nthumb	72	H6
Bingham Notts	51	P11
Bingley C Brad	58	E6

162 Binham – Bracorina

Binham Norfk 44 G3
Binley Covtry 41 J10
Binley Hants 19 M9
Binley Woods Warwks 41 K11
Binnegar Dorset 8 C9
Binniehill Falk 85 P8
Binscombe Surrey 10 F2
Binstead IoW 9 P8
Binsted Hants 10 C2
Binsted W Susx 10 F8
Binton Warwks 30 F4
Bintree Norfk 44 G5
Birch Essex 34 F11
Bircham Newton Norfk 44 C4
Bircham Tofts Norfk 44 C4
Birchanger Essex 33 N11
Birchanger Green Services Essex 33 N11
Birch Cross Staffs 40 E2
Bircher Herefs 39 J8
Birchfield Birm 40 E8
Birch Green Essex 34 F11
Birchgrove Cardif 27 N11
Birchgrove Swans 26 F8
Birchgrove W Susx 11 N4
Birchington Kent 23 P9
Birchley Heath Warwks 40 H8
Birchover Derbys 50 G8
Birch Services Rochdl 57 Q7
Birch Vale Derbys 50 D4
Birchwood Lincs 52 D9
Birch Wood Somset 16 H12
Birchwood Warrtn 57 M9
Bircotes Notts 51 N3
Birdbrook Essex 34 B8
Birdforth N York 66 C11
Birdham W Susx 10 D9
Birdingbury Warwks 31 K1
Birdlip Gloucs 29 N6
Birdsall N York 60 E2
Birds Edge Kirk 58 G11
Birds Green Essex 22 C2
Birdsgreen Shrops 39 P5
Birdsmoorgate Dorset 7 K3
Birdwell Barns 51 J1
Birgham Border 80 G6
Birichin Highld 107 M4
Birkby N York 65 N7
Birkdale Sefton 56 G6
Birkenbog Abers 102 C3
Birkenhead Wirral 56 G10
Birkenhead (Queensway) Tunnel Lpool 56 G10
Birkenhills Abers 102 F6
Birkenshaw Kirk 58 G8
Birkhall Abers 94 F4
Birkhill Angus 93 L8
Birkhill D & G 79 K6
Birkin N York 59 M8
Birley Herefs 39 J10
Birley Carr Sheff 51 J3
Birling Kent 22 D10
Birlingham Worcs 30 C5
Birmingham Birm 40 E9
Birmingham Airport Solhll 40 F10
Birnam P & K 92 F7
Birness Abers 103 K8
Birse Abers 95 J3
Birsemore Abers 95 J3
Birstall Kirk 58 G8
Birstall Leics 41 N5
Birstwith N York 58 G3
Birtley Gatesd 73 M9
Birtley Herefs 38 G8
Birtley Nthumb 72 F5
Birtley Crematorium Gatesd 73 M9
Birts Street Worcs 29 K2
Bisbrooke Rutlnd 42 C9
Biscathorpe Lincs 52 H6
Bisham W & M 20 D6
Bishampton Worcs 30 C4
Bish Mill Devon 15 M7
Bishop Auckland Dur 65 L2
Bishopbridge Lincs 52 E5
Bishopbriggs E Duns 85 K8
Bishop Burton E R Yk 60 G6
Bishop Middleham Dur 65 N2
Bishopmill Moray 101 J3
Bishop Monkton N York 59 J2
Bishop Norton Lincs 52 E5
Bishopsbourne Kent 23 M11
Bishops Cannings Wilts 18 F7
Bishop's Castle Shrops 38 G4
Bishop's Caundle Dorset 17 Q12
Bishop's Cleeve Gloucs 29 N4
Bishop's Frome Herefs 39 M11
Bishop's Green Essex 33 Q12
Bishop's Hull Somset 16 G10
Bishop's Itchington Warwks 31 K3
Bishops Lydeard Somset 16 G9
Bishop's Norton Gloucs 29 L4
Bishop's Nympton Devon 15 N7
Bishop's Offley Staffs 49 P9
Bishop's Stortford Herts 33 M11
Bishop's Sutton Hants 9 Q2
Bishop's Tachbrook Warwks 30 H2
Bishop's Tawton Devon 15 K6
Bishopsteignton Devon 6 B7
Bishopstoke Hants 9 M4
Bishopston Swans 26 D10
Bishopstone Bucks 20 C2
Bishopstone E Susx 11 P9
Bishopstone Herefs 38 H12
Bishopstone Kent 23 N9
Bishopstone Swindn 19 J4
Bishopstone Wilts 8 F3
Bishopstrow Wilts 18 D11
Bishop Sutton BaNES 17 N4
Bishop's Waltham Hants 9 P4
Bishopswood Somset 6 H1
Bishop's Wood Staffs 49 Q12
Bishopsworth Bristl 17 N3
Bishop Thornton N York 58 H2
Bishopthorpe C York 59 N5
Bishopton Darltn 65 P4
Bishopton Rens 84 G8
Bishop Wilton E R Yk 60 D3
Bishton Newpt 28 D10
Bishton Staffs 40 D4
Bisley Gloucs 29 M7
Bisley Surrey 20 F10
Bissoe Cnwll 2 H7
Bisterne Hants 8 G7
Bitchfield Lincs 42 E4
Bittadon Devon 15 J4
Bittaford Devon 5 N8
Bitterley Shrops 39 K6
Bitterne C Sotn 9 M5
Bitteswell Leics 41 M9
Bitton S Glos 17 P3
Bix Oxon 20 B6
Bixter Shet 111 k4
Blaby Leics 41 M7
Blackadder Border 80 H4
Blackawton Devon 5 Q9
Blackborough Devon 6 E2
Blackborough End Norfk 43 Q7
Black Bourton Oxon 30 H12
Blackboys E Susx 11 Q6
Blackbrook Derbys 51 J10
Blackbrook St Hel 57 K9
Blackbrook Staffs 49 N7
Blackburn Abers 102 H11
Blackburn Bl w D 57 M4
Blackburn W Loth 86 B8
Blackburn with Darwen Services Bl w D 57 M4
Blackcraig E Ayrs 77 K9
Black Crofts Ag & B 90 C8
Blackdog Abers 103 K11
Black Dog Devon 15 N9
Blackdown Dorset 7 K3
Blacker Hill Barns 51 J1
Blackfen Gt Lon 21 P8
Blackfield Hants 9 M7
Blackford P & K 85 P2
Blackford Somset 17 K6
Blackford Somset 17 P10
Blackfordby Leics 41 J4
Blackhall C Edin 86 E7
Blackhall Colliery Dur 73 Q11
Blackhall Mill Gatesd 73 K9
Blackhaugh Border 79 N2
Blackheath Gt Lon 21 M7
Blackheath Sandw 40 C9
Blackheath Suffk 35 N2
Blackheath Surrey 10 G2
Blackhill Abers 103 M4
Blackhill Abers 103 M6
Blackhill Dur 73 J9
Blackhill of Clackriach Abers 103 J6
Blackhorse Devon 6 D4
Blacklaw D & G 78 G7
Blackley Manch 57 Q8
Blackley Crematorium Manch 57 Q7
Blacklunans P & K 94 C9
Blackmarstone Herefs 28 F2
Blackmill Brdgnd 27 K10
Blackmoor Hants 10 C4
Blackmoor N Som 17 L4
Blackmoorfoot Kirk 58 E10
Blackmore Essex 22 C3
Blackmore End Essex 34 C9
Black Mountains 27 Q4
Blackness Falk 86 C6
Blacknest Hants 10 C2
Black Notley Essex 34 C11
Blacko Lancs 57 Q1
Black Pill Swans 26 E10
Blackpool Bpool 56 F2
Blackpool Devon 6 B12
Blackpool Zoo Bpool 56 G2
Blackridge W Loth 85 P9
Blackrod Bolton 57 L6
Blacksboat Moray 101 J7
Blackshaw D & G 70 G3
Blackshaw Head Calder 58 C8
Blackstone W Susx 11 K6
Black Street Suffk 45 Q11
Blackthorn Oxon 31 N9
Blackthorpe Suffk 34 E4
Blacktoft E R Yk 60 E8
Blacktop C Aber 95 P2
Black Torrington Devon 14 H10
Blackwall Derbys 50 G10
Blackwall Tunnel Gt Lon 21 M7
Blackwater Cnwll 2 H6
Blackwater Hants 20 D10
Blackwater IoW 9 N9
Blackwater Somset 16 H11
Blackwaterfoot N Ayrs 75 N6
Blackwell Cumb 71 N5
Blackwell Derbys 50 E6
Blackwell Derbys 51 K8
Blackwell Warwks 30 G5
Blackwell Worcs 40 C11
Blackwood Caerph 27 N8
Blackwood D & G 78 E10
Blackwood S Lans 77 N3
Blacon Ches W 48 H2
Bladnoch D & G 69 K8
Bladon Oxon 31 K10
Blaenannerch Cerdgn 36 D10
Blaenau Ffestiniog Gwynd 47 L3
Blaenavon Torfn 27 Q7
Blaenavon Industrial Landscape Torfn 27 P7
Blaenffos Pembks 25 L2
Blaengarw Brdgnd 27 J9
Blaengwrach Neath 27 J7
Blaengwynfi Neath 27 J9
Blaenpennal Cerdgn 37 K7
Blaenplwyf Cerdgn 37 J5
Blaenporth Cerdgn 36 D10
Blaenrhondda Rhondd 27 K8
Blaenwaun Carmth 25 L4
Blaen-y-coed Carmth 25 N4
Blaen-y-cwm Rhondd 27 K8
Blagdon N Som 17 M4
Blagdon Somset 16 G11
Blagdon Torbay 6 B9
Blagdon Hill Somset 16 G11
Blaich Highld 90 E2
Blain Highld 89 N3
Blaina Blae G 27 P7
Blair Atholl P & K 92 C3
Blair Drummond Stirlg 85 M3
Blairgowrie P & K 92 H6
Blairhall Fife 86 B5
Blairingone P & K 86 B3
Blairlogie Stirlg 85 N4
Blairmore Ag & B 84 D6
Blairmore Highld 108 D4
Blair's Ferry Ag & B 83 P8
Blaisdon Gloucs 29 J5
Blakebrook Worcs 39 P6
Blakedown Worcs 39 Q6
Blake End Essex 34 B11
Blakemere Ches W 49 K2
Blakemere Herefs 28 D1
Blakenall Heath Wsall 40 D7
Blakeney Gloucs 29 J7
Blakeney Norfk 44 G2
Blakenhall Ches E 49 N6
Blakenhall Wolves 40 B7
Blakesley Nhants 31 N4
Blanchland Nthumb 72 H10
Blandford Forum Dorset 8 C6
Blandford St Mary Dorset 8 C6
Blanefield Stirlg 85 J7
Blankney Lincs 52 F10
Blantyre S Lans 85 L10
Blàr a' Chaorainn Highld 90 F3
Blargie Highld 98 H9
Blarmachfoldach Highld 90 F3
Blaston Leics 42 B10
Blatherwycke Nhants 42 D10
Blawith Cumb 62 F5
Blawquhairn D & G 69 P3
Blaxhall Suffk 35 M5
Blaxton Donc 51 P2
Blaydon Gatesd 73 L8
Bleadney Somset 17 L7
Bleadon N Som 17 J5
Blean Kent 23 L10
Bleasby Notts 51 Q10
Blebocraigs Fife 93 M11
Bleddfa Powys 38 E8
Bledington Gloucs 30 G9
Bledlow Bucks 20 C3
Bledlow Ridge Bucks 20 C4
Blegbie E Loth 87 J9
Blencarn Cumb 64 B2
Blencogo Cumb 71 K6
Blendworth Hants 10 B7
Blenheim Palace Oxon 31 K10
Blennerhasset Cumb 71 J7
Bletchingdon Oxon 31 L9
Bletchingley Surrey 21 M12
Bletchley M Keyn 32 C9
Bletchley Shrops 49 L8
Bletchley Park Museum M Keyn 32 C9
Bletherston Pembks 25 J5
Bletsoe Bed 32 E5
Blewbury Oxon 19 N4
Blickling Norfk 45 K4
Blidworth Notts 51 N9
Blidworth Bottoms Notts 51 N9
Blindcrake Cumb 71 J8
Blindley Heath Surrey 11 M2
Blisland Cnwll 4 D5
Blissford Hants 8 H5
Bliss Gate Worcs 39 N7
Blisworth Nhants 31 Q4
Blithbury Staffs 40 E4
Blockley Gloucs 30 F7
Blofield Norfk 45 M8
Blofield Heath Norfk 45 M7
Blo Norton Norfk 34 G2
Bloomfield Border 80 D8
Blore Staffs 50 F10
Bloxham Oxon 31 K7
Bloxholm Lincs 52 F11
Bloxwich Wsall 40 D7
Bloxworth Dorset 8 C8
Blubberhouses N York 58 F3
Blue Anchor Somset 16 D7
Blue Bell Hill Kent 22 E10
Blue John Cavern Derbys 50 F4
Blundellsands Sefton 56 F8
Blundeston Suffk 45 Q10
Blunham C Beds 32 G6
Blunsdon St Andrew Swindn 18 G3
Bluntington Worcs 40 B11
Bluntisham Cambs 33 K2
Blurton C Stke 50 B11
Blyborough Lincs 52 D5
Blyford Suffk 35 N2
Blymhill Staffs 49 P11
Blyth Notts 51 N4
Blyth Nthumb 73 N5
Blyth Bridge Border 86 D12
Blythburgh Suffk 35 P2
Blyth Crematorium Nthumb 73 N5
Blythe Border 80 D4
Blythe Bridge Staffs 50 C11
Blyth Services Notts 51 N3
Blyton Lincs 52 C5
Boarhills Fife 93 P11
Boarhunt Hants 9 P6
Boarstall Bucks 31 N10
Boath Highld 107 J7
Boat of Garten Highld 99 P5
Bobbing Kent 22 H9
Bobbington Staffs 39 P4
Bocking Essex 34 C11
Bocking Churchstreet Essex 34 C10
Boddam Abers 103 M6
Boddam Shet 111 k5
Boddington Gloucs 29 M4
Bodedern IoA 54 D5
Bodelwyddan Denbgs 55 Q6
Bodenham Herefs 39 K11
Bodenham Wilts 8 H3
Bodenham Moor Herefs 39 K11
Bodewryd IoA 54 E4
Bodfari Denbgs 48 C2
Bodffordd IoA 54 F6
Bodfuan Gwynd 46 E4
Bodham Norfk 45 J3
Bodiam E Susx 12 F5
Bodicote Oxon 31 L6
Bodinnick Cnwll 4 E9
Bodle Street Green E Susx 12 D7
Bodmin Cnwll 3 N3
Bodmin Moor Cnwll 4 F5
Bodsham Kent 13 L2
Bodwen Cnwll 3 M4
Bogallan Highld 107 K11
Bogbrae Abers 103 L8
Bogend S Ayrs 76 G5
Boggs Holdings E Loth 87 J7
Boghall Mdloth 86 F8
Boghall W Loth 86 B8
Boghead S Lans 77 N3
Bogmoor Moray 101 L3
Bogmuir Abers 95 K7
Bogniebrae Abers 102 D6
Bognor Regis W Susx 10 E9
Bogroy Highld 99 N4
Bogue D & G 69 P3
Bohortha Cnwll 3 J8
Bohuntine Highld 98 D11
Bolam Dur 65 L3
Bolberry Devon 5 N11
Boldmere Birm 40 E8
Boldre Hants 9 K7
Boldron Dur 65 J5
Bole Notts 52 B6
Bolehill Derbys 50 H9
Bolham Devon 16 C12
Bolham Water Devon 6 F1
Bolingey Cnwll 2 H5
Bollington Ches E 50 C5
Bolney W Susx 11 L5
Bolnhurst Bed 32 F5
Bolnore W Susx 11 M5
Bolshan Angus 93 Q5
Bolsover Derbys 51 L6
Bolsterstone Sheff 50 H2
Boltby N York 66 C9
Boltenstone Abers 101 M12
Bolton Bolton 57 N7
Bolton Cumb 64 B3
Bolton E Loth 87 K8
Bolton E R Yk 60 D4
Bolton Nthumb 81 M10
Bolton Abbey N York 58 E4
Bolton-by-Bowland Lancs 63 P11
Boltonfellend Cumb 71 P2
Boltongate Cumb 71 K7
Bolton-le-Sands Lancs 63 J8
Bolton Low Houses Cumb 71 K6
Bolton-on-Swale N York 65 M7
Bolton Percy N York 59 M6
Bolton upon Dearne Barns 51 L1
Bolventor Cnwll 4 E5
Bomere Heath Shrops 49 J10
Bonar Bridge Highld 107 K4
Bonawe Ag & B 90 D9
Bonby N Linc 60 G10
Boncath Pembks 25 L2
Bonchester Bridge Border 80 D10
Bondleigh Devon 15 L10
Bonds Lancs 63 J12
Bo'ness Falk 86 B6
Boney Hay Staffs 40 D5
Bonhill W Duns 84 G7
Boningale Shrops 39 P2
Bonjedward Border 80 E9
Bonkle N Lans 85 P10
Bonnington Angus 93 P7
Bonnington Kent 13 K3
Bonnybank Fife 86 G2
Bonnybridge Falk 85 N7
Bonnykelly Abers 102 H5
Bonnyrigg Mdloth 86 G8
Bonnyton Angus 93 L7
Bonsall Derbys 50 H8
Bonshaw Tower D & G 71 K2
Bont-Dolgadfan Powys 47 P10
Bont-goch Cerdgn 37 L4
Bontnewydd Cerdgn 37 K7
Bontnewydd Gwynd 54 G9
Bontuchel Denbgs 48 C4
Bonvilston V Glam 16 E2
Boode Devon 15 J5
Booker Bucks 20 D5
Boon Border 80 D5
Boosbeck R & Cl 66 F4
Boose's Green Essex 34 E9
Boot Cumb 62 D3
Booth Calder 58 D8
Boothby Graffoe Lincs 52 E10
Boothby Pagnell Lincs 42 D4
Boothferry E R Yk 60 C8
Boothstown Salfd 57 N8
Bootle Cumb 62 C5
Bootle Sefton 56 G9
Boraston Shrops 39 L8
Bordeaux Guern 6 c1
Borden Kent 22 G10
Borders Crematorium Border 80 D7
Boreham Essex 22 F2
Boreham Street E Susx 12 D7
Borehamwood Herts 21 J4
Boreland D & G 79 J10
Boreraig Highld 104 B10
Borgh W Isls 111 a7
Borgh W Isls 111 d1
Borgie Highld 109 M4
Borgue D & G 69 P9
Borgue Highld 110 D9
Borley Essex 34 E7
Borneskitaig Highld 104 E7
Borness D & G 69 N9
Boroughbridge N York 59 K2
Borough Green Kent 22 C11
Borrowash Derbys 41 K1
Borrowby N York 65 Q9
Borrowstoun Falk 86 B6
Borstal Medway 22 E9
Borth Cerdgn 37 K3
Borthwickbrae Border 79 N6
Borthwickshiels Border 79 N6
Borth-y-Gest Gwynd 47 J4
Borve Highld 104 F11
Borve W Isls 111 a7
Borve W Isls 111 c3
Borve W Isls 111 d1
Borwick Lancs 63 K7
Bosbury Herefs 39 M12
Boscastle Cnwll 4 D3
Boscombe Bmouth 8 G8
Boscombe Wilts 18 H11
Bosham W Susx 10 D8
Bosherston Pembks 24 G9
Bosley Ches E 50 B7
Bossall N York 60 C3
Bossiney Cnwll 4 D3
Bossingham Kent 13 M1
Bossington Somset 16 B6
Bostock Green Ches W 49 M2
Boston Lincs 43 K2
Boston Crematorium Lincs 43 K2
Boston Spa Leeds 59 K5
Boswinger Cnwll 3 L7
Botallack Cnwll 2 B8
Botany Bay Gt Lon 21 L4
Botesdale Suffk 34 H2
Bothal Nthumb 73 M4
Bothamsall Notts 51 P6
Bothel Cumb 71 K7
Bothenhampton Dorset 7 L5
Bothwell S Lans 85 L10
Bothwell Services S Lans 85 M10
Botley Bucks 20 F3
Botley Hants 9 N5
Botley Oxon 31 L11
Botolph Claydon Bucks 31 Q8
Botolphs W Susx 11 J8
Bottesford Leics 42 B3
Bottesford N Linc 52 C3
Bottisham Cambs 33 N5
Bottomcraig Fife 93 L10
Bottoms Calder 58 B9
Botusfleming Cnwll 5 J7
Botwnnog Gwynd 46 D5
Bough Beech Kent 11 P1
Boughrood Powys 27 N2
Boughton Nhants 31 Q2
Boughton Norfk 44 B9
Boughton Notts 51 P7
Boughton Aluph Kent 13 K1
Boughton Green Kent 22 F12
Boughton Monchelsea Kent 22 F12
Boughton Street Kent 23 K10
Bouldon Shrops 39 K5
Boulmer Nthumb 81 Q10
Boultham Lincs 52 D9
Bourn Cambs 33 K5
Bourne Lincs 42 F6
Bournebridge Essex 21 P5
Bournebrook Birm 40 D10
Bourne End Bucks 20 E6
Bourne End C Beds 32 D7
Bourne End Herts 20 G3
Bournemouth Bmouth 8 G8
Bournemouth Airport Dorset 8 G7
Bournemouth Crematorium Bmouth 8 G8
Bournes Green Sthend 22 H6
Bournheath Worcs 40 C11
Bournmoor Dur 73 N9
Bournville Birm 40 D10
Bourton Dorset 8 B2
Bourton Oxon 19 J4
Bourton Shrops 39 L3
Bourton Wilts 18 F7
Bourton on Dunsmore Warwks 41 K12
Bourton-on-the-Hill Gloucs 30 F7
Bourton-on-the-Water Gloucs 30 F9
Bousd Ag & B 88 G4
Bouth Cumb 62 G5
Bouthwaite N York 65 K12
Boveridge Dorset 8 F4
Bovey Tracey Devon 5 Q5
Bovingdon Herts 20 G3
Bow Devon 15 M10
Bow Gt Lon 21 M6
Bow Ork 111 h3
Bow Brickhill M Keyn 32 C9
Bowbridge Gloucs 29 M7
Bowburn Dur 73 N12
Bowcombe IoW 9 M9
Bowd Devon 6 F5
Bowden Border 80 D7
Bowden Hill Wilts 18 D7
Bowdon Traffd 57 N10
Bower Highld 110 E3
Bowerchalke Wilts 8 F3
Bowermadden Highld 110 F3
Bowers Staffs 49 P8
Bowers Gifford Essex 22 E6
Bowershall Fife 86 C4
Bower's Row Leeds 59 K8
Bowes Dur 64 H5
Bowgreave Lancs 63 J12
Bowhouse D & G 70 G3
Bowland Border 79 P2
Bowley Herefs 39 K10
Bowlhead Green Surrey 10 E3
Bowling C Brad 58 F7
Bowling W Duns 84 G8
Bowmanstead Cumb 62 F3
Bowmore Ag & B 82 D10
Bowness-on-Solway Cumb 71 K3
Bowness-on-Windermere Cumb 62 H3
Bow of Fife Fife 93 K12
Bowriefauld Angus 93 N6
Bowsden Nthumb 81 L6
Bow Street Cerdgn 37 K4
Bowthorpe Norfk 45 K8
Box Gloucs 29 M8
Box Wilts 18 C7
Boxford Suffk 34 F8
Boxford W Berk 19 M6
Boxgrove W Susx 10 E8
Boxley Kent 22 F10
Boxmoor Herts 20 G3
Boxted Essex 34 G9
Boxted Essex 34 G9
Boxted Suffk 34 D6
Boxted Cross Essex 34 G9
Boxworth Cambs 33 K4
Boyden Gate Kent 23 N9
Boylestone Derbys 40 F1
Boyndie Abers 102 E3
Boyndlie Abers 103 J3
Boynton E R Yk 61 K1
Boysack Angus 93 Q6
Boyton Cnwll 4 H2
Boyton Suffk 35 N7
Boyton Wilts 18 D11
Boyton Cross Essex 22 D2
Boyton End Suffk 34 C7
Bozeat Nhants 32 C5
Brabourne Kent 13 L2
Brabourne Lees Kent 13 L3
Brabstermire Highld 110 G2
Bracadale Highld 96 D2
Braceborough Lincs 42 F7
Bracebridge Heath Lincs 52 E9
Bracebridge Low Fields Lincs 52 D9
Braceby Lincs 42 E3
Bracewell Lancs 63 Q11
Brackenfield Derbys 51 J8
Brackenhirst N Lans 85 M8
Brackla Brdgnd 27 K11
Bracklesham W Susx 10 D10
Brackletter Highld 98 B11
Brackley Nhants 31 N6
Bracknell Br For 20 D9
Braco P & K 85 N2
Bracobrae Moray 101 P5
Bracon Ash Norfk 45 K9
Bracora Highld 97 K10
Bracorina Highld 97 K10

Bradbourne – Buckhorn Weston 163

Bradbourne Derbys 50 G9
Bradbury Dur 65 N2
Bradden Nhants 31 N5
Bradeley C Stke 49 Q5
Bradenham Bucks 20 D4
Bradenstoke Wilts 18 E5
Bradfield Devon 6 E2
Bradfield Essex 35 J9
Bradfield Norfk 45 L4
Bradfield Sheff 50 H3
Bradfield W Berk 19 P6
Bradfield Combust Suffk 34 E5
Bradfield Green Ches E 49 M4
Bradfield Heath Essex 35 J10
Bradfield St Clare Suffk 34 E5
Bradfield St George Suffk 34 E5
Bradford C Brad 58 F7
Bradford Devon 14 G10
Bradford Abbas Dorset 17 N12
Bradford Leigh Wilts 18 C8
Bradford-on-Avon Wilts 18 C8
Bradford-on-Tone Somset 16 G10
Bradford Peverell Dorset 7 P4
Bradiford Devon 15 K5
Brading IoW 9 Q9
Bradley Derbys 50 G10
Bradley Hants 19 Q11
Bradley NE Lin 53 J3
Bradley Staffs 49 Q11
Bradley Wolves 40 C8
Bradley Worcs 30 C2
Bradley Green Worcs 30 C2
Bradley in the Moors Staffs 50 D11
Bradley Stoke S Glos 28 H11
Bradmore Notts 41 N2
Bradninch Devon 6 D3
Bradnop Staffs 50 D9
Bradpole Dorset 7 L4
Bradshaw Calder 58 E8
Bradstone Devon 4 H4
Bradwall Green Ches E 49 N3
Bradwell Derbys 50 F5
Bradwell Essex 34 D11
Bradwell M Keyn 32 B8
Bradwell Norfk 45 Q8
Bradwell Crematorium Staffs 49 Q5
Bradwell-on-Sea Essex 23 J3
Bradwell Waterside Essex 23 J2
Bradworthy Devon 14 F8
Brae Highld 107 L9
Brae Shet 111 k3
Braeface Falk 85 N7
Braehead Angus 95 L10
Braehead D & G 69 K8
Braehead S Lans 77 Q2
Braeintra Highld 97 M3
Braemar Abers 94 C4
Braemore Highld 106 C6
Braemore Highld 110 C9
Brae Roy Lodge Highld 98 D10
Braeside Inver 84 D7
Braes of Coul Angus 93 K4
Braes of Enzie Moray 101 M4
Braeswick Ork 111 i1
Braevallich Ag & B 83 P2
Brafferton Darltn 65 N4
Brafferton N York 66 B12
Brafield-on-the-Green Nhants 32 B5
Bragar W Isls 111 d1
Bragbury End Herts 33 J11
Braidwood S Lans 77 P2
Brailsford Derbys 50 G11
Braintree Essex 34 C11
Braiseworth Suffk 35 J3
Braishfield Hants 9 L3
Braithwaite Cumb 71 K10
Braithwell Donc 51 M2
Bramber W Susx 11 J7
Bramcote Warwks 41 K9
Bramcote Crematorium Notts 51 L11
Bramdean Hants 9 Q2
Bramerton Norfk 45 L8
Bramfield Herts 33 J12
Bramfield Suffk 35 N3
Bramford Suffk 35 J7
Bramhall Stockp 50 B4
Bramham Leeds 59 K5
Bramhope Leeds 58 G5
Bramley Hants 19 Q8
Bramley Leeds 58 G7
Bramley Rothm 51 L3
Bramley Surrey 10 G2
Bramley Corner Hants 19 Q8
Bramling Kent 23 N11
Brampford Speke Devon 6 C3
Brampton Cambs 32 H3
Brampton Cumb 64 C3
Brampton Cumb 71 Q4
Brampton Lincs 52 B7
Brampton Norfk 45 K5
Brampton Rothm 51 K1
Brampton Suffk 35 P1
Brampton Abbotts Herefs 28 H4
Brampton Ash Nhants 42 B11
Brampton Bryan Herefs 38 G7
Brampton-en-le-Morthen Rothm 51 L4
Bramshall Staffs 40 D2
Bramshaw Hants 9 J4
Bramshott Hants 10 D4
Bramwell Somset 17 L9
Branault Highld 89 L3
Brancaster Norfk 44 C2
Brancaster Staithe Norfk 44 D2
Brancepeth Dur 73 L12
Branchill Moray 100 G5
Branderburgh Moray 101 K2
Brandesburton E R Yk 61 J5
Brandeston Suffk 35 L5
Brandiston Norfk 45 J6
Brandon Dur 73 M11
Brandon Lincs 42 C1
Brandon Suffk 44 D11
Brandon Warwks 41 K11
Brandon Parva Norfk 44 H8
Brandsby N York 66 E11
Brandy Wharf Lincs 52 E4
Bran End Essex 33 Q10
Branksome Poole 8 F8
Branksome Park Poole 8 F8
Bransbury Hants 19 M11
Bransby Lincs 52 C7
Branscombe Devon 6 G5
Bransford Worcs 39 P10
Bransgore Hants 8 H7
Bransholme C KuH 61 J7
Bransley Shrops 39 M7
Branston Leics 42 B4
Branston Lincs 52 E9
Branston Staffs 40 G4
Branston Booths Lincs 52 F9
Branstone IoW 9 P10
Brant Broughton Lincs 52 D11
Brantham Suffk 35 J9
Branthwaite Cumb 70 H9
Branthwaite Cumb 71 L7
Brantingham E R Yk 60 G8
Branton Donc 51 N1
Branton Nthumb 81 L10
Branton Green N York 59 K2
Branxton Nthumb 81 J6
Brassington Derbys 50 G9
Brasted Kent 21 P11
Brasted Chart Kent 21 P11
Brathens Abers 95 L3
Bratoft Lincs 53 M9
Brattleby Lincs 52 D7
Bratton Wilts 18 D9
Bratton Wrekin 49 L11
Bratton Clovelly Devon 5 K2
Bratton Fleming Devon 15 L5
Bratton Seymour Somset 17 P9
Braughing Herts 33 L10
Braunston Nhants 31 M2
Braunston Rutlnd 42 B8
Braunton Devon 14 H5
Brawby N York 66 G11
Brawl Highld 109 P3
Bray W & M 20 E7
Braybrooke Nhants 41 Q9
Brayford Devon 15 M5
Bray Shop Cnwll 4 H5
Brayton N York 59 N7
Braywick W & M 20 E7
Breachwood Green Herts 32 G11
Breadsall Derbys 51 J11
Breadstone Gloucs 29 J8
Breage Cnwll 2 F9
Breakachy Highld 106 H12
Breakish Highld 97 J5
Breakspear Crematorium Gt Lon 20 H5
Brealangwell Lodge Highld 106 H4
Bream Gloucs 28 H7
Breamore Hants 8 H4
Brean Somset 16 H5
Breanais W Isls 111 b2
Brearton N York 58 H3
Breascleit W Isls 111 c2
Breasclete W Isls 111 c2
Breaston Derbys 41 L2
Brechfa Carmth 26 C3
Brechin Angus 95 K9
Breckles Norfk 44 F10
Brecon Powys 27 L3
Brecon Beacons National Park 27 L4
Bredbury Stockp 50 B3
Brede E Susx 12 G6
Bredenbury Herefs 39 L10
Bredfield Suffk 35 L6
Bredgar Kent 22 G10
Bredhurst Kent 22 F10
Bredon Worcs 29 N2
Bredon's Hardwick Worcs 29 M2
Bredon's Norton Worcs 29 N2
Bredwardine Herefs 38 G12
Breedon on the Hill Leics 41 K3
Breich W Loth 85 Q10
Breightmet Bolton 57 N7
Breighton E R Yk 60 C7
Breinton Herefs 28 F2
Bremhill Wilts 18 E6
Brenchley Kent 12 D2
Brendon Devon 15 N3
Brenfield Ag & B 83 M6
Brenish W Isls 111 b2
Brent Cross Gt Lon 21 K6
Brent Eleigh Suffk 34 F7
Brentford Gt Lon 21 J7
Brentingby Leics 42 B6
Brent Knoll Somset 17 J6
Brent Mill Devon 5 N8
Brent Pelham Herts 33 M10
Brentwood Essex 22 C5
Brenzett Kent 13 J5
Brenzett Green Kent 13 J4
Brereton Staffs 40 D4
Brereton Green Ches E 49 P3
Bressay Shet 111 k4
Bressingham Norfk 34 H1
Bretby Derbys 40 H3
Bretby Crematorium Derbys 40 H3
Bretford Warwks 41 K11
Bretforton Worcs 30 E5
Bretherton Lancs 57 J5
Breton C Pete 42 G9
Brettabister Shet 111 k4
Brettenham Norfk 44 F12
Brettenham Suffk 34 F6
Bretton Flints 48 G3
Brewood Staffs 40 B6
Briantspuddle Dorset 8 B8
Brickendon Herts 21 L2
Bricket Wood Herts 20 H3
Brick Houses Sheff 50 H5
Bricklehampton Worcs 29 N1
Bride IoM 56 e2
Bridekirk Cumb 71 J8
Bridestowe Devon 5 L3
Brideswell Abers 102 D7
Bridford Devon 5 Q3
Bridge Kent 23 M11
Bridgefoot Angus 93 L8
Bridgehampton Somset 17 N10
Bridge Hewick N York 65 N12
Bridgehill Dur 73 K9
Bridgemary Hants 9 P6
Bridgend Abers 101 P7
Bridgend Ag & B 75 M5
Bridgend Ag & B 82 E9
Bridgend Angus 95 J8
Bridgend Brdgnd 27 J11
Bridgend Cerdgn 36 C10
Bridgend D & G 78 H7
Bridgend Devon 5 L9
Bridgend Fife 93 L12
Bridgend Moray 101 M8
Bridgend P & K 92 G10
Bridgend W Loth 86 C7
Bridgend of Lintrathen Angus 93 K5
Bridge of Alford Abers 102 D10
Bridge of Allan Stirlg 85 N4
Bridge of Avon Moray 100 H10
Bridge of Avon Moray 101 J7
Bridge of Balgie P & K 91 N7
Bridge of Brewlands Angus 94 C9
Bridge of Brown Highld 100 H10
Bridge of Cally P & K 92 H5
Bridge of Canny Abers 95 K3
Bridge of Craigisla Angus 93 J5
Bridge of Dee D & G 70 C4
Bridge of Don C Aber 103 K12
Bridge of Dye Abers 95 K5
Bridge of Earn P & K 92 G11
Bridge of Ericht P & K 91 M5
Bridge of Feugh Abers 95 L3
Bridge of Gairn Abers 94 F3
Bridge of Gaur P & K 91 M5
Bridge of Marnoch Abers 102 D5
Bridge of Muchalls Abers 95 P4
Bridge of Orchy Ag & B 91 J8
Bridge of Tilt P & K 92 D3
Bridge of Tynet Moray 101 M3
Bridge of Walls Shet 111 j4
Bridge of Weir Rens 84 G9
Bridgerule Devon 14 E10
Bridge Sollers Herefs 28 E1
Bridge Street Suffk 34 E6
Bridgetown Somset 16 C9
Bridge Trafford Ches W 49 J2
Bridgham Norfk 44 F11
Bridgnorth Shrops 39 N4
Bridgwater Somset 16 H8
Bridgwater Services Somset 17 J8
Bridlington E R Yk 61 K2
Bridport Dorset 7 L4
Bridstow Herefs 28 G4
Brierfield Lancs 57 Q2
Brierley Barns 59 K11
Brierley Gloucs 28 H6
Brierley Hill Dudley 40 B9
Brigg N Linc 52 E3
Briggate Norfk 45 M5
Briggswath N York 67 J6
Brigham Cumb 70 H9
Brigham E R Yk 61 J4
Brighouse Calder 58 F9
Brighstone IoW 9 M10
Brighthampton Oxon 31 K12
Brightley Devon 15 K11
Brightling E Susx 12 D6
Brightlingsea Essex 34 H12
Brighton Br & H 11 L8
Brighton City Airport W Susx 11 K8
Brighton le Sands Sefton 56 F8
Brightons Falk 85 Q7
Brightwalton W Berk 19 M5
Brightwell Suffk 35 L7
Brightwell Baldwin Oxon 19 Q2
Brightwell-cum-Sotwell Oxon 19 P3
Brightwell Upperton Oxon 19 Q2
Brignall Dur 65 J5
Brig o'Turk Stirlg 85 J2
Brigsley NE Lin 53 J3
Brigsteer Cumb 63 J4
Brigstock Nhants 42 D11
Brill Bucks 31 P10
Brill Cnwll 2 G9
Brilley Herefs 38 F11
Brimfield Herefs 39 K8
Brimfield Cross Herefs 39 K8
Brimington Derbys 51 K6
Brimley Devon 5 Q5
Brimpsfield Gloucs 29 N6
Brimpton W Berk 19 P7
Brimscombe Gloucs 29 M8
Brimstage Wirral 56 F11
Brincliffe Sheff 51 J4
Brind E R Yk 60 C7
Brindister Shet 111 j4
Brindle Lancs 57 L4
Brineton Staffs 49 P11
Bringhurst Leics 42 B10
Bringsty Common Herefs 39 M10
Brington Cambs 32 F2
Briningham Norfk 44 G4
Brinkhill Lincs 53 L8
Brinkley Cambs 33 Q6
Brinklow Warwks 41 K10
Brinkworth Wilts 18 E4
Brinscall Lancs 57 L5
Brinsley Notts 51 L10
Brinsworth Rothm 51 K3
Brinton Norfk 44 G3
Brinyan Ork 111 h2
Brisley Norfk 44 F6
Brislington Bristl 17 N3
Brissenden Green Kent 12 H3
Bristol Bristl 17 N2
Bristol Airport N Som 17 M3
Bristol Zoo Gardens Bristl 17 N2
Briston Norfk 44 H4
Britford Wilts 8 H2
Brithdir Caerph 27 N8
Brithdir Gwynd 47 M7
British Legion Village Kent 22 E11
Briton Ferry Neath 26 G9
Britwell Salome Oxon 19 R3
Brixham Torbay 6 C10
Brixton Devon 5 L9
Brixton Gt Lon 21 L8
Brixton Deverill Wilts 18 C11
Brixworth Nhants 41 Q12
Brize Norton Oxon 30 H11
Brize Norton Airport Oxon 30 H11
Broad Alley Worcs 30 B1
Broad Blunsdon Swindn 18 G3
Broadbottom Tamesd 50 C3
Broadbridge W Susx 10 D8
Broadbridge Heath W Susx 11 J4
Broad Campden Gloucs 30 F6
Broad Carr Calder 58 E9
Broad Chalke Wilts 8 F3
Broadclyst Devon 6 D4
Broadfield Inver 84 F8
Broadford Highld 96 H5
Broadford Bridge W Susx 10 H6
Broadgairhill Border 79 K6
Broad Green Worcs 39 P10
Broadhaugh Border 81 J4
Broad Haven Pembks 24 F6
Broadheath Traffd 57 N10
Broadhembury Devon 6 E2
Broadhempston Devon 5 Q7
Broad Hinton Wilts 18 G5
Broadland Row E Susx 12 G6
Broadley Moray 101 M3
Broad Marston Worcs 30 F5
Broadmayne Dorset 7 Q5
Broad Meadow Staffs 49 Q6
Broadmoor Pembks 25 J7
Broadoak Dorset 7 L4
Broad Oak E Susx 12 C5
Broad Oak E Susx 12 G6
Broad Oak Herefs 28 F5
Broad Oak Kent 23 M10
Broad Oak St Hel 57 K9
Broadsands Torbay 6 B10
Broad's Green Essex 22 E2
Broadstairs Kent 23 Q9
Broadstone Poole 8 E8
Broadstone Shrops 39 K4
Broad Street E Susx 12 G6
Broad Street Kent 22 G11
Broad Town Wilts 18 G5
Broadwas Worcs 39 N10
Broadwater Herts 33 J11
Broadwater W Susx 11 J8
Broadwaters Worcs 39 Q6
Broadway Pembks 24 F6
Broadway Somset 17 J11
Broadway Worcs 30 E6
Broadwell Gloucs 28 G6
Broadwell Gloucs 30 G8
Broadwell Oxon 30 G12
Broadwell Warwks 31 L2
Broadwindsor Dorset 7 L3
Broadwood Kelly Devon 15 K10
Broadwoodwidger Devon 5 J3
Brochel Highld 104 H12
Brochroy Ag & B 90 D9
Brockamin Worcs 39 P10
Brockbridge Hants 9 Q4
Brockdish Norfk 35 K2
Brockenhurst Hants 9 K7
Brocketsbrae S Lans 78 D2
Brockford Street Suffk 35 J4
Brockhall Nhants 31 N2
Brockham Surrey 21 K12
Brockhampton Gloucs 30 D9
Brockhampton Hants 10 B8
Brockhampton Herefs 28 H3
Brockholes Kirk 58 F11
Brocklesby Lincs 61 K11
Brockley N Som 17 L3
Brockley Suffk 34 D3
Brockley Green Suffk 34 C7
Brockley Green Suffk 34 D6
Brockmoor Dudley 40 B9
Brockton Shrops 38 G2
Brockton Shrops 38 G5
Brockton Shrops 39 L4
Brockweir Gloucs 28 G8
Brockworth Gloucs 29 M5
Brocton Staffs 40 C4
Brodick N Ayrs 75 Q5
Brodie Moray 100 F4
Brodsworth Donc 59 L11
Brogaig Highld 104 F8
Brokenborough Wilts 18 D3
Broken Cross Ches E 50 B6
Brokerswood Wilts 18 C9
Bromborough Wirral 56 G11
Brome Suffk 35 J2
Brome Street Suffk 35 J2
Bromeswell Suffk 35 M6
Bromfield Cumb 71 J6
Bromfield Shrops 39 J6
Bromham Bed 32 E6
Bromham Wilts 18 E7
Bromley Dudley 40 B9
Bromley Gt Lon 21 N9
Bromley Shrops 39 N3
Bromley Cross Bolton 57 N6
Brompton Medway 22 F9
Brompton N York 65 P8
Brompton-by-Sawdon N York 67 K10
Brompton-on-Swale N York 65 L7
Brompton Ralph Somset 16 E9
Brompton Regis Somset 16 C9
Bromsberrow Gloucs 29 K3
Bromsberrow Heath Gloucs 29 K3
Bromsgrove Worcs 40 C12
Bromyard Herefs 39 M10
Bronant Cerdgn 37 K7
Brongest Cerdgn 36 E10
Bronington Wrexhm 49 J7
Bronllys Powys 27 N2
Bronwydd Carmth 25 P4
Bronygarth Shrops 48 F7
Brook Hants 9 J5
Brook IoW 9 L9
Brook Kent 13 K2
Brook Surrey 10 E3
Brooke Norfk 45 L9
Brooke Rutlnd 42 C8
Brookenby Lincs 52 H4
Brookfield Rens 84 G9
Brookhampton Somset 17 P9
Brook Hill Hants 9 J5
Brookhouse Lancs 63 K8
Brookhouse Rothm 51 L3
Brookhouse Green Ches E 49 P4
Brookhouses Derbys 50 D3
Brookland Kent 13 J5
Brooklands Traffd 57 P10
Brookmans Park Herts 21 K3
Brook Street Essex 22 C5
Brook Street Kent 12 H4
Brookthorpe Gloucs 29 L6
Brookwood Surrey 20 F11
Broom C Beds 32 G8
Broom Rothm 51 K3
Broom Warwks 30 E4
Broome Norfk 45 M10
Broome Shrops 38 H6
Broome Worcs 40 B10
Broomedge Warrtn 57 N10
Broomfield Essex 22 E2
Broomfield Kent 22 G11
Broomfield Kent 23 M9
Broomfield Somset 16 G9
Broomfleet E R Yk 60 F8
Broomhaugh Nthumb 72 H8
Broom Hill Barns 59 K12
Broom Hill Notts 51 M10
Broomhill Nthumb 73 M1
Broompark Dur 73 M11
Brora Highld 107 P2
Broseley Shrops 39 M2
Brotherlee Dur 72 G12
Brotherton N York 59 L8
Brotton R & Cl 66 F4
Broubster Highld 110 B4
Brough Cumb 64 E5
Brough E R Yk 60 F8
Brough Highld 110 E2
Brough Notts 52 B10
Brough Shet 111 m3
Broughall Shrops 49 K7
Brough Lodge Shet 111 m2
Brough Sowerby Cumb 64 E5
Broughton Border 78 H2
Broughton Cambs 33 J2
Broughton Flints 48 G3
Broughton Hants 9 K2
Broughton Lancs 57 K2
Broughton M Keyn 32 C8
Broughton N Linc 52 D2
Broughton N York 58 C4
Broughton N York 66 H11
Broughton Nhants 32 B2
Broughton Oxon 31 K6
Broughton Salfd 57 P8
Broughton V Glam 16 C3
Broughton Astley Leics 41 M8
Broughton Gifford Wilts 18 C7
Broughton Green Worcs 30 C2
Broughton Hackett Worcs 30 B3
Broughton-in-Furness Cumb 62 E5
Broughton Mains D & G 69 L9
Broughton Mills Cumb 62 E4
Broughton Moor Cumb 70 H8
Broughton Poggs Oxon 30 G12
Broughty Ferry C Dund 93 N9
Brown Candover Hants 19 P11
Brown Edge Staffs 50 B9
Brownhill Abers 102 H7
Brownhills Fife 93 P11
Brownhills Wsall 40 D6
Browninghill Green Hants 19 P8
Brown Lees Staffs 49 Q4
Brownsea Island Dorset 8 F9
Brown's Green Birm 40 D8
Browns Hill Gloucs 29 M8
Brownston Devon 5 N9
Broxa N York 67 K8
Broxbourne Herts 21 M3
Broxburn E Loth 87 N6
Broxburn W Loth 86 C7
Broxted Essex 33 P10
Bruan Highld 110 G7
Bruar P & K 92 C3
Bruchag Ag & B 84 B10
Bruichladdich Ag & B 82 C10
Bruisyard Suffk 35 M4
Bruisyard Street Suffk 35 M4
Brumby N Linc 52 C2
Brund Staffs 50 E8
Brundall Norfk 45 M8
Brundish Suffk 35 L3
Brundish Street Suffk 35 L3
Brunery Highld 89 P2
Brunswick Village N u Ty 73 M6
Brunthwaite C Brad 58 D5
Bruntingthorpe Leics 41 N9
Brunton Fife 93 K10
Brunton Wilts 19 J9
Brushford Devon 15 L9
Brushford Somset 16 C10
Bruton Somset 17 P8
Bryan's Green Worcs 30 B1
Bryanston Dorset 8 C6
Brydekirk D & G 71 K2
Bryher IoS 2 b2
Brympton Somset 17 M11
Bryn Carmth 26 D8
Bryn Neath 26 H9
Bryn Wigan 57 K8
Brynamman Carmth 26 F6
Brynberian Pembks 25 J2
Bryncir Gwynd 46 H3
Bryn-côch Neath 26 G8
Bryncroes Gwynd 46 D5
Bryncrug Gwynd 47 K9
Bryneglwys Denbgs 48 D6
Brynford Flints 48 D1
Bryn Gates Wigan 57 L8
Bryngwran IoA 54 D6
Bryngwyn Mons 28 D7
Bryngwyn Powys 38 E11
Bryn-Henllan Pembks 24 H2
Brynhoffnant Cerdgn 36 E9
Brynmawr Blae G 27 P6
Bryn-mawr Gwynd 46 D5
Brynmenyn Brdgnd 27 J10
Brynmill Swans 26 E9
Brynna Rhondd 27 L11
Brynrefail Gwynd 54 H8
Brynsadler Rhondd 27 L11
Bryn Saith Marchog Denbgs 48 C5
Brynsiencyn IoA 54 F7
Brynteg IoA 54 G5
Bryn-y-Maen Conwy 55 M6
Bualintur Highld 96 E5
Bubbenhall Warwks 41 J11
Bubwith E R Yk 60 C7
Buccleuch Border 79 M6
Buchanan Smithy Stirlg 84 H5
Buchanhaven Abers 103 M6
Buchanty P & K 92 D9
Buchany Stirlg 85 M3
Buchlyvie Stirlg 85 J4
Buckabank Cumb 71 M6
Buckden Cambs 32 H4
Buckden N York 64 G11
Buckenham Norfk 45 M8
Buckerell Devon 6 F3
Buckfast Devon 5 P6
Buckfastleigh Devon 5 P7
Buckhaven Fife 86 G3
Buckholt Mons 28 F5
Buckhorn Weston Dorset 17 R10

164 Buckhurst Hill – Carmyllie

Buckhurst Hill Essex 21 N5
Buckie Moray 101 M3
Buckingham Bucks 31 P7
Buckland Bucks 20 E2
Buckland Devon 5 N10
Buckland Gloucs 30 E7
Buckland Herts 33 K9
Buckland Kent 13 P2
Buckland Oxon 19 K2
Buckland Surrey 21 K12
Buckland Brewer Devon 14 G7
Buckland Common Bucks 20 E3
Buckland Dinham Somset 17 R6
Buckland Filleigh Devon 14 H9
Buckland in the Moor Devon 5 P5
Buckland Monachorum Devon 5 K6
Buckland Newton Dorset 7 P2
Buckland Ripers Dorset 7 P6
Buckland St Mary Somset 16 H12
Buckland-Tout-Saints Devon 5 P10
Bucklebury W Berk 19 P6
Bucklers Hard Hants 9 L7
Bucklesham Suffk 35 L8
Buckley Flints 48 F3
Bucklow Hill Ches E 57 N11
Buckminster Leics 42 C5
Bucknall C Stke 50 B10
Bucknall Lincs 52 G9
Bucknell Oxon 31 M8
Bucknell Shrops 38 G7
Buckpool Moray 101 M3
Bucksburn C Aber 103 J12
Buck's Cross Devon 14 F7
Bucks Green W Susx 10 H4
Buckshaw Village Lancs 57 K5
Bucks Horn Oak Hants 10 D2
Buck's Mills Devon 14 F7
Buckton E R Yk 67 P11
Buckton Nthumb 81 M6
Buckworth Cambs 32 G2
Budby Notts 51 N6
Bude Cnwll 14 D10
Budge's Shop Cnwll 4 H8
Budleigh Salterton Devon 6 E6
Budock Water Cnwll 2 H9
Buerton Ches E 49 M6
Bugbrooke Nhants 31 P3
Bugle Cnwll 3 M4
Bugley Dorset 8 B3
Bugthorpe E R Yk 60 D3
Buildwas Shrops 39 L2
Builth Wells Powys 38 B11
Bulbridge Wilts 8 G2
Bulford Wilts 18 H11
Bulkeley Ches E 49 K5
Bulkington Warwks 41 K9
Bulkington Wilts 18 D8
Bulkworthy Devon 14 G8
Bullbrook Br For 20 E9
Bullington Hants 19 M11
Bullington Lincs 52 F7
Bulmer Essex 34 D8
Bulmer N York 60 C1
Bulmer Tye Essex 34 D8
Bulphan Thurr 22 D6
Bulwark Abers 103 J6
Bulwell C Nott 51 M11
Bulwick Nhants 42 D10
Bumble's Green Essex 21 N3
Bunacaimb Highld 97 J11
Bunarkaig Highld 98 B10
Bunbury Ches E 49 K4
Bunchrew Highld 107 K12
Bundalloch Highld 97 M4
Bunessan Ag & B 89 J11
Bungay Suffk 45 M11
Bunnahabhain Ag & B 82 F8
Bunny Notts 41 N2
Buntait Highld 98 E3
Buntingford Herts 33 K10
Bunwell Norfk 45 J10
Burbage Leics 41 K8
Burbage Wilts 19 J8
Burchett's Green W & M 20 D7
Burcombe Wilts 8 F2
Burcott Bucks 32 C11
Bures Essex 34 E9
Burford Oxon 30 G10
Burford Shrops 39 L8
Burg Ag & B 88 J7
Burgates Hants 10 C4
Burgess Hill W Susx 11 L6
Burgh Suffk 35 K6
Burgh by Sands Cumb 71 M4
Burgh Castle Norfk 45 P8
Burghclere Hants 19 M8
Burghead Moray 100 H2
Burghfield W Berk 19 Q7
Burghfield Common W Berk 19 Q7
Burgh Heath Surrey 21 K10
Burghill Herefs 39 J12
Burgh Island Devon 5 M10
Burgh le Marsh Lincs 53 N9
Burgh next Aylsham Norfk 45 K5
Burgh on Bain Lincs 52 H6
Burgh St Margaret Norfk 45 P7
Burgh St Peter Norfk 45 P10
Burghwallis Donc 59 M10
Burham Kent 22 E10
Buriton Hants 10 C6
Burland Ches E 49 L5
Burlawn Cnwll 3 M2
Burleigh Gloucs 29 M8
Burlescombe Devon 16 E11
Burleston Dorset 8 B8
Burley Hants 8 H6
Burley Rutlnd 42 C7
Burleydam Ches E 49 L7
Burley Gate Herefs 39 L11
Burley in Wharfedale C Brad 58 F5
Burley Street Hants 8 H6
Burley Wood Head C Brad 58 F5
Burlton Shrops 49 J9
Burmarsh Kent 13 L4
Burmington Warwks 30 H6
Burn N York 59 N8
Burnage Manch 57 Q9
Burnaston Derbys 40 H2
Burnbrae N Lans 85 P10
Burnby E R Yk 60 E5
Burneside Cumb 63 J3
Burneston N York 65 N9
Burnett BaNES 17 P3
Burnfoot Border 79 N6
Burnfoot Border 80 C10
Burnfoot D & G 78 F9
Burnfoot D & G 79 M10
Burnfoot D & G 79 N9
Burnfoot P & K 86 B2
Burnham Bucks 20 E7
Burnham Deepdale Norfk 44 D2
Burnham Market Norfk 44 D2
Burnham Norton Norfk 44 D2
Burnham-on-Crouch Essex 23 J4
Burnham-on-Sea Somset 17 J6
Burnham Overy Norfk 44 D2
Burnham Overy Staithe Norfk 44 D2
Burnham Thorpe Norfk 44 E2
Burnhead D & G 78 E9
Burnhervie Abers 102 F10
Burnhill Green Staffs 39 P3
Burnhope Dur 73 L10
Burnhouse N Ayrs 76 G2
Burniston N York 67 L8
Burnley Lancs 57 Q3
Burnley Crematorium Lancs 57 P3
Burnmouth Border 81 K3
Burn of Cambus Stirlg 85 M3
Burnopfield Dur 73 L9
Burnsall N York 58 D2
Burnside Angus 93 M4
Burnside Angus 93 N5
Burnside Fife 86 D1
Burnside Moray 101 J2
Burnside W Loth 86 C7
Burnside of Duntrune Angus 93 M8
Burntisland Fife 86 F5
Burnton E Ayrs 76 H9
Burntwood Staffs 40 D5
Burntwood Green Staffs 40 E6
Burnt Yates N York 58 G2
Burnworthy Somset 16 G11
Burpham Surrey 20 G11
Burpham W Susx 10 G8
Burradon Nthumb 81 K11
Burrafirth Shet 111 m2
Burravoe Shet 111 k3
Burrells Cumb 64 C4
Burrelton P & K 92 H8
Burridge Devon 7 J2
Burridge Hants 9 N5
Burrill N York 65 M9
Burringham N Linc 52 B2
Burrington Devon 15 L8
Burrington Herefs 38 H7
Burrington N Som 17 L4
Burrough Green Cambs 33 Q6
Burrough on the Hill Leics 41 Q5
Burrow Lancs 63 L7
Burrow Somset 16 C7
Burrow Bridge Somset 17 J9
Burrowhill Surrey 20 F10
Burry Green Swans 26 B9
Burry Port Carmth 25 Q8
Burscough Lancs 56 H6
Burscough Bridge Lancs 57 J6
Bursea E R Yk 60 D7
Bursledon Hants 9 N5
Burslem C Stke 49 Q5
Burstall Suffk 34 H7
Burstock Dorset 7 K3
Burston Norfk 45 J12
Burstow Surrey 11 L2
Burstwick E R Yk 61 L8
Burtersett N York 64 F9
Burtholme Cumb 71 Q3
Burthorpe Green Suffk 34 C4
Burtoft Lincs 43 J3
Burton Ches W 48 G1
Burton Ches W 49 K3
Burton Dorset 8 H8
Burton Pembks 24 H7
Burton Somset 16 G7
Burton Wilts 18 B5
Burton Agnes E R Yk 61 J2
Burton Bradstock Dorset 7 L5
Burton-by-Lincoln Lincs 52 D8
Burton Coggles Lincs 42 E5
Burton End Essex 33 N11
Burton Fleming E R Yk 67 M12
Burton Hastings Warwks 41 K9
Burton-in-Kendal Cumb 63 K7
Burton-in-Kendal Services Cumb 63 K7
Burton in Lonsdale N York 63 M7
Burton Joyce Notts 51 N11
Burton Latimer Nhants 32 C2
Burton Lazars Leics 41 Q4
Burton Leonard N York 59 J2
Burton on the Wolds Leics 41 N4
Burton Overy Leics 41 P7
Burton Pedwardine Lincs 42 G2
Burton Pidsea E R Yk 61 L7
Burton Salmon N York 59 L8
Burton's Green Essex 34 D10
Burton upon Stather N Linc 60 E10
Burton upon Trent Staffs 40 G3
Burton Waters Lincs 52 D8
Burtonwood Warrtn 57 K9
Burtonwood Services Warrtn 57 L9
Burwardsley Ches W 49 K4
Burwarton Shrops 39 L5
Burwash E Susx 12 D5
Burwash Common E Susx 12 D5
Burwash Weald E Susx 12 D5
Burwell Cambs 33 P4
Burwell Lincs 53 K7
Burwen IoA 54 F3
Burwick Ork 111 h3
Bury Bury 57 P6
Bury Cambs 43 J12
Bury Somset 16 C10
Bury W Susx 10 G7
Bury Green Herts 33 M11
Bury St Edmunds Suffk 34 E4
Burythorpe N York 60 D2
Busby E Rens 85 K10
Buscot Oxon 19 J2
Bush Abers 95 M8
Bush Bank Herefs 39 J10
Bushbury Wolves 40 B7
Bushbury Crematorium Wolves 40 B6
Bushey Herts 21 J4
Bushey Heath Herts 21 J5
Bush Hill Park Gt Lon 21 M4
Bushley Worcs 29 M2
Bushmoor Shrops 38 H5
Bushton Wilts 18 F5
Bussage Gloucs 29 M7
Bussex Somset 17 J8
Butcombe N Som 17 M4
Bute Ag & B 83 Q8
Butleigh Somset 17 M9
Butleigh Wootton Somset 17 M8
Butlers Marston Warwks 30 H4
Butley Suffk 35 N6
Buttercrambe N York 60 C3
Butterdean Border 87 P8
Butterknowle Dur 65 K3
Butterleigh Devon 6 D2
Buttermere Cumb 71 J11
Buttershaw C Brad 58 F8
Butterstone P & K 92 F6
Butterton Staffs 49 P7
Butterton Staffs 50 E9
Butterwick Lincs 43 L2
Butterwick N York 66 G11
Butterwick N York 67 L12
Buttington Powys 38 F1
Buttonoak Shrops 39 N6
Buxhall Suffk 34 G5
Buxted E Susx 11 P5
Buxton Derbys 50 D6
Buxton Norfk 45 K5
Buxton Heath Norfk 45 K6
Bwlch Powys 27 N4
Bwlchgwyn Wrexhm 48 F5
Bwlchllan Cerdgn 37 J8
Bwlchtocyn Gwynd 46 E6
Bwlch-y-cibau Powys 48 D11
Bwlch-y-ffridd Powys 38 C3
Bwlch-y-groes Pembks 25 M2
Bwlch-y-sarnau Powys 38 B7
Byers Green Dur 65 L2
Byfield Nhants 31 M4
Byfleet Surrey 20 G10
Byford Herefs 38 H12
Byker N u Ty 73 M7
Bylchau Conwy 55 P8
Byley Ches W 49 N2
Byrness Nthumb 72 D1
Bystock Devon 6 D6
Bythorn Cambs 32 F2
Byton Herefs 38 G8
Bywell Nthumb 73 J8
Byworth W Susx 10 F6

C

Cabourne Lincs 52 G3
Cabrach Ag & B 82 G9
Cabrach Moray 101 M9
Cabus Lancs 63 J11
Cadbury Devon 6 C2
Cadbury World Birm 40 D10
Cadder E Duns 85 K8
Caddington C Beds 32 F11
Caddonfoot Border 79 P2
Cadeby Donc 51 L1
Cadeby Leics 41 K7
Cadeleigh Devon 6 C2
Cade Street E Susx 12 C6
Cadgwith Cnwll 2 G11
Cadham Fife 86 F2
Cadishead Salfd 57 N9
Cadle Swans 26 E9
Cadley Lancs 57 K3
Cadley Wilts 18 H7
Cadley Wilts 19 J9
Cadmore End Bucks 20 C5
Cadnam Hants 9 K5
Cadney N Linc 52 E3
Cadoxton V Glam 16 F3
Cadoxton Juxta-Neath Neath 26 G8
Caeathro Gwynd 54 G8
Caenby Lincs 52 E5
Caeo Carmth 37 L11
Caerau Brdgnd 27 J9
Caerau Cardif 16 F2
Caer Farchell Pembks 24 E4
Caergeiliog IoA 54 D6
Caergwrle Flints 48 F4
Caerlanrig Border 79 N7
Caerleon Newpt 28 D10
Caernarfon Gwynd 54 F8
Caernarfon Castle Gwynd 54 F8
Caerphilly Caerph 27 N10
Caersws Powys 38 B4
Caerwedros Cerdgn 36 F9
Caerwent Mons 28 F10
Caerwys Flints 48 D2
Cairinis W Isls 111 b5
Cairnbaan Ag & B 83 M5
Cairnbulg Abers 103 L3
Cairncross Border 81 J2
Cairncurran Inver 84 F8
Cairndow Ag & B 84 C2
Cairneyhill Fife 86 C5
Cairngarroch D & G 68 E8
Cairngorms National Park 99 N8
Cairnie Abers 101 N6
Cairnorrie Abers 102 H7
Cairnryan D & G 68 E5
Cairnty Moray 101 L5
Caister-on-Sea Norfk 45 Q7
Caistor Lincs 52 G3
Caistor St Edmund Norfk 45 K8
Calanais W Isls 111 c2
Calbourne IoW 9 M9
Calcot Flints 48 D1
Calcot Gloucs 30 E11
Calcot Row W Berk 19 R6
Calcots Moray 101 K3
Caldbeck Cumb 71 M7
Caldecote Cambs 33 K5
Caldecote Cambs 42 G11
Caldecote Highfields Cambs 33 K5
Caldecott Nhants 32 E3
Caldecott Oxon 19 N2
Caldecott Rutlnd 42 C10
Calderbank N Lans 85 M9
Calder Bridge Cumb 62 B2
Caldercruix N Lans 85 N9
Calder Grove Wakefd 58 H10
Caldermill S Lans 77 L3
Calder Vale Lancs 63 K11
Calderwood S Lans 85 L11
Caldey Island Pembks 25 K9
Caldicot Mons 28 F10
Caldmore Wsall 40 D7
Caldwell N York 65 L5
Calf of Man IoM 56 a7
Calfsound Ork 111 h1
Calgary Ag & B 89 J6
Califer Moray 100 G4
California Falk 85 Q7
California Norfk 45 Q7
Calke Derbys 41 J3
Calke Abbey Derbys 41 J3
Callakille Highld 105 K10
Callander Stirlg 85 K2
Callanish W Isls 111 c2
Callestick Cnwll 2 H6
Calligarry Highld 96 H8
Callington Cnwll 4 H6
Callow Herefs 28 F2
Callow End Worcs 39 Q11
Callow Hill Wilts 18 F4
Calmore Hants 9 K5
Calmsden Gloucs 30 D11
Calne Wilts 18 E6
Calshot Hants 9 N7
Calstock Cnwll 5 J6
Calstone Wellington Wilts 18 F7
Calthorpe Norfk 45 K4
Calthorpe Street Norfk 45 N5
Calthwaite Cumb 71 P7
Calton Staffs 50 E10
Calveley Ches E 49 L4
Calver Derbys 50 G6
Calverhall Shrops 49 L7
Calverleigh Devon 16 C12
Calverton M Keyn 32 B8
Calverton Notts 51 N10
Calvine P & K 92 B3
Calzeat Border 78 H2
Cam Gloucs 29 K8
Camasachoirce Highld 89 Q4
Camasine Highld 89 P4
Camas Luinie Highld 97 N4
Camastianavaig Highld 96 F2
Camault Muir Highld 98 G2
Camber E Susx 13 J6
Camberley Surrey 20 E10
Camberwell Gt Lon 21 L7
Camblesforth N York 59 N8
Cambo Nthumb 72 H4
Camborne Cnwll 2 F7
Camborne & Redruth Mining District Cnwll 2 F7
Cambourne Cambs 33 K5
Cambridge Cambs 33 M5
Cambridge Gloucs 29 K7
Cambridge Airport Cambs 33 M5
Cambridge City Crematorium Cambs 33 L4
Cambrose Cnwll 2 G6
Cambus Clacks 85 P4
Cambusavie Platform Highld 107 M3
Cambusbarron Stirlg 85 N5
Cambuskenneth Stirlg 85 N4
Cambuslang S Lans 85 L10
Cambus o' May Abers 94 G3
Cambuswallace S Lans 78 G2
Camden Town Gt Lon 21 L6
Cameley BaNES 17 N5
Camelford Cnwll 4 D4
Camelon Falk 85 P6
Camerory Highld 100 F8
Camerton BaNES 17 P5
Camerton Cumb 70 G8
Camghouran P & K 91 N5
Camieston Border 80 D8
Cammachmore Abers 95 P3
Cammeringham Lincs 52 D7
Camore Highld 107 N4
Campbeltown Ag & B 75 K8
Campbeltown Airport Ag & B 75 K7
Cample D & G 78 E9
Campmuir P & K 93 J7
Camps W Loth 86 C8
Campsall Donc 59 M10
Campsea Ash Suffk 35 M5
Campton C Beds 32 G8
Camptown Border 80 F10
Camrose Pembks 24 G5
Camserney P & K 92 C6
Camusnagaul Highld 90 E2
Camusnagaul Highld 105 Q5
Camusteel Highld 97 J2
Camusterrach Highld 97 J2
Canada Hants 9 K4
Candacraig Abers 94 F3
Candlesby Lincs 53 M9
Candy Mill Border 78 H1
Cane End Oxon 20 B7
Canewdon Essex 22 H5
Canford Cliffs Poole 8 F9
Canford Crematorium Bristl 28 G12
Canford Heath Poole 8 F8
Canisbay Highld 110 G2
Canley Covtry 40 H11
Canley Crematorium Covtry 40 H11
Cann Dorset 8 C3
Canna Highld 96 B8
Cann Common Dorset 8 C4
Cannich Highld 98 D3
Cannington Somset 16 H8
Canning Town Gt Lon 21 N7
Cannock Staffs 40 C5
Cannock Chase Staffs 40 C4
Cannon Bridge Herefs 28 E1
Canonbie D & G 71 N1
Canon Frome Herefs 39 M12
Canon Pyon Herefs 39 J11
Canons Ashby Nhants 31 M4
Canonstown Cnwll 2 D8
Canterbury Kent 23 M10
Canterbury Cathedral Kent 23 M10
Cantley Norfk 45 N8
Canton Cardif 16 F2
Cantraywood Highld 107 N11
Cantsfield Lancs 63 L7
Canvey Island Essex 22 F6
Canwick Lincs 52 E9
Canworthy Water Cnwll 4 F2
Caol Highld 90 F2
Caolas Scalpaigh W Isls 111 c3
Caoles Ag & B 88 D6
Caonich Highld 97 Q10
Capel Kent 12 D2
Capel Surrey 11 J2
Capel Bangor Cerdgn 37 K5
Capel Coch IoA 54 F5
Capel Curig Conwy 55 K9
Capel Dewi Carmth 26 C5
Capel Dewi Cerdgn 36 G11
Capel-Dewi Cerdgn 37 K4
Capel Garmon Conwy 55 M9
Capel Hendre Carmth 26 E6
Capel Iwan Carmth 25 M2
Capel-le-Ferne Kent 13 N3
Capel Parc IoA 54 F4
Capel St Andrew Suffk 35 N7
Capel St Mary Suffk 34 H8
Capel Seion Cerdgn 37 K5
Capelulo Conwy 55 L6
Capenhurst Ches W 48 G2
Cape Wrath Highld 108 E1
Capheaton Nthumb 73 J5
Caplaw E Rens 84 G10
Cappercleuch Border 79 K4
Capstone Medway 22 F9
Capton Devon 5 Q9
Caputh P & K 92 G7
Caradon Mining District Cnwll 4 G5
Carbeth Inn Stirlg 85 J7
Carbis Bay Cnwll 2 D7
Carbost Highld 96 D4
Carbost Highld 104 F11
Carbrook Sheff 51 J3
Carbrooke Norfk 44 F9
Car Colston Notts 51 Q11
Carcroft Donc 59 M11
Cardenden Fife 86 E4
Cardhu Moray 101 J6
Cardiff Cardif 16 G2
Cardiff Airport V Glam 16 E3
Cardiff & Glamorgan Crematorium Cardif 27 N11
Cardiff Gate Services Cardif 27 P11
Cardiff West Services Cardif 27 M11
Cardigan Cerdgn 36 C10
Cardington Bed 32 F7
Cardington Shrops 39 J3
Cardinham Cnwll 4 D6
Cardrain D & G 68 F11
Cardrona Border 79 L2
Cardross Ag & B 84 F7
Cardross Crematorium Ag & B 84 F7
Cardryne D & G 68 F11
Cardurnock Cumb 71 J4
Careby Lincs 42 E6
Careston Angus 95 J9
Carew Pembks 24 H7
Carew Cheriton Pembks 24 H8
Carew Newton Pembks 24 H7
Carey Herefs 28 G3
Carfin N Lans 85 N10
Carfraemill Border 80 C4
Cargate Green Norfk 45 N7
Cargenbridge D & G 70 F1
Cargill P & K 92 H8
Cargo Cumb 71 M4
Cargreen Cnwll 5 J7
Carham Nthumb 80 H6
Carhampton Somset 16 D7
Carharrack Cnwll 2 G7
Carie P & K 91 P5
Carinish W Isls 111 b5
Carisbrooke IoW 9 N9
Cark Cumb 62 G6
Carkeel Cnwll 5 J7
Càrlabhagh W Isls 111 c2
Carlbury Darltn 65 L4
Carlby Lincs 42 F7
Carleen Cnwll 2 F9
Carleton Crematorium Bpool 56 G2
Carleton Forehoe Norfk 44 H8
Carleton-in-Craven N York 58 C4
Carleton Rode Norfk 44 H10
Carleton St Peter Norfk 45 M9
Carlincraig Abers 102 E6
Carlingcott BaNES 17 Q5
Carlisle Cumb 71 N4
Carlisle Airport Cumb 71 P4
Carlisle Crematorium Cumb 71 N5
Carlops Border 86 D10
Carloway W Isls 111 c2
Carlton Barns 59 J11
Carlton Bed 32 D6
Carlton Cambs 33 Q6
Carlton Leeds 59 J8
Carlton Leics 41 K6
Carlton N York 59 N9
Carlton N York 65 J9
Carlton N York 66 E9
Carlton Notts 51 N11
Carlton S on T 65 P3
Carlton Suffk 35 N4
Carlton Colville Suffk 45 Q11
Carlton Curlieu Leics 41 P7
Carlton Green Cambs 33 Q6
Carlton Husthwaite N York 66 C11
Carlton-in-Cleveland N York 66 C6
Carlton in Lindrick Notts 51 N4
Carlton-le-Moorland Lincs 52 C10
Carlton Miniott N York 65 P10
Carlton-on-Trent Notts 52 B10
Carlton Scroop Lincs 42 D2
Carluke S Lans 77 P2
Carmacoup S Lans 77 N6
Carmarthen Carmth 25 P5
Carmel Carmth 26 D5
Carmel Flints 56 D12
Carmel Gwynd 54 G9
Carmichael S Lans 78 F2
Carmountside Crematorium C Stke 50 B10
Carmunnock C Glas 85 K10
Carmyle C Glas 85 L9
Carmyllie Angus 93 P7

Carnaby E R Yk....61 K2
Carnbee Fife....87 K2
Carnbo P & K....86 C2
Carn Brea Cnwll....2 G7
Carnbrogie Abers....102 H9
Carndu Highld....97 M4
Carnduff S Lans....77 L3
Carnell E Ayrs....76 H5
Carnforth Lancs....63 J7
Carn-gorm Highld....97 N5
Carnhell Green Cnwll....2 F8
Carnie Abers....95 N2
Carnkie Cnwll....2 G7
Carnkie Cnwll....2 G8
Carno Powys....47 Q11
Carnock Fife....86 C4
Carnon Downs Cnwll....3 J7
Carnousie Abers....102 E5
Carnoustie Angus....93 P8
Carnwath S Lans....86 B11
Carol Green Solhll....40 H11
Carperby N York....64 H9
Carradale Ag & B....75 M5
Carrbridge Highld....99 N4
Carrefour Jersey....7 b1
Carreglefn IoA....54 E4
Carr Gate Wakefd....58 H8
Carrhouse N Linc....60 D11
Carrick Ag & B....83 N5
Carrick Castle Ag & B....84 D4
Carriden Falk....86 B6
Carrington Mdloth....86 G9
Carrington Traffd....57 N9
Carrog Denbgs....48 C6
Carron Falk....85 P6
Carron Moray....101 J7
Carronbridge D & G....78 E8
Carron Bridge Stirlg....85 M6
Carronshore Falk....85 P6
Carr Shield Nthumb....72 E10
Carrutherstown D & G....70 H2
Carruth House Inver....84 F9
Carville Dur....73 N11
Carsaig Ag & B....89 L11
Carseriggan D & G....69 J5
Carsethorn D & G....70 G4
Carshalton Gt Lon....21 L9
Carsington Derbys....50 G9
Carskey Ag & B....75 J10
Carsluith D & G....69 L8
Carsphairn D & G....77 J11
Carstairs S Lans....77 Q3
Carstairs Junction S Lans....77 Q3
Carterton Oxon....30 H11
Carthew Cnwll....3 M5
Carthorpe N York....65 N10
Cartland S Lans....77 P3
Cartmel Cumb....62 H6
Carway Carmth....26 C7
Cashe's Green Gloucs....29 L7
Cassington Oxon....31 L11
Cassop Dur....73 N12
Castel Guern....6 b2
Casterton Cumb....63 L6
Castle Acre Norfk....44 D7
Castle Ashby Nhants....32 C5
Castlebay W Isls....111 a7
Castle Bolton N York....65 J8
Castle Bromwich Solhll....40 F9
Castle Bytham Lincs....42 E6
Castlebythe Pembks....24 H3
Castle Caereinion Powys....38 D2
Castle Camps Cambs....33 P8
Castle Carrock Cumb....71 Q5
Castlecary Falk....85 N7
Castle Cary Somset....17 P9
Castle Combe Wilts....18 C5
Castle Donington Leics....41 K3
Castle Douglas D & G....70 C3
Castle Eaton Swindn....18 G2
Castle Eden Dur....73 Q12
Castleford Wakefd....59 K8
Castle Frome Herefs....39 M11
Castle Gresley Derbys....40 H4
Castle Hedingham Essex....34 D9
Castlehill Border....79 K2
Castlehill Highld....110 E3
Castle Hill Suffk....35 J7
Castlehill W Duns....84 G7
Castle Howard N York....66 G12
Castle Kennedy D & G....68 F7
Castle Lachlan Ag & B....83 Q4
Castlemartin Pembks....24 F8
Castlemilk C Glas....85 K10
Castlemorton Worcs....29 L2
Castlemorton Common Worcs....29 K2
Castle O'er D & G....79 L9
Castle Rising Norfk....43 Q5
Castleside Dur....73 J10
Castle Stuart Highld....107 M11
Castlethorpe M Keyn....32 B7
Castleton Border....79 Q10
Castleton Derbys....50 F4
Castleton N York....66 F6
Castleton Newpt....27 Q11
Castleton Rochdl....58 B11
Castletown Highld....110 E3
Castletown IoM....56 b7
Castletown Sundld....73 P8
Castley N York....58 H5
Caston Norfk....44 F9
Castor C Pete....42 G9
Catacol N Ayrs....75 N3
Catcliffe Rothm....51 K3
Catcomb Wilts....18 E5
Catcott Somset....17 K8
Catcott Burtle Somset....17 K7
Caterham Surrey....21 M11
Catfield Norfk....45 N6
Catford Gt Lon....21 M8
Catforth Lancs....57 J2
Cathcart C Glas....85 K10
Cathedine Powys....27 N4
Catherington Hants....10 B7
Catherston Leweston Dorset....7 K4
Catisfield Hants....9 P6
Catlodge Highld....99 J9
Catmere End Essex....33 N8
Catmore W Berk....19 M5
Caton Lancs....63 K8
Caton Green Lancs....63 K8
Catrine E Ayrs....77 J6
Catsfield E Susx....12 E7
Catsgore Somset....17 M10
Catshill Worcs....40 C11
Cattadale Ag & B....75 K9
Cattal N York....59 L4
Cattawade Suffk....34 H9

Catterall Lancs....57 J1
Catterick N York....65 M7
Catterick Bridge N York....65 M7
Catterlen Cumb....71 P8
Catterline Abers....95 P6
Catterton N York....59 L5
Catteshall Surrey....10 F2
Catthorpe Leics....41 M10
Cattistock Dorset....7 N3
Catton N York....65 P10
Catton Nthumb....72 E8
Catwick E R Yk....61 J5
Catworth Cambs....32 F3
Caudle Green Gloucs....29 N6
Caulcott Oxon....31 L8
Cauldcots Angus....93 Q6
Cauldhame Stirlg....85 L4
Cauldmill Border....80 C10
Cauldon Staffs....50 E10
Cauldwell Derbys....40 G4
Caulkerbush D & G....70 F4
Caulside D & G....79 P11
Caundle Marsh Dorset....17 P12
Caunton Notts....51 Q8
Causeway End D & G....69 K7
Causeway End Essex....34 B11
Causewayend S Lans....78 G2
Causewayhead Stirlg....85 N4
Causeyend Abers....103 K10
Causey Park Bridge Nthumb....73 L2
Cavendish Suffk....34 D7
Cavenham Suffk....34 C3
Caversfield Oxon....31 M8
Caversham Readg....20 B8
Caverswall Staffs....50 C11
Caverton Mill Border....80 G8
Cawdor Highld....100 D5
Cawood N York....59 M6
Cawsand Cnwll....5 J9
Cawston Norfk....45 J5
Cawthorne Barns....58 H11
Cawton N York....66 E12
Caxton Cambs....33 K5
Caynham Shrops....39 K7
Caythorpe Lincs....42 D1
Caythorpe Notts....51 P10
Cayton N York....67 M10
Ceann a Bhaigh W Isls....111 a4
Ceannacroc Lodge Highld....98 C6
Cearsiadar W Isls....111 d2
Cefn Newpt....28 C10
Cefn-brith Conwy....55 N10
Cefn-bryn-brain Carmth....26 G6
Cefn Cribwr Brdgnd....27 J11
Cefneithin Carmth....26 D6
Cefngorwydd Powys....37 P10
Cefn-mawr Wrexhm....48 F7
Cefn-y-pant Carmth....25 L4
Cellardyke Fife....87 L2
Cellarhead Staffs....50 C10
Cemaes IoA....54 E3
Cemmaes Powys....47 N9
Cemmaes Road Powys....47 N9
Cenarth Cerdgn....36 E11
Ceres Fife....93 M12
Cerne Abbas Dorset....7 P3
Cerney Wick Gloucs....18 F2
Cerrigydrudion Conwy....55 P11
Ceunant Gwynd....54 G8
Chaceley Gloucs....29 M3
Chacewater Cnwll....2 H6
Chackmore Bucks....31 P7
Chacombe Nhants....31 L5
Chadbury Worcs....30 D5
Chadderton Oldham....58 B12
Chaddesden C Derb....51 J12
Chaddesley Corbett Worcs....40 B11
Chaddlehanger Devon....5 K5
Chaddleworth W Berk....19 M5
Chadlington Oxon....31 J9
Chadshunt Warwks....31 J4
Chadwell Leics....42 B5
Chadwell Heath Gt Lon....21 P6
Chadwell St Mary Thurr....22 D7
Chadwick Worcs....39 Q8
Chadwick End Solhll....40 G11
Chaffcombe Somset....7 J2
Chafford Hundred Thurr....22 C7
Chagford Devon....5 N3
Chailey E Susx....11 N6
Chainhurst Kent....12 E1
Chaldon Surrey....21 L11
Chaldon Herring Dorset....8 B10
Chale IoW....9 N11
Chale Green IoW....9 N10
Chalfont Common Bucks....20 G5
Chalfont St Giles Bucks....20 F5
Chalfont St Peter Bucks....20 G5
Chalford Gloucs....29 M8
Chalford Wilts....18 C10
Chalgrove Oxon....19 Q2
Chalk Kent....22 D8
Chalkwell Kent....22 H10
Challacombe Devon....15 M4
Challoch D & G....69 K5
Challock Kent....23 J12
Chalton C Beds....32 E10
Chalton Hants....10 B6
Chalvey Slough....20 F7
Chalvington E Susx....11 P8
Chandler's Cross Herts....20 H4
Chandler's Ford Hants....9 M4
Channel Tunnel Terminal Kent....13 M3
Chanterlands Crematorium C KuH....61 J7
Chantry Somset....17 Q6
Chantry Suffk....35 J7
Chapel Fife....86 F4
Chapel Allerton Leeds....58 H6
Chapel Allerton Somset....17 K6
Chapel Amble Cnwll....3 M1
Chapel Brampton Nhants....31 Q2
Chapel Chorlton Staffs....49 P7
Chapelend Way Essex....34 B8
Chapel-en-le-Frith Derbys....50 D5
Chapel Green Warwks....31 L3
Chapel Haddlesey N York....59 M8
Chapelhall N Lans....85 N9
Chapel Hill Abers....103 L8
Chapel Hill Lincs....52 H11
Chapel Hill N York....59 J5
Chapelhope Border....79 K5
Chapelknowe D & G....71 M2
Chapel Lawn Shrops....38 G6
Chapel-le-Dale N York....64 D11

Chapel Leigh Somset....16 F9
Chapel of Garioch Abers....102 F9
Chapel Rossan D & G....68 F9
Chapel Row W Berk....19 P6
Chapel St Leonards Lincs....53 N8
Chapel Stile Cumb....62 G2
Chapelton Abers....95 P4
Chapelton Angus....93 Q6
Chapelton Devon....15 M6
Chapelton S Lans....77 L2
Chapeltown Bl w D....57 N6
Chapeltown Moray....101 K10
Chapeltown Sheff....51 J2
Chapmanslade Wilts....18 C10
Chapmans Well Devon....4 H2
Chapmore End Herts....33 K12
Chappel Essex....34 E10
Chard Somset....7 J2
Chard Junction Somset....7 J2
Chardleigh Green Somset....7 J1
Chardstock Devon....7 J2
Charfield S Glos....29 J9
Charing Kent....23 J12
Charing Crematorium Kent....13 J1
Charingworth Gloucs....30 G6
Charlbury Oxon....31 J9
Charlcombe BaNES....17 Q3
Charlcutt Wilts....18 E5
Charlecote Warwks....30 H3
Charlemont Sandw....40 D8
Charles Devon....15 M5
Charleston Angus....93 L6
Charlestown C Aber....95 Q2
Charlestown C Brad....58 F6
Charlestown Calder....58 C8
Charlestown Cnwll....3 M5
Charlestown Cnwll....3 M5
Charlestown Fife....86 C5
Charlestown Highld....105 M7
Charlestown Highld....107 K11
Charlestown Salfd....57 P7
Charlestown of Aberlour Moray....101 K6
Charles Tye Suffk....34 G6
Charlesworth Derbys....50 D3
Charlinch Somset....16 H8
Charlottetown Fife....93 K12
Charlton Gt Lon....21 N7
Charlton Nhants....31 M7
Charlton Nthumb....72 E4
Charlton Oxon....19 L3
Charlton Somset....16 H10
Charlton Somset....17 P6
Charlton W Susx....10 E7
Charlton Wilts....8 D3
Charlton Wilts....18 E3
Charlton Worcs....30 D5
Charlton Wrekin....49 L12
Charlton Abbots Gloucs....30 D8
Charlton Adam Somset....17 M9
Charlton All Saints Wilts....8 H3
Charlton Down Dorset....7 P4
Charlton Horethorne Somset....17 P10
Charlton Kings Gloucs....29 N5
Charlton Mackrell Somset....17 M9
Charlton Marshall Dorset....8 D6
Charlton Musgrove Somset....17 Q9
Charlton-on-Otmoor Oxon....31 M10
Charlton on the Hill Dorset....8 D6
Charlton St Peter Wilts....18 G9
Charlwood Hants....10 A4
Charlwood Surrey....11 K2
Charminster Dorset....7 P4
Charmouth Dorset....7 J4
Charndon Bucks....31 P8
Charney Bassett Oxon....19 L2
Charnock Richard Lancs....57 K6
Charnock Richard Crematorium Lancs....57 K5
Charnock Richard Services Lancs....57 K6
Charsfield Suffk....35 L5
Charter Alley Hants....19 P8
Charterhall Border....80 G5
Charterhouse Somset....17 M5
Chartershall Stirlg....85 N5
Chartham Kent....23 L11
Chartham Hatch Kent....23 L11
Chartridge Bucks....20 E3
Chart Sutton Kent....22 F12
Charvil Wokham....20 C8
Charwelton Nhants....31 M3
Chase Terrace Staffs....40 D5
Chasetown Staffs....40 D6
Chastleton Oxon....30 G8
Chasty Devon....14 F10
Chatburn Lancs....63 P12
Chatcull Staffs....49 P8
Chatham Medway....22 F9
Chatham Green Essex....22 E1
Chathill Nthumb....81 P8
Chatsworth House Derbys....50 H6
Chattenden Medway....22 F8
Chatteris Cambs....43 L11
Chatterton Lancs....57 P5
Chattisham Suffk....34 H8
Chatto Border....80 G10
Chatton Nthumb....81 M8
Chawleigh Devon....15 M9
Chawton Hants....10 B3
Cheadle Staffs....50 D11
Cheadle Stockp....57 Q10
Cheadle Hulme Stockp....57 Q10
Cheam Gt Lon....21 K10
Chearsley Bucks....31 Q11
Chebsey Staffs....49 Q9
Checkendon Oxon....19 Q4
Checkley Ches E....49 N6
Checkley Staffs....50 D12
Chedburgh Suffk....34 D5
Cheddar Somset....17 L5
Cheddington Bucks....32 D12
Cheddleton Staffs....50 C9
Cheddon Fitzpaine Somset....16 H9
Chedgrave Norfk....45 N9
Chedington Dorset....7 L2
Chediston Suffk....35 M2
Chedworth Gloucs....30 D10
Chedzoy Somset....17 J8
Cheeseman's Green Kent....13 J3
Cheetham Hill Manch....57 Q8
Cheldon Devon....15 M9

Chelford Ches E....49 P1
Chellaston C Derb....41 J2
Chellington Bed....32 D5
Chelmarsh Shrops....39 N5
Chelmondiston Suffk....35 K8
Chelmorton Derbys....50 E6
Chelmsford Essex....22 E3
Chelmsford Crematorium Essex....22 E3
Chelmsley Wood Solhll....40 F9
Chelsea Gt Lon....21 L7
Chelsfield Gt Lon....21 P9
Chelsworth Suffk....34 G7
Cheltenham Gloucs....29 N4
Cheltenham Crematorium Gloucs....29 N4
Chelveston Nhants....32 E3
Chelvey N Som....17 L3
Chelwood BaNES....17 P4
Chelwood Gate E Susx....11 N4
Cheney Longville Shrops....38 H5
Chenies Bucks....20 G4
Chepstow Mons....28 G9
Cherhill Wilts....18 F6
Cherington Gloucs....29 M8
Cherington Warwks....30 H6
Cheriton Hants....9 P2
Cheriton Kent....13 M3
Cheriton Pembks....24 H8
Cheriton Swans....26 B9
Cheriton Bishop Devon....5 P2
Cheriton Fitzpaine Devon....15 P10
Cherrington Wrekin....49 M10
Cherry Burton E R Yk....60 G6
Cherry Hinton Cambs....33 M5
Cherry Orchard Worcs....39 Q10
Cherry Willingham Lincs....52 E8
Chertsey Surrey....20 G9
Cherwell Valley Services Oxon....31 M8
Cheselbourne Dorset....8 B7
Chesham Bucks....20 F3
Chesham Bury....57 P6
Chesham Bois Bucks....20 F4
Cheshunt Herts....21 M3
Chesil Beach Dorset....7 N6
Cheslyn Hay Staffs....40 C6
Chessetts Wood Warwks....40 F11
Chessington Gt Lon....21 J10
Chessington World of Adventures Gt Lon....21 J10
Chester Ches W....48 H3
Chesterblade Somset....17 P7
Chester Crematorium Ches W....48 H2
Chesterfield Derbys....51 J6
Chesterfield Staffs....40 E6
Chesterfield Crematorium Derbys....51 K6
Chesterhill Mdloth....86 H8
Chester-le-Street Dur....73 M9
Chester Moor Dur....73 M10
Chesters Border....80 D11
Chesters Border....80 E9
Chester Services Ches W....49 J1
Chesterton Cambs....33 M5
Chesterton Cambs....42 G10
Chesterton Gloucs....18 E1
Chesterton Oxon....31 M9
Chesterton Shrops....39 P3
Chesterton Staffs....49 P5
Chesterton Green Warwks....31 J3
Chesterwood Nthumb....72 E7
Chester Zoo Ches W....48 H2
Chestfield Kent....23 L9
Cheston Devon....5 N8
Cheswardine Shrops....49 N9
Cheswick Nthumb....81 L5
Chetnole Dorset....7 N2
Chettisham Cambs....43 N12
Chettle Dorset....8 D5
Chetton Shrops....39 M4
Chetwynd Wrekin....49 N10
Chetwynd Aston Wrekin....49 N11
Cheveley Cambs....34 B5
Chevening Kent....21 P11
Chevington Suffk....34 D5
Cheviot Hills....80 G11
Chevithorne Devon....16 D11
Chew Magna BaNES....17 N4
Chew Stoke BaNES....17 M4
Chewton Keynsham BaNES....17 P3
Chewton Mendip Somset....17 N5
Chicheley M Keyn....32 C7
Chichester W Susx....10 D8
Chichester Crematorium W Susx....10 E8
Chickerell Dorset....7 P6
Chicklade Wilts....8 D1
Chidden Hants....9 Q4
Chiddingfold Surrey....10 F3
Chiddingly E Susx....12 B7
Chiddingstone Kent....11 P2
Chiddingstone Causeway Kent....11 Q1
Chideock Dorset....7 K4
Chidham W Susx....10 C8
Chidswell Kirk....58 H9
Chieveley W Berk....19 M6
Chieveley Services W Berk....19 N6
Chignall St James Essex....22 D2
Chignall Smealy Essex....22 D2
Chigwell Essex....21 N5
Chigwell Row Essex....21 P5
Chilbolton Hants....19 L11
Chilcombe Dorset....7 M5
Chilcompton Somset....17 P5
Chilcote Leics....40 H5
Childer Thornton Ches W....56 G12
Child Okeford Dorset....8 C5
Childrey Oxon....19 L3
Child's Ercall Shrops....49 M9
Childswickham Worcs....30 D6
Childwall Lpool....56 H10
Chilfrome Dorset....7 N3
Chilgrove W Susx....10 D7
Chilham Kent....23 K11
Chillaton Devon....5 J4
Chillenden Kent....23 N11
Chillerton IoW....9 N10
Chillesford Suffk....35 N6
Chillington Devon....5 P11
Chillington Somset....7 K1
Chilmark Wilts....8 E2

Chilmington Green Kent....13 J3
Chilson Oxon....30 H9
Chilsworthy Cnwll....5 J6
Chilsworthy Devon....14 F10
Chiltern Hills....20 C4
Chilterns Crematorium Bucks....20 F4
Chilthorne Domer Somset....17 M11
Chilton Bucks....31 P10
Chilton Dur....65 M2
Chilton Oxon....19 N4
Chilton Candover Hants....19 P11
Chilton Cantelo Somset....17 N10
Chilton Foliat Wilts....19 K6
Chilton Polden Somset....17 K7
Chilton Street Suffk....34 C7
Chilton Trinity Somset....16 H8
Chilwell Notts....41 L1
Chilworth Hants....9 L4
Chilworth Surrey....10 G1
Chimney Oxon....19 L1
Chineham Hants....19 Q9
Chingford Gt Lon....21 M5
Chinley Derbys....50 D4
Chinnor Oxon....20 C3
Chipnall Shrops....49 N8
Chippenham Cambs....33 Q3
Chippenham Wilts....18 D6
Chipperfield Herts....20 G3
Chipping Herts....33 K9
Chipping Lancs....63 L12
Chipping Campden Gloucs....30 F6
Chipping Norton Oxon....30 H8
Chipping Ongar Essex....22 B3
Chipping Sodbury S Glos....29 K11
Chipping Warden Nhants....31 L5
Chipstable Somset....16 E10
Chipstead Kent....21 P11
Chipstead Surrey....21 L11
Chirbury Shrops....38 F3
Chirk Wrexhm....48 F7
Chirnside Border....81 J3
Chirnsidebridge Border....80 H3
Chirton Wilts....18 F8
Chisbury Wilts....19 J7
Chiselborough Somset....17 L12
Chiseldon Swindn....18 H5
Chiselhampton Oxon....19 P2
Chisholme Border....79 N6
Chislehurst Gt Lon....21 N9
Chislet Kent....23 N9
Chisley Calder....58 D8
Chiswell Green Herts....21 J3
Chiswick Gt Lon....21 K7
Chisworth Derbys....50 C3
Chithurst W Susx....10 D5
Chittering Cambs....33 M3
Chitterne Wilts....18 E11
Chittlehamholt Devon....15 L7
Chittlehampton Devon....15 L7
Chittoe Wilts....18 E7
Chivelstone Devon....5 Q11
Chivenor Devon....15 J5
Chlenry D & G....68 F7
Chobham Surrey....20 F10
Cholderton Wilts....19 J11
Cholesbury Bucks....20 E3
Chollerton Nthumb....72 G6
Cholsey Oxon....19 P4
Cholstrey Herefs....39 J9
Chop Gate N York....66 D7
Choppington Nthumb....73 M4
Chopwell Gatesd....73 K8
Chorley Ches E....49 K5
Chorley Lancs....57 L5
Chorley Shrops....39 M5
Chorleywood Herts....20 G4
Chorleywood West Herts....20 G4
Chorlton Ches E....49 N5
Chorlton-cum-Hardy Manch....57 P9
Chorlton Lane Ches W....49 J6
Choulton Shrops....38 H5
Chrishall Essex....33 M8
Chrisswell Inver....84 D7
Christchurch Cambs....43 M10
Christchurch Dorset....8 H8
Christchurch Newpt....28 D10
Christian Malford Wilts....18 E5
Christon N Som....17 K5
Christon Bank Nthumb....81 P9
Christow Devon....5 P4
Chudleigh Devon....6 B6
Chudleigh Knighton Devon....6 B7
Chulmleigh Devon....15 M8
Church Lancs....57 N3
Churcham Gloucs....29 K5
Church Aston Wrekin....49 N11
Church Brampton Nhants....31 Q2
Church Broughton Derbys....40 G2
Church Cove Cnwll....2 G12
Church Crookham Hants....20 D12
Churchdown Gloucs....29 M5
Church Eaton Staffs....49 Q11
Church End C Beds....32 H8
Churchend Essex....23 J9
Church End Essex....34 C10
Church End Gt Lon....21 K5
Church Green Devon....6 G4
Church Hanborough Oxon....31 K10
Church Houses N York....66 F7
Churchill Devon....6 H3
Churchill N Som....17 L4
Churchill Oxon....30 H8
Churchill Worcs....30 B4
Churchill Worcs....39 Q6
Churchinford Somset....6 H1
Church Knowle Dorset....8 D10
Church Langton Leics....41 Q8
Church Lawford Warwks....41 L11
Church Leigh Staffs....40 D1
Church Lench Worcs....30 D4
Church Mayfield Staffs....50 F11
Church Minshull Ches E....49 M4
Church Norton W Susx....10 E10
Churchover Warwks....41 L10
Church Preen Shrops....39 K3
Church Pulverbatch Shrops....38 H2
Churchstanton Somset....16 G10

Churchstoke Powys 38 F4
Churchstow Devon 5 P10
Church Stowe Nhants 31 N3
Church Street Kent 22 E8
Church Stretton Shrops 39 J4
Churchtown Cnwll 4 D1
Churchtown Derbys 50 H8
Churchtown IoM 56 d3
Churchtown Lancs 63 J12
Church Village Rhondd 27 M10
Church Warsop Notts 51 M7
Churston Ferrers Torbay 6 B10
Churt Surrey 10 D3
Churton Ches W 48 H4
Churwell Leeds 58 H8
Chwilog Gwynd 46 G4
Chyandour Cnwll 2 D9
Cilcain Flints 48 D3
Cilcennin Cerdgn 36 H8
Cilfrew Neath 26 G8
Cilfynydd Rhondd 27 M9
Cilgerran Pembks 36 C11
Cilmaengwyn Neath 26 G7
Cilmery Powys 38 B11
Cilsan Carmth 26 E4
Ciltalgarth Gwynd 47 P4
Cilycwm Carmth 37 M11
Cimla Neath 26 G9
Cinderford Gloucs 28 H6
Cinder Hill Wolves 40 B8
Cippenham Slough 20 F7
Cirencester Gloucs 18 F1
City Gt Lon 21 M7
City Airport Gt Lon 21 N7
City of London Crematorium Gt Lon 21 N6
Clabhach Ag & B 88 F5
Clachaig Ag & B 84 B6
Clachan Ag & B 83 L10
Clachan Ag & B 84 B3
Clachan Ag & B 89 Q11
Clachan Ag & B 90 B7
Clachan Highld 96 G3
Clachan-a-Luib W Isls 111 b4
Clachan Mor Ag & B 88 C6
Clachan na Luib W Isls 111 b4
Clachan of Campsie E Duns 85 K7
Clachan-Seil Ag & B 89 Q11
Clachnaharry Highld 107 K11
Clachtoll Highld 108 B9
Clackavoid P & K 94 C8
Clacket Lane Services Surrey 21 N11
Clackmannan Clacks 85 Q5
Clackmannanshire Bridge Fife 85 Q5
Clackmarras Moray 101 K4
Clacton-on-Sea Essex 23 M1
Cladich Ag & B 90 F11
Cladswell Worcs 30 D3
Claggan Highld 89 P6
Claigan Highld 104 C10
Clanfield Hants 10 B6
Clanfield Oxon 19 K1
Clanville Hants 19 K10
Clanville Somset 17 P9
Claonaig Ag & B 83 N10
Clapgate Herts 33 M10
Clapham Bed 32 E6
Clapham Gt Lon 21 L8
Clapham N York 63 N8
Clapham W Susx 10 H8
Clapton Somset 7 K2
Clapton Somset 17 P5
Clapton-in-Gordano N Som 17 L2
Clapton-on-the-Hill Gloucs 30 F9
Claravale Gatesd 73 K7
Clarbeston Pembks 25 J5
Clarbeston Road Pembks 24 H5
Clarborough Notts 51 Q4
Clare Suffk 34 C7
Clarebrand D & G 70 C3
Clarencefield D & G 70 H2
Clarilaw Border 80 C9
Clarkston E Rens 85 J10
Clashmore Highld 107 M5
Clashmore Highld 108 B9
Clashnessie Highld 108 B9
Clashnoir Moray 101 J10
Clathy P & K 92 E10
Clathymore P & K 92 F10
Clatt Abers 102 C9
Clatter Powys 38 B4
Clatworthy Somset 16 E9
Claughton Lancs 57 K1
Claughton Lancs 63 K8
Claughton Wirral 56 F10
Claverdon Warwks 30 G2
Claverham N Som 17 L3
Clavering Essex 33 M9
Claverley Shrops 39 P4
Claverton BaNES 18 B7
Clawdd-coch V Glam 27 M12
Clawdd-newydd Denbgs 48 C5
Clawton Devon 14 F11
Claxby Lincs 52 G5
Claxton N York 59 P3
Claxton Norfk 45 M9
Claybrooke Magna Leics 41 L9
Clay Coton Nhants 41 N11
Clay Cross Derbys 51 K8
Claydon Oxon 31 L4
Claydon Suffk 35 J6
Claygate D & G 79 N11
Claygate Kent 12 E2
Claygate Surrey 21 J10
Clayhall Gt Lon 21 N5
Clayhanger Devon 16 D10
Clayhidon Devon 16 F11
Clayhill E Susx 12 G5
Clayock Highld 110 D4
Claypits Gloucs 29 K7
Claypole Lincs 42 C1
Clayton C Brad 58 E7
Clayton Donc 59 L11
Clayton W Susx 11 L7
Clayton-le-Moors Lancs 57 N3
Clayton-le-Woods Lancs 57 K4
Clayton West Kirk 58 H11
Clayworth Notts 51 Q4
Cleadale Highld 96 F11
Cleadon S Tyne 73 P8
Clearbrook Devon 5 L7
Clearwell Gloucs 28 G7
Cleasby N York 65 M5
Cleat Ork 111 h3
Cleatlam Dur 65 K4

Cleator Cumb 70 G11
Cleator Moor Cumb 70 G11
Cleckheaton Kirk 58 F8
Cleehill Shrops 39 L7
Cleekhimin N Lans 85 M10
Clee St Margaret Shrops 39 K5
Cleethorpes NE Lin 53 K2
Cleeton St Mary Shrops 39 L6
Cleeve N Som 17 L3
Cleeve Oxon 19 Q5
Cleeve Hill Gloucs 29 N4
Cleeve Prior Worcs 30 E4
Cleghornie E Loth 87 L5
Clehonger Herefs 28 E2
Cleish P & K 86 C3
Cleland N Lans 85 N10
Clenamacrie Ag & B 90 C9
Clenchwarton Norfk 43 P6
Clenerty Abers 102 G3
Clent Worcs 40 B10
Cleobury Mortimer Shrops 39 M7
Cleobury North Shrops 39 L5
Cleongart Ag & B 75 K5
Clephanton Highld 107 N11
Clerkhill D & G 79 L8
Cleuch-head D & G 78 D8
Clevancy Wilts 18 F6
Clevedon N Som 17 K2
Cleveleys Lancs 62 G12
Cleverton Wilts 18 E4
Clewer Somset 17 L6
Cley next the Sea Norfk 44 H2
Cliburn Cumb 64 B3
Cliddesden Hants 19 Q10
Cliffe Medway 22 E7
Cliffe N York 59 P7
Cliff End E Susx 12 H7
Cliffe Woods Medway 22 E8
Clifford Herefs 38 E11
Clifford Leeds 59 K5
Clifford Chambers Warwks 30 G4
Clifford's Mesne Gloucs 29 J4
Clifton Bristl 17 N2
Clifton C Beds 32 G8
Clifton C Nott 41 M1
Clifton C York 59 N4
Clifton Calder 58 F9
Clifton Cumb 71 Q9
Clifton Derbys 50 F11
Clifton Devon 15 K4
Clifton Donc 51 M2
Clifton Lancs 57 J3
Clifton N York 58 F5
Clifton Oxon 31 L7
Clifton Worcs 39 Q11
Clifton Campville Staffs 40 G5
Clifton Hampden Oxon 19 P2
Clifton Reynes M Keyn 32 C6
Clifton upon Dunsmore Warwks 41 M11
Clifton upon Teme Worcs 39 N9
Cliftonville Kent 23 Q8
Climping W Susx 10 F9
Clink Somset 18 B10
Clint N York 58 H3
Clinterty C Aber 102 H11
Clint Green Norfk 44 G7
Clintmains Border 80 E7
Clippesby Norfk 45 N7
Clipsham Rutlnd 42 D6
Clipston Nhants 41 Q10
Clipston Notts 41 N1
Clipstone C Beds 32 D10
Clipstone Notts 51 N8
Clitheroe Lancs 57 N1
Clive Shrops 49 K9
Cliveden Bucks 20 E6
Clixby Lincs 52 F3
Cloatley Wilts 29 N10
Clocaenog Denbgs 48 C5
Clochan Moray 101 M3
Clodock Herefs 28 C4
Clola Abers 103 K6
Clophill C Beds 32 F8
Clopton Nhants 32 F1
Clopton Suffk 35 K6
Clopton Corner Suffk 35 K6
Clos du Valle Guern 6 c1
Closeburn D & G 78 E9
Closeburnmill D & G 78 E9
Closworth Somset 7 N2
Clothall Herts 33 J9
Clotton Ches W 49 K3
Clough Foot Calder 58 B9
Clough Head Calder 58 E9
Cloughton N York 67 L8
Clousta Shet 111 k4
Clova Angus 94 F4
Clovelly Devon 14 F7
Clovenfords Border 79 P2
Clovulin Highld 90 D4
Clowne Derbys 51 L6
Clows Top Worcs 39 N7
Cluanie Inn Highld 97 N3
Cluanie Lodge Highld 97 N3
Clugston D & G 69 J7
Clun Shrops 38 F6
Clunas Highld 100 D6
Clunbury Shrops 38 G6
Clunderwen Carmth 25 K5
Clune Highld 99 L4
Clunes Highld 98 B10
Clungunford Shrops 38 H6
Clunie P & K 92 G6
Clunton Shrops 38 G6
Cluny Fife 86 F3
Clutton BaNES 17 N4
Clutton Ches W 49 J5
Clutton Hill BaNES 17 P4
Clydach Mons 27 P6
Clydach Swans 26 G6
Clydach Vale Rhondd 27 K9
Clydebank W Duns 84 H8
Clydebank Crematorium W Duns 84 H8
Clyffe Pypard Wilts 18 F5
Clynder Ag & B 84 D6
Clyne Neath 26 H8
Clynnog-fawr Gwynd 54 E10
Clyro Powys 38 E12
Clyst Honiton Devon 6 D4
Clyst Hydon Devon 6 D3
Clyst St George Devon 6 D5
Clyst St Lawrence Devon 6 D3
Clyst St Mary Devon 6 C5
Cnoc W Isls 111 d2
Cnwch Coch Cerdgn 37 L5

Coad's Green Cnwll 4 G5
Coalburn S Lans 78 D2
Coalburns Gatesd 73 K8
Coaley Gloucs 29 K8
Coalhill Essex 22 F4
Coalpit Heath S Glos 29 J11
Coal Pool Wsall 40 D7
Coalport Wrekin 39 M2
Coalsnaughton Clacks 85 Q4
Coaltown of Balgonie Fife 86 G3
Coaltown of Wemyss Fife 86 G3
Coalville Leics 41 K5
Coanwood Nthumb 72 C8
Coat Somset 17 L11
Coatbridge N Lans 85 M9
Coatdyke N Lans 85 M9
Coate Swindn 18 H4
Coate Wilts 18 F8
Coates Cambs 43 K9
Coates Gloucs 29 N8
Coates Lincs 52 C6
Coates W Susx 10 F6
Cobbaton Devon 15 K6
Coberley Gloucs 29 N5
Cobham Kent 22 D9
Cobham Surrey 20 H10
Cobham Services Surrey 20 H11
Cobnash Herefs 39 J9
Cobo Guern 6 b1
Cobridge C Stke 50 B11
Coburby Abers 103 J3
Cockayne Hatley C Beds 33 J6
Cock Bridge Abers 101 K12
Cockburnspath Border 87 P7
Cock Clarks Essex 22 F3
Cockenzie and Port Seton E Loth 86 H7
Cockerham Lancs 63 J10
Cockermouth Cumb 71 J9
Cockernhoe Herts 32 G11
Cockett Swans 26 F9
Cockfield Dur 65 K3
Cockfield Suffk 34 E6
Cockfosters Gt Lon 21 L4
Cock Green Essex 34 B11
Cocking W Susx 10 E6
Cocking Causeway W Susx 10 E6
Cockington Torbay 6 B9
Cocklake Somset 17 L6
Cockley Cley Norfk 44 D8
Cock Marling E Susx 12 G6
Cockpole Green Wokham 20 C7
Cockshutt Shrops 48 H9
Cockthorpe Norfk 44 G2
Cockwood Devon 6 D6
Cockyard Derbys 50 D5
Coddenham Suffk 35 J6
Coddington Herefs 29 J1
Coddington Notts 52 B11
Codford St Mary Wilts 18 E11
Codford St Peter Wilts 18 E11
Codicote Herts 32 H11
Codmore Hill W Susx 10 G6
Codnor Derbys 51 K10
Codrington S Glos 29 K11
Codsall Staffs 39 Q2
Codsall Wood Staffs 39 Q2
Coedpoeth Wrexhm 48 F5
Coed Talon Flints 48 F4
Coed-y-paen Mons 28 D8
Coffinswell Devon 6 B8
Cofton Devon 6 C6
Cofton Hackett Worcs 40 D11
Cogan V Glam 16 G2
Cogenhoe Nhants 32 B5
Cogges Oxon 31 J11
Coggeshall Essex 34 E11
Coignafearn Highld 99 K5
Coilacriech Abers 94 E3
Coilantogle Stirlg 85 K2
Coillore Highld 96 D3
Coity Brdgnd 27 K11
Col W Isls 111 d2
Colaboll Highld 107 J1
Colan Cnwll 3 K4
Colaton Raleigh Devon 6 E5
Colbost Highld 104 B11
Colburn N York 65 L7
Colby Cumb 64 C4
Colby IoM 56 b6
Colchester Essex 34 G10
Colchester Crematorium Essex 34 G11
Colchester Zoo Essex 34 F11
Cold Ash W Berk 19 N6
Cold Ashby Nhants 41 P11
Cold Ashton S Glos 17 Q2
Cold Aston Gloucs 30 F9
Coldbackie Highld 109 L4
Cold Brayfield M Keyn 32 D6
Coldean Br & H 11 M8
Coldeast Devon 5 Q5
Colden Calder 58 C8
Colden Common Hants 9 N3
Cold Hanworth Lincs 52 E6
Coldharbour Surrey 11 J2
Cold Higham Nhants 31 P4
Coldingham Border 81 J2
Cold Kirby N York 66 D10
Coldmeece Staffs 49 Q8
Cold Norton Essex 22 G4
Cold Overton Leics 42 B7
Coldred Kent 13 P1
Coldridge Devon 15 M10
Coldstream Border 80 H6
Coldwaltham W Susx 10 G6
Coldwells Abers 103 K7
Cole Somset 17 P9
Colebatch Shrops 38 G5
Colebrook Devon 6 D2
Colebrooke Devon 15 N11
Coleby Lincs 52 D10
Coleby N Linc 60 F9
Coleford Devon 15 N10
Coleford Gloucs 28 G6
Coleford Somset 17 P6
Colegate End Norfk 45 K11
Colehill Dorset 8 F7
Coleman's Hatch E Susx 11 N4
Colemere Shrops 48 H8
Colemore Hants 10 B4
Colenden P & K 92 G9
Colerne Wilts 18 B6
Colesbourne Gloucs 30 D10
Coleshill Bucks 20 F4
Coleshill Oxon 19 J3
Coleshill Warwks 40 G9

Coley BaNES 17 N5
Colgate W Susx 11 K4
Colinsburgh Fife 87 J2
Colinton C Edin 86 E8
Colintraive Ag & B 83 Q7
Colkirk Norfk 44 F5
Coll Ag & B 88 F5
Coll W Isls 111 d2
Collace P & K 93 J8
Collafirth Shet 111 k3
Coll Airport Ag & B 88 E5
Collaton Devon 5 P11
Collaton St Mary Torbay 6 B10
College of Roseisle Moray 100 H3
College Town Br For 20 D10
Collessie Fife 93 K11
Collier Row Gt Lon 21 P5
Collier's End Herts 33 L11
Collier Street Kent 12 E2
Collieston Abers 103 L9
Collin D & G 70 G1
Collingbourne Ducis Wilts 19 J9
Collingbourne Kingston Wilts 19 J9
Collingham Leeds 59 K5
Collingham Notts 52 B10
Collington Herefs 39 M9
Collingtree Nhants 31 Q3
Collins Green Warrtn 57 K9
Colliston Angus 93 Q6
Colliton Devon 6 E2
Collyweston Nhants 42 E9
Colmonell S Ayrs 68 F2
Colmworth Bed 32 F5
Colnabaichin Abers 101 K12
Colnbrook Slough 20 G7
Colne Cambs 33 L2
Colne Lancs 58 B6
Colne Engaine Essex 34 E10
Colney Norfk 45 K8
Colney Heath Herts 21 K3
Coln Rogers Gloucs 30 E11
Coln St Aldwyns Suffk 30 F12
Coln St Dennis Gloucs 30 E11
Colonsay Ag & B 82 E4
Colonsay Airport Ag & B 82 E5
Colpy Abers 102 E8
Colquhar Border 79 M1
Colsterworth Lincs 42 D5
Colston Bassett Notts 41 P2
Coltfield Moray 100 H3
Coltishall Norfk 45 L6
Colton Cumb 62 G5
Colton Leeds 59 J7
Colton N York 59 M5
Colton Norfk 45 H7
Colton Staffs 40 D4
Colt's Hill Kent 12 D2
Colvend D & G 70 E5
Colwall Herefs 29 K1
Colwell Nthumb 72 G6
Colwich Staffs 40 D4
Colwinston V Glam 16 C2
Colworth W Susx 10 E9
Colwyn Bay Conwy 55 M6
Colwyn Bay Crematorium Conwy 55 M6
Colyford Devon 6 H4
Colyton Devon 6 H4
Combe Oxon 31 K10
Combe W Berk 19 L8
Combe Down BaNES 18 B8
Combe Fishacre Devon 6 A9
Combe Florey Somset 16 F9
Combe Hay BaNES 17 Q4
Combeinteignhead Devon 6 B8
Combe Martin Devon 15 K3
Combe Raleigh Devon 6 F3
Comberbach Ches W 57 M12
Comberford Staffs 40 F6
Comberton Cambs 33 L5
Comberton Herefs 39 J8
Combe St Nicholas Somset 7 J1
Combrook Warwks 30 H4
Combs Derbys 50 D5
Combs Suffk 34 H5
Combs Ford Suffk 34 H5
Combwich Somset 16 H7
Comers Abers 95 L1
Comhampton Worcs 39 Q8
Commins Coch Powys 47 N10
Commondale N York 66 F5
Common End Cumb 70 G10
Common Moor Cnwll 4 F6
Compstall Stockp 50 C3
Compton D & G 69 P8
Compton Devon 6 B9
Compton Hants 9 M3
Compton Staffs 39 P5
Compton Surrey 10 F1
Compton W Berk 19 N5
Compton W Susx 10 C7
Compton Wilts 18 G9
Compton Abbas Dorset 8 C4
Compton Abdale Gloucs 30 D10
Compton Bassett Wilts 18 F6
Compton Beauchamp Oxon 19 J4
Compton Bishop Somset 17 K5
Compton Chamberlayne Wilts 8 F2
Compton Dando BaNES 17 P4
Compton Dundon Somset 17 L9
Compton Durville Somset 17 K11
Compton Greenfield S Glos 28 G11
Compton Martin BaNES 17 M5
Compton Pauncefoot Somset 17 P10
Compton Valence Dorset 7 N4
Comrie Fife 86 B4
Comrie P & K 92 B10
Conaglen House Highld 90 E3
Conchra Highld 97 M4
Concraigie P & K 92 G6
Conderton Worcs 30 N2
Condicote Gloucs 30 F8
Condorrat N Lans 85 M8
Condover Shrops 39 J2
Coney Hill Gloucs 29 L5
Coneyhurst Common W Susx 10 H5
Coneysthorpe N York 66 G12
Coney Weston Suffk 34 F2

Congerstone Leics 41 J6
Congham Norfk 44 B5
Congleton Ches E 49 Q3
Congresbury N Som 17 L4
Conheath D & G 70 G2
Conicavel Moray 100 F5
Coningsby Lincs 52 H11
Conington Cambs 33 K4
Conington Cambs 42 H11
Conisbrough Donc 51 L2
Conisholme Lincs 53 L4
Coniston Cumb 62 F3
Coniston E R Yk 61 K7
Coniston Cold N York 58 B3
Conistone N York 58 C1
Connah's Quay Flints 48 F2
Connel Ag & B 90 C9
Connel Park E Ayrs 77 K8
Connor Downs Cnwll 2 F7
Conon Bridge Highld 107 J10
Cononley N York 58 C5
Consall Staffs 50 C10
Consett Dur 73 K10
Constable Burton N York 65 L8
Constable Lee Lancs 57 P4
Constantine Cnwll 2 H11
Constantine Bay Cnwll 3 K2
Contin Highld 106 G10
Conwy Conwy 55 L6
Conwy Castle Conwy 55 L6
Conyer's Green Suffk 34 E3
Cooden E Susx 12 E8
Cookbury Devon 14 G10
Cookham W & M 20 E6
Cookham Dean W & M 20 D6
Cookham Rise W & M 20 E6
Cookhill Worcs 30 D3
Cookley Suffk 35 M2
Cookley Worcs 39 Q6
Cookley Green Oxon 20 B5
Cookney Abers 95 P4
Cook's Green Essex 35 K11
Cooks Green Suffk 34 G6
Cooksmill Green Essex 22 D3
Coolham W Susx 10 H5
Cooling Medway 22 F8
Coombe Cnwll 3 L8
Coombe Devon 6 C7
Coombe Devon 6 E4
Coombe Gloucs 29 K9
Coombe Abbey Warwks 41 K10
Coombe Bissett Wilts 8 G3
Coombe Cellars Devon 6 B8
Coombe Hill Gloucs 29 M4
Coombe Keynes Dorset 8 C9
Coombe Pafford Torbay 6 C9
Coombes W Susx 11 J8
Coombes-Moor Herefs 38 G9
Coombeswood Dudley 40 C9
Coopersale Common Essex 21 P3
Copdock Suffk 35 J8
Copford Green Essex 34 F11
Copgrove N York 59 J2
Copister Shet 111 k3
Cople Bed 32 F7
Copley Dur 65 J3
Copmanthorpe C York 59 M5
Copmere End Staffs 49 P9
Copp Lancs 56 H2
Coppenhall Staffs 40 B4
Copperhouse Cnwll 2 E8
Coppingford Cambs 32 G2
Copplestone Devon 5 N10
Coppull Lancs 57 K6
Copsale W Susx 11 J5
Copster Green Lancs 57 M3
Copston Magna Warwks 41 L9
Cop Street Kent 23 P10
Copt Hewick N York 65 N12
Copthorne W Susx 11 L3
Copt Oak Leics 41 L5
Copythorne Hants 9 K5
Corbets Tey Gt Lon 22 C6
Corbière Jersey 7 a2
Corbridge Nthumb 72 H7
Corby Nhants 42 C11
Corby Glen Lincs 42 E5
Cordon N Ayrs 75 Q6
Coreley Shrops 39 L7
Corfe Somset 16 G11
Corfe Castle Dorset 8 E10
Corfe Mullen Dorset 8 E8
Corfton Shrops 39 J5
Corgarff Abers 94 E1
Corhampton Hants 9 Q4
Corlae D & G 77 L10
Corley Warwks 40 H9
Corley Services Warwks 40 H9
Cormuir Angus 94 E4
Cornard Tye Suffk 34 E8
Cornforth Dur 65 N1
Cornhill Abers 102 D4
Cornhill-on-Tweed Nthumb 81 J6
Cornholme Calder 58 B8
Cornoigmore Ag & B 88 C3
Cornsay Dur 73 K11
Cornsay Colliery Dur 73 L11
Corntown Highld 107 J10
Corntown V Glam 27 J12
Cornwall Airport Newquay Cnwll 3 K3
Cornwell Oxon 30 H8
Cornwood Devon 5 M8
Cornworthy Devon 6 Q8
Corpach Highld 90 F2
Corpusty Norfk 45 J4
Corrachree Abers 94 H2
Corran Highld 90 E3
Corran Highld 97 M7
Corrie D & G 79 K10
Corrie N Ayrs 75 Q4
Corriecravie N Ayrs 75 P7
Corriegills N Ayrs 75 Q5
Corriegour Lodge Hotel Highld 98 C9
Corriemoille Highld 106 F9
Corrimony Highld 98 E3
Corringham Lincs 52 C5
Corringham Thurr 22 F6
Corris Gwynd 47 M9
Corris Uchaf Gwynd 47 M9
Corrow Ag & B 84 D3
Corry Highld 96 H5
Corscombe Devon 15 L11
Corscombe Dorset 7 M2
Corse Gloucs 29 K3
Corse Lawn Gloucs 29 L3

Corsham – Daildy 167

Corsham Wilts 18 C6
Corsindae Abers 102 F12
Corsley Wilts 18 C10
Corsley Heath Wilts 18 B10
Corsock D & G 78 C12
Corston BaNES 17 Q3
Corston Wilts 18 D4
Corstorphine C Edin 86 E7
Cortachy Angus 94 F9
Corton Suffk 45 Q10
Corton Wilts 18 D11
Corton Denham Somset 17 P10
Coruanan Highld 90 E3
Corwen Denbgs 48 C6
Coryton Devon 5 K4
Coryton Thurr 22 E6
Cosby Leics 41 M8
Coseley Dudley 40 C8
Cosgrove Nhants 32 B8
Cosham C Port 9 Q6
Cosheston Pembks 24 H7
Coshieville P & K 92 B6
Cossall Notts 51 L11
Cossington Leics 41 N5
Cossington Somset 17 J7
Costessey Norfk 45 K7
Costock Notts 41 M3
Coston Leics 42 B6
Coston Norfk 44 H8
Cote Oxon 19 L1
Cotebrook Ches W 49 L3
Cotehill Cumb 71 P5
Cotes Leics 41 M4
Cotesbach Leics 41 M10
Cotford St Luke Somset 16 G9
Cotgrave Notts 41 N1
Cothal Abers 102 H11
Cotham Notts 42 B1
Cotherstone Dur 64 H4
Cothill Oxon 19 M2
Cotleigh Devon 6 G3
Cotmanhay Derbys 51 L11
Coton Cambs 33 L5
Coton Nhants 41 P12
Coton Staffs 49 P10
Coton Clanford Staffs 49 Q10
Coton Hill Shrops 49 J11
Coton in the Elms Derbys 40 G4
Cotswolds 30 C11
Cotswold Wildlife Park & Gardens Oxon 30 G11
Cott Devon 5 Q7
Cottam Lancs 57 J3
Cottam Notts 52 B7
Cottenham Cambs 33 M4
Cottered Herts 33 K10
Cotteridge Birm 40 D10
Cotterstock Nhants 42 F11
Cottesbrooke Nhants 41 P11
Cottesmore Rutlnd 42 C7
Cottingham E R Yk 60 H7
Cottingham Nhants 42 B11
Cottingley C Brad 58 E6
Cottingley Hall Crematorium Leeds 58 H7
Cottisford Oxon 31 N7
Cotton Suffk 34 H4
Cottown Abers 101 P9
Cottown Abers 102 G11
Cottown of Gight Abers 102 H7
Cotts Devon 5 J7
Coughton Warwks 30 E3
Coulaghailtro Ag & B 83 K9
Coulags Highld 97 N1
Coull Abers 94 H2
Coulport Ag & B 84 D5
Coulsdon Gt Lon 21 L10
Coulston Wilts 18 D9
Coulter S Lans 78 G3
Coulton N York 66 E11
Coultra Fife 93 L10
Cound Shrops 39 K2
Coundon Dur 65 M2
Countersett N York 64 G9
Countess Wear Devon 6 C5
Countesthorpe Leics 41 N8
Counties Crematorium Nhants 31 Q3
Countisbury Devon 15 M3
Coupar Angus P & K 93 J7
Coupland Nthumb 81 K7
Cour Ag & B 75 M3
Courteachan Highld 97 J9
Courteenhall Nhants 31 Q4
Court Henry Carmth 26 D4
Courtsend Essex 23 K5
Courtway Somset 16 G8
Cousland Mdloth 86 H8
Cousley Wood E Susx 12 D4
Cove Ag & B 84 D6
Cove Border 87 P7
Cove Devon 16 C11
Cove Hants 20 D11
Cove Highld 105 M4
Cove Bay C Aber 95 Q2
Covehithe Suffk 35 Q1
Coven Staffs 40 B6
Coveney Cambs 33 M1
Covenham St Bartholomew Lincs 53 K5
Covenham St Mary Lincs 53 K5
Coventry Covtry 41 J10
Coverack Cnwll 2 H11
Coverack Bridges Cnwll 2 G9
Coverham N York 65 K9
Covington Cambs 32 F3
Covington S Lans 78 F2
Cowan Bridge Lancs 63 L7
Cowbeech E Susx 12 C7
Cowbit Lincs 43 J6
Cowbridge V Glam 16 D2
Cowden Kent 11 P3
Cowdenbeath Fife 86 D4
Cowers Lane Derbys 50 H10
Cowes IoW 9 N8
Cowesby N York 66 C9
Cowfold W Susx 11 K5
Cowhill S Glos 28 H9
Cowie Stirlg 85 P5
Cowley Devon 6 B4
Cowley Gloucs 29 N6
Cowley Gt Lon 20 G7
Cowley Oxon 31 M12
Cowling Lancs 57 L5
Cowling N York 58 C5
Cowling N York 65 M9
Cowlinge Suffk 34 B6
Cowpen Nthumb 73 N5
Cowplain Hants 10 B7
Cowshill Dur 72 F11
Cowslip Green N Som 17 L4
Cowthorpe N York 59 K4
Coxbank Ches E 49 M7
Coxbench Derbys 51 J11
Coxford Cnwll 14 C11
Coxford Norfk 44 E4
Coxheath Kent 22 E12
Coxhoe Dur 65 N1
Coxley Somset 17 M7
Coxley Wick Somset 17 M7
Coxtie Green Essex 22 C4
Coxwold N York 66 D11
Coychurch Brdgnd 27 K11
Coychurch Crematorium Brdgnd 27 K11
Coylton S Ayrs 76 G7
Coylumbridge Highld 99 N6
Coytrahen Brdgnd 27 J10
Crabbs Cross Worcs 30 D2
Crabtree W Susx 11 K5
Crackenthorpe Cumb 64 C3
Crackington Haven Cnwll 14 C11
Crackley Staffs 49 Q5
Crackleybank Shrops 49 N12
Cracoe N York 58 C3
Craddock Devon 6 E1
Cradley Dudley 40 C9
Cradley Herefs 39 N11
Cradley Heath Sandw 40 C9
Cradoc Powys 27 L3
Crafthole Cnwll 4 H9
Craggan Highld 100 F9
Cragganmore Moray 101 J7
Craghead Dur 73 L10
Cragside House & Garden Nthumb 73 J1
Crai Powys 27 J4
Craibstone Moray 101 P4
Craichie Angus 93 N6
Craig Angus 95 L10
Craig Highld 105 Q11
Craigbank E Ayrs 77 K8
Craigburn Border 86 F10
Craigcleuch D & G 79 M10
Craigdam Abers 102 H8
Craigdhu Ag & B 83 M2
Craigearn Abers 102 F11
Craigellachie Moray 101 K6
Craigend P & K 92 G10
Craigend Rens 84 H8
Craigendoran Ag & B 84 E6
Craigends Rens 84 G9
Craighlaw D & G 69 J6
Craighouse Ag & B 82 G9
Craigie P & K 92 G7
Craigie S Ayrs 76 G5
Craigiefold Abers 103 J3
Craigley D & G 70 C4
Craig Llangiwg Neath 26 G7
Craiglockhart C Edin 86 E7
Craigmillar C Edin 86 F7
Craigneston D & G 78 C10
Craigneuk N Lans 85 N10
Craigneuk N Lans 85 N9
Craignure Ag & B 89 P8
Craigo Angus 95 L8
Craigrothie Fife 93 L12
Craigruie Stirlg 91 M11
Craigton Angus 93 N7
Craigton C Aber 95 N2
Craigton E Rens 84 H11
Craigton Crematorium C Glas 85 J9
Craigton of Airlie Angus 93 K5
Craik Border 79 M7
Crail Fife 87 L1
Crailing Border 80 F8
Craiselound N Linc 51 Q2
Crakehall N York 65 M9
Crambe N York 60 C2
Cramlington Nthumb 73 M5
Cramond C Edin 86 E7
Cramond Bridge C Edin 86 E7
Cranage Ches E 49 N2
Cranberry Staffs 49 P8
Cranborne Dorset 8 F5
Cranbourne Br For 20 E8
Cranbrook Devon 6 D4
Cranbrook Kent 12 F3
Cranfield C Beds 32 D8
Cranford Gt Lon 20 H7
Cranford St Andrew Nhants 32 D2
Cranford St John Nhants 32 D2
Cranham Gloucs 29 M6
Crank St Hel 57 J8
Cranleigh Surrey 10 G3
Cranmore Somset 17 P7
Cranoe Leics 41 Q8
Cransford Suffk 35 M4
Cranshaws Border 87 N9
Crantock Cnwll 2 H4
Cranwell Lincs 52 E12
Cranwich Norfk 44 C10
Cranworth Norfk 44 G8
Craobh Haven Ag & B 83 M2
Crarae Ag & B 83 Q4
Crask Inn Highld 109 J10
Crask of Aigas Highld 98 F1
Craster Nthumb 81 Q9
Cratfield Suffk 35 M2
Crathes Abers 95 M3
Crathes Crematorium Abers 95 M3
Crathie Abers 94 E3
Crathie Highld 98 H9
Crathorne N York 66 B6
Craven Arms Shrops 38 H5
Crawcrook Gatesd 73 K8
Crawford S Lans 78 F5
Crawfordjohn S Lans 78 E4
Crawley Hants 9 M1
Crawley Oxon 31 J10
Crawley W Susx 11 L3
Crawley Down W Susx 11 M3
Crawton Abers 95 P6
Cray N York 64 G10
Crayford Gt Lon 21 P8
Crayke N York 66 D12
Crays Hill Essex 22 E5
Creacombe Devon 15 P8
Creagan Inn Ag & B 90 D7
Creag Ghoraidh W Isls 111 b5
Creagorry W Isls 111 b5
Creaguaineach Lodge Highld 91 J3
Creaton Nhants 41 P12
Creca D & G 71 K2
Credenhill Herefs 39 J12
Crediton Devon 15 P11
Creebank D & G 69 J4
Creebridge D & G 69 K6
Creech Heathfield Somset 16 H10
Creech St Michael Somset 16 H10
Creed Cnwll 3 L6
Creekmouth Gt Lon 21 P7
Creeting St Mary Suffk 34 H5
Creeton Lincs 42 E6
Creetown D & G 69 L7
Cregneash IoM 56 a7
Creich Fife 93 K10
Creigiau Cardif 27 M11
Cremyll Cnwll 5 K9
Cressage Shrops 39 L2
Cressbrook Derbys 50 F6
Cresselly Pembks 25 J7
Cressex Bucks 20 D5
Cressing Essex 34 D11
Cresswell Nthumb 73 N3
Cresswell Pembks 25 J7
Cresswell Staffs 50 C11
Creswell Derbys 51 M6
Cretingham Suffk 35 K5
Cretshengan Ag & B 83 K9
Crewe Ches E 49 N4
Crewe-by-Farndon Ches W 48 H5
Crewe Crematorium Ches E 49 N4
Crewe Green Ches E 49 N5
Crew Green Powys 48 G11
Crewkerne Somset 7 L2
Crewton C Derb 41 J2
Crianlarich Stirlg 91 K10
Cribyn Cerdgn 36 H9
Criccieth Gwynd 46 H4
Crich Derbys 51 J9
Crichton Mdloth 86 H9
Crick Nhants 41 N11
Crickadarn Powys 27 M1
Cricket St Thomas Somset 7 K2
Crickhowell Powys 27 P5
Cricklade Wilts 18 G3
Cricklewood Gt Lon 21 K6
Crieff P & K 92 C10
Criggion Powys 48 F11
Crigglestone Wakefd 58 H10
Crimond Abers 103 L4
Crimplesham Norfk 43 Q8
Crimscote Warwks 30 G5
Crinaglack Highld 98 F2
Crinan Ag & B 83 L4
Crindledyke N Lans 85 N10
Cringleford Norfk 45 K8
Crinow Pembks 25 K6
Croachy Highld 99 J4
Crockenhill Kent 21 P9
Crocker End Oxon 20 B6
Crockernwell Devon 5 P2
Crockerton Wilts 18 C11
Crocketford D & G 70 D2
Crockham Hill Kent 21 N12
Croeserw Neath 27 J9
Croes-goch Pembks 24 E3
Croes-lan Cerdgn 36 F10
Croesor Gwynd 47 K3
Croesyceiliog Carmth 25 P5
Croesyceiliog Torfn 28 C9
Croft Leics 41 L8
Croft Lincs 53 N10
Croft Warrtn 57 L9
Croftamie Stirlg 84 H6
Crofton Wakefd 59 J9
Croft-on-Tees N York 65 M5
Croftown Highld 106 C5
Crofts Moray 101 K5
Crofts Bank Traffd 57 N9
Crofts of Dipple Moray 101 L4
Crofts of Savoch Abers 103 L4
Crofty Swans 26 C9
Croggan Ag & B 89 P10
Croglin Cumb 71 R6
Croick Highld 106 H4
Cromarty Highld 107 N8
Crombie Fife 86 C5
Cromdale Highld 100 G9
Cromer Herts 33 J10
Cromer Norfk 45 K2
Cromford Derbys 50 H9
Cromhall S Glos 29 J10
Cromor W Isls 111 d2
Cromwell Notts 52 B10
Cronberry E Ayrs 77 K6
Crondall Hants 10 C1
Cronton Knows 57 J10
Crook Cumb 63 J3
Crook Dur 65 L1
Crookedholm E Ayrs 76 H4
Crookes Sheff 51 J4
Crookham Nthumb 81 J6
Crookham W Berk 19 P7
Crookham Village Hants 20 C11
Crook Inn Border 78 H4
Crooklands Cumb 63 K5
Crook of Devon P & K 86 C3
Cropredy Oxon 31 L5
Cropston Leics 41 M5
Cropthorne Worcs 30 D5
Cropton N York 66 G9
Cropwell Bishop Notts 41 P1
Cropwell Butler Notts 51 P12
Cros W Isls 111 e1
Crosbost W Isls 111 d2
Crosby Cumb 70 H7
Crosby IoM 56 c5
Crosby N Linc 60 F10
Crosby Sefton 56 G8
Crosby Garret Cumb 63 N1
Crosby Ravensworth Cumb 64 B5
Croscombe Somset 17 N7
Cross Somset 17 K5
Crossaig Ag & B 75 M3
Crossapol Ag & B 88 C7
Cross Ash Mons 28 E5
Cross-at-Hand Kent 12 F2
Crossbost W Isls 111 d2
Crosscanonby Cumb 70 H7
Crossdale Street Norfk 45 K3
Cross Flatts C Brad 58 E6
Crossford Fife 86 C5
Crossford S Lans 77 N3
Crossgatehall E Loth 86 H8
Crossgates E Ayrs 76 F3
Crossgates Fife 86 D5
Cross Gates Leeds 59 J7
Crossgates N York 67 M10
Crossgill Lancs 63 K9
Cross Green Leeds 59 J7
Cross Green Suffk 34 E5
Cross Green Suffk 34 G6
Cross Hands Carmth 26 D6
Crosshands E Ayrs 76 H5
Crosshill Fife 86 E3
Crosshill S Ayrs 76 F9
Crosshouse E Ayrs 76 G4
Cross Houses Shrops 39 K1
Cross in Hand E Susx 12 C6
Cross Inn Cerdgn 36 F8
Cross Keys Ag & B 84 F6
Crosskeys Caerph 27 P9
Crosskirk Highld 110 B2
Cross Lane IoW 9 N9
Cross Lane Head Shrops 39 N3
Crosslee Rens 84 G9
Crossmichael D & G 70 C3
Cross of Jackston Abers 102 G8
Cross o' th' hands Derbys 50 H10
Crossroads Abers 95 J1
Crossroads Abers 95 M3
Cross Street Suffk 35 K2
Crosston Angus 93 N5
Cross Town Ches E 57 N12
Crossway Green Worcs 39 Q8
Crossways Dorset 8 B9
Crosswell Pembks 25 K2
Crosthwaite Cumb 62 H4
Croston Lancs 57 J5
Crostwick Norfk 45 L7
Crouch End Gt Lon 21 L6
Croucheston Wilts 8 F3
Crouch Hill Dorset 7 Q1
Croughton Nhants 31 M7
Crovie Abers 102 G3
Crowan Cnwll 2 F8
Crowborough E Susx 11 P4
Crowborough Warren E Susx 11 P4
Crowcombe Somset 16 F8
Crowdecote Derbys 50 E7
Crowden Derbys 50 E2
Crow Edge Barns 58 F12
Crowell Oxon 20 C4
Crowfield Suffk 35 J5
Crowhill E Loth 87 N7
Crow Hill Herefs 28 H4
Crowhurst E Susx 12 F7
Crowhurst Surrey 11 M1
Crowland Lincs 43 J7
Crowland Suffk 34 G3
Crowlas Cnwll 2 D8
Crowle N Linc 60 D10
Crowle Worcs 30 B3
Crowle Green Worcs 30 B3
Crowmarsh Gifford Oxon 19 Q3
Crown Corner Suffk 35 L3
Crownhill C Plym 5 K8
Crownhill Crematorium M Keyn 32 B8
Crownthorpe Norfk 44 H9
Crowntown Cnwll 2 F9
Crows-an-Wra Cnwll 2 B9
Crowthorne Wokham 20 D9
Crowton Ches W 49 L1
Croxdale Dur 73 M12
Croxden Staffs 50 E11
Croxley Green Herts 20 H4
Croxteth Lpool 56 H9
Croxton Cambs 33 J5
Croxton N Linc 61 J10
Croxton Norfk 44 E11
Croxton Norfk 44 G4
Croxton Staffs 49 P8
Croxton Kerrial Leics 42 B4
Croy Highld 107 N11
Croy N Lans 85 M7
Croyde Devon 14 H4
Croydon Cambs 33 K6
Croydon Gt Lon 21 L9
Croydon Crematorium Gt Lon 21 L9
Crubenmore Highld 99 K10
Cruckmeole Shrops 38 H1
Cruckton Shrops 48 H12
Cruden Bay Abers 103 M7
Crudgington Wrekin 49 L11
Crudie Abers 102 G4
Crudwell Wilts 29 N9
Crumlin Caerph 27 P8
Crumplehorn Cnwll 4 F9
Crumpsall Manch 57 Q8
Crundale Kent 13 K1
Crunwear Pembks 25 L6
Crux Easton Hants 19 M9
Crwbin Carmth 26 C6
Cryers Hill Bucks 20 E4
Crymych Pembks 25 L2
Crynant Neath 26 H7
Crystal Palace Gt Lon 21 M8
Cuaig Highld 105 K10
Cuan Ag & B 89 P12
Cubert Cnwll 2 H4
Cublington Bucks 32 B11
Cublington Herefs 28 E2
Cuckfield W Susx 11 L5
Cucklington Somset 17 R10
Cuckney Notts 51 M6
Cuddesdon Oxon 31 N12
Cuddington Bucks 31 Q11
Cuddington Ches W 49 L2
Cuddington Heath Ches W 49 J6
Cudham Gt Lon 21 N10
Cudliptown Devon 5 L4
Cudnell Bmouth 8 F7
Cudworth Barns 59 K11
Cudworth Somset 7 K1
Cuffley Herts 21 L3
Cuil Highld 90 D5
Culbokie Highld 107 K9
Culburnie Highld 98 G1
Culcabock Highld 107 L12
Culcharry Highld 100 D5
Culcheth Warrtn 57 M9
Culdrain Abers 101 P8
Culduie Highld 97 K2
Culford Suffk 34 D3
Culgaith Cumb 64 B2
Culham Oxon 19 N2
Culkein Highld 108 B8
Culkein Drumbeg Highld 108 C8
Culkerton Gloucs 29 N9
Cullen Moray 101 P2
Cullercoats N Tyne 73 P6
Cullerlie Abers 95 M2
Cullicudden Highld 107 K9
Cullingworth C Brad 58 E6
Cuillin Hills Highld 96 F5
Cullipool Ag & B 83 L1
Cullivoe Shet 111 k2
Culloden Highld 107 M12
Cullompton Devon 6 D2
Cullompton Services Devon 6 D2
Culm Davy Devon 16 F12
Culmington Shrops 39 J6
Culmstock Devon 16 E12
Culnacraig Highld 106 A2
Culnaightrie D & G 70 C5
Culnaknock Highld 104 G9
Culrain Highld 107 J4
Culross Fife 86 B5
Culroy S Ayrs 76 F8
Culsalmond Abers 102 E8
Culscadden D & G 69 L8
Culshabbin D & G 69 J8
Culswick Shet 111 j4
Cultercullen Abers 103 J9
Cults C Aber 95 P2
Culverstone Green Kent 22 D10
Culverthorpe Lincs 42 E3
Culworth Nhants 31 M5
Culzean Castle & Country Park S Ayrs 76 D8
Cumbernauld N Lans 85 M7
Cumbernauld Village N Lans 85 M7
Cumberworth Lincs 53 N8
Cuminestown Abers 102 G5
Cumledge Border 80 G3
Cummersdale Cumb 71 N5
Cummertrees D & G 71 J3
Cummingston Moray 100 H2
Cumnock E Ayrs 77 J7
Cumnor Oxon 31 L12
Cumrew Cumb 71 Q5
Cumrue D & G 78 H10
Cumwhinton Cumb 71 P5
Cumwhitton Cumb 71 Q5
Cundall N York 65 Q11
Cunninghamhead N Ayrs 76 F3
Cunningsburgh Shet 111 k4
Cupar Fife 93 L11
Cupar Muir Fife 93 L11
Curbar Derbys 50 G6
Curbridge Hants 9 N5
Curbridge Oxon 31 J11
Curdridge Hants 9 N5
Curdworth Warwks 40 F8
Curland Somset 16 H11
Curridge W Berk 19 N6
Currie C Edin 86 E8
Curry Mallet Somset 17 J10
Curry Rivel Somset 17 K10
Curtisden Green Kent 12 E3
Curtisknowle Devon 5 P9
Cury Cnwll 2 G10
Cushnie Abers 102 C11
Cusworth Donc 59 M12
Cutcloy D & G 69 L11
Cutcombe Somset 16 C8
Cuthill Highld 107 M5
Cutnall Green Worcs 39 Q8
Cutsdean Gloucs 30 E7
Cutthorpe Derbys 51 J6
Cuxham Oxon 19 Q2
Cuxton Medway 22 E9
Cuxwold Lincs 52 G4
Cwm Denbgs 56 C12
Cwmafan Neath 26 G9
Cwmaman Rhondd 27 L8
Cwmbach Carmth 25 M4
Cwmbâch Powys 27 N2
Cwmbach Rhondd 27 L8
Cwmbach Llechrhyd Powys 38 B10
Cwmbran Torfn 28 C9
Cwmcarn Caerph 27 P9
Cwmcarvan Mons 28 F7
Cwm-cou Cerdgn 36 E11
Cwm Crawnon Powys 27 N5
Cwmdare Rhondd 27 L7
Cwmdu Powys 27 P4
Cwmdu Swans 26 E9
Cwmduad Carmth 25 P3
Cwmfelin Brdgnd 27 J10
Cwmfelin Myr Td 27 M8
Cwmfelin Boeth Carmth 25 L5
Cwmfelinfach Caerph 27 P9
Cwmffrwd Carmth 25 P5
Cwmgiedd Powys 26 H6
Cwmgorse Carmth 26 F6
Cwmgwili Carmth 26 D6
Cwmhiraeth Carmth 25 N2
Cwm Llinau Powys 47 N9
Cwmllynfell Neath 26 G6
Cwmmawr Carmth 26 D6
Cwmparc Rhondd 27 K9
Cwmpengraig Carmth 25 N2
Cwmtillery Blae G 27 P7
Cwm-twrch Isaf Powys 26 G6
Cwm-twrch Uchaf Powys 26 G6
Cwm-y-glo Gwynd 54 H8
Cwmystwyth Cerdgn 37 N6
Cwrt-newydd Cerdgn 36 H10
Cyfarthfa Castle Museum Myr Td 27 L7
Cylibebyll Neath 26 G7
Cymer Neath 27 J9
Cymmer Rhondd 27 L10
Cynghordy Carmth 37 N11
Cynonville Neath 26 H9
Cynwyd Denbgs 48 C7
Cynwyl Elfed Carmth 25 P4

D

Daccombe Devon 6 B8
Dacre Cumb 71 P9
Dacre N York 58 F3
Dacre Banks N York 58 G2
Daddry Shield Dur 72 F12
Dadford Bucks 31 P6
Dadlington Leics 41 K7
Dafen Carmth 26 C8
Dagenham Gt Lon 21 P6
Daglingworth Gloucs 30 C12
Dagnall Bucks 32 E12
Dail bho Dheas W Isls 111 d1
Dailly S Ayrs 76 E10

Dairsie Fife 93 M11
Dalabrog W Isls 111 a6
Dalavich Ag & B 83 P1
Dalbeattie D & G 70 D4
Dalby IoM 56 b5
Dalby N York 66 F12
Dalcapon P & K 92 E5
Dalchalm Highld 107 Q2
Dalchreichart Highld 98 D6
Dalchruin P & K 91 Q11
Dalcrue P & K 92 F9
Dalditch Devon 6 E6
Daldowie Crematorium
 C Glas 85 L9
Dale Derbys 51 K12
Dale Pembks 24 E7
Dalelia Highld 89 P3
Dalgarven N Ayrs 76 E3
Dalgety Bay Fife 86 E5
Dalgig E Ayrs 77 J8
Dalginross P & K 92 B10
Dalguise P & K 92 E5
Dalhalvaig Highld 109 Q5
Dalham Suffk 34 C4
Daliburgh W Isls 111 a6
Dalkeith Mdloth 86 G8
Dallas Moray 100 H5
Dallinghoo Suffk 35 L6
Dallington E Susx 12 D6
Dallington Nhants 31 Q2
Dalmally Ag & B 90 G10
Dalmary Stirlg 85 J4
Dalmellington E Ayrs 76 H9
Dalmeny C Edin 86 D6
Dalmore Highld 107 L8
Dalmuir W Duns 84 H8
Dalnabreck Highld 89 P3
Dalnacardoch P & K 91 Q3
Dalnahaitnach Highld 99 M5
Dalnaspidal P & K 91 P2
Dalnawillan Lodge
 Highld 110 B7
Daloist P & K 92 B4
Dalqueich P & K 86 C2
Dalquhairn S Ayrs 76 F11
Dalreavoch Highld 107 M1
Dalry N Ayrs 76 E2
Dalrymple E Ayrs 76 F8
Dalserf S Lans 77 N2
Dalsmeran Ag & B 75 J9
Dalston Cumb 71 M5
Dalston Gt Lon 21 M6
Dalswinton D & G 78 F10
Dalton D & G 70 H2
Dalton N Ayrs 65 K6
Dalton N York 66 B11
Dalton Nthumb 73 K6
Dalton-in-Furness Cumb 62 E7
Dalton-le-Dale Dur 73 P10
Dalton-on-Tees N York 65 N6
Dalton Piercy Hartpl 66 C2
Dalveich Stirlg 91 P10
Dalwhinnie Highld 99 J11
Dalwood Devon 6 H3
Damerham Hants 8 G4
Damgate Norfk 45 N8
Damnaglaur D & G 68 F11
Danbury Essex 22 F3
Danby N York 66 G6
Danby Wiske N York 65 N7
Dandaleith Moray 101 K6
Danderhall Mdloth 86 G8
Danebridge Ches E 50 C7
Dane End Herts 33 K11
Danehill E Susx 11 N5
Dane Hills C Leic 41 M6
Dane Street Kent 23 K11
Danshillock Abers 102 F4
Danskine E Loth 87 L8
Darenth Kent 22 C8
Daresbury Halton 57 L11
Darfield Barns 59 K12
Dargate Kent 23 L10
Dargavel Rens 84 G8
Darite Cnwll 4 G6
Darland Medway 22 F9
Darlaston Wsall 40 C7
Darlaston Green Wsall 40 C7
Darley N York 58 G3
Darley Abbey C Derb 51 J12
Darley Bridge Derbys 50 H8
Darley Dale Derbys 50 H7
Darley Green Solhll 40 F11
Darleyhall Herts 32 G11
Darley Head N York 58 G3
Darlingscott Warwks 30 G6
Darlington Darltn 65 M5
Darlington
 Crematorium Darltn 65 M5
Darlton Notts 51 Q6
Darnick Border 80 D7
Darowen Powys 47 N10
Darra Abers 102 F6
Darracott Devon 14 E8
Darracott Devon 14 H4
Darras Hall Nthumb 73 K6
Darrington Wakefd 59 L9
Darsham Suffk 35 N3
Darshill Somset 17 N7
Dartford Kent 22 B8
Dartford Crossing Kent 22 C8
Dartington Devon 5 Q7
Dartmoor National Park
 Devon 5 N4
Dartmouth Devon 6 B11
Darton Barns 58 H11
Darvel E Ayrs 77 J4
Darwen Bl w D 57 M4
Datchet W & M 20 F7
Datchworth Herts 33 J11
Daubhill Bolton 57 M7
Daugh of Kinermony
 Moray 101 K7
Dauntsey Wilts 18 E4
Dava Highld 100 F7
Davenham Ches W 49 M2
Daventry Nhants 31 M2
Davidson's Mains C Edin 86 E7
Davidstow Cnwll 4 D3
Davington D & G 79 K8
Davington Hill Kent 23 J10
Daviot Abers 102 G9
Daviot Highld 99 K2
Daviot House Highld 99 K2
Davoch of Grange Moray 101 N5
Davyhulme Traffd 57 N9
Daw End Wsall 40 D7
Dawesgreen Surrey 11 K1
Dawley Wrekin 39 M1
Dawlish Devon 6 C7

Dawlish Warren Devon 6 D7
Daybrook Notts 51 M10
Daylesford Gloucs 30 G8
Deal Kent 23 Q11
Dean Cumb 70 H9
Dean Devon 5 P7
Dean Devon 15 M3
Dean Hants 9 P4
Dean Oxon 31 J9
Dean Somset 17 P7
Dean Bottom Kent 22 C9
Deanburnhaugh Border 79 N6
Deancombe Devon 5 P7
Dean Court Oxon 31 L11
Deane Bolton 57 M7
Deane Hants 19 P10
Deanhead Kirk 58 D10
Deanland Dorset 8 E4
Dean Prior Devon 5 P7
Deanraw Nthumb 72 E8
Deans W Loth 86 B8
Deanscales Cumb 70 H9
Deanshanger Nhants 31 Q6
Deanshaugh Moray 101 L5
Deanston Stirlg 85 M3
Dearham Cumb 70 H8
Debach Suffk 35 L6
Debden Essex 21 N4
Debden Essex 33 N9
Debenham Suffk 35 K4
Deblin's Green Worcs 39 P11
Dechmont W Loth 86 C7
Dechmont Road W Loth 86 B8
Deddington Oxon 31 L7
Dedham Essex 34 H9
Dedworth W & M 20 F8
Deene Nhants 42 D10
Deenethorpe Nhants 42 D10
Deepcar Sheff 50 H2
Deeping Gate C Pete 42 G8
Deeping St James Lincs 42 G8
Deeping St Nicholas
 Lincs 42 H7
Deerhurst Gloucs 29 M3
Defford Worcs 30 B5
Defynnog Powys 27 K4
Deganwy Conwy 55 L6
Degnish Ag & B 83 L1
Deighton C York 59 N5
Deighton N York 65 P7
Deiniolen Gwynd 54 H8
Delabole Cnwll 4 D4
Delamere Ches W 49 K2
Delfrigs Abers 103 K10
Delliefure Highld 100 G8
Dell Quay W Susx 10 D9
Delnabo Moray 100 H11
Delny Highld 107 M7
Delph Oldham 58 C11
Delves Dur 73 K10
Dembleby Lincs 42 E3
Denaby Donc 51 L2
Denbigh Denbgs 48 C3
Denbighshire
 Crematorium Denbgs 55 Q6
Denbrae Fife 93 L11
Denbury Devon 5 Q6
Denby Derbys 51 K10
Denby Dale Kirk 58 G11
Denchworth Oxon 19 L3
Dendron Cumb 62 E7
Denfield P & K 92 E11
Denford Nhants 32 E2
Dengie Essex 23 J3
Denham Bucks 20 G6
Denham Suffk 34 C5
Denham Suffk 35 K2
Denham Green Bucks 20 G6
Denhead Abers 103 K5
Denhead Fife 93 N11
Denhead of Gray C Dund 93 L8
Denholm Border 80 D9
Denholme C Brad 58 E7
Denmead Hants 9 Q5
Denmore C Aber 103 K11
Dennington Suffk 35 L4
Denny Falk 85 N6
Dennyloanhead Falk 85 N7
Den of Lindores Fife 93 J11
Denshaw Oldham 58 C11
Denside Abers 95 N3
Densole Kent 13 N2
Denston Suffk 34 C6
Denstone Staffs 50 E11
Denstroude Kent 23 L10
Dent Cumb 63 N5
Denton Cambs 42 G11
Denton Darltn 65 L4
Denton E Susx 11 P9
Denton Kent 13 N1
Denton Lincs 42 C4
Denton N York 58 F4
Denton Nhants 32 B5
Denton Norfk 45 L11
Denton Tamesd 50 B2
Denver Norfk 43 P9
Denwick Nthumb 81 P10
Deopham Norfk 44 H9
Deopham Green Norfk 44 H9
Deptford Gt Lon 21 M7
Deptford Wilts 18 E12
Derby C Derb 51 J1
Derby Devon 15 K5
Derbyhaven IoM 56 b7
Derculich P & K 92 D5
Dereham Norfk 44 G7
Deri Caerph 27 N8
Derringstone Kent 23 M12
Derrington Staffs 40 B3
Derriton Devon 14 E8
Derrythorpe N Linc 52 B2
Dersingham Norfk 44 B4
Dervaig Ag & B 89 J6
Derwen Denbgs 48 C5
Derwenlas Powys 47 L10
Derwent Valley Mills
 Derbys 50 H9
Derwent Water Cumb 71 L10
Desborough Nhants 42 B12
Desford Leics 41 L6
Deskford Moray 101 N3
Detling Kent 22 F10
Devauden Mons 28 F8
Devil's Bridge Cerdgn 37 M5
Devizes Wilts 18 E8
Devonport C Plym 5 K8
Devonside Clacks 85 Q4
Devoran Cnwll 2 H7
Devoran & Perran Cnwll 2 H7

Dewarton Mdloth 86 H9
Dewlish Dorset 8 B7
Dewsbury Kirk 58 H9
Dewsbury Moor Kirk 58 G9
Dewsbury Moor
 Crematorium Kirk 58 G9
Deytheur Powys 48 E11
Dibden Hants 9 L6
Dibden Purlieu Hants 9 M6
Dickleburgh Norfk 35 J1
Didbrook Gloucs 30 D7
Didcot Oxon 19 N3
Diddington Cambs 32 H4
Diddlebury Shrops 39 K5
Didling W Susx 10 D6
Didmarton Gloucs 18 B4
Didsbury Manch 57 Q9
Digby Lincs 52 F11
Digg Highld 104 F8
Diggle Oldham 58 D11
Digmoor Lancs 57 J7
Dihewyd Cerdgn 36 H9
Dilham Norfk 45 M5
Dilhorne Staffs 50 C11
Dill Hall Lancs 57 N3
Dillington Cambs 32 G4
Dilston Nthumb 72 H8
Dilton Wilts 18 C10
Dilton Marsh Wilts 18 C10
Dilwyn Herefs 38 H10
Dinas Gwynd 46 E4
Dinas Pembks 24 H2
Dinas-Mawddwy Gwynd 47 P8
Dinas Powys V Glam 16 F2
Dinder Somset 17 N7
Dinedor Herefs 28 G2
Dingestow Mons 28 E6
Dingle Lpool 56 G10
Dingley Nhants 41 Q9
Dingwall Highld 107 J9
Dinnet Abers 94 H3
Dinnington N u Ty 73 L6
Dinnington Rothm 51 M4
Dinnington Somset 17 K12
Dinorwic Gwynd 54 H8
Dinton Bucks 31 Q11
Dinton Wilts 8 E2
Dinwoodie D & G 78 H10
Dinworthy Devon 14 F8
Dipford Somset 16 G10
Dippen Ag & B 75 M5
Dippen N Ayrs 75 Q7
Dippertown Devon 5 J4
Dipple Moray 101 L4
Dipple S Ayrs 76 D10
Diptford Devon 5 P8
Dipton Dur 73 K9
Dirleton E Loth 87 K5
Dirt Pot Nthumb 72 H10
Diseworth Leics 41 L3
Dishforth N York 65 P11
Disley Ches E 50 C4
Diss Norfk 35 J1
Distington Cumb 70 G10
Distington Hall
 Crematorium Cumb 70 G10
Ditchampton Wilts 8 G2
Ditcheat Somset 17 P8
Ditchingham Norfk 45 M11
Ditchling E Susx 11 M7
Ditherington Shrops 49 J11
Ditteridge Wilts 18 B6
Dittisham Devon 6 B10
Ditton Kent 22 E10
Ditton Green Cambs 33 Q5
Ditton Priors Shrops 39 L4
Dixton Mons 28 F6
Dobcross Oldham 58 C11
Dobwalls Cnwll 4 F7
Doccombe Devon 5 Q3
Dochgarroch Highld 99 J2
Docking Norfk 44 C3
Docklow Herefs 39 K10
Dockray Cumb 71 N10
Doddinghurst Essex 22 C4
Doddington Cambs 43 L11
Doddington Kent 22 H11
Doddington Lincs 52 C9
Doddington Nthumb 81 L7
Doddington Shrops 39 L6
Doddiscombsleigh Devon 6 B5
Dodd's Green Ches E 49 L6
Dodford Nhants 31 N3
Dodford Worcs 40 C11
Dodington S Glos 29 K11
Dodington Somset 16 G7
Dodleston Ches W 48 G4
Dodside E Rens 84 H11
Dod's Leigh Staffs 40 D1
Dodworth Barns 58 H12
Doe Bank Birm 40 E7
Dogdyke Lincs 52 H11
Dogmersfield Hants 20 C11
Dogsthorpe C Pete 42 H9
Dolanog Powys 48 C11
Dolbenmaen Gwynd 46 H3
Dolfach Powys 47 P10
Dolfor Powys 38 C5
Dolgarrog Conwy 55 L7
Dolgellau Gwynd 47 M7
Doll Highld 107 P2
Dollar Clacks 85 Q4
Dollarfield Clacks 85 Q4
Dolphin Flints 48 E2
Dolphinholme Lancs 63 K10
Dolphinton S Lans 86 D11
Dolton Devon 15 K9
Dolwen Conwy 55 N6
Dolwyddelan Conwy 55 K10
Domgay Powys 48 F10
Doncaster Donc 59 M12
Doncaster North
 Services Donc 59 P11
Doncaster Sheffield
 Airport Donc 51 P2
Donhead St Andrew Wilts 8 D3
Donhead St Mary Wilts 8 D3
Donibristle Fife 86 E5
Doniford Somset 16 E7
Donington Lincs 42 H3
Donington on Bain Lincs 52 H7
Donington Park
 Services Leics 41 L3
Donisthorpe Leics 40 H5
Donkey Street Kent 13 L3
Donnington Gloucs 30 F8
Donnington Herefs 29 J3
Donnington Shrops 39 L1
Donnington W Berk 19 M7
Donnington W Susx 10 D9
Donnington Wrekin 49 N11
Donnington Wood Wrekin 49 N11

Donyatt Somset 17 J12
Doonfoot S Ayrs 76 F7
Dorback Lodge Highld 100 G11
Dorchester Dorset 7 Q5
Dorchester-on-Thames
 Oxon 19 P2
Dordon Warwks 40 H7
Dore Sheff 50 H5
Dores Highld 98 H3
Dorking Surrey 21 J12
Dormansland Surrey 11 N2
Dormington Herefs 28 G2
Dormston Worcs 30 C3
Dorney Bucks 20 E7
Dornie Highld 97 M5
Dornoch Highld 107 N4
Dornock D & G 71 K3
Dorrery Highld 110 C5
Dorridge Solhll 40 F10
Dorrington Lincs 52 F11
Dorrington Shrops 39 J2
Dorrington Shrops 49 N7
Dorsington Warwks 30 F4
Dorstone Herefs 28 C1
Dorton Bucks 31 P10
Douglas IoM 56 d6
Douglas S Lans 78 D3
Douglas and Angus
 C Dund 93 M8
Douglas Crematorium
 IoM 56 d5
Douglas Pier Ag & B 84 D3
Douglastown Angus 93 M6
Douglas Water S Lans 78 E2
Douglas West S Lans 78 D3
Doulting Somset 17 P7
Dounby Ork 111 g2
Doune Highld 106 G3
Doune Stirlg 85 M3
Dounepark S Ayrs 76 D11
Dounie Highld 107 J4
Dousland Devon 5 L6
Dove Dale Derbys 50 F9
Dove Holes Derbys 50 E5
Dovenby Cumb 70 H8
Dover Kent 13 P2
Dover Castle Kent 13 P2
Dovercourt Essex 35 L9
Doverdale Worcs 39 Q8
Doveridge Derbys 40 E1
Doversgreen Surrey 11 K1
Dowally P & K 92 E6
Dowdeswell Gloucs 30 D9
Dowlais Myr Td 27 M7
Dowland Devon 15 K9
Dowlish Wake Somset 7 K1
Down Ampney Gloucs 18 G2
Downderry Cnwll 4 G9
Downe Gt Lon 21 N10
Downend Gloucs 29 L8
Downend S Glos 28 H12
Downfield C Dund 93 L8
Downgate Cnwll 4 H5
Downham Essex 22 E4
Downham Gt Lon 21 M8
Downham Lancs 63 P12
Downham Market Norfk 43 P9
Down Hatherley Gloucs 29 M4
Downhead Somset 17 N10
Downhead Somset 17 Q7
Downhill P & K 92 G9
Downholme N York 65 K7
Downies Abers 95 Q3
Downley Bucks 20 D4
Down St Mary Devon 15 M10
Downs Crematorium
 Br & H 11 M8
Downs Crematorium
 Br & H 11 M8
Downside Surrey 20 H10
Down Thomas Devon 5 M9
Downton Wilts 8 H3
Dowsby Lincs 42 G4
Doynton S Glos 17 Q2
Draethen Caerph 27 P10
Draffan S Lans 77 N3
Drakeholes Notts 51 P3
Drakemyre N Ayrs 76 E2
Drakes Broughton Worcs 30 B4
Draughton N York 58 D4
Draughton Nhants 41 Q11
Drax N York 59 P8
Draycote Warwks 41 K12
Draycott Derbys 51 K2
Draycott Gloucs 30 F7
Draycott Somset 17 L6
Draycott in the Clay
 Staffs 40 F2
Draycott in the Moors
 Staffs 50 C11
Drayton C Port 9 R6
Drayton Leics 42 B10
Drayton Norfk 45 K7
Drayton Oxon 19 N2
Drayton Oxon 31 K6
Drayton Somset 17 K10
Drayton Worcs 40 B11
Drayton Bassett Staffs 40 G7
Drayton Beauchamp
 Bucks 20 E2
Drayton Manor Park
 Staffs 40 G7
Drayton Parslow Bucks 32 B10
Drayton St Leonard Oxon 19 P2
Dreen Hill Pembks 24 G6
Drefach Carmth 25 N2
Drefach Carmth 26 D6
Drefach Cerdgn 36 H10
Dreghorn N Ayrs 76 F4
Drellingore Kent 13 N2
Drem E Loth 87 K6
Dresden C Stke 50 B11
Drewsteignton Devon 5 P3
Driffield E R Yk 60 H3
Driffield Gloucs 18 F2
Drift Cnwll 2 C9
Drigg Cumb 62 C3
Drighlington Leeds 58 G8
Drimnin Highld 89 L5
Drimpton Dorset 7 K2
Drimsallie Highld 90 C1
Dringhouses C York 59 N4
Drinkstone Suffk 34 F5
Drinkstone Green Suffk 34 F5
Drointon Staffs 40 D3
Droitwich Spa Worcs 30 B2
Dron P & K 92 H11
Dronfield Derbys 51 J5
Drongan E Ayrs 76 H7
Dronley Angus 93 L8

Droop Dorset 7 Q2
Droxford Hants 9 Q4
Droylsden Tamesd 50 B2
Druid Denbgs 48 B6
Druidston Pembks 24 F5
Druimarbin Highld 90 E3
Druimavuic Ag & B 90 D7
Druimdrishaig Ag & B 83 L8
Druimindarroch Highld 97 J11
Drum Ag & B 83 P7
Drum P & K 86 C3
Drumalbin S Lans 78 E2
Drumbeg Highld 108 C8
Drumblade Abers 102 D7
Drumbreddon D & G 68 E9
Drumbuie Highld 97 K4
Drumburgh Cumb 71 L5
Drumburn D & G 70 E5
Drumburn D & G 70 F3
Drumchapel C Glas 85 J8
Drumchastle P & K 91 Q5
Drumclog S Lans 77 L4
Drumeldrie Fife 87 J2
Drumelzier Border 79 J3
Drumfearn Highld 97 J6
Drumfrennie Abers 95 M3
Drumgley Angus 93 M5
Drumguish Highld 99 L8
Drumin Moray 101 J8
Drumjohn D & G 77 J10
Drumlamford S Ayrs 68 H4
Drumlasie Abers 95 K2
Drumleaning Cumb 71 L5
Drumlemble Ag & B 75 K8
Drumlithie Abers 95 N6
Drummoddie D & G 69 K9
Drummore D & G 68 F10
Drummuir Moray 101 M6
Drumnadrochit Highld 98 G3
Drumnagorrach Moray 102 C5
Drumpark D & G 78 E11
Drumrunie Lodge Highld 106 C2
Drumshang S Ayrs 76 E8
Drumuie Highld 104 F11
Drumuillie Highld 99 P5
Drumvaich Stirlg 85 L3
Drunzie P & K 86 D1
Drybeck Cumb 64 C5
Drybridge Moray 101 N3
Drybridge N Ayrs 76 F4
Drybrook Gloucs 28 H5
Dryburgh Border 80 D7
Dry Doddington Lincs 42 C2
Dry Drayton Cambs 33 L4
Drymen Stirlg 84 H5
Drymuir Abers 103 J6
Drynoch Highld 96 E4
Dubford Abers 102 G3
Duchally Highld 108 G11
Ducklington Oxon 31 J11
Duddenhoe End Essex 33 M9
Duddington Nhants 42 E9
Duddlestone Somset 16 H11
Duddo Nthumb 81 K6
Duddon Ches W 49 K3
Duddleston Shrops 48 G8
Dudleston Heath Shrops 48 G8
Dudley Dudley 40 C9
Dudley N Tyne 73 M6
Dudley Port Sandw 40 C8
Dudsbury Dorset 8 F7
Duffield Derbys 51 J11
Duffryn Neath 26 H9
Dufftown Moray 101 L7
Duffus Moray 101 J2
Dufton Cumb 64 C3
Duggleby N York 60 F2
Duirinish Highld 97 L4
Duisdalemore Highld 97 J7
Duisky Highld 90 D2
Dukestown Blae G 27 N6
Duke Street Suffk 34 H8
Dukinfield Tamesd 50 C2
Dukinfield
 Crematorium Tamesd 50 C2
Dulcote Somset 17 N7
Dulford Devon 6 E2
Dull P & K 92 B6
Dullatur N Lans 85 M7
Dullingham Cambs 33 Q5
Dulnain Bridge Highld 99 P4
Duloe Bed 32 G5
Duloe Cnwll 4 F8
Dulsie Bridge Highld 100 E7
Dulverton Somset 16 C9
Dulwich Gt Lon 21 M8
Dumbarton W Duns 84 G7
Dumbleton Gloucs 30 D7
Dumfries D & G 70 F1
Dumgoyne Stirlg 85 J6
Dummer Hants 19 P10
Dumpton Kent 23 Q9
Dun Angus 95 L9
Dunalastair P & K 91 Q5
Dunan Ag & B 84 C8
Dunan Highld 96 G4
Dunan P & K 91 L5
Dunball Somset 17 J7
Dunbar E Loth 87 M6
Dunbeath Highld 110 D9
Dunbeg Ag & B 90 B9
Dunblane Stirlg 85 N3
Dunbog Fife 93 K11
Duncanston Highld 107 J10
Duncanstone Abers 102 D9
Dunchideock Devon 6 B5
Dunchurch Warwks 41 L12
Duncow D & G 78 F11
Duncrievie P & K 86 D1
Duncton W Susx 10 F6
Dundee C Dund 93 M8
Dundee Airport C Dund 93 L9
Dundee Crematorium
 C Dund 93 L8
Dundon Somset 17 L9
Dundonald S Ayrs 76 F5
Dundonnell Highld 106 B5
Dundraw Cumb 71 K5
Dundreggan Highld 98 D6
Dundrennan D & G 70 C6
Dundry N Som 17 N3
Dunecht Abers 102 G12
Dunfermline Fife 86 C5
Dunfermline
 Crematorium Fife 86 D5
Dunfield Gloucs 18 G2
Dungavel S Lans 77 L4
Dungeness Kent 13 L6

Dunham Massey – Elmswell 169

Dunham Massey Traffd 57 N10
Dunham-on-the-Hill Ches W 49 J2
Dunham-on-Trent Notts 52 B8
Dunhampton Worcs 39 Q8
Dunham Town Traffd 57 N10
Dunham Woodhouses Traffd 57 N10
Dunholme Lincs 52 E7
Dunino Fife 93 P12
Dunipace Falk 85 N6
Dunkeld P & K 92 F7
Dunkerton BaNES 17 Q4
Dunkeswell Devon 6 F2
Dunkeswick N York 58 H5
Dunkirk Kent 23 L10
Dunkirk S Glos 18 B4
Dunk's Green Kent 22 C11
Dunlappie Angus 95 K8
Dunley Worcs 39 P8
Dunlop E Ayrs 76 G2
Dunmaglass Highld 98 H5
Dunmore Falk 85 P5
Dunnet Highld 110 E2
Dunnichen Angus 93 N6
Dunning P & K 92 F11
Dunnington C York 59 P4
Dunnington E R Yk 61 K4
Dunnington Warwks 30 E4
Dunoon Ag & B 84 C7
Dunphail Moray 100 F5
Dunragit D & G 68 F7
Duns Border 80 G4
Dunsby Lincs 42 F5
Dunscore D & G 78 E11
Dunscroft Donc 59 P11
Dunsdale R & Cl 66 E4
Dunsden Green Oxon 20 B7
Dunsdon Devon 14 F9
Dunsfold Surrey 10 G3
Dunsford Devon 5 Q3
Dunshalt Fife 86 F1
Dunshillock Abers 103 K5
Dunsill Notts 51 L8
Dunsley N York 67 J5
Dunsley Staffs 39 Q5
Dunsmore Bucks 20 D3
Dunsop Bridge Lancs 63 M11
Dunstable C Beds 32 E11
Dunstall Staffs 40 F4
Dunstan Nthumb 81 Q9
Dunster Somset 16 D7
Duns Tew Oxon 31 L8
Dunston Gatesd 73 M8
Dunston Lincs 52 F10
Dunston Norfk 45 K9
Dunston Staffs 40 B4
Dunstone Devon 5 M9
Dunstone Devon 5 P5
Dunsville Donc 59 N11
Dunswell E R Yk 61 J7
Dunsyre S Lans 86 C11
Dunterton Devon 4 H4
Duntisbourne Abbots Gloucs 29 N7
Duntisbourne Rouse Gloucs 29 P7
Duntish Dorset 7 Q2
Duntocher W Duns 84 H8
Dunton Bucks 32 B11
Dunton C Beds 33 J7
Dunton Norfk 44 E4
Dunton Bassett Leics 41 M8
Dunton Green Kent 21 P11
Duntulm Highld 104 F7
Dunure S Ayrs 76 E8
Dunvant Swans 26 D9
Dunvegan Highld 104 C11
Dunwich Suffk 35 P3
Durgan Cnwll 2 H9
Durham Dur 73 M11
Durham Cathedral Dur 73 M11
Durham Crematorium Dur 73 M11
Durham Services Dur 73 N12
Durham Tees Valley Airport S on T 65 P5
Durisdeer D & G 78 E8
Durisdeermill D & G 78 E7
Durleigh Somset 16 H8
Durley Hants 9 N4
Durley Wilts 19 J7
Durley Street Hants 9 N4
Durlock Kent 23 P10
Durlock Kent 23 P9
Durness Highld 108 G3
Durno Abers 102 F9
Duror Highld 90 D5
Durran Ag & B 83 P2
Durrington W Susx 10 H8
Durrington Wilts 18 H10
Durris Abers 95 M3
Dursley Gloucs 29 K8
Dursley Cross Gloucs 29 J5
Durston Somset 16 H9
Durweston Dorset 8 C6
Duston Nhants 31 Q2
Duthil Highld 99 P4
Dutton Ches W 57 L11
Duxford Cambs 33 M7
Duxford Oxon 19 L2
Duxford IWM Cambs 33 M7
Dwygyfylchi Conwy 55 K6
Dwyran IoA 54 F8
Dyce C Aber 103 J11
Dyffryn Ardudwy Gwynd 47 J6
Dyffryn Cellwen Neath 27 J6
Dyke Lincs 42 F5
Dyke Moray 100 F4
Dykehead Angus 93 J5
Dykehead Angus 94 F9
Dykehead N Lans 85 P10
Dykehead Stirlg 85 K4
Dykelands Abers 95 L8
Dykends Angus 93 J4
Dykeside Abers 102 F6
Dymchurch Kent 13 L4
Dymock Gloucs 29 J3
Dyrham S Glos 17 Q2
Dysart Fife 86 G4
Dyserth Denbgs 56 C11

E

Eagland Hill Lancs 62 H12
Eagle Lincs 52 C9
Eaglesfield Cumb 70 H9
Eaglesfield D & G 71 K1
Eaglesham E Rens 85 J11
Eagley Bolton 57 N6
Eakring Notts 51 P8
Ealand N Linc 60 D10
Ealing Gt Lon 21 J7
Eals Nthumb 72 C9
Eamont Bridge Cumb 71 Q9
Earby Lancs 58 B5
Earcroft Bl w D 57 M4
Eardington Shrops 39 N4
Eardisland Herefs 38 H9
Eardisley Herefs 38 F11
Eardiston Shrops 48 G9
Eardiston Worcs 39 M8
Earith Cambs 33 L2
Earlestown St Hel 57 L9
Earley Wokham 20 C8
Earlham Norfk 45 K8
Earlham Crematorium Norfk 45 K8
Earlish Highld 104 E9
Earls Barton Nhants 32 C4
Earls Colne Essex 34 E10
Earls Common Worcs 30 C3
Earl's Croome Worcs 29 M1
Earlsdon Covtry 40 H10
Earlsferry Fife 87 J3
Earlsfield Gt Lon 21 K8
Earlsford Abers 102 H8
Earlsheaton Kirk 58 H9
Earl Shilton Leics 41 L7
Earl Soham Suffk 35 K4
Earl Sterndale Derbys 50 E7
Earlston Border 80 D6
Earlston E Ayrs 76 G4
Earlswood Surrey 21 L12
Earlswood Warwks 40 E11
Earnley W Susx 10 D10
Earsdon N Tyne 73 N6
Earsham Norfk 45 M11
Eartham W Susx 10 F8
Easby N York 66 E6
Easdale Ag & B 89 P11
Easebourne W Susx 10 E5
Easenhall Warwks 41 L10
Eashing Surrey 10 F2
Easington Bucks 31 P11
Easington Dur 73 P11
Easington E R Yk 61 P9
Easington R & Cl 66 G4
Easington Colliery Dur 73 Q11
Easington Lane Sundld 73 P10
Easingwold N York 59 M1
Eassie and Nevay Angus 93 L6
East Aberthaw V Glam 16 D3
East Allington Devon 5 P9
East Anstey Devon 15 P6
East Ashey IoW 9 P9
East Ashling W Susx 10 D8
East Ayton N York 67 L9
East Barkwith Lincs 52 G7
East Barming Kent 22 E11
East Barnby N York 66 H5
East Barnet Gt Lon 21 L4
East Barns E Loth 87 N7
East Barsham Norfk 44 F4
East Beckham Norfk 45 J3
East Bedfont Gt Lon 20 H8
East Bergholt Suffk 34 H9
East Bilney Norfk 44 F6
East Blatchington E Susx 11 P9
East Boldon S Tyne 73 P8
East Boldre Hants 9 L7
Eastbourne Darltn 65 N5
Eastbourne E Susx 12 C9
Eastbourne Crematorium E Susx 12 D9
East Bradenham Norfk 44 F8
East Brent Somset 17 J6
Eastbridge Suffk 35 P4
East Bridgford Notts 51 P11
East Buckland Devon 15 L6
East Budleigh Devon 6 E6
Eastburn C Brad 58 D5
Eastbury Herts 20 H5
Eastbury W Berk 19 K5
East Butterwick N Linc 52 B3
Eastby N York 58 D4
East Calder W Loth 86 C8
East Carleton Norfk 45 K9
East Carlton Leeds 58 G5
East Carlton Nhants 42 B11
East Chaldon Dorset 8 B10
East Challow Oxon 19 L3
East Charleton Devon 5 P10
East Chelborough Dorset 7 M2
East Chiltington E Susx 11 M7
East Chinnock Somset 17 L12
East Chisenbury Wilts 18 G9
Eastchurch Kent 23 J8
East Clandon Surrey 20 G11
East Claydon Bucks 31 Q8
East Coker Somset 7 M1
Eastcombe Gloucs 29 M7
East Compton Somset 17 N7
East Cornworthy Devon 6 B10
Eastcote Gt Lon 20 H6
Eastcote Nhants 31 P4
Eastcote Solhll 40 G10
Eastcott Wilts 18 F9
East Cottingwith E R Yk 60 C6
Eastcourt Wilts 19 J8
East Cowes IoW 9 N8
East Cowick E R Yk 59 P9
East Cowton N York 65 N6
East Cranmore Somset 17 P7
East Dean E Susx 12 C9
East Dean Gloucs 28 H5
East Dean Hants 9 J3
East Dean W Susx 10 E7
East Devon Crematorium Devon 6 E4
East Drayton Notts 51 Q6
East Dulwich Gt Lon 21 M8
East Dundry N Som 17 N3
East Ella C KuH 60 H8
Eastend Essex 22 H5
East End Hants 9 L7
East End Hants 19 M8
East End Kent 12 G3
East End Oxon 31 K10
East End Somset 17 P6
Easter Balmoral Abers 94 E3
Easter Compton S Glos 28 G11
Easter Dalziel Highld 107 M11
Eastergate W Susx 10 F8
Easterhouse C Glas 85 L9
Easter Howgate Mdloth 86 F9
Easter Kinkell Highld 107 J10
Easter Moniack Highld 98 H1
Eastern Green Covtry 40 H10
Easter Ord Abers 95 N2
Easter Pitkierie Fife 87 L2
Easter Skeld Shet 111 k4
Easter Softlaw Border 80 G7
Easterton Wilts 18 F9
East Everleigh Wilts 18 H9
East Farleigh Kent 22 E11
East Farndon Nhants 41 Q9
East Ferry Lincs 52 B4
Eastfield N Lans 85 P9
Eastfield N York 67 M10
East Fortune E Loth 87 K6
East Garston W Berk 19 L5
Eastgate Dur 72 G12
Eastgate Norfk 45 J5
East Goscote Leics 41 N5
East Grafton Wilts 19 J8
East Grimstead Wilts 9 J2
East Grinstead W Susx 11 N3
East Guldeford E Susx 12 H6
East Haddon Nhants 31 P1
East Hagbourne Oxon 19 N3
East Halton N Linc 61 K9
East Ham Gt Lon 21 N6
Easthampstead Park Crematorium Br For 20 D9
Easthampton Herefs 38 H9
East Hanney Oxon 19 M3
East Hanningfield Essex 22 F3
East Hardwick Wakefd 59 L9
East Harling Norfk 44 G11
East Harlsey N York 65 Q7
East Harnham Wilts 8 G2
East Harptree BaNES 17 N5
East Harting W Susx 10 C6
East Hatch Wilts 8 D2
East Hatley Cambs 33 J6
East Hauxwell N York 65 L8
East Haven Angus 93 P8
East Heckington Lincs 42 H2
East Hedleyhope Dur 73 K11
East Helmsdale Highld 110 B11
East Hendred Oxon 19 M3
East Heslerton N York 67 K11
East Hoathly E Susx 11 Q6
East Holme Dorset 8 D9
Easthope Shrops 39 K3
Easthorpe Essex 34 F11
East Horrington Somset 17 N6
East Horsley Surrey 20 H11
East Howe Bmouth 8 F8
East Huntington C York 59 N3
East Huntspill Somset 17 J7
East Ilsley W Berk 19 N5
Eastington Devon 15 M9
Eastington Gloucs 29 K7
Eastington Gloucs 30 F10
East Keal Lincs 53 L10
East Kennett Wilts 18 G7
East Keswick Leeds 59 J5
East Kilbride S Lans 85 K11
East Kirkby Lincs 53 K10
East Knighton Dorset 8 B9
East Knoyle Wilts 8 C2
East Lambrook Somset 17 L11
East Lancashire Crematorium Bury 57 P7
Eastlands D & G 70 D2
East Langdon Kent 13 P2
East Langton Leics 41 Q8
East Lavant W Susx 10 D8
East Lavington W Susx 10 F6
East Layton N York 65 L5
Eastleach Martin Gloucs 30 G12
Eastleach Turville Gloucs 30 G11
East Leake Notts 41 M3
Eastleigh Devon 14 H6
Eastleigh Hants 9 M4
East Lexham Norfk 44 E6
Eastling Kent 23 J11
East Linton E Loth 87 L6
East Lockinge Oxon 19 M4
East London Crematorium Gt Lon 21 N6
East Lound N Linc 52 B4
East Lulworth Dorset 8 C10
East Lutton N York 60 G1
East Lydford Somset 17 N9
East Malling Kent 22 E11
East Marden W Susx 10 D7
East Markham Notts 51 Q6
East Martin Hants 8 F4
East Marton N York 58 B4
East Meon Hants 10 B5
East Mersea Essex 23 K1
East Midlands Airport Leics 41 K3
East Molesey Surrey 21 J9
East Morden Dorset 8 D8
East Morton C Brad 58 E6
East Morton D & G 78 E8
East Ness N York 66 F10
Eastney C Port 9 Q7
Eastnor Herefs 29 K2
East Norton Leics 42 B9
Eastoft N Linc 60 D10
East Ogwell Devon 5 Q6
Easton Cambs 32 G3
Easton Devon 5 N3
Easton Dorset 7 Q8
Easton Hants 9 N2
Easton Lincs 42 D5
Easton Norfk 45 J7
Easton Somset 17 M6
Easton Suffk 35 L5
Easton Wilts 18 D6
Easton Grey Wilts 18 C4
Easton-in-Gordano N Som 17 M2
Easton Maudit Nhants 32 C5
Easton-on-the-Hill Nhants 42 E8
Easton Royal Wilts 18 H8
East Orchard Dorset 8 C4
East Peckham Kent 12 D1
East Pennar Pembks 24 G8
East Pennard Somset 17 N8
East Perry Cambs 32 G4
East Portlemouth Devon 5 P11
East Prawle Devon 5 Q11
East Preston W Susx 10 H9
East Putford Devon 14 G8
East Quantoxhead Somset 16 F7
East Rainton Sundld 73 N10
East Ravendale NE Lin 52 H4
East Raynham Norfk 44 E5
Eastrea Cambs 43 J10
East Riding Crematorium E R Yk 60 H1
Eastriggs D & G 71 L3
East Rigton Leeds 59 J5
Eastrington E R Yk 60 D8
Eastrop Swindn 18 H3
East Rounton N York 65 Q6
East Rudham Norfk 44 D5
East Runton Norfk 45 K2
East Ruston Norfk 45 M5
Eastry Kent 23 P11
East Saltoun E Loth 87 J8
East Sheen Gt Lon 21 K8
East Shefford W Berk 19 L6
East Stockwith Lincs 52 B5
East Stoke Dorset 8 C9
East Stoke Notts 51 Q10
East Stour Dorset 8 B3
East Stourmouth Kent 23 N10
East Stowford Devon 15 L6
East Stratton Hants 19 P11
East Studdal Kent 23 P12
East Taphouse Cnwll 4 E7
East-the-Water Devon 14 H6
East Thirston Nthumb 73 L2
East Tilbury Thurr 22 D7
East Tisted Hants 10 B4
East Torrington Lincs 52 G6
East Tuddenham Norfk 44 H7
East Tytherley Hants 9 K2
East Tytherton Wilts 18 E6
East Village Devon 15 P10
Eastville Bristl 17 N2
Eastville Lincs 53 L11
East Walton Norfk 44 C6
East Week Devon 5 N2
Eastwell Leics 41 Q2
East Wellow Hants 9 K4
East Wemyss Fife 86 G3
East Whitburn W Loth 85 Q9
Eastwick Herts 21 N2
East Wickham Gt Lon 21 P7
East Williamston Pembks 25 J7
East Winch Norfk 44 B6
East Winterslow Wilts 9 J1
East Wittering W Susx 10 C9
East Witton N York 65 K9
Eastwood Notts 51 L10
Eastwood Sthend 22 G6
East Woodburn Nthumb 72 G4
East Woodhay Hants 19 L8
East Worldham Hants 10 C3
East Wretham Norfk 44 F11
Eathorpe Warwks 31 K1
Eaton Ches E 49 Q3
Eaton Ches W 49 L3
Eaton Leics 42 B4
Eaton Norfk 45 K8
Eaton Notts 51 P5
Eaton Oxon 31 K12
Eaton Shrops 39 J4
Eaton Bray C Beds 32 D11
Eaton Constantine Shrops 39 L2
Eaton Green C Beds 32 D11
Eaton Hastings Oxon 19 J2
Eaton Mascott Shrops 39 K2
Eaton Socon Cambs 32 G5
Eaton upon Tern Shrops 49 M10
Ebberston N York 67 K10
Ebbesborne Wake Wilts 8 E3
Ebbw Vale Blae G 27 N6
Ebchester Dur 73 K9
Ebford Devon 6 D5
Ebley Gloucs 29 L7
Ebnal Ches W 49 J6
Ebrington Gloucs 30 F6
Ecchinswell Hants 19 N8
Ecclaw Border 87 P8
Ecclefechan D & G 71 K1
Eccles Border 80 G6
Eccles Kent 22 E10
Eccles Salfd 57 P8
Ecclesall Sheff 50 H4
Ecclesfield Sheff 51 J3
Eccleshall Staffs 49 P9
Eccleshill C Brad 58 F6
Ecclesmachan W Loth 86 C7
Eccles Road Norfk 44 G11
Eccleston Ches W 48 H3
Eccleston Lancs 57 K5
Eccleston St Hel 57 J9
Echt Abers 95 M2
Eckford Border 80 F8
Eckington Derbys 51 K5
Eckington Worcs 29 N1
Ecton Nhants 32 B4
Edale Derbys 50 E4
Eday Ork 111 h1
Eday Airport Ork 111 h1
Edburton W Susx 11 K7
Edderton Highld 107 L5
Eddleston Border 86 F11
Eddlewood S Lans 85 M11
Edenbridge Kent 11 N2
Edenfield Lancs 57 P5
Edenhall Cumb 71 Q8
Edenham Lincs 42 F6
Eden Park Gt Lon 21 M9
Eden Project Cnwll 3 M5
Edensor Derbys 50 G6
Edentaggart Ag & B 84 F4
Edenthorpe Donc 59 N11
Edern Gwynd 46 E4
Edgbaston Birm 40 D9
Edgcott Bucks 31 P9
Edgcott Somset 15 P4
Edge Gloucs 29 L6
Edgefield Norfk 44 H4
Edgefield Green Norfk 44 H4
Edgerton Kirk 58 F10
Edgeworth Gloucs 29 N7
Edgmond Wrekin 49 N10
Edgton Shrops 38 H5
Edgware Gt Lon 21 J5
Edgworth Bl w D 57 N5
Edinbane Highld 104 D11
Edinburgh C Edin 86 F7
Edinburgh Airport C Edin 86 D7
Edinburgh Castle C Edin 86 F7
Edinburgh Old & New Town C Edin 86 F7
Edinburgh Royal Botanic Gardens C Edin 86 F7
Edinburgh Zoo RZSS C Edin 86 E7
Edingale Staffs 40 G5
Edingham D & G 70 D3
Edingley Notts 51 P9
Edingthorpe Norfk 45 M4
Edingthorpe Green Norfk 45 M4
Edington Border 81 J3
Edington Nthumb 73 K4
Edington Somset 17 K8
Edington Wilts 18 D9
Edington Burtle Somset 17 K7
Edingworth Somset 17 J5
Edithmead Somset 17 J6
Edith Weston Rutlnd 42 D8
Edlesborough Bucks 32 D11
Edlingham Nthumb 81 M11
Edlington Lincs 52 H8
Edmondsham Dorset 8 F5
Edmondsley Dur 73 M10
Edmondthorpe Leics 42 C6
Edmonton Gt Lon 21 M5
Edmundbyers Dur 72 H10
Ednam Border 80 G6
Edradynate P & K 92 D5
Edrom Border 80 H3
Edstaston Shrops 49 K8
Edstone Warwks 30 F2
Edwalton Notts 41 N1
Edwinstowe Notts 51 N7
Edworth C Beds 32 H8
Edwyn Ralph Herefs 39 M9
Edzell Angus 95 K8
Edzell Woods Abers 95 K7
Efail-fach Neath 26 G9
Efail Isaf Rhondd 27 M11
Efailnewydd Gwynd 46 F4
Efailwen Carmth 25 K4
Efenechtyd Denbgs 48 C4
Effgill D & G 79 L9
Effingham Surrey 20 H11
Efford Crematorium C Plym 5 K8
Egerton Bolton 57 N6
Egerton Kent 12 H1
Eggborough N York 59 M9
Eggbuckland C Plym 5 K8
Eggesford Devon 15 M9
Eggington C Beds 32 D10
Egginton Derbys 40 H2
Eggleston Dur 64 H3
Egham Surrey 20 G8
Egleton Rutlnd 42 C8
Eglingham Nthumb 81 M9
Egloshayle Cnwll 3 M2
Egloskerry Cnwll 4 G3
Eglwysbach Conwy 55 L7
Eglwys Cross Wrexhm 49 J7
Eglwyswrw Pembks 25 K2
Egmanton Notts 51 Q7
Egremont Cumb 70 G12
Egremont Wirral 56 G9
Egton N York 66 H6
Egton Bridge N York 66 H6
Egypt Bucks 20 F6
Eigg Highld 96 F11
Eight Ash Green Essex 34 F10
Eilanreach Highld 97 L6
Eilean Donan Castle Highld 97 M5
Elan Valley Powys 37 P7
Elan Village Powys 37 Q7
Elberton S Glos 28 H10
Elburton C Plym 5 L9
Elcombe Swindn 18 G5
Eldersfield Worcs 29 L3
Elderslie Rens 84 H9
Eldon Dur 65 M2
Elerch Cerdgn 37 L4
Elfhill Abers 95 N5
Elford Staffs 40 F5
Elgin Moray 101 J3
Elgol Highld 96 G6
Elham Kent 13 M2
Elie Fife 87 K3
Elim IoA 54 E5
Eling Hants 9 L5
Elkesley Notts 51 P6
Elkstone Gloucs 29 N6
Ella Abers 102 E4
Ellacombe Torbay 6 C9
Elland Calder 58 E9
Ellary Ag & B 83 L7
Ellastone Staffs 50 E11
Ellel Lancs 63 J10
Ellemford Border 87 N9
Ellenabeich Ag & B 89 P11
Ellenhall Staffs 49 Q9
Ellen's Green Surrey 10 H3
Ellerbeck N York 66 B8
Ellerby N York 66 H5
Ellerdine Heath Wrekin 49 L10
Elleric Ag & B 90 E6
Ellerker E R Yk 60 F8
Ellerton E R Yk 60 C6
Ellerton N York 65 M7
Ellesborough Bucks 20 D3
Ellesmere Shrops 48 H8
Ellesmere Port Ches W 56 H12
Ellingham Norfk 45 N10
Ellingham Nthumb 81 N8
Ellingstring N York 65 L10
Ellington Cambs 32 G3
Ellington Nthumb 73 M3
Elliots Green Somset 18 B10
Ellisfield Hants 19 Q10
Ellishader Highld 104 G8
Ellistown Leics 41 K5
Ellon Abers 103 K8
Ellonby Cumb 71 N8
Elloughton E R Yk 60 G8
Ellwood Gloucs 28 G7
Elm Cambs 43 M8
Elmbridge Worcs 30 B1
Elmdon Essex 33 M8
Elmdon Solhll 40 F10
Elmer W Susx 10 F9
Elmers End Gt Lon 21 M9
Elmer's Green Lancs 57 J7
Elmesthorpe Leics 41 L8
Elmhurst Staffs 40 E5
Elmley Castle Worcs 29 N1
Elmley Lovett Worcs 39 Q8
Elmore Gloucs 29 K6
Elmore Back Gloucs 29 K5
Elm Park Gt Lon 21 Q6
Elmsett Suffk 34 H7
Elmstead Market Essex 34 H10
Elmsted Kent 13 L2
Elmstone Kent 23 N10
Elmstone Hardwicke Gloucs 29 M4
Elmswell E R Yk 60 G3

170 Elmswell – Fogo

Elmswell Suffk 34 G4
Elmton Derbys 51 L6
Elphin Highld 108 E12
Elphinstone E Loth 86 H8
Elrick Abers 95 N1
Elrig D & G 69 J9
Elrington Nthumb 72 F8
Elsdon Nthumb 72 G3
Elsenham Essex 33 N10
Elsfield Oxon 31 M11
Elsham N Linc 60 H10
Elsing Norfk 44 H6
Elslack N York 58 B4
Elson Hants 9 P7
Elsrickle S Lans 86 C12
Elstead Surrey 10 E2
Elsted W Susx 10 D6
Elsthorpe Lincs 42 F5
Elston Notts 51 Q10
Elstow Bed 32 F7
Elstree Herts 21 J4
Elstronwick E R Yk 61 L7
Elswick Lancs 56 H2
Elswick N u Ty 73 M7
Elsworth Cambs 33 K4
Elterwater Cumb 62 G2
Eltham Gt Lon 21 N8
Eltham Crematorium Gt Lon 21 N8
Eltisley Cambs 33 J5
Elton Cambs 42 F10
Elton Ches W 49 J1
Elton Derbys 50 G8
Elton Herefs 39 J7
Elton Notts 51 Q11
Elton S on T 65 P4
Eltringham Nthumb 73 J8
Elvanfoot S Lans 78 F5
Elvaston Derbys 41 K2
Elveden Suffk 34 D2
Elvetham Heath Hants 20 C11
Elvingston E Loth 87 J7
Elvington C York 60 C5
Elvington Kent 23 P12
Elwick Hartpl 66 C2
Elworth Ches E 49 N3
Elworthy Somset 16 E8
Ely Cambs 33 N1
Ely Cardif 16 F2
Emberton M Keyn 32 C6
Embleton Cumb 71 J9
Embleton Nthumb 81 P9
Embo Highld 107 N4
Emborough Somset 17 N6
Embo Street Highld 107 N4
Embsay N York 58 D4
Emery Down Hants 9 K6
Emley Kirk 58 G10
Emmington Oxon 20 C3
Emneth Norfk 43 M8
Emneth Hungate Norfk 43 N8
Empingham Rutlnd 42 D8
Empshott Hants 10 C4
Emstrey Crematorium Shrops 49 K12
Emsworth Hants 10 C8
Enborne W Berk 19 M7
Enborne Row W Berk 19 M7
Enderby Leics 41 M7
Endmoor Cumb 63 K5
Endon Staffs 50 B9
Endon Bank Staffs 50 B9
Enfield Gt Lon 21 M4
Enfield Crematorium Gt Lon 21 M4
Enfield Lock Gt Lon 21 M4
Enfield Wash Gt Lon 21 M4
Enford Wilts 18 G9
Engine Common S Glos 29 J11
Englefield W Berk 19 Q6
Englefield Green Surrey 20 F8
English Bicknor Gloucs 28 G5
Englishcombe BaNES 17 Q4
English Frankton Shrops 49 J9
Enham-Alamein Hants 19 L10
Enmore Somset 16 H8
Enmore Green Dorset 8 C3
Ennerdale Bridge Cumb 70 H11
Enochdhu P & K 92 F3
Ensay Ag & B 88 H6
Ensbury Bmouth 8 F8
Ensdon Shrops 48 H11
Enstone Oxon 31 J8
Enterkinfoot D & G 78 E7
Enville Staffs 39 P5
Eòlaigearraidh W Isls 111 a6
Eoligarry W Isls 111 a6
Epney Gloucs 29 K6
Epperstone Notts 51 P10
Epping Essex 21 P3
Epping Green Essex 21 N3
Epping Upland Essex 21 N3
Eppleby N York 65 L5
Epsom Surrey 21 K10
Epwell Oxon 31 J6
Epworth N Linc 52 A3
Erbistock Wrexhm 48 G7
Erdington Birm 40 E8
Eridge Green E Susx 12 B3
Erines Ag & B 83 N7
Eriska Ag & B 90 C7
Eriskay W Isls 111 b6
Eriswell Suffk 34 C2
Erith Gt Lon 21 P7
Erlestoke Wilts 18 E9
Ermington Devon 5 M9
Erpingham Norfk 45 K4
Errogie Highld 98 H5
Errol P & K 93 J10
Erskine Rens 84 H8
Erskine Bridge Rens 84 H8
Ervie D & G 68 D5
Erwarton Suffk 35 K9
Erwood Powys 38 C12
Eryholme N York 65 N6
Eryrys Denbgs 48 E4
Escomb Dur 65 L2
Escrick N York 59 N5
Esgairgeiliog Powys 47 M9
Esh Dur 73 L11
Esher Surrey 21 J9
Eshott Nthumb 73 L2
Esh Winning Dur 73 L11
Eskadale Highld 98 F2
Eskbank Mdloth 86 G8
Eskdale Green Cumb 62 D3
Eskdalemuir D & G 79 L8
Esprick Lancs 56 H2
Essendine Rutlnd 42 F7
Essendon Herts 21 L2
Essich Highld 99 J2
Essington Staffs 40 C6
Esslemont Abers 103 J8
Eston R & Cl 66 D4
Etal Nthumb 81 K6
Etchilhampton Wilts 18 F8
Etchingham E Susx 12 E5
Etchinghill Kent 13 M3
Etchinghill Staffs 40 D4
Eton W & M 20 F7
Eton Wick W & M 20 F7
Etruria C Stke 49 Q6
Etteridge Highld 99 K9
Ettersgill Dur 64 F2
Ettiley Heath Ches E 49 N4
Ettingshall Wolves 40 B8
Ettington Warwks 30 H4
Etton C Pete 42 G8
Etton E R Yk 60 G5
Ettrick Border 79 L6
Ettrickbridge Border 79 N4
Ettrickhill Border 79 L6
Etwall Derbys 40 H2
Euston Suffk 34 E2
Euxton Lancs 57 K5
Evanton Highld 107 K8
Evedon Lincs 42 F1
Evelix Highld 107 M4
Evenjobb Powys 38 F9
Evenley Nhants 31 N7
Evenlode Gloucs 30 G8
Evenwood Dur 65 K3
Evercreech Somset 17 P8
Everingham E R Yk 60 D6
Everleigh Wilts 18 H9
Eversholt C Beds 32 E9
Evershot Dorset 7 N2
Eversley Hants 20 C10
Eversley Cross Hants 20 C10
Everthorpe E R Yk 60 F7
Everton C Beds 32 H6
Everton Hants 9 K8
Everton Lpool 56 G9
Everton Notts 51 P3
Evertown D & G 71 M1
Evesbatch Herefs 39 M11
Evesham Worcs 30 D5
Evington C Leic 41 N6
Ewden Village Sheff 50 H2
Ewell Surrey 21 K10
Ewell Minnis Kent 13 N2
Ewelme Oxon 19 Q3
Ewen Gloucs 18 E2
Ewenny V Glam 27 J12
Ewerby Lincs 42 G1
Ewhurst Surrey 10 H3
Ewhurst Green E Susx 12 F5
Ewhurst Green Surrey 10 H3
Ewloe Flints 48 F3
Ewood Bl w D 57 M4
Eworthy Devon 5 J2
Ewshot Hants 20 D12
Ewyas Harold Herefs 28 D3
Exbourne Devon 15 K10
Exbury Hants 9 M7
Exebridge Somset 16 C10
Exelby N York 65 N9
Exeter Devon 6 C4
Exeter Airport Devon 6 D4
Exeter & Devon Crematorium Devon 6 C5
Exeter Services Devon 6 C4
Exford Somset 15 P5
Exfordsgreen Shrops 39 J2
Exhall Warwks 30 E3
Exhall Warwks 41 J9
Exlade Street Oxon 19 Q4
Exminster Devon 6 C5
Exmoor National Park 15 P4
Exmouth Devon 6 D6
Exning Suffk 33 P4
Exton Devon 6 D5
Exton Hants 9 Q4
Exton Rutlnd 42 D7
Exton Somset 16 C9
Exwick Devon 6 B4
Eyam Derbys 50 G5
Eydon Nhants 31 M4
Eye C Pete 42 H9
Eye Herefs 39 J8
Eye Suffk 35 J3
Eyemouth Border 81 K2
Eyeworth C Beds 33 J7
Eyhorne Street Kent 22 G11
Eyke Suffk 35 M6
Eynesbury Cambs 32 H5
Eynsford Kent 22 B9
Eynsham Oxon 31 K11
Eype Dorset 7 L5
Eyre Highld 104 F10
Eythorne Kent 23 P12
Eyton Herefs 39 J9
Eyton Shrops 48 H10
Eyton on Severn Shrops 39 L2
Eyton upon the Weald Moors Wrekin 49 M11

F

Faccombe Hants 19 L8
Faceby N York 66 C7
Fachwen Powys 48 B11
Faddiley Ches E 49 L5
Fadmoor N York 66 F9
Faerdre Swans 26 F8
Faifley W Duns 84 H8
Failand N Som 17 M2
Failford S Ayrs 76 H6
Failsworth Oldham 50 B1
Fairbourne Gwynd 47 K8
Fairburn N York 59 L8
Fairfield Derbys 50 E6
Fairfield Worcs 40 C11
Fairford Gloucs 18 H1
Fairgirth D & G 70 E4
Fair Green Norfk 43 Q6
Fairhaven Lancs 56 G4
Fair Isle Shet 111 m5
Fair Isle Airport Shet 111 m5
Fairlands Surrey 20 F11
Fairlie N Ayrs 84 D11
Fairlight E Susx 12 G7
Fairmile Devon 6 E4
Fairmile Surrey 20 H10
Fairnilee Border 79 P3
Fair Oak Hants 9 N4
Fairoak Staffs 49 N8
Fair Oak Green Hants 19 Q8
Fairseat Kent 22 D10
Fairstead Essex 34 C12
Fairstead Norfk 43 Q6
Fairwarp E Susx 11 P5
Fairwater Cardif 27 N12
Fairy Cross Devon 14 G7
Fakenham Norfk 44 F4
Fakenham Magna Suffk 34 E2
Fala Mdloth 87 J9
Fala Dam Mdloth 87 J9
Faldingworth Lincs 52 F6
Faldouët Jersey 7 c2
Falfield S Glos 29 J9
Falkenham Suffk 35 L8
Falkirk Falk 85 P7
Falkirk Crematorium Falk 85 P6
Falkirk Wheel Falk 85 P7
Falkland Fife 86 F2
Fallburn S Lans 78 F2
Fallin Stirlg 85 N5
Fallodon Nthumb 81 P9
Fallowfield Manch 57 Q9
Fallowfield Nthumb 72 G7
Falls of Blarghour Ag & B 83 Q1
Falmer E Susx 11 M8
Falmouth Cnwll 3 J8
Falnash Border 79 N7
Falsgrave N York 67 M9
Falstone Nthumb 72 D4
Fanagmore Highld 108 D6
Fancott C Beds 32 E10
Fanellan Highld 98 G1
Fangdale Beck N York 66 D8
Fangfoss E R Yk 60 D4
Fanmore Ag & B 89 J7
Fannich Lodge Highld 106 D8
Fans Border 80 E6
Far Bletchley M Keyn 32 C9
Farcet Cambs 42 H10
Far Cotton Nhants 31 Q3
Fareham Hants 9 P6
Farewell Staffs 40 E5
Faringdon Oxon 19 K2
Farington Lancs 57 K4
Farlam Cumb 71 Q4
Farleigh N Som 17 M3
Farleigh Surrey 21 M10
Farleigh Hungerford Somset 18 B8
Farleigh Wallop Hants 19 Q10
Farlesthorpe Lincs 53 M8
Farleton Cumb 63 K6
Farleton Lancs 63 L8
Farley Staffs 50 E11
Farley Wilts 9 J2
Farley Green Surrey 10 G2
Farley Hill Wokham 20 C9
Farleys End Gloucs 29 K6
Farlington C Port 10 B8
Farlington N York 59 N1
Farlow Shrops 39 L6
Farmborough BaNES 17 P4
Farmcote Gloucs 30 D8
Farmers Carmth 37 K10
Farmington Gloucs 30 F10
Farmoor Oxon 31 L11
Far Moor Wigan 57 K7
Farmtown Moray 101 P5
Farnborough Gt Lon 21 N9
Farnborough Hants 20 E11
Farnborough W Berk 19 M4
Farnborough Warwks 31 K4
Farnborough Park Hants 20 E11
Farncombe Surrey 10 F2
Farndish Bed 32 D4
Farndon Ches W 48 H5
Farndon Notts 51 Q9
Farne Islands Nthumb 81 P6
Farnell Angus 93 Q5
Farnham Dorset 8 E4
Farnham Essex 33 M10
Farnham N York 59 J3
Farnham Suffk 35 M5
Farnham Surrey 10 D1
Farnham Common Bucks 20 F6
Farnham Royal Bucks 20 F6
Farningham Kent 22 B9
Farnley Leeds 58 G7
Farnley N York 58 G5
Farnley Tyas Kirk 58 F10
Farnsfield Notts 51 P9
Farnworth Bolton 57 N7
Farnworth Halton 57 K10
Far Oakridge Gloucs 29 N7
Farr Highld 99 K3
Farr Highld 99 M8
Farr Highld 109 M3
Farraline Highld 98 H5
Farringdon Devon 6 D5
Farrington Gurney BaNES 17 P5
Far Sawrey Cumb 62 H3
Farthinghoe Nhants 31 M6
Farthingstone Nhants 31 N3
Fartown Kirk 58 F9
Fasnacloich Ag & B 90 D6
Fasnakyle Highld 98 D4
Fassfern Highld 90 D1
Fatfield Sundld 73 N9
Fauldhouse W Loth 85 Q10
Faulkbourne Essex 34 D12
Faulkland Somset 17 Q5
Fauls Shrops 49 L8
Faversham Kent 23 K10
Fawdington N York 66 B11
Fawdon N u Ty 73 M7
Fawkham Green Kent 22 C9
Fawler Oxon 31 J10
Fawley Bucks 20 C6
Fawley Hants 9 M6
Fawley W Berk 19 L5
Faxfleet E R Yk 60 E8
Faygate W Susx 11 K4
Fazakerley Lpool 56 G9
Fazeley Staffs 40 G7
Fearby N York 65 L10
Fearn Highld 107 N7
Fearnan P & K 91 Q7
Fearnbeg Highld 105 L9
Fearnmore Highld 105 K9
Fearnoch Ag & B 83 P7
Featherstone Staffs 40 C6
Featherstone Wakefd 59 K9
Feckenham Worcs 30 D2
Feering Essex 34 E11
Feetham N York 64 H7
Felbridge Surrey 11 M3
Felbrigg Norfk 45 K3
Felcourt Surrey 11 M2
Felindre Carmth 25 N2
Felindre Carmth 26 D5
Felindre Powys 38 D6
Felindre Swans 26 E8
Felindre Farchog Pembks 36 B11
Felingwm Isaf Carmth 26 C4
Felingwm Uchaf Carmth 26 C4
Felixkirk N York 66 C9
Felixstowe Suffk 35 L9
Felling Gatesd 73 M8
Felmersham Bed 32 E5
Felmingham Norfk 45 L4
Felpham W Susx 10 F9
Felsham Suffk 34 F5
Felsted Essex 34 B11
Feltham Gt Lon 20 H8
Felthamhill Surrey 20 H8
Felthorpe Norfk 45 J6
Felton Herefs 39 L11
Felton N Som 17 M3
Felton Nthumb 73 L2
Felton Butler Shrops 48 H11
Feltwell Norfk 44 B11
Fence Lancs 57 P2
Fence Rothm 51 K4
Fencott Oxon 31 M10
Fendike Corner Lincs 53 M10
Fen Ditton Cambs 33 M5
Fen Drayton Cambs 33 K3
Feniscliffe Bl w D 57 M4
Feniscowles Bl w D 57 M4
Feniton Devon 6 F3
Fenland Crematorium Cambs 43 L10
Fenn Green Shrops 39 P5
Fenn Street Medway 22 F8
Fenny Bentley Derbys 50 F10
Fenny Bridges Devon 6 F3
Fenny Compton Warwks 31 K4
Fenny Drayton Leics 41 J7
Fenstanton Cambs 33 K3
Fen Street Norfk 44 G10
Fenton Cambs 33 K2
Fenton Cumb 71 Q4
Fenton Lincs 52 B8
Fenton Lincs 52 C12
Fenton Notts 52 B6
Fenton Nthumb 81 K7
Fenton Barns E Loth 87 K6
Fenwick Donc 59 N10
Fenwick E Ayrs 76 H3
Fenwick Nthumb 73 J6
Fenwick Nthumb 81 M6
Feock Cnwll 3 J7
Feolin Ferry Ag & B 82 F8
Fergushill N Ayrs 76 F3
Feriniquarrie Highld 104 B11
Fern Angus 94 H9
Ferndale Rhondd 27 L9
Ferndown Dorset 8 F7
Ferness Highld 100 E6
Fernham Oxon 19 K3
Fernhill Heath Worcs 39 Q9
Fernhurst W Susx 10 E4
Fernie Fife 93 K11
Ferniegair S Lans 85 M11
Fernilea Highld 96 D3
Fernilee Derbys 50 D5
Fernwood Notts 52 B12
Ferrensby N York 59 J3
Ferrindonald Highld 97 J7
Ferring W Susx 10 H9
Ferrybridge Services Wakefd 59 L9
Ferryden Angus 95 M9
Ferryhill Dur 65 M2
Ferryhill Station Dur 65 N2
Ferry Point Highld 107 M5
Ferryside Carmth 25 N6
Ferrytown Highld 107 M5
Fersfield Norfk 44 H12
Fersit Highld 91 K2
Feshiebridge Highld 99 M8
Fetcham Surrey 21 J11
Fetlar Shet 111 m2
Fetterangus Abers 103 K5
Fettercairn Abers 95 K7
Fewston N York 58 G4
Ffairfach Carmth 26 E5
Ffair Rhos Cerdgn 37 M7
Ffestiniog Gwynd 47 L3
Ffestiniog Railway Gwynd 47 K3
Fforest Carmth 26 D7
Fforest Fach Swans 26 E9
Ffostrasol Cerdgn 36 F10
Ffrith Flints 48 F4
Ffynnongroyw Flints 56 D11
Fickleshole Surrey 21 M10
Fiddington Somset 16 G7
Fiddleford Dorset 8 B5
Fiddlers Green Cnwll 3 J5
Field Staffs 40 D2
Field Dalling Norfk 44 G3
Field Head Leics 41 L5
Fifehead Magdalen Dorset 8 B3
Fifehead Neville Dorset 8 B5
Fifehead St Quintin Dorset 8 B5
Fife Keith Moray 101 M5
Fifield Oxon 30 G9
Fifield W & M 20 E7
Figheldean Wilts 18 H10
Filby Norfk 45 P7
Filey N York 67 N10
Filgrave M Keyn 32 C7
Filkins Oxon 30 G12
Filleigh Devon 15 L6
Fillingham Lincs 52 D6
Fillongley Warwks 40 H9
Filton S Glos 28 H11
Fimber E R Yk 60 F3
Finavon Angus 93 N4
Fincham Norfk 44 B8
Finchampstead Wokham 20 C10
Fincharn Ag & B 83 N3
Finchdean Hants 10 B7
Finchingfield Essex 34 B9
Finchley Gt Lon 21 L5
Findern Derbys 40 H2
Findhorn Moray 100 G3
Findhorn Bridge Highld 99 M4
Findochty Moray 101 N2
Findo Gask P & K 92 E10
Findon Abers 95 Q3
Findon W Susx 10 H8
Findon Mains Highld 107 K9
Findrack House Abers 95 K2
Finedon Nhants 32 D3
Fingask P & K 92 H10
Fingest Bucks 20 C5
Finghall N York 65 L9
Fingland D & G 77 M7
Finglesham Kent 23 P11
Fingringhoe Essex 34 G11
Finlarig Stirlg 91 N9
Finmere Oxon 31 N7
Finnart P & K 91 M5
Finningham Suffk 34 H3
Finningley Donc 51 P2
Finsbay W Isls 111 c4
Finstall Worcs 40 C12
Finsthwaite Cumb 62 G5
Finstock Oxon 31 J10
Finstown Ork 111 h2
Fintry Abers 102 G4
Fintry Stirlg 85 K5
Finzean Abers 95 K4
Fionnphort Ag & B 88 G10
Fionnsbhagh W Isls 111 c4
Firbank Cumb 63 L4
Firbeck Rothm 51 M3
Firby N York 60 C2
Firby N York 65 M9
Firle E Susx 11 P8
Firsby Lincs 53 M10
Fir Tree Dur 65 K1
Fishbourne IoW 9 P8
Fishbourne W Susx 10 D8
Fishbourne Roman Palace W Susx 10 D8
Fishburn Dur 65 P2
Fishcross Clacks 85 P4
Fisherford Abers 102 E8
Fisherrow E Loth 86 G7
Fisher's Pond Hants 9 N4
Fisherton Highld 107 M11
Fisherton S Ayrs 76 E7
Fisherton de la Mere Wilts 18 E11
Fishery Estate W & M 20 E7
Fishguard Pembks 24 G2
Fishlake Donc 59 P10
Fishnish Pier Ag & B 89 N7
Fishponds Bristl 17 P2
Fishtoft Lincs 43 K2
Fishtoft Drove Lincs 43 K1
Fiskavaig Highld 96 D3
Fiskerton Lincs 52 F8
Fiskerton Notts 51 Q9
Fittleton Wilts 18 G10
Fittleworth W Susx 10 G6
Fitz Shrops 49 J11
Fitzhead Somset 16 F9
Fitzwilliam Wakefd 59 K10
Five Ash Down E Susx 11 P5
Five Ashes E Susx 12 B5
Fivehead Somset 17 J10
Fivelanes Cnwll 4 F4
Five Oak Green Kent 12 D2
Five Oaks Jersey 7 c2
Five Oaks W Susx 10 H4
Five Roads Carmth 26 C7
Flackwell Heath Bucks 20 E5
Fladbury Worcs 30 C5
Fladdabister Shet 111 k4
Flagg Derbys 50 F7
Flamborough E R Yk 67 Q12
Flamborough Head E R Yk 67 Q12
Flamingo Land Theme Park N York 66 H10
Flamstead Herts 20 H1
Flamstead End Herts 21 M3
Flansham W Susx 10 F9
Flanshaw Wakefd 58 H9
Flasby N York 58 C3
Flash Staffs 50 D7
Flashader Highld 104 D10
Flaunden Herts 20 G4
Flawborough Notts 42 B2
Flawith N York 59 L2
Flax Bourton N Som 17 M3
Flaxby N York 59 K3
Flaxley Gloucs 29 J6
Flaxpool Somset 16 F8
Flaxton N York 59 P2
Fleckney Leics 41 P8
Flecknoe Warwks 31 L2
Fledborough Notts 52 B8
Fleet Dorset 7 P6
Fleet Hants 20 D11
Fleet Lincs 43 L5
Fleet Hargate Lincs 43 L5
Fleet Services Hants 20 C11
Fleetwood Lancs 62 G11
Fleggburgh Norfk 45 P7
Flemingston V Glam 16 D3
Flemington S Lans 85 L10
Flempton Suffk 34 D3
Fletchertown Cumb 71 K7
Fletching E Susx 11 N5
Flexbury Cnwll 14 D10
Flexford Surrey 20 E12
Flimby Cumb 70 G8
Flimwell E Susx 12 E4
Flint Flints 48 E2
Flintham Notts 51 Q10
Flinton E R Yk 61 L7
Flitcham Norfk 44 C5
Flitton C Beds 32 F9
Flitwick C Beds 32 E9
Flixborough N Linc 60 E10
Flixborough Stather N Linc 60 E10
Flixton N York 67 M10
Flixton Suffk 45 M11
Flixton Traffd 57 N9
Flockton Kirk 58 G10
Flockton Green Kirk 58 G10
Flodigarry Highld 104 F7
Flookburgh Cumb 62 G7
Flordon Norfk 45 K10
Flore Nhants 31 N3
Flowton Suffk 34 H7
Flushing Cnwll 3 J8
Fluxton Devon 6 E4
Flyford Flavell Worcs 30 C3
Fobbing Thurr 22 E6
Fochabers Moray 101 L4
Fochriw Caerph 27 M7
Fockerby N Linc 60 E9
Foddington Somset 17 N9
Foel Powys 48 B12
Foggathorpe E R Yk 60 D6
Fogo Border 80 G4

Fogwatt – Gloucester Crematorium 171

Fogwatt Moray 101 K4
Foindle Highld 108 D6
Folda Angus 94 C8
Fole Staffs 50 D12
Foleshill Covtry 41 J10
Folke Dorset 17 P12
Folkestone Kent 13 N3
Folkingham Lincs 42 F4
Folkington E Susx 12 C8
Folksworth Cambs 42 G11
Folkton N York 67 M10
Folla Rule Abers 102 F8
Follifoot N York 59 J4
Folly Gate Devon 15 K11
Fonthill Bishop Wilts 8 D2
Fonthill Gifford Wilts 8 D2
Fontmell Magna Dorset 8 C4
Fontmell Parva Dorset 8 C5
Fontwell W Susx 10 F8
Foolow Derbys 50 F5
Forbestown Abers 101 M11
Forcett N York 65 L5
Ford Ag & B 83 N3
Ford Bucks 31 Q11
Ford Derbys 51 K5
Ford Devon 14 G7
Ford Gloucs 30 E8
Ford Nthumb 81 K6
Ford Somset 16 E9
Ford Staffs 50 E9
Ford W Susx 10 F8
Ford Wilts 18 C6
Fordcombe Kent 11 Q3
Fordell Fife 86 D5
Forden Powys 38 E2
Ford End Essex 34 B12
Forder Green Devon 5 Q6
Fordham Cambs 33 Q3
Fordham Essex 34 F10
Fordham Norfk 43 P9
Fordingbridge Hants 8 G5
Fordon E R Yk 67 M11
Fordoun Abers 95 M6
Fordstreet Essex 34 F10
Ford Street Somset 16 F11
Fordwich Kent 23 M10
Fordyce Abers 102 D3
Forebridge Staffs 40 B3
Forest Guern 6 b2
Forest Chapel Ches E 50 C6
Forest Gate Gt Lon 21 N6
Forest Green Surrey 10 H2
Forest Hall N Tyne 73 M6
Forest Hill Gt Lon 21 M8
Forest Hill Oxon 31 N11
Forest Lane Head N York 59 J3
Forest Mill Clacks 85 Q4
Forest of Bowland Lancs 63 L10
Forest of Dean Gloucs 28 H6
Forest of Dean
Crematorium Gloucs 28 H6
Forest Park
Crematorium Gt Lon 21 P5
Forest Row E Susx 11 N3
Forestside W Susx 10 C7
Forfar Angus 93 M5
Forgandenny P & K 92 G11
Forge Hammer Torfn 28 C9
Forgie Moray 101 M4
Forgieside Moray 101 M5
Forgue Abers 102 D6
Formby Sefton 56 F7
Forncett End Norfk 45 J10
Forncett St Mary Norfk 45 J10
Forncett St Peter Norfk 45 J10
Fornham All Saints Suffk 34 D4
Fornham St Martin Suffk 34 E4
Fornighty Highld 100 E5
Forres Moray 100 F4
Forsbrook Staffs 50 C11
Forse Highld 110 E8
Forsinard Highld 109 Q7
Forss Highld 110 B3
Fort Augustus Highld 98 E7
Forteviot P & K 92 F11
Forth S Lans 85 Q11
Forthampton Gloucs 29 M3
Forth Rail Bridge C Edin 86 D6
Forth Road Bridge Fife 86 D6
Fortingall P & K 91 Q6
Forton Hants 19 M11
Forton Lancs 63 J11
Forton Shrops 48 H11
Forton Somset 7 J2
Forton Staffs 49 N10
Fortrie Abers 102 E6
Fortrose Highld 107 M10
Fortuneswell Dorset 7 P7
Fort William Highld 90 F2
Forty Hill Gt Lon 21 M4
Fosbury Wilts 19 K8
Foscot Oxon 30 G9
Fosdyke Lincs 43 K4
Foss P & K 92 B4
Fossebridge Gloucs 30 E11
Foster Street Essex 21 P2
Foston Derbys 40 F2
Foston Leics 41 N8
Foston Lincs 42 C2
Foston N York 59 P2
Foston on the Wolds
E R Yk 61 J3
Fotherby Lincs 53 K5
Fotheringhay Nhants 42 F10
Foula Shet 111 j5
Foula Airport Shet 111 j5
Foulden Border 81 K3
Foulden Norfk 44 C9
Foul End Warwks 40 G8
Foulness Island Essex 23 J5
Foulon Vale
Crematorium Guern 6 b2
Foulridge Lancs 58 B6
Foulsham Norfk 44 G5
Fountainhall Border 87 J11
Four Ashes Suffk 34 G3
Four Crosses Powys 48 F10
Four Elms Kent 11 P1
Four Forks Somset 16 G8
Four Gotes Cambs 43 M6
Four Lanes Cnwll 2 G7
Four Marks Hants 9 R1
Four Mile Bridge IoA 54 C6
Four Oaks Birm 40 E7
Four Oaks Solhll 40 G10
Fourpenny Highld 107 N4
Four Roads Carmth 25 Q7
Fourstones Nthumb 72 F7
Four Throws Kent 12 F4
Fovant Wilts 8 E2
Foveran Abers 103 K9
Fowey Cnwll 4 D9
Fowlhall Kent 12 E2
Fowlis Angus 93 K8
Fowlis Wester P & K 92 D10
Fowlmere Cambs 33 L7
Fownhope Herefs 28 G3
Foxbar Rens 84 H10
Foxcote Somset 17 Q5
Foxdale IoM 56 b5
Foxearth Essex 34 D7
Foxfield Cumb 62 E5
Foxhole Cnwll 3 L5
Foxholes N York 67 L11
Foxley Norfk 44 H6
Foxt Staffs 50 D10
Foxton Cambs 33 L7
Foxton Leics 41 P9
Foxton N York 65 Q8
Foxwood Shrops 39 L6
Foy Herefs 28 H3
Foyers Highld 98 G5
Foynesfield Highld 100 D5
Fraddon Cnwll 3 K4
Fradley Staffs 40 F5
Fradswell Staffs 40 C2
Fraisthorpe E R Yk 61 K2
Framfield E Susx 11 P6
Framingham Earl Norfk 45 L9
Framingham Pigot Norfk 45 L9
Framlingham Suffk 35 L4
Frampton Dorset 7 P4
Frampton Lincs 43 K3
Frampton Cotterell
S Glos 29 J11
Frampton Mansell
Gloucs 29 N8
Frampton-on-Severn
Gloucs 29 K7
Framsden Suffk 35 K5
Framwellgate Moor Dur 73 M11
Franche Worcs 39 P6
Frankby Wirral 56 E10
Frankley Worcs 40 C10
Frankley Services Worcs 40 C10
Frankton Warwks 41 K12
Frant E Susx 12 C3
Fraserburgh Abers 103 K2
Frating Essex 34 H11
Frating Green Essex 34 H11
Fratton C Port 9 Q7
Freathy Cnwll 5 J9
Freckenham Suffk 33 Q3
Freckleton Lancs 56 H3
Freeby Leics 42 B6
Freefolk Hants 19 N10
Freeland Oxon 31 K10
Freethorpe Norfk 45 N8
Freethorpe Common
Norfk 45 N8
Freiston Lincs 43 L2
Fremington Devon 15 J6
Fremington N York 65 J7
Frenchay S Glos 28 H12
Frenich P & K 92 C4
Frensham Surrey 10 D2
Freshfield Sefton 56 F7
Freshford Wilts 18 B8
Freshwater IoW 9 K9
Fressingfield Suffk 35 L2
Freston Suffk 35 J8
Freswick Highld 110 G3
Fretherne Gloucs 29 K6
Frettenham Norfk 45 L6
Freuchie Fife 86 F2
Freystrop Pembks 24 G6
Friar Park Sandw 40 D8
Friday Bridge Cambs 43 M8
Friday Street Suffk 35 N5
Fridaythorpe E R Yk 60 E3
Friern Barnet Gt Lon 21 L5
Friesthorpe Lincs 52 F6
Frieston Lincs 42 D1
Frieth Bucks 20 C5
Frilford Oxon 19 M2
Frilsham W Berk 19 P6
Frimley Surrey 20 E10
Frindsbury Medway 22 E9
Fring Norfk 44 C3
Fringford Oxon 31 N8
Frinsted Kent 22 H11
Frinton-on-Sea Essex 35 K11
Friockheim Angus 93 Q6
Frisby on the Wreake
Leics 41 P4
Friskney Lincs 53 M11
Friston E Susx 12 B9
Friston Suffk 35 N5
Fritchley Derbys 51 J9
Fritham Hants 9 J5
Frithelstock Devon 14 H8
Frithelstock Stone
Devon 14 H8
Frithville Lincs 53 K12
Frittenden Kent 12 F2
Frittiscombe Devon 5 Q10
Fritton Norfk 45 K10
Fritton Norfk 45 P9
Fritwell Oxon 31 M8
Frizinghall C Brad 58 F7
Frizington Cumb 70 G11
Frocester Gloucs 29 K8
Frodesley Shrops 39 K2
Frodsham Ches W 57 K12
Frogden Border 80 G8
Frog End Cambs 33 L7
Froggatt Derbys 50 G5
Froghall Staffs 50 D10
Frogmore Devon 5 P10
Frognall Lincs 42 G7
Frog Pool Worcs 39 P8
Frogwell Cnwll 4 H6
Frolesworth Leics 41 L8
Frome Somset 18 B10
Frome St Quintin Dorset 7 N3
Fromes Hill Herefs 39 M11
Froncysyllte Denbgs 48 F7
Fron-goch Gwynd 47 P4
Fron Isaf Wrexhm 48 F7
Frosterley Dur 72 H12
Froxfield Wilts 19 K7
Froxfield Green Hants 10 B5
Fryern Hill Hants 9 M4
Fryerning Essex 22 D4
Fuinary Highld 89 M7
Fulbeck Lincs 52 D12
Fulbourn Cambs 33 N5
Fulbrook Oxon 30 H10
Fulflood Hants 9 M2
Fulford C York 59 N4
Fulford Somset 16 G9
Fulford Staffs 50 C12
Fulham Gt Lon 21 K8
Fulking W Susx 11 K7
Fullarton N Ayrs 76 F4
Fuller Street Essex 34 C12
Fullerton Hants 19 L11
Fulletby Lincs 53 J8
Fullready Warwks 30 H5
Full Sutton E R Yk 60 D3
Fullwood E Ayrs 76 G2
Fulmer Bucks 20 F6
Fulmodeston Norfk 44 G4
Fulnetby Lincs 52 F7
Fulney Lincs 43 J5
Fulstow Lincs 53 K4
Fulwell Sundld 73 P8
Fulwood Lancs 57 K3
Fulwood Sheff 50 H4
Fundenhall Norfk 45 J10
Funtington W Susx 10 C8
Funtullich P & K 92 B9
Furley Devon 6 H2
Furnace Ag & B 83 Q3
Furnace Carmth 26 C8
Furness Vale Derbys 50 D4
Furneux Pelham Herts 33 L10
Furzley Hants 9 K4
Fyfield Essex 22 C3
Fyfield Hants 19 K10
Fyfield Oxon 19 M2
Fyfield Wilts 18 G7
Fyfield Wilts 18 H8
Fylingthorpe N York 67 K6
Fyning W Susx 10 D5
Fyvie Abers 102 G7

G

Gabroc Hill E Ayrs 76 H2
Gaddesby Leics 41 P5
Gaddesden Row Herts 20 G2
Gadgirth S Ayrs 76 G6
Gaerllwyd Mons 28 E9
Gaerwen IoA 54 F7
Gailes N Ayrs 76 F4
Gailey Staffs 40 B5
Gainford Dur 65 L4
Gainsborough Lincs 52 B5
Gainsford End Essex 34 C9
Gairloch Highld 105 M7
Gairlochy Highld 98 B11
Gairneybridge P & K 86 D3
Gaitsgill Cumb 71 N6
Galashiels Border 80 C7
Galgate Lancs 63 J10
Galhampton Somset 17 P9
Gallanachbeg Ag & B 90 B10
Gallanachmore Ag & B 89 R10
Gallatown Fife 86 G4
Galleywood Essex 22 E3
Gallovie Highld 98 H10
Galloway Forest Park 69 L3
Gallowfauld Angus 93 M7
Gallowhill P & K 92 H8
Galltair Highld 97 L5
Galmisdale Highld 96 F11
Galmpton Devon 5 N11
Galmpton Torbay 6 B10
Galphay N York 65 M11
Galston E Ayrs 76 H4
Gamblesby Cumb 72 B11
Gamlingay Cambs 33 J6
Gamlingay Great Heath
Cambs 32 H6
Gamrie Abers 102 G3
Gamston Notts 51 N12
Gamston Notts 51 P5
Ganavan Bay Ag & B 90 B9
Ganllwyd Gwynd 47 M6
Gannachy Angus 95 K7
Ganstead E R Yk 61 K7
Ganthorpe N York 66 F12
Ganton N York 67 L11
Garbity Moray 101 L5
Garboldisham Norfk 34 G1
Garbole Highld 99 L4
Garchory Abers 101 L12
Gardeners Green
Wokham 20 D9
Garden of England
Crematorium Kent 22 H9
Gardenstown Abers 102 G3
Garden Village Sheff 50 H2
Garderhouse Shet 111 k4
Gare Hill Somset 18 B11
Garelochhead Ag & B 84 D5
Garford Oxon 19 M2
Garforth Leeds 59 K7
Gargrave N York 58 B4
Gargunnock Stirlg 85 M4
Garlic Street Norfk 45 K12
Garlieston D & G 69 L9
Garlinge Kent 23 P9
Garlinge Green Kent 23 L11
Garlogie Abers 95 M2
Garmond Abers 102 G5
Garmouth Moray 101 L3
Garmston Shrops 39 L2
Garn-Dolbenmaen
Gwynd 46 H3
Garrabost W Isls 111 e2
Garrallan E Ayrs 77 J7
Garras Cnwll 2 G10
Garreg Gwynd 47 K3
Garrigill Cumb 72 D11
Garroch D & G 69 N3
Garrochtrie D & G 68 F10
Garrochty Ag & B 84 B11
Garros Highld 104 G9
Garsdale Head Cumb 64 E8
Garsdon Wilts 18 E4
Garshall Green Staffs 40 C1
Garsington Oxon 31 M12
Garstang Lancs 63 J12
Garston Herts 20 H4
Garston Lpool 56 H11
Gartachossan Ag & B 82 E10
Gartcosh N Lans 85 L9
Garth Powys 37 Q10
Garth Wrexhm 48 F7
Garthamlock C Glas 85 L9
Garthmyl Powys 38 E3
Garthorpe Leics 42 B6
Garthorpe N Linc 60 E9
Garth Row Cumb 63 K3
Gartly Abers 102 C8
Gartmore Stirlg 85 J4
Gartness N Lans 85 N9
Gartness Stirlg 84 H5
Gartocharn W Duns 84 G6
Garton-on-the-Wolds
E R Yk 60 G3
Gartymore Highld 110 B11
Garva Bridge Highld 98 G9
Garvald E Loth 87 L7
Garvan Highld 90 D2
Garvard Ag & B 82 E5
Garve Highld 106 G9
Garvellachs Ag & B 83 K2
Garvestone Norfk 44 G8
Garvock Inver 84 E8
Garway Herefs 28 E4
Garyvard W Isls 111 d2
Gasper Wilts 8 B2
Gastard Wilts 18 C7
Gasthorpe Norfk 34 F1
Gaston Green Essex 33 N12
Gatcombe IoW 9 N9
Gate Burton Lincs 52 B7
Gateforth N York 59 M8
Gatehead E Ayrs 76 G4
Gate Helmsley N York 59 P3
Gatehouse Nthumb 72 E3
Gatehouse of Fleet
D & G 69 N7
Gateley Norfk 44 F5
Gatenby N York 65 N9
Gateshaw Border 80 G9
Gateshead Gatesd 73 M8
Gateside Angus 93 M6
Gateside E Rens 84 H10
Gateside Fife 86 E1
Gateside N Ayrs 84 F11
Gateslack D & G 78 E8
Gatley Stockp 57 Q10
Gattonside Border 80 D7
Gatwick Airport W Susx 11 L2
Gaulby Leics 41 P7
Gauldry Fife 93 L10
Gauldswell P & K 93 J5
Gautby Lincs 52 H8
Gavinton Border 80 G4
Gawcott Bucks 31 P7
Gawsworth Ches E 50 B6
Gawthrop Cumb 63 M5
Gawthwaite Cumb 62 F5
Gaydon Warwks 31 J4
Gayhurst M Keyn 32 C7
Gayle N York 64 F9
Gayles N York 65 K6
Gayton Nhants 31 P4
Gayton Norfk 44 C6
Gayton Staffs 40 C2
Gayton le Marsh Lincs 53 L6
Gayton Thorpe Norfk 44 C6
Gaywood Norfk 43 Q6
Gazeley Suffk 34 C4
Gearraidh Bhaird W Isls 111 d2
Geary Highld 104 C9
Gedding Suffk 34 F5
Geddington Nhants 42 C12
Gedling Notts 51 N11
Gedney Lincs 43 L5
Gedney Broadgate Lincs 43 L5
Gedney Drove End Lincs 43 M4
Gedney Dyke Lincs 43 L5
Gedney Hill Lincs 43 K7
Geeston Rutlnd 42 E8
Geldeston Norfk 45 N10
Gellifor Denbgs 48 D3
Gelligaer Caerph 27 N9
Gellilydan Gwynd 47 L4
Gellinudd Neath 26 G7
Gellyburn P & K 92 G7
Gellywen Carmth 25 M4
Gelston D & G 70 C4
Gelston Lincs 42 C2
Gembling E R Yk 61 J3
Gentleshaw Staffs 40 D5
Georgefield D & G 79 L9
George Green Bucks 20 F7
Georgeham Devon 14 H4
Georgemas Junction
Station Highld 110 D4
George Nympton Devon 15 M7
Georth Ork 111 h2
Germansweek Devon 5 J2
Gerrans Cnwll 3 K8
Gerrards Cross Bucks 20 G6
Gerrick R & Cl 66 G5
Gestingthorpe Essex 34 D8
Geuffordd Powys 48 E11
Gidea Park Gt Lon 21 Q5
Giffnock E Rens 85 J10
Gifford E Loth 87 K8
Giffordtown Fife 93 K12
Giggleswick N York 63 P9
Gigha Ag & B 75 J3
Gilberdyke E R Yk 60 E8
Gilchriston E Loth 87 J8
Gilcrux Cumb 70 H7
Gildersome Leeds 58 G8
Gildingwells Rothm 51 M4
Gilesgate Moor Dur 73 N11
Gileston V Glam 16 D3
Gilfach Caerph 27 N8
Gilfach Goch Brdgnd 27 K10
Gilfachrheda Cerdgn 36 G8
Gilgarran Cumb 70 G10
Gillamoor N York 66 F9
Gillen Highld 104 C9
Gillesbie D & G 79 J9
Gilling East N York 66 E11
Gillingham Dorset 8 B3
Gillingham Medway 22 F9
Gillingham Norfk 45 N10
Gilling West N York 65 L6
Gillock Highld 110 E4
Gills Highld 110 G2
Gilmanscleuch Border 79 M5
Gilmerton C Edin 86 F8
Gilmerton P & K 92 D10
Gilmonby Dur 64 H5
Gilmorton Leics 41 M9
Gilroes Crematorium
C Leic 41 M6
Gilsland Nthumb 72 B7
Gilston Border 87 J10
Gilston Herts 21 N2
Gilwern Mons 27 Q6
Gimingham Norfk 45 L3
Gipping Suffk 34 H4
Gipsey Bridge Lincs 53 J12
Girdle Toll N Ayrs 76 F3
Girlsta Shet 111 k4
Girsby N York 65 N6
Girthon D & G 69 N8
Girton Cambs 33 L4
Girton Notts 52 B9
Girvan S Ayrs 76 D10
Gisburn Lancs 63 P11
Gisleham Suffk 45 Q11
Gislingham Suffk 34 H3
Gissing Norfk 45 J11
Gittisham Devon 6 F3
Gladestry Powys 38 E10
Gladsmuir E Loth 87 J7
Glais Swans 26 F8
Glaisdale N York 66 H6
Glamis Angus 93 L6
Glanaman Carmth 26 F6
Glandford Norfk 44 H2
Glandwr Pembks 25 L3
Glandyfi Cerdgn 47 L11
Glanllynfi Brdgnd 27 J10
Glan-rhyd Powys 26 G7
Glanton Nthumb 81 M10
Glanvilles Wootton
Dorset 7 P2
Glan-y-don Flints 56 D11
Glapthorn Nhants 42 E11
Glapwell Derbys 51 L7
Glasbury Powys 27 P2
Glascote Staffs 40 G6
Glascwm Powys 38 D10
Glasfryn Conwy 55 N10
Glasgow C Glas 85 K9
Glasgow Airport Rens 84 H9
Glasgow Prestwick
Airport S Ayrs 76 F6
Glasgow Science
Centre C Glas 85 J9
Glasinfryn Gwynd 54 H7
Glasnacardoch Bay
Highld 97 J9
Glasnakille Highld 96 G7
Glassford S Lans 77 M2
Glasshouse Gloucs 29 J5
Glasshouses N York 58 F2
Glasslaw Abers 102 H4
Glasson Cumb 71 L4
Glasson Lancs 63 J10
Glassonby Cumb 72 B12
Glasterlaw Angus 93 Q5
Glaston Rutlnd 42 C9
Glastonbury Somset 17 M8
Glatton Cambs 42 G11
Glazebrook Warrtn 57 M9
Glazebury Warrtn 57 M9
Glazeley Shrops 39 N5
Gleaston Cumb 62 F7
Glebe Highld 98 G5
Gledhow Leeds 58 H6
Gledpark D & G 69 P8
Gledrid Shrops 48 F7
Glemsford Suffk 34 D7
Glenallachie Moray 101 K7
Glenancross Highld 97 J10
Glenaros House Ag & B 89 L7
Glen Auldyn IoM 56 d3
Glenbarr Ag & B 75 K5
Glenbarry Abers 102 D4
Glenbeg Highld 89 M4
Glenbervie Abers 95 M6
Glenboig N Lans 85 M8
Glenborrodale Highld 89 M4
Glenbranter Ag & B 84 B4
Glenbreck Border 78 H5
Glenbrittle Highld 96 E5
Glenbuck E Ayrs 77 M5
Glencally Angus 94 F8
Glencaple D & G 70 G2
Glencarse P & K 92 H10
Glencoe Highld 90 F5
Glencothe Border 78 H3
Glencraig Fife 86 E4
Glencrosh D & G 78 C10
Glendale Highld 104 B11
Glendaruel Ag & B 83 Q6
Glendevon P & K 86 B2
Glendoe Lodge Highld 98 E7
Glendoick P & K 93 J10
Glenduckie Fife 93 K11
Glenegedale Ag & B 74 D3
Glenelg Highld 97 L6
Glenerney Moray 100 F6
Glenfarg P & K 92 G12
Glenfield Leics 41 M6
Glenfinnan Highld 90 C1
Glenfintaig Lodge Highld 98 C10
Glenfoot P & K 92 H11
Glenfyne Lodge Ag & B 90 H12
Glengarnock N Ayrs 84 F11
Glengolly Highld 110 C3
Glengorm Castle Ag & B 89 K5
Glengrasco Highld 96 E1
Glenholm Border 78 H3
Glenhoul D & G 69 N2
Glenisla Angus 94 D9
Glenkin Ag & B 84 C7
Glenkindie Abers 101 N11
Glenlivet Moray 101 J9
Glenlochar D & G 70 C3
Glenlomond P & K 86 E2
Glenluce D & G 68 G7
Glenmassen Ag & B 84 B5
Glenmavis N Lans 85 M9
Glen Maye IoM 56 b5
Glenmore Highld 96 E2
Glenmore Lodge Highld 99 P7
Glen Nevis House Highld 90 F2
Glenochil Clacks 85 P4
Glen Parva Leics 41 M7
Glenquiech Angus 94 G9
Glenralloch Ag & B 83 M8
Glenridding Cumb 71 N11
Glenrothes Fife 86 F3
Glenshero Lodge Highld 98 H9
Glenstriven Ag & B 84 B7
Glentham Lincs 52 E5
Glentrool D & G 69 J4
Glen Trool Lodge D & G 69 K3
Glentruim Highld 99 K9
Glentworth Lincs 52 D6
Glenuig Highld 89 N2
Glenvarragill Highld 96 F2
Glen Vine IoM 56 c5
Glenwhilly D & G 68 G5
Glespin S Lans 78 D4
Glewstone Herefs 28 G4
Glinton C Pete 42 G8
Glooston Leics 41 Q8
Glossop Derbys 50 D3
Gloster Hill Nthumb 81 Q12
Gloucester Gloucs 29 L5
Gloucester
Crematorium Gloucs 29 L5

Gloucester Services
Gloucs... 29 L6
Gloucestershire Airport
Gloucs... 29 M5
Glusburn N York... 58 D5
Glutt Lodge Highld... 110 B8
Glympton Oxon... 31 K9
Glynarthen Cerdgn... 36 E10
Glyn Ceiriog Wrexhm... 48 E7
Glynde E Susx... 11 P8
Glyncorrwg Neath... 27 J8
Glyndyfrdwy Denbgs... 48 D7
Glynneath Neath... 27 J7
Glynn Valley
Crematorium Cnwll... 3 N3
Glyntaff Crematorium
Rhondd... 27 M10
Glyntawe Powys... 26 H5
Glynteg Carmth... 25 N2
Gnosall Staffs... 49 P10
Gnosall Heath Staffs... 49 P10
Goadby Leics... 41 Q7
Goadby Marwood Leics... 41 R3
Goatacre Wilts... 18 F5
Goathill Dorset... 17 P11
Goathland N York... 67 J7
Goathurst Somset... 16 H8
Gobowen Shrops... 48 F8
Godalming Surrey... 10 F2
Goddard's Green Kent... 12 G3
Godmanchester Cambs... 33 J3
Godmanstone Dorset... 7 P4
Godmersham Kent... 23 K12
Godney Somset... 17 L7
Godolphin Cross Cnwll... 2 F9
Godre'r-graig Neath... 26 G7
Godshill IoW... 9 N10
Godstone Surrey... 21 M11
Goetre Mons... 28 C7
Goff's Oak Herts... 21 M3
Gogar C Edin... 86 E7
Goginan Cerdgn... 37 L4
Golan Gwynd... 46 H3
Golant Cnwll... 4 D8
Golberdon Cnwll... 4 H6
Golborne Wigan... 57 L8
Golcar Kirk... 58 E10
Goldcliff Newpt... 28 D11
Golden Green Kent... 12 D1
Goldenhill C Stke... 49 Q5
Golden Pot Hants... 10 B2
Golders Green Gt Lon... 21 K6
Golders Green
Crematorium Gt Lon... 21 K6
Goldhanger Essex... 22 H2
Goldington Bed... 32 F6
Goldsborough N York... 59 J3
Goldsborough N York... 67 J5
Golds Green Sandw... 40 C8
Goldsithney Cnwll... 2 E9
Goldsworth Park Surrey... 20 F10
Goldthorpe Barns... 59 L12
Goldworthy Devon... 14 G7
Gollanfield Highld... 107 N10
Golspie Highld... 107 N3
Gomeldon Wilts... 8 H1
Gomshall Surrey... 10 H1
Gonalston Notts... 51 P10
Gonerby Hill Foot Lincs... 42 C3
Gonfirth Shet... 111 k3
Good Easter Essex... 22 D2
Gooderstone Norfk... 44 C9
Goodleigh Devon... 15 K5
Goodmanham E R Yk... 60 F5
Goodmayes Gt Lon... 21 P6
Goodnestone Kent... 23 K10
Goodnestone Kent... 23 N11
Goodrich Herefs... 28 G5
Goodrington Torbay... 6 B10
Goodshaw Lancs... 57 P4
Goodwick Pembks... 24 G2
Goodworth Clatford
Hants... 19 L11
Goole E R Yk... 60 C9
Goom's Hill Worcs... 30 D3
Goonbell Cnwll... 2 G6
Goonhavern Cnwll... 2 H5
Goonvrea Cnwll... 2 G6
Goosecruives Abers... 95 M5
Gooseford Devon... 5 N2
Goose Green Essex... 35 J10
Goose Green S Glos... 17 P2
Gooseham Cnwll... 14 E8
Goosey Oxon... 19 L3
Goosnargh Lancs... 57 K2
Goostrey Ches E... 49 P2
Gordano Services N Som... 17 M2
Gordon Border... 80 E5
Gordon Arms Hotel
Border... 79 L4
Gordonstown Abers... 102 D4
Gordonstown Abers... 102 F7
Gorebridge Mdloth... 86 G9
Gorefield Cambs... 43 L7
Gores Wilts... 18 G8
Gorey Jersey... 7 c2
Goring Oxon... 19 P5
Goring-by-Sea W Susx... 10 H9
Gorleston on Sea Norfk... 45 Q8
Gornal Wood
Crematorium Dudley... 40 B7
Gorrachie Abers... 102 F4
Gorran Churchtown
Cnwll... 3 M7
Gorran Haven Cnwll... 3 M7
Gorsedd Flints... 56 D12
Gorse Hill Swindn... 18 H4
Gorseinon Swans... 26 D9
Gorsgoch Cerdgn... 36 H9
Gorslas Carmth... 26 D6
Gorsley Gloucs... 29 J4
Gorsley Common Herefs... 29 J4
Gorstan Highld... 106 F9
Gorsten Ag & B... 89 P9
Gorsty Hill Staffs... 40 E2
Gorthleck Highld... 98 G5
Gorton Manch... 50 B2
Gosbeck Suffk... 35 J5
Gosberton Lincs... 43 J4
Gosfield Essex... 34 D10
Gosforth Cumb... 62 C2
Gosforth N u Ty... 73 M7
Gosport Hants... 9 Q7
Gossington Gloucs... 29 K8
Gotham Notts... 41 M2
Gotherington Gloucs... 29 N3
Gotton Somset... 16 H9
Goudhurst Kent... 12 E3
Goulceby Lincs... 53 J8
Gourdas Abers... 102 G7

Gourdie C Dund... 93 L8
Gourdon Abers... 95 N7
Gourock Inver... 84 D7
Govan C Glas... 85 J9
Goveton Devon... 5 P10
Govilon Mons... 28 B6
Gowdall E R Yk... 59 N9
Gower Highld... 106 H10
Gower Swans... 26 C10
Gowerton Swans... 26 D9
Gowkhall Fife... 86 C5
Goxhill E R Yk... 61 K5
Goxhill N Linc... 61 J3
Grabhair W Isls... 111 d3
Graffham W Susx... 10 E6
Grafham Cambs... 32 G3
Grafham Surrey... 10 G2
Grafton N York... 59 K2
Grafton Oxon... 19 J1
Grafton Shrops... 48 H10
Grafton Worcs... 29 N2
Grafton Flyford Worcs... 30 C3
Grafton Regis Nhants... 31 Q5
Grafton Underwood
Nhants... 32 D2
Grafty Green Kent... 12 G1
Graig Conwy... 55 L7
Graigfechan Denbgs... 48 D5
Grain Medway... 22 H7
Grainsby Lincs... 53 J4
Grainthorpe Lincs... 53 L4
Grampound Cnwll... 3 L6
Grampound Road Cnwll... 3 K5
Gramsdal W Isls... 111 b5
Gramsdale W Isls... 111 b5
Granborough Bucks... 31 Q8
Granby Notts... 41 Q1
Grandborough Warwks... 31 L2
Grand Chemins Jersey... 7 c2
Grandes Rocques Guern... 6 b1
Grandtully P & K... 92 D5
Grange Cumb... 71 L11
Grange Medway... 22 F9
Grange P & K... 93 K10
Grange Crossroads
Moray... 101 N4
Grange Hall Moray... 100 G3
Grangehall S Lans... 78 F1
Grange Hill Essex... 21 N5
Grangemill Derbys... 50 G8
Grange Moor Kirk... 58 G10
Grangemouth Falk... 85 Q6
Grange of Lindores Fife... 93 J11
Grange-over-Sands
Cumb... 62 H6
Grangepans Falk... 86 B6
Grange Park Nhants... 31 Q3
Grangetown R & Cl... 66 D4
Grangetown Sundld... 73 P9
Grange Villa Dur... 73 M9
Gransmoor E R Yk... 61 J3
Granston Pembks... 24 F2
Grantchester Cambs... 33 M6
Grantham Lincs... 42 D3
Grantham
Crematorium Lincs... 42 D3
Granton C Edin... 86 F6
Grantown-on-Spey
Highld... 100 F9
Grantshouse Border... 87 P8
Grasby Lincs... 52 F3
Grasmere Cumb... 62 G1
Grasscroft Oldham... 58 C12
Grassendale Lpool... 56 H10
Grassington N York... 58 D2
Grassmoor Derbys... 51 K7
Grassthorpe Notts... 52 B9
Grateley Hants... 19 J11
Graveley Cambs... 33 J4
Graveley Herts... 32 H10
Gravelly Hill Birm... 40 E8
Graveney Kent... 23 K10
Gravesend Kent... 22 D8
Gravir W Isls... 111 d3
Grayingham Lincs... 52 F3
Grayrigg Cumb... 63 L3
Grays Thurr... 22 C7
Grayshott Hants... 10 E3
Grayswood Surrey... 10 E3
Greasbrough Rothm... 51 K2
Greasby Wirral... 56 F10
Great Abington Cambs... 33 N7
Great Addington Nhants... 32 D2
Great Alne Warwks... 30 E3
Great Altcar Lancs... 56 G7
Great Amwell Herts... 21 M2
Great Asby Cumb... 64 C5
Great Ashfield Suffk... 34 G4
Great Ayton N York... 66 D5
Great Baddow Essex... 22 E3
Great Badminton S Glos... 18 B4
Great Bardfield Essex... 34 B10
Great Barford Bed... 32 G6
Great Barr Sandw... 40 D8
Great Barrington Gloucs... 30 G10
Great Barrow Ches W... 49 J2
Great Barton Suffk... 34 E4
Great Barugh N York... 66 G10
Great Bavington
Nthumb... 72 H5
Great Bealings Suffk... 35 K7
Great Bedwyn Wilts... 19 J7
Great Bentley Essex... 35 J11
Great Billing Nhants... 32 B4
Great Bircham Norfk... 44 C4
Great Blakenham Suffk... 35 J6
Great Blencow Cumb... 71 P8
Great Bolas Wrekin... 49 M10
Great Bookham Surrey... 21 J11
Great Bourton Oxon... 31 L5
Great Bowden Leics... 41 Q9
Great Bradley Suffk... 34 B6
Great Braxted Essex... 22 G1
Great Bricett Suffk... 34 G6
Great Brickhill Bucks... 32 C10
Great Bridgeford Staffs... 40 B3
Great Brington Nhants... 31 P2
Great Bromley Essex... 34 H10
Great Broughton Cumb... 70 H8
Great Broughton N York... 66 D6
Great Budworth Ches W... 57 M12
Great Burdon Darltn... 65 N4
Great Burstead Essex... 22 D5
Great Busby N York... 66 D6
Great Carlton Lincs... 53 L6
Great Casterton Rutlnd... 42 E7
Great Chalfield Wilts... 18 C7
Great Chart Kent... 13 J2
Great Chatwell Staffs... 49 P11
Great Chell C Stke... 49 Q5

Great Chesterford Essex... 33 N8
Great Cheverell Wilts... 18 E9
Great Chishill Cambs... 33 L8
Great Clacton Essex... 35 K12
Great Clifton Cumb... 70 G9
Great Coates NE Lin... 61 L11
Great Comberton Worcs... 29 N11
Great Corby Cumb... 71 P5
Great Cornard Suffk... 34 E8
Great Cowden E R Yk... 61 L6
Great Coxwell Oxon... 19 J3
Great Cransley Nhants... 32 B2
Great Cressingham
Norfk... 44 E9
Great Crosthwaite Cumb... 71 L10
Great Cubley Derbys... 50 F12
Great Cumbrae Island
N Ayrs... 84 C10
Great Dalby Leics... 41 Q5
Great Denham Bed... 32 E7
Great Doddington
Nhants... 32 C4
Great Dunham Norfk... 44 E7
Great Dunmow Essex... 33 Q11
Great Durnford Wilts... 18 G12
Great Easton Essex... 33 P10
Great Easton Leics... 42 C10
Great Eccleston Lancs... 56 H1
Great Ellingham Norfk... 44 G10
Great Elm Somset... 17 Q6
Great Everdon Nhants... 31 N3
Great Eversden Cambs... 33 K6
Greatford Lincs... 42 F7
Great Fransham Norfk... 44 E7
Great Gaddesden Herts... 20 G2
Greatgate Staffs... 50 D11
Great Gidding Cambs... 42 G12
Great Givendale E R Yk... 60 E4
Great Glemham Suffk... 35 M4
Great Glen Leics... 41 P7
Great Gonerby Lincs... 42 C3
Great Gransden Cambs... 33 J5
Great Green Cambs... 33 J7
Great Green Suffk... 34 F5
Great Habton N York... 66 G11
Great Hale Lincs... 42 G2
Great Hallingbury Essex... 33 N11
Greatham Hants... 10 C4
Greatham Hartpl... 66 C3
Greatham W Susx... 10 G6
Great Hampden Bucks... 20 D3
Great Harrowden
Nhants... 32 C3
Great Harwood Lancs... 57 N3
Great Haseley Oxon... 19 Q1
Great Hatfield E R Yk... 61 K5
Great Haywood Staffs... 40 D3
Great Heck N York... 59 N9
Great Henny Essex... 34 E8
Great Hinton Wilts... 18 D8
Great Hockham Norfk... 44 F10
Great Holland Essex... 35 K11
Great Hollands Br For... 20 D9
Great Horkesley Essex... 34 F9
Great Hormead Herts... 33 L10
Great Horton C Brad... 58 F7
Great Horwood Bucks... 31 Q7
Great Houghton Barns... 59 K11
Great Houghton Nhants... 32 B5
Great Hucklow Derbys... 50 F5
Great Kelk E R Yk... 61 J3
Great Kimble Bucks... 20 D3
Great Kingston N York... 65 N8
Great Langdale Cumb... 62 F2
Great Langton N York... 65 N8
Great Leighs Essex... 34 C12
Great Limber Lincs... 52 G2
Great Linford M Keyn... 32 C8
Great Livermere Suffk... 34 E3
Great Longstone Derbys... 50 G6
Great Lumley Dur... 73 N10
Great Malvern Worcs... 39 P11
Great Maplestead Essex... 34 D9
Great Marton Bpool... 56 G2
Great Massingham Norfk... 44 D5
Great Milton Oxon... 19 Q1
Great Missenden Bucks... 20 E3
Great Mitton Lancs... 57 N2
Great Mongeham Kent... 23 Q12
Great Moulton Norfk... 45 J11
Great Musgrave Cumb... 64 D5
Great Ness Shrops... 48 H10
Great Notley Essex... 34 C11
Great Oak Mons... 28 D6
Great Oakley Essex... 35 K10
Great Oakley Nhants... 42 C11
Great Offley Herts... 32 G10
Great Ormside Cumb... 64 C4
Great Orton Cumb... 71 M5
Great Ouseburn N York... 59 K2
Great Oxendon Nhants... 41 Q10
Great Park N u Ty... 73 L6
Great Parndon Essex... 21 N2
Great Paxton Cambs... 32 H4
Great Plumpton Lancs... 56 H3
Great Plumstead Norfk... 45 L7
Great Ponton Lincs... 42 D4
Great Preston Leeds... 59 K8
Great Raveley Cambs... 33 J1
Great Rissington Gloucs... 30 G10
Great Rollright Oxon... 31 J7
Great Ryburgh Norfk... 44 F5
Great Ryton Shrops... 39 J2
Great Saling Essex... 34 B10
Great Salkeld Cumb... 71 Q8
Great Sampford Essex... 33 Q9
Great Saughall Ches W... 48 G2
Great Shefford W Berk... 19 L6
Great Shelford Cambs... 33 M6
Great Smeaton N York... 65 N6
Great Snoring Norfk... 44 F4
Great Somerford Wilts... 18 E4
Great Soudley Shrops... 49 N8
Great Stainton Darltn... 65 N3
Great Stambridge Essex... 22 H5
Great Staughton Cambs... 32 G4
Great Steeping Lincs... 53 M9
Great Stoke S Glos... 28 H11
Greatstone-on-Sea Kent... 13 L5
Great Strickland Cumb... 71 Q10
Great Stukeley Cambs... 33 J2
Great Sturton Lincs... 52 H7
Great Swinburne
Nthumb... 72 H6
Great Tew Oxon... 31 K8
Great Tey Essex... 34 E10
Great Thurlow Suffk... 34 B6
Great Torrington Devon... 15 J8

Great Tosson Nthumb... 72 H2
Great Totham Essex... 22 G2
Great Totham Essex... 22 G2
Great Urswick Cumb... 62 F7
Great Wakering Essex... 22 H6
Great Waldingfield Suffk... 34 E7
Great Walsingham Norfk... 44 F3
Great Waltham Essex... 22 E2
Great Warley Essex... 22 C5
Great Washbourne
Gloucs... 29 N2
Great Weeke Devon... 5 P3
Great Welnetham Suffk... 34 E6
Great Wenham Suffk... 34 H8
Great Whittington
Nthumb... 72 H6
Great Wigborough Essex... 23 J1
Great Wilbraham Cambs... 33 N5
Great Wishford Wilts... 8 F1
Great Witcombe Gloucs... 29 M6
Great Witley Worcs... 39 N8
Great Wolford Warwks... 30 G7
Greatworth Nhants... 31 M6
Great Wratting Suffk... 34 B7
Great Wymondley Herts... 32 H10
Great Wyrley Staffs... 40 C6
Great Yarmouth Norfk... 45 Q8
Great Yarmouth
Crematorium Norfk... 45 Q8
Great Yeldham Essex... 34 C8
Greenburn W Loth... 85 Q10
Green End Herts... 33 K11
Green End Herts... 33 K9
Greenfield Ag & B... 84 D5
Greenfield C Beds... 32 F9
Greenfield Flints... 56 E12
Greenfield Highld... 98 B8
Greenfield Oldham... 58 C12
Greenford Gt Lon... 21 J7
Greengairs N Lans... 85 N8
Greengates C Brad... 58 G6
Greenham Somset... 16 E11
Green Hammerton N York... 59 L3
Greenhaugh Nthumb... 72 E4
Greenhead Nthumb... 72 C7
Green Heath Staffs... 40 C5
Greenhill D & G... 78 H11
Greenhill Falk... 85 N7
Greenhill Kent... 23 M9
Greenhill S Lans... 78 F3
Greenhills S Lans... 85 K11
Greenhithe Kent... 22 C8
Greenholm E Ayrs... 77 J4
Greenhouse Border... 80 D9
Greenhow Hill N York... 58 E2
Greenland Highld... 110 E3
Greenland Sheff... 51 K3
Greenlaw Border... 80 F5
Greenlea D & G... 71 Q1
Greenloaning P & K... 85 N2
Greenmount Bury... 57 P6
Greenock Inver... 84 D7
Greenodd Cumb... 62 G6
Green Ore Somset... 17 N6
Green Quarter Cumb... 63 J2
Greenshields S Lans... 86 B12
Greenside Gatesd... 73 K8
Greenside Kirk... 58 F10
Greens Norton Nhants... 31 P4
Greenstead Green Essex... 34 D10
Green Street Herts... 21 J4
Green Street Herts... 33 M11
Green Tye Herts... 33 M11
Greenway Somset... 17 J10
Greenwich Gt Lon... 21 M7
Greenwich Maritime
Gt Lon... 21 M7
Greet Gloucs... 30 D7
Greete Shrops... 39 L7
Greetham Lincs... 53 K8
Greetham Rutlnd... 42 D7
Greetland Calder... 58 E9
Greinton Somset... 17 K8
Grenaby IoM... 56 b6
Grendon Nhants... 32 C5
Grendon Warwks... 40 H7
Grendon Underwood
Bucks... 31 P9
Grenoside Sheff... 51 J3
Grenoside
Crematorium Sheff... 51 J3
Greosabhagh W Isls... 111 c3
Gresford Wrexhm... 48 G5
Gresham Norfk... 45 J3
Greshornish Highld... 104 D10
Gressenhall Norfk... 44 F7
Gressenhall Green Norfk... 44 F6
Gressingham Lancs... 63 K8
Greta Bridge Dur... 65 J5
Gretna D & G... 71 M3
Gretna Green D & G... 71 M2
Gretna Services D & G... 71 L2
Gretton Gloucs... 30 D7
Gretton Nhants... 42 C10
Gretton Shrops... 39 K3
Grewelthorpe N York... 65 M11
Greyrigg D & G... 78 H10
Greys Green Oxon... 20 B6
Greysouthen Cumb... 70 H9
Greystoke Cumb... 71 P8
Greystone Angus... 93 P7
Greywell Hants... 20 B12
Griff Warwks... 41 J9
Griffithstown Torfn... 28 C8
Grimeford Village Lancs... 57 L6
Grimesthorpe Sheff... 51 J3
Grimethorpe Barns... 59 K11
Grimley Worcs... 39 Q9
Grimmet S Ayrs... 76 F8
Grimoldby Lincs... 53 L6
Grimpo Shrops... 48 G9
Grimsargh Lancs... 57 L3
Grimsby NE Lin... 61 M11
Grimsby Crematorium
NE Lin... 53 J3
Grimscote Nhants... 31 P4
Grimscott Cnwll... 14 E10
Grimshader W Isls... 111 d2
Grimsthorpe Lincs... 42 F5
Grimston Leics... 41 P3
Grimston Norfk... 44 C5
Grimstone Dorset... 7 P4
Grimstone End Suffk... 34 F4
Grindale E R Yk... 67 N12
Grindleford Derbys... 50 G5
Grindleton Lancs... 63 N11
Grindley Brook Shrops... 49 K7
Grindlow Derbys... 50 F5
Grindon Staffs... 50 E9
Gringley on the Hill
Notts... 51 Q3

Grinsdale Cumb... 71 M4
Grinshill Shrops... 49 K10
Grinton N York... 65 J7
Griomaisiader W Isls... 111 d2
Grishipoll Ag & B... 88 C5
Gristhorpe N York... 67 M10
Griston Norfk... 44 F9
Gritley Ork... 111 h2
Grittenham Wilts... 18 F4
Grittleton Wilts... 18 C5
Grizebeck Cumb... 62 E5
Grizedale Cumb... 62 G4
Groby Leics... 41 M6
Groes Conwy... 55 Q8
Groes-faen Rhondd... 27 M11
Groeslon Gwynd... 54 F9
Groes-Wen Caerph... 27 N10
Grogarry W Isls... 111 a5
Grogport Ag & B... 75 M4
Groigearraidh W Isls... 111 a5
Gronant Flints... 56 C11
Groombridge E Susx... 11 Q3
Grosebay W Isls... 111 c3
Grosmont Mons... 28 E4
Grosmont N York... 67 J6
Groton Suffk... 34 F8
Grouville Jersey... 7 c2
Grove Notts... 51 Q5
Grove Oxon... 19 L3
Grove Green Kent... 22 F11
Grove Park Gt Lon... 21 N8
Grovesend Swans... 26 D8
Gruinard Highld... 105 P4
Gruinart Ag & B... 82 D9
Grula Highld... 96 D4
Gruline Ag & B... 89 L8
Grundisburgh Suffk... 35 K6
Gruting Shet... 111 j4
Grutness Shet... 111 k5
Gualachulain Highld... 90 F7
Guardbridge Fife... 93 M11
Guarlford Worcs... 39 P11
Guay P & K... 92 E6
Guernsey Guern... 6 b2
Guernsey Airport Guern... 6 b2
Guestling Green E Susx... 12 G7
Guestling Thorn E Susx... 12 G6
Guestwick Norfk... 44 H5
Guide Bridge Tamesd... 50 B2
Guilden Morden Cambs... 33 J7
Guilden Sutton Ches W... 49 J2
Guildford Surrey... 20 F12
Guildford Crematorium
Surrey... 10 F2
Guildtown P & K... 92 G8
Guilsborough Nhants... 41 P11
Guilsfield Powys... 48 E12
Guiltreehill S Ayrs... 76 F8
Guineaford Devon... 15 J5
Guisborough R & Cl... 66 E4
Guiseley Leeds... 58 G6
Guist Norfk... 44 G5
Guiting Power Gloucs... 30 E8
Gullane E Loth... 87 J5
Gulval Cnwll... 2 D9
Gulworthy Devon... 5 K5
Gumfreston Pembks... 25 J8
Gumley Leics... 41 P9
Gunby Lincs... 42 D6
Gunby Lincs... 53 M9
Gundleton Hants... 9 Q2
Gun Hill E Susx... 12 C7
Gunn Devon... 15 L5
Gunnerside N York... 64 G7
Gunnerton Nthumb... 72 G6
Gunness N Linc... 60 E11
Gunnislake Cnwll... 5 J6
Gunnista Shet... 111 k4
Gunthorpe C Pete... 42 H9
Gunthorpe N Linc... 52 B4
Gunthorpe Norfk... 44 G3
Gunthorpe Notts... 51 P11
Gunwalloe Cnwll... 2 F10
Gurnard IoW... 9 N8
Gurney Slade Somset... 17 N6
Gurnos Powys... 26 G7
Gussage All Saints
Dorset... 8 E5
Gussage St Andrew
Dorset... 8 E5
Gussage St Michael
Dorset... 8 E5
Guston Kent... 13 P2
Gutcher Shet... 111 k2
Guthrie Angus... 93 P5
Guyhirn Cambs... 43 L8
Guyzance Nthumb... 81 P12
Gwaenysgor Flints... 56 C11
Gwalchmai IoA... 54 E6
Gwaun-Cae-Gurwen
Carmth... 26 F6
Gweek Cnwll... 2 G9
Gwenddwr Powys... 38 C12
Gwennap Cnwll... 2 H7
Gwennap Mining
District Cnwll... 2 H7
Gwent Crematorium
Mons... 28 C8
Gwernaffield Flints... 48 E3
Gwernesney Mons... 28 E8
Gwernogle Carmth... 26 D3
Gwernymynydd Flints... 48 E3
Gwespyr Flints... 56 C11
Gwinear Cnwll... 2 E8
Gwithian Cnwll... 2 E7
Gwyddelwern Denbgs... 48 C6
Gwyddgrug Carmth... 26 C2
Gwytherin Conwy... 55 N8

H

Habberley Shrops... 38 H2
Habberley Worcs... 39 P6
Habergham Lancs... 57 P3
Habertoft Lincs... 53 N9
Habrough NE Lin... 61 K10
Hacconby Lincs... 42 F5
Haceby Lincs... 42 E3
Hacheston Suffk... 35 M5
Hackbridge Gt Lon... 21 L9
Hackenthorpe Sheff... 51 K4
Hackford Norfk... 44 H9
Hackforth N York... 65 M8
Hackland Ork... 111 h2
Hackleton Nhants... 32 B6
Hacklinge Kent... 23 Q11
Hackness N York... 67 L9
Hackney Gt Lon... 21 M6

Place	County	Page	Grid
Hackthorn	Lincs	52	E7
Hackthorpe	Cumb	71	Q10
Hadden	Border	80	G7
Haddenham	Bucks	20	B2
Haddenham	Cambs	33	M2
Haddington	E Loth	87	K7
Haddington	Lincs	52	D10
Haddiscoe	Norfk	45	P10
Haddo	Abers	102	H7
Haddon	Cambs	42	G10
Hadfield	Derbys	50	D2
Hadham Ford	Herts	33	M11
Hadleigh	Essex	22	F6
Hadleigh	Suffk	34	G8
Hadley	Worcs	39	Q8
Hadley	Wrekin	49	M12
Hadley End	Staffs	40	F4
Hadley Wood	Gt Lon	21	L4
Hadlow	Kent	22	D12
Hadlow Down	E Susx	11	Q5
Hadnall	Shrops	49	K10
Hadrian's Wall		72	G6
Hadstock	Essex	33	N7
Hadzor	Worcs	30	B2
Haggersta	Shet	111	k4
Haggerston	Nthumb	81	L5
Haggs	Falk	85	N7
Hagley	Herefs	28	G1
Hagley	Worcs	40	B10
Hagworthingham	Lincs	53	K9
Haile	Cumb	62	B1
Hailey	Oxon	31	J10
Hailsham	E Susx	12	C8
Hail Weston	Cambs	32	G4
Hainault	Gt Lon	21	P5
Hainford	Norfk	45	K6
Hainton	Lincs	52	H6
Haisthorpe	E R Yk	61	J2
Hakin	Pembks	24	F7
Halam	Notts	51	P9
Halbeath	Fife	86	D5
Halberton	Devon	6	D1
Halcro	Highld	110	E4
Hale	Cumb	63	J6
Hale	Halton	57	J11
Hale	Hants	8	H4
Hale	Surrey	10	D1
Hale	Traffd	57	P10
Halebarns	Traffd	57	P10
Hales	Norfk	45	N10
Hales	Staffs	49	N8
Halesowen	Dudley	40	C10
Hales Place	Kent	23	M10
Hale Street	Kent	22	D12
Halesworth	Suffk	35	N2
Halewood	Knows	57	J10
Halford	Devon	5	Q5
Halford	Warwks	30	H5
Halfpenny Green	Staffs	39	P4
Halfway House	Shrops	48	G12
Halfway Houses	Kent	22	H8
Halifax	Calder	58	E8
Halket	E Ayrs	84	G11
Halkirk	Highld	110	D4
Halkyn	Flints	48	E2
Hall	E Rens	84	G11
Halland	E Susx	11	P6
Hallaton	Leics	42	B10
Hallatrow	BaNES	17	P5
Hallbankgate	Cumb	72	B8
Hall Dunnerdale	Cumb	62	E3
Hallen	S Glos	28	G11
Hallgarth	Dur	73	N11
Hallglen	Falk	85	P7
Hall Green	Birm	40	E10
Hallin	Highld	104	C9
Halling	Medway	22	E10
Hallington	Lincs	53	K6
Hallington	Nthumb	72	H6
Halliwell	Bolton	57	M6
Halloughton	Notts	51	P9
Hallow	Worcs	39	P9
Hall's Green	Herts	33	J10
Hallyne	Border	79	K2
Halmore	Gloucs	29	J8
Halnaker	W Susx	10	E8
Halsall	Lancs	56	G6
Halse	Nhants	31	M6
Halse	Somset	16	F9
Halsetown	Cnwll	2	D7
Halsham	E R Yk	61	M8
Halstead	Essex	34	D10
Halstead	Kent	21	P10
Halstead	Leics	41	Q6
Halstock	Dorset	7	M2
Haltemprice Crematorium	E R Yk	60	H7
Haltham	Lincs	53	J10
Halton	Bucks	20	E2
Halton	Halton	57	K11
Halton	Lancs	63	J8
Halton	Leeds	59	J7
Halton	Nthumb	72	H7
Halton	Wrexhm	48	F7
Halton East	N York	58	D4
Halton Gill	N York	64	F11
Halton Holegate	Lincs	53	L9
Halton Lea Gate	Nthumb	72	C8
Halton Shields	Nthumb	72	H7
Halton West	N York	63	Q10
Haltwhistle	Nthumb	72	D7
Halvergate	Norfk	45	N8
Halwell	Devon	5	Q9
Halwill	Devon	14	H11
Halwill Junction	Devon	14	H11
Ham	Devon	6	H3
Ham	Gloucs	29	J8
Ham	Gt Lon	21	J8
Ham	Kent	23	P11
Ham	Somset	16	H10
Ham	Wilts	19	K8
Hambleden	Bucks	20	C6
Hambledon	Hants	9	Q4
Hambledon	Surrey	10	F3
Hamble-le-Rice	Hants	9	N6
Hambleton	Lancs	56	G1
Hambleton	N York	59	M7
Hambridge	Somset	17	K10
Hambrook	W Susx	10	C8
Hameringham	Lincs	53	K9
Hamerton	Cambs	32	G2
Ham Green	Worcs	30	D2
Hamilton	S Lans	85	M11
Hamilton Services	S Lans	85	M10
Hamlet	Dorset	7	N2
Hammersmith	Gt Lon	21	K7
Hammerwich	Staffs	40	E6
Hammoon	Dorset	8	B5
Hamnavoe	Shet	111	k4
Hampden Park	E Susx	12	C9
Hampnett	Gloucs	30	E10
Hampole	Donc	59	L11
Hampreston	Dorset	8	F7
Hampstead	Gt Lon	21	L6
Hampstead Norreys	W Berk	19	N5
Hampsthwaite	N York	58	H3
Hampton	C Pete	42	G10
Hampton	Gt Lon	21	J9
Hampton	Kent	23	M9
Hampton	Shrops	39	N5
Hampton	Swindn	18	H3
Hampton	Worcs	30	D5
Hampton Bishop	Herefs	28	G2
Hampton Court Palace	Gt Lon	21	J9
Hampton Heath	Ches W	49	J5
Hampton-in-Arden	Solhll	40	G10
Hampton Lovett	Worcs	30	B2
Hampton Lucy	Warwks	30	G3
Hampton Magna	Warwks	30	H2
Hampton Poyle	Oxon	31	L10
Hampton Wick	Gt Lon	21	J9
Hamptworth	Wilts	9	J4
Hamsey	E Susx	11	N7
Hamstall Ridware	Staffs	40	E4
Hamstead	Birm	40	D8
Hamstead Marshall	W Berk	19	M7
Hamsterley	Dur	65	K9
Hamsterley	Dur	73	K9
Hamstreet	Kent	13	J4
Ham Street	Somset	17	M8
Hamworthy	Poole	8	E8
Hanbury	Staffs	40	F2
Hanbury	Worcs	30	C2
Hanchurch	Staffs	49	Q7
Handa Island	Highld	108	C6
Hand and Pen	Devon	6	E4
Handbridge	Ches W	48	H3
Handcross	W Susx	11	L4
Handforth	Ches E	57	Q11
Handley	Ches W	49	J4
Handley	Derbys	51	J8
Handsworth	Birm	40	D9
Handsworth	Sheff	51	K4
Hanford	C Stke	49	Q7
Hanging Heaton	Kirk	58	G9
Hanging Houghton	Nhants	41	Q11
Hanging Langford	Wilts	18	F12
Hangleton	Br & H	11	L8
Hanham	S Glos	17	P2
Hankelow	Ches E	49	M6
Hankerton	Wilts	29	N9
Hanley	C Stke	50	B10
Hanley Castle	Worcs	39	Q12
Hanley Child	Worcs	39	M8
Hanley Swan	Worcs	39	P12
Hanley William	Worcs	39	M8
Hanlith	N York	58	B2
Hanmer	Wrexhm	49	J7
Hannaford	Devon	15	K6
Hannington	Hants	19	N9
Hannington	Nhants	32	B3
Hannington	Swindn	18	H3
Hannington Wick	Swindn	18	H2
Hanslope	M Keyn	32	B7
Hanthorpe	Lincs	42	F5
Hanwell	Gt Lon	21	J7
Hanwell	Oxon	31	K5
Hanwood	Shrops	49	J12
Hanworth	Gt Lon	20	H8
Hanworth	Norfk	45	K3
Happendon	S Lans	78	E3
Happendon Services	S Lans	78	D3
Happisburgh	Norfk	45	N4
Happisburgh Common	Norfk	45	N4
Hapsford	Ches W	49	J1
Hapton	Lancs	57	P3
Hapton	Norfk	45	K10
Harberton	Devon	5	Q8
Harbertonford	Devon	5	Q8
Harbledown	Kent	23	L10
Harborne	Birm	40	D10
Harborough Magna	Warwks	41	L10
Harbottle	Nthumb	81	K12
Harbourneford	Devon	5	P7
Harbury	Warwks	31	J3
Harby	Leics	41	Q2
Harby	Notts	52	C8
Harcombe	Devon	6	B6
Harcombe	Devon	6	F5
Harcombe Bottom	Devon	7	J4
Harden	C Brad	58	E6
Harden	Wsall	40	D7
Hardenhuish	Wilts	18	D6
Hardgate	Abers	95	N2
Hardgate	D & G	70	D3
Hardgate	W Duns	84	H8
Hardham	W Susx	10	G6
Hardingham	Norfk	44	H8
Hardingstone	Nhants	31	Q3
Hardington	Somset	17	Q5
Hardington Mandeville	Somset	7	M1
Hardington Marsh	Somset	7	M2
Hardington Moor	Somset	7	M1
Hardisworthy	Devon	14	E7
Hardley	Hants	9	M6
Hardley Street	Norfk	45	N9
Hardraw	N York	64	F8
Hardstoft	Derbys	51	K8
Hardway	Hants	9	Q7
Hardway	Somset	17	Q8
Hardwick	Bucks	32	B11
Hardwick	Cambs	33	L5
Hardwick	Nhants	32	C3
Hardwick	Norfk	45	K11
Hardwick	Oxon	31	J11
Hardwick	Oxon	31	M7
Hardwick	Wsall	40	E7
Hardwicke	Gloucs	29	L6
Hardwicke	Gloucs	29	M4
Hardwick Hall	Derbys	51	K7
Hardy's Green	Essex	34	F11
Hare Croft	C Brad	58	E7
Harefield	Gt Lon	20	G5
Hare Green	Essex	34	H10
Hare Hatch	Wokham	20	C7
Harehill	Derbys	40	F1
Harehills	Leeds	59	J7
Harelaw	Border	80	C9
Harelaw	D & G	79	N12
Harescombe	Gloucs	29	L6
Haresfield	Gloucs	29	L6
Harestock	Hants	9	M2
Hare Street	Essex	21	N1
Hare Street	Herts	33	L10
Harewood	Leeds	58	H5
Harewood End	Herefs	28	F4
Harford	Devon	5	M9
Hargrave	Ches W	49	J3
Hargrave	Nhants	32	E3
Hargrave	Suffk	34	C5
Harkstead	Suffk	35	K9
Harlaston	Staffs	40	G5
Harlaxton	Lincs	42	C4
Harlech	Gwynd	47	J5
Harlech Castle	Gwynd	47	J5
Harlescott	Shrops	49	J11
Harlesden	Gt Lon	21	K6
Harlesthorpe	Derbys	51	L5
Harleston	Devon	5	Q10
Harleston	Norfk	45	L12
Harleston	Suffk	34	G5
Harlestone	Nhants	31	P2
Harle Syke	Lancs	57	Q2
Harley	Rothm	51	J2
Harley	Shrops	39	L2
Harlington	C Beds	32	E10
Harlington	Donc	51	L1
Harlington	Gt Lon	20	H7
Harlosh	Highld	96	C2
Harlow	Essex	21	N2
Harlow Carr RHS	N York	58	H4
Harlow Hill	Nthumb	73	J7
Harlthorpe	E R Yk	60	C6
Harlton	Cambs	33	L6
Harlyn	Cnwll	3	K1
Harman's Cross	Dorset	8	E10
Harmby	N York	65	K9
Harmer Green	Herts	33	J12
Harmer Hill	Shrops	49	J10
Harmston	Lincs	52	D10
Harnage	Shrops	39	K2
Harnhill	Gloucs	18	F1
Harold Hill	Gt Lon	21	Q5
Haroldston West	Pembks	24	F6
Haroldswick	Shet	111	m2
Harold Wood	Gt Lon	22	B5
Harome	N York	66	F10
Harpenden	Herts	21	J1
Harpford	Devon	6	E5
Harpham	E R Yk	61	J2
Harpley	Norfk	44	D5
Harpley	Worcs	39	M9
Harpole	Nhants	31	P2
Harpsdale	Highld	110	D5
Harpswell	Lincs	52	D5
Harpurhey	Manch	57	Q8
Harraby	Cumb	71	N5
Harracott	Devon	15	K6
Harrapool	Highld	97	J5
Harrietfield	P & K	92	E9
Harrietsham	Kent	22	G11
Harringay	Gt Lon	21	L6
Harrington	Cumb	70	G9
Harrington	Lincs	53	L8
Harrington	Nhants	41	Q9
Harringworth	Nhants	42	D10
Harris	W Isls	111	c3
Harrogate	N York	58	H3
Harrogate Crematorium	N York	59	J4
Harrold	Bed	32	D5
Harrow	Gt Lon	21	J6
Harrowbarrow	Cnwll	5	J6
Harrowgate Village	Darltn	65	N4
Harrow Green	Suffk	34	E6
Harrow on the Hill	Gt Lon	21	J6
Harrow Weald	Gt Lon	21	J5
Harston	Cambs	33	L6
Harston	Leics	42	B4
Harswell	E R Yk	60	E6
Hart	Hartpl	66	C1
Hartburn	Nthumb	73	J4
Hartburn	S on T	65	Q4
Hartest	Suffk	34	D6
Hartfield	E Susx	11	P3
Hartford	Cambs	33	J3
Hartford	Ches W	49	L2
Hartfordbridge	Hants	20	C10
Hartford End	Essex	34	B12
Hartforth	N York	65	L6
Hartgrove	Dorset	8	C4
Harthill	Ches W	49	J4
Harthill	N Lans	85	Q9
Harthill	Rothm	51	L5
Hartington	Derbys	50	F8
Hartland	Devon	14	E7
Hartland Quay	Devon	14	D7
Hartlebury	Worcs	39	Q7
Hartlepool Crematorium	Hartpl	66	C2
Hartley	Cumb	64	E6
Hartley	Kent	12	F3
Hartley	Kent	22	D10
Hartley Wespall	Hants	20	B10
Hartley Wintney	Hants	20	C11
Hartlip	Kent	22	G9
Harton	N York	60	C2
Harton	S Tyne	73	P7
Hartpury	Gloucs	29	L4
Hartshead	Kirk	58	F9
Hartshead Moor Services	Calder	58	F8
Hartshill	C Stke	49	Q6
Hartshill	Warwks	41	J8
Hartshorne	Derbys	41	J4
Hartwell	Nhants	32	B6
Hartwith	N York	58	G2
Hartwood	N Lans	85	P10
Hartwoodmyres	Border	79	N4
Harvel	Kent	22	D10
Harvington	Worcs	30	D4
Harvington	Worcs	39	Q7
Harwell	Notts	51	P3
Harwell	Oxon	19	N3
Harwich	Essex	35	L9
Harwood Dale	N York	67	L8
Harwood Park Crematorium	Herts	33	J11
Harworth	Notts	51	N3
Hasbury	Dudley	40	C10
Hascombe	Surrey	10	G3
Haselbech	Nhants	41	P11
Haselbury Plucknett	Somset	7	L1
Haseley	Warwks	30	G1
Haselor	Warwks	30	E3
Hasfield	Gloucs	29	L4
Haskayne	Lancs	56	G7
Hasketon	Suffk	35	L6
Haslemere	Surrey	10	E4
Haslingden	Lancs	57	P4
Haslingfield	Cambs	33	L6
Haslington	Ches E	49	N4
Hassingham	Norfk	45	N8
Hassocks	W Susx	11	L7
Hassop	Derbys	50	G6
Haster	Highld	110	G5
Hastingleigh	Kent	13	L2
Hastings	E Susx	12	G7
Hastings Crematorium	E Susx	12	G7
Hastingwood	Essex	21	P2
Hastoe	Herts	20	F3
Haswell	Dur	73	P11
Haswell Plough	Dur	73	P11
Hatch Beauchamp	Somset	17	J11
Hatch End	Gt Lon	21	J5
Hatchmere	Ches W	49	K2
Hatcliffe	NE Lin	53	J3
Hatfield	Donc	59	P11
Hatfield	Herefs	39	L9
Hatfield	Herts	21	K2
Hatfield Broad Oak	Essex	33	N12
Hatfield Heath	Essex	21	Q1
Hatfield Peverel	Essex	22	F2
Hatfield Woodhouse	Donc	59	P11
Hatford	Oxon	19	K2
Hatherden	Hants	19	K10
Hatherleigh	Devon	15	J10
Hathern	Leics	41	L3
Hatherop	Gloucs	30	F11
Hathersage	Derbys	50	G5
Hathersage Booths	Derbys	50	G5
Hatherton	Ches E	49	M6
Hatherton	Staffs	40	C5
Hatley St George	Cambs	33	J6
Hatt	Cnwll	5	J7
Hattersley	Tamesd	50	C2
Hatton	Abers	103	L7
Hatton	Angus	93	N7
Hatton	Derbys	40	G2
Hatton	Gt Lon	20	H8
Hatton	Lincs	52	H7
Hatton	Shrops	39	J4
Hatton	Warrtn	57	L11
Hatton	Warwks	30	G1
Hatton of Fintray	Abers	102	H11
Haugh	E Ayrs	76	H6
Haugham	Lincs	53	K7
Haughead	E Duns	85	K7
Haughley	Suffk	34	G4
Haughley Green	Suffk	34	G4
Haugh of Glass	Moray	101	M7
Haugh of Urr	D & G	70	D3
Haughs of Kinnaird	Angus	93	Q4
Haughton	Ches E	49	L4
Haughton	Shrops	48	H9
Haughton	Staffs	49	Q10
Haughton le Skerne	Darltn	65	N4
Haultwick	Herts	33	K11
Haunton	Staffs	40	G5
Hauxton	Cambs	33	M6
Havant	Hants	10	B8
Havant Crematorium	Hants	10	B8
Havenstreet	IoW	9	P8
Havercroft	Wakefd	59	K10
Haverfordwest	Pembks	24	G6
Haverhill	Suffk	33	Q7
Haverigg	Cumb	62	D6
Havering-atte-Bower	Gt Lon	21	P5
Haversham	M Keyn	32	B8
Haverthwaite	Cumb	62	G5
Havyatt	N Som	17	L4
Hawarden	Flints	48	G3
Hawbush Green	Essex	34	D11
Hawen	Cerdgn	36	F10
Hawes	N York	64	F9
Hawe's Green	Norfk	45	L9
Hawford	Worcs	39	Q9
Hawick	Border	80	C10
Hawkchurch	Devon	7	J3
Hawkedon	Suffk	34	D6
Hawkeridge	Wilts	18	C9
Hawkesbury	S Glos	18	B4
Hawkesbury Upton	S Glos	18	B4
Hawkhurst	Kent	12	F4
Hawkinge	Kent	13	N3
Hawkinge Crematorium	Kent	13	M3
Hawkley	Hants	10	C4
Hawkridge	Somset	15	P6
Hawkshead	Cumb	62	G3
Hawkshead Hill	Cumb	62	G3
Hawksland	S Lans	78	D2
Hawkstone	Shrops	49	L9
Hawkswick	N York	64	G12
Hawksworth	Leeds	58	F6
Hawksworth	Notts	51	Q11
Hawkwell	Essex	22	G5
Hawley	Hants	20	D10
Hawling	Gloucs	30	D9
Hawnby	N York	66	D9
Haworth	C Brad	58	D6
Hawstead	Suffk	34	E5
Hawthorn	Dur	73	P10
Hawthorn Hill	Lincs	52	H11
Hawton	Notts	51	B12
Haxby	C York	59	N3
Haxey	N Linc	51	Q2
Haycombe Crematorium	BaNES	17	Q4
Haydock	St Hel	57	K9
Haydon Bridge	Nthumb	72	F7
Haydon Wick	Swindn	18	G4
Hayes	Gt Lon	20	H7
Hayes	Gt Lon	21	N9
Hayes End	Gt Lon	20	H7
Hayfield	Ag & B	90	E10
Hayfield	Derbys	50	D4
Hayhillock	Angus	93	N7
Hayle	Cnwll	2	E8
Hayle Port	Cnwll	2	E8
Hayley Green	Dudley	40	C10
Hayling Island	Hants	10	B9
Hayne	Devon	5	P3
Haynes (Church End)	C Beds	32	F8
Haynes (Northwood End)	C Beds	32	F8
Haynes (Silver End)	C Beds	32	F8
Haynes (West End)	C Beds	32	F8
Hay-on-Wye	Powys	27	P1
Hayscastle	Pembks	24	F4
Hayscastle Cross	Pembks	24	F4
Hay Street	Herts	33	L10
Hayton	Cumb	70	H7
Hayton	Cumb	71	Q4
Hayton	E R Yk	60	E5
Hayton	Notts	51	Q4
Haytor Vale	Devon	5	P5
Haytown	Devon	14	G8
Haywards Heath	W Susx	11	M5
Haywood	Donc	59	N10
Hazelbank	S Lans	77	P3
Hazelbury Bryan	Dorset	7	Q2
Hazeleigh	Essex	22	G3
Hazel Grove	Stockp	50	B4
Hazelton Walls	Fife	93	L10
Hazelwood	Derbys	51	J10
Hazlemere	Bucks	20	E4
Hazlerigg	N u Ty	73	M6
Hazleton	Gloucs	30	E9
Heacham	Norfk	44	B3
Headbourne Worthy	Hants	9	N2
Headcorn	Kent	12	G2
Headingley	Leeds	58	H7
Headington	Oxon	31	M11
Headlam	Dur	65	L4
Headlesscross	N Lans	85	Q10
Headless Cross	Worcs	30	D2
Headley	Hants	10	D3
Headley	Hants	19	N8
Headley	Surrey	21	K11
Headley Down	Hants	10	D3
Headon	Notts	51	Q5
Heads Nook	Cumb	71	P5
Heage	Derbys	51	J10
Healaugh	N York	59	L5
Healaugh	N York	64	H7
Heald Green	Stockp	57	Q10
Heale	Somset	16	H11
Heale	Somset	17	K10
Healey	N York	65	L10
Healeyfield	Dur	73	J10
Healing	NE Lin	61	L11
Heamoor	Cnwll	2	C9
Heanor	Derbys	51	K10
Heanton Punchardon	Devon	15	J5
Heapham	Lincs	52	C6
Heart of England Crematorium	Warwks	41	J8
Heart of Scotland Services	N Lans	85	Q9
Heasley Mill	Devon	15	M6
Heaste	Highld	96	H6
Heath	Derbys	51	K7
Heath	Wakefd	59	J9
Heath and Reach	C Beds	32	D10
Heathcote	Derbys	50	F8
Heather	Leics	41	K5
Heathfield	E Susx	12	C6
Heathfield	Somset	16	F10
Heath Green	Worcs	30	E12
Heath Hall	D & G	78	G11
Heath Hayes & Wimblebury	Staffs	40	D5
Heath Hill	Shrops	49	N11
Heathrow Airport	Gt Lon	20	H8
Heathton	Shrops	39	P4
Heath Town	Wolves	40	B7
Heatley	Warrtn	57	N10
Heaton	C Brad	58	F7
Heaton	N u Ty	73	M7
Heaton	Staffs	50	C8
Heaton Chapel	Stockp	57	Q9
Heaton Mersey	Stockp	57	Q10
Heaton Norris	Stockp	50	B3
Heaton's Bridge	Lancs	56	H6
Heaverham	Kent	22	C10
Heavitree	Devon	6	C4
Hebburn	S Tyne	73	N7
Hebden	N York	58	D2
Hebden Bridge	Calder	58	C8
Hebing End	Herts	33	K11
Hebron	Carmth	25	L4
Hebron	Nthumb	73	L3
Heckfield	Hants	20	B10
Heckfield Green	Suffk	35	K2
Heckfordbridge	Essex	34	F11
Heckington	Lincs	42	G2
Heckmondwike	Kirk	58	G9
Heddington	Wilts	18	E7
Heddon-on-the-Wall	Nthumb	73	K7
Hedenham	Norfk	45	M10
Hedge End	Hants	9	N5
Hedgerley	Bucks	20	F6
Hedging	Somset	17	J9
Hedley on the Hill	Nthumb	73	J8
Hednesford	Staffs	40	C5
Hedon	E R Yk	61	K8
Hedsor	Bucks	20	E6
Heeley	Sheff	51	J4
Heglibister	Shet	111	k4
Heighington	Darltn	65	M3
Heighington	Lincs	52	E9
Heightington	Worcs	39	N7
Heiton	Border	80	F7
Hele	Devon	6	D3
Hele	Devon	15	J3
Helensburgh	Ag & B	84	E6
Helenton	S Ayrs	76	G5
Helford	Cnwll	2	H9
Helford Passage	Cnwll	2	H9
Helhoughton	Norfk	44	E5
Helions Bumpstead	Essex	33	Q8
Helland	Cnwll	4	N2
Hellescott	Cnwll	4	G3
Hellesdon	Norfk	45	K7
Hellidon	Nhants	31	M3
Hellifield	N York	63	Q10
Hellingly	E Susx	12	C7
Helmdon	Nhants	31	N5
Helme	Kirk	58	E10
Helmingham	Suffk	35	K5
Helmsdale	Highld	110	B11
Helmshore	Lancs	57	P5
Helmsley	N York	66	E10

Helperby N York 59 K1
Helperthorpe N York 67 K12
Helpringham Lincs 42 G3
Helpston C Pete 42 G8
Helsby Ches W 49 J1
Helston Cnwll 2 F9
Helstone Cnwll 4 D4
Helton Cumb 71 Q10
Hemel Hempstead Herts 20 G2
Hemerdon Devon 5 L8
Hemingbrough N York 59 P7
Hemingby Lincs 53 J8
Hemingford Abbots
    Cambs 33 J3
Hemingford Grey Cambs 33 J3
Hemingstone Suffk 35 J6
Hemington Leics 41 L2
Hemington Nhants 42 F12
Hemington Somset 17 Q5
Hemley Suffk 35 L8
Hemlington Middsb 66 C5
Hempnall Norfk 45 L10
Hempnall Green Norfk 45 L10
Hempriggs Moray 100 H3
Hempstead Essex 33 Q8
Hempstead Medway 22 F9
Hempstead Norfk 44 H3
Hempstead Norfk 45 N5
Hempton Norfk 44 E4
Hempton Oxon 31 K7
Hemsby Norfk 45 P6
Hemswell Lincs 52 D5
Hemswell Cliff Lincs 52 D5
Hemsworth Wakefd 59 K10
Hemyock Devon 16 F12
Henbury Bristl 28 G11
Hendon Gt Lon 21 K5
Hendon Sundld 73 P9
Hendon Crematorium
    Gt Lon 21 K5
Hendy Carmth 26 D7
Henfield W Susx 11 K6
Hengoed Caerph 27 N9
Hengoed Powys 38 E10
Hengrave Suffk 34 D3
Henham Essex 33 N10
Heniarth Powys 38 D1
Henlade Somset 16 H10
Henley Dorset 7 Q2
Henley Somset 17 L9
Henley Suffk 35 J6
Henley W Susx 10 E5
Henley Green Covtry 41 J10
Henley-in-Arden Warwks 30 F2
Henley-on-Thames Oxon 20 C6
Henley's Down E Susx 12 E7
Henllan Cerdgn 36 F11
Henllan Denbgs 55 Q7
Henllys Torfn 28 B9
Henlow C Beds 32 H8
Hennock Devon 5 Q4
Henny Street Essex 34 E8
Henryd Conwy 55 L6
Henry's Moat (Castell
    Hendre) Pembks 24 H4
Hensall N York 59 N9
Henshaw Nthumb 72 D7
Hensingham Cumb 70 G11
Henstead Suffk 45 P11
Hensting Hants 9 N3
Henstridge Somset 17 Q11
Henstridge Ash Somset 17 Q11
Henton Oxon 20 C3
Henton Somset 17 L7
Henwick Worcs 39 Q10
Henwood Cnwll 4 G5
Heol-y-Cyw Brdgnd 27 K11
Hepple Nthumb 72 H1
Hepscott Nthumb 73 L4
Heptonstall Calder 58 C8
Hepworth Kirk 58 F11
Hepworth Suffk 34 G2
Herbrandston Pembks 24 F7
Hereford Herefs 28 F2
Hereford Crematorium
    Herefs 28 F2
Hereson Kent 23 Q9
Heribusta Highld 104 E8
Heriot Border 86 H10
Hermiston C Edin 86 E8
Hermitage Border 79 P9
Hermitage Dorset 7 P2
Hermitage W Berk 19 N6
Hermon Carmth 25 N3
Hermon Pembks 25 L3
Herne Kent 23 M9
Herne Bay Kent 23 M9
Herne Hill Gt Lon 21 L8
Herne Pound Kent 22 D11
Hernhill Kent 23 K10
Herodsfoot Cnwll 4 F7
Heronsford S Ayrs 68 F7
Herriard Hants 19 Q10
Herringfleet Suffk 45 P9
Herringswell Suffk 34 C3
Herringthorpe Rothm 51 K3
Herrington Sundld 73 P9
Hersden Kent 23 M10
Hersham Surrey 20 H9
Herstmonceux E Susx 12 D7
Herston Ork 111 h3
Hertford Herts 21 M2
Hertford Heath Herts 21 M2
Hertingfordbury Herts 21 L2
Hesketh Bank Lancs 57 J4
Hesketh Lane Lancs 57 L1
Hesket Newmarket
    Cumb 71 M7
Hesleden Dur 73 Q12
Heslington C York 59 N4
Hessay C York 59 M4
Hessenford Cnwll 4 G8
Hessett Suffk 34 F4
Hessle E R Yk 60 H8
Hessle Wakefd 59 K10
Hest Bank Lancs 63 J8
Heston Gt Lon 20 H7
Heston Services Gt Lon 20 H7
Hestwall Ork 111 g2
Heswall Wirral 56 F11
Hethe Oxon 31 N8
Hethersett Norfk 45 J8
Hethersgill Cumb 71 P3
Hett Dur 73 M12
Hetton N York 58 C3
Hetton-le-Hole Sundld 73 N10
Heugh Nthumb 73 J6
Heughhead Abers 101 M11
Heugh Head Border 87 Q9
Heveningham Suffk 35 M3

Hever Kent 11 P2
Heversham Cumb 63 J5
Hevingham Norfk 45 K6
Hewas Water Cnwll 3 L6
Hewelsfield Gloucs 28 G8
Hewish Somset 7 K2
Hewood Dorset 7 J3
Hexham Nthumb 72 G7
Hextable Kent 21 P8
Hexthorpe Donc 51 M1
Hexton Herts 32 F10
Hexworthy Cnwll 4 H4
Hexworthy Devon 5 N6
Heybridge Essex 22 D4
Heybridge Essex 22 G2
Heybrook Bay Devon 5 K9
Heydon Cambs 33 M8
Heydon Norfk 45 J5
Heydour Lincs 42 E3
Heylipoll Ag & B 88 B7
Heylor Shet 111 J3
Heysham Lancs 62 H9
Heyshott W Susx 10 E6
Heytesbury Wilts 18 D11
Heythrop Oxon 31 J8
Heywood Rochdl 57 Q6
Heywood Wilts 18 C9
Hibaldstow N Linc 52 D3
Hickleton Donc 59 L12
Hickling Norfk 45 N5
Hickling Notts 41 P2
Hickling Green Norfk 45 N5
Hickstead W Susx 11 L6
Hidcote Bartrim Gloucs 30 F5
Hidcote Boyce Gloucs 30 F6
High Ackworth Wakefd 59 K9
Higham Barns 58 H11
Higham Derbys 51 K8
Higham Kent 12 C1
Higham Kent 22 E8
Higham Lancs 57 P2
Higham Suffk 34 C4
Higham Suffk 34 G9
Higham Ferrers Nhants 32 D3
Higham Gobion C Beds 32 F9
Higham Hill Gt Lon 21 M5
Higham on the Hill Leics 41 J8
Highampton Devon 14 H10
Highams Park Gt Lon 21 M5
High Ardwell D & G 68 E9
High Auldgirth D & G 78 E10
High Bankhill Cumb 71 Q7
High Beach Essex 21 N4
High Bentham N York 63 M8
High Bickington Devon 15 K7
High Biggins Cumb 63 L6
High Blantyre S Lans 85 L10
High Bonnybridge Falk 85 N7
High Bray Devon 15 M5
Highbridge Somset 17 J6
Highbrook W Susx 11 M4
High Brooms Kent 12 C2
Highburton Kirk 58 F10
Highbury Gt Lon 21 L6
Highbury Somset 17 Q6
High Catton E R Yk 60 C4
Highcliffe Hants 19 M8
Highcliffe Dorset 8 H8
High Coniscliffe Darltn 65 M5
High Crosby Cumb 71 P4
High Cross E Ayrs 76 G3
High Cross Hants 10 B5
High Cross Herts 33 K11
High Cross Warwks 30 G1
High Drummore D & G 68 F11
High Easter Essex 22 C1
High Ellington N York 65 L10
Higher Ansty Dorset 8 B6
Higher Bartle Lancs 57 J3
Higher Bockhampton
    Dorset 7 Q4
Higher Brixham Torbay 6 C10
Higher Chillington
    Somset 7 K2
Higher Folds Wigan 57 M8
Higher Gabwell Devon 6 C8
Higher Heysham Lancs 62 H9
Higher Irlam Salfd 57 N9
Higher Kinnerton Flints 48 G4
Higher Muddiford Devon 15 K5
Higher Penwortham
    Lancs 57 K3
Higher Prestacott Devon 14 G11
Higher Town Cnwll 3 J6
Higher Town Cnwll 3 M4
Higher Town IoS 2 C1
Higher Walton Lancs 57 L4
Higher Walton Warrtn 57 L10
Higher Wambrook
    Somset 6 H2
Higher Waterston
    Dorset 7 Q4
Higher Wheelton Lancs 57 L4
Higher Whitley Ches W 57 L11
Higher Wincham Ches W 57 M12
Higher Wraxhall Dorset 7 N3
Higher Wych Ches W 49 J6
High Etherley Dur 65 L2
Highfield Gatesd 73 K8
Highfield N Ayrs 76 E2
High Garrett Essex 34 C10
Highgate Gt Lon 21 L6
Highgate Kent 12 F4
High Grantley N York 65 M12
High Green N York 45 J11
High Green Norfk 45 J8
High Green Sheff 51 J2
High Halden Kent 12 H3
High Halstow Medway 22 F8
High Ham Somset 17 K9
High Harrington Cumb 70 G9
High Harrogate N York 58 H3
High Hatton Shrops 49 L9
High Hauxley Nthumb 73 M1
High Hawsker N York 67 K6
High Hesket Cumb 71 P6
High Hoyland Barns 58 H11
High Hurstwood E Susx 11 P5
High Hutton N York 60 D1
High Ireby Cumb 71 K7
High Kilburn N York 66 D10
High Lands Dur 65 K3
Highlane Derbys 51 K4
High Lane Stockp 50 C4
High Lanes Cnwll 2 F8
Highleadon Gloucs 29 K4
High Legh Ches E 57 M11
Highleigh W Susx 10 D9
High Leven S on T 66 C5

Highley Shrops 39 N5
High Littleton BaNES 17 P5
High Lorton Cumb 71 J9
High Marnham Notts 52 B9
High Melton Donc 51 L1
High Mickley Nthumb 73 J8
Highmoor Oxon 20 B6
Highmoor Cross Oxon 20 B6
Highnam Gloucs 29 K5
High Newport Sundld 73 P9
High Newton Cumb 62 H5
High Nibthwaite Cumb 62 F4
High Offley Staffs 49 P9
High Ongar Essex 22 C3
High Onn Staffs 49 P11
High Park Corner Essex 34 G11
High Pennyvenie E Ayrs 76 H9
High Roding Essex 33 P12
High Salvington W Susx 10 H8
High Spen Gatesd 73 K8
Highsted Kent 22 H10
High Street Cnwll 3 L5
Highstreet Kent 23 L10
Highstreet Green Surrey 10 F3
Hightae D & G 78 H11
Highter's Heath Birm 40 E10
Hightown Sefton 56 F7
Hightown Green Suffk 34 F5
High Toynton Lincs 53 J9
High Valleyfield Fife 86 B5
Highweek Devon 6 B8
Highwood Essex 22 D3
Highwood Hill Gt Lon 21 K5
Highworth Swindn 18 H3
High Wray Cumb 62 G3
High Wych Herts 21 P1
High Wycombe Bucks 20 D5
Hilborough Norfk 44 D9
Hilcott Wilts 18 G8
Hildenborough Kent 21 R12
Hilden Park Kent 12 C1
Hildersham Cambs 33 N7
Hilderstone Staffs 40 C1
Hilderthorpe E R Yk 61 K2
Hilgay Norfk 43 P9
Hill S Glos 28 H9
Hill Warwks 31 L2
Hillam N York 59 L8
Hill Brow Hants 10 C5
Hillbutts Dorset 8 E7
Hill Chorlton Staffs 49 P7
Hillclifflane Derbys 50 H10
Hill Common Somset 16 F10
Hilldyke Lincs 43 K1
Hill End Fife 86 C3
Hillend Fife 86 D5
Hill End Gloucs 29 M2
Hillend Mdloth 86 F8
Hillend N Lans 85 N9
Hillesden Bucks 31 P8
Hillesley Gloucs 29 K10
Hillfarrance Somset 16 F10
Hill Green Kent 22 G10
Hillhead Abers 102 D8
Hill Head Hants 9 P6
Hillhead S Lans 78 F2
Hillhead of Cocklaw
    Abers 103 M6
Hilliclay Highld 110 D3
Hillingdon Gt Lon 20 H6
Hillington C Glas 85 J9
Hillington Norfk 44 C5
Hillmorton Warwks 41 M11
Hill of Beath Fife 86 D4
Hill of Fearn Highld 107 N6
Hillowton D & G 70 C3
High Ridware Staffs 40 E4
Hillside Abers 95 Q3
Hillside Angus 95 L9
Hill Side Kirk 58 F10
Hills Town Derbys 51 L6
Hillstreet Hants 9 K4
Hillswick Shet 111 J3
Hill Top Sandw 40 C8
Hill Top Wakefd 59 J10
Hillwell Shet 111 k5
Hilmarton Wilts 18 E6
Hilperton Wilts 18 C8
Hilsea C Port 9 Q6
Hilston E R Yk 61 M7
Hilton Border 81 J4
Hilton Cambs 33 J4
Hilton Cumb 64 D4
Hilton Derbys 40 G2
Hilton Dorset 8 B6
Hilton Dur 65 L3
Hilton Highld 107 P7
Hilton S on T 66 C5
Hilton Shrops 39 P3
Hilton Park Services
    Staffs 40 C6
Himbleton Worcs 30 C3
Himley Staffs 39 Q4
Hincaster Cumb 63 K5
Hinchley Wood Surrey 21 J9
Hinckley Leics 41 K8
Hinderclay Suffk 34 G2
Hinderwell N York 66 H4
Hindhead Surrey 10 E3
Hindhead Tunnel Surrey 10 E3
Hindley Wigan 57 L7
Hindlip Worcs 39 Q9
Hindolveston Norfk 44 G4
Hindon Wilts 8 D2
Hindringham Norfk 44 G3
Hingham Norfk 44 G9
Hinstock Shrops 49 M9
Hintlesham Suffk 34 H7
Hinton Herefs 28 D2
Hinton S Glos 17 Q2
Hinton Shrops 38 H1
Hinton Ampner Hants 9 P2
Hinton Blewett BaNES 17 N5
Hinton Charterhouse
    BaNES 18 B8
Hinton-in-the-Hedges
    Nhants 31 M6
Hinton Martell Dorset 8 E6
Hinton on the Green
    Worcs 30 D6
Hinton Parva Swindn 19 J4
Hinton St George
    Somset 7 K1
Hinton St Mary Dorset 8 B4
Hinton Waldrist Oxon 19 L2
Hints Staffs 40 F6
Hinwick Bed 32 D5
Hinxhill Kent 13 K2
Hinxton Cambs 33 M7
Hinxworth Herts 32 H8

Hipperholme Calder 58 E8
Hipswell N York 65 L7
Hirn Abers 95 M2
Hirnant Powys 48 B10
Hirst Nthumb 73 M4
Hirst Courtney N York 59 N8
Hirwaun Rhondd 27 K7
Hiscott Devon 15 J7
Histon Cambs 33 M4
Hitcham Suffk 34 G6
Hitcham Causeway Suffk 34 G6
Hitcham Street Suffk 34 G6
Hitchin Herts 32 H10
Hither Green Gt Lon 21 M8
Hittisleigh Devon 5 P2
Hive E R Yk 60 E7
Hixon Staffs 40 D3
Hoaden Kent 23 N10
Hoar Cross Staffs 40 F3
Hoarwithy Herefs 28 G3
Hoath Kent 23 M9
Hobarris Shrops 38 F6
Hobkirk Border 80 D11
Hobson Dur 73 L9
Hoby Leics 41 P4
Hockering Norfk 44 H7
Hockerton Notts 51 Q9
Hockley Essex 22 G5
Hockley Heath Solhll 40 F11
Hockliffe C Beds 32 D10
Hockwold cum Wilton
    Norfk 44 C11
Hockworthy Devon 16 D11
Hoddesdon Herts 21 M2
Hoddlesden Bl w D 57 N4
Hoddom Cross D & G 71 J2
Hoddom Mains D & G 71 J2
Hodgeston Pembks 24 H8
Hodnet Shrops 49 L9
Hodsock Notts 51 N4
Hodsoll Street Kent 22 D10
Hodson Swindn 18 H5
Hodthorpe Derbys 51 M5
Hoe Norfk 44 G6
Hogben's Hill Kent 23 K11
Hoggeston Bucks 32 B10
Hoggrill's End Warwks 40 G8
Hoghton Lancs 57 L4
Hognaston Derbys 50 G10
Hogsthorpe Lincs 53 N8
Holbeach Lincs 43 K5
Holbeach Bank Lincs 43 K5
Holbeach Clough Lincs 43 K5
Holbeach Drove Lincs 43 L6
Holbeach Hurn Lincs 43 L5
Holbeach St Johns Lincs 43 K6
Holbeach St Mark's Lincs 43 L4
Holbeach St Matthew
    Lincs 43 L4
Holbeck Notts 51 M6
Holberrow Green Worcs 30 D3
Holbeton Devon 5 M9
Holborn Gt Lon 21 L7
Holbrook Derbys 51 J11
Holbrook Suffk 35 J9
Holbrooks Covtry 41 J10
Holbury Hants 9 M6
Holcombe Devon 6 C7
Holcombe Somset 17 P6
Holcombe Rogus Devon 16 E11
Holcot Nhants 32 B3
Holden Lancs 63 P11
Holdenby Nhants 31 P1
Holder's Green Essex 33 Q10
Holdgate Shrops 39 K4
Holdingham Lincs 42 F1
Holditch Dorset 7 J3
Holemoor Devon 14 H10
Holford Somset 16 F7
Holgate C York 59 N4
Holker Cumb 62 G6
Holkham Norfk 44 E2
Hollacombe Devon 14 G10
Holland Fen Lincs 52 H12
Holland-on-Sea Essex 35 K12
Hollandstoun Ork 111 i1
Hollee D & G 71 L2
Hollesley Suffk 35 M7
Hollicombe Torbay 6 B9
Hollingbourne Kent 22 G11
Hollingbury Br & H 11 L8
Hollington Bucks 32 C10
Hollington Derbys 50 G11
Hollington Staffs 50 D11
Hollingworth Tamesd 50 D2
Hollinsclough Staffs 50 E7
Hollins End Sheff 51 J4
Hollins Green Warrtn 57 M10
Hollinswood Wrekin 39 N1
Hollocombe Devon 15 L9
Holloway Derbys 51 J9
Holloway Gt Lon 21 L6
Hollowell Nhants 41 P11
Hollowmoor Heath
    Ches W 49 J2
Hollows D & G 79 N12
Hollybush Caerph 27 N7
Hollybush E Ayrs 76 G8
Hollybush Herefs 29 K2
Hollym E R Yk 61 N8
Holmbridge Kirk 58 E11
Holmbury St Mary
    Surrey 10 H2
Holmbush Cnwll 3 M5
Holmcroft Staffs 40 B3
Holme Cambs 42 H11
Holme Cumb 63 K6
Holme Kirk 58 E11
Holme N York 65 P10
Holme Notts 52 B10
Holme Chapel Lancs 57 Q3
Holme Hale Norfk 44 E8
Holme Lacy Herefs 28 G2
Holme Marsh Herefs 38 G10
Holme next the Sea
    Norfk 44 B2
Holme on the Wolds
    E R Yk 60 G5
Holme Pierrepont Notts 51 N11
Holmer Herefs 28 F1
Holmer Green Bucks 20 E4
Holme St Cuthbert
    Cumb 70 H6
Holmes Chapel Ches E 49 N3
Holmesfield Derbys 50 H5
Holmeswood Lancs 56 H5
Holmethorpe Surrey 21 L12
Holme upon Spalding
    Moor E R Yk 60 D6
Holmewood Derbys 51 K7

Holmfirth Kirk 58 F11
Holmhead E Ayrs 77 J7
Holmpton E R Yk 61 N9
Holmrook Cumb 62 C3
Holmsford Bridge
    Crematorium N Ayrs 76 F4
Holmside Dur 73 L10
Holne Devon 5 N6
Holnicote Somset 16 C6
Holsworthy Devon 14 F10
Holsworthy Beacon
    Devon 14 G9
Holt Dorset 8 F6
Holt Norfk 44 H3
Holt Wilts 18 C8
Holt Worcs 39 P9
Holt Wrexhm 48 H5
Holtby C York 59 P4
Holt End Worcs 40 E12
Holt Heath Worcs 39 P9
Holton Oxon 31 N11
Holton Somset 17 P10
Holton Suffk 35 N2
Holton cum Beckering
    Lincs 52 G7
Holton le Clay Lincs 53 J3
Holton le Moor Lincs 52 F4
Holton St Mary Suffk 34 H8
Holwell Dorset 7 Q1
Holwell Herts 32 G9
Holwell Leics 41 Q3
Holwell Oxon 30 G11
Holwick Dur 64 G3
Holybourne Hants 10 B2
Holyhead IoA 54 C5
Holy Island IoA 54 C5
Holy Island Nthumb 81 N5
Holy Island Nthumb 81 N6
Holymoorside Derbys 51 J7
Holyport W & M 20 E7
Holystone Nthumb 72 G1
Holytown N Lans 85 M10
Holytown
    Crematorium N Lans 85 N10
Holywell C Beds 32 E12
Holywell Cambs 33 K3
Holywell Cnwll 2 H4
Holywell Dorset 7 N2
Holywell Flints 48 E1
Holywell Green Calder 58 E9
Holywell Lake Somset 16 F11
Holywell Row Suffk 34 B2
Holywood D & G 78 F11
Holywood Village D & G 78 F11
Homer Shrops 39 L2
Homer Green Sefton 56 G8
Homersfield Suffk 45 L11
Homington Wilts 8 G3
Honeybourne Worcs 30 E5
Honeychurch Devon 15 L10
Honeystreet Wilts 18 G8
Honey Tye Suffk 34 F9
Honiley Warwks 40 G11
Honing Norfk 45 M5
Honingham Norfk 44 H7
Honington Lincs 42 D2
Honington Suffk 34 E2
Honington Warwks 30 H5
Honiton Devon 6 F3
Honley Kirk 58 F10
Honor Oak
    Crematorium Gt Lon 21 M8
Hooe C Plym 5 M9
Hooe E Susx 12 E7
Hoo Green Ches E 57 N11
Hoohill Bpool 56 G2
Hook E R Yk 60 D8
Hook Gt Lon 21 J9
Hook Hants 20 B11
Hook Pembks 24 G6
Hook Wilts 18 F4
Hooke Dorset 7 M3
Hook Green Kent 12 D3
Hook Norton Oxon 31 J7
Hookway Devon 15 P11
Hooley Surrey 21 L11
Hoo St Werburgh
    Medway 22 F8
Hooton Levitt Rothm 51 M3
Hooton Pagnell Donc 59 L11
Hooton Roberts Rothm 51 L2
Hope Derbys 50 F4
Hope Devon 5 N11
Hope Flints 48 G4
Hope Staffs 50 E9
Hope Bagot Shrops 39 L7
Hope Bowdler Shrops 39 J4
Hopehouse Border 79 L5
Hopeman Moray 100 H2
Hope Mansell Herefs 28 H5
Hopesay Shrops 38 H5
Hope under Dinmore
    Herefs 39 K10
Hopgrove C York 59 N3
Hopperton N York 59 K3
Hopstone Shrops 39 P4
Hopton Derbys 50 H9
Hopton Shrops 40 C3
Hopton Staffs 40 C3
Hopton Cangeford
    Shrops 39 K6
Hopton Castle Shrops 38 G6
Hoptonheath Shrops 38 H6
Hopton on Sea Norfk 45 Q9
Hopton Wafers Shrops 39 M6
Hopwas Staffs 40 F6
Hopwood Worcs 40 D11
Hopwood Park
    Services Worcs 40 D11
Horam E Susx 12 C6
Horbling Lincs 42 G3
Horbury Wakefd 58 H9
Horden Dur 73 Q11
Hordle Hants 9 J8
Hordley Shrops 48 H8
Horfield Bristl 17 N2
Horham Suffk 35 K3
Horkesley Heath Essex 34 G10
Horkstow N Linc 60 G9
Horley Oxon 31 K5
Horley Surrey 11 L2
Hornblotton Green
    Somset 17 N9
Hornby Lancs 63 L8
Hornby N York 65 L8
Hornby N York 65 P6
Horncastle Lincs 53 J9
Hornchurch Gt Lon 21 Q6
Horncliffe Nthumb 81 K4
Horndean Border 81 J4

Horndean – Keir Mill 175

Horndean Hants 10 B7
Horndon Devon 5 L4
Horndon on the Hill Thurr 22 D6
Horne Surrey 11 M2
Horner Somset 16 B7
Horning Norfk 45 M6
Horninghold Leics 42 B10
Horninglow Staffs 40 G3
Horningsea Cambs 33 M4
Horningsham Wilts 18 B11
Horningtoft Norfk 44 F5
Horns Cross Devon 14 G7
Hornsea E R Yk 61 K5
Hornsey Gt Lon 21 L5
Hornton Oxon 31 K5
Horra Shet 111 k2
Horrabridge Devon 5 K6
Horringer Suffk 34 D4
Horrocksford Lancs 63 N12
Horsebridge Devon 5 J5
Horsebridge E Susx 12 C7
Horsebridge Hants 9 L2
Horsehay Wrekin 39 M1
Horseheath Cambs 33 P7
Horsehouse N York 65 J10
Horsell Surrey 20 F10
Horseman's Green Wrexhm 49 J7
Horsey Norfk 45 P5
Horsey Somset 17 J8
Horsford Norfk 45 K6
Horsforth Leeds 58 G6
Horsham W Susx 11 J4
Horsham Worcs 39 N9
Horsham St Faith Norfk 45 K7
Horsington Lincs 52 H9
Horsington Somset 17 Q10
Horsley Derbys 51 J11
Horsley Gloucs 29 L8
Horsley Nthumb 72 F2
Horsley Nthumb 73 J7
Horsleycross Street Essex 35 J10
Horsleyhill Border 80 C9
Horsley Woodhouse Derbys 51 K11
Horsmonden Kent 12 E2
Horspath Oxon 31 M12
Horstead Norfk 45 L6
Horsted Keynes W Susx 11 M5
Horton Bucks 32 D11
Horton Dorset 8 F6
Horton Lancs 63 Q11
Horton Nhants 32 B6
Horton S Glos 18 A4
Horton Somset 17 J12
Horton Staffs 50 C8
Horton Swans 26 C10
Horton W & M 20 G8
Horton Wilts 18 F7
Horton Wrekin 49 M11
Horton-cum-Studley Oxon 31 N10
Horton Green Ches W 49 J5
Horton-in-Ribblesdale N York 64 E12
Horton Kirby Kent 22 C9
Horwich Bolton 57 M6
Horwood Devon 15 J6
Hoscote Border 79 N6
Hose Leics 41 Q2
Hosh P & K 92 C10
Hoswick Shet 111 k5
Hotham E R Yk 60 F7
Hothfield Kent 13 J2
Hoton Leics 41 M3
Hough Ches E 49 N5
Hougham Lincs 42 C2
Hough Green Halton 57 J10
Hough-on-the-Hill Lincs 42 D2
Houghton Cambs 33 J3
Houghton Hants 9 K2
Houghton Pembks 24 H7
Houghton W Susx 10 G7
Houghton Conquest C Beds 32 F8
Houghton Green E Susx 12 H5
Houghton-le-Spring Sundld 73 N10
Houghton on the Hill Leics 41 P6
Houghton Regis C Beds 32 E11
Houghton St Giles Norfk 44 F3
Hound Green Hants 20 B10
Houndslow Border 80 E5
Houndwood Border 87 Q9
Hounslow Gt Lon 21 J8
Househill Highld 100 D4
Houses Hill Kirk 58 G10
Housieside Abers 103 J9
Houston Rens 84 G9
Houstry Highld 110 D8
Houton Ork 111 g2
Hove Br & H 11 L8
Hoveringham Notts 51 P10
Hoveton Norfk 45 M6
Hovingham N York 66 F11
How Caple Herefs 28 H3
Howden E R Yk 60 D8
Howden-le-Wear Dur 65 L2
Howe Highld 110 F4
Howe N York 65 P10
Howe Norfk 45 L9
Howe Bridge Crematorium Wigan 57 M8
Howe Green Essex 22 E3
Howegreen Essex 22 G3
Howell Lincs 42 G2
Howe of Teuchar Abers 102 G6
Howes D & G 71 K3
Howe Street Essex 22 E1
Howe Street Essex 34 B9
Howey Powys 38 C9
Howgate Cumb 70 G10
Howgate Mdloth 86 F10
Howick Nthumb 81 Q10
Howlett End Essex 33 P9
Howley Somset 6 H2
How Mill Cumb 71 Q4
Howmore W Isls 111 a5
Hownam Border 80 G9
Howsham N Linc 52 E3
Howsham N York 60 C2
Howtel Nthumb 81 J7
How Wood Herts 21 J3
Howwood Rens 84 G10
Hoxa Ork 111 h3
Hoxne Suffk 35 K2
Hoy Ork 111 g3
Hoylake Wirral 56 E10
Hoyland Barns 51 J1
Hoylandswaine Barns 58 H12
Hubberston Pembks 24 F7
Huby N York 58 H5
Huby N York 59 M2
Hucclecote Gloucs 29 M5
Hucking Kent 22 G10
Hucknall Notts 51 M10
Huddersfield Kirk 58 F10
Huddersfield Crematorium Kirk 58 F9
Huddington Worcs 30 C3
Hudswell N York 65 K7
Huggate E R Yk 60 F3
Hughenden Valley Bucks 20 D4
Hughley Shrops 39 K3
Hugh Town IoS 2 c2
Huish Devon 15 J9
Huish Wilts 18 G7
Huish Champflower Somset 16 E9
Huish Episcopi Somset 17 L10
Hùisinis W Isls 111 b3
Huisinish W Isls 111 b3
Hulcott Bucks 32 C12
Hulham Devon 6 D6
Hulland Derbys 50 G10
Hulland Ward Derbys 50 G10
Hullavington Wilts 18 D4
Hullbridge Essex 22 F4
Hull, Kingston upon C KuH 61 J8
Hulme Manch 57 Q9
Hulme Staffs 50 C10
Hulme Warrtn 57 L9
Hulme End Staffs 50 E8
Hulme Walfield Ches E 49 Q3
Hulverstone IoW 9 L9
Hulver Street Suffk 45 P11
Humber Bridge N Linc 60 H8
Humberside Airport N Linc 61 J11
Humberston NE Lin 53 K3
Humberstone C Leic 41 N6
Humbie E Loth 87 J9
Humbleton E R Yk 61 L7
Humby Lincs 42 E4
Hume Border 80 F6
Humshaugh Nthumb 72 G6
Huna Highld 110 G2
Huncote Leics 41 M7
Hundalee Border 80 E9
Hunderthwaite Dur 64 H4
Hundleby Lincs 53 L9
Hundleton Pembks 24 G8
Hundon Suffk 34 C7
Hundred House Powys 38 C10
Hungarton Leics 41 P6
Hungerford Somset 16 E7
Hungerford W Berk 19 K7
Hungerford Newtown W Berk 19 L6
Hungerstone Herefs 28 E2
Hunmanby N York 67 N11
Hunningham Warwks 31 J1
Hunsbury Hill Nhants 31 Q3
Hunsdon Herts 21 N1
Hunsingore N York 59 K4
Hunslet Leeds 58 H7
Hunsonby Cumb 64 B1
Hunstanton Norfk 43 Q3
Hunstanworth Dur 72 G10
Hunsterson Ches E 49 M6
Hunston Suffk 34 F3
Hunston W Susx 10 D9
Hunstrete BaNES 17 P4
Hunsworth Kirk 58 F8
Hunter's Quay Ag & B 84 C7
Huntham Somset 17 J10
Hunthill Lodge Angus 94 H7
Huntingdon Cambs 33 J3
Huntingfield Suffk 35 M2
Huntington C York 59 N3
Huntington Ches W 48 H3
Huntington E Loth 87 J7
Huntington Herefs 38 F10
Huntington Staffs 40 C5
Huntingtowerfield P & K 92 G9
Huntley Gloucs 29 J5
Huntly Abers 102 C7
Hunton Kent 22 E12
Hunton N York 65 L8
Huntscott Somset 16 C7
Huntsham Devon 16 D11
Huntshaw Devon 15 J7
Huntspill Somset 17 J7
Huntstile Somset 16 H9
Huntworth Somset 17 J8
Hunwick Dur 65 L2
Hunworth Norfk 44 H3
Hurdcott Wilts 8 H1
Hurdsfield Ches E 50 B6
Hurley W & M 20 D6
Hurley Warwks 40 G8
Hurley Common Warwks 40 G7
Hurlford E Ayrs 76 H4
Hurn Dorset 8 G7
Hursley Hants 9 M3
Hurst Wokham 20 C8
Hurstbourne Priors Hants 19 M10
Hurstbourne Tarrant Hants 19 L9
Hurst Green E Susx 12 E5
Hurst Green Essex 34 H12
Hurst Green Lancs 57 M2
Hurst Green Surrey 21 N12
Hurst Hill Dudley 40 B8
Hurstpierpoint W Susx 11 L6
Hurstwood Lancs 57 Q3
Hurtiso Ork 111 h2
Hurworth-on-Tees Darltn 65 N5
Hurworth Place Darltn 65 N5
Husbands Bosworth Leics 41 N10
Husborne Crawley C Beds 32 D9
Husthwaite N York 66 D11
Hutcliffe Wood Crematorium Sheff 51 J4
Huthwaite Notts 51 L8
Huttoft Lincs 53 N8
Hutton Border 81 J4
Hutton E R Yk 60 H4
Hutton Essex 22 D4
Hutton Lancs 57 J4
Hutton N Som 17 J4
Hutton Buscel N York 67 L10
Hutton Conyers N York 65 N11
Hutton Cranswick E R Yk 60 H4
Hutton End Cumb 71 P7
Hutton Henry Dur 65 Q1
Hutton-le-Hole N York 66 G9
Hutton Lowcross R & Cl 66 E5
Hutton Magna Dur 65 K5
Hutton Roof Cumb 63 K6
Hutton Roof Cumb 71 M8
Hutton Rudby N York 66 C6
Hutton Sessay N York 66 C11
Hutton Wandesley N York 59 L4
Huxham Devon 6 C4
Huxley Ches W 49 K3
Huyton Knows 57 J10
Hycemoor Cumb 62 C4
Hyde Tamesd 50 C2
Hyde Heath Bucks 20 E4
Hyde Lea Staffs 40 B4
Hylands House & Park Essex 22 D3
Hyndford Bridge S Lans 78 E1
Hynish Ag & B 88 C8
Hyssington Powys 38 F4
Hythe Essex 34 G10
Hythe Hants 9 M6
Hythe Kent 13 M3
Hythe End W & M 20 G8

I

Ibberton Dorset 8 B6
Ible Derbys 50 G9
Ibsley Hants 8 H5
Ibstock Leics 41 K5
Ibstone Bucks 20 C5
Ibthorpe Hants 19 L9
Iburndale N York 67 J6
Ibworth Hants 19 P9
Ichrachan Ag & B 90 D9
Ickburgh Norfk 44 D10
Ickenham Gt Lon 20 H6
Ickford Bucks 31 N11
Ickham Kent 23 N10
Ickleford Herts 32 H9
Icklesham E Susx 12 G6
Ickleton Cambs 33 M7
Icklingham Suffk 34 C3
Ickornshaw N York 58 C5
Ickwell Green C Beds 32 G7
Icomb Gloucs 30 G9
Idbury Oxon 30 G9
Iddesleigh Devon 15 K9
Ide Devon 6 B5
Ideford Devon 6 B7
Ide Hill Kent 21 P11
Iden E Susx 12 H5
Iden Green Kent 12 E3
Iden Green Kent 12 F4
Idle C Brad 58 F6
Idless Cnwll 3 J6
Idlicote Warwks 30 H5
Idmiston Wilts 18 H12
Idole Carmth 25 P6
Idridgehay Derbys 50 H10
Idrigill Highld 104 E9
Idstone Oxon 19 J4
Iffley Oxon 31 M12
Ifield W Susx 11 K3
Ifold W Susx 10 G4
Iford Bmouth 8 G8
Iford E Susx 11 N8
Ifton Mons 28 F10
Ightfield Shrops 49 L7
Ightham Kent 22 C11
Ilam Staffs 50 F10
Ilchester Somset 17 M10
Ilderton Nthumb 81 L9
Ilford Gt Lon 21 N6
Ilford Somset 17 K11
Ilfracombe Devon 15 J3
Ilkeston Derbys 51 L11
Ilketshall St Andrew Suffk 45 N11
Ilketshall St Margaret Suffk 45 M11
Ilkley C Brad 58 E5
Illand Cnwll 4 G5
Illey Dudley 40 C10
Illogan Cnwll 2 G7
Illston on the Hill Leics 41 P7
Ilmer Bucks 20 C3
Ilmington Warwks 30 G5
Ilminster Somset 17 J12
Ilsington Devon 5 Q5
Ilston Swans 26 D10
Ilton N York 65 L11
Ilton Somset 17 J11
Imachar N Ayrs 75 N4
Immingham NE Lin 61 K10
Immingham Dock NE Lin 61 K10
Impington Cambs 33 M4
Ince Ches W 57 J12
Ince Blundell Sefton 56 G8
Ince-in-Makerfield Wigan 57 L7
Inchbae Lodge Hotel Highld 106 G8
Inchbare Angus 95 K8
Inchberry Moray 101 L4
Incheril Highld 105 Q9
Inchinnan Rens 84 H8
Inchlaggan Highld 98 B8
Inchmichael P & K 93 J9
Inchmore Highld 107 J12
Inchnacardoch Hotel Highld 98 E6
Inchnadamph Highld 108 E10
Inchture P & K 93 K9
Inchvuilt Highld 98 C2
Inchyra P & K 92 H10
Indian Queens Cnwll 3 K4
Ingatestone Essex 22 D4
Ingbirchworth Barns 58 G11
Ingestre Staffs 40 C3
Ingham Lincs 52 D6
Ingham Norfk 45 N5
Ingham Suffk 34 E3
Ingham Corner Norfk 45 N5
Ingleby Derbys 41 J3
Ingleby Arncliffe N York 66 C7
Ingleby Barwick S on T 66 C5
Ingleby Greenhow N York 66 E6
Ingleigh Green Devon 15 K10
Inglesbatch BaNES 17 Q4
Inglesham Swindn 18 H2
Ingleston D & G 70 F3
Ingleton Dur 65 L4
Ingleton N York 63 M7
Inglewhite Lancs 57 K2
Ingoe Nthumb 73 J6
Ingol Lancs 57 K3
Ingoldisthorpe Norfk 44 B4
Ingoldmells Lincs 53 N9
Ingoldsby Lincs 42 E4
Ingram Nthumb 81 L10
Ingrave Essex 22 D5
Ingrow C Brad 58 D6
Ings Cumb 63 J3
Ingst S Glos 28 G10
Ingthorpe RutInd 42 E8
Ingworth Norfk 45 K4
Inkberrow Worcs 30 D3
Inkhorn Abers 103 J7
Inkpen W Berk 19 L7
Inkstack Highld 110 F2
Innellan Ag & B 84 C8
Innerleithen Border 79 M2
Innerleven Fife 86 H3
Innermessan D & G 68 E6
Innerwick E Loth 87 N7
Innesmill Moray 101 K3
Insch Abers 102 E9
Insh Highld 99 M8
Inskip Lancs 57 J2
Instow Devon 14 H6
Intake Sheff 51 K4
Inver Abers 94 D4
Inver Highld 107 P6
Inver P & K 92 F7
Inverailort Highld 97 K12
Inveralligin Highld 105 M10
Inverallochy Abers 103 L3
Inveran Highld 107 J3
Inveraray Ag & B 84 B2
Inverarish Highld 96 G3
Inverarity Angus 93 M6
Inverarnan Stirlg 91 J11
Inverasdale Highld 105 M5
Inverbeg Ag & B 84 F4
Inverbervie Abers 95 N7
Inverboyndie Abers 102 E3
Invercreran House Hotel Ag & B 90 D7
Inverdruie Highld 99 N6
Inveresk E Loth 86 G7
Inveresragan Ag & B 90 D8
Inverey Abers 94 B4
Inverfarigaig Highld 98 G4
Inverfolla Ag & B 90 C7
Invergarry Highld 98 D8
Invergeldie P & K 91 Q10
Invergloy Highld 98 C10
Invergordon Highld 107 L8
Invergowrie P & K 93 L9
Inverguseran Highld 97 K8
Inverhadden P & K 91 P5
Inverherive Hotel Stirlg 91 K10
Inverie Highld 97 K9
Inverinan Ag & B 90 D11
Inverinate Highld 97 N5
Inverkeilor Angus 93 R6
Inverkeithing Fife 86 D5
Inverkeithny Abers 102 E6
Inverkip Inver 84 D8
Inverkirkaig Highld 108 B10
Inverlael Highld 106 C5
Inverlair Highld 98 D11
Inverliever Lodge Ag & B 83 N2
Inverlochy Ag & B 90 G10
Invermark Angus 94 G6
Invermoriston Highld 98 F5
Invernaver Highld 109 M4
Inverneill Ag & B 83 M6
Inverness Highld 107 L12
Inverness Airport Highld 107 M11
Inverness Crematorium Highld 99 J1
Invernettie Abers 103 M6
Invernoaden Ag & B 84 C4
Inveroran Hotel Ag & B 90 H7
Inverquharity Angus 93 M4
Inverquhomery Abers 103 L6
Inverroy Highld 98 C11
Inversanda Highld 90 C4
Invershiel Highld 97 N6
Invershin Highld 107 J3
Invershore Highld 110 F8
Inversnaid Hotel Stirlg 84 F2
Inverugie Abers 103 M6
Inveruglas Ag & B 84 F2
Inveruglass Highld 99 M8
Inverurie Abers 102 G10
Inwardleigh Devon 15 K11
Inworth Essex 34 E12
Iochdar W Isls 111 a5
Iona Ag & B 88 G10
Iping W Susx 10 D5
iPort Logistics Park Donc 51 N2
Ipplepen Devon 5 Q7
Ipsden Oxon 19 Q4
Ipstones Staffs 50 D10
Ipswich Suffk 35 J7
Ipswich Crematorium Suffk 35 K7
Irby Wirral 56 F11
Irby in the Marsh Lincs 53 M10
Irby upon Humber NE Lin 52 H3
Irchester Nhants 32 D4
Ireby Cumb 71 K7
Ireby Lancs 63 M7
Ireleth Cumb 62 E6
Ireshopeburn Dur 72 F12
Irlam Salfd 57 N9
Irnham Lincs 42 E5
Iron Acton S Glos 29 J11
Ironbridge Wrekin 39 M2
Ironbridge Gorge Wrekin 39 M2
Ironmacannie D & G 69 P4
Ironville Derbys 51 K9
Irstead Norfk 45 M6
Irthington Cumb 71 P4
Irthlingborough Nhants 32 D3
Irton N York 67 L10
Irvine N Ayrs 76 F4
Isauld Highld 110 A3
Isbister Shet 111 k2
Isbister Shet 111 m3
Isfield E Susx 11 N6
Isham Nhants 32 C3
Isington Hants 10 C2
Islay Ag & B 82 E7
Islay Airport Ag & B 74 D3
Isle Abbotts Somset 17 J11
Isle Brewers Somset 17 K11
Isleham Cambs 33 Q2
Isle of Dogs Gt Lon 21 M7
Isle of Grain Medway 22 G7
Isle of Lewis W Isls 111 d2
Isle of Man IoM 56 c4
Isle of Man Ronaldsway Airport IoM 56 b7
Isle of Mull Ag & B 89 M8
Isle of Purbeck Dorset 8 E10
Isle of Sheppey Kent 23 J9
Isle of Skye Highld 96 E3
Isle of Thanet Kent 23 P9
Isle of Walney Cumb 62 E8
Isle of Whithorn D & G 69 L10
Isle of Wight IoW 9 N9
Isle of Wight Crematorium IoW 9 N8
Isleornsay Highld 97 J7
Isles of Scilly IoS 2 c2
Isles of Scilly St Mary's Airport IoS 2 c2
Islesteps D & G 70 F2
Isleworth Gt Lon 21 J8
Isley Walton Leics 41 K3
Islibhig W Isls 111 b2
Islington Gt Lon 21 L6
Islington Crematorium Gt Lon 21 L5
Islip Nhants 32 E2
Islip Oxon 31 M10
Islivig W Isls 111 b2
Isombridge Wrekin 49 L11
Istead Rise Kent 22 D9
Itchen Abbas Hants 9 N2
Itchen Stoke Hants 9 P2
Itchingfield W Susx 11 J4
Itteringham Norfk 45 J4
Itton Mons 28 F9
Itton Common Mons 28 F9
Ivegill Cumb 71 N6
Iver Bucks 20 G7
Iver Heath Bucks 20 G6
Iveston Dur 73 K10
Ivinghoe Bucks 32 D12
Ivinghoe Aston Bucks 32 D12
Ivington Herefs 39 J10
Ivybridge Devon 5 M8
Ivychurch Kent 13 K5
Ivy Hatch Kent 22 C11
Iwade Kent 22 H9
Iwerne Courtney Dorset 8 C5
Iwerne Minster Dorset 8 C5
Ixworth Suffk 34 F3
Ixworth Thorpe Suffk 34 F3

J

Jack-in-the-Green Devon 6 D4
Jackton S Lans 85 K11
Jacobstow Cnwll 4 F2
Jacobstowe Devon 15 K10
Jameston Pembks 25 J8
Jamestown Highld 106 H10
Jamestown W Duns 84 G6
Janetstown Highld 110 E8
Janetstown Highld 110 G5
Jardine Hall D & G 78 H10
Jarrow S Tyne 73 N7
Jasper's Green Essex 34 C10
Jawcraig Falk 85 P7
Jaywick Essex 23 M1
Jedburgh Border 80 E9
Jeffreyston Pembks 25 J7
Jemimaville Highld 107 M8
Jerbourg Guern 6 c2
Jersey Jersey 7 b1
Jersey Airport Jersey 7 a2
Jersey Crematorium Jersey 7 b2
Jesmond N u Ty 73 M7
Jevington E Susx 12 C9
Jockey End Herts 20 G1
Johnby Cumb 71 N8
John Lennon Airport Lpool 56 H11
John o' Groats Highld 110 H2
Johnshaven Abers 95 N8
Johnston Pembks 24 G6
Johnstone D & G 79 L8
Johnstone Rens 84 G9
Johnstonebridge D & G 78 H9
Johnstown Carmth 25 P5
Johnstown Wrexhm 48 F6
Joppa C Edin 86 G7
Joppa Cerdgn 37 J7
Joppa S Ayrs 76 G7
Jordanston Pembks 24 G3
Joyden's Wood Kent 21 P8
Juniper Nthumb 72 G8
Juniper Green C Edin 86 E8
Jura Ag & B 82 G6
Jurassic Coast Devon 7 J5
Jurby IoM 56 c2

K

Kaber Cumb 64 E5
Kaimend S Lans 86 B11
Kames Ag & B 83 P8
Kames E Ayrs 77 L6
Kea Cnwll 3 J7
Keadby N Linc 60 E10
Keal Cotes Lincs 53 K10
Kearsley Bolton 57 N7
Kearsney Kent 13 P2
Kearstwick Cumb 63 L6
Kedington Suffk 34 B7
Kedleston Derbys 50 H11
Keelby Lincs 61 K11
Keele Staffs 49 P6
Keele Services Staffs 49 P6
Keelham C Brad 58 E7
Keeston Pembks 24 F5
Keevil Wilts 18 D8
Kegworth Leics 41 L3
Kehelland Cnwll 2 F7
Keig Abers 102 D10
Keighley C Brad 58 D6
Keighley Crematorium C Brad 58 D6
Keilarsbrae Clacks 85 P4
Keillour P & K 92 E9
Keiloch Abers 94 C4
Keils Ag & B 82 G8
Keinton Mandeville Somset 17 M9
Keir Mill D & G 78 E9

Keisley Cumb 64 D3
Keiss Highld 110 G4
Keith Moray 101 N5
Keithick P & K 93 J7
Keithock Angus 95 K8
Keithtown Highld 106 H10
Kelbrook Lancs 58 B5
Kelby Lincs 42 E2
Keld Highld 64 F7
Kelfield N York 59 N6
Kelham Notts 51 Q9
Kelhead D & G 71 J2
Kellamergh Lancs 56 H3
Kellas Angus 93 M8
Kellas Moray 101 J5
Kellaton Devon 5 Q11
Kelling Norfk 44 H2
Kellington N York 59 M8
Kelloe Dur 73 N12
Kelloholm D & G 77 M8
Kelly Devon 5 J4
Kelmarsh Nhants 41 Q10
Kelmscott Oxon 19 J2
Kelsale Suffk 35 N4
Kelsall Ches W 49 K2
Kelshall Herts 33 K9
Kelsick Cumb 71 K5
Kelso Border 80 G7
Kelstedge Derbys 51 J7
Kelstern Lincs 53 J5
Kelston BaNES 17 Q3
Keltneyburn P & K 92 B6
Kelton D & G 70 G2
Kelty Fife 86 D4
Kelvedon Essex 34 E11
Kelvedon Hatch Essex 22 C4
Kelynack Cnwll 2 B9
Kemback Fife 93 M11
Kemberton Shrops 39 N2
Kemble Gloucs 29 P8
Kemerton Worcs 29 N2
Kemeys Commander Mons 28 D7
Kemnay Abers 102 F11
Kempley Gloucs 29 J3
Kempley Green Gloucs 29 J3
Kempsey Worcs 39 Q11
Kempsford Gloucs 18 H2
Kempshott Hants 19 P10
Kempston Bed 32 E7
Kempton Shrops 38 G5
Kemp Town Br & H 11 M8
Kemsing Kent 22 B10
Kenardington Kent 13 J4
Kenchester Herefs 38 H12
Kencot Oxon 30 G12
Kendal Cumb 63 K4
Kenfig Brdgnd 26 H11
Kenilworth Warwks 40 H12
Kenley Gt Lon 21 L10
Kenley Shrops 39 K3
Kenmore Highld 105 L10
Kenmore P & K 92 B6
Kenn Devon 6 C5
Kenn N Som 17 K3
Kennacraig Ag & B 83 M9
Kennall Vale Cnwll 2 H8
Kennerleigh Devon 15 P10
Kennessee Green Sefton 56 H8
Kennet Clacks 85 Q5
Kennethmont Abers 102 C9
Kennett Cambs 34 B3
Kennford Devon 6 C5
Kenninghall Norfk 44 G11
Kennington Kent 13 K2
Kennington Oxon 19 N1
Kennoway Fife 86 G2
Kenny Somset 17 J11
Kenny Hill Suffk 33 Q2
Kennythorpe N York 60 D2
Kenovay Ag & B 88 C7
Kensaleyre Highld 104 F11
Kensington Gt Lon 21 K7
Kensington Palace Gt Lon 21 K7
Kensworth Common C Beds 32 E12
Kentallen Highld 90 D5
Kent and Sussex Crematorium Kent 12 C3
Kentchurch Herefs 28 E4
Kentford Suffk 34 B4
Kentisbeare Devon 6 E2
Kentisbury Devon 15 L4
Kentish Town Gt Lon 21 L6
Kentmere Cumb 63 J2
Kenton Devon 6 C6
Kenton Gt Lon 21 J6
Kenton N u Ty 73 L7
Kenton Suffk 35 K4
Kenton Bankfoot N u Ty 73 L7
Kentra Highld 89 N3
Kent's Green Gloucs 29 K4
Kent's Oak Hants 9 K3
Kenwyn Cnwll 3 J6
Keoldale Highld 108 G3
Keppoch Highld 97 M5
Kepwick N York 66 C8
Keresley Covtry 40 H10
Kerrera Ag & B 89 Q10
Kerris Cnwll 2 C9
Kerry Powys 38 D4
Kerrycroy Ag & B 84 B10
Kersall Notts 51 Q8
Kersbrook Devon 6 E6
Kersey Suffk 34 G7
Kershader W Isls 111 d2
Kerswell Devon 6 E2
Kerswell Green Worcs 39 Q11
Kesgrave Suffk 35 K7
Kessingland Suffk 45 Q11
Kestle Cnwll 3 L6
Kestle Mill Cnwll 3 K4
Keston Gt Lon 21 N9
Keswick Cumb 71 L10
Keswick Norfk 45 K8
Kettering Nhants 32 C2
Kettering Crematorium Nhants 32 C2
Ketteringham Norfk 45 J9
Kettins P & K 93 J7
Kettlebaston Suffk 34 F6
Kettlebridge Fife 86 G2
Kettlebrook Staffs 40 G6
Kettleburgh Suffk 35 L5
Kettleholm D & G 79 J12
Kettleshulme Ches E 50 C5
Kettlesing N York 58 G3
Kettlesing Bottom N York 58 G3

Kettlestone Norfk 44 F4
Kettlethorpe Lincs 52 C8
Kettletoft Ork 111 i1
Kettlewell N York 64 H11
Ketton Rutlnd 42 E8
Kew Gt Lon 21 J7
Kew Royal Botanic Gardens Gt Lon 21 J7
Kewstoke N Som 17 J4
Kexby C York 60 C4
Kexby Lincs 52 C6
Key Green Ches E 50 B7
Keyham Leics 41 P6
Keyhaven Hants 9 K8
Keyingham E R Yk 61 L8
Keymer W Susx 11 L7
Keynsham BaNES 17 P3
Keysoe Bed 32 F4
Keysoe Row Bed 32 F5
Keyston Cambs 32 F2
Keyworth Notts 41 N2
Kibblesworth Gatesd 73 M9
Kibworth Beauchamp Leics 41 P8
Kibworth Harcourt Leics 41 P8
Kidbrooke Gt Lon 21 N7
Kidderminster Worcs 39 Q6
Kidlington Oxon 31 L10
Kidmore End Oxon 20 B7
Kidsdale D & G 69 L10
Kidsgrove Staffs 49 Q5
Kidwelly Carmth 25 P7
Kiel Crofts Ag & B 90 C8
Kielder Nthumb 72 B3
Kielder Forest 72 B4
Kiells Ag & B 82 F8
Kilbarchan Rens 84 G9
Kilbeg Highld 97 J8
Kilberry Ag & B 83 K9
Kilbirnie N Ayrs 84 E11
Kilbride Ag & B 83 L7
Kilbride Ag & B 83 Q9
Kilbuiack Moray 100 G4
Kilburn Derbys 51 J10
Kilburn Gt Lon 21 K6
Kilburn N York 66 D10
Kilby Leics 41 N8
Kilchamaig Ag & B 83 M10
Kilchattan Ag & B 82 E4
Kilchattan Ag & B 84 B11
Kilcheran Ag & B 89 Q8
Kilchoan Highld 89 K4
Kilchoman Ag & B 82 C9
Kilchrenan Ag & B 90 E10
Kilconquhar Fife 87 J2
Kilcot Gloucs 29 J4
Kilcoy Highld 107 J11
Kilcreggan Ag & B 84 D6
Kildale N York 66 E5
Kildalloig Ag & B 75 L8
Kildary Highld 107 M7
Kildavaig Ag & B 83 Q9
Kildavanan Ag & B 83 Q9
Kildonan Highld 109 Q10
Kildonan N Ayrs 75 Q8
Kildonan Lodge Highld 109 Q10
Kildonnan Highld 96 F11
Kildrochet House D & G 68 E7
Kildrummy Abers 101 N10
Kildwick N York 58 D5
Kilfinan Ag & B 83 P7
Kilfinnan Highld 98 C9
Kilgetty Pembks 25 K7
Kilgrammie S Ayrs 76 E10
Kilgwrrwg Common Mons 28 F8
Kilham E R Yk 60 H2
Kilkenneth Ag & B 88 B7
Kilkenzie Ag & B 75 K7
Kilkerran Ag & B 75 L8
Kilkhampton Cnwll 14 E9
Killamarsh Derbys 51 L5
Killay Swans 26 E9
Killean Ag & B 75 J6
Killearn Stirlg 85 J6
Killen Highld 107 L10
Killerby Darltn 65 L4
Killerton Devon 6 D3
Killichonan P & K 91 M5
Killiechonate Highld 98 C11
Killiechronan Ag & B 89 L7
Killiecrankie P & K 92 D3
Killilan Highld 97 N4
Killimster Highld 110 G4
Killin Stirlg 91 N9
Killinghall N York 58 H3
Killington Cumb 63 L3
Killington Lake Services Cumb 63 L4
Killingworth N Tyne 73 M6
Killochyett Border 87 J12
Kilmacolm Inver 84 F8
Kilmahog Stirlg 85 K2
Kilmahumaig Ag & B 83 L4
Kilmaluag Highld 104 F7
Kilmany Fife 93 L10
Kilmarnock E Ayrs 76 G4
Kilmartin Ag & B 83 M3
Kilmaurs E Ayrs 76 G3
Kilmelford Ag & B 83 M1
Kilmersdon Somset 17 Q6
Kilmeston Hants 9 P3
Kilmichael Ag & B 75 K7
Kilmichael Glassary Ag & B 83 N4
Kilmichael of Inverlussa Ag & B 83 L6
Kilmington Devon 6 H4
Kilmington Wilts 18 B12
Kilmington Common Wilts 8 B1
Kilmington Street Wilts 8 B1
Kilmorack Highld 106 H12
Kilmore Ag & B 90 B10
Kilmore Highld 97 J8
Kilmory Ag & B 83 K7
Kilmory Highld 89 L3
Kilmory N Ayrs 75 P7
Kilmuir Highld 104 C11
Kilmuir Highld 104 E8
Kilmuir Highld 107 L11
Kilmuir Highld 107 M7
Kilmun Ag & B 84 C6
Kilnave Ag & B 82 D8
Kilncadzow S Lans 77 P2
Kilndown Kent 12 E3
Kilninver Ag & B 89 Q11
Kilnsea E R Yk 61 P10
Kilnsey N York 58 C1
Kilnwick E R Yk 60 G4
Kiloran Ag & B 82 E4

Kilpatrick N Ayrs 75 N7
Kilpeck Herefs 28 E3
Kilpin E R Yk 60 D8
Kilrenny Fife 87 L2
Kilsby Nhants 41 M12
Kilspindie P & K 93 J9
Kilstay D & G 68 F10
Kilsyth N Lans 85 M7
Kiltarlity Highld 98 G12
Kilton R & Cl 66 F4
Kilton Thorpe R & Cl 66 F4
Kilvaxter Highld 104 E8
Kilve Somset 16 F7
Kilvington Notts 42 B2
Kilwinning N Ayrs 76 E3
Kimberley Norfk 44 H8
Kimberley Notts 51 L11
Kimberworth Rothm 51 K3
Kimblesworth Dur 73 M10
Kimbolton Cambs 32 F4
Kimbolton Herefs 39 K9
Kimcote Leics 41 N9
Kimmeridge Dorset 8 D10
Kimpton Hants 19 J10
Kimpton Herts 32 H11
Kinbrace Highld 109 Q8
Kinbuck Stirlg 85 N3
Kincaple Fife 93 N11
Kincardine Fife 85 Q5
Kincardine Highld 107 K5
Kincardine Bridge Fife 85 Q5
Kincardine O'Neil Abers 95 K3
Kinclaven P & K 92 H7
Kincorth C Aber 95 Q2
Kincorth House Moray 100 F3
Kincraig Highld 99 M7
Kincraigie P & K 92 E6
Kindallachan P & K 92 E6
Kineararch Ag & B 75 J2
Kineton Gloucs 30 E8
Kineton Warwks 31 J4
Kinfauns P & K 92 H10
Kingarth Ag & B 84 B10
Kingcausie Abers 95 P3
Kingcoed Mons 28 E7
Kingerby Lincs 52 F5
Kingham Oxon 30 H8
Kingholm Quay D & G 70 F2
Kinghorn Fife 86 F5
Kinglassie Fife 86 E3
Kingoodie P & K 93 L9
Kingsand Cnwll 5 J9
Kingsbarns Fife 93 Q12
Kingsbridge Devon 5 P10
Kingsbridge Somset 16 D8
King's Bromley Staffs 40 E4
Kingsburgh Highld 104 E10
Kingsbury Gt Lon 21 J5
Kingsbury Warwks 40 G8
Kingsbury Episcopi Somset 17 L11
King's Caple Herefs 28 G3
Kingsclere Hants 19 N8
King's Cliffe Nhants 42 E10
Kings Clipstone Notts 51 N7
Kingscote Gloucs 29 L9
Kingscott Devon 15 J8
King's Coughton Warwks 30 E3
Kingscross N Ayrs 75 Q6
Kingsdon Somset 17 M10
Kingsdown Kent 13 Q1
Kingsdown Swindn 18 H3
Kingsdown Wilts 18 B7
Kingsdown Crematorium Swindn 18 H3
Kingseat Abers 103 J10
Kingseat Fife 86 D4
Kingsey Bucks 20 C3
Kingsfold W Susx 11 J3
Kingsford C Aber 95 P1
Kingsford E Ayrs 76 H2
Kingsgate Kent 23 Q8
Kingshall Street Suffk 34 F4
King's Heath Birm 40 E10
Kings Hill Kent 22 D11
King's Hill Wsall 40 C8
Kings House Hotel Highld 90 H5
Kingshouse Hotel Stirlg 91 N11
Kingshurst Solhll 40 F9
Kingskerswell Devon 6 B8
Kingskettle Fife 86 G1
Kingsland Herefs 39 J9
Kingsland IoA 54 C5
Kings Langley Herts 21 H3
Kingsley Ches W 49 K1
Kingsley Hants 10 C3
Kingsley Staffs 50 D10
Kingsley Green W Susx 10 E4
Kingsley Park Nhants 31 Q3
King's Lynn Norfk 43 P6
Kings Meaburn Cumb 64 B4
King's Mills Guern b2
Kingsmuir Angus 93 N6
Kingsmuir Fife 87 K1
Kingsnorth Kent 13 J3
King's Norton Birm 40 D10
King's Norton Leics 41 P7
Kings Nympton Devon 15 M8
King's Pyon Herefs 38 H11
Kings Ripton Cambs 33 J2
King's Somborne Hants 9 L2
King's Stag Dorset 7 Q1
King's Stanley Gloucs 29 L7
King's Sutton Nhants 31 L6
Kingstanding Birm 40 E8
Kingsteignton Devon 6 B8
Kingsthorne Herefs 28 F3
Kingsthorpe Nhants 31 Q2
Kingston Cambs 33 K6
Kingston Cnwll 4 H5
Kingston Devon 5 M10
Kingston Devon 7 Q2
Kingston Dorset 8 C4
Kingston Dorset 8 E10
Kingston E Loth 87 K6
Kingston IoW 9 N10
Kingston Kent 23 M12
Kingston Bagpuze Oxon 19 L2
Kingston Blount Oxon 20 B4
Kingston Deverill Wilts 18 C12
Kingstone Herefs 28 E2
Kingstone Somset 17 K12
Kingstone Staffs 40 D2
Kingston Lacy House & Gardens Dorset 8 E7
Kingston Lisle Oxon 19 K4
Kingston near Lewes E Susx 11 N8
Kingston on Soar Notts 41 L2

Kingston on Spey Moray 101 L3
Kingston Russell Dorset 7 N5
Kingston St Mary Somset 16 G9
Kingston Seymour N Som 17 K3
Kingston upon Hull C KuH 61 J8
Kingston upon Thames Gt Lon 21 J9
Kingston upon Thames Crematorium Gt Lon 21 J9
King's Walden Herts 32 G11
Kingswear Devon 6 B11
Kingswells C Aber 95 P1
Kings Weston Bristl 28 G12
Kingswinford Dudley 40 B9
Kingswood Bucks 31 P9
Kingswood Gloucs 29 K9
Kingswood S Glos 17 P2
Kingswood Somset 16 F8
Kingswood Surrey 21 L11
Kingswood Warwks 40 F12
Kingswood Common Staffs 39 Q2
Kings Worthy Hants 9 N2
Kingthorpe Lincs 52 G8
Kington Herefs 38 F10
Kington S Glos 28 H10
Kington Worcs 30 C3
Kington Langley Wilts 18 D5
Kington Magna Dorset 8 B3
Kington St Michael Wilts 18 D5
Kingussie Highld 99 L8
Kingweston Somset 17 M9
Kinharrachie Abers 103 J8
Kinharvie D & G 70 F3
Kinkell Bridge P & K 92 D11
Kinknockie Abers 103 L7
Kinleith C Edin 86 E8
Kinlet Shrops 39 N6
Kinloch Highld 96 F9
Kinloch Highld 108 G8
Kinloch Highld 109 K5
Kinloch P & K 92 H6
Kinlochard Stirlg 84 H3
Kinlochbervie Highld 108 E4
Kinlocheil Highld 90 D1
Kinlochewe Highld 105 Q9
Kinloch Hourn Highld 97 N8
Kinlochlaggan Highld 98 G10
Kinlochleven Highld 90 G4
Kinlochmoidart Highld 89 P2
Kinlochnanuagh Highld 97 K11
Kinloch Rannoch P & K 91 P5
Kinloss Moray 100 G3
Kinmel Bay Conwy 55 P5
Kinmuck Abers 102 H10
Kinmundy Abers 103 J10
Kinnabus Ag & B 74 D4
Kinnadie Abers 103 K6
Kinnaird P & K 92 E4
Kinneff Abers 95 N6
Kinnelhead D & G 78 G8
Kinnell Angus 93 Q5
Kinnerley Shrops 48 G10
Kinnersley Herefs 38 G11
Kinnersley Worcs 39 Q12
Kinnerton Powys 38 E9
Kinnesswood P & K 86 E2
Kinnordy Angus 93 L5
Kinoulton Notts 41 P2
Kinross P & K 86 D2
Kinrossie P & K 92 H8
Kinross Services P & K 86 D2
Kinsham Herefs 38 G8
Kinsham Worcs 29 N2
Kinsley Wakefd 59 K10
Kinson Bmouth 8 F7
Kintail Highld 97 P6
Kintbury W Berk 19 L7
Kintessack Moray 100 F4
Kintillo P & K 92 H11
Kinton Herefs 38 H7
Kinton Shrops 48 G10
Kintore Abers 102 G11
Kintour Ag & B 74 F3
Kintra Ag & B 74 D3
Kintra Ag & B 88 H10
Kintraw Ag & B 83 M3
Kintyre Ag & B 75 L5
Kinveachy Highld 99 N5
Kinver Staffs 39 Q5
Kippax Leeds 59 K7
Kippen Stirlg 85 L4
Kippford Gloucs 70 D5
Kipping's Cross Kent 12 D3
Kirbister Ork 111 h2
Kirby Bedon Norfk 45 L9
Kirby Bellars Leics 41 Q4
Kirby Cane Norfk 45 N10
Kirby Cross Essex 35 K11
Kirby Grindalythe N York 60 F1
Kirby Hill N York 59 K1
Kirby Hill N York 65 K6
Kirby Knowle N York 66 C9
Kirby-le-Soken Essex 35 K11
Kirby Misperton N York 66 H10
Kirby Muxloe Leics 41 M6
Kirby Underdale E R Yk 60 D3
Kirby Wiske N York 65 P9
Kirdford W Susx 10 G5
Kirk Highld 110 F4
Kirkabister Shet 111 k4
Kirkandrews D & G 69 N9
Kirkandrews upon Eden Cumb 71 M4
Kirkbampton Cumb 71 L4
Kirkbean D & G 70 F4
Kirk Bramwith Donc 59 N10
Kirkbride Cumb 71 K4
Kirkbuddo Angus 93 N7
Kirkburn Border 79 L2
Kirkburn E R Yk 60 G3
Kirkburton Kirk 58 G10
Kirkby Knows 57 J8
Kirkby Lincs 52 F5
Kirkby N York 66 D6
Kirkby Fleetham N York 65 M8
Kirkby Green Lincs 52 F11
Kirkby-in-Ashfield Notts 51 L9
Kirkby-in-Furness Cumb 62 F4
Kirkby la Thorpe Lincs 42 F2
Kirkby Lonsdale Cumb 63 L6
Kirkby Malham N York 58 B3
Kirkby Mallory Leics 41 L7
Kirkby Malzeard N York 65 M11
Kirkby Overblow N York 59 J4

Kirkby Stephen Cumb 64 E6
Kirkby Thore Cumb 64 B3
Kirkby Underwood Lincs 42 F5
Kirkby Wharf N York 59 L6
Kirkcaldy Fife 86 F4
Kirkcaldy Crematorium Fife 86 F4
Kirkcambeck Cumb 71 Q2
Kirkchrist D & G 69 P8
Kirkcolm D & G 68 D5
Kirkconnel D & G 77 M8
Kirkconnell D & G 70 F2
Kirkcowan D & G 69 J7
Kirkcudbright D & G 69 P8
Kirkdale Lpool 56 G9
Kirk Deighton N York 59 K4
Kirk Ella E R Yk 60 H8
Kirkfieldbank S Lans 77 P3
Kirkgunzeon D & G 70 E3
Kirk Hallam Derbys 51 L11
Kirkham Lancs 56 H3
Kirkham N York 60 C2
Kirkhamgate Wakefd 58 H9
Kirk Hammerton N York 59 L3
Kirkhaugh Nthumb 72 C10
Kirkheaton Kirk 58 F9
Kirkheaton Nthumb 72 H5
Kirkhill Highld 107 J12
Kirkhope S Lans 78 F7
Kirkibost Highld 96 G6
Kirkinch P & K 93 K6
Kirkinner D & G 69 K8
Kirkintilloch E Duns 85 L8
Kirk Ireton Derbys 50 H10
Kirkland Cumb 70 H11
Kirkland D & G 77 M8
Kirkland D & G 78 D10
Kirkland D & G 78 G10
Kirk Langley Derbys 50 H11
Kirkleatham R & Cl 66 E3
Kirkleatham Crematorium R & Cl 66 E3
Kirklevington S on T 66 B5
Kirkley Suffk 45 Q10
Kirklington N York 65 N10
Kirklington Notts 51 P8
Kirklinton Cumb 71 N3
Kirkliston C Edin 86 D7
Kirkmabreck D & G 69 L7
Kirkmaiden D & G 68 F10
Kirk Merrington Dur 65 M2
Kirk Michael IoM 56 c4
Kirkmichael P & K 92 F3
Kirkmichael S Ayrs 76 F9
Kirkmuirhill S Lans 77 N3
Kirknewton Nthumb 81 J8
Kirknewton W Loth 86 D8
Kirkney Abers 101 P8
Kirk of Shotts N Lans 85 P9
Kirkoswald Cumb 71 Q7
Kirkoswald S Ayrs 76 D9
Kirkpatrick D & G 78 E10
Kirkpatrick Durham D & G 70 C2
Kirkpatrick-Fleming D & G 71 L2
Kirk Sandall Donc 59 N11
Kirksanton Cumb 62 D6
Kirk Smeaton N York 59 M10
Kirkstall Leeds 58 H7
Kirkstead Lincs 52 H10
Kirkstile Abers 102 C8
Kirkstile D & G 79 M10
Kirkstyle Highld 110 G2
Kirkthorpe Wakefd 59 J9
Kirkton Abers 102 E9
Kirkton D & G 78 F11
Kirkton Fife 93 L10
Kirkton Highld 97 L4
Kirkton Highld 97 N2
Kirkton Highld 97 N2
Kirkton P & K 92 F11
Kirkton Manor Border 79 K2
Kirkton of Airlie Angus 93 K5
Kirkton of Auchterhouse Angus 93 L7
Kirkton of Barevan Highld 107 L11
Kirkton of Collace P & K 92 H8
Kirkton of Glenbuchat Abers 101 M11
Kirkton of Kingoldrum Angus 93 L5
Kirkton of Logie Buchan Abers 103 K8
Kirkton of Maryculter Abers 95 P3
Kirkton of Menmuir Angus 95 J8
Kirkton of Monikie Angus 93 N7
Kirkton of Rayne Abers 102 F8
Kirkton of Skene Abers 95 N1
Kirkton of Tealing Angus 93 M7
Kirkton of Tough Abers 102 D11
Kirktown Abers 103 K3
Kirktown Abers 103 M3
Kirktown of Alvah Abers 102 E4
Kirktown of Bourtie Abers 102 G9
Kirktown of Fetteresso Abers 95 P5
Kirktown of Mortlach Moray 101 L7
Kirktown of Slains Abers 103 L9
Kirkurd Border 86 D12
Kirkwall Ork 111 h2
Kirkwall Airport Ork 111 h2
Kirkwhelpington Nthumb 72 H4
Kirk Yetholm Border 80 H8
Kirmington Linc 61 J11
Kirmond le Mire Lincs 52 H5
Kirn Ag & B 84 C7
Kirriemuir Angus 93 L5
Kirstead Green Norfk 45 L10
Kirtlebridge D & G 71 K2
Kirtling Cambs 34 B5
Kirtling Green Cambs 34 B5
Kirtlington Oxon 31 L9
Kirtomy Highld 109 N3
Kirton Lincs 43 K3
Kirton Notts 51 P7
Kirton Suffk 35 L8
Kirtonhill W Duns 84 G7
Kirton in Lindsey N Linc 52 D4
Kirwaugh D & G 69 K8
Kishorn Highld 97 L2
Kislingbury Nhants 31 P3
Kittisford Somset 16 E10
Kitt's Green Birm 40 F9

Kittybrewster C Aber 95 Q1
Kivernoll Herefs 28 F3
Kiveton Park Rothm 51 L4
Knaith Lincs 52 B6
Knap Corner Dorset 8 B3
Knaphill Surrey 20 F10
Knapp Somset 17 J10
Knapton C York 59 M4
Knapton N York 67 J11
Knapton Norfk 45 M4
Knapwell Cambs 33 K4
Knaresborough N York 59 J3
Knarsdale Nthumb 72 C9
Knaven Abers 103 J6
Knayton N York 66 B9
Knebworth Herts 33 J11
Knedlington E R Yk 60 C8
Kneesall Notts 51 P7
Kneeton Notts 51 P10
Knelston Swans 26 C10
Knenhall Staffs 50 B12
Knightcote Warwks 31 K4
Knightley Staffs 49 P9
Knighton C Leic 41 N7
Knighton Dorset 7 N1
Knighton Powys 38 F7
Knighton Somset 16 G7
Knighton Staffs 49 N7
Knighton Staffs 49 N9
Knighton on Teme
    Worcs 39 L7
Knightwick Worcs 39 N10
Knill Herefs 38 F9
Knipoch Ag & B 90 B10
Knipton Leics 42 B4
Kniveton Derbys 50 G10
Knock Cumb 64 C3
Knock Highld 97 J7
Knock Moray 102 C5
Knock W Isls 111 d2
Knockally Highld 110 D9
Knockan Highld 106 D1
Knockando Moray 101 J7
Knockbain Highld 98 H1
Knockbain Highld 107 K10
Knock Castle N Ayrs 84 D9
Knockdee Highld 110 D4
Knockdow Ag & B 84 B8
Knockdown Wilts 18 C3
Knockeen S Ayrs 76 E11
Knockenkelly N Ayrs 75 Q7
Knockentiber E Ayrs 76 G4
Knockholt Kent 21 P10
Knockholt Pound Kent 21 P10
Knockin Shrops 48 G10
Knockinlaw E Ayrs 76 G4
Knocknain D & G 68 C6
Knockrome Ag & B 82 H8
Knocksharry IoM 56 b4
Knocksheen D & G 69 N3
Knockvennie Smithy
    D & G 70 C2
Knodishall Suffk 35 N4
Knodishall Common
    Suffk 35 P5
Knole Somset 17 L10
Knolls Green Ches E 57 P11
Knolton Wrexhm 48 H7
Knook Wilts 18 D11
Knossington Leics 42 B8
Knott End-on-Sea Lancs ...62 G11
Knotting Bed 32 E4
Knotting Green Bed 32 E4
Knottingley Wakefd 59 L9
Knotty Ash Lpool 56 H9
Knowbury Shrops 39 L7
Knowe D & G 69 J5
Knowehead D & G 69 N2
Knoweside S Ayrs 76 E8
Knowle Bristl 17 N3
Knowle Devon 6 D2
Knowle Devon 6 E6
Knowle Devon 15 J5
Knowle Devon 15 N10
Knowle Shrops 39 L7
Knowle Solhll 40 F11
Knowle Somset 16 C7
Knowlefield Cumb 71 N4
Knowle Green Lancs 57 L2
Knowle St Giles Somset 7 J1
Knowl Hill W & M 20 D7
Knowsley Knows 56 H9
Knowsley Safari Park
    Knows 57 J9
Knowstone Devon 15 P7
Knox Bridge Kent 12 F2
Knoydart Highld 97 L8
Knucklas Powys 38 F7
Knuston Nhants 32 D4
Knutsford Ches E 57 N12
Knutsford Services
    Ches E 57 N12
Krumlin Calder 58 D9
Kuggar Cnwll 2 G11
Kyleakin Highld 97 K4
Kyle of Lochalsh Highld ..97 K4
Kylerhea Highld 97 L5
Kylesku Highld 108 E8
Kylesmorar Highld 97 L10
Kyles Scalpay W Isls 111 c3
Kylestrome Highld 108 E8
Kynnersley Wrekin 49 M11
Kyrewood Worcs 39 L8

L

Lacasaigh W Isls 111 d2
Lacasdal W Isls 111 d2
Laceby NE Lin 52 H3
Lacey Green Bucks 20 D4
Lach Dennis Ches W 49 N2
Lackford Suffk 34 D3
Lackford Green Suffk 34 D3
Lacock Wilts 18 D7
Ladbroke Warwks 31 K3
Laddingford Kent 12 E1
Ladock Cnwll 3 J4
Lady Ork 111 i1
Ladybank Fife 93 K12
Ladygill S Lans 78 F4
Ladykirk Border 81 J3
Ladywood Birm 40 D9
Ladywood Worcs 39 Q9
La Fontenelle Guern 6 c1
Lag D & G 78 E10
Laga Highld 89 N4
Lagavulin Ag & B 74 F4

Lagg N Ayrs 75 P7
Laggan Highld 98 D9
Laggan Highld 99 J9
Lagganlia Highld 99 M8
La Grève de Lecq Jersey ...7 a1
Laid Highld 108 H4
Laide Highld 105 N4
Laig Highld 96 F11
Laigh Clunch E Ayrs 76 H2
Laigh Fenwick E Ayrs 76 H3
Laigh Glenmuir E Ayrs 77 K7
Laighstonehall S Lans 85 M11
Laindon Essex 22 D5
Lairg Highld 107 J2
Laisterdyke C Brad 58 F7
Lake IoW 9 P10
Lake Wilts 18 G11
Lake District Cumb 71 K12
Lake District National
    Park Cumb 71 K12
Lakenheath Suffk 44 B12
Lakesend Norfk 43 N10
Laleston Brdgnd 27 J11
Lamarsh Essex 34 E9
Lamas Norfk 45 L5
Lambden Border 80 G5
Lamberhurst Kent 12 D3
Lamberhurst Down Kent 12 D3
Lamberton Border 81 K3
Lambeth Gt Lon 21 L7
Lambeth Crematorium
    Gt Lon 21 L8
Lambfair Green Suffk 34 B6
Lambley Notts 51 N10
Lambley Nthumb 72 C8
Lambourn W Berk 19 K5
Lambourne End Essex 21 P5
Lambs Green W Susx 11 K3
Lamerton Devon 5 K5
Lamesley Gatesd 73 M8
Lamington S Lans 78 F3
Lamlash N Ayrs 75 Q6
Lamonby Cumb 71 N8
Lamorna Cnwll 2 C10
Lamorran Cnwll 3 K7
Lampeter Cerdgn 37 J10
Lampeter Velfrey
    Pembks 25 K6
Lamphey Pembks 24 H8
Lamplugh Cumb 70 H10
Lamport Nhants 41 Q11
Lamyatt Somset 17 P8
Lanark S Lans 77 P3
Lancaster Lancs 63 J9
Lancaster &
    Morecambe
    Crematorium Lancs 63 J9
Lancaster Services Lancs ..63 J10
Lanchester Dur 73 L10
Lancing W Susx 11 J8
L'Ancresse Guern 6 c1
Landbeach Cambs 33 M4
Landcross Devon 14 H7
Landerberry Abers 95 M2
Landford Wilts 9 J4
Land-hallow Highld 110 E8
Landican Crematorium
    Wirral 56 F10
Landimore Swans 26 C9
Landkey Devon 15 K6
Landore Swans 26 F9
Landrake Cnwll 4 H4
Land's End Airport Cnwll ...2 B9
Landulph Cnwll 5 J7
Lane Cnwll 3 J4
Laneast Cnwll 4 F4
Lane End Bucks 20 D5
Lane End Wilts 18 B10
Lane Ends Derbys 40 G1
Laneham Notts 52 B8
Lane Head Dur 65 K5
Lanehead Dur 72 F11
Lane Head Wsall 40 C7
Lane Side Lancs 57 P4
Langal Highld 89 P3
Langaller Somset 16 H10
Langar Notts 41 Q1
Langbank Rens 84 G8
Langbar N York 58 E4
Langcliffe N York 63 P8
Langdale End N York 67 K8
Langdown Hants 9 M6
Langdyke Fife 86 G2
Langenhoe Essex 34 G11
Langford C Beds 32 H8
Langford Devon 6 D3
Langford Essex 22 G2
Langford Notts 52 B10
Langford Oxon 30 G12
Langford Budville
    Somset 16 F10
Langham Essex 34 G9
Langham Norfk 44 G2
Langham Rutlnd 42 B7
Langham Suffk 34 F3
Langho Lancs 57 N3
Langholm D & G 79 M11
Langland Swans 26 E10
Langlee Border 80 C7
Langley Hants 9 M7
Langley Herts 32 H11
Langley Kent 22 F11
Langley Nthumb 72 E8
Langley Slough 20 G7
Langley Somset 16 E9
Langley W Susx 10 D4
Langley Warwks 30 F2
Langley Burrell Wilts 18 D6
Langley Green Essex 34 E11
Langley Marsh Somset 16 E9
Langley Park Dur 73 L11
Langley Street Norfk 45 N9
Langley Upper Green
    Essex 33 M9
Langney E Susx 12 D9
Langold Notts 51 N4
Langore Cnwll 4 G3
Langport Somset 17 K10
Langrick Lincs 43 J11
Langridge BaNES 17 Q3
Langrigg Cumb 71 J6
Langrish Hants 10 B5
Langsett Barns 50 G2
Langside P & K 92 B11
Langstone Hants 10 B8
Langthorne N York 65 M8
Langthorpe N York 59 K1
Langthwaite N York 65 J7
Langtoft E R Yk 60 H2
Langtoft Lincs 42 G7

Langton Dur 65 L4
Langton Lincs 52 H9
Langton Lincs 53 L9
Langton N York 60 D2
Langton by Wragby
    Lincs 52 G7
Langton Green Kent 12 B3
Langton Herring Dorset 7 N6
Langton Matravers
    Dorset 8 E10
Langtree Devon 14 H8
Langwathby Cumb 71 R8
Langwell House Highld ...110 D10
Langwith Derbys 51 M6
Langworth Lincs 52 F8
Lanhydrock House &
    Gardens Cnwll 3 N3
Lanivet Cnwll 3 M3
Lanlivery Cnwll 3 N4
Lanner Cnwll 2 G7
Lanreath Cnwll 4 E8
Lansallos Cnwll 4 E9
Lanteglos Cnwll 4 D4
Lanteglos Highway
    Cnwll 4 E9
Lanton Border 80 E9
Lanton Nthumb 81 K7
Lapford Devon 15 M9
Laphroaig Ag & B 74 E4
Lapley Staffs 49 Q11
Lapworth Warwks 40 F12
Larachbeg Highld 89 N6
Larbert Falk 85 P6
Largie Abers 102 D8
Largiemore Ag & B 83 P6
Largoward Fife 87 J1
Largs N Ayrs 84 D10
Largybeg N Ayrs 75 Q7
Largymore N Ayrs 75 Q7
Larkfield Inver 84 D7
Larkfield Kent 22 E10
Larkhall S Lans 77 M2
Larkhill Wilts 18 G11
Larling Norfk 44 G11
La Rocque Jersey 7 c2
Lartington Dur 64 H4
Lasham Hants 19 Q11
Lasswade Mdloth 86 G8
Lastingham N York 66 G9
Latchford Warrtn 57 L10
Latchingdon Essex 22 G4
Latchley Cnwll 5 J5
Lathbury M Keyn 32 C7
Latheron Highld 110 E8
Latheronwheel Highld 110 E8
Lathones Fife 87 J1
Latimer Bucks 20 G4
Latteridge S Glos 29 J10
Lattiford Somset 17 Q10
Latton Wilts 18 G2
Lauder Border 80 C5
Laugharne Carmth 25 M6
Laughterton Lincs 52 B8
Laughton E Susx 11 P7
Laughton Leics 41 P9
Laughton Lincs 42 F4
Laughton Lincs 52 B4
Laughton-en-le-
    Morthen Rothm 51 M4
Launcekirk Abers 95 L7
Launton Oxon 31 N9
Laurencekirk Abers 95 L7
Laurieston D & G 69 P6
Laurieston Falk 85 Q7
Lavendon M Keyn 32 D6
Lavenham Suffk 34 F7
Lavernock V Glam 16 G3
Laversdale Cumb 71 P3
Laverstock Wilts 8 H2
Laverstoke Hants 19 N10
Laverton Gloucs 30 E7
Laverton N York 65 M11
Laverton Somset 18 B9
La Villette Guern 6 b2
Lavister Wrexhm 48 G4
Law S Lans 85 N11
Lawers P & K 91 Q8
Lawford Essex 34 H9
Lawford Somset 16 F8
Law Hill S Lans 85 N11
Lawhitton Cnwll 4 H4
Lawkland N York 63 P8
Lawns Wood
    Crematorium Leeds 58 H6
Lawrenny Pembks 24 H7
Lawshall Suffk 34 E6
Laxay W Isls 111 d2
Laxdale W Isls 111 d2
Laxey IoM 56 d4
Laxfield Suffk 35 L3
Laxford Bridge Highld ...108 E6
Laxo Shet 111 k3
Laxton E R Yk 60 D8
Laxton Nhants 42 D10
Laxton Notts 51 Q7
Laycock C Brad 58 D6
Layer Breton Essex 34 F12
Layer-de-la-Haye Essex ...34 F11
Layer Marney Essex 34 F12
Layham Suffk 34 G8
Laymore Dorset 7 K2
Laytham E R Yk 60 D6
Lazonby Cumb 71 Q7
Lea Derbys 51 J8
Lea Herefs 28 H4
Lea Lincs 52 B6
Lea Shrops 38 G4
Lea Wilts 18 E4
Leachkin Highld 107 K12
Leadburn Border 86 E9
Leadenham Lincs 52 D11
Leaden Roding Essex 22 C1
Leadgate Dur 73 K9
Leadhills S Lans 78 E6
Leafield Oxon 30 H10
Leagrave Luton 32 F11
Leake Common Side Lincs ..53 L11
Lealholm N York 66 G6
Lealt Highld 104 G9
Lea Marston Warwks 40 F8
Leamington Hastings
    Warwks 31 K1
Leamington Spa Warwks 30 H2
Leap Cross E Susx 12 C7
Leasgill Cumb 63 J5
Leasingham Lincs 42 F1
Leasingthorne Dur 65 M2
Leatherhead Surrey 21 J11

Leathley N York 58 G5
Leaton Shrops 49 J10
Leaveland Kent 23 J11
Leavenheath Suffk 34 F8
Leavening N York 60 D2
Leaves Green Gt Lon 21 N10
Lebberston N York 67 M10
Le Bourg Guern 6 b2
Lechlade on Thames
    Gloucs 18 H2
Lecht Gruinart Ag & B 82 D8
Leck Lancs 63 M6
Leckbuie P & K 91 Q8
Leckford Hants 19 L12
Leckhampstead Bucks 31 Q6
Leckhampstead W Berk 19 M5
Leckhampton Gloucs 29 N5
Leckmelm Highld 106 C4
Leconfield E R Yk 60 H5
Ledaig Ag & B 90 C8
Ledburn Bucks 32 C11
Ledbury Herefs 29 J2
Ledgemoor Herefs 38 H11
Ledmore Junction
    Highld 108 E12
Ledsham Leeds 59 L8
Ledston Leeds 59 K8
Ledwell Oxon 31 K8
Lee Devon 14 H3
Lee Gt Lon 21 M8
Leebotwood Shrops 39 J3
Lee Brockhurst Shrops 49 K9
Leece Cumb 62 E8
Lee Chapel Essex 22 E6
Lee Clump Bucks 20 E3
Leeds Kent 22 G11
Leeds Leeds 58 H7
Leeds Bradford Airport
    Leeds 58 G6
Leeds Castle Kent 22 G11
Leedstown Cnwll 2 E8
Leek Staffs 50 C9
Leek Wootton Warwks 30 H1
Lee Mill Devon 5 M8
Leeming N York 65 N9
Leeming Bar N York 65 M9
Lee-on-the-Solent Hants ...9 P7
Lees Derbys 50 H12
Lees Oldham 58 C12
Lees Green Derbys 50 H12
Leesthorpe Leics 42 B7
Leeswood Flints 48 F4
Leetown P & K 93 J10
Leftwich Ches W 49 M2
Legbourne Lincs 53 L6
Legerwood Border 80 D5
Legoland W & M 20 F8
Legsby Lincs 52 G6
Leicester C Leic 41 N6
Leicester Forest East
    Services Leics 41 M7
Leigh Dorset 7 N2
Leigh Gloucs 29 M4
Leigh Kent 12 B2
Leigh Surrey 11 K1
Leigh Wigan 57 M8
Leigh Wilts 18 F3
Leigh Worcs 39 P10
Leigh Beck Essex 22 F6
Leigh Delamere Wilts 18 C5
Leigh Delamere
    Services Wilts 18 D5
Leigh Green Kent 12 H4
Leigh Knoweglass S Lans ..77 K2
Leigh-on-Sea Sthend 22 G6
Leigh Park Dorset 8 F7
Leigh Park Hants 10 B8
Leigh Sinton Worcs 39 P11
Leighswood Wsall 40 D7
Leighterton Gloucs 29 L9
Leighton Powys 38 E2
Leighton Shrops 39 L2
Leighton Bromswold
    Cambs 32 G2
Leighton Buzzard C Beds ..32 D10
Leigh upon Mendip
    Somset 17 Q6
Leigh Woods N Som 17 N2
Leinthall Earls Herefs ...39 J8
Leinthall Starkes Herefs .38 H8
Leintwardine Herefs 38 H7
Leire Leics 41 M9
Leiston Suffk 35 P4
Leith C Edin 86 F7
Leitholm Border 80 G5
Lelant Cnwll 2 E8
Lelley E R Yk 61 L7
Lempitlaw Border 80 G7
Lemreway W Isls 111 d3
Lemsford Herts 21 K2
Lenchwick Worcs 30 D5
Lendalfoot S Ayrs 68 F2
Lendrick Stirlg 85 J2
Lendrum Terrace Abers ...103 M7
Lenham Kent 22 H11
Lenham Heath Kent 22 H12
Lenie Highld 98 G4
Lennel Border 80 H6
Lennox Plunton D & G 69 N7
Lennoxtown E Duns 85 K7
Lenton C Nott 51 M11
Lenton Lincs 42 E4
Lenwade Norfk 44 H6
Lenzie E Duns 85 L8
Leochel-Cushnie Abers ...102 C12
Leominster Herefs 39 J9
Leonard Stanley Gloucs ...29 L7
Lephin Highld 104 B11
Leppington N York 60 D2
Lepton Kirk 58 G10
Lerags Ag & B 90 B10
Lerryn Cnwll 4 E8
Lerwick Shet 111 k4
Lesbury Nthumb 81 P10
Leslie Abers 102 D9
Leslie Fife 86 F2
Lesmahagow S Lans 78 D3
Lesnewth Cnwll 4 E3
Les Quartiers Guern 6 c1
Les Quennevais Jersey 7 a2
Lessingham Norfk 45 N5
Lessonhall Cumb 71 J6
Leswalt D & G 68 E6
L'Etacq Jersey 7 a1
Letchmore Heath Herts 21 J4
Letchworth Garden
    City Herts 32 H9

Letcombe Bassett Oxon 19 L4
Letcombe Regis Oxon 19 L4
Letham Angus 93 P6
Letham Border 80 F11
Letham Falk 85 P6
Letham Fife 93 K11
Letham Grange Angus 93 Q6
Lethendy P & K 92 G7
Lethenty Abers 102 D10
Lethenty Abers 102 H7
Letheringham Suffk 35 L5
Letheringsett Norfk 44 H3
Letterewe Highld 105 P7
Letterfearn Highld 97 M5
Letterfinlay Lodge
    Hotel Highld 98 C10
Lettermorar Highld 97 K10
Letters Highld 106 C3
Lettershaw S Lans 78 E5
Letterston Pembks 24 G3
Lettoch Highld 99 Q5
Lettoch Highld 100 H8
Letton Herefs 38 G11
Letty Green Herts 21 L2
Letwell Rothm 51 M4
Leuchars Fife 93 M10
Leumrabhagh W Isls 111 d3
Leurbost W Isls 111 d2
Levedale Staffs 40 B4
Leven E R Yk 61 J5
Leven Fife 86 H3
Levens Cumb 63 J5
Levens Green Herts 33 K11
Levenshulme Manch 57 Q9
Levenwick Shet 111 k5
Leverburgh W Isls 111 c4
Leverington Cambs 43 M7
Leverstock Green Herts ...20 H3
Leverton Lincs 43 L1
Le Villocq Guern 6 b1
Levington Suffk 35 K8
Levisham N York 67 J8
Lew Oxon 31 J11
Lewannick Cnwll 4 G4
Lewdown Devon 5 K3
Lewes E Susx 11 N7
Leweston Pembks 24 G4
Lewisham Gt Lon 21 M8
Lewisham
    Crematorium Gt Lon 21 N8
Lewiston Highld 98 G4
Lewistown Brdgnd 27 K10
Lewknor Oxon 20 B4
Leworthy Devon 14 H3
Lewson Street Kent 23 J10
Lewtrenchard Devon 5 K3
Lexden Essex 34 F10
Lexworthy Somset 16 H8
Leybourne Kent 22 D10
Leyburn N York 65 K9
Leygreen Herts 32 G10
Ley Hill Bucks 20 F3
Leyland Lancs 57 K4
Leylodge Abers 102 G11
Leys Abers 103 K5
Leys P & K 93 J7
Leysdown-on-Sea Kent 23 K8
Leysmill Angus 93 Q6
Leys of Cossans Angus 93 L6
Leysters Herefs 39 K8
Leyton Gt Lon 21 M6
Leytonstone Gt Lon 21 N6
Lezant Cnwll 4 H4
Lhanbryde Moray 101 K3
Libanus Powys 27 L4
Libberton S Lans 78 F3
Liberton C Edin 86 F8
Lichfield Staffs 40 E5
Lichfield & District
    Crematorium Staffs 40 F5
Lickey Worcs 40 C11
Lickey End Worcs 40 C11
Lickfold W Susx 10 E5
Liddaton Highld 89 Q4
Liddington Swindn 18 H5
Lidgate Suffk 34 C5
Lidlington C Beds 32 E8
Liff Angus 93 L8
Lifford Birm 40 D10
Lifton Devon 5 J3
Liftondown Devon 4 H3
Lighthorne Warwks 31 J3
Lighthorne Heath
    Warwks 31 J3
Lightwater Surrey 20 E10
Lightwater Valley
    Theme Park N York 65 M11
Lightwood C Stke 50 B11
Lilbourne Nhants 41 M11
Lilleshall Wrekin 49 N11
Lilley Herts 32 G10
Lilliesleaf Border 80 C8
Lillingstone Dayrell
    Bucks 31 P6
Lillingstone Lovell Bucks 31 P6
Lillington Dorset 7 P1
Lilliput Poole 8 F8
Lilstock Somset 16 F7
Limbury Luton 32 F11
Limekilnburn S Lans 77 M2
Limekilns Fife 86 C5
Limerigg Falk 85 P8
Limerstone IoW 9 M10
Lime Street Worcs 29 L3
Limington Somset 17 M10
Limmerhaugh E Ayrs 77 K6
Limpenhoe Norfk 45 N8
Limpley Stoke Wilts 18 B8
Limpsfield Surrey 21 N11
Limpsfield Chart Surrey ..21 N11
Linby Notts 51 M9
Linchmere W Susx 10 D4
Lincluden D & G 78 F12
Lincoln Lincs 52 D8
Lincoln Crematorium
    Lincs 52 E8
Lincomb Worcs 39 P8
Lindale Cumb 62 H6
Lindal in Furness Cumb ...62 F7
Lindfield W Susx 11 M5
Lindford Hants 10 D4
Lindley Kirk 58 F9
Lindores Fife 93 K11
Lindridge Worcs 39 M8
Lindsell Essex 33 Q10
Lindsey Suffk 34 G7
Lindsey Tye Suffk 34 G7
Lingdale R & Cl 66 F4
Lingen Herefs 38 G8
Lingfield Surrey 11 M2
Lingwood Norfk 45 M8

Liniclate W Isls ...111 b5
Linicro Highld ...104 E8
Linkend Worcs ...29 L3
Linkenholt Hants ...19 L8
Linkinhorne Cnwll ...4 G5
Linktown Fife ...86 F4
Linkwood Moray ...101 K3
Linley Shrops ...38 G4
Linley Green Herefs ...39 M10
Linlithgow W Loth ...86 B6
Linn Crematorium
  E Rens ...85 K10
Linsidemore Highld ...107 J3
Linslade C Beds ...32 C10
Linstead Parva Suffk ...35 M2
Linstock Cumb ...71 N4
Linthurst Worcs ...40 D11
Linthwaite Kirk ...58 E10
Lintlaw Border ...87 Q9
Lintmill Moray ...101 P3
Linton Border ...80 G8
Linton Cambs ...33 P7
Linton Derbys ...40 H4
Linton Herefs ...28 H4
Linton Kent ...22 F12
Linton Leeds ...59 K5
Linton N York ...58 C2
Linton Hill Herefs ...29 J4
Linton-on-Ouse N York ...59 L3
Linwood Lincs ...52 G6
Linwood Rens ...84 H3
Lionacleit W Isls ...111 b5
Lional W Isls ...111 e1
Liphook Hants ...10 D4
Liscard Wirral ...56 F9
Liscombe Somset ...15 P5
Liskeard Cnwll ...4 G7
Lismore Ag & B ...90 B7
Liss Hants ...10 C5
Lissett E R Yk ...61 K3
Lissington Lincs ...52 G6
Lisvane Cardif ...27 P11
Liswerry Newpt ...28 D10
Litcham Norfk ...44 E6
Litchborough Nhants ...31 N4
Litchfield Hants ...19 M9
Litherland Sefton ...56 G8
Litlington Cambs ...33 K8
Litlington E Susx ...11 Q9
Little Abington Cambs ...33 N7
Little Addington Nhants ...32 D3
Little Airies D & G ...69 K9
Little Alne Warwks ...30 F2
Little Altcar Sefton ...56 F7
Little Amwell Herts ...21 M2
Little Aston Staffs ...40 E7
Little Ayton N York ...66 D5
Little Baddow Essex ...22 F2
Little Badminton S Glos ...18 B4
Little Bampton Cumb ...71 L5
Little Bardfield Essex ...33 Q9
Little Barford Bed ...32 H5
Little Barningham Norfk ...45 J4
Little Barrington Gloucs ...30 G10
Little Barrow Ches W ...49 J2
Little Bavington Nthumb ...72 H5
Little Bedwyn Wilts ...19 K7
Little Bentley Essex ...35 J10
Little Berkhamsted
  Herts ...21 L2
Little Billing Nhants ...32 B4
Little Billington C Beds ...32 D11
Little Birch Herefs ...28 F3
Little Blakenham Suffk ...34 H7
Little Blencow Cumb ...71 P8
Little Bognor W Susx ...10 G6
Little Bollington Ches E ...57 N10
Little Bookham Surrey ...20 H11
Littleborough Notts ...52 B7
Littleborough Rochdl ...58 C10
Littlebourne Kent ...23 N11
Little Bourton Oxon ...31 L6
Little Braxted Essex ...22 G1
Little Brechin Angus ...95 J9
Littlebredy Dorset ...7 N5
Little Brickhill M Keyn ...32 C9
Little Brington Nhants ...31 P2
Little Bromley Essex ...34 H10
Little Budworth Ches W ...49 L3
Littleburn Highld ...107 K10
Little Burstead Essex ...22 D5
Littlebury Essex ...33 N8
Littlebury Green Essex ...33 M8
Little Bytham Lincs ...42 E6
Little Carlton Lincs ...53 L6
Little Casterton Rutlnd ...42 E8
Little Cawthorpe Lincs ...53 K6
Little Chalfont Bucks ...20 F4
Little Chart Kent ...12 H2
Little Chesterford Essex ...33 N8
Little Cheverell Wilts ...18 E9
Little Chishill Cambs ...33 L8
Little Clacton Essex ...35 J11
Little Clifton Cumb ...70 H9
Little Coates NE Lin ...53 J2
Little Comberton Worcs ...30 C5
Little Common E Susx ...12 E8
Little Compton Warwks ...30 H7
Little Cornard Suffk ...34 E8
Little Cowarne Herefs ...39 L11
Little Coxwell Oxon ...19 K3
Little Crakehall N York ...65 M9
Little Cressingham Norfk ...44 E9
Little Crosby Sefton ...56 G8
Little Cubley Derbys ...50 F12
Little Dalby Leics ...41 Q5
Littledean Gloucs ...29 J6
Little Dewchurch Herefs ...28 F3
Little Ditton Cambs ...33 Q5
Little Downham Cambs ...43 N12
Little Driffield E R Yk ...60 H3
Little Dunham Norfk ...44 E6
Little Dunkeld P & K ...92 F7
Little Dunmow Essex ...33 Q11
Little Durnford Wilts ...8 G1
Little Easton Essex ...33 P11
Little Eaton Derbys ...51 J11
Little Ellingham Norfk ...44 G9
Little Everdon Nhants ...31 N3
Little Eversden Cambs ...33 L6
Little Faringdon Oxon ...19 J1
Little Fencote N York ...65 M9
Little Fenton N York ...59 M7
Little Fransham Norfk ...44 E7
Little Gaddesden Herts ...20 F2
Little Glemham Suffk ...35 M5
Little Gorsley Herefs ...29 J4
Little Gransden Cambs ...33 K6
Little Green Somset ...17 Q6
Little Hadham Herts ...33 M11

Little Hale Lincs ...42 G2
Little Hallam Derbys ...51 L11
Little Hallingbury Essex ...33 N12
Littleham Devon ...6 D6
Littleham Devon ...14 H7
Littlehampton W Susx ...10 G9
Little Harrowden Nhants ...32 C3
Little Haseley Oxon ...19 Q1
Little Haven Pembks ...24 F6
Littlehaven W Susx ...11 J4
Little Hay Staffs ...40 E7
Little Haywood Staffs ...40 D3
Littlehempston Devon ...5 Q7
Little Hereford Herefs ...39 K8
Little Horkesley Essex ...34 F9
Little Hormead Herts ...33 L10
Little Horsted E Susx ...11 P6
Little Horton C Brad ...58 F7
Little Horwood Bucks ...32 B10
Little Houghton Barns ...59 K11
Little Houghton Nhants ...32 B5
Little Hucklow Derbys ...50 F5
Little Hutton N York ...66 C11
Little Irchester Nhants ...32 C4
Little Keyford Somset ...18 B10
Little Kimble Bucks ...20 D3
Little Kineton Warwks ...31 J4
Little Kingshill Bucks ...20 E4
Little Knox D & G ...70 D4
Little Langdale Cumb ...62 G2
Little Langford Wilts ...18 F12
Little Leigh Ches W ...49 L1
Little Leighs Essex ...34 C12
Little Lever Bolton ...57 N7
Little Linford M Keyn ...32 B7
Little Load Somset ...17 L10
Little London Cambs ...43 L10
Little London E Susx ...12 C6
Little London Hants ...19 L10
Little London Hants ...19 Q8
Little Longstone Derbys ...50 F6
Little Maplestead Essex ...34 D9
Little Marcle Herefs ...29 J2
Little Marlow Bucks ...20 E6
Little Massingham Norfk ...44 D5
Little Melton Norfk ...45 J8
Littlemill Abers ...94 E3
Littlemill Highld ...100 E5
Little Mill Mons ...28 C8
Little Milton Oxon ...19 Q1
Little Missenden Bucks ...20 E4
Littlemore Oxon ...31 M12
Little Musgrave Cumb ...64 D5
Little Ness Shrops ...48 H10
Little Newcastle Pembks ...24 G3
Little Newsham Dur ...65 K4
Little Norton Somset ...17 L11
Little Oakley Essex ...35 K10
Little Oakley Nhants ...42 C11
Little Orton Cumb ...71 M5
Littleover C Derb ...41 J1
Little Packington
  Warwks ...40 G9
Little Paxton Cambs ...32 H4
Little Petherick Cnwll ...3 K2
Little Plumstead Norfk ...45 M7
Little Ponton Lincs ...42 D4
Littleport Cambs ...43 P11
Little Preston Nhants ...31 N4
Little Raveley Cambs ...33 J2
Little Reedness E R Yk ...60 D9
Little Ribston N York ...59 J4
Little Rissington Gloucs ...30 F9
Little Rollright Oxon ...30 H7
Little Ryburgh Norfk ...44 F5
Little Salkeld Cumb ...71 Q8
Little Sampford Essex ...33 Q9
Little Saughall Ches W ...48 G2
Little Saxham Suffk ...34 D4
Little Scatwell Highld ...106 F10
Little Shelford Cambs ...33 M6
Little Singleton Lancs ...56 G2
Little Skipwith N York ...59 P6
Little Smeaton N York ...59 M10
Little Snoring Norfk ...44 F4
Little Sodbury S Glos ...18 A4
Little Somborne Hants ...9 L2
Little Somerford Wilts ...18 E4
Little Soudley Shrops ...49 N9
Little Stainton Darltn ...65 N4
Little Stanney Ches W ...48 H1
Little Staughton Bed ...32 F4
Little Steeping Lincs ...53 M10
Little Stoke Staffs ...40 B2
Littlestone-on-Sea Kent ...13 L5
Little Stonham Suffk ...35 J5
Little Stretton Leics ...41 P7
Little Stretton Shrops ...39 J4
Little Strickland Cumb ...71 Q10
Little Stukeley Cambs ...32 H2
Little Sugnall Staffs ...49 P8
Little Swinburne
  Nthumb ...72 G5
Little Sypland D & G ...70 B5
Little Tew Oxon ...31 J8
Little Tey Essex ...34 E11
Little Thetford Cambs ...33 N2
Little Thorpe Dur ...73 Q11
Littlethorpe Leics ...41 M7
Littlethorpe N York ...59 J1
Little Thurlow Suffk ...34 B6
Little Thurrock Thurr ...22 D7
Littleton Angus ...93 L5
Littleton Ches W ...48 H3
Littleton D & G ...69 P7
Littleton Hants ...9 M2
Littleton Somset ...17 L9
Littleton Surrey ...20 H9
Littleton Drew Wilts ...18 C5
Littleton-on-Severn
  S Glos ...28 H10
Littleton Pannell Wilts ...18 E9
Little Torrington Devon ...15 J9
Littletown Dur ...73 N11
Little Town Lancs ...57 M2
Little Urswick Cumb ...62 F7
Little Wakering Essex ...22 H6
Little Walden Essex ...33 N8
Little Waldingfield Suffk ...34 F7
Little Walsingham Norfk ...44 F4
Little Waltham Essex ...22 E2
Little Weighton E R Yk ...60 G7
Little Wenlock Wrekin ...39 M2
Little Weston Somset ...17 N10
Little Whitefield IoW ...9 P9
Littlewick Green W & M ...20 D7
Little Wilbraham Cambs ...33 N5
Little Witcombe Gloucs ...29 M6
Little Witley Worcs ...39 P8
Little Wittenham Oxon ...19 P3

Little Wolford Warwks ...30 H7
Little Woodcote Gt Lon ...21 L9
Littleworth Oxon ...19 K2
Littleworth Staffs ...40 C3
Littleworth Worcs ...30 B4
Little Wymington Bed ...32 D4
Little Wymondley Herts ...32 H10
Little Wyrley Staffs ...40 D6
Little Yeldham Essex ...34 C8
Littley Green Essex ...34 B12
Litton Derbys ...50 F6
Litton N York ...64 G11
Litton Somset ...17 N5
Litton Cheney Dorset ...7 M5
Liurbost W Isls ...111 d2
Liverpool Lpool ...56 G10
Liverpool Maritime
  Mercantile City Lpool ...56 G10
Liversedge Kirk ...58 G9
Liverton Devon ...5 Q5
Liverton R & Cl ...66 G4
Livingston W Loth ...86 C8
Livingston Village
  W Loth ...86 C8
Lixwm Flints ...48 D2
Lizard Cnwll ...2 G12
Llanaelhaearn Gwynd ...46 F3
Llanafan Cerdgn ...37 L6
Llanafan-Fawr Powys ...37 Q9
Llanallgo IoA ...54 G5
Llanarmon Dyffryn
  Ceiriog Wrexhm ...48 D10
Llanarmon-yn-Ial
  Denbgs ...48 E4
Llanarth Cerdgn ...36 G8
Llanarth Mons ...28 D6
Llanarthne Carmth ...26 D5
Llanasa Flints ...56 C11
Llanbadarn Fawr Cerdgn ...37 K4
Llanbadarn Fynydd
  Powys ...38 C6
Llanbadoc Mons ...28 D8
Llanbeder Newpt ...28 D10
Llanbedr Gwynd ...47 J6
Llanbedr Powys ...27 P5
Llanbedr-Dyffryn-
  Clwyd Denbgs ...48 D4
Llanbedrgoch IoA ...54 G5
Llanbedrog Gwynd ...46 E5
Llanbedr-y-Cennin
  Conwy ...55 L7
Llanberis Gwynd ...54 H9
Llanbethery V Glam ...16 D3
Llanbister Powys ...38 C7
Llanblethian V Glam ...16 D2
Llanboidy Carmth ...25 L4
Llanbradach Caerph ...27 N10
Llanbrynmair Powys ...47 P10
Llancadle V Glam ...16 D3
Llancarfan V Glam ...16 E3
Llancloudy Herefs ...28 F5
Llandaff Cardif ...27 N12
Llandanwg Gwynd ...47 J5
Llanddaniel Fab IoA ...54 G7
Llanddarog Carmth ...26 C5
Llanddeiniol Cerdgn ...37 J6
Llanddeiniolen Gwynd ...54 G8
Llandderfel Gwynd ...47 R4
Llanddeusant Carmth ...26 F4
Llanddeusant IoA ...54 D5
Llanddew Powys ...27 M3
Llanddewi Swans ...26 B10
Llanddewi Brefi Cerdgn ...37 L9
Llanddewi Rhydderch
  Mons ...28 D6
Llanddewi Velfrey
  Pembks ...25 K5
Llanddewi Ystradenni
  Powys ...38 C8
Llanddoget Conwy ...55 L8
Llanddona IoA ...54 H5
Llanddowror Carmth ...25 M6
Llanddulas Conwy ...55 N6
Llanddwywe Gwynd ...47 J6
Llanddyfnan IoA ...54 G6
Llandefaelog-Tre'r-
  Graig Powys ...27 N3
Llandefalle Powys ...27 M2
Llandegfan IoA ...54 H6
Llandegla Denbgs ...48 E5
Llandegley Powys ...38 D9
Llandegveth Mons ...28 D9
Llandeilo Carmth ...26 E4
Llandeilo Graban Powys ...38 C12
Llandeloy Pembks ...24 F4
Llandenny Mons ...28 E7
Llandevaud Newpt ...28 E10
Llandevenny Mons ...28 E10
Llandinam Powys ...38 B5
Llandissilio Pembks ...25 K5
Llandogo Mons ...28 F7
Llandough V Glam ...16 D2
Llandough V Glam ...16 F2
Llandovery Carmth ...26 G2
Llandow V Glam ...16 C2
Llandre Carmth ...37 L11
Llandre Carmth ...37 K4
Llandre Isaf Pembks ...25 K3
Llandrillo Denbgs ...48 B7
Llandrillo-yn-Rhos
  Conwy ...55 M5
Llandrindod Wells Powys ...38 C9
Llandrinio Powys ...48 F11
Llandudno Conwy ...55 L5
Llandudno Junction
  Conwy ...55 L6
Llandulas Powys ...37 P11
Llandwrog Gwynd ...54 F9
Llandybie Carmth ...26 E6
Llandyfaelog Carmth ...25 P6
Llandyfriog Cerdgn ...36 F11
Llandygai Gwynd ...54 H7
Llandygwydd Cerdgn ...36 D11
Llandynog Denbgs ...48 E3
Llandyssil Powys ...38 E3
Llandysul Cerdgn ...36 G11
Llanedeyrn Cardif ...27 P11
Llaneglwys Powys ...27 M2
Llanegryn Gwynd ...47 K9
Llanegwad Carmth ...26 D4
Llaneilian IoA ...54 F3
Llanelian-yn-Rhôs Conwy ...55 M6
Llanelidan Denbgs ...48 D4
Llanelieu Powys ...27 P3
Llanellen Mons ...28 C6
Llanelli Carmth ...26 C8
Llanelli Crematorium
  Carmth ...26 D8
Llanelltyd Gwynd ...47 L7
Llanelwedd Powys ...38 B10
Llanenddwyn Gwynd ...47 J6

Llanengan Gwynd ...46 E6
Llanerchymedd IoA ...54 F5
Llanerfyl Powys ...38 B1
Llanfachraeth IoA ...54 D5
Llanfachreth Gwynd ...47 M6
Llanfaelog IoA ...54 D7
Llanfaelrhys Gwynd ...46 D6
Llanfaethlu IoA ...54 D4
Llanfair Gwynd ...47 J5
Llanfair Caereinion
  Powys ...38 C2
Llanfair Clydogau
  Cerdgn ...37 K9
Llanfair Dyffryn Clwyd
  Denbgs ...48 D4
Llanfairfechan Conwy ...55 K6
Llanfairpwllgwyngyll
  IoA ...54 G7
Llanfair Talhaiarn Conwy ...55 N7
Llanfair Waterdine
  Shrops ...38 E7
Llanfairynghornwy IoA ...54 D4
Llanfair-yn-Neubwll IoA ...54 D6
Llanfallteg Carmth ...25 K5
Llanfallteg West Carmth ...25 K5
Llanfarian Cerdgn ...37 J5
Llanfechain Powys ...48 E10
Llanfechell IoA ...54 E4
Llanferres Denbgs ...48 E4
Llanfihangel-ar-arth
  Carmth ...36 G11
Llanfihangel Glyn
  Myfyr Conwy ...55 P10
Llanfihangel Nant Bran
  Powys ...27 K2
Llanfihangel Rhydithon
  Powys ...38 D8
Llanfihangel Rogiet
  Mons ...28 E10
Llanfihangel-y-
  Creuddyn Cerdgn ...37 L5
Llanfihangel-yng-
  Ngwynfa Powys ...48 C11
Llanfihangel yn
  Nhowyn IoA ...54 D6
Llanfihangel-y-
  traethau Gwynd ...47 K4
Llanfilo Powys ...27 N3
Llanfoist Mons ...28 C6
Llanfor Gwynd ...47 Q4
Llanfrechfa Torfn ...28 C9
Llanfrynach Powys ...27 M4
Llanfwrog Denbgs ...48 D4
Llanfwrog IoA ...54 D5
Llanfyllin Powys ...48 D10
Llanfynydd Carmth ...26 D4
Llanfynydd Flints ...48 F4
Llanfyrnach Pembks ...25 L3
Llangadfan Powys ...48 B12
Llangadog Carmth ...26 F3
Llangadwaladr IoA ...54 E7
Llangaffo IoA ...54 F7
Llangammarch Wells
  Powys ...37 Q10
Llangan V Glam ...27 K12
Llangarron Herefs ...28 F5
Llangathen Carmth ...26 D4
Llangattock Powys ...27 P5
Llangattock Lingoed
  Mons ...28 D5
Llangedwyn Powys ...48 E10
Llangefni IoA ...54 F6
Llangeinor Brdgnd ...27 J10
Llangeitho Cerdgn ...37 K8
Llangeler Carmth ...36 F11
Llangelynin Gwynd ...47 J9
Llangendeirne Carmth ...26 B6
Llangennech Carmth ...26 D8
Llangennith Swans ...25 P9
Llangernyw Conwy ...55 N7
Llangian Gwynd ...46 E5
Llangloffan Pembks ...24 F3
Llanglydwen Carmth ...25 L4
Llangoed IoA ...54 H6
Llangollen Denbgs ...48 E7
Llangolman Pembks ...25 K4
Llangors Powys ...27 N4
Llangower Gwynd ...47 P5
Llangranog Cerdgn ...36 E9
Llangristiolus IoA ...54 F6
Llangrove Herefs ...28 F5
Llangunllo Powys ...38 E7
Llangunnor Carmth ...25 P5
Llangurig Powys ...37 P5
Llangwm Conwy ...47 Q3
Llangwm Mons ...28 E8
Llangwm Pembks ...24 H6
Llangwnnadl Gwynd ...46 D5
Llangwyryfon Cerdgn ...37 K6
Llangybi Cerdgn ...37 K9
Llangybi Gwynd ...46 G3
Llangybi Mons ...28 D9
Llangynhafal Denbgs ...48 D3
Llangynidr Powys ...27 N5
Llangynin Carmth ...25 M5
Llangynog Carmth ...25 N6
Llangynog Powys ...48 B9
Llangynwyd Brdgnd ...27 J10
Llanhamlach Powys ...27 M4
Llanharan Rhondd ...27 L11
Llanharry Rhondd ...27 L11
Llanhennock Mons ...28 D9
Llanhilleth Blae G ...27 P8
Llanidloes Powys ...37 Q4
Llaniestyn Gwynd ...46 E5
Llanigon Powys ...27 P2
Llanilar Cerdgn ...37 K5
Llanilid Rhondd ...27 K11
Llanina Cerdgn ...36 G8
Llanishen Cardif ...27 N11
Llanishen Mons ...28 F7
Llanllechid Gwynd ...55 J7
Llanllowell Mons ...28 D8
Llanllugan Powys ...38 C2
Llanllwch Carmth ...25 N5
Llanllwchaiarn Powys ...38 D4
Llanllwni Carmth ...36 H11
Llanllyfni Gwynd ...54 F10
Llanmadoc Swans ...25 Q9
Llanmaes V Glam ...16 D3
Llanmartin Newpt ...28 D10
Llanmiloe Carmth ...25 M7
Llannefydd Conwy ...55 P7
Llannon Carmth ...26 D7
Llannor Gwynd ...46 F4
Llanon Cerdgn ...36 H7
Llanover Mons ...28 C7
Llanpumsaint Carmth ...25 P3
Llanrhaeadr-ym-
  Mochnant Powys ...48 D9

Llanrhian Pembks ...24 E3
Llanrhidian Swans ...26 C9
Llanrhychwyn Conwy ...55 L8
Llanrhyddlad IoA ...54 D4
Llanrhystud Cerdgn ...37 J6
Llanrug Gwynd ...54 G8
Llanrumney Cardif ...27 P11
Llanrwst Conwy ...55 L8
Llansadurnen Carmth ...25 M6
Llansadwrn Carmth ...26 F3
Llansadwrn IoA ...54 H6
Llansaint Carmth ...25 P7
Llansamlet Swans ...26 F8
Llansanffraid Glan
  Conwy Conwy ...55 L6
Llansannan Conwy ...55 N8
Llansantffraed Powys ...27 N4
Llansantffraed-
  Cwmdeuddwr Powys ...37 Q7
Llansantffraed-in-Elvel
  Powys ...38 C10
Llansantffraid Cerdgn ...36 H7
Llansantffraid-ym-
  Mechain Powys ...48 E10
Llansawel Carmth ...26 E2
Llansilin Powys ...48 E9
Llansoy Mons ...28 E8
Llanspyddid Powys ...27 L3
Llanstadwell Pembks ...24 G7
Llansteffan Carmth ...25 N6
Llantarnam Torfn ...28 C9
Llanteg Pembks ...25 L6
Llanthewy Skirrid Mons ...28 D5
Llanthony Mons ...28 C4
Llantilio-Crossenny
  Mons ...28 D6
Llantilio Pertholey Mons ...28 C5
Llantrisant Mons ...28 D9
Llantrisant Rhondd ...27 L11
Llantrithyd V Glam ...16 E2
Llantwit Fardre Rhondd ...27 M10
Llantwit Major V Glam ...16 C3
Llanuwchllyn Gwynd ...47 P5
Llanvaches Newpt ...28 E9
Llanvair Discoed Mons ...28 E9
Llanvapley Mons ...28 D6
Llanvetherine Mons ...28 D5
Llanvihangel
  Crucorney Mons ...28 C5
Llanwddyn Powys ...48 B10
Llanweno Cerdgn ...36 H10
Llanwenarth Newpt ...28 D10
Llanwinio Carmth ...25 M4
Llanwnda Gwynd ...54 F9
Llanwnda Pembks ...24 G2
Llanwnnen Cerdgn ...37 J10
Llanwnog Powys ...38 B4
Llanwrda Carmth ...26 F3
Llanwrin Powys ...47 M9
Llanwrthwl Powys ...37 Q7
Llanwrtyd Wells Powys ...37 P10
Llanwyddelan Powys ...38 C2
Llanyblodwel Shrops ...48 E10
Llanybri Carmth ...25 N6
Llanybydder Carmth ...36 H10
Llanycefn Pembks ...25 J4
Llanychaer Pembks ...24 H2
Llanymawddwy Gwynd ...47 P7
Llanymynech Powys ...48 F10
Llanynghenedl IoA ...54 D5
Llanynys Denbgs ...48 C3
Llanyre Powys ...38 B9
Llanystumdwy Gwynd ...46 H4
Llanywern Powys ...27 M3
Llawhaden Pembks ...25 J5
Llawryglyn Powys ...37 Q3
Llay Wrexhm ...48 G4
Llechrhyd Caerph ...27 M7
Llechryd Cerdgn ...36 D11
Lledrod Cerdgn ...37 K6
Lleyn Peninsula Gwynd ...46 E4
Llithfaen Gwynd ...46 F3
Lloc Flints ...56 D12
Llowes Powys ...27 P1
Llwydcoed Rhondd ...27 L7
Llwydcoed
  Crematorium Rhondd ...27 L7
Llwydiarth Powys ...48 B11
Llwyncelyn Cerdgn ...36 G8
Llwyndafydd Cerdgn ...36 F9
Llwyngwril Gwynd ...47 J9
Llwynmawr Wrexhm ...48 E7
Llwynypia Rhondd ...27 L9
Llynclys Shrops ...48 F10
Llynfaes IoA ...54 E6
Llysfaen Conwy ...55 N6
Llyswen Powys ...27 N2
Llysworney V Glam ...16 C2
Llys-y-frân Pembks ...24 H4
Llywel Powys ...27 J3
Loan Falk ...85 Q7
Loanhead Mdloth ...86 F8
Loaningfoot D & G ...70 F4
Loans S Ayrs ...76 F5
Lobhillcross Devon ...5 K3
Lochailort Highld ...97 K12
Lochaline Highld ...89 N7
Lochans D & G ...68 E7
Locharbriggs D & G ...78 G11
Lochavich Ag & B ...90 C12
Lochawe Ag & B ...90 F10
Loch Baghasdail W Isls ...111 b6
Lochboisdale W Isls ...111 b6
Lochbuie Ag & B ...89 M10
Lochcarron Highld ...97 M2
Lochdon Ag & B ...89 P9
Lochdonhead Ag & B ...89 P9
Lochead Ag & B ...83 L7
Lochearnhead Stirlg ...91 N10
Lochee C Dund ...93 L8
Locheilside Station
  Highld ...90 D1
Lochend Highld ...98 H2
Lochfoot D & G ...70 E2
Lochgair Ag & B ...83 P5
Lochgelly Fife ...86 E4
Lochgilphead Ag & B ...83 N5
Lochgoilhead Ag & B ...84 D3
Lochieheads Fife ...93 J11
Lochill Moray ...101 K3
Lochindorb Lodge
  Highld ...100 E8
Lochinver Highld ...108 C10
Loch Lomond and The
  Trossachs National
  Park ...84 H1
Loch Loyal Lodge Highld ...109 L6
Lochluichart Highld ...106 F9

Lochmaben D & G....78 H11
Lochmaddy W Isls....111 b4
Loch nam Madadh W Isls....111 b4
Loch Ness Highld....98 G6
Lochranza N Ayrs....75 P3
Loch Sgioport W Isls....111 b5
Lochside Abers....95 M8
Lochside D & G....78 F12
Lochside Highld....107 N11
Lochskipport W Isls....111 b5
Lochslin Highld....107 N6
Lochton S Ayrs....68 H3
Lochty Angus....95 J9
Lochty Fife....87 K1
Lochuisge Highld....89 Q5
Lochwinnoch Rens....84 F10
Lochwood D & G....78 H9
Lockengate Cnwll....3 M4
Lockerbie D & G....79 J11
Lockeridge Wilts....18 G7
Lockerley Hants....9 K3
Locking N Som....17 J4
Locking Stumps Warrtn....57 M9
Lockington E R Yk....60 G5
Lockleywood Shrops....49 M9
Locksbottom Gt Lon....21 N9
Locks Heath Hants....9 N6
Lockton N York....67 J9
Loddington Leics....42 B9
Loddington Nhants....32 B2
Loddiswell Devon....5 P9
Loddon Norfk....45 M9
Lode Cambs....33 N4
Lode Heath Solhll....40 F10
Loders Dorset....7 L4
Lodge Hill
  Crematorium Birm....40 D10
Lodsworth W Susx....10 E5
Lofthouse Leeds....59 J8
Lofthouse N York....65 K11
Lofthouse Gate Wakefd....59 J8
Loftus R & Cl....66 G4
Logan E Ayrs....77 K7
Loganlea W Loth....86 B9
Loggerheads Staffs....49 N8
Logie Angus....95 L9
Logie Fife....93 M10
Logie Moray....100 F5
Logie Coldstone Abers....94 G2
Logie Newton Abers....102 E7
Logie Pert Angus....95 L8
Logierait P & K....92 E5
Logierieve Abers....103 J9
Login Carmth....25 K4
Lolworth Cambs....33 L4
Lonbain Highld....105 K10
Londesborough E R Yk....60 E5
London Gt Lon....21 M7
London Apprentice
  Cnwll....3 M6
London Colney Herts....21 J3
Londonderry N York....65 N9
London Gateway
  Services Gt Lon....21 K5
London Gatwick Airport
  W Susx....11 L2
London Heathrow
  Airport Gt Lon....20 H8
London Luton Airport
  Luton....32 G11
London Oxford Airport
  Oxon....31 L10
London Southend
  Airport Essex....22 G5
London Stansted
  Airport Essex....33 N11
Londonthorpe Lincs....42 D3
London Zoo ZSL Gt Lon....21 L6
Londubh Highld....105 M4
Lonemore Highld....105 L6
Long Ashton N Som....17 M3
Long Bank Worcs....39 N7
Long Bennington Lincs....42 B2
Longbenton N Tyne....73 M7
Longborough Gloucs....30 F8
Long Bredy Dorset....7 N5
Longbridge Birm....40 D11
Longbridge Deverill
  Wilts....18 C11
Long Buckby Nhants....31 N1
Longburton Dorset....7 P1
Long Clawson Leics....41 Q3
Longcliffe Derbys....50 G9
Longcombe Devon....5 Q8
Long Compton Staffs....49 Q10
Long Compton Warwks....30 H7
Longcot Oxon....19 J3
Long Crendon Bucks....20 B2
Long Crichel Dorset....8 E5
Longden Shrops....38 H2
Long Ditton Surrey....21 J9
Longdon Staffs....40 E5
Longdon Worcs....29 L2
Longdon Green Staffs....40 E5
Longdon upon Tern
  Wrekin....49 L11
Longdown Devon....6 B5
Longdowns Cnwll....2 H8
Long Duckmanton
  Derbys....51 K6
Long Eaton Derbys....41 L2
Longfield Kent....22 C9
Longford Covtry....41 J10
Longford Derbys....50 G12
Longford Gloucs....29 L5
Longford Shrops....49 M8
Longford Wrekin....49 N10
Longforgan P & K....93 K9
Longformacus Border....87 N10
Longframlington
  Nthumb....73 K1
Long Green Ches W....49 J2
Longham Dorset....8 F7
Longham Norfk....44 F7
Long Hanborough Oxon....31 K10
Longhaven Abers....103 M7
Longhirst Nthumb....73 L3
Longhope Gloucs....29 J5
Longhope Ork....111 g3
Longhorsley Nthumb....73 K2
Longhoughton Nthumb....81 P10
Long Itchington Warwks....31 K2
Longlane Derbys....50 G12
Long Lawford Warwks....41 L11
Longleat Safari &
  Adventure Park Wilts....18 B11
Longlevens Gloucs....29 L5
Longley P & K....93 K7
Long Load Somset....17 L10

Longmanhill Abers....102 F3
Long Marston Herts....20 E1
Long Marston N York....59 L4
Long Marston Warwks....30 F4
Longmoor Camp Hants....10 C4
Longmorn Moray....101 K4
Longmoss Ches E....50 B6
Long Newnton Gloucs....29 M9
Longnewton Border....80 D8
Long Newton E Loth....87 K8
Longnewton S on T....65 P4
Longney Gloucs....29 K6
Longniddry E Loth....87 J7
Longnor Shrops....39 J3
Longnor Staffs....50 C9
Longparish Hants....19 M10
Long Preston N York....63 Q9
Longridge Lancs....57 L2
Longridge W Loth....85 Q9
Longriggend N Lans....85 N8
Long Riston E R Yk....61 J4
Longrock Cnwll....2 D9
Longsdon Staffs....50 C9
Longside Abers....103 L6
Longstanton Cambs....33 L4
Longstock Hants....19 L12
Longstowe Cambs....33 K6
Long Stratton Norfk....45 K10
Longstreet Wilts....18 G9
Long Sutton Hants....10 B1
Long Sutton Lincs....43 L5
Long Sutton Somset....17 L10
Longthorpe C Pete....42 G9
Long Thurlow Suffk....34 G3
Longthwaite Cumb....71 N10
Longton Lancs....57 J4
Longtown Cumb....71 N2
Longtown Herefs....28 C3
Longueville Jersey....7 c2
Longville in the Dale
  Shrops....39 K4
Long Waste Wrekin....49 L11
Long Whatton Leics....41 L3
Longwick Bucks....20 C3
Long Wittenham Oxon....19 P3
Longwitton Nthumb....73 J3
Longwood D & G....70 B4
Longworth Oxon....19 L2
Longyester E Loth....87 K8
Lonmay Abers....103 L4
Lonmore Highld....104 C12
Looe Cnwll....4 F9
Loose Kent....22 F11
Loosley Row Bucks....20 D4
Lootcherbrae Abers....102 D5
Lopen Somset....17 K12
Loppington Shrops....49 J9
Lordshill C Sotn....9 L4
Lords Wood Medway....22 F10
Lornty P & K....92 H6
Loscoe Derbys....51 K10
Losgaintir W Isls....111 c3
Lossiemouth Moray....101 K2
Lostock Gralam Ches W....49 M1
Lostock Green Ches W....49 M2
Lostwithiel Cnwll....4 D8
Lothbeg Highld....107 Q1
Lothersdale N York....58 C5
Lothmore Highld....110 A12
Loudwater Bucks....20 E5
Loughborough
  Crematorium Leics....41 M4
Loughborough Leics....41 M4
Loughor Swans....26 D8
Loughton Essex....21 N4
Loughton M Keyn....32 B8
Lound Lincs....42 F6
Lound Notts....51 P4
Lound Suffk....45 Q9
Lount Leics....41 K4
Louth Lincs....53 K6
Lover Wilts....8 H4
Loversall Donc....51 M2
Loveston Pembks....25 J7
Lovington Somset....17 N9
Low Ackworth Wakefd....59 K10
Low Barbeth D & G....68 D6
Low Bentham N York....63 M8
Low Biggins Cumb....63 L6
Low Borrowbridge
  Cumb....63 L3
Low Bradfield Sheff....50 H3
Low Bradley N York....58 D5
Low Burnham N Linc....52 A3
Lowca Cumb....70 F10
Low Catton E R Yk....60 C4
Low Crosby Cumb....71 P4
Lowdham Notts....51 P10
Low Dinsdale Darltn....65 N5
Lower Aisholt Somset....16 G8
Lower Ansty Dorset....8 B6
Lower Apperley Gloucs....29 M4
Lower Ashton Devon....6 A6
Lower Assendon Oxon....20 C6
Lower Bartle Lancs....57 J3
Lower Basildon W Berk....19 Q5
Lower Beeding W Susx....11 K5
Lower Benefield Nhants....42 E11
Lower Bentley Worcs....30 C2
Lower Boddington
  Nhants....31 L4
Lower Bourne Surrey....10 D2
Lower Brailes Warwks....30 H6
Lower Breakish Highld....97 K5
Lower Broadheath
  Worcs....39 P10
Lower Broxwood Herefs....38 G10
Lower Bullingham
  Herefs....28 F2
Lower Burgate Hants....8 H4
Lower Caldecote C Beds....32 H7
Lower Chapel Powys....27 L2
Lower Chicksgrove Wilts....8 E2
Lower Chute Wilts....19 K9
Lower Clapton Gt Lon....21 M6
Lower Clent Worcs....40 B10
Lower Cumberworth
  Kirk....58 G11
Lower Darwen Bl w D....57 M4
Lower Dean Bed....32 F3
Lower Diabaig Highld....105 L9
Lower Dicker E Susx....12 B7
Lower Down Shrops....38 G5
Lower Dunsforth N York....59 K2
Lower Egleton Herefs....39 L11
Lower End M Keyn....32 D8
Lower Eythorne Kent....23 P12

Lower Failand N Som....17 M2
Lower Farringdon Hants....10 B3
Lower Feltham Gt Lon....20 H8
Lower Froyle Hants....10 C2
Lower Gabwell Devon....6 C8
Lower Gledfield Highld....107 K4
Lower Godney Somset....17 L7
Lower Gornal Dudley....40 B8
Lower Gravenhurst
  C Beds....32 G9
Lower Green Kent....12 C3
Lower Green Kent....12 D2
Lower Halliford Surrey....20 H9
Lower Halstow Kent....22 G9
Lower Hamworthy
  Poole....8 E8
Lower Hardres Kent....23 M11
Lower Hartwell Bucks....20 C2
Lower Hergest Herefs....38 F10
Lower Heyford Oxon....31 L8
Lower Heysham Lancs....62 H9
Lower Houses Kirk....58 F10
Lower Irlam Salfd....57 N9
Lower Killeyan Ag & B....74 D4
Lower Langford N Som....17 L4
Lower Largo Fife....86 H2
Lower Leigh Staffs....40 D1
Lower Loxhore Devon....15 K5
Lower Lydbrook Gloucs....28 G5
Lower Lye Herefs....38 H8
Lower Machen Newpt....27 P10
Lower Merridge Somset....16 G8
Lower Middleton
  Cheney Nhants....31 L6
Lower Moor Worcs....30 C5
Lower Morton S Glos....28 H9
Lower Nazeing Essex....21 N3
Lower Penarth V Glam....16 G3
Lower Penn Staffs....39 Q3
Lower Peover Ches E....49 N1
Lower Place Rochdl....58 B10
Lower Quinton Warwks....30 F5
Lower Raydon Suffk....34 G8
Lower Roadwater
  Somset....16 D8
Lower Seagry Wilts....18 E5
Lower Shelton C Beds....32 E8
Lower Shiplake Oxon....20 C7
Lower Shuckburgh
  Warwks....31 L2
Lower Slaughter Gloucs....30 F9
Lower Standen Kent....13 N3
Lower Stanton St
  Quintin Wilts....18 D5
Lower Stoke Medway....22 G8
Lower Stone Gloucs....29 J9
Lower Stow Bedon
  Norfk....44 F10
Lower Street Norfk....45 L3
Lower Street Suffk....35 J6
Lower Swanwick Hants....9 N5
Lower Swell Gloucs....30 F8
Lower Tean Staffs....50 D12
Lower Town Devon....5 P5
Lower Town Pembks....24 G2
Lower Upham Hants....9 N4
Lower Weare Somset....17 K5
Lower Welson Herefs....38 F11
Lower Westmancote
  Worcs....29 N2
Lower Whatley Somset....17 Q6
Lower Whitley Ches W....57 L11
Lower Wield Hants....19 Q11
Lower Willington E Susx....12 C9
Lower Withington
  Ches E....49 P2
Lower Woodford Wilts....8 G1
Lower Wraxhall Dorset....7 N3
Lowesby Leics....41 Q6
Lowestoft Suffk....45 Q10
Loweswater Cumb....71 J10
Low Fell Gatesd....73 M8
Lowfield Heath W Susx....11 L3
Low Gartachorrans Stirlg....84 H6
Low Grantley N York....65 M12
Low Ham Somset....17 L9
Low Harrogate N York....58 H3
Low Hesket Cumb....71 P6
Low Hutton N York....60 D1
Lowick Nhants....32 E1
Lowick Nthumb....81 L6
Lowick Green Cumb....62 F5
Low Lorton Cumb....71 J9
Low Marnham Notts....52 B9
Low Mill N York....66 F8
Low Moorsley Sundld....73 N10
Low Moresby Cumb....70 G10
Low Newton Cumb....62 H6
Low Row Cumb....72 B8
Low Row N York....64 H7
Low Salchrie D & G....68 D6
Low Santon N Linc....60 G10
Lowsonford Warwks....30 F1
Low Tharston Norfk....45 K10
Lowther Cumb....71 Q10
Lowthorpe E R Yk....61 J3
Lowton Somset....16 G11
Low Torry Fife....86 B5
Low Worsall N York....65 P5
Low Wray Cumb....62 G2
Loxbeare Devon....16 C11
Loxhill Surrey....10 G3
Loxhore Devon....15 K4
Loxley Warwks....30 H4
Loxton N Som....17 K5
Loxwood W Susx....10 G4
Lubenham Leics....41 P9
Luccombe Somset....16 C7
Luccombe Village IoW....9 P10
Lucker Nthumb....81 N8
Luckett Cnwll....5 J5
Lucking Street Essex....34 D9
Luckington Wilts....18 C4
Lucklawhill Fife....93 M10
Luckwell Bridge Somset....16 B8
Lucton Herefs....38 H8
Ludag W Isls....111 b6
Ludborough Lincs....53 J4
Ludbrook Devon....5 N8
Ludchurch Pembks....25 K6
Luddenden Calder....58 D8
Luddenden Foot Calder....58 D8
Luddesdown Kent....22 D9
Luddington N Linc....60 E10
Luddington Warwks....30 F4
Luddington in the
  Brook Nhants....42 F12
Ludford Lincs....52 H5
Ludford Shrops....39 K7
Ludgershall Bucks....31 P10

Ludgershall Wilts....19 J9
Ludgvan Cnwll....2 D8
Ludham Norfk....45 N6
Ludlow Shrops....39 K7
Ludney Somset....7 K1
Ludwell Wilts....8 D3
Ludworth Dur....73 P11
Luffness E Loth....87 J6
Lugar E Ayrs....77 K7
Luggate Burn E Loth....87 L7
Luggiebank N Lans....85 M8
Lugton E Ayrs....84 G11
Lugwardine Herefs....28 G1
Luib Highld....96 G4
Luing Ag & B....83 L2
Lulham Herefs....28 E1
Lullington Derbys....40 G5
Lullington Somset....18 B9
Lulsgate Bottom N Som....17 M3
Lulsley Worcs....39 N10
Lumb Calder....58 D9
Lumburn Devon....5 L7
Lumby N York....59 L7
Lumloch E Duns....85 K8
Lumphanan Abers....95 J2
Lumphinnans Fife....86 E4
Lumsden Abers....101 N10
Lunan Angus....95 L10
Lunanhead Angus....93 N5
Luncarty P & K....92 G9
Lund E R Yk....60 G5
Lund N York....59 P7
Lundie Angus....93 K8
Lundin Links Fife....86 H2
Lundin Mill Fife....86 H2
Lundy Devon....14 C3
Lunga Ag & B....83 K2
Lunna Shet....111 k3
Lunsford Kent....22 E10
Lunsford's Cross E Susx....12 E7
Lunt Sefton....56 G8
Luppitt Devon....6 F2
Lupset Wakefd....58 H9
Lupton Cumb....63 K6
Lurgashall W Susx....10 F5
Lurley Devon....16 C12
Luscombe Devon....5 Q8
Luss Ag & B....84 F4
Lussagiven Ag & B....83 J6
Lusta Highld....104 C10
Lustleigh Devon....5 Q4
Luston Herefs....39 J9
Luthermuir Abers....95 L8
Luthrie Fife....93 K10
Luton Devon....6 B7
Luton Devon....6 E3
Luton Luton....32 F11
Luton Medway....22 F9
Luton Airport Luton....32 G11
Lutterworth Leics....41 M9
Lutton Devon....5 M8
Lutton Devon....5 N7
Lutton Lincs....43 M5
Lutton Nhants....42 G11
Luxborough Somset....16 D8
Luxulyan Cnwll....3 M4
Luxulyan Valley Cnwll....3 N4
Lybster Highld....110 F7
Lydbury North Shrops....38 G5
Lydd Kent....13 K6
Lydd Airport Kent....13 K6
Lydden Kent....13 N2
Lydden Kent....23 Q9
Lyddington Rutlnd....42 C10
Lydeard St Lawrence
  Somset....16 F9
Lydford Devon....5 K3
Lydford on Fosse
  Somset....17 N9
Lydgate Calder....58 B8
Lydham Shrops....38 G4
Lydiard Millicent Wilts....18 G4
Lydiard Tregoze Swindn....18 G4
Lydiate Sefton....56 G7
Lydiate Ash Worcs....40 C11
Lydlinch Dorset....17 Q12
Lydney Gloucs....28 H7
Lydstep Pembks....25 J8
Lye Dudley....40 B10
Lye Green E Susx....11 P4
Lye Green Warwks....30 G2
Lye's Green Wilts....18 B10
Lyford Oxon....19 L2
Lymbridge Green Kent....13 L2
Lyme Regis Dorset....7 J4
Lyminge Kent....13 M2
Lymington Hants....9 K8
Lyminster W Susx....10 G8
Lymm Warrtn....57 M10
Lymm Services Warrtn....57 M11
Lympne Kent....13 L3
Lympsham Somset....17 J5
Lympstone Devon....6 D6
Lynchat Highld....99 L8
Lynch Green Norfk....45 J8
Lyndhurst Hants....9 K6
Lyndon Rutlnd....42 C8
Lyndon Green Birm....40 F9
Lyne Border....79 K1
Lyne Surrey....20 G9
Lyneal Shrops....49 J8
Lyneham Oxon....30 H9
Lyneham Wilts....18 F5
Lynemouth Nthumb....73 N3
Lyne of Skene Abers....102 G12
Lyness Ork....111 g3
Lyng Norfk....44 H6
Lyng Somset....17 J9
Lynmouth Devon....15 M3
Lynsted Kent....22 H10
Lynton Devon....15 M3
Lyon's Gate Dorset....7 P2
Lyonshall Herefs....38 G10

Macharioch Ag & B....75 L9
Machen Caerph....27 P10
Machrie N Ayrs....75 N5
Machrihanish Ag & B....75 J8
Machrins Ag & B....82 E4
Machynlleth Powys....47 M10
Machynys Carmth....26 C8
Mackworth Derbys....50 H12
Macmerry E Loth....87 J7
Madderty P & K....92 E10
Maddiston Falk....85 Q7
Madeley Staffs....49 P6
Madeley Wrekin....39 M2
Madingley Cambs....33 L5
Madley Herefs....28 E2
Madresfield Worcs....39 P11
Madron Cnwll....2 C9
Maenclochog Pembks....25 J4
Maendy V Glam....16 D2
Maentwrog Gwynd....47 L3
Maen-y-groes Cerdgn....36 F8
Maer Staffs....49 P7
Maerdy Rhondd....27 K8
Maesbrook Shrops....48 F10
Maesbury Shrops....48 F9
Maesbury Marsh Shrops....48 G9
Maesllyn Cerdgn....36 F10
Maesteg Brdgnd....27 J10
Maesybont Carmth....26 D5
Maesycwmmer Caerph....27 N9
Maggieknockater Moray....101 L6
Magham Down E Susx....12 C7
Maghull Sefton....56 G8
Magna Park Leics....41 L9
Magor Mons....28 E10
Magor Services Mons....28 E10
Maidenbower W Susx....11 L3
Maiden Bradley Wilts....18 B11
Maidencombe Torbay....6 C8
Maidenhayne Devon....6 H4
Maiden Head N Som....17 N3
Maidenhead W & M....20 E7
Maiden Newton Dorset....7 N4
Maidens S Ayrs....76 D9
Maiden's Green Br For....20 E8
Maiden Wells Pembks....24 G8
Maidford Nhants....31 N4
Maids Moreton Bucks....31 P7
Maidstone Kent....22 F11
Maidstone Services Kent....22 G11
Maidwell Nhants....41 Q11
Mail Shet....111 k4
Maindee Newpt....28 C10
Mainland Ork....111 h2
Mainland Shet....111 k4
Mainsforth Dur....65 N2
Mains of Balhall Angus....94 H8
Mains of Balnakettle
  Abers....95 K7
Mains of Dalvey Highld....100 H8
Mains of Haulkerton
  Abers....95 L7
Mains of Lesmoir Abers....101 N9
Mains of Melgunds
  Angus....93 P5
Mainsriddle D & G....70 F4
Mainstone Shrops....38 F5
Maisemore Gloucs....29 L5
Major's Green Worcs....40 E11
Malborough Devon....5 P11
Maldon Essex....22 G3
Malham N York....58 B2
Maligar Highld....104 G9
Mallaig Highld....97 J9
Mallaigvaig Highld....97 J9
Malleny Mills C Edin....86 E8
Malltraeth IoA....54 E7
Mallwyd Gwynd....47 P8
Malmesbury Wilts....18 D4
Malmsmead Devon....15 N3
Malpas Ches W....49 J6
Malpas Cnwll....3 J7
Malpas Newpt....28 C10
Maltby Rothm....51 M3
Maltby S on T....65 C5
Maltby le Marsh Lincs....53 M7
Maltman's Hill Kent....12 H2
Malton N York....66 H12
Malvern Worcs....39 P11
Malvern Hills....39 P12
Malvern Link Worcs....39 P11
Malvern Wells Worcs....29 K1
Mamble Worcs....39 M7
Mamhilad Mons....28 C7
Manaccan Cnwll....2 H10
Manafon Powys....38 C2
Manais W Isls....111 c3
Manaton Devon....5 P4
Manby Lincs....53 L6
Mancetter Warwks....40 H7
Manchester Manch....57 Q8
Manchester Airport
  Manch....57 P11
Manchester
  Crematorium Manch....57 P9
Mancot Flints....48 G3
Mandally Highld....98 D8
Manea Cambs....43 M11
Maney Birm....40 E8
Manfield N York....65 L5
Mangotsfield S Glos....17 P2
Manish W Isls....111 c3
Manley Ches W....49 J2
Manmoel Caerph....27 P7
Mannal Ag & B....88 C8
Manningford Bohune
  Wilts....18 G8
Manningford Bruce Wilts....18 G8
Manningham C Brad....58 F7
Mannings Heath W Susx....11 K4
Mannington Dorset....8 F6
Manningtree Essex....34 H9
Mannofield C Aber....95 Q2
Manorbier Pembks....25 J8
Manorbier Newton
  Pembks....24 H8
Manorhill Border....80 F7
Manorowen Pembks....24 G2
Manor Park Gt Lon....21 N6
Manor Park
  Crematorium Gt Lon....21 N6
Mansell Gamage Herefs....38 H12
Mansell Lacy Herefs....38 H11
Mansfield E Ayrs....77 K8
Mansfield Notts....51 M8
Mansfield & District
  Crematorium Notts....51 M8
Mansfield Woodhouse
  Notts....51 M7
Manston Dorset....8 B4

M

Mabe Burnthouse Cnwll....2 H8
Mablethorpe Lincs....53 N6
Macclesfield Ches E....50 B6
Macclesfield
  Crematorium Ches E....50 B6
Macduff Abers....102 F3

Manston Kent....23 Q9
Manston Leeds....59 J7
Manswood Dorset....8 E6
Manthorpe Lincs....42 F7
Manton N Linc....52 D3
Manton Rutlnd....42 C8
Manton Wilts....18 H7
Manuden Essex....33 M10
Maperton Somset....17 P10
Maplebeck Notts....51 P8
Mapledurham Oxon....19 R5
Mapledurwell Hants....20 B12
Maplehurst W Susx....11 J5
Maplescombe Kent....22 C9
Mapleton Derbys....50 F10
Mapperley Derbys....51 K11
Mapperley Park C Nott....51 M11
Mapperton Dorset....7 M3
Mappleborough Green
Warwks....30 E2
Mappleton E R Yk....61 L5
Mapplewell Barns....59 J11
Mappowder Dorset....7 Q2
Marazion Cnwll....2 D9
Marbury Ches E....49 K6
March Cambs....43 L10
March S Lans....78 G6
Marcham Oxon....19 M2
Marchamley Shrops....49 L9
Marchington Staffs....40 F2
Marchros Gwynd....46 E6
Marchwiel Wrexhm....48 G6
Marchwood Hants....9 L5
Marcross V Glam....16 C3
Marden Herefs....39 K11
Marden Kent....12 E2
Marden Wilts....18 G8
Marden Thorn Kent....12 F2
Mardy Mons....28 C5
Mareham le Fen Lincs....53 J10
Mareham on the Hill
Lincs....53 J9
Marehill W Susx....10 G6
Maresfield E Susx....11 P5
Marfleet C KuH....61 K8
Marford Wrexhm....48 G4
Margam Neath....26 G10
Margam Crematorium
Neath....26 H10
Margaret Marsh Dorset....8 B4
Margaretting Essex....22 D3
Margaretting Tye Essex....22 D4
Margate Kent....23 Q8
Margnaheglish N Ayrs....75 Q6
Margrie D & G....69 N8
Margrove Park R & Cl....66 F4
Marham Norfk....44 B7
Marhamchurch Cnwll....14 D10
Marholm C Pete....42 G9
Mariansleigh Devon....15 M7
Marine Town Kent....22 H8
Marionburgh Abers....95 L1
Marishader Highld....104 G9
Maristow Devon....5 K7
Marjoriebanks D & G....78 H11
Mark Somset....17 K6
Markbeech Kent....11 P2
Markby Lincs....53 M7
Mark Cross E Susx....12 C4
Markeaton
Crematorium C Derb....51 J12
Market Bosworth Leics....41 K6
Market Deeping Lincs....42 G8
Market Drayton Shrops....49 M8
Market Harborough
Leics....41 Q9
Market Lavington Wilts....18 E9
Market Overton Rutlnd....42 C6
Market Rasen Lincs....52 G5
Market Stainton Lincs....52 H7
Market Warsop Notts....51 M7
Market Weighton E R Yk....60 F6
Market Weston Suffk....34 G2
Markfield Leics....41 L5
Markham Caerph....27 N8
Markham Moor Notts....51 Q6
Markinch Fife....86 G2
Markington N York....58 H2
Markle E Loth....87 L6
Marksbury BaNES....17 P4
Marks Tey Essex....34 E11
Markyate Herts....32 F12
Marlborough Wilts....18 H7
Marlcliff Warwks....30 E4
Marldon Devon....6 B9
Marlesford Suffk....35 M5
Marlingford Norfk....45 J8
Marloes Pembks....24 E7
Marlow Bucks....20 D6
Marlow Bottom Bucks....20 D6
Marlpit Hill Kent....11 N1
Marnhull Dorset....8 B4
Marple Stockp....50 C3
Marr Donc....59 L12
Marrick N York....65 J7
Marsden Kirk....58 D10
Marsden S Tyne....73 P7
Marshalswick Herts....21 J2
Marsham Norfk....45 K5
Marsh Baldon Oxon....19 P2
Marshborough Kent....23 P11
Marshbrook Shrops....38 H4
Marshchapel Lincs....53 K4
Marsh Farm Luton....32 F10
Marshfield Newpt....28 B11
Marshfield S Glos....18 B6
Marshgate Cnwll....4 E2
Marsh Gibbon Bucks....31 N9
Marsh Green Devon....6 E4
Marsh Green Kent....11 N2
Marshland St James
Norfk....43 N8
Marsh Lane Derbys....51 K5
Marsh Street Somset....16 D7
Marshwood Dorset....7 J3
Marske N York....65 K7
Marske-by-the-Sea
R & Cl....66 E3
Marston Herefs....38 G10
Marston Lincs....42 C2
Marston Oxon....31 M11
Marston Staffs....40 B3
Marston Wilts....18 E9
Marston Green Solhll....40 F9
Marston Magna Somset....17 N10
Marston Meysey Wilts....18 G2
Marston Montgomery
Derbys....50 F12
Marston Moretaine
C Beds....32 E8

Marston on Dove Derbys....40 G2
Marston St Lawrence
Nhants....31 M6
Marston Trussell Nhants....41 P9
Marstow Herefs....28 G5
Marsworth Bucks....20 E1
Marten Wilts....19 K8
Martham Norfk....45 P6
Martin Hants....8 F4
Martin Kent....13 Q1
Martin Lincs....52 G10
Martinhoe Devon....15 L3
Martin Hussingtree
Worcs....39 Q9
Martinstown Dorset....7 P5
Martlesham Suffk....35 L7
Martlesham Heath Suffk....35 L7
Martletwy Pembks....24 H6
Martley Worcs....39 N9
Martock Somset....17 L11
Marton Ches E....49 Q2
Marton E R Yk....61 K6
Marton Lincs....52 B7
Marton Middsb....66 D4
Marton N York....59 K2
Marton N York....66 G10
Marton Shrops....38 F2
Marton Warwks....31 K1
Marton-le-Moor N York....65 P12
Martyr Worthy Hants....9 N1
Marwell Wildlife Hants....9 N3
Marwick Ork....111 g2
Marwood Devon....15 J5
Marybank Highld....106 H10
Maryburgh Highld....107 J10
Marygold Border....87 P9
Maryhill C Glas....85 J8
Maryhill Crematorium
C Glas....85 J8
Marykirk Abers....95 L8
Marylebone Gt Lon....21 L7
Marylebone Wigan....57 L7
Marypark Moray....101 J7
Maryport Cumb....70 G8
Maryport D & G....68 F11
Marystow Devon....5 K4
Mary Tavy Devon....5 K4
Maryton Angus....95 L10
Marywell Abers....95 J3
Marywell Abers....95 Q3
Marywell Angus....93 Q6
Masham N York....65 L10
Masongill N York....63 M7
Masonhill Crematorium
S Ayrs....76 F7
Mastin Moor Derbys....51 L5
Matching Green Essex....21 Q2
Matching Tye Essex....21 P2
Matfen Nthumb....73 J6
Matfield Kent....12 D2
Mathern Mons....28 F9
Mathon Herefs....39 N11
Mathry Pembks....24 F3
Matlask Norfk....45 J3
Matlock Derbys....50 H8
Matlock Bath Derbys....50 H8
Matson Gloucs....29 L5
Mattersey Notts....51 P3
Mattingley Hants....20 B10
Mattishall Norfk....44 H7
Mattishall Burgh Norfk....44 H7
Mauchline E Ayrs....76 H6
Maud Abers....103 J6
Maugersbury Gloucs....30 G8
Maughold IoM....56 e3
Mauld Highld....98 E2
Maulden C Beds....32 F8
Maulds Meaburn Cumb....64 B4
Maunby N York....65 N9
Maundown Somset....16 E9
Mautby Norfk....45 P7
Mavesyn Ridware Staffs....40 E4
Mavis Enderby Lincs....53 K9
Mawbray Cumb....70 H6
Mawdesley Lancs....57 J6
Mawdlam Brdgnd....26 H11
Mawgan Cnwll....2 G10
Mawgan Porth Cnwll....3 J3
Mawla Cnwll....2 G6
Mawnan Cnwll....3 J9
Mawnan Smith Cnwll....2 H9
Mawsley Nhants....32 B2
Maxey C Pete....42 G8
Maxstoke Warwks....40 G9
Maxton Border....80 E7
Maxton Kent....13 P2
Maxwelltown D & G....70 F1
Maxworthy Cnwll....4 G2
May Bank Staffs....49 Q6
Maybole S Ayrs....76 E8
Maybury Surrey....20 G10
Mayfield E Susx....12 C5
Mayfield Mdloth....86 G8
Mayfield Staffs....50 F10
Mayford Surrey....20 F11
May Hill Gloucs....29 J5
Mayland Essex....22 H3
Maylandsea Essex....22 H3
Maynard's Green E Susx....12 C6
Maypole Birm....40 E10
Maypole Green Norfk....45 N10
Maypole Green Suffk....34 F5
Meadgate BaNES....17 P5
Meadle Bucks....20 C3
Meadowfield Dur....73 M11
Meadwell Devon....5 J4
Meaford Staffs....49 Q5
Mealsgate Cumb....71 J7
Meanwood Leeds....58 H6
Meare Somset....17 L7
Meare Green Somset....16 H10
Meare Green Somset....17 J10
Mearns E Rens....85 J11
Mears Ashby Nhants....32 B4
Measham Leics....41 J5
Meath Green Surrey....11 L2
Meathop Cumb....62 H6
Meavaig W Isls....111 c2
Meavy Devon....5 L6
Medbourne Leics....42 B9
Meddon Devon....14 E8
Meden Vale Notts....51 M6
Medmenham Bucks....20 D6
Medomsley Dur....73 K9
Medstead Hants....19 Q12
Medway Crematorium
Kent....22 E10
Medway Services
Medway....22 G10
Meerbrook Staffs....50 C8
Meesden Herts....33 L9

Meeth Devon....15 J9
Meeting House Hill Norfk....45 M5
Meidrim Carmth....25 M5
Meifod Powys....48 D11
Meigle P & K....93 K6
Meikle Carco D & G....77 N8
Meikle Earnock S Lans....85 M11
Meikle Kilmory Ag & B....83 R10
Meikle Obney P & K....92 F8
Meikleour P & K....92 H7
Meikle Wartle Abers....102 F8
Meinciau Carmth....26 B6
Meir C Stke....50 C11
Melbourn Cambs....33 L7
Melbourne Derbys....41 J3
Melbourne E R Yk....60 D5
Melbury Abbas Dorset....8 C4
Melbury Bubb Dorset....7 N2
Melbury Osmond Dorset....7 N2
Melchbourne Bed....32 E4
Melcombe Bingham
Dorset....8 B6
Meldon Devon....5 L2
Meldon Nthumb....73 K4
Meldreth Cambs....33 L7
Meldrum Stirlg....85 M3
Melfort Ag & B....90 B12
Meliden Denbgs....56 C11
Melin-y-wig Denbgs....48 B6
Melkinthorpe Cumb....71 Q9
Melkridge Nthumb....72 D7
Melksham Wilts....18 D7
Melling Lancs....63 L7
Melling Sefton....56 H8
Mellis Suffk....34 H2
Mellon Charles Highld....105 M4
Mellon Udrigle Highld....105 N3
Mellor Lancs....57 M3
Mellor Stockp....50 C3
Mellor Brook Lancs....57 M3
Mells Somset....17 Q6
Melmerby Cumb....72 B12
Melmerby N York....65 J9
Melmerby N York....65 N10
Melness Highld....109 K4
Melplash Dorset....7 L3
Melrose Border....80 D7
Melsetter Ork....111 g3
Melsonby N York....65 L6
Meltham Kirk....58 E11
Melton E R Yk....60 G8
Melton Suffk....35 L6
Melton Constable Norfk....44 H4
Melton Mowbray Leics....41 Q4
Melton Ross N Linc....60 H11
Melvaig Highld....105 L5
Melverley Shrops....48 G11
Melvich Highld....109 Q3
Membury Devon....6 H3
Membury Services
W Berk....19 K5
Memsie Abers....103 K3
Memus Angus....93 M4
Menai Bridge IoA....54 H7
Mendham Suffk....45 L12
Mendip Crematorium
Somset....17 N7
Mendip Hills....17 M5
Mendlesham Suffk....34 H4
Mendlesham Green
Suffk....34 H4
Menheniot Cnwll....4 G7
Mennock D & G....77 N9
Menston C Brad....58 F5
Menstrie Clacks....85 P4
Mentmore Bucks....32 C11
Meoble Highld....97 L11
Meole Brace Shrops....49 J12
Meonstoke Hants....9 Q4
Meopham Kent....22 D9
Mepal Cambs....33 M1
Meppershall C Beds....32 G9
Mere Ches E....57 N11
Mere Wilts....8 B2
Mere Brow Lancs....56 H5
Mereclough Lancs....57 Q3
Mere Green Birm....40 E7
Mereworth Kent....22 D11
Meriden Solhll....40 G10
Merkadale Highld....96 D4
Merley Poole....8 F8
Merrion Pembks....24 G8
Merriott Somset....7 L1
Merrow Surrey....20 G12
Merry Hill Herts....21 J5
Merryhill Wolves....40 B7
Merrymeet Cnwll....4 G7
Mersea Island Essex....23 K1
Mersey Crossing Halton....57 K11
Mersham Kent....13 K3
Merstham Surrey....21 L11
Merston W Susx....10 E9
Merstone IoW....9 N9
Merthyr Cynog Powys....27 L2
Merthyr Mawr Brdgnd....27 J12
Merthyr Tydfil Myr Td....27 M7
Merthyr Vale Myr Td....27 M8
Merton Devon....15 J9
Merton Gt Lon....21 K9
Merton Norfk....44 E9
Merton Oxon....31 M9
Meshaw Devon....15 N8
Messing Essex....34 E11
Messingham N Linc....52 C3
Metfield Suffk....35 L1
Metherell Cnwll....5 J6
Metheringham Lincs....52 F10
Methil Fife....86 H3
Methilhill Fife....86 G3
Methlick Abers....102 H7
Methley Leeds....59 J8
Methven P & K....92 F9
Methwold Norfk....44 C10
Methwold Hythe Norfk....44 B10
Mettingham Suffk....45 M11
Metton Norfk....45 K3
Mevagissey Cnwll....3 M6
Mexborough Donc....51 L12
Mey Highld....110 F2
Meysey Hampton Gloucs....18 G1
Miabhaig W Isls....111 c2
Michaelchurch Herefs....28 F4
Michaelchurch Escley
Herefs....28 C3
Michaelchurch-y-Fedw
Newpt....27 P11
Michaelston-le-Pit
V Glam....16 F2
Michaelstow Cnwll....4 D4
Michaelwood Services
Gloucs....29 J9

Micheldever Hants....19 N11
Micheldever Station
Hants....19 N11
Michelmersh Hants....9 L3
Mickfield Suffk....35 J4
Micklebring Donc....51 L2
Mickleby N York....66 H5
Micklefield Leeds....59 K7
Mickleham Surrey....21 J11
Mickleover C Derb....40 H1
Mickleton Dur....64 H3
Mickleton Gloucs....30 F5
Mickletown Leeds....59 K8
Mickle Trafford Ches W....49 J2
Mickley N York....65 M11
Mickley Square Nthumb....73 J8
Mid Ardlaw Abers....103 K3
Midbea Ork....111 h1
Mid Beltie Abers....95 K2
Mid Calder W Loth....86 C8
Mid Clyth Highld....110 F8
Mid Culbeuchly Abers....102 E3
Middle Aston Oxon....31 L8
Middle Barton Oxon....31 K8
Middlebie D & G....71 K1
Middlebridge P & K....92 D3
Middle Chinnock Somset....7 L1
Middle Claydon Bucks....31 Q8
Middleham N York....65 K9
Middle Handley Derbys....51 K5
Middlehill Wilts....18 B7
Middlehope Shrops....39 J4
Middle Kames Ag & B....83 N5
Middle Littleton Worcs....30 E5
Middlemarsh Dorset....7 P2
Middle Mayfield Staffs....50 F10
Middle Rasen Lincs....52 F5
Middle Rocombe Devon....6 B8
Middlesbrough Middsb....66 C4
Middlesham Cumb....63 K4
Middlesmoor N York....65 J11
Middle Stoke Medway....22 G8
Middlestone Dur....65 M2
Middlestown Wakefd....58 H10
Middlethird Border....80 F5
Middleton Ag & B....88 B7
Middleton Derbys....50 G8
Middleton Derbys....50 H9
Middleton Essex....34 E8
Middleton Hants....19 M11
Middleton Herefs....39 K8
Middleton Leeds....58 H8
Middleton N York....58 C4
Middleton N York....66 H9
Middleton Nhants....42 B11
Middleton Norfk....43 Q6
Middleton Nthumb....73 J4
Middleton P & K....86 D2
Middleton Rochdl....57 Q7
Middleton Shrops....39 K6
Middleton Suffk....35 N3
Middleton Swans....25 P10
Middleton Warwks....40 F7
Middleton Cheney
Nhants....31 L6
Middleton
Crematorium Rochdl....58 B11
Middleton-in-Teesdale
Dur....64 G3
Middleton Moor Suffk....35 N4
Middleton One Row
Darltn....65 P5
Middleton-on-Sea
W Susx....10 F9
Middleton on the Hill
Herefs....39 K8
Middleton on the
Wolds E R Yk....60 G4
Middleton Park C Aber....103 J11
Middleton Quernhow
N York....65 N10
Middleton St George
Darltn....65 N5
Middleton Scriven
Shrops....39 M5
Middleton Stoney Oxon....31 M9
Middleton Tyas N York....65 M6
Middle Town IoS....2 b3
Middletown Powys....48 F11
Middle Tysoe Warwks....31 J5
Middle Wallop Hants....19 K12
Middlewich Ches E....49 N3
Middle Winterslow Wilts....9 J2
Middlewood Cnwll....4 G5
Middle Woodford Wilts....18 G12
Middlewood Green Suffk....34 H5
Middleyard E Ayrs....77 J5
Middlezoy Somset....17 K9
Midford BaNES....18 B8
Midgham W Berk....19 P7
Midgley Calder....58 D8
Midgley Wakefd....58 H10
Midhopestones Sheff....50 G2
Midhurst W Susx....10 D6
Mid Lavant W Susx....10 D8
Midlem Border....80 C8
Mid Mains Highld....98 F2
Midpark Ag & B....83 Q10
Midsomer Norton BaNES....17 P5
Midtown Highld....109 K4
Mid Warwickshire
Crematorium Warwks....30 H3
Mid Yell Shet....111 k2
Migvie Abers....94 G1
Milborne Port Somset....17 P11
Milborne St Andrew
Dorset....8 B7
Milborne Wick Somset....17 P11
Milbourne Nthumb....73 K6
Milbourne Wilts....18 D4
Milburn Cumb....64 C2
Milbury Heath S Glos....29 J10
Milby N York....59 K1
Milcombe Oxon....31 K7
Milden Suffk....34 F7
Mildenhall Suffk....34 B2
Mildenhall Wilts....18 H6
Mileham Norfk....44 F6
Mile Oak Br & H....11 K8
Milesmark Fife....86 C5
Miles Platting Manch....57 Q8
Mile Town Kent....22 H8
Milfield Nthumb....81 K7
Milford Derbys....51 J10
Milford Devon....14 E7
Milford Staffs....40 C4
Milford Surrey....10 F2
Milford Haven Pembks....24 G7
Milford on Sea Hants....9 K8
Milkwall Gloucs....28 G7

Milland W Susx....10 D4
Mill Bank Calder....58 D8
Millbreck Abers....103 K6
Millbridge Surrey....10 D2
Millbrook C Beds....32 E8
Millbrook C Sotn....9 L5
Millbrook Cnwll....5 J9
Millbrook Jersey....7 b2
Mill Brow Stockp....50 C3
Millbuie Abers....102 G12
Millbuie Highld....107 J11
Millcorner E Susx....12 G5
Millcraig Highld....107 L7
Milldale Staffs....50 F9
Mill End Bucks....20 C6
Mill End Herts....33 K9
Millerhill Mdloth....86 G8
Miller's Dale Derbys....50 F6
Millerston C Glas....85 L9
Mill Green Cambs....33 P7
Mill Green Essex....22 D3
Mill Green Lincs....42 H5
Mill Green Suffk....34 F8
Mill Green Suffk....34 G5
Mill Green Suffk....35 J5
Millhalf Herefs....38 F11
Millheugh S Lans....77 M2
Mill Hill Gt Lon....21 K5
Millhouse Ag & B....83 P8
Millhousebridge D & G....78 H10
Millhouse Green Barns....58 G12
Millhouses Sheff....51 J4
Milliken Park Rens....84 G9
Millington E R Yk....60 E4
Millmeece Staffs....49 Q8
Mill of Drummond P & K....92 C11
Mill of Haldane W Duns....84 G6
Millom Cumb....62 D6
Millport N Ayrs....84 C11
Mill Street Suffk....34 H3
Millthrop Cumb....63 M4
Milltimber C Aber....95 P2
Milltown Abers....101 K12
Milltown Abers....101 N11
Milltown D & G....71 M1
Milltown Devon....15 K4
Milltown of
Auchindoun Moray....101 L7
Milltown of Campfield
Abers....95 L2
Milltown of Edinville
Moray....101 K7
Milltown of Learney
Abers....95 K2
Milltown of Rothiemay
Moray....102 D5
Milnathort P & K....86 D2
Milngavie E Duns....85 J7
Milnrow Rochdl....58 B10
Milnthorpe Cumb....63 J6
Milovaig Highld....104 B11
Milson Shrops....39 M7
Milstead Kent....22 H10
Milston Wilts....18 H10
Milthorpe Nhants....31 N5
Milton C Stke....50 B10
Milton Cambs....33 M4
Milton Cumb....71 Q4
Milton D & G....68 G8
Milton D & G....70 D2
Milton Derbys....40 H3
Milton Highld....97 J3
Milton Highld....98 G3
Milton Highld....107 J11
Milton Highld....107 M7
Milton Highld....110 G5
Milton Inver....84 F8
Milton Kent....22 D8
Milton Moray....101 J10
Milton Moray....101 P3
Milton N Som....17 J4
Milton Notts....51 P6
Milton Oxon....19 N3
Milton Oxon....31 L7
Milton P & K....94 B9
Milton Pembks....24 H8
Milton Somset....17 L10
Milton Stirlg....84 H3
Milton W Duns....84 G7
Milton Abbas Dorset....8 B7
Milton Abbot Devon....5 J4
Milton Bridge Mdloth....86 F9
Milton Bryan C Beds....32 D10
Milton Clevedon Somset....17 P8
Milton Combe Devon....5 K7
Milton Damerel Devon....14 G9
Milton Ernest Bed....32 E5
Milton Green Ches W....49 J4
Milton Hill Oxon....19 M3
Milton Keynes M Keyn....32 C8
Milton Lilbourne Wilts....18 H8
Milton Malsor Nhants....31 Q3
Milton Morenish P & K....91 P8
Milton of Auchinhove
Abers....95 J2
Milton of Balgonie Fife....86 G3
Milton of Buchanan
Stirlg....84 G5
Milton of Campsie
E Duns....85 L7
Milton of Finavon Angus....93 N4
Milton of Leys Highld....99 K3
Milton of Murtle C Aber....95 P2
Milton on Stour Dorset....8 B2
Milton Regis Kent....22 H9
Milton-under-
Wychwood Oxon....30 H9
Milverton Somset....16 F10
Milverton Warwks....30 H2
Milwich Staffs....40 C2
Minard Ag & B....83 P4
Minchinhampton Gloucs....29 M8
Minehead Somset....16 C6
Minera Wrexhm....48 F5
Minety Wilts....18 F3
Minffordd Gwynd....47 J4
Mingarrypark Highld....89 N3
Miningsby Lincs....53 K10
Minions Cnwll....4 G6
Minishant S Ayrs....76 F7
Minllyn Gwynd....47 P8
Minnigaff D & G....69 K6
Minnonie Abers....102 G4
Minskip N York....59 K2
Minstead Hants....9 K5
Minsted W Susx....10 D6
Minster Kent....23 P9
Minsterley Shrops....38 G2
Minster Lovell Oxon....30 H10
Minster-on-Sea Kent....23 J8

Minsterworth Gloucs 29 K5
Minterne Magna Dorset 7 P2
Minting Lincs 52 H8
Mintlaw Abers 103 K6
Mintlyn Crematorium Norfk 43 Q6
Minto Border 80 D9
Minton Shrops 38 H4
Mirehouse Cumb 70 F11
Mireland Highld 110 G4
Mirfield Kirk 58 G9
Miserden Gloucs 29 N7
Miskin Rhondd 27 L11
Misson Notts 51 P2
Misterton Notts 51 Q2
Misterton Somset 7 L2
Mistley Essex 35 J9
Mitcham Gt Lon 21 K9
Mitcheldean Gloucs 29 J5
Mitchell Cnwll 3 J5
Mitchellslacks D & G 78 F9
Mitchel Troy Mons 28 F6
Mitford Nthumb 73 L4
Mithian Cnwll 2 H5
Mixbury Oxon 31 N7
Mobberley Ches E 57 P11
Mobberley Staffs 50 D11
Mochdre Powys 38 C4
Mockbeggar Kent 12 E1
Mockerkin Cumb 70 H10
Modbury Devon 5 N9
Moddershall Staffs 50 B12
Moelfre IoA 54 G4
Moelfre Powys 48 E9
Moffat D & G 78 H7
Moggerhanger C Beds 32 G6
Moira Leics 40 H4
Molash Kent 23 K11
Mol-chlach Highld 96 E7
Mold Flints 48 E3
Moldgreen Kirk 58 F10
Molehill Green Essex 33 P10
Molescroft E R Yk 60 H6
Molesworth Cambs 32 F2
Moll Highld 96 G4
Molland Devon 15 N6
Mollington Ches W 48 H2
Mollington Oxon 31 K5
Mollinsburn N Lans 85 M8
Mondynes Abers 95 M6
Monewden Suffk 35 L5
Moneydie P & K 92 F9
Moniaive D & G 78 C10
Monifieth Angus 93 N8
Monikie Angus 93 N7
Monimail Fife 93 K11
Monken Hadley Gt Lon 21 K4
Monk Fryston N York 59 L8
Monkhide Herefs 39 L12
Monkhill Cumb 71 M4
Monkhopton Shrops 39 L4
Monkland Herefs 39 J10
Monkleigh Devon 14 H7
Monknash V Glam 16 C3
Monkokehampton Devon 15 K10
Monkseaton N Tyne 73 N6
Monks Eleigh Suffk 34 F7
Monk's Gate W Susx 11 K5
Monks Heath Ches E 49 Q1
Monk Sherborne Hants 19 Q9
Monksilver Somset 16 E8
Monks Kirby Warwks 41 L10
Monk Soham Suffk 35 K4
Monks Risborough Bucks 20 D3
Monksthorpe Lincs 53 M9
Monk Street Essex 33 P10
Monkswood Mons 28 D8
Monkton Devon 6 G3
Monkton Kent 23 P9
Monkton S Ayrs 76 F6
Monkton S Tyne 73 N8
Monkton Combe BaNES 18 B8
Monkton Deverill Wilts 18 C12
Monkton Farleigh Wilts 18 B7
Monkton Heathfield Somset 16 H10
Monkton Wyld Dorset 7 J4
Monkwearmouth Sundld 73 P8
Monkwood Hants 9 Q2
Monmore Green Wolves 40 B7
Monmouth Mons 28 F6
Monnington on Wye Herefs 38 G12
Monreith D & G 69 J10
Montacute Somset 17 M11
Montford Shrops 48 H11
Montford Bridge Shrops 48 H11
Montgarrie Abers 102 D10
Montgomery Powys 38 E3
Montrose Angus 95 L9
Mont Saint Guern 6 b2
Monxton Hants 19 K11
Monyash Derbys 50 F7
Monymusk Abers 102 F11
Monzie P & K 92 C9
Moodiesburn N Lans 85 L8
Moonzie Fife 93 L11
Moor Allerton Leeds 58 H6
Moorby Lincs 53 J10
Moor Crichel Dorset 8 E6
Moordown Bmouth 8 G8
Moore Halton 57 L11
Moor End Calder 58 E8
Moorends Donc 59 P10
Moorhead C Brad 58 F6
Moorhouse Cumb 71 M4
Moorhouse Notts 51 Q7
Moorhouse Bank Surrey 21 N11
Moorlinch Somset 17 K8
Moor Monkton N York 59 L3
Moorsholm R & Cl 66 F5
Moorside Dorset 8 B4
Moorswater Cnwll 4 F7
Moorthorpe Wakefd 59 L11
Moortown Leeds 58 H6
Moortown Lincs 52 F4
Morangie Highld 107 M5
Morar Highld 97 J10
Moray Crematorium Moray 101 M3
Morborne Cambs 42 G10
Morchard Bishop Devon 15 N10
Morcombelake Dorset 7 K4
Morcott Rutlnd 42 D9
Morda Shrops 48 F9
Morden Dorset 8 D8

Morden Gt Lon 21 K9
Mordiford Herefs 28 G2
Mordon Dur 65 N3
More Shrops 38 G4
Morebath Devon 16 C10
Morebattle Border 80 G8
Morecambe Lancs 62 H8
Moredon Swindn 18 G4
Morefield Highld 106 B4
Morehall Kent 13 N3
Moreleigh Devon 5 P9
Morenish P & K 91 N8
Morestead Hants 9 N3
Moreton Dorset 8 B9
Moreton Essex 21 Q3
Moreton Herefs 39 J8
Moreton Oxon 20 B3
Moreton Wirral 56 F10
Moreton Corbet Shrops 49 K10
Moretonhampstead Devon 5 P3
Moreton-in-Marsh Gloucs 30 G2
Moreton Jeffries Herefs 39 L11
Moreton Morrell Warwks 30 H3
Moreton on Lugg Herefs 39 J11
Moreton Pinkney Nhants 31 M4
Moreton Say Shrops 49 L8
Moreton Valence Gloucs 29 K6
Morfa Nefyn Gwynd 46 E4
Morham E Loth 87 K7
Morland Cumb 64 B3
Morley Ches E 57 P11
Morley Derbys 51 K11
Morley Leeds 58 H8
Morley Green Ches E 57 P11
Morley St Botolph Norfk 44 H9
Morningside C Edin 86 F7
Morningside N Lans 85 N11
Morningthorpe Norfk 45 K10
Morphie Abers 95 L8
Morrey Staffs 40 E4
Morriston Swans 26 F8
Morston Norfk 44 G2
Mortehoe Devon 14 H3
Morthen Rothm 51 L3
Mortimer W Berk 19 Q7
Mortimer West End Hants 19 Q7
Mortlake Gt Lon 21 K8
Mortlake Crematorium Gt Lon 21 K8
Morton Cumb 71 N5
Morton Derbys 51 K8
Morton Lincs 42 F5
Morton Lincs 52 B5
Morton Notts 51 Q9
Morton Shrops 48 F9
Mortonhall Crematorium C Edin 86 F8
Morton-on-Swale N York 65 N8
Morton on the Hill Norfk 45 J6
Morvah Cnwll 2 B8
Morvich Highld 97 N5
Morville Shrops 39 M4
Morwenstow Cnwll 14 D8
Mosborough Sheff 51 K5
Moscow E Ayrs 76 H4
Moseley Birm 40 E10
Moseley Wolves 40 C7
Moseley Worcs 39 P9
Moss Ag & B 88 B7
Moss Donc 59 N10
Mossat Abers 101 N10
Mossbank Shet 111 k3
Moss Bank St Hel 57 K8
Mossbay Cumb 70 G9
Mossblown S Ayrs 76 G6
Mossburnford Border 80 F10
Moss Edge Lancs 62 H12
Mossley Tamesd 50 C1
Moss-side Highld 100 D4
Mosstodloch Moray 101 L4
Mossyard D & G 69 M8
Mossy Lea Lancs 57 K6
Mosterton Dorset 7 L2
Moston Manch 57 Q8
Mostyn Flints 56 D11
Motcombe Dorset 8 C3
Mothecombe Devon 5 M10
Motherby Cumb 71 N9
Motherwell N Lans 85 M10
Motspur Park Gt Lon 21 K9
Mottingham Gt Lon 21 N8
Mottisfont Hants 9 K3
Mottisfont Hants 9 K3
Mottistone IoW 9 L10
Mottram in Longdendale Tamesd 50 C12
Mottram St Andrew Ches E 57 Q12
Mouldsworth Ches W 49 J2
Moulin P & K 92 E4
Moulsecoomb Br & H 11 M8
Moulsford Oxon 19 P4
Moulsoe M Keyn 32 C8
Moultavie Highld 107 K7
Moulton Ches W 49 M2
Moulton Lincs 43 K5
Moulton N York 65 M6
Moulton Nhants 32 B4
Moulton Suffk 34 B4
Moulton V Glam 16 E3
Moulton Chapel Lincs 43 J6
Moulton St Mary Norfk 45 N8
Moulton Seas End Lincs 43 K5
Mount Cnwll 4 E6
Mountain C Brad 58 E7
Mountain Ash Rhondd 27 L8
Mountain Cross Border 86 D11
Mount Ambrose Cnwll 2 G7
Mount Bures Essex 34 E9
Mountfield E Susx 12 E6
Mountgerald Highld 107 J9
Mount Hawke Cnwll 2 G6
Mountjoy Cnwll 3 K4
Mount Lothian Mdloth 86 F10
Mountnessing Essex 22 D4
Mounton Mons 28 G9
Mount Pleasant Derbys 51 J10
Mount Pleasant Suffk 34 C7
Mountsett Crematorium Dur 73 L9
Mountsorrel Leics 41 M5
Mount Tabor Calder 58 D8

Mousehole Cnwll 2 C9
Mouswald D & G 70 H2
Mow Cop Ches E 49 Q4
Mowhaugh Border 80 H9
Mowmacre Hill C Leic 41 N6
Mowsley Leics 41 N9
Moy Highld 98 F11
Moy Highld 99 L3
Moyle Highld 97 M6
Moylegrove Pembks 36 B10
Muasdale Ag & B 75 K4
Muchalls Abers 95 P4
Much Birch Herefs 28 F3
Much Cowarne Herefs 39 L11
Much Dewchurch Herefs 28 F3
Muchelney Somset 17 K10
Muchelney Ham Somset 17 L10
Much Hadham Herts 33 L11
Much Hoole Lancs 57 J4
Muchlarnick Cnwll 4 F8
Much Marcle Herefs 28 H3
Much Wenlock Shrops 39 L3
Muck Highld 89 J1
Muckleburgh Collection Norfk 44 H2
Mucklestone Staffs 49 N7
Muckton Lincs 53 L7
Muddiford Devon 15 K5
Muddles Green E Susx 12 B7
Mudeford Dorset 8 H8
Mudford Somset 17 N11
Mudford Sock Somset 17 N11
Mugdock Stirlg 85 J7
Mugeary Highld 96 E2
Mugginton Derbys 50 H11
Muirden Abers 102 F5
Muirdrum Angus 93 P8
Muiresk Abers 102 F5
Muirhead Angus 93 L8
Muirhead Fife 86 F2
Muirhead N Lans 85 L8
Muirkirk E Ayrs 77 L6
Muirmill Stirlg 85 M6
Muir of Fowlis Abers 102 D11
Muir of Miltonduff Moray 101 J4
Muir of Ord Highld 107 J11
Muirshearlich Highld 98 A11
Muirtack Abers 103 K7
Muirton P & K 85 Q1
Muirton Mains Highld 106 H10
Muirton of Ardblair P & K 92 H7
Muker N York 64 G7
Mulbarton Norfk 45 K9
Mulben Moray 101 L5
Mull Ag & B 89 M8
Mullion Cnwll 2 G11
Mullion Cove Cnwll 2 F11
Mumby Lincs 53 N8
Munderfield Row Herefs 39 M10
Munderfield Stocks Herefs 39 M11
Mundesley Norfk 45 M3
Mundford Norfk 44 D10
Mundham Norfk 45 M9
Mundon Hill Essex 22 G3
Mungrisdale Cumb 71 M9
Munlochy Highld 107 K10
Munnoch N Ayrs 76 E2
Munsley Herefs 29 J1
Munslow Shrops 39 K5
Murchington Devon 5 N3
Murcott Oxon 31 N10
Murkle Highld 110 D3
Murlaggan Highld 97 P10
Murroes Angus 93 N8
Murrow Cambs 43 L8
Mursley Bucks 32 B10
Murthill Angus 93 N4
Murthly P & K 92 G7
Murton C York 59 P4
Murton Cumb 64 D3
Murton Dur 73 P10
Murton Nthumb 81 K5
Musbury Devon 6 H4
Musselburgh E Loth 86 G7
Muston Leics 42 B3
Muston N York 67 N10
Muswell Hill Gt Lon 21 L5
Mutehill D & G 69 P8
Mutford Suffk 45 P11
Muthill P & K 92 C11
Mybster Highld 110 D5
Myddfai Carmth 26 G3
Myddle Shrops 49 J10
Mydroilyn Cerdgn 36 G9
Mylor Cnwll 3 J8
Mylor Bridge Cnwll 3 J8
Mynachlog ddu Pembks 25 K3
Mynydd-bach Mons 28 F9
Mynydd-Bach Swans 26 E8
Mynyddgarreg Carmth 25 P7
Mynydd Isa Flints 48 F3
Myrebird Abers 95 M3
Myredykes Border 72 B2
Mytchett Surrey 20 E11
Mytholm Calder 58 C8
Mytholmroyd Calder 58 D8
Myton-on-Swale N York 59 K2

N

Naast Highld 105 M6
Na Buirgh W Isls 111 c3
Naburn C York 59 N5
Nab Wood Crematorium C Brad 58 E6
Nackington Kent 23 M11
Nacton Suffk 35 K8
Nafferton E R Yk 60 H3
Nailbourne Somset 16 G9
Nailsea N Som 17 L3
Nailstone Leics 41 K6
Nailsworth Gloucs 29 L8
Nairn Highld 100 D4
Nannerch Flints 48 D2
Nanpantan Leics 41 L4
Nanpean Cnwll 3 L5
Nanstallon Cnwll 3 M3
Nanternis Cerdgn 36 F8
Nantgaredig Carmth 26 C5
Nantglyn Denbgs 55 Q8
Nantmel Powys 38 B8
Nantmor Gwynd 47 K3
Nant Peris Gwynd 54 H9
Nantwich Ches E 49 M5
Nantyglo Blae G 27 P6

Nant-y-moel Brdgnd 27 K9
Naphill Bucks 20 D4
Napton on the Hill Warwks 31 L2
Narberth Pembks 25 J6
Narborough Leics 41 M7
Narborough Norfk 44 C7
Nasareth Gwynd 54 F10
Naseby Nhants 41 P10
Nash Bucks 32 B9
Nash Newpt 28 D11
Nash Shrops 39 L7
Nassington Nhants 42 F10
Nateby Cumb 64 E6
Nateby Lancs 63 J12
National Memorial Arboretum Staffs 40 F5
National Motor Museum (Beaulieu) Hants 9 L6
National Space Centre C Leic 41 N6
Natland Cumb 63 K4
Naughton Suffk 34 G7
Naunton Gloucs 30 E9
Naunton Worcs 29 M2
Naunton Beauchamp Worcs 30 C4
Navenby Lincs 52 E10
Navestock Essex 21 Q4
Navestock Side Essex 22 C4
Navidale Highld 110 B11
Navity Highld 107 N8
Nawton N York 66 F9
Nayland Suffk 34 F9
Nazeing Essex 21 N3
Neap Shet 111 k4
Near Cotton Staffs 50 E10
Near Sawrey Cumb 62 G3
Neasden Gt Lon 21 K6
Neasham Darltn 65 N5
Neath Neath 26 G8
Neatham Hants 10 C3
Neatishead Norfk 45 M6
Nebo Cerdgn 37 J7
Nebo Conwy 55 M9
Nebo Gwynd 54 F10
Nebo IoA 54 F4
Necton Norfk 44 E8
Nedd Highld 108 C8
Nedging Suffk 34 G7
Nedging Tye Suffk 34 G6
Needham Norfk 45 K11
Needham Market Suffk 34 H6
Needingworth Cambs 33 K3
Neen Savage Shrops 39 M6
Neen Sollars Shrops 39 M7
Neenton Shrops 39 M5
Nefyn Gwynd 46 E4
Neilston E Rens 84 H10
Nelson Caerph 27 M9
Nelson Lancs 57 Q2
Nemphlar S Lans 77 P3
Nempnett Thrubwell BaNES 17 M4
Nenthead Cumb 72 E11
Nenthorn Border 80 F6
Nercwys Flints 48 E4
Nereabolls Ag & B 82 C11
Nerston S Lans 85 L10
Nesbit Nthumb 81 K7
Nesfield N York 58 E4
Nesscliffe Shrops 48 H10
Neston Ches W 56 F12
Neston Wilts 18 C7
Netchwood Shrops 39 L4
Nether Alderley Ches E 49 Q1
Netheravon Wilts 18 G10
Nether Blainslie Border 80 D5
Netherbrae Abers 102 G4
Nether Broughton Leics 41 P3
Netherburn S Lans 77 N2
Netherbury Dorset 7 L3
Netherby N York 59 J5
Nether Cerne Dorset 7 P3
Nethercleuch D & G 79 J10
Nether Compton Dorset 17 N11
Nether Crimond Abers 102 H10
Nether Dallachy Moray 101 M3
Netherend Gloucs 28 G8
Netherfield E Susx 12 E6
Netherfield Notts 51 N11
Nether Fingland S Lans 78 F6
Nether Handwick Angus 93 L7
Nether Haugh Rothm 51 K2
Netherhay Dorset 7 K2
Nether Headon Notts 51 Q5
Nether Heage Derbys 51 J10
Nether Heyford Nhants 31 P3
Nether Howcleugh S Lans 78 G6
Nether Kellet Lancs 63 J8
Nether Kinmundy Abers 103 L6
Nether Langwith Notts 51 M6
Netherlaw D & G 70 C6
Netherley Abers 95 P4
Nethermill D & G 78 G10
Nethermuir Abers 103 J6
Netherne-on-the-Hill Surrey 21 L11
Netheroyd Hill Kirk 58 F9
Nether Padley Derbys 50 G5
Nether Poppleton C York 59 M4
Netherseal Derbys 40 H5
Nether Silton N York 66 C8
Nether Stowey Somset 16 G8
Netherthong Kirk 58 F11
Netherton Angus 93 M4
Netherton Devon 6 B8
Netherton Dudley 40 C9
Netherton Herefs 28 F3
Netherton Kirk 58 F10
Netherton N Lans 85 M11
Netherton Nthumb 81 K11
Netherton P & K 92 H5
Netherton Sefton 56 G8
Netherton Stirlg 85 J7
Netherton Wakefd 58 H10
Nethertown Cumb 62 C3
Nethertown Highld 110 G1
Nethertown Staffs 40 E4
Netherurd Border 86 D12
Nether Wallop Hants 19 K12
Nether Wasdale Cumb 62 D3
Nether Westcote Gloucs 30 G9
Nether Whitacre Warwks 40 G8
Nether Whitecleuch S Lans 78 D5
Nether Winchendon Bucks 31 Q10

Netherwitton Nthumb 73 K3
Nethy Bridge Highld 99 Q5
Netley Hants 9 M6
Netley Marsh Hants 9 K5
Nettlebed Oxon 20 B6
Nettlebridge Somset 17 P6
Nettlecombe Dorset 7 M4
Nettleden Herts 20 G2
Nettleham Lincs 52 E8
Nettlestead Kent 22 D11
Nettlestead Green Kent 22 D12
Nettlestone IoW 9 Q8
Nettlesworth Dur 73 M10
Nettleton Lincs 52 G4
Nettleton Wilts 18 B5
Netton Wilts 18 G12
Nevern Pembks 36 B11
Nevill Holt Leics 42 B10
New Abbey D & G 70 F3
New Aberdour Abers 103 J3
New Addington Gt Lon 21 M10
Newall Leeds 58 G5
New Alresford Hants 9 P2
New Alyth P & K 93 J6
Newark C Pete 42 H9
Newark Ork 111 i1
Newark-on-Trent Notts 52 B11
Newarthill N Lans 85 N10
New Ash Green Kent 22 C9
New Balderton Notts 52 B11
New Barn Kent 22 C9
New Barnet Gt Lon 21 L4
Newbattle Mdloth 86 G8
New Bewick Nthumb 81 M9
Newbie D & G 71 K3
Newbiggin Cumb 64 B2
Newbiggin Cumb 71 P9
Newbiggin Cumb 71 Q6
Newbiggin Dur 64 G3
Newbiggin N u Ty 64 H9
Newbiggin-by-the-Sea Nthumb 73 N4
Newbigging Angus 93 K7
Newbigging Angus 93 M8
Newbigging Angus 93 N8
Newbigging S Lans 86 B11
Newbiggin-on-Lune Cumb 63 N2
New Bilton Warwks 41 L11
Newbold Derbys 51 J6
Newbold on Avon Warwks 41 L11
Newbold on Stour Warwks 30 G5
Newbold Pacey Warwks 30 H3
Newbold Verdon Leics 41 K6
New Bolingbroke Lincs 53 K11
Newborough C Pete 42 H8
Newborough IoA 54 F8
Newborough Staffs 40 F3
New Boultham Lincs 52 D8
Newbourne Suffk 35 L8
New Bradwell M Keyn 32 B7
New Brampton Derbys 51 J6
New Brancepeth Dur 73 M11
Newbridge C Edin 86 D7
Newbridge Caerph 27 P8
Newbridge Cnwll 2 C9
Newbridge D & G 78 F11
Newbridge Hants 9 K4
Newbridge IoW 9 M9
Newbridge Green Worcs 29 L2
Newbridge-on-Wye Powys 38 B9
New Brighton Wirral 56 F9
Newbrough Nthumb 72 F7
New Buckenham Norfk 44 H11
Newbuildings Devon 15 N10
Newburgh Abers 103 K4
Newburgh Abers 103 K3
Newburgh Fife 93 J11
Newburgh Lancs 57 J6
Newburgh Priory N York 66 D11
Newburn N u Ty 73 L7
Newbury Somset 17 Q6
Newbury W Berk 19 M7
Newbury Park Gt Lon 21 N6
Newby Cumb 64 B4
Newby Lancs 63 P11
Newby N York 63 N8
Newby N York 66 C5
Newby Bridge Cumb 62 G5
Newby East Cumb 71 P4
New Byth Abers 102 H5
Newby West Cumb 71 M5
Newcastle Mons 28 E5
Newcastle Shrops 38 F5
Newcastle Airport Nthumb 73 L6
Newcastle Emlyn Carmth 36 E11
Newcastleton Border 79 P10
Newcastle-under-Lyme Staffs 49 Q6
Newcastle upon Tyne N u Ty 73 M7
Newchapel Pembks 36 D11
Newchapel Surrey 11 M2
Newchurch IoW 9 P9
Newchurch Kent 13 K4
Newchurch Mons 28 E8
Newchurch Powys 38 E11
Newchurch Staffs 40 F3
New Costessey Norfk 45 K7
Newcraighall C Edin 86 G7
New Crofton Wakefd 59 K10
New Cross Gt Lon 21 M7
New Cross Somset 17 K11
New Cumnock E Ayrs 77 K8
New Deer Abers 103 J6
New Denham Bucks 20 G4
Newdigate Surrey 11 K2
New Duston Nhants 31 Q2
New Earswick C York 59 N3
New Edlington Donc 51 M2
New Elgin Moray 101 J3
New Ellerby E R Yk 61 K6
Newell Green Br For 20 E8
New Eltham Gt Lon 21 N8
New End Worcs 30 D3
Newenden Kent 12 G5
New England C Pete 42 H9
Newent Gloucs 29 J4
New Ferry Wirral 56 G10
Newfield Dur 65 L2
Newfield Highld 107 N7
New Fletton C Pete 42 H9
New Forest National Park Hants 9 K6
Newgale Pembks 24 E4

182 New Galloway - Odsal

New Galloway D & G 69 P4
Newgate Street Herts 21 L3
New Gilston Fife 87 J1
New Grimsby IoS 2 b1
Newhall Ches E 49 L6
New Hartley Nthumb 73 N5
Newhaven C Edin 86 F7
Newhaven E Susx 11 N9
New Haw Surrey 20 G10
New Hedges Pembks 25 K8
New Holland N Linc 61 J9
Newholm N York 67 J5
New Houghton Derbys 51 L7
New Houghton Norfk 44 D5
Newhouse N Lans 85 N10
New Hutton Cumb 63 K4
Newick E Susx 11 N6
Newington Kent 13 M3
Newington Kent 22 G9
Newington Oxon 19 Q2
New Inn Carmth 26 C2
New Inn Torfn 28 C8
New Invention Shrops 38 F6
New Lakenham Norfk 45 K8
New Lanark S Lans 78 E1
New Lanark Village S Lans 78 E1
Newland C KuH 61 J7
Newland Gloucs 28 G6
Newland N York 59 P8
Newland Somset 15 P5
Newland Worcs 39 P11
Newlandrig Mdloth 86 H9
Newlands Border 79 Q9
Newlands Nthumb 73 J9
Newlands of Dundurcas Moray 101 L5
New Langholm D & G 79 M11
New Leake Lincs 53 L11
New Leeds Abers 103 K4
New Lodge Barns 59 J11
New Longton Lancs 57 K4
New Luce D & G 68 G6
Newlyn Cnwll 2 C9
Newmachar Abers 103 J10
Newmains N Lans 85 N10
New Malden Gt Lon 21 K9
Newman's Green Suffk 34 E7
Newmarket Suffk 33 Q4
Newmarket W Isls 111 d2
New Marske R & Cl 66 E4
New Marston Oxon 31 M11
New Mill Abers 95 N5
Newmill Border 79 P6
New Mill Cnwll 2 C8
New Mill Kirk 58 F11
Newmill Moray 101 N5
Newmillerdam Wakefd 59 J10
Newmill of Inshewan Angus 94 G9
Newmills C Edin 86 E8
New Mills Derbys 50 D4
Newmills Fife 86 B5
Newmills Mons 28 F7
New Mills Powys 38 C2
Newmiln P & K 92 G9
Newmilns E Ayrs 77 J4
New Milton Hants 9 J8
New Mistley Essex 35 J9
New Moat Pembks 25 J4
Newney Green Essex 22 D3
Newnham Hants 20 B11
Newnham Herts 33 J8
Newnham Kent 23 J11
Newnham Nhants 31 M3
Newnham Bridge Worcs 39 M8
Newnham on Severn Gloucs 29 J6
New Ollerton Notts 51 P7
New Oscott Birm 40 E8
New Pitsligo Abers 103 J4
Newport Cnwll 4 H3
Newport E R Yk 60 E7
Newport Essex 33 N9
Newport Gloucs 29 J8
Newport Highld 110 D10
Newport IoW 9 N9
Newport Newpt 28 C10
Newport Pembks 25 J2
Newport Wrekin 49 N10
Newport-on-Tay Fife 93 M9
Newport Pagnell M Keyn 32 C7
Newport Pagnell Services M Keyn 32 C7
New Prestwick S Ayrs 76 F6
New Quay Cerdgn 36 F8
Newquay Cnwll 3 J4
Newquay Zoo Cnwll 3 J4
New Rackheath Norfk 45 L7
New Radnor Powys 38 E9
New Ridley Nthumb 73 J8
New Romney Kent 13 K5
New Rossington Donc 51 N2
New Sauchie Clacks 85 P4
Newseat Abers 102 F8
Newsham Lancs 57 K2
Newsham N York 65 K5
Newsham N York 65 P9
Newsham Nthumb 73 N5
New Sharlston Wakefd 59 J9
Newsholme E R Yk 60 C8
New Silksworth Sundld 73 P9
Newsome Kirk 58 F10
New Somerby Lincs 42 D3
New Southgate Crematorium Gt Lon 21 L5
Newstead Border 80 D7
Newstead Notts 51 L9
Newstead Nthumb 81 N8
New Stevenston N Lans 85 M10
Newthorpe Notts 51 L10
New Thundersley Essex 22 F5
Newton Ag & B 83 Q4
Newton Border 80 E9
Newton Brdgnd 26 H12
Newton C Beds 32 H7
Newton Cambs 33 M6
Newton Cambs 43 M7
Newton Ches W 48 H2
Newton Ches W 49 J4
Newton Cumb 62 E7
Newton Derbys 51 K8
Newton Herefs 28 D3
Newton Herefs 39 K10
Newton Highld 107 J11
Newton Highld 107 M11
Newton Highld 107 M8
Newton Highld 110 G6
Newton Lincs 42 F3
Newton Mdloth 86 G8
Newton Moray 100 H3
Newton Moray 101 L3
Newton Nhants 42 C12
Newton Norfk 44 D7
Newton Notts 51 P11
Newton Nthumb 73 J7
Newton S Lans 78 F3
Newton S Lans 85 L10
Newton Sandw 40 D8
Newton Staffs 40 D3
Newton Suffk 34 F8
Newton W Loth 86 C6
Newton Warwks 41 M10
Newton Abbot Devon 6 B8
Newton Arlosh Cumb 71 K5
Newton Aycliffe Dur 65 M3
Newton Bewley Hartpl 66 C3
Newton Blossomville M Keyn 32 D6
Newton Bromswold Nhants 32 E4
Newton Burgoland Leics 41 J6
Newton-by-the-Sea Nthumb 81 P8
Newton by Toft Lincs 52 F6
Newton Ferrers Devon 5 L9
Newton Ferry W Isls 111 b4
Newton Flotman Norfk 45 K9
Newtongrange Mdloth 86 G8
Newton Green Mons 28 F9
Newton Harcourt Leics 41 N7
Newton Heath Manch 57 Q8
Newtonhill Abers 95 P4
Newton-in-Bowland Lancs 63 M11
Newton Kyme N York 59 L5
Newton-le-Willows N York 65 L9
Newton-le-Willows St Hel 57 L9
Newtonloan Mdloth 86 G9
Newton Longville Bucks 32 C9
Newton Mearns E Rens 85 J11
Newtonmill Angus 95 K8
Newtonmore Highld 99 K8
Newton Morrell N York 65 M5
Newton of Balcanquhal P & K 92 H12
Newton of Balcormo Fife 87 K2
Newton-on-Ouse N York 59 L3
Newton-on-Rawcliffe N York 66 H9
Newton-on-the-Moor Nthumb 81 N12
Newton on Trent Lincs 52 B8
Newton Poppleford Devon 6 E5
Newton Purcell Oxon 31 N7
Newton Regis Warwks 40 H6
Newton Reigny Cumb 71 P8
Newton St Cyres Devon 15 Q11
Newton St Faith Norfk 45 K6
Newton St Loe BaNES 17 Q3
Newton St Petrock Devon 14 G9
Newton Solney Derbys 40 H3
Newton Stacey Hants 19 M11
Newton Stewart D & G 69 K6
Newton Tony Wilts 19 J11
Newton Tracey Devon 15 J6
Newton under Roseberry R & Cl 66 D5
Newton upon Derwent E R Yk 60 C4
Newton Valence Hants 10 B4
Newton Wamphray D & G 78 H9
Newton with Scales Lancs 57 J3
Newtown Cumb 70 H6
Newtown Cumb 71 P3
Newtown D & G 77 N8
Newtown Devon 6 E3
Newtown Devon 15 N7
New Town E Susx 11 P6
Newtown Gloucs 29 J8
Newtown Hants 9 Q5
Newtown Herefs 39 L12
Newtown Highld 98 E7
Newtown IoW 9 M8
Newtown Nthumb 81 L8
Newtown Poole 8 F8
Newtown Powys 38 C4
Newtown Shrops 49 J8
Newtown Somset 6 H1
Newtown Staffs 50 B8
Newtown Wigan 57 K7
Newtown Worcs 39 Q10
Newtown Linford Leics 41 M5
Newtown of Beltrees Rens 84 F10
Newtown St Boswells Border 80 D7
New Tredegar Caerph 27 N8
New Trows S Lans 77 N4
Newtyle Angus 93 K7
New Walsoken Cambs 43 M8
New Waltham NE Lin 53 J3
New Winton E Loth 87 J7
Newyork Ag & B 83 P2
New York Lincs 53 J11
New York N Tyne 73 N6
Neyland Pembks 24 G7
Nicholashayne Devon 16 E11
Nicholaston Swans 26 C10
Nidd N York 58 H3
Nigg C Aber 95 Q2
Nigg Highld 107 N7
Nigg Ferry Highld 107 N8
Ninebanks Nthumb 72 E9
Nine Elms Swindn 18 G4
Ninfield E Susx 12 E7
Ningwood IoW 9 L9
Nisbet Border 80 F8
Nisbet Hill Border 80 H4
Niton IoW 9 N11
Nitshill C Glas 85 J10
Nocton Lincs 52 F10
Noke Oxon 31 M10
Nolton Pembks 24 F5
Nolton Haven Pembks 24 F5
No Man's Heath Ches W 49 K6
No Man's Heath Warwks 40 H6
Nomansland Devon 15 P9
Nomansland Wilts 9 J4
Noneley Shrops 49 J9
Nonington Kent 23 N11
Nook Cumb 63 K6
Norbiton Gt Lon 21 K9
Norbury Ches E 49 K6
Norbury Derbys 50 F11
Norbury Gt Lon 21 L9
Norbury Shrops 38 G4
Norbury Staffs 49 P10
Norchard Worcs 39 Q8
Nordelph Norfk 43 N9
Nordley Shrops 39 M3
Norfolk Broads Norfk 45 P8
Norham Nthumb 81 J5
Norley Ches W 49 K2
Norleywood Hants 9 L7
Normanby Lincs 52 E6
Normanby N Linc 60 F10
Normanby N York 66 G10
Normanby R & Cl 66 D4
Normanby le Wold Lincs 52 G5
Normandy Surrey 20 E11
Norman's Green Devon 6 E3
Normanton C Derb 41 J2
Normanton Leics 42 B2
Normanton Notts 51 P9
Normanton Wakefd 59 J9
Normanton le Heath Leics 41 J5
Normanton on Cliffe Lincs 42 D2
Normanton on Soar Notts 41 L3
Normanton on the Wolds Notts 41 N2
Normanton on Trent Notts 52 B9
Norris Green Lpool 56 H9
Norris Hill Leics 41 J4
Norristhorpe Kirk 58 G9
Northall Bucks 32 D11
Northallerton N York 65 P8
Northam C Sotn 9 M5
Northam Devon 14 H6
Northampton Nhants 31 Q2
Northampton Worcs 39 Q8
Northampton Services Nhants 31 Q3
North Anston Rothm 51 M4
North Ascot Br For 20 E9
North Aston Oxon 31 L8
Northaw Herts 21 L3
Northay Somset 6 H1
North Baddesley Hants 9 L4
North Ballachulish Highld 90 E4
North Barrow Somset 17 N9
North Barsham Norfk 44 F3
Northbay W Isls 111 a7
North Benfleet Essex 22 F5
North Berwick E Loth 87 K5
North Boarhunt Hants 9 P5
Northborough C Pete 42 G8
Northbourne Kent 23 P11
North Bovey Devon 5 P4
North Bradley Wilts 18 C9
North Brentor Devon 5 K4
North Brewham Somset 17 Q8
Northbrook Hants 19 N11
North Buckland Devon 14 H4
North Burlingham Norfk 45 N7
North Cadbury Somset 17 P10
North Carlton Lincs 52 D7
North Carlton Notts 51 N4
North Cave E R Yk 60 F7
North Cerney Gloucs 30 D11
North Chailey E Susx 11 N6
Northchapel W Susx 10 F4
North Charford Hants 8 H4
North Charlton Nthumb 81 N9
North Cheam Gt Lon 21 K9
North Cheriton Somset 17 Q10
North Chideock Dorset 7 K4
Northchurch Herts 20 F2
North Cliffe E R Yk 60 E6
North Clifton Notts 52 B8
North Cockerington Lincs 53 L5
North Connel Ag & B 90 C9
North Cornelly Brdgnd 26 H11
North Cotes Lincs 53 K4
Northcott Devon 4 H2
Northcourt Oxon 19 N2
North Cove Suffk 45 P11
North Cowton N York 65 M6
North Crawley M Keyn 32 D7
North Creake Norfk 44 E3
North Curry Somset 17 J10
North Dalton E R Yk 60 F4
North Deighton N York 59 K4
North Devon Crematorium Devon 15 J6
Northdown Kent 23 Q8
North Downs 22 H11
North Duffield N York 59 P6
North East Surrey Crematorium Gt Lon 21 K9
North Elmham Norfk 44 G6
North Elmsall Wakefd 59 L10
North End C Port 9 Q7
North End Essex 33 Q11
North End Hants 8 G4
North End Nhants 32 D3
North End W Susx 10 F8
Northend Warwks 31 K4
Northenden Manch 57 P10
North Erradale Highld 105 L6
North Evington C Leic 41 N6
North Fambridge Essex 22 G4
North Ferriby E R Yk 60 G8
Northfield Birm 40 D10
Northfield C Aber 95 P1
Northfield E R Yk 60 H8
Northfields Lincs 42 E8
Northfleet Kent 22 D8
North Frodingham E R Yk 61 J4
North Gorley Hants 8 H5
North Green Suffk 35 M4
North Greetwell Lincs 52 E8
North Grimston N York 60 E1
North Haven Shet 111 m5
North Hayling Hants 10 B9
North Hertfordshire Memorial Park & Crematorium Herts 32 H9
North Hill Cnwll 4 G5
North Hillingdon Gt Lon 20 H6
North Hinksey Village Oxon 31 L11
North Holmwood Surrey 11 J1
North Huish Devon 5 P8
North Hykeham Lincs 52 D9
Northiam E Susx 12 G5
Northill C Beds 32 G7
Northington Hants 19 P12
North Kelsey Lincs 52 F3
North Kessock Highld 107 L11
North Killingholme N Linc 61 K10
North Kilvington N York 65 Q9
North Kilworth Leics 41 N10
North Kyme Lincs 52 G11
North Landing E R Yk 67 Q12
Northlands Lincs 53 K11
Northleach Gloucs 30 E10
North Lee Bucks 20 D2
Northleigh Devon 6 G4
North Leigh Oxon 31 K10
North Leverton with Habblesthorpe Notts 52 B7
Northlew Devon 15 J11
North Littleton Worcs 30 E5
North Lopham Norfk 44 G12
North Luffenham Rutlnd 42 D9
North Marden W Susx 10 D6
North Marston Bucks 31 Q9
North Middleton Mdloth 86 G9
North Millbrex Abers 102 H6
North Milmain D & G 68 E8
North Molton Devon 15 M6
Northmoor Oxon 19 M1
North Moreton Oxon 19 P3
Northmuir Angus 93 L5
North Mundham W Susx 10 E9
North Muskham Notts 52 B10
North Newbald E R Yk 60 F6
North Newington Oxon 31 K6
North Newnton Wilts 18 G8
North Newton Somset 17 J9
Northney Hants 10 B8
North Nibley Gloucs 29 K9
Northolt Gt Lon 21 J6
Northolt Airport Gt Lon 20 H6
Northop Flints 48 E2
Northop Hall Flints 48 F2
North Ormesby Middsb 66 D4
North Ormsby Lincs 53 J5
Northorpe Kirk 58 G9
Northorpe Lincs 42 H3
Northorpe Lincs 52 C4
North Otterington N York 65 P9
North Owersby Lincs 52 F5
Northowram Calder 58 E8
North Perrott Somset 7 L2
North Petherton Somset 16 H9
North Petherwin Cnwll 4 G3
North Pickenham Norfk 44 E8
North Piddle Worcs 30 C3
North Poorton Dorset 7 M3
Northport Dorset 8 D9
North Queensferry Fife 86 D6
North Rauceby Lincs 42 E2
Northrepps Norfk 45 L3
North Reston Lincs 53 L6
North Rigton N York 58 H4
North Rode Ches E 50 B7
North Ronaldsay Ork 111 i1
North Ronaldsay Airport Ork 111 i1
North Runcton Norfk 43 Q6
North Scarle Lincs 52 C9
North Shian Ag & B 90 C7
North Shields N Tyne 73 N7
North Shoebury Sthend 22 H6
North Shore Bpool 56 F2
North Side C Pete 43 J9
North Somercotes Lincs 53 L4
North Stainley N York 65 M11
North Stifford Thurr 22 C7
North Stoke BaNES 17 Q3
North Stoke Oxon 19 Q4
North Stoke W Susx 10 G7
North Street Kent 23 K10
North Street W Berk 19 Q6
North Sunderland Nthumb 81 P7
North Tamerton Cnwll 14 F11
North Tawton Devon 15 L10
North Third Stirlg 85 M5
North Thoresby Lincs 53 J4
North Tolsta W Isls 111 e1
Northton W Isls 111 b3
North Town Devon 15 J9
North Town Somset 17 N7
North Town W & M 20 E7
North Tuddenham Norfk 44 G7
North Uist W Isls 111 a4
Northumberland National Park Nthumb 72 F1
North Walsham Norfk 45 L4
North Waltham Hants 19 P10
North Warnborough Hants 20 B12
North Weald Bassett Essex 21 P3
North Wheatley Notts 51 Q4
Northwich Ches W 49 M2
Northwick Worcs 39 Q9
North Widcombe BaNES 17 N5
North Willingham Lincs 52 G6
North Wingfield Derbys 51 K7
North Witham Lincs 42 D6
Northwold Norfk 44 C10
Northwood C Stke 50 B10
Northwood Gt Lon 20 H5
Northwood IoW 9 N8
Northwood Shrops 49 J8
Northwood Green Gloucs 29 J5
North Wootton Dorset 17 P12
North Wootton Norfk 43 Q5
North Wootton Somset 17 N7
North Wraxall Wilts 18 B6
North York Moors National Park 66 G7
Norton Donc 59 M10
Norton E Susx 11 P9
Norton Gloucs 29 M4
Norton Halton 57 K11
Norton Nhants 31 N2
Norton Notts 51 M6
Norton Powys 38 F8
Norton S on T 66 C3
Norton Shrops 39 N3
Norton Suffk 34 F4
Norton Swans 26 E10
Norton W Susx 10 E8
Norton Wilts 18 C4
Norton Worcs 30 D5
Norton Worcs 39 Q11
Norton Bavant Wilts 18 D11
Norton Canes Staffs 40 D6
Norton Canes Services Staffs 40 D6
Norton Canon Herefs 38 H11
Norton Disney Lincs 52 C10
Norton Fitzwarren Somset 16 G10
Norton Green IoW 9 K9
Norton Hawkfield BaNES 17 N4
Norton Heath Essex 22 C3
Norton in Hales Shrops 49 N7
Norton-Juxta-Twycross Leics 41 J6
Norton-le-Clay N York 65 P12
Norton-le-Moors C Stke 50 B9
Norton Lindsey Warwks 30 G2
Norton Little Green Suffk 34 F4
Norton Malreward BaNES 17 N3
Norton-on-Derwent N York 66 H12
Norton St Philip Somset 18 B9
Norton Subcourse Norfk 45 N9
Norton sub Hamdon Somset 17 L11
Norwell Notts 51 Q8
Norwell Woodhouse Notts 51 Q8
Norwich Norfk 45 K8
Norwich Airport Norfk 45 K7
Norwich (St Faith) Crematorium Norfk 45 K7
Norwick Shet 111 m2
Norwood Clacks 85 P4
Norwood Green Gt Lon 21 J7
Norwood Hill Surrey 11 K2
Norwoodside Cambs 43 L9
Noss Mayo Devon 5 L10
Nosterfield N York 65 M10
Nostie Highld 97 M4
Notgrove Gloucs 30 E9
Nottage Brdgnd 26 H12
Nottingham C Nott 51 M11
Notton Wakefd 59 J10
Notton Wilts 18 D6
Noutard's Green Worcs 39 P8
Nuffield Oxon 19 Q4
Nunburnholme E R Yk 60 E5
Nuneaton Warwks 41 J8
Nunhead Gt Lon 21 M8
Nun Monkton N York 59 L3
Nunney Somset 17 Q7
Nunnington N York 66 F10
Nunsthorpe NE Lin 53 J2
Nunthorpe C York 59 N4
Nunthorpe Middsb 66 D5
Nunthorpe Village Middsb 66 D5
Nunton Wilts 8 H3
Nunwick N York 65 N11
Nursling Hants 9 L4
Nutbourne W Susx 10 C8
Nutbourne W Susx 10 H6
Nutfield Surrey 21 L12
Nuthall Notts 51 M11
Nuthampstead Herts 33 L9
Nuthurst W Susx 11 J5
Nutley E Susx 11 N5
Nuttall Bury 57 P5
Nybster Highld 110 G3
Nyetimber W Susx 10 E9
Nyewood W Susx 10 C6
Nymans W Susx 11 L4
Nymet Rowland Devon 15 M9
Nymet Tracey Devon 15 M11
Nympsfield Gloucs 29 L8
Nynehead Somset 16 F10
Nyton W Susx 10 E8

O

Oadby Leics 41 N7
Oad Street Kent 22 G10
Oakamoor Staffs 50 D11
Oakbank W Loth 86 C8
Oak Cross Devon 15 J11
Oakdale Caerph 27 P8
Oake Somset 16 F10
Oaken Staffs 39 Q2
Oakenclough Lancs 63 K11
Oakengates Wrekin 49 M12
Oakenshaw Dur 73 L12
Oakenshaw Kirk 58 F8
Oakford Cerdgn 36 G8
Oakford Devon 16 C11
Oakham Rutlnd 42 C8
Oakhanger Hants 10 C3
Oakhill Somset 17 P6
Oakington Cambs 33 L4
Oakle Street Gloucs 29 K5
Oakley Bed 32 E6
Oakley Bucks 31 N10
Oakley Fife 86 B4
Oakley Hants 19 P9
Oakley Suffk 35 J2
Oakridge Lynch Gloucs 29 M7
Oaksey Wilts 29 P9
Oakthorpe Leics 40 H5
Oakwood C Derb 51 J12
Oakworth C Brad 58 D6
Oare Kent 23 J10
Oare Somset 15 N3
Oare Wilts 18 H7
Oasby Lincs 42 E3
Oath Somset 17 K10
Oathlaw Angus 93 N4
Oatlands Park Surrey 20 H9
Oban Ag & B 90 B9
Oban Airport Ag & B 90 C8
Obley Shrops 38 G6
Obney P & K 92 F8
Oborne Dorset 17 P11
Occold Suffk 35 J3
Occumster Highld 110 F8
Ochiltree E Ayrs 76 H7
Ockbrook Derbys 41 K1
Ocker Hill Sandw 40 C8
Ockham Surrey 20 H11
Ockle Highld 89 L3
Ockley Surrey 11 J3
Ocle Pychard Herefs 39 L11
Odcombe Somset 17 M11
Odd Down BaNES 17 Q4
Oddingley Worcs 30 B3
Oddington Gloucs 30 G8
Oddington Oxon 31 M10
Odell Bed 32 D5
Odiham Hants 20 C12
Odsal C Brad 58 F8

Odsey Cambs 33 J8
Odstock Wilts 8 G3
Odstone Leics 41 K6
Offchurch Warwks ...31 J2
Offenham Worcs 30 D5
Offerton Stockp 50 B3
Offham E Susx 11 N7
Offham Kent 22 D11
Offham W Susx 10 G8
Offord Cluny Cambs .32 H4
Offord D'Arcy Cambs .32 H4
Offton Suffk 34 H6
Offwell Devon 6 G3
Ogbourne Maizey Wilts .18 H6
Ogbourne St Andrew
Wilts 18 H6
Ogbourne St George
Wilts 18 H6
Ogle Nthumb 73 K5
Oglet Lpool 56 H11
Ogmore V Glam 16 B2
Ogmore-by-Sea V Glam .16 B2
Ogmore Vale Brdgnd ..27 K10
Okeford Fitzpaine
Dorset 8 B5
Okehampton Devon 5 M2
Oker Side Derbys 50 H8
Okewood Hill Surrey ..11 J3
Old Nhants 32 B3
Old Aberdeen C Aber ..95 Q1
Old Alresford Hants ...9 P1
Oldany Highld 108 C8
Old Auchenbrack D & G .77 M11
Old Basford C Nott ...51 M11
Old Basing Hants 19 Q9
Old Beetley Norfk 44 F6
Oldberrow Warwks 30 E2
Old Bewick Nthumb ...81 M9
Old Bolingbroke Lincs .53 L9
Old Bramhope Leeds ...58 G5
Old Brampton Derbys ..51 J6
Old Bridge of Urr D & G .70 C3
Old Buckenham Norfk .44 H10
Old Burghclere Hants ..19 M8
Oldbury Sandw 40 C9
Oldbury Shrops 39 N4
Oldbury Warwks 40 H8
Oldbury-on-Severn
S Glos 28 H9
Oldbury on the Hill
Gloucs 18 B3
Old Byland N York 66 D9
Old Cantley Donc 51 N1
Oldcastle Mons 28 C4
Old Catton Norfk 45 K7
Old Clee NE Lin 53 J2
Old Cleeve Somset 16 E7
Old Colwyn Conwy 55 M6
Oldcotes Notts 51 N3
Old Coulsdon Gt Lon ..21 L11
Old Dailly S Ayrs 76 D10
Old Dalby Leics 41 P3
Old Deer Abers 103 K6
Old Edlington Donc ...51 M2
Old Ellerby E R Yk ...61 K6
Old Felixstowe Suffk ..35 M9
Oldfield Worcs 39 Q8
Old Fletton C Pete 42 H10
Oldford Somset 18 B10
Old Forge Herefs 28 G5
Old Grimsby IoS 2 b1
Old Hall Green Herts ..33 L11
Oldham Oldham 58 B12
Oldham Crematorium
Oldham 50 B1
Oldhamstocks E Loth ..87 N7
Old Harlow Essex 21 P2
Old Hunstanton Norfk .44 B2
Old Hurst Cambs 33 J2
Old Hutton Cumb 63 K5
Old Inns Services N Lans .85 N7
Old Kilpatrick W Duns .84 H8
Old Knebworth Herts ..32 H11
Old Lakenham Norfk ..45 K8
Oldland S Glos 17 P2
Old Langho Lancs 57 M2
Old Leake Lincs 53 L12
Old Malton N York ...66 H11
Oldmeldrum Abers ...102 H9
Oldmill Cnwll 4 H5
Old Milverton Warwks .30 H1
Oldmixon N Som 17 J5
Old Newton Suffk 34 H4
Old Portlethen Abers ..95 Q3
Old Radford C Nott ...51 M11
Old Rayne Abers 102 F9
Old Romney Kent 13 K5
Old Shoreham W Susx .11 K8
Oldshoremore Highld .108 H4
Old Sodbury S Glos ..29 K11
Old Somerby Lincs ...42 D4
Oldstead N York 66 D10
Old Stratford Nhants ..31 Q6
Old Struan P & K 92 C3
Old Swinford Dudley ..40 B10
Old Thirsk N York 66 B10
Old Town Cumb 63 L5
Old Town E Susx 12 C9
Old Town IoS 2 C2
Old Trafford Traffd ...57 P9
Oldwall Cumb 71 P4
Oldwalls Swans 26 C9
Old Warden C Beds ...32 G7
Old Weston Cambs 32 F2
Old Wick Highld 110 G6
Old Windsor W & M ..20 F8
Old Wives Lees Kent ..23 K11
Old Woking Surrey ...20 G11
Olgrinmore Highld ...110 C5
Olive Green Staffs 40 E4
Oliver's Battery Hants ..9 M2
Ollaberry Shet 111 k3
Ollach Highld 96 F3
Ollerton Ches E 57 P12
Ollerton Notts 51 P7
Ollerton Shrops 49 M9
Olney M Keyn 32 C6
Olrig House Highld ..110 E3
Olton Solhil 40 F10
Olveston S Glos 28 H10
Ombersley Worcs 39 Q8
Ompton Notts 51 P7
Onchan IoM 56 d5
Onecote Staffs 50 D9
Onibury Shrops 38 H6
Onich Highld 90 E4
Onllwyn Neath 26 H6
Onneley Staffs 49 N6
Onslow Green Essex ..33 Q12

Onslow Village Surrey .20 F12
Onston Ches W 49 L1
Opinan Highld 105 L7
Orbliston Moray 101 L4
Orbost Highld 96 B2
Orby Lincs 53 M9
Orchard Portman
Somset 16 H10
Orcheston Wilts 18 F10
Orcop Herefs 28 F4
Orcop Hill Herefs 28 F4
Ord Abers 102 E4
Ordhead Abers 102 E12
Ordie Abers 94 G2
Ordiequish Moray ...101 N11
Ordsall Notts 51 P5
Ore E Susx 12 G7
Orford Suffk 35 N6
Orford Warrtn 57 L10
Organford Dorset 8 D9
Orkney Islands Ork ..111 h2
Orkney Neolithic Ork .111 g2
Orlestone Kent 13 J3
Orleton Herefs 39 J8
Orleton Worcs 39 M8
Orlingbury Nhants 32 C3
Ormesby R & Cl 66 D4
Ormesby St Margaret
Norfk 45 P7
Ormesby St Michael
Norfk 45 P7
Ormiscaig Highld ...105 M4
Ormiston E Loth 86 H8
Ormsaigmore Highld ..89 K4
Ormsary Ag & B 83 L8
Ormskirk Lancs 56 H7
Oronsay Ag & B 82 E5
Orphir Ork 111 h2
Orpington Gt Lon 21 P9
Orrell Sefton 56 G9
Orrell Wigan 57 K7
Orroland D & G 70 C5
Orsett Thurr 22 D7
Orslow Staffs 49 P11
Orston Notts 51 Q11
Orton Cumb 63 L1
Orton Nhants 32 B2
Orton Staffs 39 Q3
Orton Longueville C Pete .42 G10
Orton-on-the-Hill Leics .40 H6
Orton Waterville C Pete .42 G10
Orwell Cambs 33 K6
Osbaldeston Lancs ...57 M3
Osbaldwick C York ...59 N4
Osbaston Leics 41 K6
Osbaston Shrops 48 G10
Osbournby Lincs 42 F3
Oscroft Ches W 49 J3
Ose Highld 96 C2
Osgathorpe Leics 41 K4
Osgodby Lincs 52 F5
Osgodby N York 59 N7
Osgodby N York 67 M9
Oskaig Highld 96 G3
Oskamull Ag & B 89 K8
Osmaston Derbys 50 G11
Osmington Dorset 7 Q6
Osmington Mills Dorset .7 Q6
Osmondthorpe Leeds ..59 J7
Osmotherley N York ..66 C7
Osney Oxon 31 L11
Ospringe Kent 23 J10
Ossett Wakefd 58 H9
Ossington Notts 51 Q7
Osterley Gt Lon 21 J7
Oswaldkirk N York ...66 E10
Oswaldtwistle Lancs ..57 N4
Oswestry Shrops 48 F9
Otford Kent 21 Q10
Otham Kent 22 F11
Othery Somset 17 K9
Otley Leeds 58 G5
Otley Suffk 35 K5
Otterbourne Hants 9 M3
Otterburn N York 63 Q9
Otterburn Nthumb 72 F3
Otter Ferry Ag & B ...83 P6
Otterham Cnwll 4 E3
Otterhampton Somset .16 H7
Otternish W Isls 111 b4
Ottershaw Surrey 20 C9
Otterswick Shet 111 k3
Otterton Devon 6 E6
Ottery St Mary Devon ..6 E4
Ottinge Kent 13 M2
Ottringham E R Yk 61 M8
Oughterby Cumb 71 J7
Oughtibridge Sheff ...50 H3
Oughtrington Warrtn ..57 M10
Oulston N York 66 D11
Oulton Cumb 71 K5
Oulton Norfk 45 J4
Oulton Staffs 40 C3
Oulton Suffk 45 Q10
Oulton Broad Suffk ...45 Q10
Oulton Street Norfk ...45 J5
Oundle Nhants 42 E11
Ounsdale Staffs 39 Q4
Our Dynamic Earth
C Edin 86 F7
Ousby Cumb 64 B1
Ousden Suffk 34 C5
Ousefleet E R Yk 60 E9
Ouston Dur 73 M9
Outgate Cumb 62 G3
Outhgill Cumb 64 E7
Outhill Warwks 30 E2
Outlane Kirk 58 E9
Out Rawcliffe Lancs ..56 H1
Outwell Norfk 43 N8
Outwood Surrey 11 L2
Outwoods Staffs 49 P10
Ouzlewell Green Leeds .59 J8
Over Cambs 33 L3
Overbury Worcs 29 N2
Overcombe Dorset 7 Q6
Over Compton Dorset .17 N11
Overdale Crematorium
Bolton 57 M7
Over Haddon Derbys ..50 G7
Over Kellet Lancs 63 K7
Over Kiddington Oxon .31 K9
Overleigh Somset 17 L8
Over Norton Oxon 30 H8
Over Peover Ches E ...49 P1
Overpool Ches W 56 F12
Overscaig Highld 108 H10
Overseal Derbys 40 H4
Over Silton N York ...66 C8

Oversland Kent 23 K11
Overstone Nhants 32 B4
Over Stowey Somset ..16 G8
Overstrand Norfk 45 L3
Over Stratton Somset .17 L11
Overthorpe Nhants ...31 L6
Overton C Aber 102 H11
Overton Hants 19 N10
Overton Lancs 62 H9
Overton N York 59 M3
Overton Shrops 39 J7
Overton Swans 26 B10
Overton Wakefd 58 H10
Overton Wrexhm 48 G7
Overtown N Lans 85 N11
Over Wallop Hants ...19 K11
Over Whitacre Warwks .40 G8
Over Worton Oxon 31 K8
Oving Bucks 32 A11
Oving W Susx 10 E8
Ovingdean Br & H 11 M8
Ovingham Nthumb ...73 J7
Ovington Dur 65 K5
Ovington Essex 34 C1
Ovington Hants 9 P2
Ovington Norfk 44 F9
Ovington Nthumb 73 J7
Ower Hants 9 K4
Owermoigne Dorset ...8 B9
Owlerton Sheff 51 J3
Owlsmoor Br For 20 D10
Owlswick Bucks 20 C3
Owmby Lincs 52 E6
Owmby Lincs 52 F3
Owslebury Hants 9 N3
Owston Donc 59 M11
Owston Leics 41 Q6
Owston Ferry N Linc .52 B4
Owstwick E R Yk 61 N7
Owthorne E R Yk 61 N8
Owthorpe Notts 41 P2
Owton Manor Hartpl ..66 C2
Oxborough Norfk 44 C9
Oxcombe Lincs 53 K7
Oxenholme Cumb 63 K4
Oxenhope C Brad 58 D7
Oxen Park Cumb 62 G5
Oxenpill Somset 17 L7
Oxenton Gloucs 29 N3
Oxenwood Wilts 19 K8
Oxford Oxon 31 L11
Oxford Airport Oxon ..31 L10
Oxford Crematorium
Oxon 31 M11
Oxford Services Oxon .31 N12
Oxhey Herts 20 H4
Oxhill Warwks 30 H5
Oxley Wolves 40 B7
Oxley Green Essex ...22 H1
Oxlode Cambs 43 M11
Oxnam Border 80 F9
Oxnead Norfk 45 K5
Oxshott Surrey 21 J10
Oxspring Barns 50 H1
Oxted Surrey 21 N11
Oxton Border 80 C4
Oxton N York 59 L5
Oxton Notts 51 N9
Oxton Wirral 56 F10
Oxwich Swans 26 C10
Oxwich Green Swans .26 C10
Oykel Bridge Highld .106 F3
Oyne Abers 102 G9
Oystermouth Swans ..26 E10

P

Pabail W Isls 111 e2
Packington Leics 41 J5
Packmoor C Stke 49 Q5
Padanaram Angus 93 M5
Padbury Bucks 31 Q7
Paddington Gt Lon ...21 L7
Paddlesworth Kent ...13 M3
Paddlesworth Kent ...22 D10
Paddock Wood Kent ..12 D2
Padiham Lancs 57 P3
Padside N York 58 H3
Padstow Cnwll 3 K1
Padworth W Berk 19 Q7
Pagham W Susx 10 E9
Paglesham Essex 22 H5
Paignton Torbay 6 B10
Pailton Warwks 41 L10
Painscastle Powys 38 D11
Painshawfield Nthumb .73 J8
Painsthorpe E R Yk ..60 E3
Painswick Gloucs 29 M6
Painter's Forstal Kent .23 J10
Paisley Rens 84 H9
Paisley Woodside
Crematorium Rens ..84 H9
Pakefield Suffk 45 Q11
Pakenham Suffk 34 F4
Paley Street W & M ..20 E7
Palfrey Wsall 40 D7
Palgrave Suffk 35 J2
Pallington Dorset 8 B8
Palmersbridge Cnwll ..4 H7
Palmerston E Ayrs ...76 H7
Palnackie D & G 70 D4
Palnure D & G 69 L6
Palterton Derbys 51 L7
Pamber End Hants ...19 Q8
Pamber Green Hants ..19 Q8
Pamber Heath Hants ..19 Q8
Pamington Gloucs 29 N3
Pamphill Dorset 8 E7
Pampisford Cambs ...33 N7
Panbride Angus 93 P8
Pancrasweek Devon ..14 F10
Pandy Mons 28 D4
Pandy Tudur Conwy ..55 M8
Panfield Essex 34 C10
Pangbourne W Berk ..19 Q5
Pangdean W Susx 11 L7
Pannal N York 58 H4
Pannal Ash N York ...58 H4
Pant Shrops 48 F10
Pantasaph Flints 48 D1
Pant-ffrwyth Brdgnd ..27 K11
Pant Glas Gwynd 46 H3
Pantglas Powys 47 M10
Panton Lincs 52 H7
Pant-y-dwr Powys ...37 R6
Pant-y-mwyn Flints ..48 E3
Panxworth Norfk 45 M7
Papa Stour Airport Shet .111 j4
Papa Westray Airport Ork .111 h1
Pen-allt Herefs 28 G3

Papcastle Cumb 70 H8
Papigoe Highld 110 H5
Papple E Loth 87 L7
Papplewick Notts 51 M9
Papworth Everard
Cambs 33 J4
Papworth St Agnes
Cambs 33 J4
Par Cnwll 3 N5
Parbold Lancs 57 J6
Parbrook Somset 17 N8
Parc Gwynd 47 P5
Parc Gwyn
Crematorium Pembks .25 K6
Parc Seymour Newpt ..28 E9
Pardshaw Cumb 70 H9
Parham Suffk 35 M5
Park Nthumb 72 C8
Park D & G 78 E10
Park Corner Oxon 20 B6
Park Crematorium Hants .10 E1
Park Crematorium Lancs .56 G3
Parkend Gloucs 28 H7
Parker's Green Kent ..12 C1
Park Farm Kent 13 J3
Parkgate Ches W 56 F12
Parkgate D & G 78 G10
Park Gate Hants 9 N6
Park Gate Leeds 58 F6
Parkgate Surrey 11 K2
Parkgrove
Crematorium Angus .93 Q6
Parkhall W Duns 84 H8
Parkham Devon 14 G7
Parkmill Swans 26 D10
Park Royal Gt Lon 21 K7
Parkside Dur 73 Q10
Parkside N Lans 85 N10
Parkstone Poole 8 F8
Park Street Herts 21 J3
Park Wood
Crematorium Calder .58 E9
Parndon Wood
Crematorium Essex ..21 N3
Parracombe Devon ...15 L3
Parson Drove Cambs .43 L8
Parson's Heath Essex .34 G10
Partick C Glas 85 J9
Partington Traffd 57 N9
Partney Lincs 53 L9
Parton Cumb 70 F10
Partridge Green W Susx .11 J6
Parwich Derbys 50 F9
Passenham Nhants ...32 A8
Paston C Pete 42 H9
Paston Norfk 45 M4
Patcham Br & H 11 L8
Patching W Susx 10 H8
Patchway S Glos 28 H11
Pateley Bridge N York .58 F2
Pathhead Fife 86 F4
Pathhead Mdloth 86 H9
Path of Condie P & K .92 G12
Patna E Ayrs 76 G8
Patney Wilts 18 F8
Patrick IoM 56 b5
Patrick Brompton
N York 65 L8
Patricroft Salfd 57 N8
Patrington E R Yk 61 N9
Patrington Haven E R Yk .61 M9
Patrixbourne Kent ...23 M11
Patterdale Cumb 71 N11
Pattingham Staffs 39 P3
Pattishall Nhants 31 P4
Pattiswick Green Essex .34 D11
Paul Cnwll 2 C9
Paulerspury Nhants ..31 Q5
Paull E R Yk 61 K8
Paulton BaNES 17 P5
Pauperhaugh Nthumb .73 K2
Pavenham Bed 32 E5
Pawlett Somset 16 H7
Paxford Gloucs 30 F6
Paxton Border 81 K4
Payhembury Devon ...6 E3
Paythorne Lancs 63 P10
Peacehaven E Susx ..11 N9
Peak District National
Park 50 F3
Peak Forest Derbys ..50 E5
Peakirk C Pete 42 G8
Peasedown St John
BaNES 17 Q5
Peasemore W Berk ...19 M5
Peasenhall Suffk 35 M3
Pease Pottage W Susx .11 L4
Pease Pottage Services
W Susx 11 L4
Peaslake Surrey 10 H2
Peasley Cross St Hel .57 K9
Peasmarsh E Susx ...12 H5
Peathill Abers 103 J3
Peat Inn Fife 87 J1
Peatling Magna Leics .41 N8
Peatling Parva Leics ..41 N9
Pebmarsh Essex 34 E9
Pebsham E Susx 12 F8
Pebworth Worcs 30 F5
Pecket Well Calder ...58 C8
Peckforton Ches E ...49 K4
Peckham Gt Lon 21 M8
Peckleton Leics 41 L7
Pedlinge Kent 13 L3
Pedmore Dudley 40 B10
Pedwell Somset 17 K8
Peebles Border 79 L2
Peel IoM 56 b4
Peel Green
Crematorium Salfd ..57 N8
Peene Kent 13 M3
Pegsdon C Beds 32 G9
Pegswood Nthumb ...73 M4
Pegwell Kent 23 Q9
Peinchorran Highld ...96 G3
Peinlich Highld 104 F10
Peldon Essex 34 G12
Pelsall Wsall 40 D6
Pelton Dur 73 M9
Pelynt Cnwll 4 H5
Pemberton Carmth ...26 D8
Pemberton Wigan 57 K7
Pembrey Carmth 25 P8
Pembridge Herefs ...38 H9
Pembroke Pembks ...24 H8
Pembroke Dock Pembks .24 H8
Pembrokeshire Coast
National Park Pembks .24 E5
Pembury Kent 12 D2
Pen-allt Herefs 28 G3

Penallt Mons 28 F6
Penally Pembks 25 K8
Penarth V Glam 16 G2
Pen-bont
Rhydybeddau Cerdgn .37 L4
Penbryn Cerdgn 36 E9
Pencader Carmth 25 Q2
Pencaitland E Loth ...87 J8
Pencarnisiog IoA 54 D6
Pencarreg Carmth 37 J10
Pencelli Powys 27 M4
Penclawdd Swans 26 D9
Pencoed Brdgnd 27 K11
Pencombe Herefs 39 L10
Pencraig Herefs 28 C5
Pencraig Powys 48 B9
Pendeen Cnwll 2 B8
Penderyn Rhondd 27 K7
Pendine Carmth 25 L7
Pendlebury Salfd 57 P8
Pendleton Lancs 57 N2
Pendock Worcs 29 K3
Pendoggett Cnwll 4 C4
Pendomer Somset 7 M1
Pendoylan V Glam ...16 E2
Penegoes Powys 47 M10
Pen-ffordd Pembks ...25 J4
Pengam Caerph 27 N8
Pengam Cardif 27 P12
Penge Gt Lon 21 M8
Pengelly Cnwll 4 D4
Penhallow Cnwll 2 H5
Penhalvean Cnwll 2 G8
Penhill Swindn 18 H3
Penhow Newpt 28 E10
Penicuik Mdloth 86 F9
Penifiler Highld 96 F2
Peninver Ag & B 75 L7
Penistone Barns 50 G1
Penkill S Ayrs 76 D10
Penkridge Staffs 40 B5
Penley Wrexhm 48 H7
Penllyn V Glam 16 C2
Penmachno Conwy ...55 L10
Penmaen Caerph 27 N8
Penmaen Swans 26 D10
Penmaenmawr Conwy .55 K6
Penmaenpool Gwynd .47 L7
Penmark V Glam 16 E3
Penmount
Crematorium Cnwll ...3 J6
Penmynydd IoA 54 G6
Pennal Gwynd 47 L10
Pennan Abers 102 H3
Pennant Powys 47 P10
Pennerley Shrops 38 G3
Pennines 58 C7
Pennington Cumb 62 F6
Pennorth Powys 27 M4
Penn Street Bucks ...20 E4
Penny Bridge Cumb ..62 F5
Pennycross Ag & B ...89 L10
Pennyghael Ag & B ..89 L10
Pennyglen S Ayrs 76 E8
Pennymoor Devon ...15 P9
Pennywell Sundld 73 P9
Penparc Cerdgn 36 D10
Penperlleni Mons 28 C7
Penpoll Cnwll 4 E8
Penponds Cnwll 2 F7
Penpont D & G 78 D9
Pen-rhew Pembks ...36 D11
Penrhiwceiber Rhondd .27 M8
Pen Rhiwfawr Neath ..26 G6
Penrhiwllan Cerdgn ..36 F11
Penrhiw-pal Cerdgn ..36 F10
Penrhos Gwynd 46 F5
Penrhos Mons 28 E6
Penrhyn Bay Conwy ..55 M5
Penrhyn-coch Cerdgn .37 K4
Penrhyndeudraeth
Gwynd 47 K4
Penrice Swans 26 C10
Penrioch N Ayrs 75 N4
Penrith Cumb 71 Q9
Penrose Cnwll 3 K2
Penruddock Cumb ...71 N9
Penryn Cnwll 2 H8
Pensarn Conwy 55 P6
Pensax Worcs 39 N8
Penselwood Somset ..17 R9
Pensford BaNES 17 N4
Pensham Worcs 30 C5
Penshaw Sundld 73 N9
Penshurst Kent 11 Q2
Pensilva Cnwll 4 H6
Pensnett Dudley 40 B9
Pentewan Cnwll 3 M6
Pentir Gwynd 54 H8
Pentire Cnwll 2 H4
Pentlow Essex 34 D7
Pentney Norfk 44 C7
Penton Mewsey Hants .19 K10
Pentraeth IoA 54 G6
Pentre Mons 28 E8
Pentre Rhondd 27 K9
Pentre Shrops 48 G11
Pentrebach Myr Td ..27 M7
Pentre-bach Powys ..27 J3
Pentre Berw IoA 54 F7
Pentrebychan
Crematorium
Wrexhm 48 F6
Pentrecelyn Denbgs ..48 D5
Pentre-celyn Powys ..47 P9
Pentre-chwyth Swans .26 F9
Pentre-cwrt Carmth ..25 P2
Pentredwr Denbgs ...48 E6
Pentrefelin Gwynd ...47 J4
Pentrefoelas Conwy ..55 M10
Pentregat Cerdgn 36 F9
Pentre-Gwenlais Carmth .26 E5
Pentre Hodrey Shrops .38 G6
Pentre Llanrhaeadr
Denbgs 48 C3
Pentre Meyrick V Glam .16 C2
Pentre-tafarn-y-fedw
Conwy 55 M8
Pentrich Derbys 51 K9
Pentridge Dorset 8 F4
Pent-twyn Mons 28 F7
Pentwynmaur Caerph .27 P9
Pentyrch Cardif 27 M11
Penwithick Cnwll 3 M5
Penybanc Carmth 26 E4
Penybont Powys 38 C8
Pen-y-bont-fawr Powys .48 C9
Pen-y-bryn Pembks ..36 C11

184 Penycae – Quidenham

Penycae Wrexhm 48 F6
Pen-y-clawdd Mons 28 E7
Pen-y-coedcae Rhondd 27 M10
Penycwn Pembks 24 E4
Pen-y-felin Flints 48 D2
Penyffordd Flints 48 F4
Pen-y-Garnedd Powys 48 C10
Pen-y-graig Gwynd 46 C5
Penygraig Rhondd 27 L10
Penygroes Carmth 26 D6
Penygroes Gwynd 54 F10
Pen-y-Mynydd Carmth 26 C7
Penymynydd Flints 48 F3
Penysarn IoA 54 F4
Pen-y-stryt Denbgs 48 E5
Penywaun Rhondd 27 K7
Penzance Cnwll 2 D9
Peopleton Worcs 30 C4
Peplow Shrops 49 L9
Perceton N Ayrs 76 F4
Percyhorner Abers 103 K3
Perham Down Wilts 19 J10
Periton Somset 16 C7
Perivale Gt Lon 21 J6
Perkins Village Devon 6 D5
Perlethorpe Notts 51 N6
Perranarworthal Cnwll 2 H7
Perranporth Cnwll 2 H5
Perranuthnoe Cnwll 2 D9
Perranwell Cnwll 2 H7
Perranzabuloe Cnwll 2 H5
Perry Birm 40 E8
Perry Barr Birm 40 E8
Perry Barr Crematorium Birm 40 E8
Perry Green Wilts 18 E3
Pershall Staffs 49 P9
Pershore Worcs 30 C5
Pertenhall Bed 32 F4
Perth P & K 92 G10
Perth Crematorium P & K 92 G9
Perthy Shrops 48 G8
Perton Herefs 28 H2
Perton Staffs 39 Q3
Peterborough C Pete 42 H9
Peterborough Crematorium C Pete 42 G9
Peterborough Services Cambs 42 G10
Peterchurch Herefs 28 D2
Peterculter C Aber 95 N2
Peterhead Abers 103 M6
Peterlee Dur 73 Q11
Petersfield Hants 10 C5
Peter's Green Herts 32 G11
Petersham Gt Lon 21 J8
Peters Marland Devon 14 H9
Peterstone Wentlooge Newpt 28 B11
Peterston-super-Ely V Glam 16 E2
Peterstow Herefs 28 G4
Peter Tavy Devon 5 K5
Petham Kent 23 L12
Petherwin Gate Cnwll 4 G3
Petrockstow Devon 15 J9
Pett E Susx 12 G7
Pettaugh Suffk 35 J5
Petterden Angus 93 M7
Pettinain S Lans 77 Q3
Pettistree Suffk 35 L6
Petton Devon 16 D10
Petts Wood Gt Lon 21 N9
Pettycur Fife 86 F5
Pettymuk Abers 103 J9
Petworth W Susx 10 F6
Pevensey E Susx 12 D8
Pevensey Bay E Susx 12 D8
Pewsey Wilts 18 H8
Phepson Worcs 30 C3
Philham Devon 14 E7
Philiphaugh Border 79 N4
Phillack Cnwll 2 E7
Philleigh Cnwll 3 K7
Philpstoun W Loth 86 C6
Phoenix Green Hants 20 C11
Pibsbury Somset 17 L10
Pickburn Donc 59 L11
Pickering N York 66 H10
Pickford Covtry 40 H10
Pickhill N York 65 N10
Picklescott Shrops 38 H3
Pickmere Ches E 57 M12
Pickney Somset 16 G9
Pickwell Leics 42 B7
Pickworth Lincs 42 F4
Pickworth Rutlnd 42 E7
Picton Ches W 48 H2
Picton N York 65 P6
Piddinghoe E Susx 11 N9
Piddington Nhants 32 B6
Piddington Oxon 31 N10
Piddlehinton Dorset 7 Q4
Piddletrenthide Dorset 7 Q3
Pidley Cambs 33 K2
Piercebridge Darltn 65 L4
Pierowall Ork 111 h1
Pilgrims Hatch Essex 22 C4
Pilham Lincs 52 C5
Pillaton Cnwll 4 H7
Pillerton Hersey Warwks 30 H4
Pillerton Priors Warwks 30 H5
Pilley Barns 51 J1
Pilley Hants 9 K7
Pillgwenlly Newpt 28 C10
Pilling Lancs 62 H11
Pilning S Glos 28 G10
Pilsbury Derbys 50 E7
Pilsdon Dorset 7 K3
Pilsley Derbys 50 G6
Pilsley Derbys 51 K8
Pilson Green Norfk 45 N7
Piltdown E Susx 11 N5
Pilton Devon 15 K5
Pilton Nhants 42 E12
Pilton Rutlnd 42 D9
Pilton Somset 17 N7
Pimlico Herts 20 H3
Pimperne Dorset 8 D5
Pinchbeck Lincs 43 J5
Pin Green Herts 33 J10
Pinhoe Devon 6 C4
Pinley Green Warwks 30 G2
Pinminnoch S Ayrs 76 D11
Pinmore S Ayrs 76 D11
Pinn Devon 6 E5
Pinner Gt Lon 20 H5
Pinner Green Gt Lon 20 H5
Pinvin Worcs 30 C4
Pinwherry S Ayrs 68 G2
Pinxton Derbys 51 L9
Pipe and Lyde Herefs 39 J12
Pipe Aston Herefs 39 J7
Pipe Gate Shrops 49 N7
Piperhill Highld 100 D5
Pipewell Nhants 42 B11
Pirbright Surrey 20 F11
Pirnie Border 80 E8
Pirnmill N Ayrs 75 N4
Pirton Herts 32 G9
Pishill Oxon 20 B5
Pistyll Gwynd 46 E3
Pitblae Abers 103 K3
Pitcairngreen P & K 92 F9
Pitcalnie Highld 107 N7
Pitcaple Abers 102 F9
Pitcarity Angus 94 F8
Pitchcombe Gloucs 29 L7
Pitchcott Bucks 31 Q9
Pitchford Shrops 39 K2
Pitch Green Bucks 20 C3
Pitchroy Moray 101 J7
Pitcombe Somset 17 P9
Pitcox E Loth 87 M7
Pitfichie Abers 102 E11
Pitglassie Abers 102 F6
Pitgrudy Highld 107 N4
Pitlessie Fife 86 G1
Pitlochry P & K 92 D4
Pitmachie Abers 102 E9
Pitmain Highld 99 L8
Pitmedden Abers 103 J9
Pitmedden Garden Abers 103 J9
Pitminster Somset 16 G11
Pitmuies Angus 93 P6
Pitmunie Abers 102 E11
Pitney Somset 17 L9
Pitroddie P & K 93 J10
Pitscottie Fife 93 M11
Pitsea Essex 22 E6
Pitsford Nhants 31 Q1
Pitstone Bucks 20 F1
Pittarrow Abers 95 M7
Pittenweem Fife 87 K2
Pitteuchar Fife 86 F3
Pittington Dur 73 N11
Pittodrie House Hotel Abers 102 F9
Pitton Wilts 8 H2
Pittulie Abers 103 K2
Pity Me Dur 73 M10
Pixham Surrey 21 J12
Plains N Lans 85 N9
Plaish Shrops 39 K3
Plaistow Gt Lon 21 N6
Plaistow W Susx 10 G4
Plaitford Hants 9 J4
Plawsworth Dur 73 M10
Plaxtol Kent 22 C11
Playden E Susx 12 H6
Playford Suffk 35 K7
Play Hatch Oxon 20 B7
Playing Place Cnwll 3 J7
Playley Green Gloucs 29 K3
Plealey Shrops 38 H2
Plean Stirlg 85 P5
Pleasance Fife 93 J12
Pleasington Bl w D 57 M4
Pleasington Crematorium Bl w D 57 M4
Pleasley Derbys 51 L7
Pleasurewood Hills Suffk 45 Q10
Plemstall Ches W 49 J2
Pleshey Essex 22 D1
Plockton Highld 97 L3
Plowden Shrops 38 H5
Pluckley Kent 12 H2
Pluckley Thorne Kent 12 H2
Plumbland Cumb 71 J7
Plumley Ches E 49 N1
Plumpton Cumb 71 P7
Plumpton E Susx 11 M7
Plumpton Nhants 31 N5
Plumpton Green E Susx 11 M6
Plumstead Gt Lon 21 N7
Plumstead Norfk 45 J3
Plumtree Notts 41 N2
Plungar Leics 41 Q1
Plurenden Kent 12 H3
Plush Dorset 7 Q3
Plwmp Cerdgn 36 F9
Plymouth C Plym 5 K8
Plympton C Plym 5 L8
Plymstock C Plym 5 L9
Plymtree Devon 6 E3
Pockley N York 66 F9
Pocklington E R Yk 60 D4
Podimore Somset 17 M10
Podington Bed 32 D4
Podmore Staffs 49 P8
Pointon Lincs 42 G4
Pokesdown Bmouth 8 G8
Polbain Highld 105 Q1
Polbathic Cnwll 4 H8
Polbeth W Loth 86 B9
Poldark Mine Cnwll 2 G9
Polebrook Nhants 42 F11
Polegate E Susx 12 C8
Polesden Lacey Surrey 21 J11
Polesworth Warwks 40 H7
Polglass Highld 105 Q2
Polgooth Cnwll 3 M5
Polgown D & G 77 M9
Poling W Susx 10 G8
Poling Corner W Susx 10 G8
Polkerris Cnwll 4 D9
Pollington E R Yk 59 N9
Polloch Highld 89 Q3
Pollokshaws C Glas 85 J10
Pollokshields C Glas 85 J9
Polmassick Cnwll 3 L6
Polmont Falk 85 Q7
Polnish Highld 97 K12
Polperro Cnwll 4 F9
Polruan Cnwll 4 E9
Polstead Suffk 34 G8
Poltalloch Ag & B 83 M4
Poltimore Devon 6 C4
Polton Mdloth 86 F8
Polwarth Border 80 G4
Polyphant Cnwll 4 G4
Polzeath Cnwll 4 B4
Pomathorn Mdloth 86 F9
Pondersbridge Cambs 43 J10
Ponders End Gt Lon 21 M4
Ponsanooth Cnwll 2 H8
Ponsworthy Devon 5 N5
Pont Abraham Services Carmth 26 D7
Pontantwn Carmth 25 Q6
Pontardawe Neath 26 F7
Pontarddulais Swans 26 D7
Pont-ar-gothi Carmth 26 C5
Pontarsais Carmth 25 Q3
Pontblyddyn Flints 48 F4
Pontcysyllte Aqueduct Wrexhm 48 F7
Pontefract Wakefd 59 L9
Pontefract Crematorium Wakefd 59 K9
Ponteland Nthumb 73 L6
Ponterwyd Cerdgn 37 M4
Pontesbury Shrops 38 H2
Pontesford Shrops 38 H2
Pontfadog Wrexhm 48 E7
Pontfaen Pembks 24 H3
Pont-faen Powys 27 L3
Pontgarreg Cerdgn 36 F9
Ponthenri Carmth 26 C7
Ponthir Torfn 28 C9
Ponthirwaun Cerdgn 36 D10
Pontllanfraith Caerph 27 P9
Pontlliw Swans 26 E8
Pontlottyn Caerph 27 N7
Pontlyfni Gwynd 54 F10
Pontneddfechan Neath 27 J7
Pontnewydd Torfn 28 C9
Pontrhydfendigaid Cerdgn 37 M7
Pont-rhyd-y-fen Neath 26 H9
Pontrhydygroes Cerdgn 37 M6
Pontrilas Herefs 28 D4
Pont Robert Powys 48 C11
Pontshaen Cerdgn 36 G10
Pontsticill Myr Td 27 M6
Pontwelly Carmth 36 G11
Pontyates Carmth 26 C7
Pontyberem Carmth 26 C6
Pontybodkin Flints 48 F4
Pontyclun Rhondd 27 L11
Pontycymer Brdgnd 27 J9
Pont-y-pant Conwy 55 L10
Pontypool Torfn 28 C8
Pontypridd Rhondd 27 M10
Pontywaun Caerph 27 P9
Pool Cnwll 2 G7
Poole Poole 8 E8
Poole Crematorium Poole 8 E8
Poole Keynes Gloucs 18 E2
Poolewe Highld 105 M6
Pooley Bridge Cumb 71 P10
Poolfold Staffs 50 B8
Poolhill Gloucs 29 K3
Pool in Wharfedale Leeds 58 G5
Pool of Muckhart Clacks 86 B3
Pool Street Essex 34 C8
Poplar Gt Lon 21 M7
Porchfield IoW 9 M8
Poringland Norfk 45 L9
Porkellis Cnwll 2 G8
Porlock Somset 15 Q3
Porlock Weir Somset 15 P3
Portachoillan Ag & B 83 L10
Port-an-Eorna Highld 97 K4
Port Appin Ag & B 90 C7
Port Askaig Ag & B 82 F8
Portavadie Ag & B 83 P8
Port Bannatyne Ag & B 84 B9
Portbury N Som 17 M2
Port Carlisle Cumb 71 K3
Port Charlotte Ag & B 82 C10
Portchester Hants 9 Q6
Portchester Crematorium Hants 9 Q6
Port Driseach Ag & B 83 Q8
Port Ellen Ag & B 74 E4
Port Elphinstone Abers 102 G10
Portencalzie D & G 68 D5
Portencross N Ayrs 76 C2
Port Erin IoM 56 a6
Portesham Dorset 7 N5
Portessie Moray 101 N3
Port Eynon Swans 26 C10
Portfield Gate Pembks 24 G6
Portgate Devon 5 J3
Port Gaverne Cnwll 4 C4
Port Glasgow Inver 84 F7
Portgordon Moray 101 M3
Portgower Highld 110 B11
Porth Cnwll 3 J4
Porth Rhondd 27 L9
Porthallow Cnwll 2 H10
Porthallow Cnwll 4 F9
Porthcawl Brdgnd 26 H12
Porthcothan Cnwll 3 K2
Porthcurno Cnwll 2 B10
Port Henderson Highld 105 L7
Porthgain Pembks 24 E3
Porthgwarra Cnwll 2 B10
Porthill Staffs 49 Q6
Porthkerry V Glam 16 E3
Porthleven Cnwll 2 F9
Porthmadog Gwynd 47 J4
Porth Navas Cnwll 2 H9
Porthoustock Cnwll 3 J10
Porthpean Cnwll 3 M5
Porthtowan Cnwll 2 G6
Porthyrhyd Carmth 26 C5
Portincaple Ag & B 84 D4
Portington E R Yk 60 D7
Portinnisherrich Ag & B 83 P2
Portinscale Cumb 71 L10
Port Isaac Cnwll 4 C4
Portishead N Som 17 L2
Portknockie Moray 101 N2
Portland Dorset 7 P8
Portlethen Abers 95 Q3
Portling D & G 70 E5
Portloe Cnwll 3 L7
Port Logan D & G 68 E10
Portmahomack Highld 107 Q5
Portmeirion Gwynd 47 J4
Portmellon Cnwll 3 M7
Port Mòr Highld 89 J1
Portnacroish Ag & B 90 C6
Portnaguran W Isls 111 e2
Portnahaven Ag & B 74 B2
Portnalong Highld 96 D3
Port nan Giùran W Isls 111 e2
Port nan Long W Isls 111 b4
Port Nis W Isls 111 e1
Portobello C Edin 86 G7
Portobello Wolves 40 C7
Port of Menteith Stirlg 85 K3
Port of Ness W Isls 111 e1
Porton Wilts 18 H12
Portpatrick D & G 68 D8
Port Quin Cnwll 4 B4
Port Ramsay Ag & B 90 B7
Portreath Cnwll 2 F6
Portreath Harbour Cnwll 2 F6
Portree Highld 96 F2
Port Righ Ag & B 75 M5
Port St Mary IoM 56 b7
Portscatho Cnwll 3 K8
Portsea C Port 9 Q7
Portskerra Highld 109 Q3
Portskewett Mons 28 F10
Portslade Br & H 11 K8
Portslade-by-Sea Br & H 11 L8
Portslogan D & G 68 D7
Portsmouth C Port 9 Q7
Portsmouth Calder 58 B8
Portsmouth Dockyard C Port 9 Q7
Port Soderick IoM 56 c6
Portsonachan Hotel Ag & B 90 E11
Portsoy Abers 102 D3
Port Sunlight Wirral 56 G11
Portswood C Sotn 9 M5
Port Talbot Neath 26 G10
Port Tennant Swans 26 F9
Portuairk Highld 89 K3
Portway Sandw 40 C9
Portway Worcs 40 E11
Port Wemyss Ag & B 74 B3
Port William D & G 69 J9
Portwrinkle Cnwll 4 H9
Portyerrock D & G 69 L10
Poslingford Suffk 34 C7
Posso Border 79 K3
Postbridge Devon 5 N4
Postcombe Oxon 20 B4
Postling Kent 13 M3
Postwick Norfk 45 L8
Potarch Abers 95 K3
Potten End Herts 20 G2
Potter Brompton N York 67 L11
Potterhanworth Lincs 52 F9
Potterhanworth Booths Lincs 52 F9
Potter Heigham Norfk 45 N6
Potterne Wilts 18 E8
Potterne Wick Wilts 18 E8
Potters Bar Herts 21 K3
Potters Crouch Herts 20 H3
Potters Green Covtry 41 J10
Potters Marston Leics 41 L8
Potterspury Nhants 31 Q5
Potter Street Essex 21 P2
Potterton Abers 103 K11
Potto N York 66 C6
Potton C Beds 32 H6
Pott Shrigley Ches E 50 C5
Poughill Cnwll 14 D10
Poughill Devon 15 P9
Poulner Hants 8 H6
Poulshot Wilts 18 E8
Poulton Gloucs 18 G1
Poulton Wirral 56 F10
Poulton-le-Fylde Lancs 56 G2
Poundbury Dorset 7 P5
Poundffald Swans 26 D9
Pound Green E Susx 11 P5
Pound Green Suffk 34 C6
Pound Hill W Susx 11 L3
Poundon Bucks 31 N8
Poundsgate Devon 5 N6
Poundstock Cnwll 14 D11
Pouton D & G 69 L9
Povey Cross Surrey 11 L2
Powburn Nthumb 81 M10
Powderham Devon 6 C6
Powerstock Dorset 7 M4
Powfoot D & G 71 J3
Powick Worcs 39 Q10
Powmill P & K 86 B3
Poxwell Dorset 7 Q6
Poyle Slough 20 G7
Poynings W Susx 11 L7
Poyntington Dorset 17 P11
Poynton Ches E 50 B4
Poynton Green Wrekin 49 K10
Praa Sands Cnwll 2 E9
Praze-an-Beeble Cnwll 2 F8
Prees Shrops 49 K8
Preesall Lancs 62 G11
Prees Green Shrops 49 K8
Prees Heath Shrops 49 K7
Prees Higher Heath Shrops 49 K8
Pren-gwyn Cerdgn 36 G10
Prenteg Gwynd 47 J3
Prescot Knows 57 J9
Prescott Devon 16 E12
Presnerb Angus 94 C8
Prestatyn Denbgs 56 C11
Prestbury Ches E 50 B5
Prestbury Gloucs 29 N4
Presteigne Powys 38 G8
Prestleigh Somset 17 P7
Preston Border 87 P10
Preston Br & H 11 L8
Preston Devon 6 B7
Preston Dorset 7 Q6
Preston E R Yk 61 K7
Preston Gloucs 18 F1
Preston Herts 32 H10
Preston Kent 23 K10
Preston Kent 23 N10
Preston Lancs 57 K3
Preston Nthumb 81 P8
Preston Rutlnd 42 C9
Preston Somset 16 E8
Preston Torbay 6 B9
Preston Wilts 18 F5
Preston Bagot Warwks 30 F2
Preston Bissett Bucks 31 P8
Preston Bowyer Somset 16 F10
Preston Brockhurst Shrops 49 K9
Preston Brook Halton 57 K11
Preston Candover Hants 19 Q11
Preston Capes Nhants 31 M3
Preston Crematorium Lancs 57 L3
Preston Green Warwks 30 F2
Preston Gubbals Shrops 49 J10
Preston on Stour Warwks 30 G4
Preston on the Hill Halton 57 K11
Preston on Wye Herefs 28 D1
Prestonpans E Loth 86 H7
Preston Patrick Cumb 63 K5
Preston Plucknett Somset 17 M11
Preston St Mary Suffk 34 F6
Preston-under-Scar N York 65 J8
Preston upon the Weald Moors Wrekin 49 M11
Preston Wynne Herefs 39 K11
Prestwich Bury 57 P7
Prestwick S Ayrs 76 F6
Prestwick Airport S Ayrs 76 F6
Prestwood Bucks 20 E4
Prickwillow Cambs 33 P1
Priddy Somset 17 M6
Priest Hutton Lancs 63 K7
Priestland E Ayrs 77 J4
Priest Weston Shrops 38 F3
Primrosehill Border 87 P10
Primrose Hill Dudley 40 C9
Primsidemill Border 80 H8
Princes Risborough Bucks 20 D3
Princethorpe Warwks 41 K12
Princetown Devon 5 M5
Priors Hardwick Warwks 31 L3
Priorslee Wrekin 49 N12
Priors Marston Warwks 31 L3
Priors Norton Gloucs 29 M4
Priston BaNES 17 Q4
Prittlewell Sthend 22 G6
Privett Hants 10 B5
Prixford Devon 15 J5
Probus Cnwll 3 K6
Prora E Loth 87 K6
Prospect Cumb 71 J7
Prospidnick Cnwll 2 F9
Protstonhill Abers 102 H3
Prudhoe Nthumb 73 K8
Publow BaNES 17 P4
Puckeridge Herts 33 L11
Puckington Somset 17 K11
Pucklechurch S Glos 17 Q2
Puddington Ches W 48 G2
Puddington Devon 15 P9
Puddletown Dorset 7 Q4
Pudsey Leeds 58 G7
Pulborough W Susx 10 G6
Pulford Ches W 48 G4
Pulham Dorset 7 Q2
Pulham Market Norfk 45 K11
Pulham St Mary Norfk 45 K11
Pulloxhill C Beds 32 F9
Pulverbatch Shrops 38 H2
Pumpherston W Loth 86 C8
Pumsaint Carmth 37 K11
Puncheston Pembks 24 H3
Puncknowle Dorset 7 M5
Punnett's Town E Susx 12 C6
Purbrook Hants 10 A8
Purfleet Thurr 22 B7
Puriton Somset 17 J7
Purleigh Essex 22 G3
Purley Gt Lon 21 L10
Purley W Berk 19 Q5
Purse Caundle Dorset 17 Q11
Purtington Somset 7 K2
Purton Gloucs 29 J7
Purton Gloucs 29 J7
Purton Wilts 18 G4
Purton Stoke Wilts 18 G3
Pury End Nhants 31 P5
Pusey Oxon 19 L2
Putley Herefs 28 H2
Putley Green Herefs 28 H2
Putney Gt Lon 21 K8
Putney Vale Crematorium Gt Lon 21 K8
Puttenham Surrey 10 E1
Puxley Nhants 31 Q6
Puxton N Som 17 K4
Pwll Carmth 26 C8
Pwll-glâs Denbgs 48 C5
Pwllgloyw Powys 27 L3
Pwllheli Gwynd 46 F4
Pwllmeyric Mons 28 F9
Pwll-trap Carmth 25 M5
Pwll-y-glaw Neath 26 H9
Pye Bridge Derbys 51 K9
Pyecombe W Susx 11 L7
Pyle Brdgnd 26 H11
Pyleigh Somset 16 F9
Pylle Somset 17 N8
Pymoor Cambs 43 M11
Pymore Dorset 7 L4
Pyrford Surrey 20 G10
Pyrton Oxon 20 B4
Pytchley Nhants 32 C2
Pyworthy Devon 14 F10

Q

Quadring Lincs 42 H4
Quadring Eaudike Lincs 43 J4
Quainton Bucks 31 Q9
Quantock Hills Somset 16 G8
Quarff Shet 111 k4
Quarley Hants 19 J11
Quarndon Derbys 51 J11
Quarrier's Village Inver 84 F9
Quarrington Lincs 42 F2
Quarrington Hill Dur 73 N12
Quarry Bank Dudley 40 B9
Quarrywood Moray 101 J3
Quarter N Ayrs 84 D10
Quarter S Lans 85 M11
Quatford Shrops 39 N4
Quatt Shrops 39 N5
Quebec Dur 73 L11
Quedgeley Gloucs 29 L6
Queen Adelaide Cambs 33 P1
Queen Camel Somset 17 N10
Queen Charlton BaNES 17 P3
Queen Elizabeth Forest Park Stirlg 84 H3
Queenhill Worcs 29 M2
Queen Oak Dorset 8 B2
Queen's Bower IoW 9 P9
Queensbury C Brad 58 E7
Queensferry Flints 48 G2
Queensferry Crossing Fife 86 D6
Queenslie C Glas 85 L9
Queen's Park Bed 32 E6
Queenzieburn N Lans 85 L7
Quendon Essex 33 N10
Queniborough Leics 41 N5
Quenington Gloucs 30 F12
Queslett Birm 40 E8
Quethiock Cnwll 4 G7
Quidenham Norfk 44 G11

Quidhampton Wilts ...8 G2
Quinton Nhants ...31 R4
Quintrell Downs Cnwll ...3 J4
Quixwood Border ...87 P9
Quoig P & K ...92 C10
Quorn Leics ...41 M4
Quothquan S Lans ...78 G2
Quoyburray Ork ...111 h2
Quoyloo Ork ...111 g2

R

Raasay Highld ...96 G2
Rachan Mill Border ...79 J3
Rachub Gwynd ...55 J7
Rackenford Devon ...15 P8
Rackham W Susx ...10 G7
Rackheath Norfk ...45 L7
Racks D & G ...70 G1
Rackwick Ork ...111 g3
Radbourne Derbys ...40 H1
Radcliffe Bury ...57 P7
Radcliffe on Trent Notts ...51 N11
Radclive Bucks ...31 P7
Raddery Highld ...107 L9
Radernie Fife ...87 J1
Radford Covtry ...41 J10
Radford Semele Warwks ...31 J2
Radlett Herts ...21 J4
Radley Oxon ...19 N2
Radley Green Essex ...22 D3
Radnage Bucks ...20 C4
Radstock BaNES ...17 P5
Radstone Nhants ...31 N6
Radway Warwks ...31 J5
Radwell Bed ...32 E5
Radwell Herts ...32 H9
Radwinter Essex ...33 P8
Radyr Cardif ...27 N11
Rafford Moray ...100 G4
RAF Museum Cosford Shrops ...39 P2
RAF Museum Hendon Gt Lon ...21 K5
Ragdale Leics ...41 P4
Raglan Mons ...28 E7
Ragnall Notts ...52 B8
Raigbeg Highld ...99 M4
Rainbow Hill Worcs ...39 Q10
Rainford St Hel ...57 J8
Rainham Gt Lon ...21 Q7
Rainham Medway ...22 F9
Rainhill St Hel ...57 J9
Rainhill Stoops St Hel ...57 J10
Rainow Ches E ...50 C6
Rainsbrook Crematorium Warwks ...41 L11
Rainton N York ...65 P11
Rainworth Notts ...51 N8
Rait P & K ...93 J3
Raithby Lincs ...53 K6
Raithby Lincs ...53 L9
Rake Hants ...10 C5
Ralia Highld ...99 K9
Ramasaig Highld ...96 A2
Rame Cnwll ...2 G8
Rame Cnwll ...5 J9
Rampisham Dorset ...7 N3
Rampside Cumb ...62 E8
Rampton Cambs ...33 L3
Rampton Notts ...52 B7
Ramsbottom Bury ...57 P5
Ramsbury Wilts ...19 J6
Ramscraigs Highld ...110 D9
Ramsdean Hants ...10 B5
Ramsdell Hants ...19 P8
Ramsden Oxon ...31 J10
Ramsden Bellhouse Essex ...22 E5
Ramsey Cambs ...43 J11
Ramsey Essex ...35 K10
Ramsey IoM ...56 e3
Ramsey Forty Foot Cambs ...43 K11
Ramsey Heights Cambs ...43 J12
Ramsey Island Essex ...23 J3
Ramsey Island Pembks ...24 C4
Ramsey Mereside Cambs ...43 J11
Ramsey St Mary's Cambs ...43 J11
Ramsgate Kent ...23 Q9
Ramsgill N York ...65 K12
Ramshope Nthumb ...80 G12
Ramshorn Staffs ...50 E10
Ramsnest Common Surrey ...10 F4
Ranby Lincs ...52 H7
Ranby Notts ...51 P5
Rand Lincs ...52 G7
Randalls Park Crematorium Surrey ...21 J11
Randwick Gloucs ...29 L7
Ranfurly Rens ...84 G9
Rangemore Staffs ...40 F3
Rangeworthy S Glos ...29 J10
Rankinston E Ayrs ...76 H8
Rannoch Station P & K ...91 L5
Ranscombe Somset ...16 C7
Ranskill Notts ...51 P4
Ranton Staffs ...49 Q10
Ranton Green Staffs ...49 Q10
Ranworth Norfk ...45 M7
Raploch Stirlg ...85 N4
Rapness Ork ...111 h1
Rascarrel D & G ...70 D6
Rashfield Ag & B ...84 C6
Rashwood Worcs ...30 B2
Raskelf N York ...66 C12
Rastrick Calder ...58 F9
Ratagan Highld ...97 N6
Ratby Leics ...41 L6
Ratcliffe Culey Leics ...41 J7
Ratcliffe on Soar Notts ...41 L2
Ratcliffe on the Wreake Leics ...41 N5
Rathen Abers ...103 K3
Rathillet Fife ...93 L10
Rathmell N York ...63 P9
Ratho C Edin ...86 D7
Ratho Station C Edin ...86 D7
Rathven Moray ...101 M3
Ratley Warwks ...31 J5
Ratling Kent ...23 N11
Ratlinghope Shrops ...38 H3
Rattar Highld ...110 F2
Rattery Devon ...5 P7
Rattlesden Suffk ...34 F5
Ratton Village E Susx ...12 C9
Rattray P & K ...92 H6

Raunds Nhants ...32 E3
Ravenfield Rothm ...51 L2
Ravenglass Cumb ...62 C3
Raveningham Norfk ...45 N10
Ravenscar N York ...67 L7
Ravenscraig N Lans ...85 N10
Ravensden Bed ...32 F6
Ravenshead Notts ...51 M9
Ravensthorpe Kirk ...58 G9
Ravensthorpe Nhants ...41 P12
Ravenstone Leics ...41 K5
Ravenstone M Keyn ...32 C6
Ravenstonedale Cumb ...63 N2
Ravenstruther S Lans ...77 Q3
Ravensworth N York ...65 K6
Rawcliffe C York ...59 M4
Rawcliffe E R Yk ...59 P9
Rawdon Leeds ...58 G6
Rawdon Crematorium Leeds ...58 G6
Rawling Street Kent ...22 H10
Rawmarsh Rothm ...51 K2
Rawreth Essex ...22 F5
Rawridge Devon ...6 G2
Rawtenstall Lancs ...57 P4
Raydon Suffk ...34 H8
Rayleigh Essex ...22 F5
Rayne Essex ...34 C11
Raynes Park Gt Lon ...21 K9
Reach Cambs ...33 P4
Read Lancs ...57 P2
Reading Readg ...20 B8
Reading Crematorium Readg ...20 B8
Reading Services W Berk ...20 A9
Reading Street Kent ...12 H4
Reading Street Kent ...23 Q9
Reagill Cumb ...64 B4
Realwa Cnwll ...2 H5
Rearquhar Highld ...107 M4
Rearsby Leics ...41 P5
Reay Highld ...110 A3
Reculver Kent ...23 N9
Red Ball Devon ...16 E11
Redberth Pembks ...25 J7
Redbourn Herts ...20 H2
Redbourne N Linc ...52 D4
Redbrook Gloucs ...28 G6
Redbrook Wrexhm ...49 K7
Redbrook Street Kent ...12 H3
Redburn Highld ...100 H6
Redcar R & Cl ...66 E3
Redcastle D & G ...70 D3
Redcastle Highld ...107 J11
Redding Falk ...85 Q7
Reddingmuirhead Falk ...85 Q7
Reddish Stockp ...50 B3
Redditch Worcs ...30 D1
Redditch Crematorium Worcs ...30 D1
Rede Suffk ...34 D5
Redenhall Norfk ...45 L12
Redesmouth Nthumb ...72 F5
Redford Abers ...95 M7
Redford Angus ...93 P6
Redford W Susx ...10 D5
Redfordgreen Border ...79 M6
Redgorton P & K ...92 G9
Redgrave Suffk ...34 H2
Redhill Abers ...95 M2
Red Hill Bmouth ...8 G8
Redhill Herts ...33 J9
Redhill N Som ...17 M4
Redhill Surrey ...21 L12
Redisham Suffk ...45 N12
Redland Bristl ...17 N2
Redland Ork ...111 h2
Redlingfield Suffk ...35 K3
Redlingfield Green Suffk ...35 K3
Red Lodge Suffk ...34 B3
Redlynch Somset ...17 Q9
Redlynch Wilts ...8 H3
Redmarley Worcs ...39 N8
Redmarley D'Abitot Gloucs ...29 K3
Redmarshall S on T ...65 P4
Redmile Leics ...42 B3
Redmire N York ...65 J8
Redmyre Abers ...95 M6
Rednal Shrops ...48 G9
Redpath Border ...80 D7
Redpoint Highld ...105 K3
Red Roses Carmth ...25 L6
Red Row Nthumb ...73 M2
Redruth Cnwll ...2 G7
Redstone P & K ...92 H8
Red Street Staffs ...49 P5
Red Wharf Bay IoA ...54 G5
Redwick Newpt ...28 E11
Redwick S Glos ...28 G10
Redworth Darltn ...65 M3
Reed Herts ...33 K9
Reedham Norfk ...45 N9
Reedness E R Yk ...60 D9
Reeds Holme Lancs ...57 P4
Reepham Lincs ...52 E8
Reepham Norfk ...44 H5
Reeth N York ...65 J7
Reeves Green Solhll ...40 H11
Regil N Som ...17 M4
Reiff Highld ...108 A11
Reigate Surrey ...21 K12
Reighton N York ...67 N11
Reisque Abers ...103 J10
Reiss Highld ...110 G5
Relubbus Cnwll ...2 E8
Relugas Moray ...100 F5
Remenham Wokham ...20 C6
Remenham Hill Wokham ...20 C6
Rempstone Notts ...41 M3
Rendcomb Gloucs ...30 D11
Rendham Suffk ...35 M4
Rendlesham Suffk ...35 M6
Renfrew Rens ...84 H9
Renhold Bed ...32 F6
Renishaw Derbys ...51 K5
Rennington Nthumb ...81 P9
Renton W Duns ...84 G7
Renwick Cumb ...72 B11
Repps Norfk ...45 N6
Repton Derbys ...40 H3
Reraig Highld ...97 L4
Resaurie Highld ...107 L12
Resipole Burn Highld ...89 Q4
Reskadinnick Cnwll ...2 F7
Resolis Highld ...107 L8
Resolven Neath ...26 H8
Rest and be thankful Ag & B ...84 D2
Reston Border ...87 R9

Reswallie Angus ...93 N5
Retford Notts ...51 P5
Rettendon Essex ...22 F4
Revesby Lincs ...53 J10
Rewe Devon ...6 C3
Rew Street IoW ...9 M8
Reymerston Norfk ...44 G8
Reynalton Pembks ...25 J7
Reynoldston Swans ...26 C10
Rezare Cnwll ...4 H5
Rhandirmwyn Carmth ...37 M11
Rhayader Powys ...37 Q7
Rheindown Highld ...106 H11
Rhes-y-cae Flints ...48 E2
Rhewl Denbgs ...48 C4
Rhewl Denbgs ...48 D6
Rhicarn Highld ...108 C10
Rhiconich Highld ...108 E5
Rhicullen Highld ...107 L7
Rhigos Rhondd ...27 K7
Rhireavach Highld ...105 Q4
Rhives Highld ...107 N3
Rhiwbina Cardif ...27 N11
Rhiwderyn Newpt ...28 B10
Rhiwlas Gwynd ...54 H8
Rhoden Green Kent ...12 D2
Rhodes Minnis Kent ...13 M2
Rhodiad-y-brenin Pembks ...24 D4
Rhonehouse D & G ...70 C4
Rhoose V Glam ...16 E3
Rhos Carmth ...25 P2
Rhos Neath ...26 G8
Rhoscolyn IoA ...54 C6
Rhoscrowther Pembks ...24 F8
Rhosesmor Flints ...48 E2
Rhosgoch Powys ...38 E11
Rhoshill Pembks ...36 C11
Rhoshirwaun Gwynd ...46 C5
Rhoslefain Gwynd ...47 J9
Rhoslanerchrugog Wrexhm ...48 F6
Rhosmeirch IoA ...54 F6
Rhosneigr IoA ...54 D7
Rhosnesni Wrexhm ...48 G5
Rhôs-on-Sea Conwy ...55 M5
Rhossili Swans ...25 P10
Rhostryfan Gwynd ...54 G9
Rhostyllen Wrexhm ...48 F6
Rhosybol IoA ...54 F4
Rhos-y-gwaliau Gwynd ...47 Q4
Rhosymedre Wrexhm ...48 F7
Rhu Ag & B ...84 E6
Rhuallt Denbgs ...48 C1
Rhubodach Ag & B ...83 Q8
Rhuddlan Denbgs ...55 Q6
Rhunahaorine Ag & B ...75 K3
Rhyd Gwynd ...47 K3
Rhydargaeau Carmth ...25 Q4
Rhydcymerau Carmth ...26 D2
Rhyd-Ddu Gwynd ...54 H10
Rhydlewis Cerdgn ...36 F10
Rhydowen Cerdgn ...36 G10
Rhyd-uchaf Gwynd ...47 P4
Rhyd-y-clafdy Gwynd ...46 E4
Rhyd-y-foel Conwy ...55 N6
Rhydyfro Neath ...26 F7
Rhyd-y-groes Gwynd ...54 H8
Rhyd-y-pennau Cerdgn ...37 K4
Rhyl Denbgs ...55 Q5
Rhymney Caerph ...27 N7
Rhynd P & K ...92 H10
Rhynie Abers ...101 P9
Rhynie Highld ...107 P6
Ribbesford Worcs ...39 P7
Ribbleton Lancs ...57 K3
Ribchester Lancs ...57 M2
Riby Lincs ...52 H3
Riccall N York ...59 N6
Riccarton Border ...79 Q9
Riccarton E Ayrs ...76 G4
Richards Castle Herefs ...39 J8
Richmond Gt Lon ...21 J8
Richmond N York ...65 L7
Richmond Sheff ...51 K4
Rickerscote Staffs ...40 B4
Rickford N Som ...17 L4
Rickham Devon ...5 P11
Rickinghall Suffk ...34 H2
Rickling Green Essex ...33 N10
Rickmansworth Herts ...20 G5
Riddell Border ...80 C8
Riddlecombe Devon ...15 K8
Riddlesden C Brad ...58 E6
Ridge Dorset ...8 D9
Ridge Herts ...21 K4
Ridge Wilts ...8 D2
Ridge Lane Warwks ...40 H8
Ridgeway Derbys ...51 K5
Ridgewell Essex ...34 C8
Ridgewood E Susx ...11 P6
Ridgmont C Beds ...32 D9
Riding Mill Nthumb ...72 H8
Ridlington Norfk ...45 M4
Ridlington Rutlnd ...42 C9
Ridsdale Nthumb ...72 G4
Rievaulx N York ...66 E9
Rigg D & G ...71 L3
Riggend N Lans ...85 M8
Righoul Highld ...100 D5
Rigsby Lincs ...53 L8
Rigside S Lans ...78 E2
Riley Green Lancs ...57 L4
Rilla Mill Cnwll ...4 G5
Rillington N York ...67 J11
Rimington Lancs ...63 P11
Rimpton Somset ...17 N10
Rimswell E R Yk ...61 M8
Rinaston Pembks ...24 H4
Ringford D & G ...69 Q7
Ringland Norfk ...45 J7
Ringmer E Susx ...11 N7
Ringmore Devon ...5 N10
Ringmore Devon ...6 C7
Ringorm Moray ...101 K6
Ringsfield Suffk ...45 N11
Ringsfield Corner Suffk ...45 N11
Ringshall Herts ...20 F1
Ringshall Suffk ...34 G6
Ringshall Stocks Suffk ...34 H6
Ringstead Nhants ...32 E2
Ringstead Norfk ...44 B3
Ringwood Hants ...8 H6
Ringwould Kent ...13 Q1
Rinmore Abers ...101 M11
Ripe E Susx ...11 P7
Ripley Derbys ...51 K9
Ripley Hants ...8 H7
Ripley N York ...58 H3

Ripley Surrey ...20 G11
Riplington Hants ...9 Q3
Ripon N York ...65 N12
Rippingale Lincs ...42 F5
Ripple Kent ...23 Q12
Ripple Worcs ...29 M2
Ripponden Calder ...58 D9
Risabus Ag & B ...74 D4
Risbury Herefs ...39 K10
Risby Suffk ...34 D4
Risca Caerph ...27 P9
Rise E R Yk ...61 K6
Risegate Lincs ...42 H4
Riseley Bed ...32 F4
Riseley Wokham ...20 B10
Rishangles Suffk ...35 J3
Rishton Lancs ...57 N3
Rishworth Calder ...58 D9
Risley Derbys ...41 L1
Risley Warrtn ...57 M9
Risplith N York ...58 G1
River Kent ...13 P2
River W Susx ...10 F5
Riverford Highld ...107 J10
Riverhead Kent ...21 P11
Rivington Lancs ...57 L6
Rivington Services Lancs ...57 L6
Roade Nhants ...31 Q4
Roadmeetings S Lans ...77 P2
Roadside E Ayrs ...77 K7
Roadside Highld ...110 D4
Roadwater Somset ...16 D8
Roag Highld ...96 C2
Roan of Craigoch S Ayrs ...76 E9
Roath Cardif ...27 P12
Roberton Border ...79 N6
Roberton S Lans ...78 F3
Robertsbridge E Susx ...12 E5
Roberttown Kirk ...58 G9
Robeston Wathen Pembks ...25 J5
Robgill Tower D & G ...71 L2
Robin Hood Crematorium Solhll ...40 E10
Robin Hood's Bay N York ...67 K6
Roborough Devon ...5 K7
Roborough Devon ...15 K8
Robroyston C Glas ...85 K8
Roby Knows ...56 H10
Rocester Staffs ...50 E11
Roch Pembks ...24 F5
Rochdale Rochdl ...58 B10
Rochdale Crematorium Rochdl ...57 Q6
Roche Cnwll ...3 L4
Rochester Medway ...22 E9
Rochester Nthumb ...72 E2
Rochford Essex ...22 G5
Rochford Worcs ...39 L8
Rock Cnwll ...3 L4
Rock Nthumb ...81 P9
Rock Worcs ...39 N7
Rockbeare Devon ...6 D4
Rockbourne Hants ...8 G4
Rockcliffe Cumb ...71 M4
Rockcliffe D & G ...70 D5
Rockend Torbay ...6 C9
Rock Ferry Wirral ...56 G10
Rockfield Highld ...107 Q6
Rockfield Mons ...28 F6
Rockford Devon ...15 N3
Rockhampton S Glos ...28 H9
Rockhill Shrops ...38 F6
Rockingham Nhants ...42 C10
Rockland All Saints Norfk ...44 G10
Rockland St Mary Norfk ...45 M8
Rockland St Peter Norfk ...44 G9
Rockley Notts ...51 Q6
Rockville Ag & B ...84 D5
Rockwell End Bucks ...20 C6
Rodborough Gloucs ...29 L7
Rodbourne Swindn ...18 G4
Rodbourne Wilts ...18 D4
Rodden Dorset ...7 N6
Rode Somset ...18 B9
Rode Heath Ches E ...49 Q4
Rodel W Isls ...111 c4
Roden Wrekin ...49 L10
Rodhuish Somset ...16 D8
Rodington Wrekin ...49 L11
Rodington Heath Wrekin ...49 L11
Rodley Gloucs ...29 K6
Rodmarton Gloucs ...29 N8
Rodmell E Susx ...11 N8
Rodmersham Kent ...22 H10
Rodmersham Green Kent ...22 H10
Rodney Stoke Somset ...17 L6
Rodsley Derbys ...50 G11
Roecliffe N York ...59 J2
Roe Green Herts ...21 K2
Roe Green Herts ...33 K9
Roehampton Gt Lon ...21 K8
Roffey W Susx ...11 K4
Rogart Highld ...107 M2
Rogate W Susx ...10 D5
Rogerstone Newpt ...28 C10
Roghadal W Isls ...111 c4
Rogiet Mons ...28 E10
Roke Oxon ...19 Q3
Roker Sundld ...73 P8
Rollesby Norfk ...45 P7
Rolleston Leics ...41 Q7
Rolleston Notts ...51 Q9
Rolleston on Dove Staffs ...40 G3
Rolston E R Yk ...61 L5
Rolvenden Kent ...12 G4
Rolvenden Layne Kent ...12 G4
Romaldkirk Dur ...64 H3
Romanby N York ...65 P8
Romanno Bridge Border ...86 D11
Romansleigh Devon ...15 M7
Romesdal Highld ...104 E10
Romford Dorset ...8 F5
Romford Gt Lon ...21 P5
Romiley Stockp ...50 C3
Romsey Cambs ...33 M5
Romsey Hants ...9 L3
Romsley Shrops ...39 P5
Romsley Worcs ...40 C10
Rona Highld ...105 J10
Ronachan Ag & B ...83 L11
Rookhope Dur ...72 G11
Rookley IoW ...9 N9
Rooks Bridge Somset ...17 K5
Rooks Nest Somset ...16 E9
Rookwith N York ...65 L9
Roos E R Yk ...61 M7
Roothams Green Bed ...32 F5

Ropley Hants ...9 Q2
Ropley Dean Hants ...9 Q2
Ropsley Lincs ...42 E4
Rora Abers ...103 L5
Rorrington Shrops ...38 F3
Rosarie Moray ...101 M5
Rose Cnwll ...2 H5
Rose Ash Devon ...15 N7
Rosebank S Lans ...77 N2
Rosebush Pembks ...25 J3
Rosedale Abbey N York ...66 G8
Rose Green Essex ...34 E10
Rose Green Suffk ...34 F7
Rose Green Suffk ...34 F8
Rose Green W Susx ...10 E9
Rosehall Highld ...106 H2
Rosehearty Abers ...103 J3
Rose Hill Lancs ...57 P3
Rose Hill Crematorium Donc ...51 N1
Roseisle Moray ...100 H2
Roselands E Susx ...12 C9
Rosemarket Pembks ...24 G7
Rosemarkie Highld ...107 M10
Rosemary Lane Devon ...16 F12
Rosemount P & K ...92 H7
Rosenannon Cnwll ...3 L3
Rosewell Mdloth ...86 F9
Roseworth S on T ...65 Q3
Rosgill Cumb ...71 Q11
Roskhill Highld ...96 C1
Rosley Cumb ...71 M6
Roslin Mdloth ...86 F9
Rosliston Derbys ...40 G4
Rosneath Ag & B ...84 E6
Ross D & G ...69 P9
Rossett Wrexhm ...48 G4
Rossett Green N York ...58 H4
Rossington Donc ...51 N2
Ross-on-Wye Herefs ...28 H4
Roster Highld ...110 F7
Rostherne Ches E ...57 N11
Rosthwaite Cumb ...71 L11
Roston Derbys ...50 F11
Rosyth Fife ...86 D5
Rothbury Nthumb ...73 J1
Rotherby Leics ...41 P4
Rotherfield E Susx ...12 B4
Rotherfield Greys Oxon ...20 B7
Rotherfield Peppard Oxon ...20 B7
Rotherham Rothm ...51 K3
Rotherham Crematorium Rothm ...51 L3
Rothersthorpe Nhants ...31 Q3
Rotherwick Hants ...20 B11
Rothes Moray ...101 K5
Rothesay Ag & B ...84 B9
Rothiebrisbane Abers ...102 G7
Rothiemurchus Lodge Highld ...99 P7
Rothienorman Abers ...102 F7
Rothley Leics ...41 N5
Rothmaise Abers ...102 F8
Rothwell Leeds ...59 J8
Rothwell Lincs ...52 G4
Rothwell Nhants ...32 B1
Rottal Lodge Angus ...94 F7
Rottingdean Br & H ...11 M9
Rottington Cumb ...70 F11
Roucan D & G ...78 G12
Roucan Loch Crematorium D & G ...78 G12
Rougham Norfk ...44 D6
Rougham Suffk ...34 E4
Rough Common Kent ...23 L10
Roughpark Abers ...101 L11
Roughton Lincs ...53 J9
Roughton Norfk ...45 K3
Roughton Shrops ...39 N4
Roundbush Green Essex ...22 C1
Round Green Luton ...32 F11
Roundham Somset ...7 K2
Roundhay Leeds ...59 J6
Rounds Green Sandw ...40 C9
Roundswell Devon ...15 J6
Roundway Wilts ...18 E7
Roundyhill Angus ...93 L5
Rousay Ork ...111 h1
Rousdon Devon ...6 H5
Rousham Oxon ...31 L8
Rous Lench Worcs ...30 D4
Routenburn N Ayrs ...84 D10
Routh E R Yk ...61 J4
Row Cumb ...63 J4
Rowanburn D & G ...79 N12
Rowardennan Stirlg ...84 F4
Rowarth Derbys ...50 D3
Rowberrow Somset ...17 L5
Rowde Wilts ...18 E8
Rowen Conwy ...55 L7
Rowfoot Nthumb ...72 C8
Rowhedge Essex ...34 G11
Rowington Warwks ...30 G1
Rowland Derbys ...50 G6
Rowland's Castle Hants ...10 B7
Rowlands Gill Gatesd ...73 L8
Rowledge Surrey ...10 D2
Rowley Dur ...73 J10
Rowley Regis Sandw ...40 C9
Rowley Regis Crematorium Sandw ...40 C9
Rowlstone Herefs ...28 D4
Rowly Surrey ...10 G2
Rowner Hants ...9 P7
Rowney Green Worcs ...40 D12
Rownhams Hants ...9 L4
Rownhams Services Hants ...9 L4
Rowrah Cumb ...70 H10
Rowsham Bucks ...32 C12
Rowsley Derbys ...50 G7
Rowston Lincs ...52 F11
Rowton Ches W ...49 J3
Rowton Wrekin ...49 L10
Roxburgh Border ...80 F7
Roxby N Linc ...60 F10
Roxton Bed ...32 G6
Roxwell Essex ...22 D2
Royal Leamington Spa Warwks ...30 H2
Royal Sutton Coldfield Birm ...40 E8
Royal Tunbridge Wells Kent ...12 C3
Royal Wootton Bassett Wilts ...18 F4
Royal Yacht Britannia C Edin ...86 F6
Roy Bridge Highld ...98 C11

Roydon Essex 21 N2
Roydon Norfk 34 H1
Roydon Norfk 44 B5
Roydon Hamlet Essex 21 N2
Royston Barns 59 J11
Royston Herts 33 K8
Royton Oldham 58 B11
Rozel Jersey 7 c1
Ruabon Wrexhm 48 F6
Ruaig Ag & B 88 D6
Ruan Lanihorne Cnwll 3 K7
Ruan Major Cnwll 2 G11
Ruan Minor Cnwll 2 G11
Ruardean Gloucs 28 H5
Ruardean Hill Gloucs 28 H5
Ruardean Woodside
    Gloucs 28 H5
Rubery Birm 40 C11
Rubha Ban W Isls 111 b6
Ruckhall Herefs 28 E2
Ruckinge Kent 13 K4
Ruckley Shrops 39 K3
Rudby N York 66 C6
Rudchester Nthumb 73 K7
Ruddington Notts 41 M2
Rudge Somset 18 C9
Rudgeway S Glos 28 H10
Rudgwick W Susx 10 H4
Rudheath Ches W 49 M2
Rudley Green Essex 22 G3
Rudloe Wilts 18 C6
Rudry Caerph 27 P10
Rudston E R Yk 61 J1
Rudyard Staffs 50 C8
Ruecastle Border 80 E9
Rufford Lancs 57 J6
Rufford Abbey Notts 51 N7
Rufforth C York 59 M4
Rugby Warwks 41 L11
Rugeley Staffs 40 D4
Ruishton Somset 16 H10
Ruislip Gt Lon 20 H6
Rùm Highld 96 D9
Rumbach Moray 101 M5
Rumbling Bridge P & K 86 B3
Rumburgh Suffk 35 M1
Rumford Cnwll 3 K2
Rumford Falk 85 Q7
Rumney Cardif 27 P11
Runcorn Halton 57 K11
Runcton W Susx 10 E9
Runcton Holme Norfk 43 P8
Runfold Surrey 10 D1
Runhall Norfk 44 H8
Runham Norfk 45 P7
Runnington Somset 16 F10
Runswick N York 66 H4
Runtaleave Angus 94 E8
Runwell Essex 22 F5
Ruscombe Wokham 20 C8
Rushall Herefs 28 H2
Rushall Norfk 45 K12
Rushall Wilts 18 G9
Rushall Wsall 40 D7
Rushbrooke Suffk 34 E5
Rushbury Shrops 39 K4
Rushden Herts 33 K9
Rushden Nhants 32 D4
Rushenden Kent 22 H8
Rushford Norfk 34 F1
Rush Green Essex 23 M1
Rush Green Gt Lon 21 P6
Rush Green Warrtn 57 M10
Rushlake Green E Susx 12 D6
Rushmere Suffk 45 P11
Rushmoor Surrey 10 E3
Rushock Worcs 40 B12
Rusholme Manch 57 Q9
Rushton Nhants 42 B12
Rushton Spencer Staffs 50 C8
Rushwick Worcs 39 P10
Rushyford Dur 65 M2
Ruskie Stirlg 85 K3
Ruskington Lincs 52 F12
Rusland Cross Cumb 62 G5
Rusper W Susx 11 K3
Ruspidge Gloucs 29 J6
Russell's Water Oxon 20 B5
Russ Hill Surrey 11 K3
Rusthall Kent 12 C3
Rustington W Susx 10 G9
Ruston N York 67 K10
Ruston Parva E R Yk 60 H2
Ruswarp N York 67 J5
Rutherford Border 80 E7
Rutherglen S Lans 85 K10
Ruthernbridge Cnwll 3 M3
Ruthin Denbgs 48 D4
Ruthrieston C Aber 95 Q2
Ruthven Abers 101 P6
Ruthven Angus 93 K6
Ruthven Highld 99 L8
Ruthven Highld 99 M3
Ruthvoes Cnwll 3 K4
Ruthwell D & G 70 H3
Ruyton-XI-Towns Shrops 48 H10
Ryal Nthumb 72 H6
Ryall Dorset 7 K4
Ryall Worcs 29 M1
Ryarsh Kent 22 D10
Rydal Cumb 62 G2
Ryde IoW 9 P8
Rye E Susx 12 H6
Rye Foreign E Susx 12 H5
Rye Street Worcs 29 K2
Ryhall Rutlnd 42 E7
Ryhill Wakefd 59 J10
Ryhope Sundld 73 P9
Ryland Lincs 52 E7
Rylands Notts 41 M1
Rylstone N York 58 C2
Ryme Intrinseca Dorset 7 N1
Ryther N York 59 M6
Ryton Gatesd 73 K7
Ryton Shrops 39 N2
Ryton-on-Dunsmore
    Warwks 41 J11
RZSS Edinburgh Zoo
    C Edin 86 E7

S

Sabden Lancs 57 P2
Sacombe Herts 33 K11
Sacriston Dur 73 M10
Sadberge Darltn 65 N4
Saddell Ag & B 75 L6
Saddington Leics 41 P8

Saddlebow Norfk 43 P7
Saddlescombe W Susx 11 L7
Saffron Walden Essex 33 N8
Sageston Pembks 25 J7
Saham Hills Norfk 44 E9
Saham Toney Norfk 44 E9
Saighton Ches W 49 J3
St Abbs Border 81 J1
St Agnes Border 87 M6
St Agnes Cnwll 2 G5
St Agnes IoS 2 b3
St Agnes Mining
    District Cnwll 2 G6
St Albans Herts 21 J2
St Allen Cnwll 3 J5
St Andrew Guern 6 b2
St Andrews Fife 93 N11
St Andrews Botanic
    Garden Fife 93 N11
St Andrews Major
    V Glam 16 F2
St Andrews Well Dorset 7 L4
St Anne's Lancs 56 G3
St Ann's D & G 78 H9
St Ann's Chapel Cnwll 5 J6
St Ann's Chapel Devon 5 N10
St Anthony-in-
    Meneage Cnwll 2 H10
St Anthony's Hill E Susx 12 D9
St Arvans Mons 28 F9
St Asaph Denbgs 48 B1
St Athan V Glam 16 D3
St Aubin Jersey 7 b2
St Austell Cnwll 3 M5
St Bees Cumb 70 F12
St Blazey Cnwll 3 N5
St Boswells Border 80 D7
St Brelade Jersey 7 a2
St Brelade's Bay Jersey 7 a2
St Breock Cnwll 3 L2
St Breward Cnwll 4 D5
St Briavels Gloucs 28 G7
St Bride's Major V Glam 16 B2
St Brides-super-Ely
    V Glam 27 M12
St Brides Wentlooge
    Newpt 28 C11
St Budeaux C Plym 5 K8
Saintbury Gloucs 30 E6
St Buryan Cnwll 2 C9
St Catherines Ag & B 84 C2
St Chloe Gloucs 29 L8
St Clears Carmth 25 M5
St Cleer Cnwll 4 F6
St Clement Cnwll 3 J7
St Clement Jersey 7 c2
St Clether Cnwll 4 F4
St Colmac Ag & B 83 Q9
St Columb Major Cnwll 3 K3
St Columb Minor Cnwll 3 K3
St Columb Road Cnwll 3 K4
St Combs Abers 103 L3
St Cross South Elmham
    Suffk 45 L12
St Cyrus Abers 95 M8
St David's P & K 92 E10
St Davids Pembks 24 D4
St Davids Cathedral
    Pembks 24 D4
St Day Cnwll 2 G7
St Dennis Cnwll 3 L4
St Dogmaels Pembks 36 C10
St Dominick Cnwll 5 J6
St Donats V Glam 16 C3
St Endellion Cnwll 4 C5
St Enoder Cnwll 3 K4
St Erme Cnwll 3 J6
St Erney Cnwll 4 H8
St Erth Cnwll 2 E8
St Erth Praze Cnwll 2 E8
St Ervan Cnwll 3 K2
St Eval Cnwll 3 K3
St Ewe Cnwll 3 L6
St Fagans Cardif 27 N12
St Fagans: National
    History Museum
    Cardif 27 N12
St Fergus Abers 103 M5
St Fillans P & K 91 Q10
St Florence Pembks 25 J8
St Gennys Cnwll 4 C11
St George Conwy 55 P6
St Georges N Som 17 K4
St George's V Glam 16 E2
St Germans Cnwll 4 H8
St Giles in the Wood
    Devon 15 J8
St Giles-on-the-Heath
    Devon 4 H3
St Harmon Powys 38 B7
St Helen Auckland Dur 65 L3
St Helen's E Susx 12 G7
St Helens IoW 9 Q9
St Helens St Hel 57 K9
St Helens Crematorium
    St Hel 57 J9
St Helier Gt Lon 21 L9
St Helier Jersey 7 b2
St Hilary Cnwll 2 E9
St Hilary V Glam 16 D2
St Ippollitts Herts 32 H10
St Ishmael's Pembks 24 E7
St Issey Cnwll 3 L2
St Ive Cnwll 4 G6
St Ives Cambs 33 K3
St Ives Cnwll 2 D7
St James's End Nhants 31 Q3
St James South
    Elmham Suffk 35 M4
St Jidgey Cnwll 3 L2
St John Cnwll 5 J9
St John Jersey 7 b1
St John's E Susx 11 P4
St John's IoM 56 b5
St John's Kent 21 Q11
St Johns Surrey 20 F10
St Johns Worcs 39 Q10
St John's Chapel Devon 15 J6
St John's Chapel Dur 72 F12
St John's Fen End Norfk 43 N7
St John's Kirk S Lans 78 F2
St John's Town of Dalry
    D & G 69 N3
St John's Wood Gt Lon 21 L6
St Judes IoM 56 d3
St Just Cnwll 2 B9
St Just-in-Roseland
    Cnwll 3 J8
St Just Mining District
    Cnwll 2 B8

St Katherines Abers 102 G8
St Keverne Cnwll 2 H10
St Kew Cnwll 3 M1
St Kew Highway Cnwll 3 M1
St Keyne Cnwll 4 F7
St Lawrence Essex 23 J3
St Lawrence IoW 9 N11
St Lawrence Jersey 7 b1
St Lawrence Kent 23 Q9
St Leonards Bucks 20 E3
St Leonards Dorset 8 G6
St Leonards E Susx 12 F8
St Levan Cnwll 2 B10
St Lythans V Glam 16 F2
St Mabyn Cnwll 3 M2
St Madoes P & K 92 H10
St Margarets Herefs 28 D3
St Margarets Herts 21 M2
St Margaret's at Cliffe
    Kent 13 Q2
St Margaret's Hope Ork 111 h3
St Margaret South
    Elmham Suffk 45 M12
St Marks IoM 56 c6
St Martin Cnwll 2 H10
St Martin Cnwll 4 G8
St Martin Guern 6 b2
St Martin Jersey 7 c1
St Martin's IoS 2 c1
St Martin's P & K 92 H9
St Martin's Shrops 48 G8
St Mary Jersey 7 a1
St Mary Bourne Hants 19 M10
St Marychurch Torbay 6 C9
St Mary Church V Glam 16 D2
St Mary Cray Gt Lon 21 P9
St Mary in the Marsh
    Kent 13 K5
St Marylebone
    Crematorium Gt Lon 21 L5
St Mary's Cnwll 2 c2
St Mary's Ork 111 h2
St Mary's Bay Kent 13 L5
St Mary's Hoo Medway 22 F7
St Mary's Platt Kent 22 D11
St Maughans Green
    Mons 28 F5
St Mawes Cnwll 3 J8
St Mawgan Cnwll 3 K3
St Mellion Cnwll 5 J7
St Mellons Cardif 27 P11
St Merryn Cnwll 3 K2
St Michael Caerhays
    Cnwll 3 L7
St Michael Church
    Somset 17 J9
St Michael Penkevil
    Cnwll 3 J7
St Michaels Kent 12 H3
St Michaels Worcs 39 L8
St Michael's Mount Cnwll 2 D9
St Michael's on Wyre
    Lancs 57 J1
St Minver Cnwll 3 L1
St Monans Fife 87 K2
St Neot Cnwll 4 E6
St Neots Cambs 32 H5
St Newlyn East Cnwll 3 J5
St Nicholas Pembks 24 F2
St Nicholas V Glam 16 E2
St Nicholas-at-Wade
    Kent 23 N9
St Ninians Stirlg 85 N5
St Olaves Norfk 45 P9
St Osyth Essex 23 L1
St Ouen Jersey 7 a1
St Owen's Cross Herefs 28 G4
St Paul's Cray Gt Lon 21 P9
St Paul's Walden Herts 32 H11
St Peter Jersey 7 a1
St Peter Port Guern 6 c2
St Peter's Guern 6 b2
St Peter's Kent 23 Q9
St Peter's Hill Cambs 33 J3
St Pinnock Cnwll 4 F7
St Quivox S Ayrs 76 F6
St Sampson Guern 6 c1
St Saviour Guern 6 b2
St Saviour Jersey 7 b2
St Stephen Cnwll 3 L5
St Stephens Cnwll 4 H3
St Stephens Cnwll 5 J8
St Teath Cnwll 4 D4
St Thomas Devon 6 B5
St Tudy Cnwll 3 N1
St Twynnells Pembks 24 G8
St Veep Cnwll 4 E8
St Vigeans Angus 93 Q7
St Wenn Cnwll 3 L3
St Weonards Herefs 28 F4
Salcombe Devon 5 P11
Salcombe Regis Devon 6 F5
Salcott-cum-Virley Essex 23 J1
Sale Traffd 57 P9
Saleby Lincs 53 M7
Sale Green Worcs 30 B3
Salehurst E Susx 12 E5
Salem Cerdgn 37 L4
Salen Ag & B 89 M7
Salen Highld 89 N4
Salford C Beds 32 D8
Salford Oxon 30 H8
Salford Salfd 57 P8
Salford Priors Warwks 30 E4
Salfords Surrey 11 L2
Salhouse Norfk 45 M7
Saline Fife 86 B4
Salisbury Wilts 8 G2
Salisbury Crematorium
    Wilts 8 H2
Salisbury Plain Wilts 18 F10
Salkeld Dykes Cumb 71 Q7
Salle Norfk 45 J5
Salmonby Lincs 53 K8
Salperton Gloucs 30 E9
Salph End Bed 32 F6
Salsburgh N Lans 85 N9
Salt Staffs 40 C2
Saltaire C Brad 58 F6
Saltaire C Brad 58 F6
Saltash Cnwll 5 J8
Saltburn Highld 107 N10
Saltburn-by-the-Sea
    R & Cl 66 F4
Saltby Leics 42 C5
Saltcoats N Ayrs 76 D3
Saltdean Br & H 11 M9
Salterbeck Cumb 70 G9
Salterforth Lancs 58 B5
Salterton Wilts 8 G12
Saltfleet Lincs 53 M5

Saltfleetby All Saints
    Lincs 53 M5
Saltfleetby St Clement
    Lincs 53 M5
Saltfleetby St Peter
    Lincs 53 M5
Salford BaNES 17 P3
Salthouse Norfk 44 H2
Saltley Birm 40 E9
Saltmarshe E R Yk 60 D8
Saltney Flints 48 H3
Salton N York 66 G10
Saltrens Devon 14 H7
Saltwell Crematorium
    Gatesd 73 M8
Saltwood Kent 13 M3
Salvington W Susx 10 H8
Salwarpe Worcs 39 Q9
Salway Ash Dorset 7 L4
Sambourne Warwks 30 D2
Sambrook Wrekin 49 N9
Sampford Arundel
    Somset 16 F11
Sampford Brett Somset 16 E7
Sampford Courtenay
    Devon 15 L11
Sampford Moor Somset 16 F11
Sampford Peverell
    Devon 16 D12
Sampford Spiney Devon 5 L6
Samsonlane Ork 111 i2
Samuelston E Loth 87 J7
Sanaigmore Ag & B 82 C8
Sancreed Cnwll 2 C9
Sancton E R Yk 60 F6
Sandaig Highld 97 K8
Sandal Magna Wakefd 59 J9
Sanday Ork 111 i1
Sanday Airport Ork 111 i1
Sandbach Ches E 49 N4
Sandbach Services
    Ches E 49 P4
Sandbank Ag & B 84 C6
Sandbanks Poole 8 F9
Sandend Abers 102 D3
Sanderstead Gt Lon 21 M10
Sandford Cumb 64 D4
Sandford Devon 15 P10
Sandford Dorset 8 D9
Sandford Hants 8 H7
Sandford IoW 9 N10
Sandford N Som 17 K4
Sandford S Lans 77 M3
Sandford-on-Thames
    Oxon 19 N1
Sandford Orcas Dorset 17 P11
Sandford St Martin Oxon 31 K8
Sandgate Kent 13 M3
Sandhaven Abers 103 K2
Sandhead D & G 68 E8
Sand Hills Leeds 59 J6
Sandhills Oxon 31 M10
Sandhills Surrey 10 F3
Sandhoe Nthumb 72 H7
Sandhole Ag & B 83 Q4
Sand Hole E R Yk 60 D6
Sandholme E R Yk 60 E7
Sandhurst Br For 20 D10
Sandhurst Gloucs 29 L4
Sandhurst Kent 12 F4
Sand Hutton N York 59 P3
Sandhutton N York 65 P10
Sandiacre Derbys 51 L12
Sandilands Lincs 53 N7
Sandleheath Hants 8 G4
Sandleigh Oxon 19 M1
Sandley Dorset 8 B3
Sandness Shet 111 j4
Sandon Essex 22 E3
Sandon Herts 33 K9
Sandon Staffs 40 C2
Sandon Bank Staffs 40 C2
Sandown IoW 9 Q10
Sandplace Cnwll 4 F8
Sandridge Herts 21 J2
Sandringham Norfk 44 B4
Sandsend N York 67 J5
Sandtoft N Linc 60 D11
Sandway Kent 22 H12
Sandwell Valley
    Crematorium Sandw 40 D8
Sandwich Kent 23 P10
Sandwick Shet 111 k5
Sandwick W Isls 111 d2
Sandwith Cumb 70 F11
Sandy C Beds 32 G7
Sandyford D & G 79 K9
Sandygate Devon 6 B7
Sandygate IoM 56 d3
Sandyhills D & G 70 E5
Sandylands Lancs 62 H9
Sandy Lane Wilts 18 E7
Sandy Park Devon 5 P3
Sangobeg Highld 108 H3
Sangomore Highld 108 H3
Sankyn's Green Worcs 39 P9
Sanna Highld 89 K3
Sanndabhaig W Isls 111 d2
Sannox N Ayrs 75 Q4
Sanquhar D & G 77 N8
Santon Bridge Cumb 62 C2
Santon Downham Suffk 44 D11
Sapcote Leics 41 L8
Sapey Common Herefs 39 M8
Sapiston Suffk 34 F2
Sapperton Gloucs 29 N7
Sapperton Lincs 42 E4
Saracen's Head Lincs 43 K5
Sarclet Highld 110 G7
Sarisbury Hants 9 N5
Sarn Powys 38 F4
Sarn Powys 47 Q10
Sarnau Cerdgn 36 F9
Sarnau Powys 48 E11
Sarn Meyllteyrn Gwynd 46 D5
Sarn Park Services
    Brdgnd 27 J11
Saron Carmth 26 E6
Saron Gwynd 54 G8
Sarratt Herts 20 G4
Sarre Kent 23 N9
Sarsden Oxon 30 H9
Satley Dur 73 K11
Satterleigh Devon 15 L7
Satterthwaite Cumb 62 G4
Sauchen Abers 102 F11
Saucher P & K 92 H8
Sauchieburn Abers 95 L12
Saul Gloucs 29 K7
Saundby Notts 52 B6

Saundersfoot Pembks 25 K7
Saunderton Bucks 20 C3
Saunton Devon 14 H5
Sausthorpe Lincs 53 L9
Savile Town Kirk 58 G9
Sawbridge Warwks 31 L2
Sawbridgeworth Herts 21 P3
Sawdon N York 67 K9
Sawley Lancs 63 P11
Sawley N York 58 G1
Sawston Cambs 33 M7
Sawtry Cambs 42 G12
Saxby Leics 42 B6
Saxby Lincs 52 E6
Saxby All Saints N Linc 60 G10
Saxelbye Leics 41 P4
Saxham Street Suffk 34 H5
Saxilby Lincs 52 C8
Saxlingham Norfk 44 G3
Saxlingham Green Norfk 45 L10
Saxlingham
    Nethergate Norfk 45 K10
Saxlingham Thorpe
    Norfk 45 K9
Saxmundham Suffk 35 N4
Saxondale Notts 51 P11
Saxon Street Cambs 34 B5
Saxtead Suffk 35 L4
Saxtead Green Suffk 35 L4
Saxtead Little Green
    Suffk 35 L4
Saxthorpe Norfk 45 J4
Saxton N York 59 L6
Sayers Common W Susx 11 L6
Scackleton N York 66 F11
Scafell Pike Cumb 62 E2
Scaftworth Notts 51 P3
Scagglethorpe N York 67 J11
Scalasaig Ag & B 82 E4
Scalby E R Yk 60 E8
Scalby N York 67 L9
Scaldwell Nhants 41 Q11
Scaleby Cumb 71 P3
Scalebyhill Cumb 71 P3
Scales Cumb 62 F7
Scales Cumb 71 M9
Scalford Leics 41 Q3
Scaling N York 66 G5
Scalloway Shet 111 k4
Scalpay Highld 96 H4
Scambie sby Lincs 53 J7
Scamodale Highld 90 B2
Scampston N York 67 J10
Scampton Lincs 52 D7
Scaniport Highld 99 J2
Scapegoat Hill Kirk 58 E10
Scarba Ag & B 83 K3
Scarborough N York 67 M9
Scarcewater Cnwll 3 K5
Scarcliffe Derbys 51 L7
Scarcroft Leeds 59 J6
Scarfskerry Highld 110 F2
Scarinish Ag & B 88 C7
Scarisbrick Lancs 56 H6
Scarning Norfk 44 F7
Scarrington Notts 51 Q11
Scartho NE Lin 53 J3
Scatsta Airport Shet 111 k3
Scaur D & G 70 D5
Scawby N Linc 52 D3
Scawsby Donc 59 M12
Scawthorpe Donc 59 M11
Scawton N York 66 D10
Scayne's Hill W Susx 11 M5
Scethrog Powys 27 M4
Scholar Green Ches E 49 Q4
Scholemoor
    Crematorium C Brad 58 F7
Scholes Kirk 58 F11
Scholes Leeds 59 J6
Scholes Rothm 51 K2
Scholes Wigan 57 L7
Scissett Kirk 58 G11
Scleddau Pembks 24 G2
Scofton Notts 51 N5
Scole Norfk 35 J2
Scone P & K 92 H9
Sconser Highld 96 F4
Scoonie Fife 86 H2
Scopwick Lincs 52 F11
Scoraig Highld 105 Q3
Scorborough E R Yk 60 H5
Scorrier Cnwll 2 G7
Scorton Lancs 63 J11
Scorton N York 65 M7
Scotby Cumb 71 P5
Scotch Corner N York 65 L6
Scotch Corner Rest
    Area N York 65 L6
Scotforth Lancs 63 J9
Scothern Lincs 52 E7
Scotlandwell P & K 86 E2
Scotscalder Station
    Highld 110 C5
Scotsmill Abers 102 D10
Scotstoun C Glas 85 J9
Scotswood N u Ty 73 L7
Scotter Lincs 52 C4
Scotterthorpe Lincs 52 C3
Scottish Seabird Centre
    E Loth 87 K5
Scottish Wool Centre
    Stirlg 85 J3
Scotton Lincs 52 C4
Scotton N York 59 J3
Scotton N York 65 L8
Scoulton Norfk 44 G9
Scourie Highld 108 D7
Scourie More Highld 108 D7
Scousburgh Shet 111 k5
Scrabster Highld 110 C2
Scraesburgh Border 80 F9
Scrane End Lincs 43 L2
Scraptoft Leics 41 P6
Scratby Norfk 45 Q7
Scrayingham N York 60 C3
Scredington Lincs 42 F3
Scremby Lincs 53 M9
Scremerston Nthumb 81 L4
Screveton Notts 51 Q11
Scriven N York 59 J3
Scrooby Notts 51 P3
Scropton Derbys 40 G2
Scrub Hill Lincs 52 H11
Scruton N York 65 N8
Scullomie Highld 109 L4
Sculthorpe Norfk 44 E4
Scunthorpe N Linc 52 B2
Seaborough Dorset 7 K2

Place	Pg	Grid
Seabridge Staffs	49	Q6
Seabrook Kent	13	M3
Seaburn Sundld	73	P8
Seacombe Wirral	56	G10
Seacroft Leeds	59	J7
Seafield W Loth	86	B8
Seafield Crematorium C Edin	86	F7
Seaford E Susx	11	P9
Seaforth Sefton	56	G9
Seagrave Leics	41	N4
Seaham Dur	73	P10
Seahouses Nthumb	81	P7
Seal Kent	22	B11
Sealand Flints	48	G2
Seale Surrey	10	E1
Seamer N York	66	C5
Seamer N York	67	L10
Seamill N Ayrs	76	D2
Sea Palling Norfk	45	N5
Searby Lincs	52	F3
Seasalter Kent	23	L9
Seascale Cumb	62	B3
Seathwaite Cumb	62	E3
Seatoller Cumb	71	L11
Seaton Cnwll	4	G8
Seaton Devon	6	H5
Seaton E R Yk	61	K5
Seaton Kent	23	N10
Seaton Nthumb	73	N5
Seaton Rutlnd	42	C9
Seaton Carew Hartpl	66	D2
Seaton Delaval Nthumb	73	N6
Seaton Ross E R Yk	60	D6
Seaton Sluice Nthumb	73	N5
Seatown Dorset	7	K4
Seave Green N York	66	D7
Seaview IoW	9	Q8
Seaville Cumb	71	J5
Seavington St Mary Somset	17	K12
Seavington St Michael Somset	17	K12
Sebergham Cumb	71	M7
Seckington Warwks	40	H6
Second Severn Crossing Mons	28	F10
Sedbergh Cumb	63	M4
Sedbury Gloucs	28	G9
Sedbusk N York	64	F8
Sedgeberrow Worcs	30	D6
Sedgebrook Lincs	42	C3
Sedgefield Dur	65	P2
Sedgeford Norfk	44	B3
Sedgehill Wilts	8	C2
Sedgemoor Crematorium Somset	16	H7
Sedgemoor Services Somset	17	J5
Sedgley Dudley	40	B8
Sedgley Park Bury	57	P8
Sedgwick Cumb	63	K5
Sedlescombe E Susx	12	F6
Sedrup Bucks	20	C2
Seend Wilts	18	D8
Seend Cleeve Wilts	18	D8
Seer Green Bucks	20	F5
Seething Norfk	45	M9
Sefton Sefton	56	G8
Seighford Staffs	49	Q9
Seion Gwynd	54	H8
Seisdon Staffs	39	Q3
Selattyn Shrops	48	F8
Selborne Hants	10	C4
Selby N York	59	N7
Selham W Susx	10	E6
Selhurst Gt Lon	21	M9
Selkirk Border	79	P3
Sellack Herefs	28	G4
Sellafield Station Cumb	62	B2
Sellafirth Shet	111	k2
Sellindge Kent	13	L3
Selling Kent	23	K11
Sells Green Wilts	18	D8
Selly Oak Birm	40	D10
Selmeston E Susx	11	P8
Selsdon Gt Lon	21	M10
Selsey W Susx	10	D10
Selside N York	64	E11
Selsley Gloucs	29	L7
Selsted Kent	13	N2
Selston Notts	51	L9
Selworthy Somset	16	C6
Semer Suffk	34	G7
Semington Wilts	18	D8
Semley Wilts	8	D3
Send Surrey	20	G11
Senghenydd Caerph	27	N10
Sennen Cnwll	2	B10
Sennen Cove Cnwll	2	B9
Sennybridge Powys	27	K3
Sessay N York	66	C11
Setchey Norfk	43	Q7
Seton Mains E Loth	87	J7
Settle N York	63	P9
Settrington N York	67	J12
Sevenhampton Gloucs	30	D9
Sevenhampton Swindn	18	H3
Seven Hills Crematorium Suffk	35	K8
Seven Kings Gt Lon	21	N6
Sevenoaks Kent	21	Q11
Sevenoaks Weald Kent	21	Q12
Seven Sisters Neath	26	H7
Seven Star Green Essex	34	F10
Severn Beach S Glos	28	G10
Severn Bridge S Glos	28	G10
Severn Stoke Worcs	39	Q12
Severn View Services S Glos	28	G10
Sevington Kent	13	K2
Sewards End Essex	33	P8
Sewell C Beds	32	E11
Sewerby E R Yk	61	L1
Seworgan Cnwll	2	G9
Sewstern Leics	42	C6
Sgiogarstaigh W Isls	111	e1
Shabbington Bucks	31	P11
Shackerstone Leics	41	J6
Shackleford Surrey	10	E2
Shader W Isls	111	d1
Shadforth Dur	73	N11
Shadingfield Suffk	45	P12
Shadoxhurst Kent	13	J3
Shadwell Leeds	59	J6
Shadwell Norfk	44	F12
Shaftenhoe End Herts	33	L8
Shaftesbury Dorset	8	C3
Shafton Barns	59	K11
Shakerley Wigan	57	M8
Shalbourne Wilts	19	K7
Shalden Hants	10	B2
Shaldon Devon	6	C8
Shalfleet IoW	9	M9
Shalford Essex	34	C10
Shalford Surrey	10	G1
Shalford Green Essex	34	B10
Shalmsford Street Kent	23	L11
Shalstone Bucks	31	N6
Shamley Green Surrey	10	G2
Shandford Angus	94	H9
Shandon Ag & B	84	E6
Shandwick Highld	107	P7
Shangton Leics	41	Q8
Shanklin IoW	9	P10
Shantron Ag & B	84	F5
Shap Cumb	71	Q11
Shapinsay Ork	111	h2
Shapwick Dorset	8	D7
Shapwick Somset	17	K8
Shard End Birm	40	F9
Shardlow Derbys	41	K2
Shareshill Staffs	40	C6
Sharlston Wakefd	59	K9
Sharman's Cross Solhll	40	F10
Sharnbrook Bed	32	E5
Sharnford Leics	41	L8
Sharoe Green Lancs	57	K3
Sharow N York	65	N12
Sharpenhoe C Beds	32	F10
Sharperton Nthumb	81	K12
Sharpness Gloucs	29	J8
Sharrington Norfk	44	G3
Shatterford Worcs	39	P6
Shaugh Prior Devon	5	L7
Shavington Ches E	49	M5
Shaw Oldham	58	C11
Shaw Swindn	18	G4
Shaw W Berk	19	N7
Shaw Wilts	18	D7
Shawbirch Wrekin	49	M11
Shawbost W Isls	111	d1
Shawbury Shrops	49	K10
Shawell Leics	41	M10
Shawford Hants	9	M3
Shawhead D & G	70	E1
Shaw Mills N York	58	G2
Shawsburn S Lans	77	N2
Shearington D & G	70	G3
Shearsby Leics	41	N8
Shearston Somset	16	H9
Shebbear Devon	14	H9
Shebdon Staffs	49	N9
Shebster Highld	110	B3
Sheddens E Rens	85	J10
Shedfield Hants	9	P5
Sheen Staffs	50	E8
Sheepridge Kirk	58	F9
Sheepscar Leeds	58	H7
Sheepscombe Gloucs	29	M6
Sheepstor Devon	5	L6
Sheepwash Devon	14	H10
Sheepy Magna Leics	41	J7
Sheepy Parva Leics	41	J7
Sheering Essex	21	P1
Sheerness Kent	22	H8
Sheerwater Surrey	20	G10
Sheet Hants	10	C5
Sheffield Sheff	51	J4
Sheffield City Road Crematorium Sheff	51	J4
Sheffield Park E Susx	11	N5
Shefford C Beds	32	G8
Sheigra Highld	108	D4
Sheinton Shrops	39	L2
Shelderton Shrops	38	H6
Sheldon Birm	40	F9
Sheldon Derbys	50	F7
Sheldon Devon	6	F2
Sheldwich Kent	23	K11
Shelfanger Norfk	45	J12
Shelford Notts	51	P11
Shelley Kirk	58	G11
Shelley Suffk	34	G8
Shellingford Oxon	19	K3
Shellow Bowells Essex	22	C2
Shelsley Beauchamp Worcs	39	N9
Shelsley Walsh Worcs	39	N9
Shelton Bed	32	E3
Shelton Norfk	45	K11
Shelton Notts	42	B2
Shelton Lock C Derb	41	J2
Shelton Under Harley Staffs	49	P7
Shelve Shrops	38	G3
Shelwick Herefs	28	F1
Shenfield Essex	22	C4
Shenington Oxon	31	J5
Shenley Herts	21	J4
Shenley Brook End M Keyn	32	B9
Shenley Church End M Keyn	32	B9
Shenmore Herefs	28	D2
Shennanton D & G	69	J6
Shenstone Staffs	40	E6
Shenstone Worcs	39	Q7
Shenton Leics	41	J7
Shenval Moray	101	J8
Shephall Herts	33	J11
Shepherd's Bush Gt Lon	21	K7
Shepherdswell Kent	13	N1
Shepley Kirk	58	G11
Shepperton Surrey	20	H9
Shepreth Cambs	33	L7
Shepshed Leics	41	L4
Shepton Beauchamp Somset	17	K11
Shepton Mallet Somset	17	N7
Shepton Montague Somset	17	P9
Shepway Kent	22	F11
Sheraton Dur	66	C1
Sherborne Dorset	17	P11
Sherborne Gloucs	30	F10
Sherborne Somset	17	N5
Sherborne St John Hants	19	Q9
Sherbourne Warwks	30	H2
Sherburn Dur	73	N11
Sherburn N York	67	K11
Sherburn Hill Dur	73	N11
Sherburn in Elmet N York	59	L7
Shere Surrey	10	H1
Shereford Norfk	44	E4
Sherfield English Hants	9	K3
Sherfield on Loddon Hants	20	B10
Sherford Devon	5	Q10
Sheriffhales Shrops	49	N11
Sheriff Hutton N York	59	P2
Sheringham Norfk	45	J2
Sherington M Keyn	32	C7
Shernborne Norfk	44	B4
Sherrington Wilts	18	E11
Sherston Wilts	18	C4
Sherwood C Nott	51	M11
Sherwood Forest Notts	51	N8
Sherwood Forest Crematorium Notts	51	P7
Shetland Islands Shet	111	k4
Shettleston C Glas	85	L9
Shevington Wigan	57	K7
Sheviock Cnwll	4	H8
Shibden Head C Brad	58	E8
Shide IoW	9	N9
Shidlaw Nthumb	80	H6
Shiel Bridge Highld	97	N6
Shieldaig Highld	105	M10
Shieldhill D & G	78	G11
Shieldhill Falk	85	P7
Shieldhill House Hotel S Lans	78	G2
Shields N Lans	85	N11
Shielfoot Highld	89	N3
Shielhill Angus	93	M4
Shielhill Inver	84	D8
Shifnal Shrops	39	N1
Shilbottle Nthumb	81	P11
Shildon Dur	65	M3
Shillford E Rens	84	H10
Shillingford Devon	16	D10
Shillingford Oxon	19	P3
Shillingford Abbot Devon	6	B5
Shillingford St George Devon	6	B5
Shillingstone Dorset	8	C5
Shillington C Beds	32	G9
Shilton Oxon	30	H11
Shilton Warwks	41	K9
Shimpling Norfk	45	J12
Shimpling Suffk	34	E6
Shimpling Street Suffk	34	E6
Shincliffe Dur	73	N11
Shiney Row Sundld	73	N9
Shinfield Wokham	20	B9
Shinness Highld	109	J11
Shipbourne Kent	22	C11
Shipdham Norfk	44	F8
Shipham Somset	17	L5
Shiphay Torbay	6	B9
Shiplake Oxon	20	C7
Shipley C Brad	58	F6
Shipley W Susx	11	J6
Shipley Bridge Surrey	11	L3
Shipmeadow Suffk	45	N11
Shippon Oxon	19	N2
Shipston-on-Stour Warwks	30	G6
Shipton Gloucs	30	D9
Shipton N York	59	M3
Shipton Shrops	39	K4
Shipton Bellinger Hants	19	J10
Shipton Gorge Dorset	7	M5
Shipton Green W Susx	10	C9
Shipton Moyne Gloucs	29	M10
Shipton-on-Cherwell Oxon	31	L10
Shiptonthorpe E R Yk	60	E5
Shipton-under-Wychwood Oxon	30	H9
Shirburn Oxon	20	B4
Shirdley Hill Lancs	56	G6
Shirebrook Derbys	51	M7
Shiregreen Sheff	51	J3
Shirehampton Bristl	28	G12
Shiremoor N Tyne	73	N6
Shirenewton Mons	28	F9
Shireoaks Notts	51	M5
Shirland Derbys	51	K8
Shirley C Sotn	9	L5
Shirley Derbys	50	G11
Shirley Gt Lon	21	M9
Shirley Solhll	40	E10
Shirrell Heath Hants	9	P5
Shirvan Ag & B	83	N6
Shirwell Devon	15	K5
Shiskine N Ayrs	75	N6
Shobdon Herefs	38	H9
Shobrooke Devon	15	P11
Shoby Leics	41	P4
Shocklach Ches W	48	H5
Shoeburyness Sthend	22	H6
Sholden Kent	23	Q11
Sholing C Sotn	9	M5
Shop Cnwll	14	E8
Shoreditch Gt Lon	21	M6
Shoreditch Somset	16	H10
Shoreham Kent	21	P10
Shoreham-by-Sea W Susx	11	K8
Shorley Hants	9	P3
Shorne Kent	22	E8
Shortgate E Susx	11	P7
Short Heath Birm	40	E8
Short Heath Wsall	40	C7
Shortlanesend Cnwll	3	J6
Shortlees E Ayrs	76	G4
Shorwell IoW	9	M10
Shoscombe BaNES	17	Q5
Shotesham Norfk	45	L9
Shotgate Essex	22	F5
Shotley Suffk	35	K9
Shotley Bridge Dur	73	J9
Shotley Gate Suffk	35	L9
Shotley Street Suffk	35	K9
Shottenden Kent	23	K11
Shottery Warwks	30	F3
Shotteswell Warwks	31	K5
Shottisham Suffk	35	M7
Shottlegate Derbys	50	H10
Shotton Dur	73	N11
Shotton Flints	48	F2
Shotton Colliery Dur	73	N11
Shotts N Lans	85	P10
Shotwick Ches W	48	G2
Shougle Moray	101	J4
Shouldham Norfk	44	B8
Shouldham Thorpe Norfk	43	Q8
Shoulton Worcs	39	P9
Shover's Green E Susx	12	C3
Shraleybrook Staffs	49	P5
Shrawardine Shrops	48	H11
Shrawley Worcs	39	P8
Shreding Green Bucks	20	G7
Shrewley Warwks	30	H1
Shrewsbury Shrops	49	J11
Shrewton Wilts	18	F11
Shripney W Susx	10	F9
Shrivenham Oxon	19	J3
Shropham Norfk	44	G10
Shroton Dorset	8	C5
Shucknall Herefs	28	G1
Shudy Camps Cambs	33	P7
Shuna Ag & B	83	L2
Shurdington Gloucs	29	N5
Shurlock Row W & M	20	D8
Shurrery Highld	110	B4
Shurrery Lodge Highld	110	B4
Shurton Somset	16	G7
Shustoke Warwks	40	G8
Shute Devon	6	H4
Shute Devon	15	Q11
Shutford Oxon	31	J6
Shut Heath Staffs	49	Q10
Shuthonger Gloucs	29	M2
Shutlanger Nhants	31	Q4
Shuttington Warwks	40	H6
Shuttlewood Derbys	51	L6
Shuttleworth Bury	57	P5
Siabost W Isls	111	d1
Siadar W Isls	111	d1
Sibbertoft Nhants	41	P10
Sibford Ferris Oxon	31	J6
Sibford Gower Oxon	31	J6
Sible Hedingham Essex	34	C9
Sibley's Green Essex	33	P10
Sibsey Lincs	53	K12
Sibson Cambs	42	F10
Sibson Leics	41	J7
Sibster Highld	110	G5
Sibthorpe Notts	51	Q10
Sibthorpe Notts	51	Q6
Sibton Suffk	35	M3
Sicklesmere Suffk	34	E5
Sicklinghall N York	59	J5
Sidbury Devon	6	F4
Sidbury Shrops	39	M5
Sidcot N Som	17	K5
Sidcup Gt Lon	21	P8
Siddington Ches E	49	Q2
Siddington Gloucs	18	F2
Sidestrand Norfk	45	L3
Sidford Devon	6	F4
Sidlesham W Susx	10	D9
Sidley E Susx	12	E8
Sidmouth Devon	6	F5
Sigglesthorne E R Yk	61	K5
Sigingstone V Glam	16	C2
Silchester Hants	19	Q8
Sileby Leics	41	N5
Silecroft Cumb	62	D6
Silfield Norfk	45	J9
Silkstone Barns	58	H11
Silkstone Common Barns	58	H12
Silk Willoughby Lincs	42	F2
Silloth Cumb	70	H5
Silpho N York	67	L8
Silsden C Brad	58	D5
Silsoe C Beds	32	F9
Silton Dorset	8	B2
Silverburn Mdloth	86	E9
Silverdale Lancs	63	J7
Silverdale Staffs	49	P6
Silver End Essex	34	D11
Silverford Abers	102	G3
Silverstone Nhants	31	P5
Silverton Devon	6	C3
Silvington Shrops	39	L6
Simonburn Nthumb	72	F6
Simonsbath Somset	15	N4
Simonstone Lancs	57	P3
Simprim Border	80	H5
Simpson M Keyn	32	C9
Simpson Cross Pembks	24	F5
Sinclair's Hill Border	80	H4
Sinclairston E Ayrs	76	H7
Sinderby N York	65	N10
Sinderland Green Traffd	57	N10
Sindlesham Wokham	20	C9
Sinfin C Derb	41	J2
Singleton Kent	13	L3
Singleton Lancs	56	H2
Singleton W Susx	10	E7
Singlewell Kent	22	D8
Sinnarhard Abers	101	K11
Sinnington N York	66	G9
Sinton Worcs	39	P9
Sinton Worcs	39	Q9
Sinton Green Worcs	39	P9
Sissinghurst Kent	12	F3
Siston S Glos	17	P2
Sithney Cnwll	2	F9
Sittingbourne Kent	22	H10
Six Ashes Shrops	39	P4
Sixhills Lincs	52	G6
Six Mile Bottom Cambs	33	P5
Sixpenny Handley Dorset	8	E4
Skaill Ork	111	h2
Skara Brae Ork	111	g2
Skares E Ayrs	77	J7
Skateraw Abers	95	P4
Skateraw E Loth	87	N7
Skeabost Highld	104	F11
Skeeby N York	65	L7
Skeffington Leics	41	Q7
Skeffling E R Yk	61	N9
Skegby Notts	51	L8
Skegby Notts	52	B9
Skegness Lincs	53	P10
Skelbo Highld	107	N4
Skelbo Street Highld	107	N4
Skelbrooke Donc	59	L10
Skeldyke Lincs	43	K3
Skellingthorpe Lincs	52	D8
Skellow Donc	59	M11
Skelmanthorpe Kirk	58	G11
Skelmersdale Lancs	57	J7
Skelmorlie N Ayrs	84	D9
Skelpick Highld	109	M5
Skelton C York	59	M3
Skelton Cumb	71	N8
Skelton E R Yk	60	D8
Skelton R & Cl	66	F4
Skelton on Ure N York	59	J1
Skelwith Bridge Cumb	62	G2
Skendleby Lincs	53	M9
Skene House Abers	102	G12
Skenfrith Mons	28	E5
Skerne E R Yk	60	H3
Skerray Highld	109	L3
Skerricha Highld	108	E5
Skerries Airport Shet	111	m3
Skerton Lancs	63	J9
Sketchley Leics	41	K8
Sketty Swans	26	E9
Skewsby N York	66	E12
Skiall Highld	110	B3
Skidby E R Yk	60	H7
Skigersta W Isls	111	e1
Skilgate Somset	16	D10
Skillington Lincs	42	C5
Skinburness Cumb	71	J4
Skinflats Falk	85	Q6
Skinidin Highld	104	C11
Skipness Ag & B	83	N10
Skipper's Bridge D & G	79	M11
Skipsea E R Yk	61	K3
Skipton N York	58	C4
Skipton-on-Swale N York	65	P10
Skipwith N York	59	P6
Skirlaugh E R Yk	61	K6
Skirling Border	78	H2
Skirmett Bucks	20	C5
Skirpenbeck E R Yk	60	D3
Skirwith Cumb	64	B2
Skirza Highld	110	H3
Skokholm Island Pembks	24	D7
Skomer Island Pembks	24	D7
Skulamus Highld	97	J5
Skye Green Essex	34	E11
Skye of Curr Highld	99	P4
Slack Calder	58	C8
Slacks of Cairnbanno Abers	102	H6
Slad Gloucs	29	M7
Slade Devon	15	J3
Slade Green Gt Lon	21	Q7
Slade Hooton Rothm	51	M3
Slaggyford Nthumb	72	C9
Slaidburn Lancs	63	N10
Slaithwaite Kirk	58	E10
Slaley Nthumb	72	H8
Slamannan Falk	85	P8
Slapton Bucks	32	D11
Slapton Devon	5	Q10
Slapton Nhants	31	N5
Slaugham W Susx	11	K5
Slaughterford Wilts	18	C6
Slawston Leics	41	R8
Sleaford Hants	10	C3
Sleaford Lincs	42	F2
Sleagill Cumb	64	B4
Sleapford Wrekin	49	L11
Sleasdairidh Highld	107	K3
Sledmere E R Yk	60	F2
Sleetbeck Cumb	79	P12
Sleights N York	67	J6
Slickly Highld	110	F3
Sliddery N Ayrs	75	P7
Sligachan Highld	96	F4
Sligrachan Ag & B	84	C5
Slimbridge Gloucs	29	K7
Slindon Staffs	49	P8
Slindon W Susx	10	F8
Slinfold W Susx	10	H4
Slingsby N York	66	F11
Slip End C Beds	32	F11
Slip End Herts	33	J8
Slipton Nhants	32	D2
Slitting Mill Staffs	40	D4
Slockavullin Ag & B	83	M4
Sloncombe Devon	5	P3
Sloothby Lincs	53	M8
Slough Slough	20	F7
Slough Crematorium Bucks	20	L6
Slough Green Somset	16	H11
Slumbay Highld	97	M2
Slyne Lancs	63	J8
Smailholm Border	80	E7
Smallburgh Norfk	45	M5
Small Dole W Susx	11	K7
Smalley Derbys	51	K11
Smallfield Surrey	11	L2
Small Heath Birm	40	E9
Small Hythe Kent	12	H4
Smallridge Devon	7	J3
Smallthorne C Stke	50	B10
Smallworth Norfk	34	G1
Smannell Hants	19	L10
Smarden Kent	12	G2
Smarden Bell Kent	12	G2
Smart's Hill Kent	11	Q2
Smearisary Highld	89	N2
Smeatharpe Devon	6	G2
Smeeth Kent	13	K3
Smeeton Westerby Leics	41	P8
Smerral Highld	110	D8
Smestow Staffs	39	Q4
Smethwick Sandw	40	D9
Smisby Derbys	41	J4
Smithfield Cumb	71	P3
Smith's Green Essex	33	Q8
Smithstown Highld	105	L6
Smithton Highld	107	L12
Smoo Highld	108	H3
Smythe's Green Essex	34	F11
Snade D & G	78	D10
Snailbeach Shrops	38	G2
Snailwell Cambs	33	Q4
Snainton N York	67	K10
Snaith E R Yk	59	N9
Snape N York	65	M10
Snape Suffk	35	N5
Snape Street Suffk	35	N5
Snaresbrook Gt Lon	21	N5
Snarestone Leics	41	J5
Snarford Lincs	52	F7
Snargate Kent	13	J4
Snave Kent	13	K4
Sneaton N York	67	J6
Snelland Lincs	52	F7
Snelston Derbys	50	F11
Snetterton Norfk	44	G11
Snettisham Norfk	44	B4
Snitter Nthumb	81	L12
Snitterby Lincs	52	E5
Snitterfield Warwks	30	G3
Snitton Shrops	39	K7
Snodland Kent	22	E10
Snowdon Gwynd	54	H10
Snowdonia National Park	47	N5
Snow End Herts	33	L9
Snowshill Gloucs	30	E7
Soake Hants	9	Q5
Soay Highld	96	F7
Soberton Hants	9	Q4
Soberton Heath Hants	9	P5
Sockburn Darltn	65	N6
Soham Cambs	33	P3
Solas W Isls	111	b4
Soldridge Hants	9	Q1
Sole Street Kent	22	D9
Sole Street Kent	23	L12
Solihull Solhll	40	F10

Sollers Dilwyn Herefs....38 H10
Sollers Hope Herefs....28 H3
Solva Pembks....24 E4
Solwaybank D & G....79 L12
Somerby Leics....41 R5
Somerby Lincs....52 F3
Somercotes Derbys....51 K9
Somerford Dorset....8 H8
Somerford Keynes
  Gloucs....18 E2
Somerley W Susx....10 D9
Somerleyton Suffk....45 P10
Somersal Herbert Derbys....40 F1
Somersby Lincs....53 K8
Somersham Cambs....33 K2
Somersham Suffk....34 H7
Somerton Oxon....31 L8
Somerton Somset....17 L9
Somerton Suffk....34 D6
Sompting W Susx....11 J8
Sonning Wokham....20 C8
Sonning Common Oxon....20 B7
Sopley Hants....8 H7
Sopwell Herts....21 J3
Sopworth Wilts....18 C4
Sorbie D & G....69 L9
Sordale Highld....110 D4
Sorisdale Ag & B....88 G4
Sorn E Ayrs....77 J6
Sortat Highld....110 F3
Sotby Lincs....52 H7
Sotterley Suffk....45 P12
Soughton Flints....48 E3
Soulbury Bucks....32 C10
Soulby Cumb....64 D5
Souldern Oxon....31 M7
Souldrop Bed....32 E4
Sound Ches E....49 L6
Sound Muir Moray....101 M5
Soundwell S Glos....17 P2
Sourton Devon....5 L3
Soutergate Cumb....62 E6
South Acre Norfk....44 D7
South Alkham Kent....13 N2
Southall Gt Lon....20 H7
South Allington Devon....5 Q11
South Alloa Falk....85 P5
Southam Gloucs....29 N4
Southam Warwks....31 K2
South Ambersham
  W Susx....10 E6
Southampton C Sotn....9 M5
Southampton Airport
  Hants....9 M4
Southampton
  Crematorium Hants....9 M4
South Anston Rothm....51 L4
South Ashford Kent....13 J2
South Baddesley Hants....9 L7
South Ballachulish
  Highld....90 E5
South Bank C York....59 N4
South Barrow Somset....17 N9
South Beddington
  Gt Lon....21 L10
South Benfleet Essex....22 F6
Southborough Gt Lon....21 N9
Southborough Kent....12 C2
Southbourne Bmouth....8 G8
Southbourne W Susx....10 C8
South Bramwith Donc....59 N11
South Brent Devon....5 N8
South Brewham Somset....17 Q8
South Bristol
  Crematorium Bristl....17 N3
South Broomhill
  Nthumb....73 M2
Southburgh Norfk....44 G8
South Burlingham Norfk....45 N8
Southburn E R Yk....60 G4
South Cadbury Somset....17 P10
South Carlton Lincs....52 D8
South Carlton Notts....51 N4
South Cave E R Yk....60 F7
South Cerney Gloucs....18 F2
South Chailey E Susx....11 N6
South Charlton Nthumb....81 N9
South Cheriton Somset....17 Q10
South Church Dur....65 L2
Southchurch Sthend....22 H6
South Cliffe E R Yk....60 F7
South Clifton Notts....52 B9
South Cockerington
  Lincs....53 L6
South Cornelly Brdgnd....26 H11
Southcott Cnwll....4 F2
Southcott Devon....5 P4
Southcourt Bucks....20 D2
South Cove Suffk....35 P1
South Creake Norfk....44 E3
South Croxton Leics....41 P5
South Dalton E R Yk....60 G5
South Darenth Kent....22 C9
South Dell W Isls....111 d1
South Downs National
  Park....11 M8
South Duffield N York....59 P7
South Earlswood Surrey....11 L1
Southease E Susx....11 N8
South Elkington Lincs....53 J6
South Elmsall Wakefd....59 L11
Southend Ag & B....75 K10
Southend Airport Essex....22 G5
Southend
  Crematorium Sthend....22 H6
Southend-on-Sea
  Sthend....22 H6
Southerndown V Glam....16 B2
Southerness D & G....70 F5
South Erradale Highld....105 L7
Southerton Devon....6 E5
Southery Norfk....43 P10
South Essex
  Crematorium Gt Lon....22 C6
South Fambridge Essex....22 G5
South Ferriby N Linc....60 G9
South Field E R Yk....60 H8
Southfield Falk....85 P8
Southfleet Kent....22 C8
Southgate Gt Lon....21 L5
Southgate Swans....26 D10
South Gorley Hants....8 H5
South Gosforth N u Ty....73 M7
South Green Essex....22 D5
South Green Kent....22 G10
South Green Norfk....44 H7
South Gyle C Edin....86 E7
South Hanningfield
  Essex....22 E4
South Harting W Susx....10 C6

South Hayling Hants....10 B9
South Heath Bucks....20 E3
South Heighton E Susx....11 N9
South Hetton Dur....73 P10
South Hiendley Wakefd....59 K10
South Hill Cnwll....4 H9
South Hinksey Oxon....31 L12
South Holmwood Surrey....11 J2
South Hornchurch
  Gt Lon....21 P6
South Huish Devon....5 N11
South Hykeham Lincs....52 D9
South Hylton Sundld....73 P9
Southill C Beds....32 G8
Southington Hants....19 N10
South Kelsey Lincs....52 E4
South Kessock Highld....107 L11
South Killingholme
  N Linc....61 N10
South Kilvington N York....65 Q10
South Kilworth Leics....41 N10
South Kirkby Wakefd....59 K11
South Kyme Lincs....52 G12
South Lanarkshire
  Crematorium S Lans....85 L10
South Leicestershire
  Crematorium Leics....41 N8
Southleigh Devon....6 G4
South Leigh Oxon....31 K11
South Leverton Notts....52 A7
South Lincolnshire
  Crematorium Lincs....43 J4
South Littleton Worcs....30 E5
South London
  Crematorium Gt Lon....21 L9
South Lopham Norfk....34 G1
South Luffenham Rutlnd....42 D9
South Lynn Norfk....43 P6
South Malling E Susx....11 N7
South Marston Swindn....18 H3
South Merstham Surrey....21 L11
South Milford N York....59 L7
South Milton Devon....5 N10
South Mimms Herts....21 K3
South Mimms Services
  Herts....21 K4
Southminster Essex....23 J4
South Molton Devon....15 M7
South Moor Dur....73 L9
Southmoor Oxon....19 L2
South Moreton Oxon....19 P3
Southmuir Angus....93 L5
South Mundham W Susx....10 E9
South Newbald E R Yk....60 F7
South Newington Oxon....31 K7
South Newton Wilts....8 G1
South Normanton
  Derbys....51 K9
South Norwood Gt Lon....21 M9
South Ockendon Thurr....22 C6
Southoe Cambs....32 H4
Southolt Suffk....35 K3
South Ormsby Lincs....53 L8
Southorpe C Pete....42 F9
South Otterington
  N York....65 P9
Southover Dorset....7 N4
South Owersby Lincs....52 F5
Southowram Calder....58 E9
South Oxfordshire
  Crematorium Oxon....19 M2
South Park Surrey....11 K1
South Perrott Dorset....7 L2
South Petherton Somset....17 L11
South Petherwin Cnwll....4 G4
South Pickenham Norfk....44 D8
South Pill Cnwll....5 J8
South Pool Devon....5 Q11
South Poorton Dorset....7 M4
Southport Sefton....56 G5
Southport
  Crematorium Lancs....56 G6
South Queensferry
  C Edin....86 D6
South Raynham Norfk....44 E5
South Reddish Stockp....50 B3
Southrepps Norfk....45 L3
South Reston Lincs....53 L6
Southrey Lincs....52 G9
South Ronaldsay Ork....111 h3
Southrop Gloucs....30 G12
Southrope Hants....19 Q10
South Runcton Norfk....43 Q8
South Scarle Notts....52 B10
Southsea C Port....9 Q7
South Shian Ag & B....90 C7
South Shields S Tyne....73 P7
South Shields
  Crematorium S Tyne....73 N8
South Shore Bpool....56 F3
Southside Dur....65 K3
South Stainley N York....58 H2
South Stifford Thurr....22 C7
South Stoke BaNES....17 Q4
South Stoke Oxon....19 P4
South Stoke W Susx....10 G7
South Street Kent....23 K10
South Street Kent....23 L9
South Tarbrax S Lans....86 B10
South Tawton Devon....5 N2
South Tehidy Cnwll....2 F7
South Thoresby Lincs....53 L7
Southtown Norfk....45 Q8
South Uist W Isls....111 b5
Southwaite Cumb....71 P6
Southwaite Services
  Cumb....71 P6
South Walsham Norfk....45 M7
Southwark Gt Lon....21 L7
South Warnborough
  Hants....10 B1
Southwater W Susx....11 J5
South Weald Essex....22 C5
Southwell Notts....51 P9
South West Middlesex
  Crematorium Gt Lon....20 H8
South Weston Oxon....20 B4
South Wheatley Notts....51 Q4
Southwick Hants....9 Q6
Southwick Nhants....42 E10
Southwick Sundld....73 P8
Southwick W Susx....11 K8
Southwick Wilts....18 C9
South Widcombe BaNES....17 N5
South Wigston Leics....41 N7
South Willesborough
  Kent....13 K2
South Willingham Lincs....52 H6
South Wingfield Derbys....51 J9

South Witham Lincs....42 D6
Southwold Suffk....35 Q2
South Woodham
  Ferrers Essex....22 F4
South Wootton Norfk....43 Q5
South Wraxall Wilts....18 C7
South Zeal Devon....5 N2
Sovereign Harbour
  E Susx....12 D9
Sowerby Calder....58 D9
Sowerby N York....66 B10
Sowerby Bridge Calder....58 D9
Sowood Calder....58 E9
Sowton Devon....6 K7
Sowton Devon....5 N8
Soyland Town Calder....58 D9
Spain's End Essex....33 Q8
Spalding Lincs....43 J5
Spaldington E R Yk....60 D7
Spaldwick Cambs....32 G3
Spalford Notts....52 B9
Spanby Lincs....42 F3
Sparham Norfk....44 H6
Spark Bridge Cumb....62 F5
Sparkford Somset....17 N10
Sparkhill Birm....40 E10
Sparkwell Devon....5 M8
Sparrowpit Derbys....50 E5
Sparrows Green E Susx....12 D4
Sparsholt Hants....9 M2
Sparsholt Oxon....19 L4
Spaunton N York....66 G9
Spaxton Somset....16 G8
Spean Bridge Highld....98 C11
Spearywell Hants....9 K2
Speen Bucks....20 D4
Speen W Berk....19 M7
Speeton N York....67 N11
Speke Lpool....56 H11
Speldhurst Kent....12 B2
Spellbrook Herts....33 M12
Spencers Wood Wokham....20 B9
Spen Green Ches E....49 P4
Spennithorne N York....65 K9
Spennymoor Dur....65 M2
Spetchley Worcs....30 B4
Spetisbury Dorset....8 D7
Spexhall Suffk....35 N2
Spey Bay Moray....101 L3
Speybridge Highld....100 G9
Speyview Moray....101 K6
Spilsby Lincs....53 L9
Spinkhill Derbys....51 L5
Spinningdale Highld....107 L4
Spital Wirral....56 G11
Spital Hill Donc....51 N3
Spittal E Loth....87 J4
Spittal Highld....110 D5
Spittal Nthumb....81 L4
Spittal Pembks....24 G4
Spittalfield P & K....92 G7
Spittal of Glenmuick
  Abers....94 E5
Spittal of Glenshee P & K....94 B7
Spittal-on-Rule Border....80 D9
Spixworth Norfk....45 L7
Splatt Devon....15 K10
Splayne's Green E Susx....11 N5
Splottlands Cardif....27 P12
Spofforth N York....59 J4
Spondon C Derb....41 K1
Spooner Row Norfk....44 H10
Sporle Norfk....44 E7
Spott E Loth....87 M7
Spottiswoode Border....80 E4
Spratton Nhants....41 Q12
Spreakley Surrey....10 D2
Spreyton Devon....15 M11
Spriddlestone Devon....5 L9
Spridlington Lincs....52 E6
Springburn C Glas....85 K8
Springfield D & G....71 M2
Springfield Essex....22 E2
Springfield Fife....93 L12
Springholm D & G....70 D2
Springside N Ayrs....76 F4
Springthorpe Lincs....52 C5
Springwell Sundld....73 M8
Springwood
  Crematorium Lpool....56 H10
Sproatley E R Yk....61 K7
Sproston Green Ches W....49 N3
Sprotbrough Donc....51 M1
Sproughton Suffk....35 J7
Sprouston Border....80 G7
Sprowston Norfk....45 L7
Sproxton Leics....42 C5
Sproxton N York....66 E10
Spurstow Ches E....49 K4
Spyway Dorset....7 M4
Stableford Shrops....39 N3
Stacey Bank Sheff....50 H3
Stackhouse N York....63 P8
Stackpole Pembks....24 H9
Stackpole Elidor Pembks....24 H8
Staddiscombe C Plym....5 M9
Stadhampton Oxon....19 Q2
Stadhlaigearraidh W Isls....111 a6
Staffield Cumb....71 Q7
Staffin Highld....104 G8
Stafford Staffs....40 B3
Stafford Crematorium
  Staffs....40 C3
Stafford Services
  (northbound) Staffs....40 B2
Stafford Services
  (southbound) Staffs....40 B2
Stagsden Bed....32 E7
Stainburn Cumb....70 G9
Stainby Lincs....42 C5
Staincross Barns....59 J11
Staindrop Dur....65 K4
Staines-upon-Thames
  Surrey....20 G8
Stainforth Donc....59 N10
Stainforth N York....63 P8
Staining Lancs....56 G2
Stainland Calder....58 E9
Stainsacre N York....67 K6
Stainton Cumb....63 K5
Stainton Cumb....71 P9
Stainton Donc....51 M3
Stainton Dur....65 J4
Stainton Middsb....66 C5
Stainton by Langworth
  Lincs....52 F7
Staintondale N York....67 L7
Stainton le Vale Lincs....52 H5
Stainton with Adgarley
  Cumb....62 F7

Stair E Ayrs....76 G6
Stairhaven D & G....68 G8
Staithes N York....66 H4
Stakes Hants....10 B8
Stalbridge Dorset....17 Q11
Stalbridge Weston
  Dorset....17 Q11
Stalham Norfk....45 N5
Stalisfield Green Kent....23 J11
Stallen Dorset....17 N11
Stallingborough NE Lin....61 K11
Stalmine Lancs....62 G12
Stalybridge Tamesd....50 C2
Stambourne Essex....34 C8
Stambourne Green
  Essex....34 B8
Stamford Lincs....42 E8
Stamford Nthumb....81 P9
Stamford Bridge Ches W....49 J2
Stamford Bridge E R Yk....60 C3
Stamfordham Nthumb....73 J6
Stamford Hill Gt Lon....21 M6
Stanbridge C Beds....32 D11
Stanbury C Brad....58 D6
Stand N Lans....85 M8
Standburn Falk....85 Q7
Standeford Staffs....40 B6
Standen Kent....12 G3
Standerwick Somset....18 B10
Standford Hants....10 D3
Standingstone Cumb....70 H8
Standish Wigan....57 K6
Standlake Oxon....31 K12
Standon Hants....9 M3
Standon Herts....33 L11
Standon Staffs....49 P6
Stane N Lans....85 P10
Stanfield Norfk....44 F6
Stanford C Beds....32 G8
Stanford Kent....13 L3
Stanford Bishop Herefs....39 M10
Stanford Bridge Worcs....39 N8
Stanford Dingley W Berk....19 P6
Stanford in the Vale
  Oxon....19 K3
Stanford le Hope Thurr....22 D7
Stanford on Avon
  Nhants....41 N10
Stanford on Soar Notts....41 M3
Stanford on Teme Worcs....39 N8
Stanfree Derbys....51 L6
Stanghow R & Cl....66 F4
Stanground C Pete....42 H10
Stanhoe Norfk....44 D3
Stanhope Border....79 J3
Stanhope Dur....72 H11
Stanhope Kent....13 J2
Stanion Nhants....42 D11
Stanley Derbys....51 K11
Stanley Dur....73 L9
Stanley P & K....92 G8
Stanley Staffs....50 B9
Stanley Crook Dur....73 L12
Stanley Pontlarge
  Gloucs....30 D7
Stanmer Br & H....11 M7
Stanmore Gt Lon....21 J5
Stanmore Hants....9 M2
Stannersburn Nthumb....72 D4
Stanningfield Suffk....34 E5
Stannington Nthumb....73 L5
Stannington Sheff....50 H4
Stannington Station
  Nthumb....73 L5
Stansbatch Herefs....38 G9
Stansfield Suffk....34 D6
Stanstead Suffk....34 D7
Stanstead Abbotts Herts....21 M2
Stansted Kent....22 C10
Stansted Airport Essex....33 N11
Stansted Mountfitchet
  Essex....33 N10
Stanton Gloucs....30 E7
Stanton N York....73 K3
Stanton Staffs....50 E10
Stanton Suffk....34 F3
Stanton by Bridge
  Derbys....41 J3
Stanton by Dale Derbys....51 L12
Stanton Drew BaNES....17 N4
Stanton Fitzwarren
  Swindn....18 H3
Stanton Harcourt Oxon....31 K11
Stanton in Peak Derbys....50 G7
Stanton Lacy Shrops....39 J6
Stanton Lees Derbys....50 G8
Stanton Long Shrops....39 L4
Stanton-on-the-Wolds
  Notts....41 N2
Stanton Prior BaNES....17 P4
Stanton St Bernard Wilts....18 G8
Stanton St John Oxon....31 M11
Stanton St Quintin Wilts....18 D5
Stanton Street Suffk....34 F4
Stanton under Bardon
  Leics....41 L5
Stanton upon Hine
  Heath Shrops....49 K10
Stanton Wick BaNES....17 N4
Stanway Essex....34 F11
Stanway Gloucs....30 D7
Stanwell Surrey....20 G8
Stanwick Nhants....32 E3
Stanwix Cumb....71 N4
Staoinebrig W Isls....111 a5
Stape N York....66 H8
Stapeley Ches E....49 M5
Stapenhill Staffs....40 G3
Staple Kent....23 P11
Staple Cross Devon....16 D11
Staplecross E Susx....12 F5
Staplefield W Susx....11 L5
Staple Fitzpaine Somset....16 H11
Stapleford Cambs....33 M6
Stapleford Herts....33 K12
Stapleford Leics....42 B6
Stapleford Lincs....52 C11
Stapleford Notts....51 L12
Stapleford Wilts....18 F12
Stapleford Abbotts
  Essex....21 P5
Staplegrove Somset....16 G10
Staplehay Somset....16 G10
Staplehurst Kent....12 F2
Staplers IoW....9 N9
Staplestreet Kent....23 K10
Stapleton Herefs....38 G8
Stapleton Leics....41 K7
Stapleton N York....65 M5
Stapleton Shrops....39 J2

Stapleton Somset....17 L11
Stapley Somset....16 G12
Staploe Bed....32 G5
Staplow Herefs....29 J1
Star Fife....86 G2
Star Pembks....25 M2
Star Somset....17 L5
Starbeck N York....59 J3
Starbotton N York....64 G11
Starcross Devon....6 C6
Stareton Warwks....41 J12
Starlings Green Essex....33 M9
Starston Norfk....45 K12
Startforth Dur....65 J4
Startley Wilts....18 D4
Statenborough Kent....23 P11
Statham Warrtn....57 M10
Stathe Somset....17 K9
Stathern Leics....41 Q2
Staughton Green Cambs....32 G4
Staunton Gloucs....28 G6
Staunton Gloucs....29 K3
Staunton on Arrow
  Herefs....38 G9
Staunton on Wye Herefs....38 G12
Staveley Cumb....63 J3
Staveley Derbys....51 K6
Staveley N York....59 J2
Staveley-in-Cartmel
  Cumb....62 H5
Staverton Devon....5 Q7
Staverton Gloucs....29 M4
Staverton Nhants....31 M2
Staverton Wilts....18 C8
Stawell Somset....17 K8
Stawley Somset....16 E10
Staxigoe Highld....110 H5
Staxton N York....67 L10
Staynall Lancs....62 G12
Stean N York....65 J11
Stearsby N York....66 E12
Steart Somset....16 H7
Stebbing Essex....33 Q11
Stechford Birm....40 F9
Stedham W Susx....10 D5
Steelend Fife....86 B4
Steele Road Border....79 Q9
Steen's Bridge Herefs....39 K10
Steep Hants....10 C5
Steep Lane Calder....58 D9
Steeple Dorset....8 D10
Steeple Essex....22 H3
Steeple Ashton Wilts....18 D9
Steeple Aston Oxon....31 L8
Steeple Bumpstead
  Essex....34 B8
Steeple Claydon Bucks....31 P8
Steeple Gidding Cambs....32 G1
Steeple Langford Wilts....18 F12
Steeple Morden Cambs....33 J8
Steeton C Brad....58 D5
Stein Highld....104 C10
Stelling Minnis Kent....13 M1
Stembridge Somset....17 K11
Stenalees Cnwll....3 M4
Stenhouse D & G....77 N11
Stenhousemuir Falk....85 P6
Stenscholl Highld....104 F8
Stenson Fields Derbys....41 J2
Stenton E Loth....87 M7
Steornabhagh W Isls....111 d2
Stepaside Pembks....25 K7
Stepford D & G....78 E11
Stepney Gt Lon....21 M7
Steppingley C Beds....32 E9
Stepps N Lans....85 L8
Sternfield Suffk....35 N5
Stert Wilts....18 F8
Stetchworth Cambs....33 Q5
Stevenage Herts....32 H10
Stevenston N Ayrs....76 E3
Steventon Hants....19 P10
Steventon Oxon....19 M3
Steventon End Essex....33 P8
Stevington Bed....32 E6
Stewartby Bed....32 E8
Stewartfield S Lans....85 K11
Stewarton Ag & B....75 K8
Stewarton E Ayrs....76 G3
Stewkley Bucks....32 C10
Stewley Somset....17 J11
Steyning W Susx....11 J7
Steynton Pembks....24 G7
Stibb Cnwll....14 D9
Stibbard Norfk....44 G4
Stibb Cross Devon....14 H8
Stibb Green Wilts....19 J8
Stibbington Cambs....42 F9
Stichill Border....80 F6
Sticker Cnwll....3 L6
Stickford Lincs....53 K10
Sticklepath Devon....5 M2
Stickney Lincs....53 K11
Stiffkey Norfk....44 F2
Stifford Clays Thurr....22 C7
Stilligarry W Isls....111 a5
Stillingfleet N York....59 N6
Stillington N York....66 N1
Stillington S on T....65 P3
Stilton Cambs....42 G11
Stinchcombe Gloucs....29 K8
Stinsford Dorset....7 Q5
Stiperstones Shrops....38 G3
Stirchley Wrekin....39 M1
Stirling Abers....103 M6
Stirling Stirlg....85 N4
Stirling Castle Stirlg....85 N4
Stirling Services Stirlg....85 N5
Stirtloe Cambs....32 H4
Stirton N York....58 C4
Stisted Essex....34 D10
Stithians Cnwll....2 G9
Stivichall Covtry....41 J11
Stixwould Lincs....52 H9
St Michaels Fife....93 M10
Stoak Ches W....48 H2
Stobo Border....79 K2
Stoborough Dorset....8 D9
Stobs Castle Border....80 C11
Stobswood Nthumb....73 L2
Stock Essex....22 E4
Stock N Som....17 L4
Stockbridge Hants....9 L1
Stockbriggs S Lans....77 N4
Stockbury Kent....22 G10
Stockcross W Berk....19 M7
Stockerston Leics....42 B9
Stock Green Worcs....30 C3
Stocking Herefs....28 H3
Stockingford Warwks....41 J8
Stocking Pelham Herts....33 M10

Place	Area	Page	Grid
Stockland	Devon	6	H2
Stockland Bristol	Somset	16	H7
Stockleigh English	Devon	15	P10
Stockleigh Pomeroy	Devon	15	P10
Stockley	Wilts	18	E7
Stocklinch	Somset	17	K11
Stockport	Stockp	50	B3
Stockport Crematorium	Stockp	50	B3
Stocksbridge	Sheff	50	H2
Stocksfield	Nthumb	73	J8
Stockton	Herefs	39	K9
Stockton	Norfk	45	N10
Stockton	Shrops	39	N3
Stockton	Warwks	31	K2
Stockton	Wilts	18	E12
Stockton	Wrekin	49	P11
Stockton Brook	Staffs	50	B9
Stockton Heath	Warrtn	57	L10
Stockton-on-Tees	S on T	66	C4
Stockton on Teme	Worcs	39	N8
Stockton on the Forest	C York	59	P3
Stockwell End	Wolves	40	B7
Stockwood	Bristl	17	P3
Stockwood	Dorset	7	N2
Stock Wood	Worcs	30	D3
Stodmarsh	Kent	23	N10
Stody	Norfk	44	H3
Stoer	Highld	108	B9
Stoford	Somset	17	N12
Stoford	Wilts	8	F1
Stogumber	Somset	16	E8
Stogursey	Somset	16	G7
Stoke	Covtry	41	J10
Stoke	Devon	14	E7
Stoke	Hants	10	B9
Stoke	Hants	19	L9
Stoke	Medway	22	G8
Stoke Abbott	Dorset	7	L3
Stoke Albany	Nhants	42	B11
Stoke Ash	Suffk	35	J3
Stoke Bardolph	Notts	51	N11
Stoke Bliss	Worcs	39	M9
Stoke Bruerne	Nhants	31	Q4
Stoke-by-Clare	Suffk	34	C7
Stoke-by-Nayland	Suffk	34	G9
Stoke Canon	Devon	6	C3
Stoke Charity	Hants	19	N11
Stoke Climsland	Cnwll	4	H5
Stoke Cross	Herefs	39	L11
Stoke D'Abernon	Surrey	20	H10
Stoke Doyle	Nhants	42	E11
Stoke Dry	Rutlnd	42	C10
Stoke Edith	Herefs	28	H1
Stoke Farthing	Wilts	8	F3
Stoke Ferry	Norfk	44	B9
Stoke Fleming	Devon	6	B11
Stokeford	Dorset	8	C9
Stoke Gabriel	Devon	6	B10
Stoke Gifford	S Glos	28	H11
Stoke Golding	Leics	41	K7
Stoke Goldington	M Keyn	32	B7
Stokeham	Notts	52	A7
Stoke Hammond	Bucks	32	C10
Stoke Holy Cross	Norfk	45	K9
Stokeinteignhead	Devon	6	C8
Stoke Lacy	Herefs	39	L11
Stoke Lyne	Oxon	31	M8
Stoke Mandeville	Bucks	20	D2
Stokenchurch	Bucks	20	C4
Stoke Newington	Gt Lon	21	M6
Stokenham	Devon	5	Q10
Stoke-on-Trent	C Stke	50	B10
Stoke Orchard	Gloucs	29	M3
Stoke Poges	Bucks	20	F6
Stoke Prior	Herefs	39	K10
Stoke Prior	Worcs	30	C1
Stoke Rivers	Devon	15	L5
Stoke Rochford	Lincs	42	D5
Stoke Row	Oxon	20	B6
Stoke St Gregory	Somset	17	J10
Stoke St Mary	Somset	16	H10
Stoke St Michael	Somset	17	P6
Stoke St Milborough	Shrops	39	K5
Stokesby	Norfk	45	N7
Stokesley	N York	66	D6
Stoke sub Hamdon	Somset	17	L11
Stoke Talmage	Oxon	20	B4
Stoke Trister	Somset	17	Q9
Stoke upon Tern	Shrops	49	M9
Stolford	Somset	16	G7
Stondon Massey	Essex	22	C4
Stone	Bucks	20	C2
Stone	Gloucs	29	J9
Stone	Rothm	51	M3
Stone	Staffs	40	B1
Stone	Worcs	39	Q7
Stone Allerton	Somset	17	K4
Ston Easton	Somset	17	N5
Stonebridge	N Som	17	K4
Stonebridge	Warwks	40	G10
Stonebroom	Derbys	51	K8
Stone Cross	Kent	23	P11
Stonecrouch	Kent	12	E4
Stoneferry	C KuH	61	J7
Stonefield Castle Hotel	Ag & B	83	N8
Stonegate	E Susx	12	D4
Stonegrave	N York	66	F11
Stonehaven	Abers	95	P5
Stonehenge	Wilts	18	G11
Stonehouse	C Plym	5	K9
Stonehouse	Gloucs	29	L7
Stonehouse	S Lans	77	M3
Stone in Oxney	Kent	12	H5
Stoneleigh	Warwks	41	J11
Stonesby	Leics	42	B5
Stonesfield	Oxon	31	K10
Stones Green	Essex	35	J10
Stone Street	Kent	22	C11
Stone Street	Suffk	35	N1
Stonewells	Moray	101	K3
Stoneybridge	W Isls	111	a5
Stoneyburn	W Loth	86	B9
Stoneygate	C Leic	41	N7
Stoneykirk	D & G	68	E8
Stoney Middleton	Derbys	50	G6
Stoney Stanton	Leics	41	L8
Stoney Stoke	Somset	17	Q8
Stoney Stratton	Somset	17	P8
Stoneywood	C Aber	103	J11
Stoneywood	Falk	85	N6
Stonham Aspal	Suffk	35	J5
Stonnall	Staffs	40	E6
Stonor	Oxon	20	B6
Stonton Wyville	Leics	41	Q8
Stony Houghton	Derbys	51	L7
Stony Stratford	M Keyn	32	B8
Stoodleigh	Devon	15	L6
Stoodleigh	Devon	16	C11
Stop 24 Services	Kent	13	L3
Stopham	W Susx	10	G6
Stopsley	Luton	32	F11
Stornoway	W Isls	111	d2
Stornoway Airport	W Isls	111	d2
Storrington	W Susx	10	H7
Storth	Cumb	63	J6
Storwood	E R Yk	60	C5
Stotfield	Moray	101	J2
Stotfold	C Beds	32	H9
Stottesdon	Shrops	39	M5
Stoughton	Leics	41	N7
Stoughton	Surrey	20	F12
Stoughton	W Susx	10	C7
Stoulton	Worcs	30	B4
Stourbridge	Dudley	40	B10
Stourbridge Crematorium	Dudley	40	B10
Stourhead	Wilts	8	B1
Stourpaine	Dorset	8	C5
Stourport-on-Severn	Worcs	39	P7
Stour Provost	Dorset	8	B3
Stour Row	Dorset	8	B3
Stourton	Staffs	39	Q5
Stourton	Warwks	30	H6
Stourton	Wilts	8	B1
Stourton Caundle	Dorset	17	Q12
Stove	Shet	111	k5
Stoven	Suffk	35	P1
Stow	Border	87	J12
Stow	Lincs	52	C7
Stow Bardolph	Norfk	43	P8
Stow Bedon	Norfk	44	F10
Stowbridge	Norfk	43	P8
Stow-cum-Quy	Cambs	33	N5
Stowe	Shrops	38	F7
Stowe by Chartley	Staffs	40	D3
Stowell	Somset	17	P10
Stowey	BaNES	17	N4
Stowford	Devon	5	J3
Stowlangtoft	Suffk	34	F3
Stow Longa	Cambs	32	G3
Stow Maries	Essex	22	G4
Stowmarket	Suffk	34	H5
Stow-on-the-Wold	Gloucs	30	F8
Stowting	Kent	13	L2
Stowupland	Suffk	34	H5
Straanruie	Highld	99	P6
Strachan	Abers	95	L4
Strachur	Ag & B	84	B3
Stradbroke	Suffk	35	K3
Stradishall	Suffk	34	C6
Stradsett	Norfk	43	Q8
Stragglethorpe	Lincs	52	C11
Straiton	Mdloth	86	F8
Straiton	S Ayrs	76	G9
Straloch	Abers	102	H10
Straloch	P & K	92	F3
Stramshall	Staffs	40	E1
Strang	IoM	56	c5
Strangeways	Salfd	57	N8
Strangford	Herefs	28	G4
Stranraer	D & G	68	E7
Stratfield Mortimer	W Berk	19	Q7
Stratfield Saye	Hants	20	B10
Stratfield Turgis	Hants	20	B10
Stratford	Gt Lon	21	M6
Stratford St Andrew	Suffk	35	M5
Stratford St Mary	Suffk	34	H9
Stratford sub Castle	Wilts	8	G2
Stratford Tony	Wilts	8	G3
Stratford-upon-Avon	Warwks	30	G3
Strath	Highld	105	L6
Strathan	Highld	108	C10
Strathan	Highld	109	K3
Strathaven	S Lans	77	L3
Strathblane	Stirlg	85	J7
Strathcanaird	Highld	106	C3
Strathcarron	Highld	97	N2
Strathcoil	Ag & B	89	N9
Strathdon	Abers	101	L11
Strathkinness	Fife	93	M11
Strathloanhead	W Loth	85	Q8
Strathmashie House	Highld	98	H10
Strathmiglo	Fife	86	E1
Strathpeffer	Highld	106	H10
Strathtay	P & K	92	D5
Strathwhillan	N Ayrs	75	Q5
Strathy	Highld	109	P3
Strathy Inn	Highld	109	P3
Strathyre	Stirlg	91	N11
Stratton	Cnwll	14	D10
Stratton	Dorset	7	P4
Stratton	Gloucs	30	D12
Stratton Audley	Oxon	31	N8
Stratton-on-the-Fosse	Somset	17	P6
Stratton St Margaret	Swindn	18	H4
Stratton St Michael	Norfk	45	K10
Stratton Strawless	Norfk	45	K6
Streat	E Susx	11	M7
Streatham	Gt Lon	21	L8
Streatley	C Beds	32	F10
Streatley	W Berk	19	P5
Street	Devon	6	G5
Street	Somset	17	L8
Street Ashton	Warwks	41	L10
Street Dinas	Shrops	48	G7
Street End	Kent	23	M11
Street End	W Susx	10	D9
Streethay	Staffs	40	F5
Streetlam	N York	65	N7
Streetly Crematorium	Wsall	40	E7
Streetly End	Cambs	33	P7
Street on the Fosse	Somset	17	N8
Strelitz	P & K	92	H8
Strelley	Notts	51	L11
Strensall	C York	59	N3
Strensham Services (northbound)	Worcs	29	M1
Strensham Services (southbound)	Worcs	29	M2
Stretcholt	Somset	16	H7
Strete	Devon	5	R10
Stretford	Traffd	57	P9
Strethall	Essex	33	M8
Stretham	Cambs	33	N2
Strettington	W Susx	10	E8
Stretton	Derbys	51	K8
Stretton	Rutlnd	42	D7
Stretton	Staffs	40	B5
Stretton	Staffs	40	G3
Stretton	Warrtn	57	L11
Stretton Grandison	Herefs	39	L12
Stretton-on-Dunsmore	Warwks	41	K11
Stretton on Fosse	Warwks	30	G6
Stretton Sugwas	Herefs	28	E1
Stretton under Fosse	Warwks	41	L10
Stretton Westwood	Shrops	39	L3
Strichen	Abers	103	K4
Stringston	Somset	16	G7
Strixton	Nhants	32	C4
Stroat	Gloucs	28	G8
Strollamus	Highld	96	H4
Stroma	Highld	110	G1
Stromeferry	Highld	97	M3
Stromness	Ork	111	g2
Stronaba	Highld	98	B11
Stronachlachar	Stirlg	84	G2
Stronafian	Ag & B	83	Q6
Stronchrubie	Highld	108	E11
Strone	Ag & B	84	D6
Strone	Highld	98	A11
Strone	Highld	98	G4
Stronmilchan	Ag & B	90	F10
Stronsay	Ork	111	i2
Stronsay Airport	Ork	111	i2
Strontian	Highld	89	Q4
Strood	Medway	22	E9
Stroud	Gloucs	29	L7
Stroud	Hants	10	B5
Stroud Green	Gloucs	29	L7
Stroxton	Lincs	42	C4
Struan	Highld	96	D3
Struan	P & K	92	B3
Strumpshaw	Norfk	45	M8
Strutherhill	S Lans	77	M2
Struthers	Fife	86	H1
Struy	Highld	98	E2
Stuartfield	Abers	103	K6
Stubbers Green	Wsall	40	D7
Stubbington	Hants	9	Q6
Stubbins	Lancs	57	P5
Stubton	Lincs	42	C1
Stuckton	Hants	8	H5
Studham	C Beds	32	E12
Studland	Dorset	8	F10
Studley	Warwks	30	E2
Studley	Wilts	18	E6
Studley Roger	N York	65	M12
Studley Royal	N York	65	M12
Studley Royal Park & Fountains Abbey	N York	58	H1
Stuntney	Cambs	33	N2
Sturmer	Essex	34	B7
Sturminster Common	Dorset	8	B5
Sturminster Marshall	Dorset	8	D7
Sturminster Newton	Dorset	8	B5
Sturry	Kent	23	M10
Sturton	N Linc	52	D3
Sturton by Stow	Lincs	52	C7
Sturton le Steeple	Notts	52	B6
Stuston	Suffk	35	J2
Stutton	N York	59	L6
Stutton	Suffk	35	J9
Styal	Ches E	57	Q11
Stynie	Moray	101	L3
Styrrup	Notts	51	N3
Succoth	Ag & B	84	E2
Suckley	Worcs	39	N10
Sudborough	Nhants	32	D1
Sudbourne	Suffk	35	N6
Sudbrook	Lincs	42	D2
Sudbrook	Mons	28	F10
Sudbrooke	Lincs	52	E8
Sudbury	Derbys	40	F2
Sudbury	Gt Lon	21	J6
Sudbury	Suffk	34	E8
Suffield	N York	67	L8
Suffield	Norfk	45	K4
Sugnall	Staffs	49	P8
Sugwas Pool	Herefs	28	E1
Suisnish	Highld	96	H6
Sulby	IoM	56	d3
Sulgrave	Nhants	31	M5
Sulham	W Berk	19	Q6
Sulhamstead	W Berk	19	Q7
Sullom	Shet	111	k3
Sullom Voe	Shet	111	k3
Sully	V Glam	16	F3
Sumburgh Airport	Shet	111	k5
Summerbridge	N York	58	G2
Summercourt	Cnwll	3	L4
Summerfield	Norfk	44	C3
Summerhill	Pembks	25	K7
Summerhouse	Darltn	65	L14
Summersdale	W Susx	10	D8
Summerseat	Bury	57	P6
Summertown	Oxon	31	L11
Sunbury-on-Thames	Surrey	20	H9
Sundaywell	D & G	78	D13
Sunderland	Ag & B	82	C9
Sunderland	Cumb	71	J8
Sunderland	Lancs	62	H10
Sunderland	Sundld	73	P9
Sunderland Bridge	Dur	73	M12
Sunderland Crematorium	Sundld	73	P9
Sundhope	Border	79	M4
Sundon Park	Luton	32	F10
Sundridge	Kent	21	P11
Sunningdale	W & M	20	F9
Sunninghill	W & M	20	F9
Sunningwell	Oxon	19	N1
Sunniside	Dur	73	K12
Sunniside	Gatesd	73	L8
Sunnyhill	C Derb	41	J2
Sunnyhurst	Bl w D	57	M4
Sunnylaw	Stirlg	85	N4
Sunnymead	Oxon	31	L11
Surbiton	Gt Lon	21	J9
Surfleet	Lincs	43	J5
Surlingham	Norfk	45	M8
Surrex	Essex	34	E11
Surrey & Sussex Crematorium	W Susx	11	L3
Sustead	Norfk	45	K3
Susworth	Lincs	52	B3
Sutcombe	Devon	14	F9
Sutcombemill	Devon	14	F9
Sutterby	Lincs	53	L8
Sutterton	Lincs	43	J3
Sutton	C Beds	32	H7
Sutton	C Pete	42	F9
Sutton	Cambs	33	M2
Sutton	Devon	5	N10
Sutton	E Susx	11	P9
Sutton	Gt Lon	21	K9
Sutton	Kent	23	P12
Sutton	N York	59	L8
Sutton	Norfk	45	N5
Sutton	Notts	51	Q12
Sutton	Oxon	31	K11
Sutton	Shrops	39	N5
Sutton	Shrops	49	J12
Sutton	Staffs	49	N10
Sutton	Suffk	35	M7
Sutton	W Susx	10	F7
Sutton-at-Hone	Kent	22	B9
Sutton Bassett	Nhants	41	Q9
Sutton Benger	Wilts	18	D5
Sutton Bonington	Notts	41	L3
Sutton Bridge	Lincs	43	M6
Sutton Cheney	Leics	41	K7
Sutton Coldfield	Birm	40	E8
Sutton Coldfield Crematorium	Birm	40	F7
Sutton Courtenay	Oxon	19	N2
Sutton cum Lound	Notts	51	P4
Sutton Green	Surrey	20	G11
Sutton Howgrave	N York	65	N10
Sutton-in-Ashfield	Notts	51	L8
Sutton-in-Craven	N York	58	D5
Sutton Maddock	Shrops	39	N2
Sutton Mallet	Somset	17	K8
Sutton Mandeville	Wilts	8	E2
Sutton Montis	Somset	17	P10
Sutton-on-Hull	C KuH	61	J7
Sutton on Sea	Lincs	53	N7
Sutton-on-the-Forest	N York	59	M2
Sutton on the Hill	Derbys	40	G2
Sutton on Trent	Notts	52	B9
Sutton St Edmund	Lincs	43	L7
Sutton St James	Lincs	43	L6
Sutton St Nicholas	Herefs	39	K11
Sutton Scotney	Hants	19	M11
Sutton-under-Brailes	Warwks	30	H6
Sutton-under-Whitestonecliffe	N York	66	C10
Sutton upon Derwent	E R Yk	60	C5
Sutton Valence	Kent	12	F1
Sutton Veny	Wilts	18	D11
Sutton Waldron	Dorset	8	C4
Sutton Weaver	Ches W	57	K11
Sutton Wick	BaNES	17	N4
Sutton Wick	Oxon	19	N2
Swaby	Lincs	53	L7
Swadlincote	Derbys	40	H4
Swaffham	Norfk	44	D8
Swaffham Bulbeck	Cambs	33	N4
Swaffham Prior	Cambs	33	P4
Swafield	Norfk	45	L4
Swainby	N York	66	C7
Swainsthorpe	Norfk	45	K9
Swainswick	BaNES	18	B7
Swalcliffe	Oxon	31	J6
Swalecliffe	Kent	23	L9
Swallow	Lincs	52	H3
Swallow Beck	Lincs	52	D9
Swallowcliffe	Wilts	8	E3
Swallowfield	Wokham	20	B9
Swanage	Dorset	8	F10
Swanbourne	Bucks	32	B10
Swan Green	Ches W	49	N2
Swanland	E R Yk	60	G8
Swanley	Kent	21	P9
Swanley Village	Kent	21	Q9
Swanmore	Hants	9	P4
Swannington	Leics	41	K4
Swannington	Norfk	45	J6
Swanpool	Lincs	52	D9
Swanscombe	Kent	22	C8
Swansea	Swans	26	E9
Swansea Airport	Swans	26	D9
Swansea Crematorium	Swans	26	E8
Swansea West Services	Swans	26	E8
Swanton Abbot	Norfk	45	L5
Swanton Morley	Norfk	44	G6
Swanton Novers	Norfk	44	G4
Swan Village	Sandw	40	C8
Swanwick	Derbys	51	K9
Swanwick	Hants	9	N5
Swarby	Lincs	42	F3
Swardeston	Norfk	45	K9
Swarkestone	Derbys	41	J2
Swarland	Nthumb	81	N12
Swarraton	Hants	19	P12
Swarthmoor	Cumb	62	F6
Swaton	Lincs	42	G3
Swavesey	Cambs	33	K3
Sway	Hants	9	J7
Swayfield	Lincs	42	E5
Swaythling	C Sotn	9	M4
Sweetham	Devon	15	Q11
Sweethaws	E Susx	11	P4
Sweets	Cnwll	4	E2
Sweetshouse	Cnwll	3	N4
Swefling	Suffk	35	M4
Swepstone	Leics	41	J5
Swerford	Oxon	31	J7
Swettenham	Ches E	49	P3
Swilland	Suffk	35	K6
Swillington	Leeds	59	J7
Swimbridge	Devon	15	L6
Swimbridge Newland	Devon	15	K6
Swinbrook	Oxon	30	H10
Swincliffe	N York	58	G3
Swinderby	Lincs	52	C10
Swindon	Gloucs	29	N4
Swindon	Staffs	39	Q4
Swindon	Swindn	18	G4
Swine	E R Yk	61	K7
Swinefleet	E R Yk	60	D9
Swineshead	Bed	32	F4
Swineshead	Lincs	43	J3
Swiney	Highld	110	E8
Swinford	Leics	41	M10
Swingfield Minnis	Kent	13	N2
Swingfield Street	Kent	13	N2
Swingleton Green	Suffk	34	F7
Swinhoe	Nthumb	81	P8
Swinithwaite	N York	65	J9
Swinside	Cumb	71	K10
Swinstead	Lincs	42	E5
Swinton	Border	80	H5
Swinton	N York	65	L10
Swinton	N York	66	G11
Swinton	Rothm	51	K2
Swinton	Salfd	57	P8
Swithland	Leics	41	M5
Swordale	Highld	107	J8
Swordland	Highld	97	L10
Swordly	Highld	109	N3
Swynnerton	Staffs	49	Q8
Swyre	Dorset	7	M5
Sychtyn	Powys	38	B1
Syde	Gloucs	29	N6
Sydenham	Gt Lon	21	M8
Sydenham	Oxon	20	B3
Sydenham Damerel	Devon	5	J5
Syderstone	Norfk	44	D4
Sydling St Nicholas	Dorset	7	P3
Sydmonton	Hants	19	N8
Syerston	Notts	51	Q10
Sykehouse	Donc	59	N10
Symbister	Shet	111	k3
Symington	S Ayrs	76	G5
Symington	S Lans	78	G2
Symondsbury	Dorset	7	L4
Symonds Yat (West)	Herefs	28	G5
Syre	Highld	109	M7
Syreford	Gloucs	30	D9
Syresham	Nhants	31	N6
Syston	Leics	41	N5
Syston	Lincs	42	D2
Sytchampton	Worcs	39	Q8
Sywell	Nhants	32	B4

T

Place	Area	Page	Grid
Tackley	Oxon	31	L9
Tacolneston	Norfk	45	J10
Tadcaster	N York	59	L5
Taddington	Derbys	50	F6
Tadley	Hants	19	P8
Tadlow	Cambs	33	J7
Tadmarton	Oxon	31	K6
Tadworth	Surrey	21	K11
Taff's Well	Rhondd	27	N11
Taibach	Neath	26	G10
Tain	Highld	107	M6
Tain	Highld	110	E3
Tairbeart	W Isls	111	c3
Takeley	Essex	33	P11
Takeley Street	Essex	33	N11
Talaton	Devon	6	E3
Talbenny	Pembks	24	E6
Talbot Village	Bmouth	8	F8
Taleford	Devon	6	E4
Talerddig	Powys	47	Q10
Talgarreg	Cerdgn	36	G9
Talgarth	Powys	27	N3
Talisker	Highld	96	D4
Talke	Staffs	49	P5
Talke Pits	Staffs	49	P5
Talkin	Cumb	71	Q4
Talladale	Highld	105	N8
Talla Linnfoots	Border	79	J5
Tallaminnock	S Ayrs	76	G10
Tallarn Green	Wrexhm	49	J6
Tallentire	Cumb	70	H8
Talley	Carmth	26	E3
Tallington	Lincs	42	F8
Talmine	Highld	109	K3
Talog	Carmth	25	N4
Talsarn	Cerdgn	37	J9
Talsarnau	Gwynd	47	K4
Talskiddy	Cnwll	3	K3
Talwrn	IoA	54	G6
Tal-y-bont	Cerdgn	37	K3
Tal-y-Bont	Conwy	55	L7
Tal-y-bont	Gwynd	47	J7
Tal-y-bont	Gwynd	54	H7
Talybont-on-Usk	Powys	27	N4
Tal-y-Cafn	Conwy	55	L7
Tal-y-coed	Mons	28	E6
Talysarn	Gwynd	54	G10
Tamar Valley Mining District	Devon	5	J7
Tamerton Foliot	C Plym	5	K7
Tamworth	Staffs	40	G6
Tamworth Services	Warwks	40	G7
Tandridge	Surrey	21	M12
Tanfield	Dur	73	L9
Tanfield Lea	Dur	73	L9
Tangasdale	W Isls	111	a7
Tangley	Hants	19	K9
Tangmere	W Susx	10	E8
Tankerness	Ork	111	h2
Tankersley	Barns	51	J2
Tankerton	Kent	23	L9
Tannach	Highld	110	G6
Tannachie	Abers	95	N5
Tannadice	Angus	93	N5
Tanner's Green	Worcs	40	E11
Tannington	Suffk	35	L4
Tannochside	N Lans	85	L10
Tansley	Derbys	51	J8
Tansor	Nhants	42	F11
Tantobie	Dur	73	L9
Tanworth in Arden	Warwks	40	E12
Tan-y-groes	Cerdgn	36	E10
Taobh Tuath	W Isls	111	b3
Taplow	Bucks	20	E7
Tarbert	Ag & B	75	J3
Tarbert	Ag & B	83	N8
Tarbert	W Isls	111	c3
Tarbet	Ag & B	84	F3
Tarbet	Highld	97	L10
Tarbet	Highld	108	D6
Tarbolton	S Ayrs	76	G6
Tarbrax	S Lans	86	B10
Tardebigge	Worcs	30	D1
Tarfside	Angus	94	H6
Tarland	Abers	94	H2
Tarleton	Lancs	57	J5

190 Tarlton – Tortworth

Tarlton Gloucs 29 N8
Tarnock Somset 17 K5
Tarporley Ches W 49 K3
Tarrant Crawford Dorset 8 D6
Tarrant Gunville Dorset 8 D5
Tarrant Hinton Dorset 8 D5
Tarrant Keyneston Dorset 8 D6
Tarrant Launceston Dorset 8 D5
Tarrant Monkton Dorset 8 D6
Tarrant Rawston Dorset 8 D6
Tarrant Rushton Dorset 8 D6
Tarring Neville E Susx 11 N8
Tarrington Herefs 28 H1
Tarskavaig Highld 96 H7
Tarves Abers 102 H8
Tarvin Ches W 49 J3
Tasburgh Norfk 45 K10
Tatenhill Staffs 40 G3
Tathwell Lincs 53 K6
Tatsfield Surrey 21 N11
Tattenhall Ches W 49 J4
Tatterford Norfk 44 E5
Tattersett Norfk 44 E4
Tattershall Lincs 52 H11
Tattershall Thorpe Lincs 52 H10
Tattingstone Suffk 35 J8
Tattingstone White Horse Suffk 35 J8
Tatton Park Ches E 57 N11
Tatworth Somset 7 J2
Tauchers Moray 101 M5
Taunton Somset 16 G10
Taunton Deane Crematorium Somset 16 G10
Taunton Deane Services Somset 16 G11
Taverham Norfk 45 J7
Tavernspite Pembks 25 L6
Tavistock Devon 5 K5
Tavistock Devon 5 K5
Taw Green Devon 15 L11
Tawstock Devon 15 K6
Taxal Derbys 50 D5
Tay Bridge C Dund 93 M9
Taychreggan Hotel Ag & B 90 E11
Tay Forest Park P & K 92 B4
Tayinloan Ag & B 75 K4
Taynton Gloucs 29 J4
Taynton Oxon 30 G10
Taynuilt Ag & B 90 D9
Tayport Fife 93 M9
Tayvallich Ag & B 83 L5
Tealby Lincs 52 G5
Tealing Angus 93 M7
Team Valley Gatesd 73 M8
Teangue Highld 97 J7
Teanord Highld 107 K9
Tebay Cumb 63 L2
Tebay Services Cumb 63 L2
Tebworth C Beds 32 E10
Tedburn St Mary Devon 5 Q2
Teddington Gloucs 29 N3
Teddington Gt Lon 21 J8
Tedstone Delamere Herefs 39 M9
Tedstone Wafer Herefs 39 M9
Teesside Crematorium Middsb 66 C4
Teeton Nhants 41 P12
Teffont Evias Wilts 8 E2
Teffont Magna Wilts 8 E2
Tegryn Pembks 25 L3
Teigh Rutlnd 42 C7
Teigngrace Devon 6 B7
Teignmouth Devon 6 C8
Teindside Border 79 P7
Telford Wrekin 39 M1
Telford Crematorium Wrekin 49 N12
Telford Services Shrops 39 N1
Tellisford Somset 18 B9
Telscombe E Susx 11 N8
Tempar P & K 91 Q5
Templand D & G 78 H10
Temple Cnwll 4 E5
Temple Mdloth 86 G9
Temple Bar Cerdgn 37 J9
Temple Cloud BaNES 17 P5
Templecombe Somset 17 Q10
Temple Grafton Warwks 30 E3
Temple Guiting Gloucs 30 E8
Temple Hirst N York 59 N8
Temple Normanton Derbys 51 K7
Temple of Fiddes Abers 95 N5
Temple Sowerby Cumb 64 B3
Templeton Devon 15 Q9
Templeton Pembks 25 K6
Templetown Dur 73 K10
Tempsford C Beds 32 G6
Tenbury Wells Worcs 39 L8
Tenby Pembks 25 K8
Tendring Essex 35 J11
Tendring Green Essex 35 J10
Tendring Heath Essex 35 J10
Ten Mile Bank Norfk 43 P10
Tenterden Kent 12 H4
Terling Essex 22 F1
Ternhill Shrops 49 L8
Terregles D & G 78 F12
Terrington N York 66 F12
Terrington St Clement Norfk 43 N6
Terrington St John Norfk 43 N7
Teston Kent 22 E11
Testwood Hants 9 L5
Tetbury Gloucs 29 M9
Tetchill Shrops 48 H8
Tetcott Devon 14 F11
Tetford Lincs 53 K8
Tetney Lincs 53 K4
Tetsworth Oxon 20 B3
Tettenhall Wolves 40 B7
Tettenhall Wood Wolves 39 Q3
Teversal Notts 51 L8
Teversham Cambs 33 M5
Teviothead Border 79 N7
Tewin Herts 21 L1
Tewkesbury Gloucs 29 M3
Teynham Kent 23 J10
Thackley C Brad 58 F6
Thainstone Abers 102 G10
Thakeham W Susx 10 H6
Thame Oxon 20 B3
Thames Ditton Surrey 21 J9
Thamesmead Gt Lon 21 P7
Thamesport Medway 22 G8
Thanet Crematorium Kent 23 Q9
Thanington Kent 23 L11
Thankerton S Lans 78 F2
Tharston Norfk 45 K10
Thatcham W Berk 19 N7
Thaxted Essex 33 P9
Theakston N York 65 N9
Thealby N Linc 60 F9
Theale Somset 17 L7
Theale W Berk 19 Q6
Thearne E R Yk 61 J6
The Beeches Gloucs 18 F1
Theberton Suffk 35 P4
The Braes Highld 96 G3
The Broads 45 P8
The Brunt E Loth 87 M7
The Bungalow IoM 56 d4
The Burf Worcs 39 P8
The City Bucks 20 C4
The Common Wilts 9 J2
Theddingworth Leics 41 P9
Theddlethorpe All Saints Lincs 53 M6
Theddlethorpe St Helen Lincs 53 M6
The Deep C KuH 61 J8
The Den N Ayrs 76 F2
The Forstal Kent 13 K3
The Green Cumb 62 D5
The Green Essex 34 C11
The Green N York 66 H6
The Green Wilts 8 C2
The Headland Hartpl 66 D1
The Hill Cumb 62 D5
The Lee Bucks 20 E3
The Lhen IoM 56 d2
Thelnetham Suffk 34 G2
The Lochs Moray 101 L3
Thelveton Norfk 35 J1
Thelwall Warrtn 57 M10
Themelthorpe Norfk 44 H5
The Middles Dur 73 L9
The Moor Kent 12 F4
The Mumbles Swans 26 E10
The Murray S Lans 85 K11
The Neuk Abers 95 M3
Thenford Nhants 31 M6
The Reddings Gloucs 29 M5
Therfield Herts 33 K8
The Ross P & K 92 B10
The Spring Warwks 40 H11
The Stocks Kent 12 H5
The Strand Wilts 18 D8
Thetford Norfk 44 E12
Thetford Forest Park 44 D11
Theydon Bois Essex 21 N4
Thickwood Wilts 18 C6
Thimbleby Lincs 53 J9
Thimbleby N York 66 C8
Thingwall Wirral 56 F11
Thirkleby N York 66 C10
Thirlby N York 66 C10
Thirlestane Border 80 D5
Thirn N York 65 L9
Thirsk N York 65 Q10
Thistleton Lancs 56 H2
Thistleton Rutlnd 42 D6
Thistley Green Suffk 33 Q2
Thixendale N York 60 E3
Thockrington Nthumb 72 G5
Tholomas Drove Cambs 43 L8
Tholthorpe N York 59 L2
Thomastown Abers 102 D7
Thompson Norfk 44 F10
Thongsbridge Kirk 58 F11
Thoralby N York 64 H9
Thoresway Lincs 52 G4
Thorganby Lincs 52 H4
Thorganby N York 59 P6
Thorgill N York 66 G7
Thorington Suffk 35 N2
Thorington Street Suffk 34 G9
Thorlby N York 58 C4
Thorley Herts 33 M11
Thorley Street IoW 9 L9
Thormanby N York 66 C11
Thornaby-on-Tees S on T 66 C4
Thornage Norfk 44 H3
Thornborough Bucks 31 Q7
Thornborough N York 65 N10
Thornbury C Brad 58 G7
Thornbury Devon 14 G9
Thornbury Herefs 39 L9
Thornbury S Glos 28 H10
Thornby Nhants 41 P11
Thorncliff Staffs 50 D8
Thorncliffe Crematorium Cumb 62 E7
Thorncombe Dorset 7 K3
Thorndon Suffk 35 J3
Thorndon Cross Devon 5 L2
Thorne Donc 59 P10
Thorner Leeds 59 J6
Thorne St Margaret Somset 16 E11
Thorney C Pete 43 J8
Thorney Notts 52 C8
Thorney Somset 17 K10
Thorney Hill Hants 8 H7
Thorney Island W Susx 10 C9
Thornfalcon Somset 16 H10
Thornford Dorset 17 N12
Thorngrafton Nthumb 72 E7
Thorngumbald E R Yk 61 L8
Thornham Norfk 44 C2
Thornham Magna Suffk 34 H3
Thornham Parva Suffk 35 J3
Thornhaugh C Pete 42 F9
Thornhill C Sotn 9 M5
Thornhill Cumb 62 B1
Thornhill D & G 78 E9
Thornhill Derbys 50 G4
Thornhill Kirk 58 G9
Thornhill Stirlg 85 L3
Thornholme E R Yk 61 J2
Thornicombe Dorset 8 C6
Thornington Nthumb 81 J7
Thornley Dur 73 K12
Thornley Dur 73 P11
Thornliebank E Rens 85 J10
Thorns Suffk 34 C6
Thornsett Derbys 50 D4
Thornthwaite Cumb 71 K9
Thornthwaite N York 58 F3
Thornton Angus 93 M6
Thornton Bucks 31 Q7
Thornton C Brad 58 E7
Thornton E R Yk 60 D5
Thornton Fife 86 F3
Thornton Lancs 56 G1
Thornton Leics 41 L6
Thornton Middsb 66 C5
Thornton Nthumb 81 K5
Thornton Curtis N Linc 61 J9
Thornton Garden of Rest Crematorium Sefton 56 G8
Thorntonhall S Lans 85 K11
Thornton Heath Gt Lon 21 L9
Thornton Hough Wirral 56 F11
Thornton-in-Craven N York 58 B5
Thornton in Lonsdale N York 63 M7
Thornton-le-Beans N York 65 P9
Thornton-le-Clay N York 59 P2
Thornton-le-Dale N York 67 J10
Thornton le Moor Lincs 52 F4
Thornton-le-Moor N York 65 P9
Thornton-le-Moors Ches W 48 H1
Thornton-le-Street N York 65 P9
Thorntonloch E Loth 87 N7
Thornton Rust N York 64 G9
Thornton Steward N York 65 L9
Thornton Watlass N York 65 M9
Thornydykes Border 80 E5
Thornythwaite Cumb 71 N10
Thoroton Notts 51 Q11
Thorp Arch Leeds 59 K5
Thorpe Derbys 50 F10
Thorpe E R Yk 60 G5
Thorpe N York 58 D2
Thorpe Notts 51 Q10
Thorpe Surrey 20 G9
Thorpe Abbotts Norfk 35 K2
Thorpe Arnold Leics 41 Q4
Thorpe Audlin Wakefd 59 L10
Thorpe Bassett N York 67 J11
Thorpe Bay Sthend 22 H6
Thorpe by Water Rutlnd 42 C10
Thorpe Constantine Staffs 40 H6
Thorpe End Norfk 45 L7
Thorpe Green Essex 35 J11
Thorpe Green Suffk 34 F6
Thorpe Hesley Rothm 51 J2
Thorpe in Balne Donc 59 N11
Thorpe Langton Leics 41 Q8
Thorpe Lea Surrey 20 G8
Thorpe-le-Soken Essex 35 K11
Thorpe le Street E R Yk 60 E5
Thorpe Malsor Nhants 32 B2
Thorpe Mandeville Nhants 31 M5
Thorpe Market Norfk 45 L3
Thorpe Marriot Norfk 45 K7
Thorpe Morieux Suffk 34 F6
Thorpeness Suffk 35 P5
Thorpe on the Hill Lincs 52 C9
Thorpe Park Surrey 20 G9
Thorpe St Andrew Norfk 45 L8
Thorpe St Peter Lincs 53 M10
Thorpe Salvin Rothm 51 M5
Thorpe Satchville Leics 41 Q5
Thorpe Thewles S on T 65 P3
Thorpe Tilney Lincs 52 G11
Thorpe Underwood N York 59 L3
Thorpe Waterville Nhants 32 E1
Thorpe Willoughby N York 59 M7
Thorrington Essex 34 H11
Thorverton Devon 6 C3
Thrandeston Suffk 35 J2
Thrapston Nhants 32 E2
Threapwood Ches W 48 H6
Threapwood Staffs 50 D11
Threave S Ayrs 76 F9
Three Bridges W Susx 11 L3
Three Chimneys Kent 12 G3
Three Cocks Powys 27 N2
Three Counties Crematorium Essex 34 D10
Three Crosses Swans 26 D9
Three Cups Corner E Susx 12 D6
Threekingham Lincs 42 F3
Three Leg Cross E Susx 12 D4
Three Legged Cross Dorset 8 F6
Three Mile Cross Wokham 20 B9
Threemilestone Cnwll 2 H6
Threemiletown W Loth 86 C7
Three Oaks E Susx 12 G7
Threlkeld Cumb 71 M9
Threshers Bush Essex 21 P2
Threshfield N York 58 C2
Thrigby Norfk 45 P7
Thrintoft N York 65 N8
Thriplow Cambs 33 M7
Throcking Herts 33 K10
Throckley N u Ty 73 K7
Throckmorton Worcs 30 C4
Throop Bmouth 8 G8
Thropton Nthumb 72 H1
Throsk Stirlg 85 P5
Throughgate D & G 78 E11
Throwleigh Devon 5 N3
Throwley Forstal Kent 23 J11
Thrumpton Notts 41 L2
Thrumster Highld 110 G6
Thrunscoe NE Lin 53 K2
Thrupp Gloucs 29 M7
Thrussington Leics 41 P4
Thruxton Hants 19 K10
Thruxton Herefs 28 E2
Thrybergh Rothm 51 L2
Thulston Derbys 41 K2
Thundersley Essex 22 F6
Thurcaston Leics 41 M5
Thurcroft Rothm 51 L3
Thurgarton Norfk 45 K3
Thurgarton Notts 51 P10
Thurgoland Barns 50 H1
Thurlaston Leics 41 L7
Thurlaston Warwks 41 L12
Thurlbear Somset 16 H11
Thurlby Lincs 42 F6
Thurlby Lincs 52 C10
Thurlby Lincs 53 M8
Thurleigh Bed 32 F5
Thurlestone Devon 5 N10
Thurloxton Somset 16 H9
Thurlstone Barns 58 G12
Thurlton Norfk 45 N9
Thurmaston Leics 41 N5
Thurnby Leics 41 N6
Thurne Norfk 45 N7
Thurnham Kent 22 F11
Thurning Nhants 42 F12
Thurning Norfk 44 H4
Thurnscoe Barns 59 L11
Thurrock Services Thurr 22 C7
Thursby Cumb 71 M5
Thursford Norfk 44 G4
Thursley Surrey 10 E3
Thurso Highld 110 D3
Thurstaston Wirral 56 F11
Thurston Suffk 34 F4
Thurstonfield Cumb 71 M4
Thurstonland Kirk 58 F11
Thurton Norfk 45 M9
Thurvaston Derbys 50 G12
Thuxton Norfk 44 G8
Thwaite N York 64 F7
Thwaite Suffk 35 J3
Thwaite Head Cumb 62 G4
Thwaite St Mary Norfk 45 M10
Thwing E R Yk 67 M12
Tibbermore P & K 92 F10
Tibbers D & G 78 E9
Tibberton Gloucs 29 K4
Tibberton Worcs 30 B3
Tibberton Wrekin 49 M10
Tibbie Shiels Inn Border 79 K5
Tibenham Norfk 45 J11
Tibshelf Derbys 51 K8
Tibshelf Services Derbys 51 K8
Tibthorpe E R Yk 60 G3
Ticehurst E Susx 12 E4
Tichborne Hants 9 P2
Tickencote Rutlnd 42 E8
Tickenham N Som 17 L2
Tickhill Donc 51 N3
Ticklerton Shrops 39 J4
Ticknall Derbys 41 J3
Tickton E R Yk 60 H6
Tidcombe Wilts 19 K8
Tiddington Oxon 31 P12
Tiddington Warwks 30 G3
Tidebrook E Susx 12 C4
Tideford Cnwll 4 H8
Tidenham Gloucs 28 G9
Tideswell Derbys 50 F6
Tidmarsh W Berk 19 Q6
Tidmington Warwks 30 H6
Tidworth Wilts 19 J10
Tiers Cross Pembks 24 F6
Tiffield Nhants 31 P4
Tigerton Angus 95 J8
Tigh a' Ghearraidh W Isls 111 a4
Tigharry W Isls 111 a4
Tighnabruaich Ag & B 83 P8
Tigley Devon 5 P7
Tilbrook Cambs 32 F3
Tilbury Thurr 22 D8
Tile Cross Birm 40 F9
Tile Hill Covtry 40 H11
Tilehurst Readg 19 Q6
Tilford Surrey 10 E2
Tilgate W Susx 11 L3
Tilham Street Somset 17 M8
Tillicoultry Clacks 85 Q4
Tillietudlem S Lans 77 N3
Tillingham Essex 23 J3
Tillington Herefs 39 J12
Tillington W Susx 10 F6
Tillington Common Herefs 39 J11
Tillybirloch Abers 95 L1
Tillyfourie Abers 102 E11
Tillygreig Abers 103 J10
Tillyrie P & K 86 D2
Tilmanstone Kent 23 P12
Tilney All Saints Norfk 43 P6
Tilney High End Norfk 43 N6
Tilney St Lawrence Norfk 43 N7
Tilshead Wilts 18 F10
Tilstock Shrops 49 K7
Tilston Ches W 49 J5
Tilstone Fearnall Ches W 49 K4
Tilsworth C Beds 32 E11
Tilton on the Hill Leics 41 Q6
Tiltups End Gloucs 29 L8
Timberland Lincs 52 G10
Timbersbrook Ches E 50 B8
Timberscombe Somset 16 C7
Timble N York 58 F4
Timpanheck D & G 71 M1
Timperley Traffd 57 P10
Timsbury BaNES 17 P4
Timsbury Hants 9 L3
Timsgarry W Isls 111 c2
Timsgearraidh W Isls 111 c2
Timworth Suffk 34 E3
Timworth Green Suffk 34 E3
Tincleton Dorset 8 B8
Tindale Cumb 72 B8
Tingewick Bucks 31 P7
Tingrith C Beds 32 E9
Tingwall Airport Shet 111 k4
Tingwell Ork 111 h2
Tinhay Devon 5 J3
Tinsley Sheff 51 K3
Tinsley Green W Susx 11 L3
Tintagel Cnwll 4 C3
Tintern Mons 28 F8
Tintinhull Somset 17 M11
Tintwistle Derbys 50 D2
Tinwald D & G 78 G11
Tinwell Rutlnd 42 E8
Tipton Sandw 40 C8
Tipton Green Sandw 40 C8
Tipton St John Devon 6 E5
Tiptree Essex 34 E12
Tiptree Heath Essex 22 G1
Tirabad Powys 37 P11
Tiree Ag & B 88 C7
Tiree Airport Ag & B 88 C7
Tiretigan Ag & B 83 K9
Tirley Gloucs 29 L3
Tiroran Ag & B 89 K10
Tirphil Caerph 27 N7
Tirril Cumb 71 P9
Tisbury Wilts 8 D2
Tissington Derbys 50 F9
Titchberry Devon 14 E6
Titchfield Hants 9 P6
Titchmarsh Nhants 32 E2
Titchwell Norfk 44 C2
Tithby Notts 51 P12
Titley Herefs 38 G9
Titsey Surrey 21 N11
Titson Cnwll 14 E10
Tittensor Staffs 49 Q7
Tittleshall Norfk 44 E6
Titton Worcs 39 P7
Tiverton Ches W 49 K4
Tiverton Devon 6 C1
Tivetshall St Margaret Norfk 45 K11
Tivetshall St Mary Norfk 45 J11
Tixall Staffs 40 C3
Tixover Rutlnd 42 D9
Toab Shet 111 k5
Tobermory Ag & B 89 L5
Toberonochy Ag & B 83 L2
Tobha Mòr W Isls 111 a5
Tocher Abers 102 F8
Tochieneal Moray 101 P3
Tockenham Wilts 18 F5
Tockholes Bl w D 57 M4
Tockington S Glos 28 H10
Tockwith N York 59 L4
Todber Dorset 8 B4
Toddington C Beds 32 E10
Toddington Gloucs 30 D7
Toddington Services C Beds 32 E10
Todenham Gloucs 30 G7
Todhills Angus 93 M7
Todhills Rest Area Cumb 71 N3
Todmorden Calder 58 C8
Todwick Rothm 51 L4
Toft Cambs 33 K5
Toft Lincs 42 F6
Toft Shet 111 k3
Toft Hill Dur 65 K2
Toft Monks Norfk 45 N10
Toft next Newton Lincs 52 E6
Toftrees Norfk 44 E5
Togston Nthumb 73 M1
Tokavaig Highld 96 H7
Tokers Green Oxon 20 B7
Tolastadh bho Thuath W Isls 111 e1
Tolland Somset 16 E9
Tollard Royal Wilts 8 D4
Toll Bar Donc 59 M11
Toller Fratrum Dorset 7 N4
Toller Porcorum Dorset 7 N3
Tollerton N York 59 L2
Tollerton Notts 41 N1
Tollesbury Essex 23 J2
Tolleshunt D'Arcy Essex 22 H2
Tolleshunt Knights Essex 22 H1
Tolleshunt Major Essex 22 H2
Toll of Birness Abers 103 K8
Tolpuddle Dorset 8 B8
Tolworth Gt Lon 21 J9
Tomatin Highld 99 M4
Tomchrasky Highld 98 C6
Tomdoun Highld 98 B8
Tomich Highld 98 D4
Tomich Highld 107 J11
Tomich Highld 107 K2
Tomich Highld 107 L8
Tomintoul Moray 101 J10
Tomnacross Highld 98 G2
Tomnavoulin Moray 101 J9
Tonbridge Kent 12 C2
Tondu Brdgnd 27 J11
Tonedale Somset 16 F11
Tong C Brad 58 G7
Tong Kent 23 J11
Tong Shrops 39 P1
Tong W Isls 111 d2
Tonge Leics 41 K3
Tongham Surrey 10 E1
Tongland D & G 69 Q8
Tong Norton Shrops 39 P1
Tongue Highld 109 K4
Tongwynlais Cardif 27 N11
Tonmawr Neath 26 H9
Tonna Neath 26 G8
Tonwell Herts 33 K12
Tonypandy Rhondd 27 L9
Tonyrefail Rhondd 27 L10
Toot Baldon Oxon 19 P1
Toot Hill Essex 21 P3
Toothill Swindn 18 G4
Tooting Gt Lon 21 L8
Tooting Bec Gt Lon 21 L8
Topcliffe N York 65 P11
Topcroft Norfk 45 L10
Topcroft Street Norfk 45 L10
Toppesfield Essex 34 C8
Toprow Norfk 45 J9
Topsham Devon 6 C5
Torbeg N Ayrs 75 N6
Torboll Highld 107 M3
Torbreck Highld 99 J2
Torbryan Devon 5 Q6
Torcastle Highld 90 F1
Torcross Devon 5 Q10
Tore Highld 107 K10
Torinturk Ag & B 83 M9
Torksey Lincs 52 B7
Torlundy Highld 90 F2
Tormarton S Glos 18 B5
Tormore N Ayrs 75 N6
Tornagrain Highld 107 M11
Tornaveen Abers 95 K2
Torness Highld 98 H4
Toronto Dur 65 L2
Torpenhow Cumb 71 K7
Torphichen W Loth 86 A7
Torphins Abers 95 K2
Torpoint Cnwll 5 J8
Torquay Torbay 6 C9
Torquay Crematorium Torbay 6 B9
Torquhan Border 87 J11
Torran Highld 104 H11
Torrance E Duns 85 K8
Torranyard N Ayrs 76 F3
Torridon Highld 105 N10
Torridon House Highld 105 M10
Torrin Highld 96 G5
Torrisdale Ag & B 75 M5
Torrisdale Highld 109 M4
Torrish Highld 110 A11
Torrisholme Lancs 63 J9
Torrobull Highld 107 K2
Torry C Aber 95 Q2
Torryburn Fife 86 B5
Torteval Guern 6 a2
Torthorwald D & G 78 G12
Tortington W Susx 10 G8
Torton Worcs 39 Q7
Tortworth S Glos 29 J9

Torvaig Highld 96 F2
Torver Cumb 62 F4
Torwood Falk 85 P6
Torwoodlee Border 79 P2
Torworth Notts 51 P4
Toscaig Highld 97 J3
Toseland Cambs 33 J4
Tosside Lancs 63 P10
Tostock Suffk 34 F4
Totaig Highld 104 B11
Tote Highld 104 F11
Tote Highld 104 G9
Totland IoW 9 K9
Totley Sheff 50 H5
Totnes Devon 5 Q7
Toton Notts 41 L1
Totronald Ag & B 88 E5
Totscore Highld 104 E8
Tottenham Gt Lon 21 M5
Tottenhill Norfk 43 Q7
Totteridge Gt Lon 21 K5
Totternhoe C Beds 32 E11
Tottington Bury 57 P6
Totton Hants 9 L5
Toulton Somset 16 G9
Toulvaddie Highld 107 P6
Tovil Kent 22 F11
Toward Ag & B 84 C8
Toward Quay Ag & B 84 B9
Towcester Nhants 31 P4
Towednack Cnwll 2 D7
Tower of London Gt Lon 21 M7
Towersey Oxon 20 B3
Towie Abers 101 N11
Tow Law Dur 73 K11
Town End Cambs 43 L10
Townend W Duns 84 G7
Townhead Barns 50 F1
Townhead D & G 78 G10
Townhead of Greenlaw
D & G 70 C3
Townhill Fife 86 D4
Town Littleworth E Susx 11 N6
Towns End Hants 19 P8
Townshend Cnwll 2 E8
Town Street Suffk 44 C11
Town Yetholm Border 80 H8
Towthorpe C York 59 N3
Towton N York 59 L6
Towyn Conwy 55 P6
Toxteth Lpool 56 G10
Toynton All Saints Lincs 53 L10
Toy's Hill Kent 21 P12
Trabboch E Ayrs 76 G7
Trabbochburn E Ayrs 76 H7
Tradespark Highld 100 D4
Trafford Park Traffd 57 P9
Trallong Powys 27 K3
Tranent E Loth 86 H7
Tranmere Wirral 56 G10
Trantelbeg Highld 109 Q5
Trantlemore Highld 109 Q5
Trap Carmth 26 E5
Traprain E Loth 87 L7
Traquair Border 79 M3
Trawden Lancs 58 B6
Trawsfynydd Gwynd 47 L4
Trealaw Rhondd 27 L9
Treales Lancs 56 H3
Trearddur Bay IoA 54 C6
Treaslane Highld 104 E10
Trebetherick Cnwll 4 H5
Treborough Somset 16 D8
Trebullett Cnwll 4 H5
Treburley Cnwll 4 H5
Trecastle Powys 27 J3
Trecwn Pembks 24 G3
Trecynon Rhondd 27 L7
Tredegar Blae G 27 N7
Tredington Gloucs 29 M3
Tredington Warwks 30 H5
Tredunnock Mons 28 D9
Treen Cnwll 2 B10
Treeton Rothm 51 K4
Trefasser Pembks 24 F2
Trefecca Powys 27 N3
Trefeglwys Powys 37 Q3
Treffgarne Pembks 24 G4
Treffgarne Owen
Pembks 24 F4
Trefforest Rhondd 27 M10
Trefilan Cerdgn 37 J8
Trefin Pembks 24 E3
Trefnant Denbgs 48 B2
Trefonen Shrops 48 F9
Trefor Gwynd 46 F3
Trefriw Conwy 55 L8
Tregadillett Cnwll 4 G4
Tregare Mons 28 E6
Tregaron Cerdgn 37 L8
Tregarth Gwynd 54 H7
Tregeare Cnwll 4 F3
Tregeiriog Wrexhm 48 D8
Tregele IoA 54 E3
Treglemais Pembks 24 E3
Tregonetha Cnwll 3 L3
Tregonning & Gwinear
Mining District Cnwll 2 E9
Tregony Cnwll 3 K6
Tregorrick Cnwll 3 M5
Tregoyd Powys 27 P2
Tre-groes Cerdgn 36 G10
Tregynon Powys 38 C3
Tre-gynwr Carmth 25 P5
Trehafod Rhondd 27 L10
Trehan Cnwll 5 J8
Treharris Myr Td 27 M9
Treherbert Rhondd 27 K8
Trekenner Cnwll 4 H5
Treknow Cnwll 4 C3
Trelawnyd Flints 56 C11
Trelech Carmth 25 M3
Treleddyd-fawr Pembks 24 D3
Trelewis Myr Td 27 M9
Trelights Cnwll 4 B4
Trelill Cnwll 4 C5
Trelleck Mons 28 F7
Trelogan Flints 56 D11
Tremadog Gwynd 47 J4
Tremail Cnwll 4 E3
Tremain Cerdgn 36 D10
Tremaine Cnwll 4 F3
Tremar Cnwll 4 G6
Trematon Cnwll 5 J8
Tremeirchion Denbgs 48 C2
Trenance Cnwll 3 J3
Trenance Cnwll 3 L2
Trench Wrekin 49 M11
Trenear Cnwll 2 G9
Treneglos Cnwll 4 F3

Trent Dorset 17 N11
Trentham C Stke 49 Q5
Trentishoe Devon 15 L3
Trent Vale C Stke 49 Q6
Treoes V Glam 27 K12
Treorchy Rhondd 27 K8
Trequite Cnwll 3 M1
Trerhyngyll V Glam 27 L12
Trerulefoot Cnwll 4 H8
Tresaith Cerdgn 36 E9
Tresco IoS 2 b2
Trescowe Cnwll 2 E9
Tresean Cnwll 2 H4
Tresham Gloucs 29 L9
Treshnish Isles Ag & B 88 G2
Tresillian Cnwll 3 K6
Treskinnick Cross Cnwll 14 D11
Tresmeer Cnwll 4 F3
Tresparrett Cnwll 4 E2
Tressait P & K 92 C4
Tresta Shet 111 k4
Tresta Shet 111 m2
Treswell Notts 52 A7
Treswithian Downs
Crematorium Cnwll 2 F7
Tre Taliesin Cerdgn 37 L3
Trethevey Cnwll 4 D3
Trethewey Cnwll 2 B10
Trethurgy Cnwll 3 M5
Tretire Herefs 28 F4
Tretower Powys 27 P5
Treuddyn Flints 48 F4
Trevalga Cnwll 4 D3
Trevalyn Wrexhm 48 H4
Trevarrian Cnwll 3 J3
Treveal Cnwll 2 H4
Treveighan Cnwll 4 D4
Trevellas Downs Cnwll 2 H5
Trevelmond Cnwll 4 F7
Treverva Cnwll 2 H9
Trevescan Cnwll 2 B10
Treviscoe Cnwll 3 L5
Trevone Cnwll 3 K1
Trevor Wrexhm 48 F7
Trewalder Cnwll 4 D4
Trewarmett Cnwll 4 D3
Trewavas Mining
District Cnwll 2 E9
Trewen Cnwll 4 F4
Trewint Cnwll 4 F4
Trewithian Cnwll 3 K8
Trewoon Cnwll 3 L5
Treyford W Susx 10 D6
Trimdon Dur 65 P1
Trimdon Colliery Dur 65 P1
Trimdon Grange Dur 65 P1
Trimingham Norfk 45 L3
Trimley St Martin Suffk 35 L8
Trimley St Mary Suffk 35 L8
Trimsaran Carmth 26 B7
Trimstone Devon 15 J4
Trinafour P & K 91 Q4
Tring Herts 20 E2
Trinity Angus 95 K9
Trinity Jersey 7 b1
Trinity Gask P & K 92 E11
Triscombe Somset 16 F8
Trislaig Highld 90 E2
Trispen Cnwll 3 J6
Tritlington Nthumb 73 L3
Trochry P & K 92 E7
Troedyraur Cerdgn 36 E10
Troedyrhiw Myr Td 27 M8
Troon Cnwll 2 F8
Troon S Ayrs 76 F5
Tropical World
Roundhay Park Leeds 59 J6
Trossachs Stirlg 84 H2
Trossachs Pier Stirlg 84 H2
Troston Suffk 34 E3
Trotshill Worcs 30 B3
Trottiscliffe Kent 22 D10
Trotton W Susx 10 D5
Troutbeck Cumb 62 H3
Troutbeck Bridge Cumb 62 H3
Troway Derbys 51 K5
Trowbridge Wilts 18 C8
Trowell Notts 51 L11
Trowell Services Notts 51 L11
Trowse Newton Norfk 45 L8
Trudoxhill Somset 17 Q7
Trull Somset 16 G10
Trumpan Highld 104 C9
Trumpet Herefs 28 H2
Trumpington Cambs 33 M6
Trunch Norfk 45 L3
Truro Cnwll 3 J6
Trusham Devon 5 B6
Trusley Derbys 40 G1
Trusthorpe Lincs 53 N6
Trysull Staffs 39 Q4
Tubney Oxon 19 M2
Tuckenhay Devon 5 Q8
Tuckhill Shrops 39 P5
Tuckingmill Cnwll 2 F7
Tuckingmill Wilts 8 D2
Tuckton Bmouth 8 G8
Tuddenham Suffk 34 C3
Tuddenham Suffk 35 K7
Tudeley Kent 12 C2
Tudhoe Dur 65 M1
Tudweiliog Gwynd 46 D4
Tuffley Gloucs 29 L6
Tufton Hants 19 M10
Tufton Pembks 24 H3
Tugby Leics 41 Q7
Tugford Shrops 39 K5
Tughall Nthumb 81 P8
Tullibody Clacks 85 P4
Tullich Abers 94 F3
Tullich Highld 99 J4
Tullich Highld 107 P7
Tulliemet P & K 92 E5
Tulloch Abers 102 G8
Tullochgorm Ag & B 83 P4
Tulloch Station Highld 98 E11
Tullymurdoch P & K 92 H5
Tullynessle Abers 102 D10
Tulse Hill Gt Lon 21 L8
Tumble Carmth 26 D6
Tumby Lincs 53 J10
Tumby Woodside Lincs 53 J11
Tummel Bridge P & K 92 B4
Tunbridge Wells Kent 12 C3
Tundergarth D & G 79 J11
Tunga W Isls 111 d2
Tunley BaNES 17 Q4
Tunstall E R Yk 61 M7
Tunstall Kent 22 H10
Tunstall Lancs 63 L7

Tunstall N York 65 L8
Tunstall Norfk 45 N8
Tunstall Staffs 49 P9
Tunstall Suffk 35 M6
Tunstall Sundld 73 P9
Tunstead Derbys 50 E6
Tunstead Norfk 45 L6
Tunstead Milton Derbys 50 D5
Tupsley Herefs 28 G2
Turkdean Gloucs 30 E9
Tur Langton Leics 41 Q8
Turleigh Wilts 18 B8
Turnastone Herefs 28 D2
Turnberry S Ayrs 76 D9
Turnditch Derbys 50 H10
Turner's Hill W Susx 11 M3
Turnhouse C Edin 86 D7
Turnworth Dorset 8 B6
Turriff Abers 102 F5
Turton Bottoms Bl w D 57 N6
Turves Cambs 43 K10
Turvey Bed 32 D6
Turville Bucks 20 C5
Turweston Bucks 31 M6
Tushielaw Inn Border 79 L5
Tutbury Staffs 40 G2
Tutshill Gloucs 28 G9
Tuttington Norfk 45 K5
Tuxford Notts 51 Q6
Twatt Ork 111 g2
Twatt Shet 111 k4
Twechar E Duns 85 L7
Tweedbank Border 80 C7
Tweedmouth Nthumb 81 L4
Tweedsmuir Border 78 H4
Twelveheads Cnwll 2 H7
Twemlow Green Ches E 49 P2
Twenty Lincs 42 G6
Twerton BaNES 17 Q4
Twickenham Gt Lon 21 J8
Twigworth Gloucs 29 L4
Twineham W Susx 11 K6
Twinstead Essex 34 E9
Twitchen Devon 15 N6
Two Dales Derbys 50 H8
Two Gates Staffs 40 G7
Two Waters Herts 20 G3
Twycross Leics 41 J6
Twycross Zoo Leics 40 H6
Twyford Bucks 31 P8
Twyford Hants 9 N3
Twyford Leics 41 Q5
Twyford Norfk 44 G5
Twyford Wokham 20 C8
Twynholm D & G 69 P8
Twyning Green Gloucs 29 M2
Twynllanan Carmth 26 G4
Twywell Nhants 32 D2
Tyberton Herefs 28 D2
Tyburn Birm 40 F8
Tycroes Carmth 26 E6
Tycrwyn Powys 48 C10
Tydd Gote Lincs 43 M6
Tydd St Giles Cambs 43 L6
Tydd St Mary Lincs 43 M6
Tye Green Essex 33 P9
Tyldesley Wigan 57 M8
Tyler Hill Kent 23 L10
Tylorstown Rhondd 27 L9
Ty-nant Conwy 48 B6
Tyndrum Stirlg 91 J9
Ty'n-dwr Denbgs 48 E7
Tynemouth N Tyne 73 P7
Tynemouth
Crematorium N Tyne 73 N7
Tyne Tunnel S Tyne 73 N7
Tyninghame E Loth 87 L6
Tynron D & G 77 N11
Tyn-y-dwr Denbgs 37 L6
Ty'n-y-Groes Conwy 55 L7
Tyn-y-nant Rhondd 27 M10
Tyrie Abers 103 J3
Tyringham M Keyn 32 C7
Tyseley Birm 40 E9
Tythegston Brdgnd 27 J11
Tytherington Ches E 50 B6
Tytherington S Glos 29 J10
Tytherington Wilts 18 D11
Tytherleigh Devon 7 J3
Tytherton Lucas Wilts 18 D6
Tywardreath Cnwll 3 N5
Tywyn Gwynd 47 J10

U

Ubbeston Green Suffk 35 M3
Ubley BaNES 17 M5
Uckfield E Susx 11 P6
Uckinghall Worcs 29 M2
Uckington Gloucs 29 M4
Uddingston S Lans 85 L10
Uddington S Lans 78 E3
Udimore E Susx 12 G6
Udny Green Abers 103 J9
Udny Station Abers 103 J9
Uffculme Devon 16 E12
Uffington Lincs 42 F8
Uffington Oxon 19 K3
Uffington Shrops 49 K11
Ufford C Pete 42 F8
Ufford Suffk 35 L6
Ufton Warwks 31 J2
Ufton Nervet W Berk 19 Q7
Ugadale Ag & B 75 L6
Ugborough Devon 5 N8
Uggeshall Suffk 35 P2
Ugglebarnby N York 67 J6
Ughill Sheff 50 G3
Ugley Essex 33 N10
Ugley Green Essex 33 N10
Ugthorpe N York 66 H5
Uibhist A Deas W Isls 111 b6
Uibhist A Tuath W Isls 111 a4
Uig Ag & B 88 E5
Uig Highld 104 B10
Uig Highld 104 E9
Uig W Isls 111 c2
Uigshader Highld 104 F12
Uisken Ag & B 89 J11
Ulbster Highld 110 G7
Ulceby Lincs 53 L8
Ulceby N Linc 61 J10
Ulceby Skitter N Linc 61 K10
Ulcombe Kent 12 G1
Uldale Cumb 71 L7
Uley Gloucs 29 K8
Ulgham Nthumb 73 M3

Ullapool Highld 106 B4
Ullenhall Warwks 30 E1
Ulleskelf N York 59 M6
Ullesthorpe Leics 41 L9
Ulley Rothm 51 L4
Ullingswick Herefs 39 L11
Ullinish Lodge Hotel
Highld 96 C3
Ullock Cumb 70 H10
Ullswater Cumb 71 N10
Ullswater Steamers
Cumb 71 N11
Ulpha Cumb 62 E4
Ulrome E R Yk 61 K3
Ulsta Shet 111 k3
Ulva Ag & B 89 J8
Ulverley Green Solhll 40 F10
Ulverston Cumb 62 F6
Ulwell Dorset 8 F10
Ulzieside D & G 77 N9
Umberleigh Devon 15 K7
Unapool Highld 108 E8
Underbarrow Cumb 63 J4
Under Burnmouth
Border 79 P11
Undercliffe C Brad 58 F7
Underdale Shrops 49 J11
Underriver Kent 22 B11
Underwood Notts 51 L10
Undy Mons 28 E10
Union Mills IoM 56 c5
Unst Shet 111 m2
Unstone Derbys 51 J5
Upavon Wilts 18 G9
Upchurch Kent 22 G9
Upcott Devon 15 N6
Up Exe Devon 6 C3
Upgate Norfk 45 J6
Uphall Dorset 7 M3
Uphall W Loth 86 C7
Upham Devon 15 Q9
Upham Hants 9 N4
Uphampton Herefs 38 H9
Uphampton Worcs 39 Q8
Uphill N Som 17 J5
Up Holland Lancs 57 K7
Uplawmoor E Rens 84 G11
Upleadon Gloucs 29 K4
Upleatham R & Cl 66 E4
Uploders Dorset 7 M4
Uplowman Devon 16 D11
Uplyme Devon 7 J4
Up Marden W Susx 10 C7
Upminster Gt Lon 22 C6
Up Mudford Somset 17 N11
Up Nately Hants 20 B11
Upottery Devon 6 G2
Upper Affcot Shrops 39 J5
Upper Ardchronie Highld 107 K5
Upper Arley Worcs 39 N6
Upper Basildon W Berk 19 P5
Upper Beeding W Susx 11 K7
Upper Benefield Nhants 42 E11
Upper Bentley Worcs 30 C2
Upper Bighouse Highld 109 Q4
Upper Boddington
Nhants 31 L4
Upper Brailes Warwks 30 H6
Upper Broadheath
Worcs 39 P10
Upper Broughton Notts 41 P3
Upper Bucklebury W Berk 19 P7
Upper Burgate Hants 8 H4
Upperby Cumb 71 N5
Upper Caldecote C Beds 32 G7
Upper Chapel Powys 27 L1
Upper Chicksgrove Wilts 8 E2
Upper Chute Wilts 19 K9
Upper Clapton Gt Lon 21 M6
Upper Clatford Hants 19 L11
Upper Cound Shrops 39 K2
Upper Cumberworth
Kirk 58 G11
Upper Dallachy Moray 101 M3
Upper Deal Kent 23 Q11
Upper Dean Bed 32 F4
Upper Denby Kirk 58 G11
Upper Dicker E Susx 12 B7
Upper Dounreay Highld 110 B3
Upper Dovercourt Essex 35 K9
Upper Drumbane Stirlg 85 L2
Upper Dunsforth N York 59 K2
Upper Eashing Surrey 10 F2
Upper Eathie Highld 107 M9
Upper Egleton Herefs 39 M12
Upper Elkstone Staffs 50 D8
Upper Ellastone Staffs 50 E11
Upper Farmcote Shrops 39 P3
Upper Farringdon Hants 10 B3
Upper Framilode Gloucs 29 K6
Upper Froyle Hants 10 C2
Upperglen Highld 104 D11
Upper Godney Somset 17 L7
Upper Gravenhurst
C Beds 32 G9
Upper Green W Berk 19 L7
Upper Grove Common
Herefs 28 G4
Upper Hale Surrey 10 D1
Upper Halliford Surrey 20 H9
Upper Hambleton Rutlnd 42 C8
Upper Harbledown Kent 23 L10
Upper Hartfield E Susx 11 P3
Upper Hatherley Gloucs 29 M5
Upper Heaton Kirk 58 F9
Upper Helmsley N York 59 P3
Upper Hergest Herefs 38 F10
Upper Heyford Nhants 31 P3
Upper Heyford Oxon 31 L8
Upper Hill Herefs 39 J9
Upper Hopton Kirk 58 G9
Upper Hulme Staffs 50 D8
Upper Inglesham Swindn 18 H2
Upper Killay Swans 26 D9
Upper Kinchrackine
Ag & B 90 G10
Upper Knockando Moray 101 J6
Upper Lambourn W Berk 19 K5
Upper Landywood Staffs 40 C6
Upper Langford N Som 17 L4
Upper Langwith Derbys 51 L6
Upper Largo Fife 87 J2
Upper Leigh Staffs 50 D12
Upper Lochton Abers 95 L3
Upper Longdon Staffs 40 D5
Upper & Lower
Stondon C Beds 32 G9
Upper Lybster Highld 110 F8
Upper Lydbrook Gloucs 28 H6
Upper Lye Herefs 38 H8
Uppermill Oldham 58 C11

Ullapool Highld 106 B4
Upper Milton Worcs 39 P7
Upper Minety Wilts 18 E3
Upper Mulben Moray 101 L5
Upper Netchwood
Shrops 39 L4
Upper Nobut Staffs 40 D1
Upper Norwood W Susx 10 F6
Upper Poppleton C York 59 M4
Upper Ratley Hants 9 K3
Upper Rissington Gloucs 30 G9
Upper Rochford Worcs 39 L8
Upper Ruscoe D & G 69 N6
Upper Sapey Herefs 39 M8
Upper Seagry Wilts 18 D5
Upper Shelton C Beds 32 E7
Upper Sheringham
Norfk 45 J2
Upper Skelmorlie N Ayrs 84 D9
Upper Slaughter Gloucs 30 F9
Upper Soudley Gloucs 28 H6
Upper Standen Kent 13 N3
Upper Stoke Norfk 45 L9
Upper Stowe Nhants 31 N3
Upper Street Hants 8 H4
Upper Street Norfk 45 M6
Upper Street Norfk 45 M6
Upper Street Suffk 34 C6
Upper Street Suffk 34 H6
Upper Sundon C Beds 32 F10
Upper Swell Gloucs 30 F8
Upper Tasburgh Norfk 45 K10
Upper Tean Staffs 50 D11
Upperthong Kirk 58 F11
Upperton W Susx 10 F5
Uppertown Highld 110 G1
Upper Town N Som 17 M3
Upper Town Herefs 39 L11
Upper Town Suffk 34 F4
Upper Tumble Carmth 26 D6
Upper Tysoe Warwks 31 J5
Upper Victoria Angus 93 P8
Upper Wardington Oxon 31 L5
Upper Welland Worcs 29 K1
Upper Wellingham
E Susx 11 N7
Upper Weybread Suffk 35 K2
Upper Wield Hants 19 Q11
Upper Winchendon
Bucks 31 Q10
Upper Woodford Wilts 18 G12
Upper Wraxall Wilts 18 B6
Uppington Shrops 39 L1
Upsall N York 66 C9
Upsettlington Border 81 J5
Upshire Essex 21 N4
Up Somborne Hants 9 L2
Upstreet Kent 23 N10
Upton Bucks 31 Q10
Upton C Pete 42 G9
Upton Cambs 32 H2
Upton Ches W 48 H2
Upton Cnwll 4 G6
Upton Devon 5 N10
Upton Devon 6 E3
Upton Dorset 7 Q6
Upton Dorset 8 E8
Upton Halton 57 J10
Upton Hants 9 L4
Upton Hants 19 L9
Upton Leics 41 J7
Upton Lincs 52 C6
Upton Norfk 45 N7
Upton Notts 51 Q5
Upton Notts 51 Q9
Upton Oxon 19 N4
Upton Slough 20 F7
Upton Somset 16 D9
Upton Somset 17 L10
Upton Wakefd 59 L10
Upton Wirral 56 F10
Upton Bishop Herefs 28 H4
Upton Cheyney S Glos 17 Q3
Upton Cressett Shrops 39 M4
Upton Grey Hants 10 B1
Upton Hellions Devon 15 P10
Upton Lovell Wilts 18 D11
Upton Magna Shrops 49 K11
Upton Noble Somset 17 Q8
Upton Pyne Devon 6 C3
Upton St Leonards
Gloucs 29 M6
Upton Scudamore Wilts 18 C10
Upton Snodsbury Worcs 30 C4
Upton-upon-Severn
Worcs 29 L1
Upton Warren Worcs 30 B1
Upwaltham W Susx 10 F7
Upwell Norfk 43 N9
Upwood Cambs 43 J12
Urchfont Wilts 18 F8
Urmston Traffd 57 P9
Urquhart Moray 101 K3
Urquhart Castle Highld 98 G4
Urra N York 66 D7
Urray Highld 106 H10
Usan Angus 95 M10
Ushaw Moor Dur 73 M11
Usk Mons 28 D8
Usselby Lincs 52 F5
Usworth Sundld 73 N8
Utkinton Ches W 49 K3
Utley C Brad 58 D5
Uton Devon 15 P11
Utterby Lincs 53 K5
Uttoxeter Staffs 40 E2
Uxbridge Gt Lon 20 G7
Uyeasound Shet 111 m2
Uzmaston Pembks 24 G6

V

Vale Guern 6 c1
Vale Crematorium Luton 32 G10
Vale of Glamorgan
Crematorium V Glam 16 F3
Valley IoA 54 D6
Valtos Highld 104 G9
Valtos W Isls 111 c2
Vange Essex 22 E6
Vatsetter Shet 111 k2
Vatten Highld 96 C2
Vaynor Myr Td 27 L6
Veensgarth Shet 111 k4
Velindre Powys 27 P2
Venngreen Devon 14 G9
Venn Ottery Devon 6 E5
Ventnor IoW 9 P11

Venton Devon............5 M8
Vernham Dean Hants......19 K9
Vernham Street Hants.....19 L8
Verwood Dorset...........8 G5
Veryan Cnwll.............3 K7
Vickerstown Cumb........62 E8
Victoria Cnwll...........3 L4
Vidlin Shet.............111 k3
Viewfield Moray.........101 K3
Viewpark N Lans.........85 M10
Vigo Kent...............22 D10
Village de Putron Guern...6 C2
Vines Cross E Susx......12 C6
Vinters Park
    Crematorium Kent....22 F11
Virginia Water Surrey...20 G9
Virginstow Devon.........4 H2
Vobster Somset..........17 Q6
Voe Shet...............111 k3
Vowchurch Herefs........28 D2

W

Waberthwaite Cumb.......62 C4
Wackerfield Dur.........65 K3
Wacton Norfk............45 K10
Wadborough Worcs........30 B5
Waddesdon Bucks.........31 Q10
Waddesdon Manor
    Bucks...............31 Q10
Waddeton Devon...........6 B10
Waddingham Lincs........52 E4
Waddington Lancs........63 N12
Waddington Lincs........52 D9
Waddon Gt Lon...........21 L9
Wadebridge Cnwll.........3 L2
Wadeford Somset..........7 J1
Wadenhoe Nhants.........42 E12
Wadesmill Herts.........33 K12
Wadhurst E Susx.........12 D4
Wadshelf Derbys.........50 H6
Wadworth Donc...........51 L1
Wainfleet All Saints Lincs.53 N10
Wainfleet St Mary Lincs..53 M10
Wainhouse Corner Cnwll...4 E2
Wainscott Medway........22 E8
Wainstalls Calder.......58 D8
Waitby Cumb.............64 D6
Waithe Lincs............53 J4
Wakefield Wakefd........59 J9
Wakefield
    Crematorium Wakefd..58 H10
Wake Green Birm.........40 E10
Wakerley Nhants.........42 D9
Wakerhurst Place W Susx.11 M4
Wakerley Nhants.........42 D9
Wakes Colne Essex.......34 E10
Walberswick Suffk.......35 P2
Walberton W Susx........10 F8
Walbutt D & G...........70 C2
Walcombe Somset.........17 M6
Walcot Lincs............42 F3
Walcot Shrops...........49 L11
Walcot Swindn...........18 H4
Walcote Leics...........41 M10
Walcot Green Norfk......35 J1
Walcott Lincs...........52 G11
Walcott Norfk...........45 M4
Walden Stubbs N York....59 M10
Walderslade Medway......22 F10
Walderton W Susx........10 C7
Walditch Dorset..........7 L4
Waldridge Dur...........73 M10
Waldringfield Suffk.....35 L7
Waldron E Susx..........12 B6
Wales Rothm.............51 L4
Wales Somset............17 N10
Walesby Lincs...........52 G5
Walesby Notts...........51 P6
Walford Herefs..........28 G5
Walford Herefs..........38 H7
Walford Heath Shrops....49 J10
Walgherton Ches E.......49 M6
Walgrave Nhants.........32 B3
Walkden Salfd...........57 N8
Walker N u Ty...........73 M7
Walkerburn Border.......79 M2
Walkeringham Notts......51 Q3
Walkerith Lincs.........52 B5
Walkern Herts...........33 J10
Walker's Heath Birm.....40 D10
Walkerton Fife..........86 F3
Walkford Dorset..........8 H8
Walkhampton Devon.......5 L6
Walkington E R Yk.......60 G6
Walkley Sheff...........51 J3
Walk Mill Lancs.........57 Q3
Walkwood Worcs..........30 D2
Wall Nthumb.............72 G7
Wall Staffs.............40 E6
Wallacetown S Ayrs......76 E10
Wallacetown S Ayrs......76 F6
Wallands Park E Susx....11 N7
Wallasey Wirral.........56 F9
Wallasey (Kingsway)
    Tunnel Wirral.......56 G9
Wall Heath Dudley.......40 B9
Wallingford Oxon........19 P3
Wallington Gt Lon.......21 L9
Wallington Hants.........9 P6
Wallington Herts........33 J9
Wallisdown Poole.........8 F8
Walliswood Surrey.......10 H3
Walls Shet.............111 j4
Wallsend N Tyne.........73 N7
Wallyford E Loth........86 H7
Walmer Kent.............23 Q12
Walmer Bridge Lancs.....57 J4
Walmley Birm............40 F8
Walmley Ash Birm........40 F8
Walpole Suffk...........35 M2
Walpole Cross Keys
    Norfk...............43 N6
Walpole Highway Norfk...43 N7
Walpole St Andrew
    Norfk...............43 N6
Walpole St Peter Norfk..43 N6
Walsall Wsall...........40 D7
Walsden Calder..........58 C9
Walsgrave on Sowe
    Covtry..............41 J10
Walsham le Willows
    Suffk...............34 G3
Walshford N York........59 K4
Walsoken Norfk..........43 M7
Walston S Lans..........86 C12
Walsworth Herts.........32 H10
Walter's Ash Bucks......20 D4
Waltham Kent............13 L1

Waltham NE Lin..........53 J3
Waltham Abbey Essex.....21 M4
Waltham Chase Hants......9 P4
Waltham Cross Herts.....21 M4
Waltham on the Wolds
    Leics...............42 B5
Waltham St Lawrence
    W & M...............20 D7
Walthamstow Gt Lon......21 M5
Walton C Pete...........42 H9
Walton Cumb.............71 Q3
Walton Derbys...........51 J7
Walton Leeds............59 K5
Walton Leics............41 N9
Walton M Keyn...........32 C9
Walton Powys............38 F9
Walton Somset...........17 L8
Walton Suffk............35 L9
Walton W Susx...........10 D8
Walton Wakefd..........59 J10
Walton Wrekin..........49 L10
Walton Cardiff Gloucs...29 M3
Walton East Pembks......24 H4
Walton Highway Norfk....43 M7
Walton-in-Gordano
    N Som...............17 K2
Walton Lea
    Crematorium Warrtn..57 L10
Walton-le-Dale Lancs....57 K4
Walton-on-Thames
    Surrey..............20 H9
Walton-on-the-Hill Staffs.40 C4
Walton on the Hill Surrey.21 K11
Walton-on-the-Naze
    Essex...............35 L11
Walton on the Wolds
    Leics...............41 N4
Walton-on-Trent Derbys..40 G4
Walton Park N Som.......17 K2
Walton West Pembks......24 F6
Waltonwrays
    Crematorium N York..58 C4
Walworth Darltn.........65 M4
Walworth Gt Lon.........21 M7
Walwyn's Castle Pembks..24 F6
Wambrook Somset..........6 H2
Wanborough Surrey.......10 E1
Wanborough Swindn.......18 H4
Wandsworth Gt Lon.......21 K8
Wangford Suffk..........35 P2
Wanlip Leics............41 N5
Wanlockhead D & G.......78 E6
Wannock E Susx..........12 C8
Wansford C Pete.........42 F9
Wansford E R Yk.........60 H3
Wanshurst Green Kent....12 F2
Wanstead Gt Lon.........21 N6
Wanstrow Somset.........17 Q6
Wanswell Gloucs.........29 J8
Wantage Oxon............19 L3
Wappenbury Warwks.......41 J12
Wappenham Nhants........31 N5
Warbleton E Susx........12 C6
Warborough Oxon........19 P3
Warboys Cambs...........33 K2
Warbreck Bpool..........56 G2
Warbstow Cnwll...........4 F3
Warburton Traffd........57 M10
Warcop Cumb.............64 D5
Warden Nthumb...........72 G7
Ward End Birm...........40 E9
Wardington Oxon.........31 L5
Wardle Ches E...........49 L4
Wardle Rochdl...........58 B10
Wardley Gatesd..........73 N8
Wardley Rutlnd..........42 B9
Wardlow Derbys..........50 F6
Wardy Hill Cambs........33 M1
Ware Herts..............21 M1
Wareham Dorset...........8 D9
Warehorne Kent..........13 J4
Warenford Nthumb........81 N8
Wareside Herts..........21 N1
Waresley Cambs..........33 J6
Warfield Br For.........20 E8
Warfleet Devon...........6 B11
Wargrave Wokham.........20 C7
Warham Norfk............44 F2
Wark Nthumb.............72 F5
Wark Nthumb.............80 H6
Warkleigh Devon.........15 L7
Warkton Nhants..........32 C2
Warkworth Nhants........31 L6
Warkworth Nthumb........81 P11
Warlaby N York..........65 N8
Warleggan Cnwll..........4 E6
Warley Town Calder......58 D8
Warlingham Surrey.......21 M10
Warmfield Wakefd........59 J9
Warmingham Ches E.......49 N4
Warmington Nhants.......42 F11
Warmington Warwks.......31 K5
Warminster Wilts........18 C10
Warmley S Glos..........17 P2
Warmsworth Donc.........51 M1
Warmwell Dorset..........7 Q5
Warner Bros. Studio
    Tour Herts..........20 H4
Warnford Hants...........9 Q3
Warnham W Susx..........11 J4
Warningcamp W Susx......10 G8
Warninglid W Susx.......11 K5
Warren Ches E...........50 B6
Warren Pembks...........24 G8
Warrenhill S Lans.......78 F2
Warren Row W & M........20 D7
Warren Street Kent......22 H11
Warrington M Keyn.......32 C6
Warrington Warrtn.......57 L10
Warriston C Edin........86 F7
Warriston
    Crematorium C Edin..86 F7
Warsash Hants............9 N6
Warslow Staffs..........50 E8
Warter E R Yk...........60 E4
Warthermaske N York.....65 L10
Warthill N York.........59 P3
Wartling E Susx.........12 D8
Wartnaby Leics..........41 P3
Warton Lancs............56 H3
Warton Lancs............63 J7
Warton Warwks...........40 H6
Warwick Warwks..........30 H2
Warwick Bridge Cumb.....71 P4
Warwick Castle Warwks...30 H2
Warwick Services
    Warwks..............31 J3
Wasbister Ork..........111 h1
Wasdale Head Cumb.......62 E1
Washaway Cnwll...........3 M2

Washbourne Devon.........5 Q8
Washbrook Suffk.........35 J8
Washfield Devon.........16 C11
Washford Somset.........16 E7
Washford Pyne Devon.....15 N9
Washingborough Lincs....52 E8
Washington Sundld.......73 N9
Washington W Susx.......10 H7
Washington Services
    Gatesd..............73 M9
Washwood Heath Birm.....40 E9
Wasperton Warwks........30 H3
Wass N York.............66 D10
Wast Water Cumb.........62 D2
Watchet Somset..........16 E7
Watchfield Oxon.........19 J3
Watchgate Cumb..........63 K3
Water Devon..............5 P4
Waterbeach Cambs........33 M4
Waterbeach W Susx.......10 E8
Waterbeck D & G.........79 L12
Water End E R Yk........60 D3
Waterfall Staffs........50 E9
Waterfoot Ag & B........75 M5
Waterfoot E Rens........85 J11
Waterford Herts.........21 L1
Waterheads Border.......86 F11
Waterhouses Staffs......50 E10
Wateringbury Kent.......22 E11
Waterloo Highld.........97 J5
Waterloo N Lans.........85 N11
Waterloo P & K..........92 F8
Waterloo Pembks.........24 G7
Waterloo Sefton.........56 G8
Waterlooville Hants.....10 B7
Watermead Bucks.........20 D1
Watermillock Cumb.......71 P10
Water Newton Cambs......42 G10
Water Orton Warwks......40 F9
Waterrow Somset.........16 E10
Watersfield W Susx......10 G6
Waterside Bl w D........57 N4
Waterside E Ayrs........76 G9
Waterside E Ayrs........76 H3
Waterside E Duns........85 L8
Waterstein Highld......104 A11
Waterstock Oxon.........31 N11
Waterston Pembks........24 G7
Water Stratford Bucks...31 P7
Waters Upton Wrekin.....49 L10
Watford Herts...........20 H4
Watford Nhants..........31 N1
Watford Gap Services
    Nhants..............31 N1
Wath N York.............58 F1
Wath N York.............65 N11
Wath upon Dearne
    Rothm...............51 K1
Watlington Norfk........43 P8
Watlington Oxon.........20 B5
Watten Highld..........110 F5
Wattisfield Suffk.......34 G2
Wattisham Suffk.........34 G6
Watton Dorset............7 L4
Watton E R Yk...........60 H4
Watton Norfk............44 F9
Watton-at-Stone Herts...33 K11
Wattston N Lans.........85 N8
Wattsville Caerph.......27 P9
Waulkmill Abers.........95 K4
Waunarlwydd Swans.......26 E9
Waunfawr Cerdgn.........37 K4
Waunfawr Gwynd..........54 G9
Wavendon M Keyn.........32 C8
Waveney Crematorium
    Suffk...............45 P11
Waverbridge Cumb........71 K6
Waverton Ches W.........49 J3
Waverton Cumb...........71 K6
Wawne E R Yk............61 J6
Waxham Norfk............45 P5
Wayford Somset...........7 K2
Waytown Dorset...........7 L4
Way Village Devon.......15 Q9
Weacombe Somset.........16 F7
Weald Oxon..............19 K1
Wealdstone Gt Lon.......21 J5
Weardley Leeds..........58 H5
Weare Somset............17 K5
Weare Giffard Devon.....14 H7
Wearhead Dur............72 F11
Wearne Somset...........17 K9
Wear Valley
    Crematorium Dur.....65 M2
Weasenham All Saints
    Norfk...............44 E6
Weasenham St Peter
    Norfk...............44 E5
Weaste Salfd............57 P8
Weaverham Ches W........49 L1
Weaverthorpe N York.....67 L12
Webheath Worcs..........30 D2
Wedderlairs Abers......102 H4
Weddington Warwks.......41 J8
Wedhampton Wilts........18 F8
Wedmore Somset..........17 L6
Wednesbury Sandw........40 C8
Wednesfield Wolves......40 C7
Weedon Bucks............32 B12
Weedon Bec Nhants.......31 N3
Weedon Lois Nhants......31 N5
Weeford Staffs..........40 F6
Weeke Hants..............9 M2
Weekley Nhants..........32 C1
Week St Mary Cnwll......14 E11
Weel E R Yk.............60 H6
Weeley Essex............35 J11
Weeley Crematorium
    Essex...............35 J11
Weeley Heath Essex......35 J11
Weem P & K..............92 C6
Weethley Warwks.........30 D3
Weeting Norfk...........44 C11
Weeton E R Yk...........61 N9
Weeton Lancs............56 H2
Weeton N York...........58 H5
Weetwood Leeds..........58 H6
Weir Lancs..............57 Q4
Weir Quay Devon..........5 J7
Weisdale Shet..........111 k4
Welborne Norfk..........44 H7
Welbourn Lincs..........52 D11
Welburn N York..........60 C1
Welburn N York..........66 E12
Welbury N York..........65 P7
Welby Lincs.............42 D3
Welcombe Devon..........14 E8
Weldon Nhants...........42 D11
Welford Nhants..........41 N10
Welford W Berk..........19 L6

Welford-on-Avon
    Warwks..............30 F4
Welham Leics............41 Q8
Welham Notts............51 Q5
Welham Green Herts......21 K3
Well Hants..............10 C2
Well Lincs..............53 M8
Well N York.............65 M10
Welland Worcs...........29 L2
Wellbank Angus..........93 N8
Wellesbourne Warwks.....30 H3
Well Head Herts.........32 H10
Welling Gt Lon..........21 P8
Wellingborough Nhants...32 C3
Wellingham Norfk........44 E6
Wellingore Lincs........52 E11
Wellington Cumb.........62 C2
Wellington Herefs.......39 J11
Wellington Somset.......16 F11
Wellington Wrekin.......49 M12
Wellington Heath Herefs.29 J1
Wellow BaNES............17 Q5
Wellow IoW...............9 L9
Wellow Notts............51 P7
Wells Somset............17 M7
Wells-next-the-Sea
    Norfk...............44 F2
Wellstye Green Essex....33 Q11
Welltree P & K..........92 E10
Wellwood Fife...........86 C5
Welney Norfk............43 N10
Welshampton Shrops......48 H8
Welsh Frankton Shrops...48 G8
Welsh Newton Herefs.....28 F5
Welshpool Powys.........38 E1
Welsh St Donats V Glam..16 D2
Welton Cumb.............71 M6
Welton E R Yk...........60 G8
Welton Lincs............52 E7
Welton Nhants...........31 M2
Welton le Marsh Lincs...53 M9
Welton le Wold Lincs....53 J6
Welwick E R Yk..........61 N9
Welwyn Herts............32 H12
Welwyn Garden City
    Herts...............21 K2
Wem Shrops..............49 K9
Wembdon Somset..........16 H8
Wembley Gt Lon..........21 J6
Wembury Devon............5 L9
Wemworthy Devon.........15 L9
Wemyss Bay Inver........84 D8
Wendens Ambo Essex......33 N9
Wendlebury Oxon.........31 M9
Wendling Norfk..........44 F7
Wendover Bucks..........20 D2
Wendron Cnwll............2 G9
Wendron Mining
    District Cnwll.......2 G9
Wendy Cambs.............33 K7
Wenhaston Suffk.........35 N2
Wennington Cambs........33 J2
Wennington Gt Lon.......22 B7
Wennington Lancs........63 L8
Wensley Derbys..........50 H8
Wensley N York..........65 J9
Wentbridge Wakefd.......59 L10
Wentnor Shrops..........38 H4
Wentworth Cambs.........33 M2
Wentworth Rothm.........51 J2
Wenvoe V Glam...........16 F2
Weobley Herefs..........38 H10
Weobley Marsh Herefs....38 H10
Wepham W Susx...........10 G8
Wereham Norfk...........44 B9
Werrington C Pete.......42 G9
Werrington Cnwll.........4 H3
Wervin Ches W...........48 H2
Wesham Lancs............56 H3
Wessex Vale
    Crematorium Hants....9 N4
Wessington Derbys.......51 J8
West Acre Norfk.........44 C7
West Alvington Devon.....5 P10
West Anstey Devon.......15 P6
West Ashby Lincs........53 J8
West Ashling W Susx.....10 D8
West Ashton Wilts.......18 C9
West Auckland Dur.......65 L3
West Ayton N York.......67 L9
West Bagborough
    Somset..............16 G9
West Bank Halton........57 K11
West Barkwith Lincs.....52 G7
West Barnby N York......66 H5
West Barns E Loth.......87 M6
West Barsham Norfk......44 E4
West Bay Dorset..........7 L5
West Beckham Norfk......45 J3
West Bedfont Surrey.....20 H8
Westbere Kent...........23 M10
West Bergholt Essex.....34 F10
West Berkshire
    Crematorium W Berk..19 P7
West Bexington Dorset....7 M5
West Bilney Norfk.......44 B7
West Blatchington
    Br & H..............11 L8
West Boldon S Tyne......73 P8
Westborough Lincs.......42 C2
Westbourne Bmouth........8 F8
Westbourne W Susx.......10 C8
West Bowling C Brad.....58 F7
West Bradenham Norfk....44 F8
West Bradford Lancs.....63 N12
West Bradley Somset.....17 M8
West Bretton Wakefd.....58 H10
West Bridgford Notts....51 N12
West Bromwich Sandw.....40 D8
Westbrook Kent..........23 Q8
Westbrook W Berk........19 M6
West Buckland Devon.....15 M5
West Buckland Somset....16 G11
West Burrafirth Shet...111 j4
West Burton N York......64 H9
Westbury Bucks..........31 N7
Westbury Shrops.........38 G1
Westbury Wilts..........18 C9
Westbury Leigh Wilts....18 C10
Westbury-on-Severn
    Gloucs..............29 J6
Westbury-on-Trym Bristl.28 G12
Westbury-sub-Mendip
    Somset..............17 M6
West Butterwick N Linc..52 B3
Westby Lancs............56 H3
West Byfleet Surrey.....20 G10
West Cairngaan D & G....68 F11
West Caister Norfk......45 Q7
West Calder W Loth......86 B9
West Camel Somset.......17 N10

West Chaldon Dorset......8 B10
West Challow Oxon.......19 L3
West Charleton Devon.....5 P10
West Chiltington W Susx.10 H6
West Chinnock Somset....17 L12
West Clandon Surrey.....20 G11
West Cliffe Kent........13 Q3
Westcliff-on-Sea Sthend.22 G6
West Coker Somset.......17 M12
Westcombe Somset.......17 P8
West Compton Somset.....17 N7
West Compton Abbas
    Dorset...............7 N4
Westcote Gloucs.........30 G9
Westcote Barton Oxon....31 K8
Westcott Bucks..........31 Q10
Westcott Devon...........6 D2
Westcott Surrey.........11 J1
West Cottingwith N York.59 P6
Westcourt Wilts.........19 J8
West Cowick E R Yk......59 P9
West Cross Swans........26 E10
West Curthwaite Cumb....71 M6
West Dean E Susx........11 Q9
West Dean W Susx........10 D7
West Dean Wilts..........9 J3
West Deeping Lincs......42 G8
West Derby Lpool........56 H9
West Dereham Norfk......43 Q9
West Down Devon.........15 J4
Westdowns Cnwll..........4 C4
West Drayton Gt Lon.....20 G7
West Drayton Notts......51 P6
West Dunnet Highld.....110 E2
West Ella E R Yk........60 H8
West End Bed............32 E6
West End Hants...........9 M5
West End N Som..........17 L3
West End Norfk..........45 Q7
West End Surrey.........20 F10
West End Surrey.........20 H10
West End Wilts...........8 E3
West End Green Hants....19 Q8
Wester Aberchalder
    Highld..............98 H5
Westerdale Highld......110 D5
Westerdale N York.......66 F6
Westerfield Suffk.......35 K7
Westergate W Susx.......10 F8
Westerham Kent..........21 N11
Westerhope N u Ty.......73 L7
Westerland Devon.........6 B9
Westerleigh S Glos......29 J11
Westerleigh
    Crematorium S Glos..29 J12
Western Isles W Isls...111 c3
Wester Ochiltree W Loth.86 B7
Wester Pitkierie Fife...87 K2
Wester Ross Highld.....105 P6
Westerton of Rossie
    Angus...............93 R5
Westerwick Shet........111 j4
West Farleigh Kent......22 E11
West Farndon Nhants.....31 M4
West Felton Shrops......48 G9
Westfield BaNES.........17 P5
Westfield Cumb..........70 G9
Westfield E Susx........12 F7
Westfield Highld.......110 C3
Westfield N Lans........85 M8
Westfield Norfk.........44 G8
Westfield W Loth........85 Q8
Westfields Herefs.......28 F1
Westfields of Rattray
    P & K...............92 H6
Westgate Dur............72 G12
Westgate N Linc.........60 D11
Westgate-on-Sea Kent....23 P8
West Grafton Wilts......19 J8
West Green Hants........20 C11
West Grimstead Wilts.....8 H3
West Grinstead W Susx...11 J5
West Haddlesey N York...59 M8
West Haddon Nhants......41 N12
West Hagbourne Oxon.....19 N3
West Hagley Worcs.......40 B10
Westhall Suffk..........35 N1
West Hallam Derbys......51 K11
West Halton N Linc......60 F9
West Ham Gt Lon.........21 N6
Westham Dorset...........7 P7
Westham E Susx..........12 D8
West Ham Gt Lon.........21 N6
Westham Somset.........17 K6
Westhampnett W Susx.....10 E8
West Handley Derbys.....51 K5
West Hanney Oxon........19 L3
West Hanningfield Essex.22 E4
West Harnham Wilts.......8 G2
West Harptree BaNES.....17 M5
West Harting W Susx.....10 C6
West Hatch Somset.......16 H11
West Hatch Wilts.........8 D2
West Haven Angus........93 P8
Westhay Somset..........17 L7
West Heath Birm.........40 D11
West Helmsdale Highld..110 B10
West Hendred Oxon.......19 M3
West Hertfordshire
    Crematorium Herts...20 H3
West Heslerton N York...67 K11
West Hewish N Som.......17 K4
Westhide Herefs.........39 L12
Westhill Abers..........95 N1
West Hill Devon..........6 E4
West Hoathly W Susx.....11 M4
West Holme Dorset........8 C9
Westhope Herefs.........39 J11
Westhope Shrops.........39 J5
West Horndon Essex......22 D6
Westhorpe Lincs.........42 H4
Westhorpe Suffk.........34 H3
West Horrington Somset..17 N6
West Horsley Surrey.....20 H11
West Hougham Kent.......13 N3
Westhoughton Bolton.....57 M7
Westhouse N York........63 M7
Westhouses Derbys.......51 K8
West Howe Bmouth.........8 F8
Westhumble Surrey.......21 J11
West Huntingtower
    P & K...............92 G10
West Huntspill Somset...17 J6
West Hythe Kent.........13 L3
West Ilsley W Berk......19 M4
West Itchenor W Susx....10 C9
West Kennett Wilts......18 G7
West Kilbride N Ayrs....76 D2
West Kingsdown Kent.....22 C9
West Kington Wilts......18 B5
West Kirby Wirral.......56 F10

West Knapton – Wingerworth 193

West Knapton N York 67 J11
West Knighton Dorset 7 Q5
West Knoyle Wilts 8 C2
Westlake Devon 5 M9
West Lambrook Somset 17 K11
West Lancashire Crematorium Lancs 56 H6
West Langdon Kent 13 P1
West Lavington W Susx 10 E6
West Lavington Wilts 18 E9
West Layton N York 65 K5
West Leake Notts 41 M3
Westleigh Devon 14 H6
Westleigh Devon 16 E11
West Leigh Somset 16 F9
Westleton Suffk 35 P3
West Lexham Norfk 44 D6
Westley Suffk 34 D4
Westley Waterless Cambs 33 P5
West Lilling N York 59 P2
Westlington Bucks 31 Q11
West Linton Border 86 D10
Westlinton Cumb 71 N3
West Littleton S Glos 18 B5
West Lockinge Oxon 19 M4
West London Crematorium Gt Lon 21 K7
West Lothian Crematorium W Loth 86 B8
West Lulworth Dorset 8 B10
West Lutton N York 60 F1
West Lydford Somset 17 N9
West Lyng Somset 17 J9
West Lynn Norfk 43 P6
West Malling Kent 22 D10
West Malvern Worcs 39 N11
West Marden W Susx 10 C7
West Markham Notts 51 Q6
Westmarsh Kent 23 P10
West Marsh NE Lin 61 L11
West Marton N York 58 B4
West Melbury Dorset 8 C4
West Meon Hants 9 Q3
West Mersea Essex 23 J2
Westmeston E Susx 11 M7
West Midland Safari Park Worcs 39 P7
Westmill Herts 33 K10
West Milton Dorset 7 M4
Westminster Gt Lon 21 L7
Westminster Abbey & Palace Gt Lon 21 L7
West Molesey Surrey 21 J9
West Monkton Somset 16 H9
West Moors Dorset 8 F6
West Morden Dorset 8 D8
West Morriston Border 80 E6
West Mudford Somset 17 N11
Westmuir Angus 93 L5
West Ness N York 66 F10
Westnewton Cumb 71 J6
West Newton E R Yk 61 L6
West Newton Norfk 44 B5
West Newton Somset 16 H9
West Norwood Gt Lon 21 L8
West Norwood Crematorium Gt Lon 21 L8
Westoe S Tyne 73 P7
West Ogwell Devon 5 Q6
Weston BaNES 17 Q3
Weston Ches E 49 N5
Weston Devon 6 F3
Weston Devon 6 F5
Weston Hants 10 B6
Weston Herts 33 J10
Weston Lincs 43 J5
Weston N York 58 F5
Weston Nhants 31 N5
Weston Notts 51 Q7
Weston Shrops 39 L4
Weston Shrops 48 F9
Weston Staffs 40 C3
Weston W Berk 19 L6
Weston Beggard Herefs 28 G1
Westonbirt Gloucs 18 C3
Weston by Welland Nhants 41 Q8
Weston Colville Cambs 33 P6
Weston Corbett Hants 10 B1
Weston Coyney C Stke 50 C11
Weston Favell Nhants 32 B4
Weston Green Cambs 33 P6
Weston Heath Shrops 49 P11
Westoning C Beds 32 E9
Weston-in-Gordano N Som 17 L2
Weston Jones Staffs 49 N10
Weston Longville Norfk 45 J7
Weston Lullingfields Shrops 48 H9
Weston Mill Crematorium C Plym 5 K8
Weston-on-the-Green Oxon 31 M9
Weston Park Staffs 49 P12
Weston Patrick Hants 10 B1
Weston Rhyn Shrops 48 F8
Weston-sub-Edge Gloucs 30 E6
Weston-super-Mare N Som 17 J4
Weston-super-Mare Crematorium N Som 17 J4
Weston Turville Bucks 20 D2
Weston-under-Lizard Staffs 49 P12
Weston under Penyard Herefs 28 H4
Weston-under-Redcastle Shrops 49 K9
Weston under Wetherley Warwks 41 J12
Weston Underwood Derbys 50 H11
Weston Underwood M Keyn 32 C6
Weston-upon-Trent Derbys 41 K2
Westonzoyland Somset 17 J8
West Orchard Dorset 8 B4
West Overton Wilts 18 G7
Westow N York 60 D2
West Park Abers 95 N3
West Parley Dorset 8 G7
West Peckham Kent 22 D11
West Pelton Dur 73 M9
West Pennard Somset 17 M8
West Pentire Cnwll 2 H4
West Perry Cambs 32 G4
West Porlock Somset 15 P3
Westport Somset 17 K11
West Putford Devon 14 G8
West Quantoxhead Somset 16 F7
Westquarter Falk 85 Q7
West Rainton Dur 73 N10
West Rasen Lincs 52 F5
Westray Ork 111 h1
Westray Airport Ork 111 h1
West Raynham Norfk 44 E5
Westrigg W Loth 85 Q9
West Road Crematorium N u Ty 73 L7
Westrop Swindn 18 H3
West Rounton N York 65 P6
West Row Suffk 34 B2
West Rudham Norfk 44 D5
West Runton Norfk 45 K2
Westruther Border 80 E4
Westry Cambs 43 L9
West Saltoun E Loth 87 J8
West Sandford Devon 15 N10
West Sandwick Shet 111 k3
West Scrafton N York 65 J10
West Stafford Dorset 7 Q5
West Stockwith Notts 52 B5
West Stoke W Susx 10 D8
West Stour Dorset 8 B3
West Stourmouth Kent 23 N10
West Stow Suffk 34 D3
West Stowell Wilts 18 G8
West Street Suffk 34 G3
West Suffolk Crematorium Suffk 34 D4
West Tanfield N York 65 M10
West Taphouse Cnwll 4 E7
West Tarbert Ag & B 83 M9
West Tarring W Susx 10 H8
West Thirston Nthumb 73 L2
West Thorney W Susx 10 C9
West Thorpe Notts 41 N3
West Thurrock Thurr 22 C7
West Tilbury Thurr 22 D7
West Tisted Hants 9 Q2
West Torrington Lincs 52 G7
West Town Hants 10 B9
West Town N Som 17 L3
West Tytherley Hants 9 J2
West Walton Norfk 43 M7
Westward Cumb 71 L6
Westward Ho! Devon 14 H6
Westwell Kent 13 J1
Westwell Oxon 30 G11
Westwell Leacon Kent 13 J1
West Wellow Hants 9 K4
West Wembury Devon 5 L9
West Wemyss Fife 86 G4
Westwick Cambs 33 L4
West Wickham Cambs 33 P6
West Wickham Gt Lon 21 M9
West Williamston Pembks 24 H7
West Wiltshire Crematorium Wilts 18 D8
West Winch Norfk 43 Q6
West Winterslow Wilts 9 J2
West Wittering W Susx 10 C9
West Witton N York 65 J9
Westwood Devon 6 D3
Westwood Kent 23 Q9
Westwood Wilts 18 B8
West Woodburn Nthumb 72 F4
West Woodhay W Berk 19 L8
Westwoodside N Linc 51 Q2
West Worldham Hants 10 C3
West Worthing W Susx 11 J9
West Wratting Cambs 33 P6
West Wylam Nthumb 73 K8
Wetheral Cumb 71 P5
Wetherby Leeds 59 K5
Wetherby Services N York 59 K4
Wetherden Suffk 34 G4
Wetheringsett Suffk 35 J4
Wethersfield Essex 34 B9
Wetherup Street Suffk 35 J4
Wetley Rocks Staffs 50 C10
Wettenhall Ches E 49 L4
Wetton Staffs 50 E9
Wetwang E R Yk 60 F3
Wetwood Staffs 49 P8
Wexcombe Wilts 19 J8
Weybourne Norfk 45 J2
Weybourne Surrey 10 D1
Weybread Suffk 35 L1
Weybread Street Suffk 35 L2
Weybridge Surrey 20 H9
Weycroft Devon 7 J3
Weydale Highld 110 D3
Weyhill Hants 19 K10
Weymouth Dorset 7 P7
Weymouth Crematorium Dorset 7 P7
Whaddon Bucks 32 B9
Whaddon Cambs 33 K7
Whaddon Gloucs 29 L6
Whaddon Wilts 8 H3
Whaddon Wilts 18 C8
Whaley Derbys 51 L6
Whaley Bridge Derbys 50 D5
Whaley Thorns Derbys 51 M6
Whaligoe Highld 110 G7
Whalley Lancs 57 N2
Whalsay Shet 111 m3
Whalton Nthumb 73 K5
Whaplode Lincs 43 K5
Whaplode Drove Lincs 43 K7
Wharf Warwks 31 K4
Wharfe N York 63 P8
Wharles Lancs 57 J2
Wharley End C Beds 32 D7
Wharncliffe Side Sheff 50 H2
Wharram-le-Street N York 60 E2
Wharton Herefs 39 J10
Whashton N York 65 K6
Whasset Cumb 63 K6
Whatcote Warwks 30 H5
Whateley Warwks 40 G7
Whatfield Suffk 34 G7
Whatley Somset 7 J2
Whatley Somset 17 Q6
Whatlington E Susx 12 F6
Whatton Notts 51 Q11
Whauphill D & G 69 K8
Wheal Peevor Cnwll 2 G6
Wheatacre Norfk 45 P10
Wheathampstead Herts 21 J1
Wheatley Hants 10 C3
Wheatley Oxon 31 N11
Wheatley Hill Dur 73 P11
Wheatley Hills Donc 59 N12
Wheaton Aston Staffs 49 Q11
Wheddon Cross Somset 16 C8
Wheelock Ches E 49 N4
Wheelton Lancs 57 L5
Wheldrake C York 59 P5
Whelford Gloucs 18 H2
Whelpley Hill Bucks 20 F3
Whempstead Herts 33 K11
Whenby N York 66 E12
Whepstead Suffk 34 D5
Wherstead Suffk 35 J8
Wherwell Hants 19 L11
Wheston Derbys 50 F5
Whetsted Kent 12 D2
Whetstone Leics 41 M7
Whicham Cumb 62 D6
Whichford Warwks 30 H7
Whickham Gatesd 73 L8
Whiddon Down Devon 5 N2
Whigstreet Angus 93 N6
Whilton Nhants 31 N2
Whimple Devon 6 E4
Whimpwell Green Norfk 45 N4
Whinburgh Norfk 44 G8
Whinnieliggate D & G 70 B5
Whinnyfold Abers 103 M8
Whippingham IoW 9 N8
Whipsnade C Beds 32 E12
Whipsnade Zoo ZSL C Beds 32 E12
Whipton Devon 6 C4
Whisby Lincs 52 C9
Whissendine Rutlnd 42 B7
Whissonsett Norfk 44 F5
Whistlefield Ag & B 84 D4
Whistlefield Inn Ag & B 84 C4
Whistley Green Wokham 20 C8
Whiston Knows 57 J9
Whiston Nhants 32 C5
Whiston Rothm 51 K3
Whiston Staffs 40 B5
Whiston Staffs 50 D10
Whitbeck Cumb 62 D5
Whitbourne Herefs 39 N10
Whitburn S Tyne 73 P8
Whitburn W Loth 85 Q9
Whitby N York 67 J5
Whitchester Border 87 N9
Whitchurch BaNES 17 N3
Whitchurch Bucks 32 B11
Whitchurch Cardif 27 N11
Whitchurch Devon 5 K5
Whitchurch Hants 19 M10
Whitchurch Herefs 28 G5
Whitchurch Oxon 19 Q5
Whitchurch Pembks 24 E4
Whitchurch Shrops 49 K7
Whitchurch Canonicorum Dorset 7 K4
Whitchurch Hill Oxon 19 Q5
Whitcombe Dorset 7 Q5
Whitcot Shrops 38 H4
Whitcott Keysett Shrops 38 F5
Whiteacre Heath Warwks 40 G8
White Ball Somset 16 E11
Whitebridge Highld 98 G6
Whitebrook Mons 28 G7
Whitebushes Surrey 11 L1
Whitecairns Abers 103 J10
Whitechapel Gt Lon 21 M7
White Chapel Lancs 57 K1
Whitecliffe Gloucs 28 G6
White Colne Essex 34 E10
Whitecraig E Loth 86 G8
Whitecrook D & G 68 F7
White Cross Cnwll 2 G10
Whitecross Falk 85 R7
Whiteface Highld 107 L5
Whitefarland N Ayrs 75 N4
Whitefaulds S Ayrs 76 E8
Whitefield Bury 57 P7
Whitefield Somset 16 E9
Whiteford Abers 102 F9
Whitegate Ches W 49 L2
Whitehall Ork 111 i2
Whitehaven Cumb 70 F11
Whitehill and Bordon Hants 10 C4
Whitehills Abers 102 E3
Whitehouse Abers 102 E11
Whitehouse Ag & B 83 M10
Whitehouse Common Birm 40 F7
Whitekirk E Loth 87 L6
White Lackington Dorset 7 Q3
Whitelackington Somset 17 K11
White Ladies Aston Worcs 30 B4
Whiteleaf Bucks 20 D3
Whiteley Hants 9 N5
Whiteley Bank IoW 9 P10
Whitemire Moray 100 F5
Whitemoor C Nott 51 M11
Whitemoor Cnwll 3 L4
Whiteness Shet 111 k4
White Notley Essex 34 D11
Whiteparish Wilts 9 J3
White Pit Lincs 53 L7
Whiterashes Abers 102 H9
White Roding Essex 22 C1
Whiterow Highld 110 G6
Whiterow Moray 100 F4
Whiteshill Gloucs 29 L7
Whitesmith E Susx 11 Q7
Whitestaunton Somset 6 H1
Whitestone Cross Devon 6 B4
White Waltham W & M 20 D7
Whitewell Lancs 63 M11
Whitfield C Dund 93 M8
Whitfield Kent 13 P2
Whitfield Nhants 31 N6
Whitfield Nthumb 72 E8
Whitfield S Glos 29 J9
Whitford Devon 6 H4
Whitford Flints 56 D12
Whitgift E R Yk 60 E9
Whitgreave Staffs 40 B2
Whithorn D & G 69 L10
Whiting Bay N Ayrs 75 Q7
Whitkirk Leeds 59 J7
Whitland Carmth 25 L5
Whitlaw Border 80 C10
Whitletts S Ayrs 76 F6
Whitley N York 59 M9
Whitley Readg 20 B8
Whitley Sheff 51 J2
Whitley Wilts 18 C7
Whitley Bay N Tyne 73 N6
Whitley Bay Crematorium N Tyne 73 N6
Whitley Chapel Nthumb 72 G8
Whitley Lower Kirk 58 G10
Whitminster Gloucs 29 K7
Whitmore Staffs 49 P7
Whitnage Devon 16 D11
Whitnash Warwks 31 J2
Whitney-on-Wye Herefs 38 F11
Whitsbury Hants 8 G4
Whitsome Border 81 J4
Whitson Newpt 28 D11
Whitstable Kent 23 L9
Whitstone Cnwll 14 E11
Whittingham Nthumb 81 M10
Whittingslow Shrops 38 H4
Whittington Derbys 51 J6
Whittington Gloucs 30 D9
Whittington Lancs 63 L7
Whittington Norfk 44 B9
Whittington Shrops 48 G8
Whittington Staffs 39 Q5
Whittington Staffs 40 F6
Whittington Warwks 40 H7
Whittington Worcs 39 Q10
Whittlebury Nhants 31 P5
Whittle-le-Woods Lancs 57 L5
Whittlesey Cambs 43 J10
Whittlesford Cambs 33 M7
Whitton N Linc 60 F8
Whitton Nthumb 73 J1
Whitton Powys 38 F8
Whitton S on T 65 P3
Whitton Shrops 39 L7
Whittonstall Nthumb 73 J9
Whitway Hants 19 M8
Whitwell Derbys 51 M5
Whitwell Herts 32 H11
Whitwell IoW 9 N10
Whitwell N York 65 M7
Whitwell Rutlnd 42 D8
Whitwell-on-the-Hill N York 60 C2
Whitwell Street Norfk 44 H6
Whitwick Leics 41 K4
Whitworth Lancs 58 B9
Whixall Shrops 49 K8
Whixley N York 59 K3
Whorlton Dur 65 K5
Whyle Herefs 39 K9
Whyteleafe Surrey 21 M10
Wibsey C Brad 58 F7
Wibtoft Warwks 41 L9
Wichenford Worcs 39 P9
Wichling Kent 22 H11
Wick Bmouth 8 H8
Wick Highld 110 G5
Wick S Glos 17 Q2
Wick V Glam 16 C2
Wick W Susx 10 G8
Wick Worcs 30 C5
Wicken Cambs 33 P3
Wicken Nhants 31 Q6
Wicken Bonhunt Essex 33 N9
Wickenby Lincs 52 F7
Wicken Green Village Norfk 44 D4
Wickersley Rothm 51 L3
Wicker Street Green Suffk 34 F8
Wickford Essex 22 E5
Wickham Hants 9 P5
Wickham W Berk 19 L6
Wickham Bishops Essex 22 G2
Wickhambreaux Kent 23 N10
Wickhambrook Suffk 34 C6
Wickhamford Worcs 30 E6
Wickham Green Suffk 34 H3
Wickham Market Suffk 35 M5
Wickhampton Norfk 45 N8
Wickham St Paul Essex 34 D9
Wickham Skeith Suffk 34 H3
Wickham Street Suffk 34 H3
Wick John o' Groats Airport Highld 110 G5
Wicklewood Norfk 44 H9
Wickmere Norfk 45 J4
Wick St Lawrence N Som 17 K3
Wicksteed Park Nhants 32 C2
Wickwar S Glos 29 J10
Widdington Essex 33 N9
Widdrington Nthumb 73 M2
Widdrington Station Nthumb 73 M3
Widecombe in the Moor Devon 5 P5
Widegates Cnwll 4 G8
Widemouth Bay Cnwll 14 D10
Wide Open N Tyne 73 M6
Widford Essex 22 E3
Widford Herts 33 L12
Widmer End Bucks 20 E4
Widmerpool Notts 41 N2
Widmore Gt Lon 21 N9
Widnes Halton 57 K10
Widnes Crematorium Halton 57 K10
Widworthy Devon 6 G3
Wigan Wigan 57 L7
Wigan Crematorium Wigan 57 L7
Wigborough Somset 17 L12
Wiggaton Devon 6 E4
Wiggenhall St Germans Norfk 43 P7
Wiggenhall St Mary Magdalen Norfk 43 P7
Wiggenhall St Mary the Virgin Norfk 43 P7
Wigginton C York 59 N3
Wigginton Herts 20 F2
Wigginton Oxon 31 K7
Wigginton Staffs 40 G6
Wigglesworth N York 63 P10
Wiggonby Cumb 71 L5
Wighill N York 59 L5
Wighton Norfk 44 F3
Wightwick Wolves 39 Q3
Wigley Hants 9 K4
Wigmore Herefs 38 H8
Wigmore Medway 22 F9
Wigsley Notts 52 C9
Wigsthorpe Nhants 42 F12
Wigston Leics 41 N7
Wigston Fields Leics 41 N7
Wigston Parva Leics 41 L9
Wigthorpe Notts 51 N4
Wigtoft Lincs 43 J3
Wigton Cumb 71 L6
Wigtown D & G 69 L7
Wike Leeds 59 J5
Wilbarston Nhants 42 B11
Wilberfoss E R Yk 60 C4
Wilburton Cambs 33 M2
Wilby Nhants 32 C4
Wilby Norfk 44 G11
Wilby Suffk 35 L3
Wilcot Wilts 18 G8
Wilcott Shrops 48 H10
Wildboarclough Ches E 50 C7
Wilden Bed 32 F6
Wilden Worcs 39 P7
Wildmanbridge S Lans 85 N11
Wildmoor Worcs 40 C11
Wildsworth Lincs 52 B4
Wilford C Nott 51 M12
Wilford Hill Crematorium Notts 41 M1
Wilkesley Ches E 49 L7
Wilkhaven Highld 107 Q5
Wilkieston W Loth 86 D8
Willand Devon 6 D1
Willaston Ches E 49 M5
Willaston Ches W 56 G12
Willen M Keyn 32 C8
Willenhall Covtry 41 J11
Willenhall Wsall 40 C7
Willerby E R Yk 60 H7
Willerby N York 67 L10
Willersey Gloucs 30 E6
Willersley Herefs 38 G11
Willesborough Kent 13 K2
Willesborough Lees Kent 13 K2
Willesden Gt Lon 21 K6
Willesley Wilts 18 C3
Willett Somset 16 F9
Willey Shrops 39 M3
Willey Warwks 41 L9
Willey Green Surrey 20 F12
Williamscot Oxon 31 L5
Willian Herts 32 H9
Willingale Essex 22 C2
Willingdon E Susx 12 C9
Willingham Cambs 33 L3
Willingham by Stow Lincs 52 C6
Willington Bed 32 G6
Willington Derbys 40 H2
Willington Dur 65 L1
Willington Kent 22 F11
Willington N Tyne 73 N7
Willington Warwks 30 H6
Willitoft E R Yk 60 C7
Williton Somset 16 E7
Willoughby Lincs 53 M8
Willoughby Warwks 31 M1
Willoughby-on-the-Wolds Notts 41 N3
Willoughby Waterleys Leics 41 M8
Willoughton Lincs 52 D5
Willows Green Essex 34 C11
Willtown Somset 17 K10
Wilmcote Warwks 30 F3
Wilmington Devon 6 G3
Wilmington E Susx 12 B8
Wilmington Kent 21 Q8
Wilmslow Ches E 57 Q11
Wilpshire Lancs 57 M3
Wilsden C Brad 58 E6
Wilsford Lincs 42 E2
Wilsford Wilts 18 G11
Wilsford Wilts 18 G8
Wilshaw Kirk 58 E11
Wilsill N York 58 F2
Wilson Leics 41 K3
Wilsontown S Lans 85 Q11
Wilstead Bed 32 F7
Wilsthorpe Lincs 42 F7
Wilstone Herts 20 E1
Wilton Herefs 28 G4
Wilton N York 67 J10
Wilton R & Cl 66 E4
Wilton Wilts 8 G2
Wilton Wilts 19 J8
Wilton Dean Border 80 C10
Wimbish Green Essex 33 P9
Wimbledon Gt Lon 21 K8
Wimblington Cambs 43 L10
Wimboldsley Ches W 49 M3
Wimborne Minster Dorset 8 E7
Wimborne St Giles Dorset 8 F5
Wimbotsham Norfk 43 P8
Wimpole Cambs 33 K6
Wimpstone Warwks 30 G4
Wincanton Somset 17 Q9
Winchburgh W Loth 86 C7
Winchcombe Gloucs 30 D8
Winchelsea E Susx 12 H6
Winchester Hants 9 N2
Winchester Services Hants 9 N1
Winchet Hill Kent 12 E2
Winchfield Hants 20 C11
Winchmore Hill Bucks 20 E4
Winchmore Hill Gt Lon 21 L5
Wincle Ches E 50 C7
Wincobank Sheff 51 J3
Windermere Cumb 62 H3
Windermere Steamboats & Museum Cumb 62 H3
Winderton Warwks 31 J6
Windhill Highld 107 J11
Windlesham Surrey 20 E9
Windmill Cnwll 3 K2
Windmill Hill E Susx 12 D7
Windmill Hill Somset 17 J11
Windrush Gloucs 30 F10
Windsole Abers 102 D4
Windsor W & M 20 F7
Windsor Castle W & M 20 F7
Windsoredge Gloucs 29 L8
Windsor Green Suffk 34 E6
Windygates Fife 86 G3
Wineham W Susx 11 K6
Winestead E R Yk 61 M8
Winfarthing Norfk 45 J11
Winford IoW 9 P9
Winford N Som 17 M3
Winforton Herefs 38 F11
Winfrith Newburgh Dorset 8 B9
Wing Bucks 32 C11
Wing Rutlnd 42 C9
Wingate Dur 73 P12
Wingerworth Derbys 51 J7

Wingfield C Beds........32 E10
Wingfield Suffk........35 K2
Wingfield Wilts........18 B9
Wingham Kent........23 N11
Wingrave Bucks........32 C11
Winkburn Notts........51 P8
Winkfield Br For........20 E8
Winkfield Row Br For........20 E8
Winkhill Staffs........50 D9
Winkleigh Devon........15 L9
Winksley N York........65 M12
Winlaton Gatesd........73 L8
Winless Highld........110 G5
Winmarleigh Lancs........63 J11
Winnall Hants........9 N5
Winnersh Wokham........20 C8
Winnington Ches W........49 M1
Winscombe N Som........17 K5
Winsford Ches W........49 M3
Winsford Somset........16 B8
Winsham Somset........7 K2
Winshill Staffs........40 H3
Winshwen Swans........26 F9
Winskill Cumb........64 B1
Winsley Wilts........18 B8
Winslow Bucks........31 Q8
Winson Gloucs........30 E11
Winsor Hants........9 K5
Winster Cumb........62 H4
Winster Derbys........50 F8
Winston Dur........65 K4
Winston Suffk........35 K5
Winstone Gloucs........29 N6
Winswell Devon........15 J9
Winterborne Came
   Dorset........7 Q5
Winterborne Clenston
   Dorset........8 C6
Winterborne
   Houghton Dorset........8 B6
Winterborne Kingston
   Dorset........8 C7
Winterborne Monkton
   Dorset........7 P5
Winterborne Stickland
   Dorset........8 C6
Winterborne
   Whitchurch Dorset........8 C7
Winterborne Zelston
   Dorset........8 D7
Winterbourne S Glos........28 H11
Winterbourne W Berk........19 M6
Winterbourne Abbas
   Dorset........7 N5
Winterbourne Bassett
   Wilts........18 G6
Winterbourne
   Dauntsey Wilts........8 H1
Winterbourne Earls Wilts........8 H1
Winterbourne Gunner
   Wilts........8 H1
Winterbourne
   Monkton Wilts........18 G6
Winterbourne
   Steepleton Dorset........7 P5
Winterbourne Stoke
   Wilts........18 F11
Winterburn N York........58 C3
Winteringham N Linc........60 F9
Winterley Ches E........49 N4
Winterslow Wilts........9 J2
Winterton N Linc........60 F9
Winterton-on-Sea Norfk........45 P6
Winthorpe Notts........52 B11
Winton Bmouth........8 G8
Winton Cumb........64 E5
Wintringham N York........67 J11
Winwick Cambs........32 F1
Winwick Nhants........41 N11
Winwick Warrtn........57 L9
Wirksworth Derbys........50 H9
Wirral........56 F10
Wirswall Ches E........49 K6
Wisbech Cambs........43 M8
Wisbech St Mary Cambs........43 L8
Wisborough Green
   W Susx........10 G5
Wiseman's Bridge
   Pembks........25 K7
Wiseton Notts........51 Q3
Wishaw N Lans........85 N11
Wisley Garden RHS
   Surrey........20 G10
Wispington Lincs........52 H8
Wissett Suffk........35 M2
Wissington Suffk........34 F9
Wistanstow Shrops........38 H5
Wistanswick Shrops........49 M9
Wistaston Ches E........49 M5
Wistaston Green Ches E........49 M5
Wiston Pembks........24 H5
Wiston S Lans........78 F3
Wiston W Susx........11 J7
Wistow Cambs........33 J1
Wistow N York........59 N7
Wiswell Lancs........57 N2
Witcham Cambs........33 M2
Witchampton Dorset........8 E6
Witchford Cambs........33 N2
Witcombe Somset........17 L10
Withcall Lincs........53 J6
Withdean Br & H........11 L8
Witherenden Hill E Susx........12 D5
Witheridge Devon........15 N8
Witherley Leics........41 J7
Withern Lincs........53 L7
Withernsea E R Yk........61 N8
Withernwick E R Yk........61 K6
Withersdale Street Suffk........35 L1
Withersfield Suffk........33 Q7
Witherslack Cumb........62 H5
Withiel Cnwll........3 M3
Withiel Florey Somset........16 D9
Withington Gloucs........30 D10
Withington Herefs........39 K12
Withington Manch........57 Q9
Withington Shrops........49 L11
Withington Staffs........40 D1
Withleigh Devon........6 B1
Withnell Lancs........57 L4
Withybed Green Worcs........40 D11
Withybrook Warwks........41 K10
Withycombe Somset........16 D7
Witham E Susx........11 P3
Withypool Somset........15 P5
Withywood Bristl........17 N3
Witley Surrey........10 F3

Witnesham Suffk........35 K6
Witney Oxon........31 J11
Wittering C Pete........42 F9
Wittersham Kent........12 H5
Witton Birm........40 E8
Witton Norfk........45 M4
Witton Norfk........45 M8
Witton Gilbert Dur........73 M10
Witton le Wear Dur........65 K2
Witton Park Dur........65 L2
Wiveliscombe Somset........16 E9
Wivelrod Hants........19 R12
Wivelsfield E Susx........11 M6
Wivelsfield Green E Susx........11 M6
Wivenhoe Essex........34 G11
Wiveton Norfk........44 G2
Wix Essex........35 J10
Wixams Bed........32 F7
Wixford Warwks........30 E3
Wixoe Suffk........34 C8
Woburn C Beds........32 D9
Woburn Safari Park
   C Beds........32 D9
Woburn Sands M Keyn........32 D9
Woking Surrey........20 G10
Woking Crematorium
   Surrey........20 F11
Wokingham Wokham........20 D9
Woldingham Surrey........21 M11
Wold Newton E R Yk........67 M11
Wold Newton NE Lin........53 J4
Wolfclyde S Lans........78 G2
Wolferton Norfk........43 Q4
Wolfhill P & K........92 H8
Wolf's Castle Pembks........24 G4
Wolfsdale Pembks........24 G5
Wollaston Dudley........40 B9
Wollaston Nhants........32 C4
Wollaston Shrops........48 G11
Wollaton C Nott........51 M11
Wollaton Hall & Park
   C Nott........51 M11
Wollerton Shrops........49 L9
Wollescote Dudley........40 B10
Wolseley Bridge Staffs........40 D4
Wolsingham Dur........73 J12
Wolstanton Staffs........49 Q6
Wolston Warwks........41 K11
Wolvercote Oxon........31 L11
Wolverhampton Wolves........40 B7
Wolverhampton
   Halfpenny Green
   Airport Staffs........39 P4
Wolverley Worcs........39 P6
Wolverton Hants........19 P8
Wolverton M Keyn........32 B8
Wolverton Warwks........30 G2
Wolverton Wilts........8 B2
Wolvesnewton Mons........28 E8
Wolvey Warwks........41 K9
Wolvey Heath Warwks........41 K9
Wolviston S on T........66 C3
Wombleton N York........66 F10
Wombourne Staffs........39 Q4
Wombwell Barns........51 K1
Womenswold Kent........23 N12
Womersley N York........59 M9
Wonersh Surrey........10 G2
Wonford Devon........6 C4
Wonston Dorset........7 Q2
Wonston Hants........19 M11
Wooburn Green Bucks........20 E6
Woodacott Devon........14 G9
Woodall Rothm........51 L5
Woodall Services Rothm........51 L5
Woodbastwick Norfk........45 M7
Wood Bevington Warwks........30 D4
Woodborough Notts........51 N10
Woodborough Wilts........18 G8
Woodbridge Suffk........35 L7
Woodbury Devon........6 D5
Woodbury Salterton
   Devon........6 D5
Woodchester Gloucs........29 L8
Woodchurch Kent........12 H3
Woodcombe Somset........16 C6
Woodcote Gt Lon........21 L10
Woodcote Oxon........19 Q4
Woodcote Wrekin........49 P11
Woodcroft Gloucs........28 G9
Wood Dalling Norfk........44 H5
Woodditton Cambs........33 Q5
Woodeaton Oxon........31 M10
Wood End Gt Lon........20 H7
Wood End Herts........33 K10
Woodend Highld........89 Q4
Woodend Nhants........31 N4
Wood End W Loth........85 Q8
Wood End W Susx........10 D8
Wood End Warwks........40 E11
Wood End Wolves........40 C7
Wood Enderby Lincs........53 J10
Woodfalls Wilts........8 H4
Woodford Cnwll........14 D9
Woodford Gloucs........29 J9
Woodford Gt Lon........21 N5
Woodford Nhants........32 D2
Woodford Stockp........56 B4
Woodford Bridge Gt Lon........21 N5
Woodford Green Gt Lon........21 N5
Woodford Halse Nhants........31 M4
Woodford Wells Gt Lon........21 N5
Woodgate Birm........40 D10
Woodgate Devon........16 E12
Woodgate W Susx........10 F8
Woodgate Worcs........30 C2
Wood Green Gt Lon........21 L5
Woodgreen Hants........8 H4
Woodhall N York........64 H9
Woodhall Spa Lincs........52 H10
Woodham Surrey........20 G10
Woodham Ferrers Essex........22 F4
Woodham Mortimer
   Essex........22 F3
Woodham Walter Essex........22 F3
Wood Hayes Wolves........40 C7
Woodhead Abers........102 G7
Woodhill Shrops........39 N5
Woodhill Somset........17 J10
Woodhorn Nthumb........73 N3
Woodhouse Leeds........58 H7
Woodhouse Leics........41 M6
Woodhouse Sheff........51 K4
Woodhouse Wakefd........59 J9
Woodhouse Eaves Leics........41 M5
Woodhouselee Mdloth........86 F8
Woodhouselees D & G........71 N1
Woodhouses Oldham........50 B1
Woodhouses Staffs........40 F4

Woodhurst Cambs........33 K2
Woodingdean Br & H........11 M8
Woodkirk Leeds........58 H8
Woodland Abers........103 J9
Woodland Devon........5 M8
Woodland Devon........5 Q6
Woodland Dur........65 J3
Woodland S Ayrs........76 C11
Woodlands Abers........95 N3
Woodlands Donc........59 M11
Woodlands Dorset........8 F5
Woodlands Hants........9 K5
Woodlands N York........59 J3
Woodlands (Coleshill)
   Crematorium Warwks........40 F9
Woodlands Park W & M........20 D7
Woodlands
   (Scarborough)
   Crematorium N York........67 L9
Woodlands
   (Scunthorpe)
   Crematorium N Linc........60 F11
Woodleigh Devon........5 M9
Woodley Wokham........20 C8
Woodmancote Gloucs........29 K8
Woodmancote Gloucs........29 N4
Woodmancote Gloucs........30 D11
Woodmancote W Susx........10 C8
Woodmancote W Susx........11 K7
Woodmancott Hants........19 P11
Woodmansey E R Yk........60 H6
Woodmansgreen W Susx........10 D5
Woodmansterne Surrey........21 L10
Woodmanton Devon........6 D5
Woodnesborough Kent........23 P11
Woodnewton Nhants........42 E10
Wood Norton Norfk........44 G5
Woodplumpton Lancs........57 J2
Woodrising Norfk........44 G9
Wood's Corner E Susx........12 D6
Woodseaves Staffs........49 P9
Woodsetts Rothm........51 M4
Woodsford Dorset........8 A8
Wood's Green E Susx........12 D4
Woodside Br For........20 E8
Woodside Fife........86 H1
Woodside Gt Lon........21 M9
Woodside P & K........93 J7
Woodside
   Crematorium Inver........84 E7
Woodstock Oxon........31 K10
Woodston C Pete........42 H10
Wood Street Norfk........45 N6
Wood Street Village
   Surrey........20 F12
Woodton Norfk........45 L10
Woodtown Devon........14 G7
Woodvale
   Crematorium Br & H........11 L8
Woodville Derbys........40 H4
Wood Walton Cambs........32 H1
Woofferton Shrops........39 K8
Wookey Somset........17 M7
Wookey Hole Somset........17 M6
Wool Dorset........8 C9
Woolacombe Devon........14 H4
Woolage Green Kent........23 N12
Woolaston Gloucs........28 G8
Woolaston Common
   Gloucs........28 G8
Woolavington Somset........17 J7
Woolbeding W Susx........10 E5
Woolbrook Devon........6 F5
Wooler Nthumb........81 L8
Woolfardisworthy
   Devon........14 F7
Woolfardisworthy
   Devon........15 P9
Woolfords S Lans........86 B10
Woolhampton W Berk........19 P7
Woolhope Herefs........28 H2
Woolland Dorset........8 B6
Woolley BaNES........17 Q3
Woolley Cambs........32 G2
Woolley Wakefd........58 H10
Woolley Edge Services
   Wakefd........58 H10
Woolmere Green Worcs........30 C2
Woolmer Green Herts........33 J11
Woolminstone Somset........7 K2
Woolpit Suffk........34 F4
Woolstaston Shrops........39 J3
Woolsthorpe Lincs........42 B4
Woolsthorpe-by-
   Colsterworth Lincs........42 D6
Woolston C Sotn........9 M5
Woolston Shrops........48 G9
Woolston Somset........16 E8
Woolston Somset........17 P9
Woolston Warrtn........57 M10
Woolstone Gloucs........29 N3
Woolstone M Keyn........32 C8
Woolstone Oxon........19 K4
Woolston Green Devon........5 Q7
Woolton Lpool........56 H10
Woolton Hill Hants........19 M8
Woolverstone Suffk........35 K8
Woolverton Somset........18 B9
Woolwich Gt Lon........21 N7
Woonton Herefs........38 G10
Woore Shrops........49 N7
Wooton Green Suffk........35 K8
Wootton Bed........32 E7
Wootton Kent........13 N2
Wootton N Linc........61 J10
Wootton Nhants........31 Q3
Wootton Oxon........19 N1
Wootton Oxon........31 K9
Wootton Staffs........50 E10
Wootton Bassett Wilts........18 F4
Wootton Bridge IoW........9 P8
Wootton Courtenay
   Somset........16 C7
Wootton Fitzpaine
   Dorset........7 K4
Wootton Rivers Wilts........18 H8
Wootton St Lawrence
   Hants........19 P9
Wootton Wawen
   Warwks........30 F2
Worcester Worcs........39 Q10
Worcester
   Crematorium Worcs........39 Q10
Worcester Park Gt Lon........21 K9
Wordsley Dudley........40 B9
Worfield Shrops........39 N3
Workington Cumb........70 G9
Worksop Notts........51 N5
Worlaby N Linc........60 H10
Worlds End Hants........9 Q5

Worlds End W Susx........11 L6
Worle N Som........17 J4
Worleston Ches E........49 M4
Worlingham Suffk........45 P11
Worlington Devon........15 N9
Worlington Suffk........34 B3
Worlingworth Suffk........35 K3
Wormbridge Herefs........28 E3
Wormegay Norfk........43 Q7
Wormelow Tump
   Herefs........28 F3
Wormhill Derbys........50 E6
Wormingford Essex........34 F9
Worminghall Bucks........31 N11
Wormington Gloucs........30 D6
Wormit Fife........93 M9
Wormleighton Warwks........31 K4
Wormley Herts........21 M3
Wormley Surrey........10 F3
Wormshill Kent........22 G11
Wormsley Herefs........38 H11
Worplesdon Surrey........20 F11
Worrall Sheff........50 H3
Worsbrough Barns........51 J1
Worsbrough Bridge
   Barns........59 J12
Worsbrough Dale Barns........59 J12
Worsley Salfd........57 N8
Worstead Norfk........45 M5
Worsthorne Lancs........57 Q3
Worston Devon........5 M9
Worston Lancs........57 P1
Worth Kent........23 P11
Wortham Suffk........34 H2
Worthen Shrops........38 G2
Worthenbury Wrexhm........48 H6
Worthing Norfk........44 G6
Worthing W Susx........11 J9
Worthing Crematorium
   W Susx........10 H8
Worthington Leics........41 K4
Worth Matravers Dorset........8 E11
Wortley Barns........50 H2
Wortley Leeds........58 H7
Worton N York........64 G9
Worton Wilts........18 E8
Wortwell Norfk........45 L12
Wotton-under-Edge
   Gloucs........29 K9
Wotton Underwood
   Bucks........31 P10
Woughton on the
   Green M Keyn........32 C8
Wouldham Kent........22 E9
Wrabness Essex........35 K9
Wrafton Devon........15 J5
Wragby Lincs........52 G7
Wragby Wakefd........59 K10
Wrangaton Devon........5 N9
Wrangle Lincs........53 L12
Wrangway Somset........16 F11
Wrantage Somset........17 J10
Wrawby N Linc........52 G2
Wraxall N Som........17 L2
Wraxall Somset........17 N8
Wray Lancs........63 L8
Wraysbury W & M........20 G8
Wrayton Lancs........63 L7
Wrea Green Lancs........56 H3
Wreay Cumb........71 N6
Wrecclesham Surrey........10 D2
Wrekenton Gatesd........73 M8
Wrelton N York........66 G9
Wrenbury Ches E........49 L6
Wreningham Norfk........45 J9
Wrentham Suffk........45 Q12
Wrenthall Shrops........38 H2
Wressle E R Yk........60 C7
Wressle N Linc........52 D2
Wrestlingworth C Beds........33 J7
Wretton Norfk........44 B9
Wrexham Wrexhm........48 G5
Wrexham Industrial
   Estate Wrexhm........48 H5
Wribbenhall Worcs........39 P7
Wrinehill Staffs........49 N6
Wrington N Som........17 L4
Writhlington BaNES........17 Q5
Writtle Essex........22 D3
Wrockwardine Wrekin........49 L11
Wroot N Linc........60 C12
Wrose C Brad........58 F6
Wrotham Kent........22 C10
Wroughton Swindn........18 G5
Wroxall IoW........9 P10
Wroxall Warwks........40 G12
Wroxeter Shrops........39 K1
Wroxham Norfk........45 L6
Wroxton Oxon........31 K6
Wyaston Derbys........50 F11
Wyberton East Lincs........43 K3
Wyboston Bed........32 G5
Wybunbury Ches E........49 M5
Wychbold Worcs........30 B2
Wychnor Staffs........40 F4
Wyck Rissington Gloucs........30 F9
Wycliffe Dur........65 K5
Wycoller Lancs........58 C6
Wycomb Leics........41 Q3
Wycombe Marsh Bucks........20 E5
Wyddial Herts........33 L9
Wye Kent........13 K1
Wyke C Brad........58 F8
Wyke Dorset........17 Q10
Wyke Champflower
   Somset........17 P8
Wykeham N York........67 L10
Wyken Covtry........41 J10
Wyken Shrops........39 N3
Wyke Regis Dorset........7 P7
Wykey Shrops........48 H9
Wylam Nthumb........73 K7
Wylde Green Birm........40 E8
Wylye Wilts........18 E12
Wymeswold Leics........41 N3
Wymington Bed........32 D4
Wymondham Leics........42 C6
Wymondham Norfk........45 J9
Wynford Eagle Dorset........7 N4
Wyre Forest
   Crematorium Worcs........39 P7
Wyre Piddle Worcs........30 C5
Wysall Notts........41 N3
Wythall Worcs........40 E11
Wytham Oxon........31 L11
Wythenshawe Manch........57 P10
Wyton Cambs........33 J3
Wyton E R Yk........61 K7
Wyverstone Suffk........34 G3
Wyverstone Street Suffk........34 G4

Y

Yaddlethorpe N Linc........52 C3
Yafforth N York........65 N8
Yalberton Torbay........6 B10
Yalding Kent........22 E12
Yanwath Cumb........71 Q9
Yanworth Gloucs........30 E10
Yapham E R Yk........60 D4
Yapton W Susx........10 F9
Yarborough N Som........17 K5
Yarburgh Lincs........53 K5
Yarcombe Devon........6 H2
Yard Devon........15 N7
Yardley Birm........40 F9
Yardley Crematorium
   Birm........40 F9
Yardley Gobion Nhants........31 Q5
Yardley Hastings Nhants........32 C5
Yardley Wood Birm........40 E10
Yarkhill Herefs........39 L12
Yarley Somset........17 M7
Yarlington Somset........17 P9
Yarm S on T........65 P5
Yarmouth IoW........9 L9
Yarnbrook Wilts........18 C9
Yarnfield Staffs........49 Q8
Yarnscombe Devon........15 K7
Yarnton Oxon........31 L10
Yarpole Herefs........39 J8
Yarrow Border........79 M4
Yarrow Feus Border........79 M4
Yarrowford Border........79 N3
Yarwell Nhants........42 F9
Yate S Glos........29 J11
Yateley Hants........20 D10
Yatesbury Wilts........18 F6
Yattendon W Berk........19 P6
Yatton Herefs........38 H8
Yatton N Som........17 L3
Yatton Keynell Wilts........18 C5
Yaverland IoW........9 Q9
Yaxham Norfk........44 G7
Yaxley Cambs........42 H10
Yaxley Suffk........35 J2
Yazor Herefs........38 H11
Yeading Gt Lon........20 H7
Yeadon Leeds........58 G6
Yealand Conyers Lancs........63 J7
Yealand Redmayne
   Lancs........63 J7
Yealmpton Devon........5 M9
Yearsley N York........66 E11
Yeaton Shrops........48 H10
Yeaveley Derbys........50 F11
Yeavering Nthumb........81 K7
Yedingham N York........67 J10
Yelford Oxon........31 J12
Yell Shet........111 k3
Yelling Cambs........33 J4
Yelvertoft Nhants........41 N11
Yelverton Devon........5 L6
Yelverton Norfk........45 L9
Yenston Somset........17 Q11
Yeoford Devon........15 N11
Yeolmbridge Cnwll........4 G3
Yeovil Somset........17 M11
Yeovil Crematorium
   Somset........17 M11
Yeovil Marsh Somset........17 M11
Yeovilton Somset........17 M10
Yesnaby Ork........111 g2
Yetminster Dorset........7 N1
Yettington Devon........6 E5
Yetts o'Muckhart Clacks........86 B2
Yew Tree Sandw........40 D8
Y Felinheli Gwynd........54 G7
Y Ferwig Cerdgn........36 C10
Y Ffor Gwynd........46 G4
Y Gyffylliog Denbgs........48 C4
Yielden Bed........32 E4
Yieldshields S Lans........77 P2
Yiewsley Gt Lon........20 G7
Y Maerdy Conwy........48 B6
Ynysboeth Rhondd........27 M9
Ynysddu Caerph........27 P9
Ynyshir Rhondd........27 L9
Ynystawe Swans........26 F8
Ynysybwl Rhondd........27 M9
Yockleton Shrops........48 H12
Yokefleet E R Yk........60 E8
Yoker C Glas........84 H8
York C York........59 N4
York City Crematorium
   C York........59 N5
Yorkletts Kent........23 L10
Yorkley Gloucs........28 H7
Yorkshire Dales National
   Park........64 F11
York Town Surrey........20 D10
Youlgreave Derbys........50 G7
Youlthorpe E R Yk........60 D3
Youlton N York........59 L2
Yoxall Staffs........40 F4
Yoxford Suffk........35 N3
Y Rhiw Gwynd........46 D6
Ysbyty Ifan Conwy........55 M10
Ysbyty Ystwyth Cerdgn........37 M6
Ysceifiog Flints........48 D2
Ystalyfera Neath........26 G7
Ystrad Rhondd........27 L9
Ystrad Aeron Cerdgn........36 H9
Ystradfellte Powys........27 K6
Ystradgynlais Powys........26 H6
Ystrad Meurig Cerdgn........37 L7
Ystrad Mynach Caerph........27 N9
Ystradowen V Glam........27 L12
Ythanbank Abers........103 J8
Ythanwells Abers........102 E7
Ythsie Abers........103 J8

Z

Zeal Monachorum
   Devon........15 M10
Zeals Wilts........8 B2
Zelah Cnwll........3 J5
Zennor Cnwll........2 C7
Zouch Notts........41 L3
ZSL London Zoo Gt Lon........21 L6
ZSL Whipsnade Zoo
   C Beds........32 E12